BUSINESS,
GOVERNMENT,
AND SOCIETY

Newman S. Peery, Jr.

School of Business and Public Administration
University of the Pacific, Stockton, California

BUSINESS, GOVERNMENT, AND SOCIETY

MANAGING COMPETITIVENESS, ETHICS, AND SOCIAL ISSUES

PRENTICE HALL, Englewood Cliffs, New Jersey 07632

Library of Congress Cataloging-in-Publication Data

Peery, Newman S.
    Business, government, and society: managing competitiveness,
ethics, and social issues / Newman S. Peery.
        p.   cm.
    Includes bibliographic references and index.
    ISBN: 0-02-393401-8
    1. Industry—Social aspects—United States.   2. Industry and state—United States.   3.
Trade regulation—United States.
    I. Title.
HD60.5.U5P377 1995
306.3'6'0973—dc20   93-46304
                                                                                       CIP

Editor: Natalie Anderson
Production Supervisor: Dora Rizzuto
Production Manager: Francesca Drago
Electronic Text Manager: Kurt Scherwatzky
Electronic Pager: Elyse Chapman
Text and Cover Designer: Robert Freese
Cover Illustration: Tom Post

© 1995 by Prentice-Hall, Inc.
A Division of Simon and Schuster, Inc.
Englewood Cliffs, New Jersey 07632

Printed in the United States of America

10 9 8 7 6 5 4 3 2 1

0-02-393401-8

Prentice-Hall International (UK) Limited, *London*
Prentice-Hall of Australia Pty. Limited, *Sydney*
Prentice-Hall Canada Inc., *Toronto*
Prentice-Hall Hispanoamericana, S.A., *Mexico*
Prentice-Hall of India Private Limited, *New Delhi*
Prentice-Hall of Japan, Inc., *Tokyo*
Simon & Schuster Asia Pte. Ltd., *Singapore*
Editora Prentice-Hall do Brasil, Ltda., *Rio de Janeiro*

This book is dedicated to my wife
Candace Caron Peery

PREFACE

This book was written for the undergraduate course in business, government, and society and can also be used for graduate-level courses in business and public policy. It includes an integrating model of business performance and another model for social change and control of business that complement one another. It offers insights for the student, the practicing manager, and the government regulator who seek to better understand the dynamic business-government-society relationship. Although it provides a unifying interdisciplinary framework, it is applications-oriented. Also included are short discussion cases and longer integrative cases to explore the practical implications for key concepts and issues.

Business, government, and society has become a recognized academic field during the past two decades. A respectable literature now supports the interdisciplinary area and several excellent texts are available. I respectfully follow in the furrows of many who have plowed this fertile field before me. This contribution represents over a decade of work and includes a rich context for intellectual and ideological history that is missing from most other books in the field. This should make the reader aware of the changing economic, social, and political environment of business and the need for managers to constantly adapt to new realities.

Business, Government, and Society: Managing Competitiveness, Ethics, and Social Issues offers a number of important features for students and to the practicing manager.

1. Business, government, and culture provide the three interacting subsystems of society within which managers must operate. This book places managers and business within a complex, threefold society: (1) Business is examined within the context of market competitiveness though other systems of political economy are discussed; (2) government is examined in the context of the democratic and pluralistic public policy process leading to the legal environment of business; and (3) Culture provides the basis for values, ethics, and ideas concerning social justice. Intellectual history and cultural change provide the backdrop for a discussion about how ideologies influence our ideas about justice, public policies, and the appropriate role of government.

2. The business social performance model includes the four dimensions of economic, ethical, political, and legal performance. Part One argues that business is the primary economic instrument for maintaining the standard of living within society. Society includes business operating within market competition, government shaped by pluralistic democracy, and a diverse culture. Managers can adopt several institutional orientations to the environment including (1) defensive and reactive, (2) anticipatory and socially responsible, or (3) proactive and politically responsive.

3. Strategic management of economic performance includes forming and implementing generic and global strategies to achieve high economic performance. Chapter 1 discusses strategic management in terms of the generic strategies of differentiation, low-cost leadership, and focus or target marketing. To these, a discussion of global strategies in Chapters 4 and 5 incorporate global strategies to include the competitive demands of a global marketplace.

4. Political performance requires the effective strategic management of public issues. This requires an understanding of the issue life cycle, the mapping of stakeholder interests, and carefully designed and implemented corporate political strategy. Strategic management of public issues is discussed in Chapter 3.

5. The necessary conditions of a competitive market are central to understanding how a market-oriented society functions. Competitive market conditions are first introduced in Chapter 2 to explain how failures in market functioning lead to the public debates that define the role of government. Market conditions are later related to economic justice in Chapter 8, to types of government regulation of business in Chapter 11, and to the ethics of exchange in Chapter 15.

6. Globalized markets increase the importance of international competitiveness and define the emerging multinational business-government relationship. Chapters 4 and 5 present competitiveness in a global market. Businesses and governments must now think globally, respond to the demands of regional economic cooperation, compete with the global firm, and deal with highly globalized capital markets. Globalization also shapes the task of government as it seeks to protect its citizens, to maintain a level playing field for fair competition, to make treaties with other countries, to establish areas of regional economic cooperation, and to generally provide a positive economic environment supportive of growth and prosperity. If business managers fulfill the demands of global competitiveness, then society's standard of living can be maintained or enhanced and the economic performance of business assured.

7. Business ethics has become increasingly important in considering the demands of competing stakeholders of business. Managers are pressed with many harsh realities of global competition, with conflicting demands from various stakeholders, and with the complexity of managing professionals and high technology with organizations. Four chapters deal with the ethical performance and the social responsibility of business managers. Chapter 6 demonstrates the links among moral judgment, corporate culture, and moral behavior. Chapter 7 provides an integrative framework for ethical analysis. Chapter 8 reviews the major approaches to economic justice by which the fairness of a business decision for various stakeholders can be evaluated. Chapter 9 integrates the material on moral judgment with the social performance model to increase our understanding of social responsibility.

8. The public policy process and the legal environment of business define the business-government relationship. Four chapters are devoted to public policy including Chapter 10, which describes how the public policy process operates to form the legal environment of business. Also, Chapter 10 extends the discussion of ideology to show how it influences the public policy debate and concepts concerning the appropriate role of government. Chapter 11 shows how the various types of government regulation of business relate to the conditions necessary for market competition. Chapter 12 shows how government regulation can also fail and reviews the historical attempts at regulatory reform and the deregulation movement that began in the 1970s. Chapter 13 provides an overview of antitrust law and how the deregulation movement influenced the antitrust enforcement strategies of the government.

9. The management of stakeholder issues includes owners and other investors, customers, employees, and ecology and the physical environment. Part Five (the last four chapters) applies the central themes of business and society: (1) business social performance model, (2) the issue life cycle model, and (3) the model of social change and control to business. Major stakeholder groups, treated as important dimensions of the environment of business, are considered within the context of social performance. Chapter 14 is concerned with stockholders and investor stakeholders and deals with organizational governance. Chapter 15 reviews consumer stakeholder issues and covers the ethics of exchange and product liability law.

Chapters 16 and 17 are devoted to employee stakeholder issues. Chapter 16 reviews the issues of technology and empowerment, job safety, downsizing, and work-family conflicts. Chapter 17 reviews the ethics of equality and discrimination as well as recent developments in this area including the Americans with Disabilities Act, the Civil Rights Act of 1991, and sexual discrimination. Chapter 18 considers the physical environment, including the effects of industrialization and modern technology, ecological problems, the regulation of the environment, and the prospects of sustainable economic development.

10. Applications-oriented discussion cases and longer integrative cases are provided throughout the book. Each chapter includes short cases for discussion. Sometimes the chapter begins with a short case, and sometimes another case is available at the end of the chapter. Most chapters illustrate the concepts with case examples that can focus class discussions on key issues. At the end of each part, integrative cases are available for discussion of the key concepts and controversies presented in that part. These cases form an important part of the book because they bring to life issues that might otherwise not be revealed by the discussion of the various theories within business, government, and society.

What economic, political, and social changes affect economic performance? What are the salient social values and how do they relate to the legitimacy for different management practices? What are the key trends in the legal environment and how can business best respond to government regulatory changes? What are the ethical considerations and how can managers use their moral imagination to balance the interests and respect the rights of diverse stakeholders when important decisions are to be made? What are the key issues within each stakeholder area and how have they unfolded within the issue life cycle? Such questions guide the reader in considering each of these important stakeholder groups.

ACKNOWLEDGMENTS

As is true for all books, the completion of this one was made possible with the help of numerous persons. Some have influenced my thinking, others provided emotional and financial support, colleagues reviewed earlier drafts, students class-tested the material, and many scholars have created the field of business and society that forms the foundation for this work.

The interdisciplinary perspective used here owes much to my graduate work at the University of Washington. It was at UW where an economist, lawyers specializing in antitrust law and the legal environment of business, an anthropologist, a business historian, and a social scientist were grouped together in one of the first Departments of Business and Society to create an interdisciplinary approach to this new field. This business-and-society book seeks to integrate the disciplines of economics, political science, business ethics, and the legal environment into one framework. Thanks especially go to William G. Scott at the University of Washington, who encouraged me to consider organizations as political systems and to study their governance.

The importance of public policy for the environment of business was clarified to me at the 1979 conference on business and public policy jointly sponsored by George Steiner at UCLA and the American Association of College Schools of Business (AACSB). The insights of Rogene Buchholz and Graham Molitar made available at this conference and in the literature contributed greatly to my understanding of the public policy process and the issue life cycle that are basic to the framework offered in this book.

My sabbatical year as a Kent Post-doctoral fellow at the University of Southern California in 1980 enabled me to develop the necessary background for business ethics and social responsibility. I want to recognize the generosity of the Dansforth Foundation for their financial support of the Kent Post-

doctoral Program at USC. My special appreciation and thanks go to William May for his insights into business ethics and to John Orr, who introduced me to the important theories of economic justice and social ethics. John Orr also made me aware of the ethical writing of Adam Smith, who not only was the father of modern economics (*Wealth of Nations*) but also contributed much to our understanding of virtues necessary for a good society (*Theory of Moral Sentiments*). Market competitiveness, evolving concepts of moral sentiments within society, and the concept of a good society first developed by Adam Smith form a unifying theme in business, government, and society.

Also, beginning with the sabbatical year at USC, other work proved central to this book: (1) the study of moral development from a psychological perspective and its influence on corporate cultures, (2) the intellectual history of the United States and its influence on both ideology and cultural values, and (3) the philosophy of Rudolf Steiner, who, early in this century, provided a dynamic model of society. Steiner's threefold society model includes the economic sphere, which produces the goods and services necessary for society; the political-governmental sphere, which defines and protects rights; and the spiritual–cultural sphere, which creates knowledge and sustains social values that, in turn, inspire public policy and define market demand.

Special thanks go to the reviewers of this manuscript, who made numerous comments and offered useful ideas that helped me to strengthen the book: Norma Carr-Ruffino, San Francisco State University; David M. Flynn, Hofstra University; W. Benoy Joseph, Cleveland State University; D. Jeffery Lenn, George Washington University; Martin K. Marsh, California State University at Bakersfield; William W. May, University of Southern California; Harvey Nussbaum, Wayne State University; David R. Palmer, Santa Clara University; Bill Shaw, University of Texas; Bong Shin, Boise State University;

Janet Stern Solomon, Towson State University; and Jonathan P. West, University of Miami.

Though I benefited from their suggestions, I am responsible for any limitations that may remain. I am indebted to the many students who class-tested earlier drafts of the book. Recognition and thanks are offered for the tireless effort of the office staff at the University of the Pacific, including Karen Hope, Barbara Garcia, and Becky Armstrong, who helped with the typing of the manuscript, the fig- ures, and the tables used in the book. I thank my colleagues who provided support and encourage- ment and to express gratitude to the University of the Pacific for a sabbatical that enabled me to complete the project. Lastly, I thank my wife, Can- dace, for her encouragement and patience and our children, whose father was often not available for family activities while writing the book.

N. S. P.

CONTENTS

CHAPTER 3   **The Strategic Management of Public Issues**   49

PART TWO **International Dimensions of Business and Society**   97

CHAPTER 4   **Competitiveness in a Global Marketplace**   99

CHAPTER 5   **Multinational Business-Government Relations**   **125**

PART THREE Ethical and Moral Dimensions of Business   175

CHAPTER 6 Moral Reasoning and Organizational Culture   177

CHAPTER 7   **Ethical Decision Making**   **203**

CHAPTER 9 **Business Social Performance and Social Responsibility**   **255**

PART FOUR **The Legal and Regulatory Environment of Business** 307

CHAPTER 10 **The Public Policy Process and Legal Environment of Business** 309

CHAPTER 11 **Government Regulation of Business**   **331**

CHAPTER 13 **Antitrust Law**   **391**

PART ONE

Business Performance, Social Control, and Strategic Management of Public Issues

CHAPTER 1

Business Social Performance in a Threefold Society

CHAPTER OBJECTIVES

1. Explain the key role that competitiveness and economic performance plays in achieving business social performance.
2. Show why legitimacy and political performance are important for business.
3. Introduce the basic approaches to ethical decision making for social performance.
4. Define three orientations business can have in developing responses to social issues.
5. Discuss the threefold society with interrelations among business, government, and culture.
6. Outline three key virtues needed for a civilized society.

Introductory Case _____

The Poletown Case

During the early 1980s, the unemployment rate in Detroit was very high. Automobile manufacturers who were major employers in Detroit faced stiff

SOURCE: Case adapted from John J. Bukowczyk, "The Decline and Fall of a Detroit Neighborhood," *Washington and Lee Law Review* 41 (1984); Joseph Auerbach, "The Poletown Dilemma," *Harvard Business Review* (May-June 1985): 93–99 and several issues of the Detroit newspapers including *Detroit News,* September 16, 1986; *Detroit Free Press,* September 23, 1984; March 18, 1985; September 28, 1986; and December 4, 1986; and *Wall Street Journal,* March 13, 1986, p. 1.

international competition. Their manufacturing plants were old and outmoded; their production costs were high; and their models were in need of redesign. The quality of life in Detroit was suffering because of the city's inability to maintain social services and because unemployment had reduced the standard of living. If more businesses moved out of Detroit, unemployment would increase from its already high levels and the city government would have even more difficulty financing required city services. However, making room for manufacturing plants might displace neighborhoods, and painful disruption would be the result.

General Motors' Needs

General Motors had reported its largest financial loss in its history, as was the pattern for other major U.S. automobile manufacturers. Keeping costs down and successfully meeting foreign competition was vital to the company's future. This required the closing of two obsolete plants in Detroit and implementing plans to construct a new, efficiently designed plant somewhere in the United States. This efficient, "new generation" automobile plant would accommodate the new technologies and designs for the automobiles of the 1980s. GM considered a "greenfield" site that required a standardized facility plan and no demolition or clearing of the land to be the most cost-effective for future assembly plants. GM managers calculated that the new plant would require 3 million square feet on a cleared site of nearly 500 acres, with access to freeways and railroads to enhance efficiency in manufacturing and logistics. It appeared that the most economical decision would be to move the Cadillac and Fisher Body operations from Detroit to a greenfield site in another part of the country.

The Problems of the City Government of Detroit

Removal of the GM operations from the City of Detroit would result in the loss of 6,150 jobs. During the last ten years, Detroit's total land area had remained the same, but the population had declined by nearly 40 percent because of declining economic conditions. The unemployment rate was 18 percent in Detroit (30 percent among African Americans). Demand on city government to provide services such as police, fire protection, sewage, street repairs, and social assistance pro-

grams were unchanged despite rapidly declining revenues from real estate and income taxes. Detroit could not afford to lose more jobs. Mr. Coleman Young, the mayor of Detroit, asked the automobile manufacturers and other businesses to provide information in advance about plant location and relocation needs so that appropriate locations could be found within the city.

Actively competing with other cities, Detroit was prepared to offer businesses various incentives to stay. These incentives included reduced taxes, a commitment to use the law of imminent domain to condemn property if necessary so that a greenfield site could be made available within the city limits. Such a site would resemble the green fields available in the Southern states that allowed efficient plants to be constructed at low cost with sufficient space to accommodate future expansion.

Poletown

The site for the new GM plant chosen by the City of Detroit was a neighborhood historically settled by people of Polish descent and was known as Poletown. This area had several schools, churches, a hospital, and businesses. Many families had lived there for several generations, and its residents had provided workers for the Chrysler plant, which had recently closed. Condemning property in Poletown for the public policy of keeping jobs in Detroit helped the overall situation in the city but resulted in the displacement of some 3,500 persons and destruction of 1,176 houses to make room for the new GM plant. The property was professionally appraised and the owners were compensated for their losses. Over 80 percent of the people willingly sold their homes and moved, but the others were forced to comply with the decision through the law of imminent domain. Psychological turmoil and the deterioration of ethnic identity resulted from the city's decision.

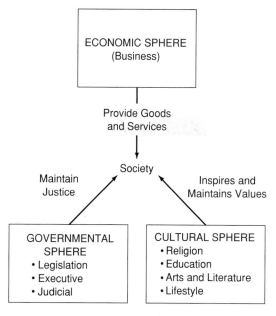

FIGURE 1–1 The Threefold Society

Business, Government, and Culture

The Poletown case illustrates some of the relationships among business, government, and culture. A major purpose of this book is to explain the relationships among the three spheres of society: the economic sphere, the political-governmental sphere, and the spiritual-cultural sphere.[1] Each of these spheres has its unique institutions and role within society, as outlined in Figure 1–1. Business is the major institution of the economic sphere and its key role is to provide the goods and services needed to maintain the standard of living within society. In a market-oriented society, businesses compete with one another to satisfy the needs and demands of customers.

The key role of government is to maintain justice within society and protect the rights of citizens by creating and enforcing laws that regulate business and cultural activities. The United States is a pluralistic society in which many interest groups compete for the popular support needed to influ-

ence public policy. Public debates are a central part of the public policy process that culminates in the passage of laws and regulations. Through this process, individual rights become legally defined before they can be protected by the government through the rule of law. The government also provides services in areas where public policy determines that competitive market forces would not be appropriate. For example, the government provides a public highway system, public safety, national defense, and various social programs that assure legally sanctioned entitlements to citizens.

The cultural sphere includes the institutions of religion, education, the arts, and many interest group organizations that sponsor lifestyles, values, or social causes. Cultural institutions provide the wellspring of the intellectual and artistic life needed for civilization and are the custodian of values within society. The task of this spiritual-cultural sphere is to inspire and legitimize values that guide the public policy process in the political sphere and are expressed as market demands in the economic sphere. Also culture defines norms of behavior within the social institutions of the other two spheres.

IDEALS, VIRTUES, AND RIGHTS IN A GOOD SOCIETY

Ideally our understanding of the role of business in society should be based on some idea of what a "good society" should be. Certain historical ideals guide every society. The purpose of this section is to briefly outline some of these ideals and explain how they form a part of the framework for understanding the threefold social order. Table 1–1 shows how the ideals of liberty, equality, and fraternity and the rights of life, liberty, and the pursuit of happiness relate to the three spheres within society.

Ideals of Liberty, Equality, and Fraternity

In European history, the key ideals for civilization arising out of the French Revolution were liberty, equality, and fraternity. *Liberty* was sought in France so that neither the established church nor the monarchy could arbitrarily constrain cultural freedom. *Political equality* was needed to protect individual rights so members of the privileged classes did not receive preferential treatment before the law. *Fraternity* was needed in an ideal society because individuals share a kinship with one another based on the common experience of the human condition.

Because of the commonly experienced interdependence within modern society, we share a certain kinship or fraternity. When we need a coat in winter, we go to the nearby store or shopping cen-

TABLE 1–1
Ideals, Virtues, and Rights in the Threefold Society

	Economic– Business Sphere	Political– Governmental Sphere	Spiritual– Cultural Sphere
Principal Role	• Produce goods and services • Provide for material welfare	• Maintain justice • Protect rights • Establish public policy	• Maintain culture • Guard values • Inspire and legitimize social institutions
Guiding Ideal	Fraternity in mutual service	Equality before the law	Cultural Freedom
Key Virtue	Prudent exchange	Required justice	Freely given beneficence
Central Right	Pursuit of happiness	Life	Liberty

SOURCE: Adapted from Rudolf Steiner, *The Threefold Social Order* (New York: Anthroposophic Press, 1966); Adam Smith, *The Theory of Moral Sentiments* (Indianapolis: Liberty Classics, 1976), based on the 1853 edition; and the Declaration of Independence.

ter and buy one. The coat may be manufactured in Korea with cloth made in Hong Kong and buttons from Japan. It is shipped to the United States on a Greek-owned ship and delivered to an American retail store. When we buy an automobile, we might consider an American brand with an engine produced in Japan and a transmission manufactured in Germany and assembled in the United States.

Human potential can be best realized when individuals were free to think, to express themselves, and to follow their chosen values. These three ideals of fraternity in mutual service, political equality before the law, and cultural freedom capture the core rights needed by the threefold social order. These rights are more likely to be realized when certain human ideals are honored.

Human Rights Established by the Declaration of Independence

The American Revolutionary War was launched in 1776 with the Declaration of Independence, which was premised on the belief that people had inalienable rights. These rights were life, liberty, and the pursuit of happiness. The *pursuit of happiness* is made possible by the effective operation of a market system in the context of economic and cultural freedom.[2] Life is protected by a government that maintains justice, protects rights necessary for life, and provides for the safety of its citizens. Liberty affords the opportunity to engage in intellectual and spiritual activity needed to develop and sustain the values, ideals, and knowledge needed for the advancement of society.

Social Virtues of Prudence, Justice, and Beneficence

These ideals of the French Revolution and the rights asserted in the American Declaration of Independence parallel the virtues of prudence, justice, and beneficence suggested in 1759 by Adam Smith as the basis for a good society.[3] Smith, considered by many to be the father of modern capitalism, argued that prudent exchanges based on individual self-interest would lead to greater wealth and higher living standards within society.

Government was needed to protect the rights of individuals, including businesses, so that self-interested behavior in market exchanges would not lead to undesirable consequences. However, beneficence, that is, behavior that transcends self-interest, in caring for the needs of others was needed for a worthy civilization.

The Economic Sphere

Business is the major social institution in the economic sphere. Its primary task is to provide goods and services to society. In a *market system*, these goods and services are freely exchanged within a competitive environment of buyers and sellers.[4] Under competitive conditions, exchanges are likely to occur voluntarily only if they benefit both parties. Successful businesses earn profits for their services and buyers are able to satisfy their needs and wants. Markets are needed to satisfy needs under the conditions of interdependence in technologically advanced societies. However, the guiding principle of market interdependence should be service based on fraternity. The central role of business is to serve customers. Industries are created when businesses serve the expressed needs of customers in the marketplace, and businesses thereby receive profits as a natural reward for service.

The place of profit in the market system has long been debated. Some argue that the primary goal or responsibility of business is to make profits.[5] Others point out that while profit maximization may not be the primary goal of business, profits are a prerequisite for sustaining or increasing a business's ability to provide future goods and services for society. Also, profits are a just reward to those who invest in business and an incentive for stockholders to continue fulfilling this important social role.[6] However, we argue that profits should come as a result of successfully satisfying market demands by satisfying customers. When profits are placed first in the minds of managers, the focus on the customer is blurred and market performance declines.

James O'Toole has criticized "old guard" businesses whose goal is profit maximization. He

BOX 1–1 On Adam Smith: The Good Society Has a Balance of Three Virtues

Three virtues should be balanced in a good society: prudence, justice, and beneficence. Prudence is based on the idea of self- interest. In his book *Wealth of Nations,* (originally published in 1776), Adam Smith showed how an economic system based on the virtue of prudent exchange could provide the basis for wealth and a high standard of living. In his earlier book *Theory of Moral Sentiments* (originally published in 1759), Smith outlined a sequence for the development of morality. A person begins with self-interest and in pursuing it, it is not long before he or she conflicts with the interests of others. To balance the interests of everyone, governments are formed to enforce legal systems of justice. For Smith, justice meant simply that a person obeyed the law. If a person was unjust, that is, if that person disobeyed the law, then the government could and should force obedience.

Unfortunately, a system based solely on the two virtues of prudence and justice leads to a society characterized by cold, calculating, impersonal exchanges. Such a society is tolerable if it has a high living standard, but it can scarcely be called a civilization. The quality of life is likely to be poor because the society is mean-spirited and without art and culture. To obtain a civilized society, another virtue is needed. According to Smith's developmental sequence, once a person gets to know others, a moral sentiment based on love appears. This love is first felt for oneself in the form of prudence. Then love is felt for one's kin, and later this warm sentiment is felt for others within the society.

Beneficence, unlike justice, cannot be forced; it can only be given freely. Thus a good society is based on three equally balanced virtues: prudent exchanges, enforced justice, and freely given beneficence. A society short of any of these virtues is unlikely to be a good society. Insufficient prudence leads to bankruptcy and poverty. Insufficient justice leads to violation of each other's rights as everyone tries to "prudently" beggar his or her neighbor and also to some citizens harming others. A lack of beneficence yields a cold, calculating, impersonal society based on mercenary exchanges among selfish individuals.

---

pointed out that focus on profit as a goal can distract from the real goal of providing goods and services to customers.[7] Similarly, excellent companies have been found to be those that stay close to their customers by anticipating and responding to their needs through committed service.[8] Thus high performing and competitive firms usually do not have profits as their primary goal. Rather, excellent businesses tend to stress satisfying the real needs of their customers expressed as market demand. Firms that stress the goal of profits in the absence of a commitment to service are usually less profitable. Those that focus on customers' needs first and let the rewards follow naturally from a job well done are more likely to achieve high levels of long-term economic performance.

Business Social Performance

The four dimensions of business social performance are concerned with four questions:

Economic Performance:	What is competitive?
	What works?
Ethical Performance:	What is right?
Legal Performance:	What is legal?
Political Performance:	What is politically wise?

Each of these questions is basic to understanding the social performance of business in a society. The answers to these questions draw on a number of disciplines including economics, ethics, law, and politics. While the economic responsibility of business is of paramount importance, effective managers need to fulfill their economic role within the context of competing demands. This book is about those demands and seeks to provide a framework for practicing managers and business students that will enable them to achieve effective social performance.

These concepts are a major part of the business social performance model developed in this chapter. *Organizational effectiveness* involves the developing and achieving of organizational goals for high performance on these four dimensions. An organization can sometimes increase its profits by violating the law or by unethical behavior, or by disregarding the values and concerns of the society. However, such behavior is shortsighted and is likely to lead to low levels of organizational effectiveness. For example, management within E. F. Hutton was able to achieve high levels of performance in the financial services industry through an illegal check kiting scheme. Key managers within the investment banking firm Drexel, Burnham, Lambert were able to reap substantial benefits through insider trading but eventually paid a $650 million fine and lost credibility with important clients in the banking industry. Their competitive position slipped from around 70 percent market share to bankruptcy.

Organizational effectiveness therefore requires high performance in its economic activity as well as in ethical behavior, compliance with laws and regulations, and maintaining social and political support within the society. Answering the four basic questions posed by these dimensions of social performance is somewhat complex and takes considerable skill. The answers are not always clear; some alternatives developed by managers will score high on some dimensions but unacceptably low in others. The high-performing manager needs to grapple with all four dimensions and strive to find imaginative approaches that integrate the requirements of all these dimensions while fulfilling the mission of the organization.

The key concepts of business social performance include competitiveness, responsibility, legality, and legitimacy.[9] These concepts parallel the four questions outlined above. Economic performance requires competitiveness; ethical performance requires responsibility in seeking to do what is right; legality requires compliance with the laws and regulations that apply to the business situation; and legitimacy requires sensitivity to the political context of the situation so that the political and social support necessary for a favorable business climate can be maintained.

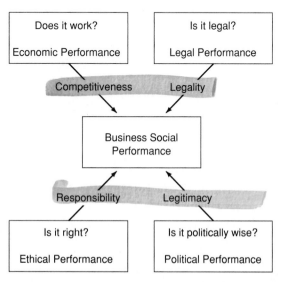

FIGURE 1–2 Key Concepts of Social Performance

ECONOMIC PERFORMANCE AND COMPETITIVE STRATEGIES

Competitiveness is concerned with the economic or market performance of an enterprise relative to other firms within the industry. It is concerned with the question, What works? The key concept in economics is rationality. *Rationality* is a way of thinking, usually described as instrumental. Decision makers rationally choose means perceived as the most likely to lead to their goals. A goal could relate to the technical implementation of a competitive strategy; it could relate to the administrative approaches to organizing; or a goal might relate to the way an organization is governed.[10]

Competitive strategy of a business can be based on low costs and low prices, differentiation of products, or focusing on a well-defined customer group.[11] Competitive pricing is usually based on some cost advantage or the *efficiency* of an organization. Efficiency is a term from the disciplines of economics and engineering and is defined as the ratio of outputs to inputs:

$$\text{Efficiency} = \frac{\text{Outputs}}{\text{Inputs}}$$

Low-cost Strategy

Outputs could be profits and inputs the investment in plant and equipment in the business. Output could be a unit produced by an organization while input could be the amount of material or the cost of labor used to produce that unit. Businesses produce goods or services and require various inputs to produce them. The more efficient an organization, the lower its cost per unit. Thus the more efficient an organization, the greater will be the ratio of outputs, however measured, to the inputs used in the production of the good or service by the organization. A business that is more efficient than its competitors is likely also to have *lower costs* that enable it to compete on the basis of lower prices.

However, there is more to competitiveness than keeping costs down so that lower prices than those of competitors can be charged. Customer satisfaction can be missed by too much attention to efficiency if this means lower quality and service. Customers who purchase automobiles are often very sensitive to the quality of the car, to the technical performance, to the styling, and to any of a number of features that suit the particular tastes of the purchaser.

Differentiation Strategy

Differentiation is a unique feature or characteristic that makes a business's product or service more desirable to the customer and a basis for sustainable competitive advantage. Thus, competition is also based on differentiation that customers use as a criterion other than price to select a good or service over alternatives. For example, European luxury automobiles are sold in the United States at relatively high prices but are preferred because of their styling and engineering. Automobiles like the Mercedes Benz are sought because of their perceived ability to confer social status.

Focus Strategy

A business can also *focus* on a particular group of buyers or target market. This targeted market may be users of a specialized product line within a specific geographic region that the competitive form is particularly able to serve. For example, a manufacturing firm in California produces electronic devices tailored to the needs of the handicapped. They market a camera that can transmit electronic impulses to a user, which enables a blind person to sense distant objects. In this case the basis of focus is on both a particular group of buyers and their specialized product needs. Another example of using a focus strategy as the basis of competition is Zenith, which produces laptop microcomputers for traveling businesspeople.

ETHICAL RESPONSIBILITY

The second major dimension of business social performance is *responsibility,* which is concerned with the ethical performance of an enterprise. It relates to the questions What is right? and What is good? Businesses are faced with many nonmarket demands that are often contradictory. For example, John Zaccaro, husband of the 1984 vice presidential candidate Geraldine A. Ferraro, was the manager of a trust fund. As such he was responsible for managing the fund on behalf of an elderly woman. He invested some money in one of his own business projects because it seemed secure and offered more return than alternative financial opportunities. However, a court found this to be a conflict of interests and a breach of professional ethics, and therefore illegal.[12]

As the example above suggests, what is right or good may not always be clear. Different persons can reach different conclusions when responding to similar situations. The purpose of ethical analysis in business is to improve the ethical behavior and therefore the responsibility of the practicing manager. The point is not to find the *one* right answer that is ethical. Rather, the point is to improve problem-solving skills of developing and considering alternatives that are ethically acceptable. Ethically acceptable alternatives would avoid the pitfall of conflicts of interest, violating another person's rights, and would need to be fair to those affected by the decision.

Ethical people often disagree with one another about specific issues, but such disagreement need not point toward the perceived futility of ethical analysis. Ethical analysis can eliminate unethical alternatives, sensitize managers to ethical pitfalls that could be anticipated and avoided, and provide a basis for identifying the most ethical alternative from among a list of alternatives that are acceptable on economic, legal, and political grounds. It is sometimes said that a really good manager can usually find at least three ways to accomplish something. Ethical analysis can help to encourage the manager to go further to find ethically acceptable alternatives or to select the most ethical option from a set of possibilities.

Ethical analysis is concerned with the process of making judgments about the moral correctness of a decision. There are many different approaches to ethics, including utilitarian, rights and duties, and justice.

Utilitarian analysis focuses on the value of the consequences or outcomes of a decision.[13] According to this approach, a decision is ethical if the results yield the greatest happiness to society. In business decisions, utilitarianism takes the form of cost-benefit analysis. This application of utilitarianism accepts alternatives as ethical if the ratio of costs to benefits is negative.[14] Business managers begin with this approach to ethics because they are normally concerned with reducing costs of operations or with improving profitability. Analysis of the economic consequences of a decision or policy closely parallels utilitarian approaches to ethics. If something is not economically worthwhile, then a manager is likely to consider it as unethical on the basis of utilitarian reasoning.

Other approaches to ethical analysis are concerned with whether an action is inherently right or wrong regardless of the results. For example some would argue that it is wrong to tell a lie even if lying appeared to have beneficial results.[15] In contrast, a manager considering only consequences might tell a person going into a job interview that he or she looks "great" even if that did not seem to be true. A person might justify a lie in this case because of the positive effect a word of encouragement might have on the applicant. Others may argue that it is never ethical to be untruthful.

Rights and Duties

A second approach to ethical analysis focuses on the *rights* of those involved. Rights are moral or legal entitlement such as a property right or the right of self-expression. According to this approach it is inherently unethical to violate the rights of another.[16] However, many rights are debatable, and sometimes one right contradicts other rights, as would be the case in the debate between pro-choice and pro-life advocates in the controversy over abortion.

Typically rights are counterbalanced by duties. A *duty* is a legal or moral responsibility to honor the rights of another person. As an employee of an organization, a person has a duty to work to achieve the purposes of the organization. It can be argued that one has a moral duty to tell the truth, to keep confidences, and to avoid harming others.[17] As in the case of rights, some duties are also debatable, and sometimes one duty contradicts another.

For example, should you keep a secret of a fellow employee even if it seems not to be in the best interests of your employer? A fellow employee secretly looking for other job opportunities may be offered a promotion that would not have been offered had the employer known of planned career changes. Would you have a duty to inform your boss? Would you have a greater duty to keep a secret given in trust and confidence by a fellow employee?

Economic justice is concerned with the fairness with which benefits and burdens like these are distributed within a society or among organizational stakeholders. *Stakeholders* are those who are affected by a decision or action made by managers within an organization. They include everyone who has a stake in the outcome of organizational activity. Thus stockholders, employees, managers, customers, suppliers, residents in the communities surrounding facilities, and others affected by the consequences of managerial decisions could all be considered stakeholders of the organization.

Are the consequences of the business activities received by persons inside and outside business organizations fair? The utilization of a new technology may put many people out of work while increasing the appeal of a company's product. A top manager in the United States may receive, on average, 100 times the earnings of the lowest-level employee. In Japan the highest-paid manager receives, on average, around 20 times the earnings of the lowest-level employee. On what basis are earnings differences justified?

The sale of a dangerous product like pesticides in the Third World might have such benefits as improved agricultural productivity and increased profits for the company and stockholder wealth, but it may adversely affect the health of farm workers, food processors, and consumers. The questions posed by utilitarian analysis, rights and duties, and economic justice are all matters of ethical analysis. The responsible manager seeks to make decisions that can be considered both ethical and economically competitive.

LEGALITY

Legality is defined as compliance with the laws and regulations of society. Businesses must comply with the laws passed at the local, state, and federal levels. Managers must also obey international treaties and comply with the laws of the countries in which they do business. It is assumed here that social performance requires obeying the law of the land.

Legal performance also requires that organizations be aware of regulations developed by such federal agencies as the Environmental Protection Agency (EPA), the Food and Drug Administration (FDA), the Equal Employment Opportunity Commission (EEOC), the Consumer Products Safety Commission (CPSC), the Occupational Safety and Health Administration (OSHA), the Internal Revenue Service (IRS), and many others. Much of the legal environment of business is concerned with the administrative law of various regulatory agencies that seek to control certain aspects of business behavior.

For example, an automobile repair shop owner needs to be aware of the EPA standards and requirements for disposal of paint thinner and solvents considered to be toxic wastes. A contractor needs to know how to follow nondiscriminatory employment practices regulated by the EEOC. A manager needs to know what records should be maintained for the IRS for tax purposes. Managers in a chemical company need to design their factory with proper ventilation so the workplace is safe for employees, as required by OSHA.

It could be argued that many of these things should be done because they are the ethical thing to do. However, society does not believe that all managers operating in a highly competitive environment will behave ethically, and so the government has a role in providing guidance in certain areas. Thus, the legal and regulatory environment is an important aspect of the business in society relationships and is a third major aspect of business social performance.

POLITICAL PERFORMANCE AND LEGITIMACY

Legitimacy is relevant social and political support for business as an institution and for a particular industry or business. Legitimacy is fundamentally a *political*, rather than a legal, concept. Through the political process, support is mobilized for a particular value or social policy. Business has the authority to operate within the confines of the law and regulatory system. If the public feels that business is acting irresponsibly, the political and social support for business in general or for a particular practice declines. This can set in motion a political process yielding a public policy or law that constrains business behavior.

For example, at one time it was not illegal to dump waste into rivers. As many businesses used the waterways to dispose of waste, environmental degradation resulted. Public awareness followed by concerned political activities led to the passage of laws and the creation of the Environmental Protection Agency within the federal government to regulate business behavior in this area. In contrast, public accounting practices are regulated by an independent private governing board formed by certified public accounting firms. The public is willing to allow the accounting industry to engage in self-regulation through its industry association because the industry has maintained its legitimacy and is perceived as responsible by society.

Institutional Orientation and Business Social Performance

Institutional orientation is the pattern of interaction between business and its environment. According to Sethi's framework outlined in Table 1–2, this capacity includes the perceptions of managers about the legitimate role of business in society. Institutional orientation also includes the operating strategy of the business, business responses to social pressures and changing social expectations, corporate political activities and governmental actions, and philanthropy.

The *institutional orientation* of a business is the pattern of responsiveness to (external legal, political, ethical, and economic) issues facing the organization. Sethi has developed a framework shown in Table 1–2 for classifying corporate behavior that can be useful in understanding three types of institutional orientation. Type-one organizations, called defensive and reactive, seek to maximize

profits within the boundary defined by law. Litigation is likely to be used as a tactic to delay implementation of new regulatory requirements or to avoid compliance with new laws considered unfavorable to the organization. Type-two organizations anticipate social change and seek to be socially responsible. This type of business seeks to include both economic and ethical considerations in defining what is required to be a good corporate citizen. Type-three organizations are characterized as proactive and responsive. Managers in these type of organizations seek to achieve economic performance and are sensitive to actions that might adversely affect their political legitimacy.

TYPE ONE: DEFENSIVE AND REACTIVE

A type-one institutional orientation can be described as defensive and reactive. Managers with this response pattern believe that legitimate actions are narrowly confined to their economic role within the limits set by the law. They may seek to maximize profits even if it means they should be exploitive and use litigation to delay the enforcement of laws and regulation that seek to protect the public. The social performance approach used by type-one managers is likely to emphasize the economic dimension, to comply minimally with the law, to ignore ethical considerations, and to be insensitive to political issues that influence their business.

A case illustrating a type-one institutional orientation concerns a door fabrication business in the Los Angeles area. This company had been in business for around 20 years and had annual sales of around $15 million. The owner, Jack Nelson, had started the business after leaving the armed forces. He began by making kitchen cabinets in his garage and later was able to buy half a block near a residential area in south Los Angeles. He decided to specialize in making doors and moved his business into a metal warehouse constructed on his property. Initially most of the property was used to store materials and for employee parking.

Because of his skill and response to the needs of the marketplace, his company quickly grew to over $1 million in sales per month. Construction com-

TABLE 1–2
A Three-Type Schema for Classifying Institutional Behavior

Dimensions of Behavior	Type One: Defensive & Reactive	Type Two: Anticipatory and Socially Responsible	Type Three: Proactive and Politically Responsive
Search for Legitimacy	Confines legitimacy to legal and economic criteria only; does not violate laws; equates profitable operations with fulfilling social expectations.	Accepts the reality of limited relevance of legal and manual criteria of legitimacy in actual practice. Willing to consider and accept broader—extralegal and extramarket—criteria for measuring corporate performance and social role.	Accepts its role as defined by the social system and therefore subject to change; recognizes importance to profitable operations but includes other criteria.
Ethical Norms	Considers business value managers expected to behave according to their own ethical standards.	Defines norms in community relaxed terms, i.e., good corporate citizen. Avoids taking moral stand on issues which may harm its economic interests or go against prevailing social norms (majority views).	Takes definite stand on issues of public concern; advocates institutional ethical norms even though they may seem detrimental to its immediate economic interest or prevailing social norms.
Social Accountability for Corporate Actions	Construes narrowly as limited to stockholders; jealously guards its prerogatives against outsiders.	Individual managers responsible not only for their own ethical standards but also for the collectivity of the corporation. Construed narrowly for legal purposes, but broadened to include groups affected by its actions; management more outward-looking.	Willing to account for its actions to other groups, even those not directly affected by its actions.

Dimensions of Behavior	Type One: Defensive & Reactive	Type Two: Anticipatory and Socially Responsible	Type Three: Proactive and Politically Responsive
Operating Strategy	Exploitative and defensive adaptation. Maximum externalization of costs.	Reactive adaptation. Where identifiable, internalizes previously external costs. Maintains current standards of physical and social environment. Compensates victims of pollution and other corporate-related activities even in the absence of clearly established legal grounds. Develops industrywide standards.	Proactive adaptation. Takes lead in overcoming and adapting new technology for environmental protectors. Evaluates side effects of corporate actions and eliminates them prior to the action being taken. Anticipates future social changes and develops internal structures to cope with them.
Response to Social Pressures	Maintain low public profile, but, if attacked, uses PR methods to upgrade its public satisfaction on ignorance or failure to understand corporate functions; discloses information only where legally required.	Accepts responsibility for solving current problems; admits deficiencies in former public that its current practices meet social norms: attitude toward critics conciliatory; freer information disclosures than state one.	Willingly discusses activities with outside groups; makes information freely available to public; accepts formal and informal inputs from outside groups in decision making; is willing to be publicly evaluated for its various activities.
Activities Pertaining to Governmental Actions	Strongly resists any regulation of its activities except when it needs help to protect its market position; avoids contact; resists any demands for information beyond that legally required.	Preserves management discretion in corporate decisions, but cooperates with government in research to improve industrywide standards; participates in political processes and encourages employees to do likewise.	Openly communicates with government; assists in enforcing existing laws and overcoming evaluations of business practices; objects publicly to governmental activities that it feels are detrimental to the public good.

TABLE 1–2   (CONTINUED)

Dimensions of Behavior	Type One: Defensive & Reactive	Type Two: Anticipatory and Socially Responsible	Type Three: Proactive and Politically Responsive
Legislative and Political Activities	Seeks to maintain status quo; actively opposes law that would internalize any previously externalized costs; seeks to keep lobbying activities secret.	Willing to work with outside groups for good environmental laws; concedes need for change in some existing laws; less secrecy in lobbying than state one.	Avoids meddling in politics and does not pursue special interest laws; assists legislative lobbies in developing better laws where relevant; promotes honesty and openness in government and in its own lobbying activities.
Philanthropy	Contributes only when direct benefit to it clearly shown: otherwise, views contributions as responsibility of individual employees.	Contributes to non-controversial and established causes; matches employee contributions.	Activities of state two, plus support and contributions to new, controversial groups whose needs it sees as unfilled and increasingly important.

SOURCE: Adapted from S. Prakash Sethi, "A Conceptual Framework for Environmental Analysis of Social Issues and Evaluation of Business Response Patterns," *Academy of Management Review* 4 (1979): 67–68.

panies would give him any dimension of door, in any quantity, from the standardized styles in his catalog and he could fabricate and ship the order anywhere in California and Oregon within two weeks. This differentiation strategy implemented through attention to high quality, competitive prices, and reliable delivery times was significantly better than that of any other competitor in this particular business.

As Nelson's success continued, he hired a few more people and built another building. His employees began to park on the street. This process continued until his sales reached the $15 million level, his employees numbered over 300, and work was done in five buildings that covered most of his property, leaving little room for parking. His neighbors began to complain. Their lawns were covered with sawdust and there was little

parking space on the streets of the neighborhood. A complaint was filed with local environmental officials. In response to this complaint, Nelson installed a filtering system to trap the sawdust. However, the strong smell of sawdust continued for miles around the factory. Complaints began to increase from neighbors that they were tired of his employees blocking their driveways. Traffic congestion increased, and parking grew even scarcer as the business grew.

The city planners and council informed him he was violating the city codes concerning required off-street parking space. Nelson instructed his lawyer to petition the city to grant a one-year extension of enforcing the parking requirement. The city officials approved the delay. Business continued as usual for another year. A year later Nelson petitioned the city for another one-year extension, indicating he had been unable to resolve the problem but that action was underway to find suitable parking spaces. A second extension was approved and another year passed with more rapid growth in the business but no action taken to find more off-street parking facilities or to relocate the business to a more suitable area.

At the end of the third year Nelson again directed his attorney to petition the city for another one-year extension. By this time the residents in the surrounding area were complaining loudly and the matter had become a local political controversy. When the third request for delay was received, city officials were dismayed and angry. They gave Nelson 60 days to comply with the law or close his business.

Nelson urgently began to search for available alternative building sites. He bought one in another city and had a building remodeled at a very high price under emergency conditions. Most of his employees didn't have transportation and could not transfer to the new plant location. Only 50 percent of his employees remained, and he had to replace and train half his workforce. In the meantime, during all the transforming, moving from one facility to another, he was behind schedule on deliveries, and quality declined momentarily while he was doing the substantial task of hiring and training new employees.

Six to eight months later, after paying a relatively high price for the new building, he was relocated in another town and his business was doing well. This is an example of a successful small business person responding well economically to the market but operating as type one in terms of institutional orientation, as outlined in Table 1–2.

TYPE TWO: ANTICIPATORY
AND SOCIALLY RESPONSIBLE

The Jack Nelson Company could have responded differently. A type-two response would have been to accept a broader concept of social responsibility, anticipate changing social expectations, and make planned changes in the operations. This business

took over ten years to grow from a small new enterprise start-up to 300 employees, and from one metal building to five buildings. The history of complaints from the neighbors didn't happen all at once but started about six years before his ultimate move and were increasing in number and anger every year. What could Nelson have done if he had realized how he was affecting his local community's quality of life by responding to economic development and population growth with a superior product? With watchful anticipation, Nelson might have realized that his facility needs could have been accommodated with economic success.

If Nelson had demonstrated a type-two institutional orientation, he would have anticipated changes and made plans to adapt to the changing conditions in his environment. He could have gone to the city managers before there were many complaints. He might have retained a real estate agent to search for other available sites; he could have engaged in negotiations with industrial parks for either a long-term lease or purchase of an adequate facility with an acceptable location.

He could have avoided many difficulties simply by understanding what was going on: by accepting nonmarket expectations as an aspect of social performance; by considering the declining local support for his industrial activity in a residential area; by planning for his growth needs for facilities in an expanding market; and by incorporating those requirements into the plan. The key to a type-two institutional orientation is to anticipate change and then to respond to this change in a planned way.

A business using a type-two institutional orientation in Table 1–2 can be described as anticipatory and responsible in its social response. The economic role continues to be important for the business, but responsibility for a broader social role is accepted by managers. They wish the business to be viewed as a good corporate citizen. Social or community norms and ethical considerations are more likely to influence decisions as they seek to fulfill the economic role of the business. Rather than actively resisting social trends and implementation of laws, managers using a type-two response pattern are more likely to incorporate anticipated legal requirements into their corporate planning process.

Another example of a type-two response to changing social expectations is Pepperidge Farm, a subsidiary of the Campbell Soup Company. Several years ago, Mr. G. Robert McGovern, who was president of Pepperidge Farm, made a presentation to a university class. He discussed social changes and how Pepperidge Farm was responding to its changing environment. He was commenting that over 50 percent of the employees at Pepperidge Farm were women when a woman in the audience asked, "How many women executives do you have?" He said that was a very good question but that there were no women executives at that time. He added that there were two very firm policies within Pepperidge Farm. The first was that only qualified persons were promoted to top levels, and the second was that Pepperidge Farm promoted only from within the company.

Promotion was viewed within Campbell Soup as a key element in motivating employees because it encouraged self-development. The internal promotion philosophy was embraced by the company because performance is better when employees learn the company from the bottom up and are highly motivated. If employees know that only competent people are promoted to the top of the organization, the system will be perceived as fair, it will be motivational, and it will increase the competitiveness of the organization.

The requirements for affirmative action programs and antidiscrimination litigation were gaining momentum. Pepperidge Farm was a defense contractor because it sold a substantial number of cookies and bakery products to the United States armed services each year. Company analysts predicted that it would be unlikely that Pepperidge Farm would lose any major contracts for at least five years because of its top management employment profile. This meant that the company probably had five years to work on this social issue. To maintain its policy of promotion from within based on merit, Pepperidge Farm developed an approach to human resource development to (1) recruit and develop capable women and minorities through

careful selection and (2) make job assignments that involved rapid transfers to quickly build the breadth of experience necessary for upper-management responsibilities.

The type-two institutional orientation of the company resulted in a strategic plan that followed the policies of merit and internal promotion while insuring that positions of higher-level management would be available to these groups within five years. The company did not try legal or political activities to change or delay affirmative action laws. Rather, management recognized its responsibility to comply with the law but took advantage of enforcement lead time. The management of this company followed established policies but anticipated and planned for changes and incorporated them in the planning and administrative process.

TYPE THREE: PROACTIVE AND POLITICALLY RESPONSIVE

A type-three institutional orientation begins with management awareness of changing social expectations of business. Competitiveness in its economic tasks continues to be of central importance, and the organization is likely to be sensitive to the implications of environmental changes in all spheres of society for its operations. Management of organizations with type-three institutional orientation are more likely to take a definite position on evolving social and political issues.

Changes are anticipated but management sometimes seeks to be proactive in influencing public policy processes so that the effect of the change on the business will be desirable. Companies with this type of institutional orientation are more likely to engage in political strategy or to interact with the environment as they communicate with the government or community groups to reach mutually agreeable solutions to social issues. Strategic issues management (SIM) becomes a part of the long-range planning process.

In the Jack Nelson case, Nelson could have used a type-three response similar to that of General Motors when he recognized that he was outgrowing his facilities. Because he knew this community in California had a high unemployment rate, he could have recognized that he was an important employer in the area. He could have been more effective in responding to the social and political concerns of the community. Instead of trying to block indefinitely public reaction in the courts to the problems of congestion and sawdust pollution, he could have responded in terms more favorable to his company and to the community. He could have avoided a situation in which he became very angry and relocated his business, saying:

I don't know what's wrong with this town. I employ over 300 people and they need the jobs. And yet they don't care about economic development, and the city treated me really shabbily and I'm glad to be gone.

He could have avoided the crisis and the controversy by going to the city planners and stating:

I really like this city, I like my workers, and they like to work for my business. I've got over 300 people employed and I would really like to stay here. I appreciate your concern about traffic congestion, parking in residential streets, and sawdust. I would like to find a way to be a good citizen while being successful in my business. Given the current city planning policies and regulations, I don't know if I can continue to operate in your city. Would you help me out? I will do what I can to cooperate.

That would have began a public dialogue with the town council. The city planners probably would have attempted to cooperate with the Jack Nelson Company similarly to the way Detroit responded to the employment needs of its citizens and the site needs of a major employer. Instead of ultimatums and eviction notices, cooperative behavior in searching for mutually acceptable alternatives might have been possible if a type-three institutional orientation had been used.

The controversial Poletown case could be interpreted as an example of a type-three response pattern by the City of Detroit. The city government sought to stop the exodus of businesses from Detroit by trying to influence plant location deci-

sions. The City of Detroit negotiated with General Motors and offered incentives that encouraged GM to construct its new manufacturing facility there.[18] GM needed to compete in the highly competitive international automobile market and in its view, competitiveness required a low-cost state-of-the-art assembly plant. It responded to the city's request by providing specifications for such a plant to the mayor of Detroit. GM indicated that if a suitable low-cost sight were not available within the city, the plant would probably relocate.

By letting city officials know their requirements, they enabled Detroit to consider them in making city policy. Because Detroit was competing against other cities and felt that having the plant was in the best interests of its citizens, it was decided to find or make a space for a new GM plant. The neighborhood called Poletown, because its residents were primarily of Polish descent, was cleared as churches, schools, hospitals, and homes were demolished to make room for the new plant. City officials moved quickly to persuade GM to locate its new assembly plant there.

According to Table 1–2, GM's behavior could be considered proactive and responsive. The company anticipated the change and was proactive by making its needs known to the local and regional political environment, and this action ultimately influenced the decisions of the mayor and development officials in Detroit. But GM did not necessarily recognize any responsibility to its stakeholder other than the interests of its shareholders. This suggests a key distinction between a type-two institutional orientation that embraces the ethical concept of *social responsibility* and the type-two orientation that draws on the political concept of *social responsiveness*.

Institutional Orientation and Social Responsibility

In type-one organizations, managers' perceptions of responsibility is limited to the owners of the business. A type-one orientation is likely to emphasize profit maximization, even if externalities detrimental to society are the result. The type-one–oriented manager is likely to suggest that if society does not like the externality, then the government should pass laws against it.

Type-two organizations broaden their concept of accountability to include other stakeholders within society. For example, managers in type-two organizations understand public concerns about the quality of life and accept responsibility for *externalities* like pollution that involve outcomes of business activity external to market transactions. A manager with a type-three orientation may recognize an externality such as water pollution but seek to influence the public policy process so that laws and regulations are passed that are technologically and economically feasible.

The debate over institutional orientation is often argued in terms of social responsibility and discussed along ideological lines.[19] Many writers argue that the interdependent complexity of our modern technological society requires managers to strive to behave ethically and to assume moral responsibility for the consequences of their actions.[20] According to this view, managers should assume moral responsibility for their actions and broaden their activities beyond those required by the competitive market if modern society is to survive.

Other writers such as Sethi suggest that the emphasis on corporate social responsibility as an ethical problem facing management misses an important point. The issue is not ideology nor a matter of ethics; institutional orientation is seen as not primarily one of moral responsibility. Rather, the issue is one of legitimacy and political support. The key to business social performance through institutional orientation is developing and maintaining social and political support for business practices.

According to this view, a business that operates with a type-one institutional orientation, as shown in Table 1–2, is likely to take a defensive and proscriptive approach to public issues. Such a business is likely to be considered irresponsible and exploitative by the public. As a controversy develops, type-one actions lead to a loss of public support for its activities. In contrast, a business with a type-two institutional orientation seeks to act ethically by

anticipating social, political, and legal changes and adapting its plans to include changing operations to coincide with changing public expectations that are considered reasonable. Type-two orientation leads to orderly adaptation, but the required changes may not be influenced by managers who must respond to changing requirements.

The business with a type-three institutional orientation attempts to influence its social-political environment by providing input that can be considered when changing expectations are transformed into laws and regulations. Those organizations with type-two or type-three institutional orientations are more likely to maintain legitimacy for business practices. Such businesses are more likely to (1) obtain the relevant social support leading to (2) favorable laws and regulations so that it can (3) operate in the competitive market. Also firms perceived as ethical are more likely to enjoy public support than those whose managers are widely regarded as dishonest and unethical. The critical factor concerning institutional orientation is the need to be sensitive to the ethical, political, and legal context of management decisions, as well as the economic outcomes of business behavior.

As implied in Table 1–2, legitimacy as a political concept is of central importance in evaluating corporate responsibility or responsiveness. However, the capacity to respond need not be considered as an either-or proposition. *Responsiveness* should include all four dimensions of corporate social performance. The survival and prosperity of business and society is not a question of competitiveness or ethics; it is not a question of morality or political action. Rather, successful businesses must be competitive, incorporate changing legal and regulatory trends into their long-range planning, and make themselves effective as moral, political, and economic agents within society if they are to prosper in the long term.

Strategic Issues Management and Business Social Performance

The third major aspect of business social performance is *strategic issues management* (SIM), the process of identifying important strategic issues, evaluating their potential impact on the business, and formulating a strategic response.[21] Figure 1–3 identifies the various stages in the process beginning with an *environmental assessment* of the legal, social, technological, and competitive trends facing the business. Some trends are more likely to affect a business than others. For example, a trend toward greater social concern about the health problems involved in smoking may greatly affect restaurants that may be required to offer nonsmoking areas to their customers in the future. In contrast, a technological trend in automobile design may have little foreseeable effect on restaurants but were thought to have a major impact on General Motors in the Poletown case. In addition, some developments are more likely than others.

Trends identified in the environmental assessment are analyzed in the context of the organization's *capabilities profile*. Capabilities include the technological, financial, managerial, and political resources available to the business. General Motors needed a technologically modern plant if it was to meet foreign competition. GM management felt they had the financial and managerial capabilities to meet the competition if a new plant were added to their production system. This would require the cooperation of the City of Detroit.

A comparison of the environmental trends and the organizational capabilities enables managers to identify the strategic problems that need attention. *Issue analysis* involves the development and evaluation of available alternatives. In the Poletown case, GM had several alternative plant locations available that would meet the technological and economic needs of the organization. However, action would be required if the cooperation of city and regional governments was to become a reality.

Response development includes the choice of a particular alternative and implementing the strategy selected. Organizations then evaluate the results of the strategic issues management process to determine whether the process should be continued for that issue.

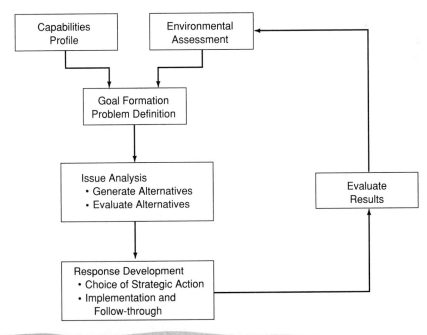

FIGURE 1–3 Strategic Issues Management Process

Summary

The business social performance model includes the performance of an organization that considers (1) the key areas of social performance including economics, ethics, politics, and the law; (2) the institutional orientation of the organization; and (3) the strategic issues management process used within the organization. Each of these dimensions is directed at a different aspect of managing the relationship between business and its environment as suggested by Table 1–3.

Dimensions of Business Social Performance

The key social performance dimensions are economic, ethical, political, and legal. These roles are directed respectively at the roles of business as (1) the primary provider of goods and services, (2) a moral agent within society, the social contract that defines society's moral and legal expectations of business.

Institutional Orientation

The capacity to respond to social expectations as a moral agent and as the provider of goods and services is influenced by the institutional orienta-tion of business. The institutional orientation enables the organization to respond to the social and political issues in a way that yields effective-ness in the key areas of economics, ethics, politics, and the law. The three types of response patterns found in business organizations include (1) reac-tive and defensive, (2) anticipatory and socially responsible, and (3) proactive and politically responsive. These types emphasize, respectively, the economic, the ethical, and the political dimensions of business social performance. Insti-tutional orientation also includes the elements of organization values, executive leadership, and cor-porate culture.

Strategic Issues Management

The third aspect of the business performance model is the strategic issues management (SIM) process used within the organization. SIM includes (1) issues identification, (2) development of a strategy to respond effectively to a crisis situation of public interest, and (3) the implementation and evaluation of the strategy. The SIM process is directed at analysis and planning that minimize surprises. In the earlier case illustrations, Jack Nel-

TABLE 1–3
The Business Social Performance Model

Key Social Performance Dimensions	Institutional Orientation	Strategic Issues Management Process
1. Economic	1. Defensive and reactive	1. Issues identification
2. Legal	2. Anticipative and responsible	2. Issues analysis
3. Ethical	3. Proactive and responsive	3. Response development
4. Political		
Directed at:	Directed at:	Directed at:
1. The social contract of business	1. Response capacity to changing society	1. Minimizing "surprises"
2. Business as a moral agent	2. Maintaining legitimacy	2. Determining effective corporate social policies
3. Business as producers of goods and services	3. Corporate culture	

SOURCE: Adapted from S.L. Wartick and P.L. Cochran, "The Evolution of the Corporate Social Performance Model," *Academy of Management Review* 10 (1985): 767.

son should not have been surprised by the actions of city managers. The planning process at Pepperidge Farm enabled the business to effectively respond to changing social expectations and legal requirements in the area of employment.

Outline of This Book

This book is concerned with business social performance in a threefold society. Thus it is organized around the key dimensions of social performance as shown in Figure 1–2. Economic performance through competitiveness is a basic concept covered in Parts 1 and 2. Chapter 1 covered the basic concepts of the threefold social order including business, government, and society. Also, the basic dimensions of social performance, institutional orientation, and the strategic issues management process are introduced.

The theme of competitiveness extended in Chapter 2 outlines a framework for the analysis of social change and control of business in a market-oriented system. This framework parallels the social performance model but looks at these dimensions from the point of view of society rather than from a manager's perspective. The primary instruments of social control of business parallel the threefold social order and include the economic control by market competition and strategy; the governmental control by laws, regulations, and political process; and the cultural control by social norms and business ethics. The conclusion of the presentation of competitiveness is presented in Part 2, which is concerned with global competitiveness (Chapter 4) and the multinational business-government interrelationship (Chapter 5).

Chapter 3 completes the discussion of business social performance with a discussion of the strategic issues management process. The issues life cycle, a systematic pattern describing the unfolding of public issues, serves as the guiding framework for the strategic issues management process. Also included in this chapter is stakeholder analysis.

Responsibility and Ethical Performance

Part 3 is concerned with the issue of responsibility and ethical performance of business. The four chapters in this part discuss the role of self-regulation through the ethical behavior of management as a major alternative for the social control of business. Chapter 6 is concerned with the role of corporate culture and moral reasoning in responsible organizational behavior. Also considered is the issue of accountability from both a moral and legal perspective. Can an organization be held morally or legally responsible for its actions? When is an individual responsible for the result of an organizational practice? Chapter 7 offers analytical approaches to managers interested in making ethical decisions. Approaches that include (1) utilitarian and cost-benefit analysis and (2) deontological analysis including consideration of competing rights and duties are introduced to enable the reader to develop analytical skills for ethical decision making.

Chapter 8 reviews the basic theories of justice currently being debated within society. These theories are then applied to the management decision process. Chapter 9 reviews the long-standing debate about the proper role of business within society and outlines a model for understanding social responsibility.

Public Policy, Government Regulation, and Regulatory Reform

Part 4 deals with the public policy process and the changing legal environment of business. Chapter 10 reviews the public policy process that creates the legal environment of business. Chapter 11 shows how market failures result in specific regulatory responses developed by society to correct them. These governmental responses include (1) antitrust law, (2) economic regulation of selected industries, and (3) social regulation of business functions such as finance, marketing, production, and human resource management.

Chapter 12 reviews the regulatory failure that has led to the regulatory reform and industry deregulation. Industries that have been deregulated since 1978 include airlines, financial services, telecommunications, and trucking. Chapter 13 is concerned with attempts to restore competition and to prohibit anticompetitive behavior with antitrust law. Enforcement trends, the economic basis of this regulation, and a discussion of the implications for management are a part of this chapter.

Part 5 applies the social performance model to major stakeholder areas. Chapter 14 discusses organizational governance and investor stakeholder issues; Chapter 15 reviews consumer issues; Chapter 16 and 17 discuss employee stakeholder issues, and Chapter 18 considers ecology and the environment.

Discussion Questions

1. What is the primary role of business in a three-fold social order? Does the adoption of different institutional orientations change the fundamental role of business? Explain.
2. What basic rights are considered inherent within a threefold society? How do these rights relate to the three spheres of society?
3. What are the key dimensions in business social performance? What central concept defines performance in each dimension?
4. Read a popular magazine or newspaper and find a current issue facing a business. From the article selected, briefly describe the issue and discuss the actions of business in terms of institutional orientation. Which orientation does the business seem to follow? What is the result in terms of social performance? Is the tone of the article generally supportive or critical of business? Discuss in terms of the information reported about the institutional orientation.
5. What is the difference between legality and legitimacy?
6. What are the key virtues of a good society suggested by Adam Smith? How do these virtues relate to the three spheres of society?

Notes

1. Rudolf Steiner, *The Threefold Social Order* (New York: Anthroposophic Press, 1972).
2. Milton Friedman and Rose Friedman, *Free to Choose* (New York: Avon Books, 1979), and Milton Friedman, *Capitalism and Freedom* (Chicago: University of Chicago Press, 1962).
3. Adam Smith, *The Theory of Moral Sentiments* (Indianapolis: Liberty Press, 1976), originally published in 1759, and Adam Smith, *The Wealth of Nations* (originally published in 1776), ed. Edwin Cannan, 5th ed. (London: Methuen, 1930).
4. Friedman and Friedman, *Free to Choose.*
5. See the classic article by Milton Friedman, "A Friedman Doctrine: The Social Responsibility of Business Is to Increase Its Profits," *New York Times Magazine*, September 13, 1970.
6. Francis W. Steckmest, *Corporate Performance: The Key to Public Trust, with a Resource and Review Committee for the Business Roundtable* (New York: McGraw-Hill, 1982), chap. 4.
7. James O'Toole, *Vanguard Management: Redesigning the Corporate Future* (Garden City, N.Y.: Doubleday, 1985).
8. Thomas J. Peters and Robert H. Waterman, Jr., *In Search of Excellence: Lessons from America's Best-Run Companies* (New York: Harper and Row, 1982).
9. See Edwin M. Epstein and Dow Votow, eds., *Rationality, Legitimacy, and Responsibility: The Search for New Directions in Business and Society* (Santa Monica, Calif.: Goodyear, 1978); Archie B. Carroll, "A Three-Dimensional Conceptual Model of Corporate Performance," *Academy of Management Review* 4, no. 4 (October 1979): 497–505; and Steven L. Wartick and Philip L. Cochran, "The Evolution of the Corporate Social Performance Model," *Academy of Management Review* 10, no. 4. (1985): 758–69.
10. William G. Scott, Terence R. Mitchell, and Newman S. Peery, "Organizational Governance," in *Handbook of Organizational Design*, Vol. 2, ed. Paul C. Nystrom and William H. Starbuck (London: Oxford University Press, 1981), pp. 135–51.
11. Michael Porter, *Competitive Strategy* (New York: Free Press, 1980); and Michael Porter, *Competitive Advantage* (New York: Free Press, 1985).
12. Tom L. Beacheaum and Norman E. Bowie, *Ethical Theory and Business,* 3d ed. (Englewood Cliffs, N.J.: Prentice-Hall, 1988), p. 30.
13. John Stuart Mill, *Utilitarianism* (Indianapolis: Bobbs-Merrill Educational Publishing, 1957).
14. Richard T. DeGeorge, *Business Ethics* (New York: Macmillan, 1982), chap. 3.
15. Sissela Bok, *Lying: Moral Choice in Public and Private Life* (New York: Vintage Books, 1978).
16. Manual Valesquez, *Business Ethics*, 2d ed. (Englewood Cliffs, N.J.: Prentice-Hall, 1988), chap. 2.

17. James F. Smurl, *A Primer in Ethics* (Bristol, Ind.: Wyndham Hall Press, 1985).

18. Joseph Auerbach, "The Poletown Dilemma," *Harvard Business Review* (May-June 1985): 93–99. For readers' reactions see, *Harvard Business Review* (January-February 1986): 185–86.

19. See Part 3 of this book, especially Chapter 9, for a more complete discussion. Also see Thomas M. Jones, "Corporate Social Responsibility Revisited, Redefined," *California Management Review* 22, no. 2 (Spring 1980): 59–67; William C. Frederick, "Free Market vs. Social Responsibility: Decision Time at the CED," *California Management Review* 23, no. 3 (Spring 1981): 20–28.

20. Henry Mintzberg, "The Case for Corporate Social Responsibility," *Journal of Business Strategy* 4 (Fall 1983): 3–15.

21. S. L. Wartick and P. L. Cochran, "The Evolution of the Corporate Social Performance Model," *Academy of Management Review* 19 (1985): 758–69; S. L. Wartick and R. E. Rude, "Issues Management: Corporate Fad or Corporate Function," *California Management Review* 29 (1986): 124–40.

CHAPTER 2

Change and Control of Business in a Market-oriented Society

CHAPTER OBJECTIVES

1. Explain how forces within the market economy, the culture, and the government influence the behavior of business.

2. Describe the necessary conditions required by a competitive market to produce desirable economic performance.

3. Describe how voluntary exchange leads to cooperative behavior and high economic performance in the production of desirable goods and services.

4. Discuss how market failures sometimes lead to socially undesirable results.

5. Show how the three spheres of society interact to control business behavior to achieve goals and fulfill social needs.

6. Discuss the alternative systems of political economy and briefly review current international trends in political economy.

Introductory Case _____

The Story of the Pencil

A delightful story called "I, Pencil: My Family Tree as Told to Leonard E. Read" dramatizes vividly how voluntary exchange enables millions of people to cooperate with one another. Mr. Read, in a voice of the "lead Pencil—the ordinary wooden pencil familiar to all boys and girls and adults who can read and write," starts his story with the fantastic statement, "not a single person. . .knows how to make me." Then he proceeds to tell about all the things that go into making a pencil. First,

the wood comes from a tree, "a cedar of straight grain that grows in Northern California and Oregon." To cut down the tree and cart the logs to the railroad siding requires "saws and trucks and rope and. . .countless other gear." Many persons and numerous skills are involved in their fabrication: in "the mining of ore, the making of steel and its refinement into saws, axes, motors; the growing of hemp and bringing it through all the stages to heavy and strong rope; the logging camps with their beds and mess halls. . .untold thousands of persons had a hand in every cup of coffee the loggers drink!"

And so Mr. Read goes on to the bringing of the logs to the mill, the millwork involved in converting the logs to slats, and the transportation of the slats from California to Wilkes-Barre, where the particular pencil that tells the story was manufactured. And so far we have only the outside wood of the pencil. The "lead" center is not really lead at all. It starts as graphite mined in Sri Lanka. After many complicated processes it ends up as the "lead" in the center of the pencil.

The bit of metal—the ferrule—near the top of the pencil is brass. "Think of all the persons," he says "who mine zinc and copper and those who have the skills to make sheet brass from these products of nature." What we call the eraser is known in the trade as "the plug." It is thought to be rubber. But Mr. Read tells us the rubber is only for binding purposes. The erasing is actually done by "factice," a rubberlike product made by reacting rapeseed oil from the Dutch East Indies (now Indonesia) with sulfur chloride.

After all of this, says the pencil, "does anyone wish to challenge my earlier assertion that no single person on the face of this earth knows how to make me?" None of the thousands of persons involved in producing the pencil performed this task because he or she wanted a pencil. Some among them had never seen a pencil and would not know what it is for. All saw their work as a way to get the goods and services they wanted—goods and services we produced to get the pencil we wanted. Every time we buy a pencil, we are exchanging a little bit of our services for the infinitesimal amount of services that each of the thousands contributed toward producing the pencil.

It is even more astounding that the pencil was ever produced. No one sitting in a central office gave orders to these thousands of workers. No military police enforced the orders that were not given. These people live in many lands, speak different languages, practice different religions, may even hate one another—yet none of these differences prevented them from cooperating to produce a pencil. How did it happen? Adam Smith gave us the answer two hundred years ago.[1]

Introduction

How does society insure that its material needs are provided? How does it encourage business to provide goods and services in a way that is consistent with the goals and values of the society? What is the appropriate role of the cultural and political spheres in ensuring that business fulfills its social tasks? Does the market mechanism itself provide sufficient incentives and controls to insure that business accomplishes its broader social purpose? If not, how can the government ensure that the market forces result in socially desirable outcomes? If market discipline is weak, can industry standards, self-management of business, or business ethics practiced by managers supplement market forces to guide business decision making? These are the central questions of this chapter.

Change and Control Mechanisms in a Threefold Society

Business is the major institution within the economic sphere of society. Its key task is to provide for the needs of society by producing the goods and services desired by the members of society. As discussed in Chapter 1, two other spheres exist within society: the political and the cultural. Each sphere contributes to the control of economic activity in a way that relates to the particular sphere's social function or purpose.[2]

As discussed in Chapter 1, the cultural sphere sustains social values and ideals and provides the context for economic activity. The political sphere protects the rights of owners, sellers, and buyers, and the rights of citizens affected by economic activity. All three spheres fulfill a key social role and interact as subsystems to bring about the goals of society. Cultural and technological changes affect lifestyles and lead to changes in values, to social and political problems, and controversy. Business activities occur within a dynamic environment in which constant changes influence the interrelationships among business, government, and society.

The political sphere includes the government that traditionally provides for national security and public safety, protects the rights of citizens, and provides certain public services. In accomplishing its purpose, institutions within the political sphere interact with those in the cultural and economic spheres. The laws of society usually reflect the central values of the pluralistic culture and constrain both lifestyles and economic activity to protect legally sanctioned rights. Laws control or prohibit the use of certain drugs; safety regulations require maintenance standards in the operation of airlines; and elaborate licensing procedures are required in some communities for such economic activities as residential development or the location of a manufacturing facility.

The cultural sphere generates and sustains values and ideas that reflect the intellectual and religious life of society. Social values are institutionalized by political processes that yield legal sanctions guiding business behavior. The public policy process is influenced by competing social values that are driving forces behind political controversies. The end results are laws made within the political sphere.

For example, in the United States, individual freedom and respect for the dignity of the individual are among the highest values. Such values have led to the development of legal rights such as equal economic opportunity protecting persons from discrimination on the basis of sex, race, and religion. Popular support of private enterprise also has its roots in these cultural values of individual dignity and private property. Laws concerning contracts, privacy, employment, and fair competition reflect these values.

In his book *Politics and Markets*, Charles Lindblom identified five different types of social con-

trol.[3] He emphasized external aspects of control that included (1) market exchange, (2) authority of laws, regulations, and public policy, (3) custom, and (4) persuasion. The mechanisms for dealing with social change and control parallel the dimensions of the threefold social order outlined in Chapter 1. Economic controls include external market competition and strategic management. Political control includes the public policy process and government laws and regulations. Cultural controls include customs and cultural norms of behavior and business ethics practiced by managers. Also, persuasion of interest groups who threaten to boycott can exercise a strong influence on business behavior.

Social controls can be viewed as either external or internal to the business organization. External controls are forces that constrain or preclude the exercise of discretion by the practicing managers. Internal controls are those aspects of control where there is a substantial amount of managerial discretion. Managers typically have little control over (1) competitive markets, (2) government laws and regulations of business behavior, and (3) cultural norms and values. They are more likely to have substantial control over (1) strategic management of economic opportunities, (2) strategic issues management directed at influencing the public policy process, and (3) ethical practices of business employees.

SOCIAL CHANGE AND THE EXTERNAL CONTROL OF BUSINESS BEHAVIOR

Voluntary exchange is the primary control mechanism of market economies. As the case of the pencil at the beginning of the chapter suggests, individuals voluntarily produce, exchange, and consume the goods and services of a market economy. However, markets must possess the characteristics of competition (discussed below) if high economic performance is to be achieved. As society changes, different goods and services that express changing needs and lifestyles are demanded in the marketplace. Buyers and sellers voluntarily exchange these goods and services, responding to changing conditions.

The *authority* of the government in controlling business behavior is exercised in the enforcement of laws and regulations as well as the operations of the courts, which settle disagreements concerning the law. Laws and regulations are established by the public policy process through political behavior of various interest groups in a pluralistic society like that of the United States. In market economies, the primary purpose of governmental authority as it relates to the economic sphere is to protect property and other rights needed for the proper functioning of the market. As long as such private actions lead to high economic performance and are consistent with cultural values and the goals of society, there is a strong argument against government intervention in market processes.[4] However, as society changes, the concepts of rights and entitlements also change and the government's role changes as well.

Custom refers to the values and cultural practices within society. These can be of key importance to the control of business in less developed countries. For example, the religious values present in the Islamic countries of the Persian Gulf states largely account for the illegality of alcoholic beverages in those countries. Similarly, religious values against the charging of interest have resulted in unique banking practices in Saudi Arabia. Rather than charge interest on loans, banks become part owners of businesses as a condition for making funds available to them. The bank then shares in the profits and risk of loss if the business fails. The secularization of market economies and establishment of governmental bureaucracies have largely displaced custom and traditional values as a means of social control of business in Western society.[5]

Persuasion, according to Lindblom, includes the use of behavioral techniques and propaganda by the government to shape the values prevalent within society. These values are then said to dominate such characteristics as individuality, self-interest, privacy, and freedom, which serve as the core of a market system. Lindblom darkly suggested that persuasion might conceivably serve as a cul-

tural dimension of social control in totalitarian societies, where the political sphere totally overwhelms cultural values. Political functionaries would control cultural institutions that develop and communicate values so that citizens could be indoctrinated, if not brainwashed, into internalizing politically desirable values.

Fascist Germany, Stalinist Russia, and the Cultural Revolution of the People's Republic of China are all examples in this century of attempts to rely on persuasion as a major mechanism of social control. In all these cases, there was little independence of the three spheres of society. In each of these three cases, the political sphere overwhelmed both the economic and the cultural spheres, leading to the collapse of performance in each, that is, to the decline of civilized values within the culture and poor economic productivity.

Another aspect of persuasion found in market-oriented societies is from interest groups that are independent of the government. Private interest groups can communicate with business and, in the extreme, threaten boycotts as a means of persuading business to change its behavior. For example, church organizations organized a boycott against Nestlé to pressure the company to change its policies in the export of infant formula to Third World countries. Nestlé, a Swiss-based global company, made substantial changes and the boycott ended in 1984.

CHANGE AND INTERNAL CONTROL OF BUSINESS BEHAVIOR

Additional control mechanisms that can influence business behavior include internal controls, which can be considered such because a substantial amount of discretion can be exercised by management in each of these areas. When strong external forces are absent, managers are in a position to exercise more self-control. This self-control can be directed at developing competitive strategies in the economic sphere, strategic issues management in the political sphere, and/or ethical behavior derived from the cultural sphere.

1. *Strategic management* of decisions in the economic sphere. Competitive strategies of low cost, differentiation, and focus are intended to establish sustainable competitive advantage in the marketplace. When these strategies are directed toward serving the customer, they can add to the dynamic performance of the market. If strategic management exploits market failures, leading to dysfunctions, the result is likely to be controversy that finds its way into the public policy process.

2. *Strategic issues management* (SIM) in the political sphere through corporate political strategies designed to influence the public policy process through responsive behavior. Media relations managed by the corporate public affairs office are also directed at maintaining organizational legitimacy and to forestall punitive government laws and regulations. SIM is discussed in the next chapter.

3. *Morality and business ethics* (discussed in Part 3) in the cultural sphere based upon self-control and can be effective when managers use ethics to guide their behavior. Morality can be based upon the religious convictions or philosophies of ethical behavior. When markets are uncompetitive, laws and regulations are undeveloped or not enforced, and customs provide weak or unclear guidance for acceptable behavior; business managers are left to their own devices to control decisions. A major thesis of this book is that managers *do* have a substantial amount of discretion over decisions in many areas. A manager can develop and use a moral imagination by striving to be ethical in exercising self-control in the many discretionary areas that exist.

A *moral act,* according to Etzioni, is characterized by (1) an imperative feeling by individuals that they must act in a certain way, (2) symmetry in behavior and expectations, and (3) intrinsic motivation. Symmetry involves the capacity to generalize that results in "a willingness to accord other comparable people, under comparable circumstances, the same standing or right." Intrinsic motivation involves an inner commitment that is affirmed or expressed and that may be stronger

than the impulse to achieve pleasure by consuming an externally available good or service.[6] In other words, a moral act concerns something important enough for a person to feel strongly about; moral situations often involve mutual interactions and expectations about proper behavior; and people often feel good about doing what they think is the right thing.

Although managers must respond to the competitive forces of the marketplace, there are many situations in which moral acts form the basis of self-control of business behavior. Thus, *business ethics* is the organized study of applying morality and moral reasoning to problems within the economic sphere of society.

Lindblom argued that morality tends to be an unreliable basis for social control because the temptations to be immoral are too great when self-interest is involved.[7] Similarly, Maitland has suggested that professional managers who have internalized the value of self-interest and profit maximization assumed in market economies will not have sufficient self-control.[8] He suggested that self-regulation would be successful only if it were in the individual self-interest of all those who agree to be a part of industrywide self-regulation agreements. If economic reasons seem to justify violating an agreement, then cheating will occur because economic self-interest is a stronger inducement than morality.

Strategic Management of Competitiveness

Cartels and monopolies provide an example where self-control is based upon self-interested economic reasoning. Cartels provide an example of the failure of both market competition and ethical self-control. For example, the Oil Producing and Exporting Countries (OPEC) were able to control the worldwide price of oil by agreeing to limit production to reduce the supply of oil during most of the 1970s. The economic conspiracy, legal in the international community, was intended to yield higher oil prices and more profits for member nations. However, as OPEC members found it in their economic interest to violate the agreement, widespread cheating occurred and a worldwide oil glut developed that forced down the price of oil during the 1980s.

Another example of a self-control failure where business ethics might apply is the management of investments. Though there are ethical standards of confidentiality as well as laws against insider trading, there appears to have been widespread use of insider information by certain members of the financial community during the 1980s.[9] Nevertheless, the possibility of ethical behavior should not be abandoned as an option for shaping business behavior. One of the themes of this book argues that although business ethics alone may not be sufficient and reliable as a basis of control, ethical self-control does supplement other mechanisms of social control found in the economic and political spheres of society, as outlined in Table 2–1.

Systems of Political Economy

The central defining criteria of systems of political economy include the type of government and the relative emphasis on the market system.

POLITICAL SYSTEMS

Political systems can be organized in many ways. To simplify our discussion, we will juxtapose systems of democratic representation with authoritarian systems. Democracies like those of North America typically have two or more political parties that offer candidates in general election. Democratic governments emphasize individual liberties and rights and seek to maintain social justice. Thus the primary role of the government in the economic sphere is focused on the issues of consumer and employee rights, regulating the competitive market, and insuring social and economic justice within the society

Democratic societies are usually *pluralistic* because a plurality of interest groups forms around issues. For example, there are environmentalists opposed to cutting old-growth timber in the Northwest because it threatens wildlife habitat. The timber

industry and those in favor of unlimited economic development of natural resources would like to harvest these timber resources, which would last another ten years if unlimited cutting were allowed. There is a bitter controversy over abortion with the pro-life forces on one side and the pro-choice on the other.

Interest groups often have divergent values and incompatible goals. Many interest groups are concerned with a single issue like abortion, opposition to nuclear energy, protecting the environment, or gun control. Organizations tend to polarize around these single issues, but often a majority of interest groups at any one time does not take a position concerning the majority of issues. For example, in confirmation hearings of a Supreme Court appointment, concerned interest groups carefully screen the candidate primarily from the prospective of a single issue.

Authoritarian societies tend to be dominated by a single political party that offers candidates to the electorate. For example, in the Soviet Union prior to the 1990s, nearly all candidates in elections were members of the Communist Party. Authoritarian societies are much less likely to protect individual political rights like freedom of expression, freedom of assembly, and freedom of religion. In an extreme form of organization, totalitarian governments control every aspect of society. As Friedreich has defined such a society, "Everything that is not forbidden is obligatory." Examples of totalitarian societies are Nazi Germany, the Soviet Union under Stalin, and the People's Republic of China under Mao Tse-tung.

ECONOMIC SYSTEMS

Economic systems can be market-oriented with minimum government interference, they can rely primarily upon the forces of market competition with substantial government regulation, or they can be characterized as command economies. *Market economies* use the forces of market competition to make decisions about what goods are produced and how they are distributed within the society. The consumer is sovereign because the demands

Table 2–1
Mechanisms of Social Control of Business

	External	Internal
Economic	Market Competition • Voluntary exchange • Prudent decision making • Adequacy of information • Mobility of resources • No market power • Market-determined production and returns	Strategic Management • Strategic planning • Management control systems • Cartels and monopolization
Political/Legal	Laws and Regulation • Antitrust law • Economic regulation of industry • Social regulation of business functions	Public Policy Process
	Courts and Litigation • Lawsuits • Consent decrees • Contractual agreements • Government prosecution	Strategic management of public issues • Corporate political strategy • Governmental relations • Interest group relations • Media relations
Cultural	Customs • Social values • Ideology • Conventional practices • Industry standards	Business Ethics & Morality • Utilitarian analysis • Rights and duties • Justice • Moral reasoning • Social responsibility
	Persuasion • Consumer boycotts • Indoctrination • Propaganda	

made by consumers in the marketplace serve as the driving force within the economy.

A *mixed economy* relies heavily upon the workings of the competitive marketplace, but the government may decide who can compete, what is produced, and the terms of the exchange. Which goods can be offered for sale is regulated through product standards, which firms can compete may be controlled through licensing restrictions, and economic activity may be influenced by the government in other ways through monetary and fiscal policy. Also, in a mixed economy, the government may own some businesses. For example, the French government owns a petroleum company, an automobile manufacturing organization, and many businesses in other key industries.

A *command economy* is characterized by the dominance of the political sphere in all aspects of the economic sphere. Economic central planners, usually controlled by the dominant political party, decide what should be produced, where, and by whom. For example, the Soviet Union under Stalin had five-year plans that identified economic priorities, production schedules, and logistics arrangements that were developed and implemented during each five-year period.

Eastern European countries after World War II had command economies where the government owned all businesses and central planners made all economic decisions. Prices were controlled and goods were distributed primarily through the government-controlled channels of distribution. During the late 1980s these economies had such poor economic performance that many sought to move their economies more to a market-based system. This was the case for the People's Republic of China (PRC), the USSR, and most of Eastern Europe. The move toward a market economy was accompanied by the collapse of communism, the breakup of the USSR, and the reassertion of their independence from the USSR by Eastern European countries.

SYSTEMS OF POLITICAL ECONOMY

Systems of political economy are the social arrangements by which a society determines how to accomplish the activities of the political and economic spheres. A typology of political economy shown in Table 2–2 classifies (1) the political dimension as democratic or authoritarian, and (2) the economic dimension as market-oriented versus a centralized or command economy.

Democratic Capitalism

The United States, as a system of democratic capitalism, would occupy cell one. Such countries have pluralistic values in the cultural sphere that translate into a multiparty system with interest group politics in the political sphere. Individual rights,

particularly equality before the law, are a key aspect of the political sphere. The economic sphere is dominated by a market system in which consumer sovereignty is expressed through voluntary exchange under the conditions of competition.

Totalitarian Society

Opposite to democratic capitalism is the totalitarian communism of cell 4 of Table 2–2. This system is characterized by a single political party (e.g., Communist), which dominates all three spheres of society. Market forces are used in a limited manner to ration what has been produced by the government's factories and sources of supply. Prices are likely to be determined by government rather than market forces of supply and demand. Political liberties are limited and human rights violations are common.

Democratic Socialism

These societies are democratic in the political sphere and have extensive government involvement in the economic sphere. France and Great Britain have experimented with this form of political economy since the 1940s, and industries have been nationalized by one administration and subsequently "privatized" by the next. Democratic socialism is perhaps an abstract classification because most countries so designated, like Sweden, in fact have both government and private ownership of industry. The concept of "mixed systems" might be more accurate for countries that are not purely socialistic or capitalistic.

Authoritarian Capitalism

The People's Republic of China attempted to implement reforms in the political economy during the 1980s. The leaders were concerned about economic performance and attempted to improve it by relying more on market forces. However, they were not willing to change the Communist Party's dominance of the political sphere and tried to develop what might be called authoritarian capitalism. These economic reforms raised expectations by citizens, especially students, for political reforms leading to greater liberty and freedom of expression to coincide with increasing freedoms of economic choice.

These rising expectations in the PRC led to demonstrations and a brutal suppression by the government, which ordered the killing of many at Tiananmen Square in June 1989. The aftermath of the demonstrations was the continued crackdown on freedom of expression and the arresting and imprisonment of those who had called for more political freedom. This discouraged international investment in the country by those who had wished to take advantage of a more market-oriented society. It is not yet known what type of political economy China will adopt. However, this

TABLE 2–2
Systems of Political-Economy

Economic Systems	Political Systems	
	Democratic	Authoritarian
Market Oriented	1. Democratic Capitalism • Pluralistic values in cultural sphere • Multiparty system in politics • Market competition in economy • Individual rights protected • Consumer sovereignty Most of North America	2. Authoritarian Market System • Single political party • Central planners regulate economy • Market system used to allocate available goods • Few individual rights Goal of Reformers in People's Republic of China Latin America, New African Nations, Non-communist Asia, except Japan
Centralized Authority	3. Democratic Socialism • Publicly and privately owned enterprise • Multiparty political system • Individual rights protected • Government provides many goals and services Poland under Solidarity, Sweden, France	4. Totalitarism Society • Single political party dominates economic, political, and cultural spheres • Rationing and quotas emphasized • Limited use of market system • Centralized planning controls economy Formally, Soviet Union and People's Republic of China under communism Fascism (Nazi Germany)

SOURCE: Based on Charles E. Lindblom, *Politics and Markets* (New York: Basic Books, 1977).

experience has led some to suspect that a political economy of authoritarian capitalism is not possible because of the inherent instability of sanctioning freedom in the economic sphere and suppressing it in the other two spheres.

The Soviet Union under Gorbachev also changed dramatically during the 1980s. Unlike the PRC, the Soviet Union emphasized political reforms as an integral part of its change in political economy. Widespread demonstrations particularly in Lithuania, which had been seized by the Soviet Union during the 1940s, led to a declaration of independence. There were widespread strikes by Soviet workers followed by a rather conciliatory response by the government. This upset hardliners in the government who tried to overthrow Gorbachev and restore the policies of previous administrations. The coup failed when Boris Yeltsin resisted the plotters and the people rallied behind Yeltsin. As president of Russia, Yeltsin sought to move the country toward democratic capitalism. The result was the outlawing of the Communist Party, the collapse of the Soviet Union, and reforms designed to move the system of political economy to democratic capitalism.

The reforms in political economy that were begun in the Soviet Union expanded into Eastern Europe, which experienced the collapse of communism and a move toward market economies. Political reforms led to an election upset for the Communists in Poland, Hungary, and several other countries. Economic reforms toward a market system have been began in Eastern European countries as well as in the Soviet Union.

However, political instability has characterized the 1990s in some countries. Czechoslovakia broke into the Czech Republic and Slovakia. Also, Yugoslavia fragmented into smaller republics warring with one another.

In Great Britain and France, the government has begun to relinquish ownership of key industries and has moved the economy more toward a purely market system from a mixed system of political economy. In conclusion, market competition has increased widely as a feature of political economic systems throughout the world during the past decade.

The Economic Sphere and Control by Market Competition

Society depends upon business, as the major institution in the economic sphere, to provide goods and services for its members. A market where voluntary exchange occurs under competitive conditions is a major instrument for the social control of business. In this sense, control means that the goals of providing for the material welfare of society are achieved as the task of the economic sphere is accomplished. Such goals include maintaining a high standard of living, achieving economic productivity, controlling inflation, and maintaining high levels of employment. Successful social performance requires that this task be accomplished efficiently and reliably so that the wealth of the nation can be increased and the standard of living of its citizens improved.

Adam Smith first argued in 1776 in his *Wealth of Nations* that the material welfare of society could best be accomplished by private businesses operating in a competitive market. Most discussions of market forces of control begin with Smith's idea of an "invisible hand," first described in 1776.[10] For example, in perfectly competitive markets, management must respond to market competition when making decisions about products to produce and prices to charge. Businesses, seeking their own self-interest, can serve customers and achieve profitability if they cooperate with market demand. Market forces can explain the complicated chain of events that go into the production and distribution of all of the products that make up a pencil, as discussed at the beginning of the chapter.

Because of the invisible hand of competition, businesses that depart from the signals and controls of the market mechanism suffer from increased costs, reduced sales, and declining profitability. This invisible hand is said to work best in controlling the

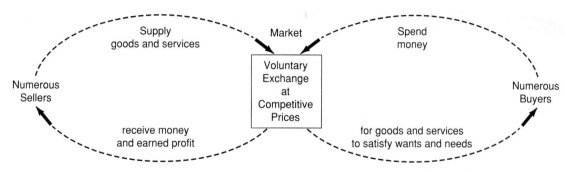

FIGURE 2–1 Cooperation Through Voluntary Exchange

behavior of businesses in competitive markets. The classical economists developed a model of perfect competition to explain logically the necessary conditions. Central to this model were the ideas of private property, self-interested behavior on the part of both buyers and sellers, and a laissez-faire government, that is, a minimal amount of government interference with the market exchange process.

Necessary Conditions for a Competitive Market

The classic model of perfect competition attempted to identify the characteristics necessary to insure that competition would lead to economic efficiency. The model of perfect competition has undergone much refinement over the past 200 years and can be characterized as having the following eight elements:

1. *Voluntary exchange.* If an exchange between individuals is voluntary, it will not occur unless both buyer and seller believe they will benefit from it.[11] Sellers make goods and services available to buyers expecting to exchange them at a price that allows for a profit. Buyers spend their money expecting to obtain goods or services that satisfy their needs or wants, as shown in Figure 2–1.

2. *Minimum governmental interference.* Because both parties to the exchange experience a benefit, market exchange promotes cooperation without extensive involvement by government. However, later in this chapter we will see that when competition is not present, undesirable consequences result, and government action is used to restore competitive conditions. Also, when a voluntary transaction harms people who are not parties to the transaction, as in the case of pollution, the government may issue regulations to protect rights.

3. *Prudent behavior* is based upon self-interest. As discussed in Chapter 1, Adam Smith argued that prudence is one of the three virtues basic to civilization, along with justice and beneficence. Economic theorists have interpreted prudence, or self-interested behavior, to mean profit maximization by businesses that sell goods and services, income maximization by employees, and maximization of satisfaction or utility by buyers. Prudence, in the long run, is enlightened self-interest because long-term economic success may mean that a business rationally forgoes short-term profits and the exploitation of certain advantages for long-term market position.

4. *Privately owned property.* Private ownership provides a built-in incentive to manage efficiently when motivated by self-interest. Self-interest combined with voluntary exchange leads to cooperative systems where everyone ideally benefits from exchanges. However, self-interest is likely to provide a stronger incentive in a competitive market if the benefits of the exchange go directly to the seller and buyer because of an ownership stake in the outcome of a market transaction.

5. *Knowledgeability and adequacy of information.* The classical model assumes that both buyers and sellers are knowledgeable about the offers available in the marketplace and about the characteristics of the goods and services available from sellers and desired by buyers. The people who transmit the information have an incentive to search out the people who can use it and they are in a position to do so. People who can use the information have an incentive to get it and they are in a position to do so.

6. *No restraints on trade and mobility of resources.* This assumption means that factor inputs can be moved from one use to another. Also, there are no barriers to entering or exiting from an economic activity that would interfere with mobility of resources and market participants. Thus, it is assumed that potential competitors are not arbitrarily excluded from a market. Discrimination that precludes participation by workers of a particular race, religion, or ethnic group would be a restraint on trade that inhibits mobility. Also, restrictive systems of apprenticeship and certification restrain trade and thus interfere with market competition.

7. *No market power by individual buyers and sellers.* The classical model of market competition assumes there are sufficient numbers of buyers and sellers so that no single party to an exchange has the power to set the price and terms of exchange. Some writers also assume that products are homogeneous, that is, products are not differentiated so that a particular producer is not preferred over others. A differentiated product might provide some preference on the part of buyers that could be used as a basis for market power by sellers of the uniquely different product or service.

8. *Market-determined prices and returns.* Milton and Rose Friedman have stated that prices perform three interdependent functions: (1) they transmit important market information, (2) they offer an incentive to adopt efficient methods of production for the most value-adding products or services, and (3) they determine the amount of income received by those involved in market exchange.[12]

The market in the classical sense is not a place of personal rivalry. Prices are set by impersonal interaction of supply and demand for a particular product or service. Those who wish to sell a product voluntarily make an offer consistent with their knowledge of orders revealing price and preferences of buyers and the perception that it is in their interest to sell. Buyers and sellers are free to enter the market, but they are not powerful enough to control the price or terms of trade. The seller willingly makes a good or service available at the going rate determined by the market forces.

If the seller is efficient and offers a service to a willing buyer, a profit can be earned and the amount of the profit or return going to the seller is also determined by the market. In a *perfectly competitive market,* products and services are very similar and there is little or no room for differentiation and little basis exists for market power. In the long run, all producers have the same cost structures and there are no barriers to entry because of large capital investment requirements. And perfectly informed competitors make a focus strategy theoretically impossible. Thus, the invisible hand of the market forces impersonally and externally controls the behavior of business to bring about the social goal of providing for the material welfare of society.

The ideal outcomes of the classical model of perfect competition are economic efficiency leading to high standards of living and full employment. These outcomes are consistent with the cultural value of freedom and are fair to all concerned without the extensive intervention of the government to protect individual rights.

The Economic Sphere and Self-control by Competitive Strategies

The classical model of competition can be considered an ideal by which actual markets are analyzed and evaluated. Because the conditions of the classical model rarely exist in actual markets, the consequences theorized by the classical economists do not always occur. Market forces often do exist and provide a powerful influence on business behavior.

Businesses that ignore signals from the market can lose market position, profitability, and suffer other consequences.

The classical model assumes that the forces of the market determine business behavior completely. There is no room for discretionary behavior on the part of the manager, and thus there is no room for either competitive strategies or the moral act of business ethics. However, as Chapter 1 suggested, managers seek strategies to improve the competitive position of their business. Generic strategies included activities achieving (1) lower-cost capabilities than competitors that support price leadership, (2) differentiation through a uniquely desirable product or service, and (3) focus on a particular market niche or customer group that may be a submarket less accessible to potential competitors and a large market share position can be obtained.[13]

In other words, a key to competitive strategy is to develop a distinctive or sustainable strategic advantage by adapting to market conditions that are not perfectly competitive. Such advantages might be based upon market power that rises from having a dominant market share or competitive position.[14] Market power can be based upon advantages in information or the ability to develop differentiated products or lower costs. However, such advantages are usually temporary and markets can continue to be highly competitive because most competing businesses can eventually achieve comparable cost structures and differentiated products, and can find favorable market segments if the business is managed well.

Sometimes the results of market competition have led to *oligopolistic* markets controlled by few dominant firms whose managers have considerable discretion in developing competitive strategies.[15] In these markets many of the assumptions of perfect competition may not be valid, and management discretion for mapping out strategic plans and management control systems can be substantial. Recent battles between Burger King and McDonald's in the fast-food industry or the battles between Coca-Cola and Pepsi in the soft

drink industry testify to the intensity of competition in oligopolistic markets. Price wars are common and the proliferation of new and unique products continues as these large firms seek to gain competitive advantage.

VIDEO EQUIPMENT IN THE CONSUMER ELECTRONIC INDUSTRY

Competitors in oligopolistic markets cannot ignore the signals from their customers or the strategic moves by competitors if they are to prosper. For example, consider the battle between the once dominant Sony and its competitors in the video player market. Sony developed a technologically superior video player, called the beta, but refused to add the capability of recording from television to its product. Other video equipment manufacturers developed a competing technology, the VHS video recorder and player, and came to dominate the market despite Sony's early lead. Customers preferred equipment that would both record and play video films. Market forces that reflected such preferences resulted in the VHS type of video machine becoming the industry standard.

Market forces are similarly influencing the development of technologies that record music. However, the control of business behavior in this market has also felt the effects of political controversy and the threat of regulatory control. The vinyl disk recordings that once dominated the music recording market now account for less than 10 percent of industry sales. Records have been largely replaced by the tape recorder, first by the eight-track tape player followed by the cassette tape players. The compact disc (CD) is fast becoming the new industry standard.

Like the beta technology, the CD can be played, but the user cannot record on the disk. However, an alternative technology to the CD is already available in Japan, the digital audio tape player (DAT). Unlike the CD, which shares the feature of the Beta video players of not recording, the DAT can reproduce high-quality stereo sound as well as play musical recordings purchased at the local music store. However, the forces of competition are being challenged in the DAT case by an issue over rights of performing artists to the music they create.

Musicians and the music industry in general argue that those who buy DAT recorders will not purchase music recorded on vinyl recorders, cassette tapes, or compact discs. Instead, it is argued that copies of music will be unfairly pirated by listeners if market forces are allowed to operate unrestrained. The music industry wants the government to protect its property rights against the misuse of DAT recorders. Thus, the political controversy has delayed the competitive introduction of the DAT technology as laws and regulations are developed to control its sale and distribution.[16]

One technological control being proposed is the "notching" of authorized recordings of music and placing a control device within the DAT recorders to prevent the recording of music with this technological signal. Customers argue that such "notching" lowers the quality of the music that is legally available on the DAT technology. The suppliers of DAT technology argue that this regulation artificially lowers the quality, and thus the competitiveness, of their product.

When Market Competition Fails to Control Business

It is sometimes argued that market forces do not adequately control business. In these situations, it is the task of the political sphere through the public policy process and the enforcement of laws and regulations to protect rights. As the brief example of the DAT technology shows, there are usually competing rights argued by the various constituencies within society. Nevertheless, once laws and regulations are passed, they constrain business behavior. They provide an external means of social control of economic activity that can complement, supplement, or be an alternative to market competition.

Robert Harris and James Carmen developed a topology of market failure that can occur when one or more of the conditions necessary for market competition are weak or absent.[17] Table 2–3 indicates that market behavior can lead to undesirable consequences when the following conditions exist:

1. Imperfect or too little competition
2. Anticompetitive behavior
3. Too much, unstable, or redundant competition
4. Imperfect information
5. Side effects or externalities
6. Demerit goods
7. Income maldistribution

IMPERFECT COMPETITION AND ANTICOMPETITIVE BEHAVIOR

Types of imperfect competition include *monopolistic competition* when products are differentiated enough for consumers to have preferences. *Oligopolistic competition* exists when a few firms dominate an industry. This can develop when significant barriers to entry develop that discourage potential competitors from entering a market. The existence of large-scale factories that result in low production costs but require substantial capital investments are sometimes a barrier. The requirements for large-scale distribution systems, promotion capabilities, or research laboratories can all discourage smaller businesses from entering a market. *Monopoly* exists when there is only one seller in a particular market. Sometimes monopolies are considered "natural," as in the case of public utilities, waste management operations, and local telephone services. In the case of utilities, regulatory agencies and industry rate review boards negotiate with the businesses in the utility industry to set the rates rather than rely on market forces to determine prices.

As noted above, imperfect competition can concentrate substantial market power in the hands of a few competitors. While competition may exist in oligopolistic markets, there is often a temptation to engage in anticompetitive behavior like price-fixing or conspiracy in restraint of trade.[18] According to the economic theory of industrial organization, the structure of a market leads to the type of competitive behavior found in that market, which, in turn, leads to market performance.

TABLE 2–3
Types of Market Failures

Type of Failure	Nature of Failure	Examples of Failure

Imperfect competition
  Natural monopoly
  Monopoly (sony)
  Oligopoly (sony)
Competition
	Economies of scale
	Bargaining power
	Interdependent conduct
	Transactions costs; excess
	  capacity
		Electric utilities
		Standard Oil (pre-1912)
		Tobacco
		Retail sale of convenience goods

Excessive competition	Fluctuating supply/demand	Trucking
Anticompetitive conduct	Collusion; predation	OPEC cartel; AT&T; MCI

Imperfect information
  Bounded rationality
  Information costs
  Asymmetric information
  Misinformation
Lack of information
	Uninformed exchange
	Uninformed exchange
	Unequal bargaining
	Misinformed exchange
	Uninformed exchange
		Professional services
		Life insurance
		"Lemons"
		Wonder Bread
		New therapeutic drugs

Side Effects
  Internalities
 	
  Negative externalities
 	
  Positive externalities
	Transmittal of costs to
	  nonsubjects
	Overconsumption; costs
	  imposed on nonsubjects
	Underconsumption; benefits
	  accrue to nonsubjects
		Health effects of tobacco
		
		Air pollution; communicable
		  diseases
		Inoculations against communica-
		  ble diseases

Public goods	Indivisibility; nonexcludability;
	  zero MC
		Street lighting; parks; national
		  defense

(De)merit goods	Divergence of private wants, social values	Education; (gambling)

Income maldistribution
  Factor market failures
  Economic vs. social value
	Any of the above
	Earned income not equal to
	  social worth
		Employee discrimination
		Children; disabled; "superstars"

Intergenerational transfers	Inconsistency with value that
	  income be "earned"
		Inheritances; socially
		  advantaged upbringing

SOURCE: Robert G. Harris and James M. Carman, "Public Regulation of Marketing Activity: Part I: Institutional Typology of Market Failure," *Journal of Macromarketing* 3, no. 1 (Spring 1983).

In other words, when the conditions of competition exist, market control successfully leads to both economic efficiency and fair profits and returns to all parties to an exchange. Highly competitive markets with many buyers and sellers, low barriers to entry, and mobility of resources lead to independent behavior and market-based prices, production, and returns, as discussed earlier in the chapter. In contrast, where the conditions of market competition are not present, market failure occurs. Highly concentrated markets are more likely to lead to such behaviors as price fixing by the few firms that dominate the market. This theory and the regulatory response of antitrust laws are discussed in Chapter 13.

REDUNDANT OR UNSTABLE COMPETITION

The opposite of the problem of monopolistic practices in imperfectly competitive markets is competition so intense that it is believed to yield socially undesirable results. According to Harris and Carman,

If supply and demand fluctuate unpredictably over time, there may be excessive entry by producers during peak demand, resulting in excess capacity during off-peak demand. Furthermore, capital is specialized, supply adjustments may take longer than the duration of the fluctuation and prices will be driven below the long-run average costs. Or if storage costs are high, producers may sell output below costs to avoid those costs. In addition to the instability in supply and loss of income by producers, excessive competition may induce producers to reduce the quality of their service with jeopardy to consumers.[19]

Industries like agriculture, banking, communications, trucking, and airlines have traditionally been regulated to avoid some of these undesirable results of excessive competition. Regulatory agencies have been created for specific industries to regulate access to the industry by competitors, prices charged, and the type of products, or in the case of transportation, the routes allowed. Since 1978, there has been a trend to deregulation in the United States. This trend and its results are discussed in Chapter 12.

IMPERFECT INFORMATION

The classical model of competition assumes that buyers and sellers are fully informed about the prices, condition, and locations of goods and services offered for exchange. However, information may in actuality be imperfect and costly to obtain. Industrialized multinational markets are geographically dispersed and information is often highly technical, difficult to acquire, and/or of varying quality. Exchanges are thus often characterized by asymmetric information in which one party knows a great deal more than the other. Or it may be too costly to become informed and decisions are based upon uninformed or misinformed buyers or sellers.

For example, it is difficult for some buyers to understand the technical characteristics of complex equipment like computer systems, test equipment, or even some automobiles. Manufacturers must develop sophisticated technological expertise in several scientific fields to develop and produce these items. There is an economic incentive to become an expert because the knowledge can lead to more efficient facilities or superior products. In contrast, the buyer may not have as much of an incentive to know about the technology of computing because the use of the technology is less central to his or her profession. This leads to an asymmetric or unbalanced condition in the relative knowledge about the product by buyers and sellers.

Producers may strive to help a buyer to be informed to increase the chances of a successful sale, as a matter of ethics, or because it is required by law in certain circumstances (as discussed in Chapter 15). Because there is an economic incentive to make a sale, there may be a temptation to misinform the buyer. Stories of misinformation provided by used car dealers abound. Sometimes marketing managers are criticized for false or misleading advertising, as in the case of "The Great American Health Pitch." Because of the increased consciousness about health, the demand for health foods has grown rapidly. Some food producers have responded by augmenting their product lines to include foods that are advertised as less likely to cause cancer, heart trouble, or other illnesses.

The absence of knowledgeable buyers and sellers can lead to imprudent or even harmful decisions that undermine the economic performance and later the legitimacy of a market. The response is then likely to be (1) attempts by business to establish industry standards and to behave ethically, or (2) political controversy and public policy processes leading to laws and regulations concerning truth in advertising and proper labeling of products.

SIDE EFFECTS AND EXTERNALITIES

Ideally all the costs of a transaction are paid voluntarily by the buyers and sellers who are directly involved in it. Unfortunately, some costs have *side effects* that can include positive or negative externalities as outlined in Table 2–3. A *negative externality* occurs when costs are imposed on someone not a party to a market transaction. For example, nonsmokers in the proximity of tobacco smoke have been known to contract cancer. This is especially true when nonsmokers work or live with heavy smokers. The market transaction is between the person buying the cigarettes and the retail establishment selling tobacco products. The consumer of the cigarettes then smokes the product and persons in the proximity of the smoking can suffer negative health effects like cancer, heart ailments, or other disease.

In other cases of negative externality, the costs of air pollution and cleanup of toxic wastes or polluted water systems are imposed on those who may not be directly involved with the transaction. Toxic waste like certain solvents could be a by-product of a manufacturing facility. If these waste products are not disposed of safely, the result could be pollution of a city water supply. It would be costly for the business to dispose of this waste, and thus costs and sales prices for the product would be lower if the solvent were dumped into the water supply. However, the solvent would then have to be removed at a much greater cost by someone not a party to the transaction between the manufacturer and the customer.

Because the market demand of a good is based upon the selling price, the negative externality leads to overconsumption of the product because some of its true costs are external to the transaction. Thus negative externalities can lead to the deterioration of the physical environment and the quality of life because the discipline inherent in market competition does not work in this case. Such externalities are an unintended consequence of economic activity not controlled by market competition. In areas where market competition fails to control the behavior of business, alternative mechanisms of social control become necessary. Market-oriented control must be augmented by government regulation, industry standards and practice, and the ethical behavior of managers if the goals of society are to be achieved.

DEMERIT GOODS

Demerit goods exist when there is a divergence between private wants and social values. For example, the United States has been ravaged by substance abuse. Babies are born addicted to crack cocaine, drug dealers are terrorizing cities and schools, and addicts seem to be able to exercise little self-control over their lives. Market competition in this illegal industry is characterized by armed dealers protecting their sales territories by gunning down rival suppliers in many cities. The economic and cultural consequences of drug abuse are substantial and are disruptive to accepted values and the goals of society. Thus drugs are demerit goods not subject to the normal controls of market competition, and some other form of social control is needed in these situations.

INCOME MALDISTRIBUTION

As noted earlier, one of the conditions of market competition is freedom of entry and exit, prudent behavior, no market power, and market-set prices. These conditions and others listed above lead to economic efficiency and a justifiable distribution of profits and returns to those involved in economic activity. *Income maldistribution* exists when the results of market competition do not lead to economic efficiency and/or just returns because these necessary conditions are not present. For example, employee discrimination exists when hiring, promotion, training, or decisions regarding pay are made on the basis of the race, ethnic origin, religion, sex, or some other unjustifiable basis. Freedom of entry in the market does not exist when members of some groups are not allowed the equal opportunity to compete.

The Political Sphere and Control by Law and Public Policy

As noted above, the political sphere, through laws and regulations, is used to protect the rights of people when market forces fail to honor such rights. Antitrust laws are used to reestablish competitive conditions and behavior when too little or imperfect competition exists. The economic regulation of selected industries is used to control excessive or inappropriate competition. Deregulation, a social experiment of the past decade, represents a reconsideration of the idea that limiting competition is in the best interest of society.

The social regulation of such business functions as marketing, employment, finance, production, distribution, and product development is often targeted to overcome market failures related to information, side-effects like pollution, maldistribution of inputs, discrimination, and demerit goods. Laws, regulations, and public policy provide major alternatives for the control of business behavior when the forces of market competition lead to undesirable consequences. Attempts to regulate business through laws and regulations seek to restore the necessary requirements and behaviors of market competition. Carman and Harris have identified the various types of regulations used by government to respond to the limitations in the operations of market exchange.

Regulatory responses by the government include the following.

1. *Laws that sanction certain rights and liabilities.* These include ordinances that forbid smoking in public places. Such laws seek to prevent an externality. Laws exist that enforce employees' right to privacy. Other laws sanction the right to know the side effects of medicine, the dangers surrounding the use of certain products, and the true finance charges involved in loan agreements. Antidiscrimination laws seek to guarantee equality of opportunity to correct the maldistribution of opportunity and income resulting from discriminatory practices. Bankruptcy laws limit the liability of individuals and businesses so that they will not face permanent economic ruin from a business failure.

2. *Government-imposed standards* enforce safety in such areas as aircraft maintenance, automobile emission requirements, and product safety standards. Market incentives may exist to supply unsafe products, or products that cause externalities like pollution, or negative incentive to invest in safe work sites. Standards are an option to require socially desirable behavior when market incentives, by themselves, lead to a less desirable outcome.

3. *Regulations that require the disclosure of information* in such areas as packaging and truth in lending. The ingredients for most foods are required to be written on the label. It is illegal to engage in false advertising for a product. Maintenance records for aircraft must be maintained and disclosed upon request to government inspectors.

4. *Taxes and subsidies* to offset market forces that encourage or discourage certain types of behavior. For example tax exemptions for nonprofit organizations encourage the creation of private schools and certain charities. Alternatively, alcoholic beverages and tobacco products are subject to "sin

taxes" to discourage consumption. Tax laws covering depreciation can stimulate business investment, and capital gains tax policy can encourage the financing of new venture start-ups.

5. *Licensing requirements that control allocation and entry* into certain markets. Special licenses are required to operate television stations, to drill offshore, to operate a business, to drive taxis, to practice law or medicine, and to perform many other activities. Cities require liscenses and have zoning laws to control entry by business.

6. *Public provision.* In cases where certain goods are needed by society but it is impractical for market competition to provide them, the government often provides them as public services. For example, highways, parks, national forests, public schools and social welfare programs, and insurance programs protecting banking deposits are all provided by the government. During the 1980s, some attempts were made to privatize certain public services like waste collection and public security in some communities.

Problems and Failures of Law and Regulation

Although law and regulation are a major alternative for the social control of business used when market competition leads to undesirable results, government intervention is not without its difficulties, as outlined in Chapter 12. The goal of the political sphere is to protect the rights of citizens and to provide for justice. Thus the key criterion of politics and government decision making involves the protection of rights, equity, and justice; consideration of economic efficiency is secondary.

Regulatory Costs

A regulatory agency might be formed to protect consumers from unsafe products or employees from unsafe working conditions. The agency may achieve the regulatory task to some degree but at considerable cost. Weidenbaum has documented the rapid growth in the number and costs of regulatory agencies.[20] Furthermore, the cost to comply with the regulation is often ten times greater than the cost of administrating it. Also, the costs of regulation are rarely borne by those who benefit from the regulation. Thus, an externality of a different sort is inherent in many regulatory activities.

Bureaucratic Failures

Agencies sometimes regulate activities across state lines, and the jurisdiction of an agency may not be congruent with a problem. For example, pollution, like the acid rain problem, cuts across political jurisdictions in a way that makes the administration by an agency very difficult or impossible. Also, agencies suffer from limitations in information and may not be fully knowledgeable about a particular market failure or about the technological dimensions of administration of that failure. For example, what are the key sources of pollution and the best way to deal with the problem? In an attempt to regulate, an agency's search for alternatives may be very costly because of problems of information, jurisdiction, and technology. Because the government agency is more likely to use rights related to public health or other similar areas as its guide, it is not as sensitive to costs as an organization facing the pressures of a competitive market.

Sometimes bureaucratic regulatory agencies are accused of maximizing their budgets rather than being cost-conscious. This may be due to the different goals, values, and decision-making criteria used within the two spheres of politics and economics. In their study of regulatory failure, Carman and Harris conclude:

Regulatory change is driven by shifts in the general conditions of the economy. While market failures can be costly in human terms, regulation can be costly in economic terms. As a society, we are continually confronted with the choice of whether to regulate, but, more fundamentally, how much can we afford to regulate. As the Unites States has declined from its former position as a dominant world economic power, we have had to confront the ultimate economic choice: of deciding how much public provision of goods, and how much public protection from bad, we are willing to pay for. That is a central source of the tension and the vitality of a democratic society.

Summary

This chapter began by raising a number of questions about how society can make sure that social goals and values are achieved within the economic sphere by business behavior. The mechanisms of social control tend to emphasize forces external to business organizations. These include the forces of market competition in the economic sphere; laws and regulations as major external constraints in the political sphere; and customs and industry standards in the cultural sphere. However, business managers can also exercise self-control through competitive strategies, strategic issues management in the public policy process, and morality and business ethics.

Different societies approach this problem of social control of economic activity in different ways through the development of unique systems of political economy. Systems of political economy focus on the relative emphasis on political and market-oriented means to control economic activity. Political systems can be democratic or authoritarian. Economic systems can rely on the competitive market system or adopt a command economy. Thus, the four major archetypes of political economies include democratic capitalism, democratic socialism, totalitarian systems, and authoritarian market systems. The United States is an example of democratic capitalism.

The primary way in which business behavior is controlled in democratic capitalism is through the forces of market competition. The conditions necessary for market competition include (1) voluntary exchange, (2) prudent behavior, (3) adequacy of information by both buyers and sellers, (4) mobility of resources and freedom of entry and exit, (5) no (or very limited) market power so that (6) prices, profits, and returns can be automatically determined by the operation of the competitive market, (7) private property, and (8) limited interference in the economic sphere by the government.

Unfortunately, the conditions needed for competitive markets to properly control economic activity do not always exist. These limitations cause a number of undesirable consequences, and thus a search for alternatives to supplement market competition is necessary. These forces include government laws and regulations that seek to regulate the management behavior in specific functional areas; antitrust laws that seek to reestablish competitive market structures and behaviors; and the adoption of industry standards, self-regulation by businesses, and business ethics.

The government uses a number of different regulatory approaches in its effort to control business behavior. However, just as markets fail when conditions for competition are not present, other approaches to the control of business also fail. For example, the cost of government regulations has grown enormously in recent years, and the costs incurred by business in complying with the numerous regulations have grown even faster. Also, sometimes businesses do not comply with industry standards and managers act unethically at times.

Conclusions

The political economy of the United States is a mixed system of democratic capitalism with a substantial infrastructure of government regulation. This system also uses other alternatives to control the economic behavior of business to ensure that it is consistent with the values and goals of society. A pluralistic society has many divergent views held by interest groups with competing values. The competition is evident in the shortcomings in business behavior, in political controversy, and in the decision making of managers seeking to act morally in a highly competitive climate.

In a democracy the government represents the pluralism inherent in society. Also, government, as the primary instrument of the political sphere, is concerned with the key task of protecting rights and maintaining justice. Performance goals of the government are to satisfy a pluralistic constituency while insuring the protection of rights and justice. Economic efficiency is an objective of public administration, but this is secondary to concerns of equity, rights, and justice. Thus attempts by government to regulate business are criticized for inefficiency.

The economic sphere has as its key instrument the business enterprise. The task of business is rationality and efficiency in the pursuit of satisfying customers in the competitive marketplace. Business is less sensitive to the issue of rights and justice than to economic performance. Thus, business is often criticized for violating the rights of employees and customers, particularly when the conditions of competition are absent.

It is the task of government to protect rights and insure justice in the context of the competitive striving of business. Also, it is a task of business with its knowledge of efficiency to encourage the efficient administration of laws and regulations. However, each sphere tends to emphasize its unique tasks, values, and performance criteria and can thus counterbalance the shortcomings of the other spheres in this context of social control.

Meanwhile, the cultural sphere provides the intellectual sustenance and values for both the economic and the political spheres. The pluralistic values of culture find their way into the public policy debates that ultimately yield laws and regulations. The individualistic lifestyle values of the cultural sphere find expression in market demand for particular goods and services. The hope of society is that the culture through its expression of values and ideals will influence both business and political behavior in a positive direction.

Discussion Questions

1. What are the conditions necessary for competitive markets? What are the results expected when these conditions exist?

2. What is the primary instrument used by society to insure that business behavior is consistent with its values, expectations, and goals?

3. How are the goals of society determined in a pluralistic society?

4. Briefly define the alternative systems of political economy.

5. What problems did the People's Republic of China experience when trying social reform intended to result in authoritarian capitalism?

6. Under what conditions are the limitations of competition likely to lead to undesirable results?

7. How are laws and regulations used by society to control business behavior?

8. What types of failure can be experienced when the political/governmental sphere is used to control the behavior of business?

9. What is a moral act? Can businesspeople be expected to engage in moral acts? Explain.

10. How do the dimensions of social control parallel the threefold social order?

11. What are the primary external types of social control mechanisms used to influence business behavior?

12. What are the primary types of self-control used by managers to influence business behavior?

Notes

1. From Milton Friedman and Rose Friedman, *Free to Choose* (New York: Harcourt, Brace, Jovanovich, 1980), pp. 3–5.

2. Rudolf Steiner, *The Threefold Social Order* (New York: Anthroposophic Press, 1972).

3. Charles E. Lindblom, *Politics and Markets: The World's Political Economic Systems* (New York: Basic Books, 1977).

4. Robert G. Harris and James M. Carman, "The Political Economy of Regulation: Analysis of Market Failures," in *Business and Society: Dimensions of Conflict and Cooperation*, ed. S. Prakash Sethi and Cecilia M. Falbe (Lexington, Mass.: Lexington Books, 1987), pp. 177–91.

5. See Sheldon Wolin, *Politics and Vision: Continuity and Innovation in Western Political Thought* (Boston: Little, Brown, 1960); Alasdair MacIntyre, *After Virtue: A Study in Moral Theory* (London: Duckworth, 1981).

6. Amitai Etzioni, *The Moral Dimension: Toward a New Economics* (New York: Free Press, 1988), pp. 41–43.

7. Lindblom, *Politics and Markets.*

8. Ian Maitland, "The Limits of Business Self-Regulation," *California Management Review* 27, no. 3 (Spring 1985): 132–47.

9. "Suddenly the Fish Get Bigger," *Business Week,* March 2, 1987, pp. 28–33.

10. Adam Smith, *An Inquiry into the Nature and Causes of the Wealth of Nations* (New York: Modern Library, 1937). First published in 1776.

11. Friedman and Friedman, *Free to Choose,* p. 5.

12. Friedman and Friedman, *Free to Choose,* p. 6

13. See Robert D. Buzzell and Bradley T. Gale, *The PIMS (Profit Impact of Market Strategy) Principles Linking Strategy to Performance* (New York: Free Press, 1987); Michael E. Porter, *Competitive Strategy* (New York:The Free Press, 1980); and Michael E. Porter, *Competitive Advantage: Creating and Sustaining Superior Performance* (New York: Free Press, 1985).

14. Porter, *Competitive Strategy* and *Competitive Advantage,* chap. 1.

15. For early writings on the theory of oligopoly and imperfect competition, see George J. Stigler, *The Organization of Industry* (Homewood, Ill.: Irwin, 1968); George J. Stigler and Kenneth E. Boulding, eds., *Readings in Price Theory* (Homewood, Ill.: Irwin, 1952).

16. *USA Today,* "The Long-Awaited Debut of the DAT," June 22, 1990, p. D1.

17. Robert G. Harris and James M. Carman, "The Political Economy of Regulation: An Analysis of Market Failures," in *Business and Society: Dimensions of Conflict and Cooperation,* ed. S. Prakash Sethi and Cecilia M. Falbe (Lexington, Mass.: Lexington Books, 1987), pp. 177–90.

18. Joe Bain, *Industrial Organization* (New York: Wiley, 1959); Richard Caves, *American Industry: Structure, Conduct, Performance,* 4th ed. (Englewood Cliffs, N.J.: Prentice-Hall, 1977); Walter Adams, ed., *The Structure of American Industry,* 6th ed. (New York: Macmillan, 1982); and Douglas F. Greer, *Business, Government, and Society* (New York: Macmillan, 1987).

19. Harris and Carman, "The Political Economy of Regulation," p. 183.

20. Murray L. Weidenbaum and Robert De Fina, *The Rising Costs of Government Regulation* (St. Louis, Mo.: Washington Center for the Study of American Business, 1977).

CHAPTER 3

The Strategic Management of Public Issues

CHAPTER OBJECTIVES

1. Discuss the political dimension of corporate social performance.
2. Show how public issues develop through a number of distinct phases that parallel the public policy process.
3. Explain the strategic management process as it relates to public issues.
4. Develop a framework for analyzing public issues within an issue life cycle that can guide the strategic management process.

Business Social Performance and Social Control Mechanisms

The basic concept for business social performance in the political sphere is *legitimacy*—maintaining the appropriate level of cultural and political support for its activities. The legitimacy of business is reflected in society's confidence in the ability of market competition to respond to changing social needs. It is influenced by the degree to which business is perceived as being ethically responsible, by the political responsiveness of businesses to public issues as they develop over time, and by whether social expectations are met.

Effective business performance includes *political responsiveness* as well as *social responsibility*. Social responsibility requires a business to behave ethically, to be a good corporate citizen, and to consider the appropriate interests of stakeholders when decisions are made. Political responsiveness is enhanced by two things: the strategic management of public issues and the institutional orientation of the business.

For example, the pricing of home heating oil became controversial during a particularly cold winter in the eastern and southeastern parts of the United States in the winter of 1990. Cold weather resulted in a sharp increase in the demand for electricity and heating oil, and an immediate price increase nearly doubled the cost to consumers. Petroleum companies were accused of price gouging and exploiting their advantageous position at the expense of consumers, who desperately needed to warm their homes. Even when the public generally opposes government regulation, it may call for specific regulations to counter perceived failures of the market or abuse by managers, as this incident of the oil price increase suggests.

A national debate began over whether to pass laws to control the price of home heating oil. Consumer groups called for laws. Congress called for investigations. Petroleum companies were caught in a position of having to defend their behavior as their legitimacy was threatened on all fronts. They were generally viewed as being defensive and reactive in their institutional orientation, as exploitative in their economic strategy, and as shortsighted and unfair in their pricing policies.

THE CONTROL CYCLE. The control cycle is the dynamic sequence of events that activates the control mechanisms discussed in the last chapter and shown in Table 3-1. This control cycle sequence begins (1) with some sort of market failure (2) that is exploited by management, leading to (3) a controversy triggering a public policy debate, leading to (4) an acceptable socially responsible action by management or (5) the continuing of the public policy process until government laws and regulations control business or (6) direct action by interest group persuades business to change its behavior.

When public confidence in market competition drops, the legitimacy of businesses involved or in business as an institution also drops. The drop in confidence is caused by the perception that a social problem was the result of a market failure irresponsibly exploited by management. If the public perception is widespread, controversy results and a control cycle continues.

The public policy process occurs in phase three of a control cycle shown in Table 3–1. The *public policy process* begins with political debate and the subsequent passing of laws, forming of agencies, and agency development and enforcement of regulations to implement the law. If business is to maintain its legitimacy, it must effectively communicate the reasons for controversial actions or change its behavior. It needs to become involved in public debates that can constrain economic activities and affect its business social performance.

Public issues normally are the substance of the public policy process. Public policy debates can be viewed as a trigger that can lead the resolution of a controversy in a variety of ways. How business deals with a controversy can influence which alternative social control mechanism is called into play. These resolutions to a controversy include social responsibility by business, regulation by government, or actions by interest group as suggested in Table 3–1.

TABLE 3–1
Strategic Management of Public Issues and the Dynamics of the Social Control Cycle

Sphere of Activity	External Control Measures on Business	Discretionary Behavior by Business
Economic	**Market Failure.** Dynamics of market competition leading to market failure 1	**Strategic Management.** Decisions that exploit market situation 2
Political/ Governmental	**Government laws or regulations** that constrain business behavior 6	**Public Policy Process and Strategic Management of Public Issue.** Management responds to public controversy, leading to some type of resolution or/and 3
Cultural	**Interest Group Persuasion.** Business is persuaded to change its behavior by interest group threats of a boycott or direct interest group protests 5	**Social Responsibility.** Business displays social responsibility by ethical behavior, which is effectively communicated to the public 4

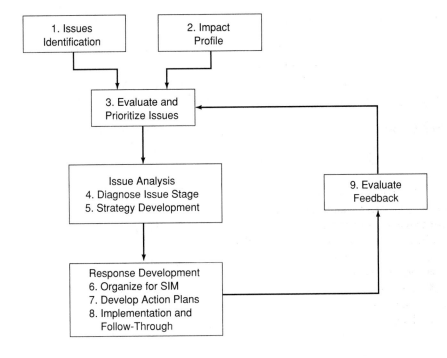

FIGURE 3–1 The Strategic Management Process for Public Issues

1. *Social responsibility.* In phase four of the control cycle, business can seek to behave in an ethically responsible manner and then communicate its position in response to its critics. Sometimes such actions do not satisfy interest groups concerned about a social problem and the issue is recycled back to phase three of the control cycle, then the controversy continues.

2. *Government laws and regulations.* If the public is not satisfied with the actions of managers, the public policy process continues to phase six of the control cycle. Government laws and regulations are passed that restrict business practices. Sometimes the corporate political behavior is successful in influencing the legislation.

3. *Persuasion by direct interest group actions.* In phase five of the control cycle, protest groups can bypass the public policy process and move to direct actions against the business in the form of consumer boycotts or other protest activity. Such activity can sometimes produce a dialogue within management. Critics of business then negotiate for changes in

management behavior. Sometimes protest movements are ineffective in bringing about the objectives of interest groups concerned about a social problem or controversial issue. The issue is then recycled if sufficient support is available to keep it on the public policy agenda.

Strategic Issues Management

Managers have used strategic issues management (SIM) as a method for dealing with the changing sociopolitical environment for the past decade.[1] A strategic issue is a condition whose outcomes (1) have a high impact on organizational performance, (2) are likely to be controversial, and (3) have consequences for the organization, resulting in the need for modifying strategies.[2]

SIM is the process of identifying important sociopolitical issues, evaluating their potential impact on the business, and formulating a strategic response and implementing the strategy. Figure 3–1 shows the nine steps or stages of the SIM process.

1. *Issues identification.* Monitoring, forecasting, identifying, and tracking social trends, political controversies, and technological developments that might become of concern to a business are the initial activities needed for issues identification.

2. *Impact profile assessment.* Developments in the technological, social, and political environment have varying effects on a particular business or industry. This stage is concerned with relating the issues that have been identified and are being monitored to the interests of a specific business organization or industry interested in developing an effective response capability for the issue.

3. *Evaluation and prioritizing of issues.* Issues are categorized depending upon the magnitude of impact and probability of strategic impact on the operations of the business. Table 3–2 illustrates the categorization framework. Research key issues thoroughly using company and outside information. Involve functional areas where necessary.

4. *Diagnosis of issue stage.* Issues pass through a six-stage issue life cycle (ILC), and response plans need to fit the requirements of each stage. This step enables managers to consider an issue broadly according to its ILC stage once an issue has been designated as a high priority.

5. *Strategy development.* The strategic objective, strategic approach, types of expertise, influence,

and action plans vary, depending upon the issue stage. Depending upon ILC stage, adopt a broad strategy such as (1) education and communication, (2) participation and involvement with other organizations, (3) support and facilitation of a public policy or a private agreement with interest groups, (4) negotiation and/or build consensus, (5) influence agency administration, and (6) litigation.

6. *Organization for strategic management of public issues.* The strategic management process has to be managed by specific departments or individuals within the company if it is to be accomplished in a reliable and effective way. Options include choice of elaborate staff coverage versus making decisions about issues management within line management.

7. *Development of action plans.* Action plans include committing resources for specific activities to manage public issues. Actions are based upon the broad strategy option previously selected. The action could be to sponsor research, issue a press release, support a political action committee, attend a hearing, offer technical support to regulators, or do "damage control" through litigation.

8. *Implementation and follow-through of the planned response.* Implementation includes the coordinated response of public statements with activities underway by the organization. Also, coordinated activities with outside groups like industry associations may be involved.

9. *Evaluation of feedback from results.* Some assessment of the effectiveness of the attempt to manage

TABLE 3–2
Classifying the Strategic Impact of Issues

	Relative Impact of the Issue		
Probability of Development	Low	Medium	High
Low			
Medium			
High			

the public issue is necessary to see if it resulted in the desired outcome. If not, then another iteration of the process may be required.

Mapping the Issues

Business organizations need to be able to identify issues and map their relative strategic importance to the business and to external stakeholders. The same issue can have a very different impact on businesses that operate in different industries. For example, foreign trade barriers that make it difficult to operate in Japanese markets may pose a significant threat to U.S.-based telecommunications companies and for agriculture exports. However, these barriers tend not to be problems for the textile industry, which exports a relatively small amount of its production. For textiles, the issue is more likely to be how to deal with fabrics imported into the United States.

Because monitoring issues and developing plans to respond to them can be costly, most businesses need to be selective in dealing with issues. Some determination must be made about the likely relative magnitude of impact of a particular issue and the probability of its developing to the point where it will be important. Mapping issues can help to answer the following questions[3]:

1. Are the issues of importance for a company the same or different from the issues important for the industry?
2. How widespread is the issue? Does it impact primarily on one set of customers? or on many different industries? Is the issue confined to one locality, or is it global in its implications?
3. To what extent is the concept of "emerging issue" useful or misleading for an industry or company? Will immediate action be needed or does there seem to be several years of lead time before action will be needed?
4. Does the stakeholder mapping of an industry's problem have specific implications for a company? Who are the stakeholders? Are these stakeholders

especially important and powerful, or do they represent a very narrowly defined interest?
5. Does the stakeholder mapping have specific implications for industrial associations? Is the issue of importance to a particular industry? Would collective action by the industry association be useful?
6. Do people inside and outside an industry perceive the same issues in the same way? Does the top management see the issue in ideological terms, while interest groups view it as a public health issue? Differences in perceptions concerning an issue lead to differences in perceptions concerning its relative importance, to why it is a controversial problems, and to what sort of resolution might be acceptable to various parties.

Issues can be identified and categorized by size of impact and the probability of an impact upon the company or a division within it, or upon some specific site. Table 3-2 suggests how this might be done. Issues that should receive the most management attention are those changes in the technological, scientific, cultural, and political areas likely to have a medium to high impact, with medium to high probability of developing into an issue. In contrast, events that have low impact and low probability of further development should be only occasionally monitored.

The monitoring capability is likely to vary with the size and resources of an organization. A small business needs to keep track of important issues likely to influence it but cannot afford an extensive research operation. Thus, small businesses may monitor their environment by joining their industry association and local chamber of commerce. Also, a careful reading of the local newspaper is essential for monitoring changes that will affect the business.

For example, a shop that does automobile painting and body work could be surprised by developments in the toxic waste area. Several of the substances used by these businesses are carcinogenic and must be used and disposed of carefully. Thus the OSHA regulations concerning job safety and EPA regulations concerning the disposal of various substances can be extensive and subject to change.

Publications of trade associations can help the small business to keep abreast of developments regarding alternative substances, state-of-the-art practices for technical processes and for toxic waste disposal requirements, and new technologies available in this line of business. Also, local zoning ordinances and county long-range planning documents have implications for where future customers are likely to live and for areas in which future business operations will be allowed to locate.

These same issues are likely to affect large petroleum companies, but the size of impact and the probabilities are likely to be different. In this case, the toxic waste problem concerning a petroleum refinery is likely to be larger and more complex. However, the possibility of reusing toxic substances by altering the chemistry and developing alternative products increases the range of available alternatives for larger businesses. With its large size and widespread operations, both the diversity and magnitude of strategic options concerning the toxic waste issue in petrochemicals is likely to be significantly different.

A small business that is an end user of the product will have fewer resources to research technological alternatives and may have more difficulty making itself heard in public debate. Larger companies may have full-time staff operations using numerous outside sources of information to track the developments in this issue.

Both large and small companies should monitor their environments and determine the relative impact and probability of issue development considered to be of strategic importance. The larger the scale of operations, the more extensive and sophisticated will be the social issues management process.

The Life Cycle of Sociopolitical Issues

The issues life cycle (ILC) is a descriptive framework designed to help in understanding how society is likely to respond to some technological or sociopolitical development over time.[4] This ILC is the general pattern followed by the public policy process that *is independent of* the strategic issues management process used by business decision makers.

We propose that strategic issues management (SIM) used by business decision makers will vary systematically with an issue's stage in the ILC as it unfolds in the public policy process. Furthermore, the management activities are most effective when their objective, strategy, and action plans are congruent with the stage of the ILC. Historically issues have unfolded slowly over several decades, as in the case of demographic, workforce, and diversity issues[5]. In recent years issues have seemed to develop at an accelerated pace fraught with uncertainty.

This ILC framework suggests a way to classify issues and to develop management actions that are likely to be the most useful. Every issue manifests itself to an organization with a unique set of circumstances, and the consequences of timing and substance of specific management actions are often highly unpredictable. Thus, the ILC framework should not be used in a deterministic way. Situations can change quickly at the tactical level in a turbulent environment. However, the pattern of strategic response is likely to follow the general pattern offered below within a given ILC stage in effective organizations.

The six stages of the ILC, as shown in Figure 3–2 are:

1. *Sociopolitical change occurs.* Generally, an issue emerges from sociotechnical, legal-political, and cultural changes. Examples are major trends including globalization, changing workforce characteristics, technological change, and the aftermath of corporate restructuring of the 1990s. The difficulties resulting from such trends, as well as the sociopolitical issues emerging from them, slowly come to public awareness. As a change issue becomes more visible, it is researched by experts and later becomes increasingly understood, and ultimately it is reported in the popular media.

2. *A public problem is defined.* Difficulties arising from the sociopolitical changes then are framed in various ways that serve to define the public policy

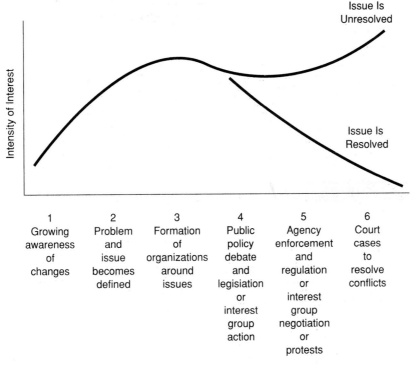

FIGURE 3–2 The Issue Life Cycle

SOURCE: Adapted from Grover Starling, *The Changing Environment of Business*, Third Ed. (Boston: PWS-Kent Publishing, 1988), p. 214.

agenda. For example, many companies are grappling presently with shaping smoking policies within their organizations. This smoking issue can be framed in terms of being a public health issue, a way to cut costs of health benefits, a matter of personal choice, and even an issue of worker productivity.

3. *Interest groups and organizations are formed.* Interest groups form around various problem definitions and, thus, can be supportive of or antagonistic to the interests of business with respect to a particular issue. As noted earlier, these interest groups might press for laws constraining offensive behavior, or they might seek to persuade business through other approaches.

For example, in the abortion controversy, pro-life interest groups sought to overturn the Supreme Court ruling that permits abortion, have laws changed, and close abortion clinics through

public protests. Pro-choice interest groups sought to sustain the views of the Court, to stop laws that limit the right to an abortion through increasing the legitimacy of abortion within society. Also, they sought police protection against pro-life demonstrators.

4. *The public policy agenda and debate are set.* Public policy alternatives are developed and different solutions are debated by lawmakers and interest groups before they are legitimized into law or public policy.

5. *Laws and regulations are passed.* The legislative and regulatory processes typically make the administration of a policy routine. Government agencies routinely administer regulations that directly affect human resource development, such as workplace health and safety (OSHA), discrimination and employment opportunity (EEOC), and safety standards and training requirements for handling various substances found in the workplace (EPA).

Business has both an external and internal task at this stage. Externally, there is a need to work with corporate public affairs to communicate the industry and company position (1) to relevant lawmakers and regulators and (2) to interest groups to obtain a favorable public policy solution to an issue. Also, management needs to become informed about the regulations once they are established. Internally, management needs to shape company policies to anticipate and respond effectively to evolving issues to ensure economic performance and legal compliance.

6. *Litigation takes place in the courts.* Remaining conflicts concerning sociopolitical issues are resolved through litigation. At this stage the management professional seeks to insure legal compliance within the organization. Litigation in the areas of wrongful discharge, sexual harassment, and privacy have dramatically increased in recent years, and company programs can help avoid lawsuits in such areas by administering human resource development programs.

Obviously, not every issue goes or should go through all six stages of the ILC. One of the objectives of SIM is to respond effectively to issues at early stages so that they do not result in needless or harmful laws, regulations, and litigation as they unfold through the ILC. The key task for strategic managers wishing to respond to an issue is to consider carefully the stage in the ILC before defining the strategic problem or adopting a broad strategic approach for responding to it. If an issue is just beginning to enter into the public's consciousness, problem-solving strategies based upon cooperation are best. For example, the development of an effective solution to the day care problem or a policy concerning parental leave could forestall harmful and possibly ineffective government intervention in this area.

Similarly, research to establish credibility followed by an effective communication of the company's position is appropriate early in the cycle. Companies that take a defensive and reactive institutional orientation through legalistic blocking approaches in the early stages will have such undesirable results as

1. Not being fully informed before taking a position
2. Being publicly perceived as obstructionist, uncaring, and exploitive
3. Being likely to assist in the political momentum of adversaries who might call for public policy that is unfavorable to the organization.[6]

The following section illustrates the interaction between SIM and the ILC framework. These examples are meant to provide managers with a useful framework for effective management of emerging issues of the 1990s.

Issue Identification and the Issue Life Cycle

The first phase of the SIM process is to diagnose the issue so that an organization can determine whether a developing situation is likely to be of strategic importance.[7] As part of this diagnosis, an issue can be categorized as a threat or an opportunity for the organization.[8] Such categorization schemes trigger different sequences of information processes and are likely to influence the motivation patterns of key organizational decision makers. Managers who feel unjustifiably threatened by an issue spend their energy in protecting themselves rather than using such problem-solving approaches as carefully listening to market concerns and redesigning the product or reaching a conciliatory relationship with regulators or major customers.

Because managerial discretion is likely to be greater at the earlier stages of the ILC[9], the perceived harmful effects of an issue are likely to increase as the issue progresses through the life cycle. Thus, a misstep in strategic issues management in the early stages of the ILC can lead to the adoption of costly, inflexible positions from which it can be difficult to withdraw.

As an issue unfolds, the nature of the strategic objectives and problems posed by it to organizations varies with each ILC stage, as outlined in Table 3–3. Individual corporate interests vary from company to company and from industry to industry. Each has a unique strategic objective and problem definition within the general pattern.

ILC Stage One: Sociopolitical Changes Occur

Changes in demography, workforce characteristics, technology, and international competitiveness do occur and do give rise to public issues. However, it is usually a long time before the problems resulting from such changes are generally known. The SIM objective in ILC stage one is not to be caught by surprise. Thus, early issue identification through monitoring the environment, doing research, and forecasting social changes is of key importance. One way to predict future sociopolitical issues needing strategic attention is tracking professional interest in issues through various journals and periodicals.

As companies tend to have more discretion at the early stages of an issue, as indicated earlier, companies that perceive emerging issues early tend to have more policy options that are also likely to be less costly in responding effectively. For example, the U.S. standard of living has been declining since around 1972. This has resulted in a trend of two-

TABLE 3–3
Issue Life Cycle, Objectives, and Problem Identification

Phase One of the SIM Process		
Issue Life Cycle Stage	Description of Problem Situation	Strategic Objective
1. Sociopolitical changes occur	Scarce and/or inaccurate information	Anticipate emergence of issue
2. Problem becomes defined	Public policy issue is not defined yet	Define problem advantageously
3. Organizations are established	New interest groups emerge, and/or established interest groups adopt issue; political coalitions develop; focal organization facing external resistance	Steer and guide public policy alternatives
4. Policy agenda is set	Resolution of problem in political arena	Influence favorable policy
5. Public policy is formalized	Public agencies are developing regulations and implementing	Influence favorable administration of the solution
6. Public enforcement becomes routine	Precedents exist; litigation frequently used to change administration of solution advantageously to focal organization	"Damage control"

family wage earners and dual-career couples during the past two decades. This long-term trend is now posing serious issues with work-family conflicts that are being defined as ILC stage-two social problems. Work-family conflicts have manifested themselves as new demands for parental or family leave, day care, and flexible work scheduling in the 1990s.

ILC Stage Two: Issue and Problem Definition

The SIM objective here is to define the issue advantageously. Policy problems can be defined in a number of ways once an issue has been identified, for example, the broad issue of international competitiveness in agriculture. In 1988 the European Community (EC) prohibited the importation of beef from cattle that had been treated with growth hormones. American agricultural interests sought to define this as an unfair market barrier. EC members sought to define the problem as a health issue. If U.S. producers could define the problem in the way they desired, they could continue to produce lower-cost beef through the use of growth hormones. If the problem was defined as a health problem, then industry practices would have to change, cost advantages would shift, and the competitive position of firms in the market would undergo sizable adjustments.

This pattern of individualistic definition of strategies and problems has long been evident in the strategic response to issues, as has been documented by Wood in her research of corporate responses to the regulatory episodes of the Progressive Era.[10] In a more recent case, consider the issue of international competitiveness. Manufacturing businesses that have weak competitive positions are likely to seek to define the problem in terms of unfair foreign competition and push for government protection. Retailing businesses benefiting from the inexpensive imported goods are likely to define the problem in terms of lower cost to their customers and thus favor a free-trade policy.

ILC Stage Three: The Establishment of Organizations

Organizations tend to form spontaneously around problem definitions once the interest in a public issue is heightened. Here the key SIM strategy for businesses is to seek support from available organizations to steer and guide policy alternatives in a way that is favorable to the organization. For example, gay rights groups are concerned about human resource policies covering health care coverage, privacy, and life-threatening disease in the workplace. Women's groups, minority groups, retirees, unions, and a host of other interest groups also are vitally concerned with public policy in the area of human resources. If industry groups can form cooperative strategic alliances with groups compatible with business interests, then public policy outcomes (i.e., laws and regulations) are more likely to be faborable for business.

ILC Stage Four: Debates over Public Policy

In this stage, public debates in Congress and state legislatures end with the adoption of legal remedies. The SIM objective at this point is to influence policy so that the new laws are consistent with organizational interests. For example, new legislation has caused the cost of pension benefits and workers' compensation insurance to be out of reach of most small businesses. It is in business's interest to outline benefit proposals or concepts that will strike a balance between employee interests and the economic limitations inherent in an internationally competitive marketplace.

Alternatively, the debates can take the form of negotiations between a business and its stakeholders, or between a global business and host country governments. The outcomes of this type of debate or negotiation are not likely to result in a law or public policy. Rather, the policy agreement would take the form of an arrangement between the company and its stakeholders. These groups could be formed by a legal contract or by an informal agreement. For example, a company would then change its product designs to comply with an international agreement on industry standards.

ILC Stage Five: Interpretation and Implementation of Public Policy

Once a law has been passed, its implementation is normally relegated to various public agencies.

These agencies obtain budgets, staffing, and a legal mandate to enforce the law. Regulations are developed and enforcement patterns are implemented by government regulators. The SIM objective of business in this stage of the ILC is to obtain a favorable administration of the formalized public policy.

ILC Stage Six: Public Enforcement of Policy by the Courts

Most of the litigation occurs within the context of administrative law under the jurisdiction of various regulatory agencies. Agencies monitor compliance, hold hearings, call witnesses, and issue fines in a quasi-judicial setting. Also, various legal entities can sue a business for the results of its actions or practices. The legal standards used to judge violations and to determine damages are based upon the laws and regulations developed up to this point. In fully developed issues in stage six, corporations seek legal compliance or legal exceptions to the public policy through litigation. As noted above, regulation is expected to increase in the area of leave policy, retirement benefits, and discrimination against disabled employees.

Issue Analysis, Management Actions, and the Issue Life Cycle

As a major social change results in the unfolding of an issue of public concern, public policy change needs to be congruent with the stage in the issue's development. Similarly, business organizations can adapt similar strategic patterns appropriate to the various stages in the ILC, as shown in Table 3–4.

1. *Education and communication.* In the early stages of the development of an issue, education and communication are necessary to bring significant sociopolitical changes to the consciousness of the general public. Companies need to monitor the environment, do strategically targeted research, and forecast trends so they are not caught unprepared for issues. For example, the rapid restructuring of U.S. industry and the increased global competition of the 1980s have made downsizing and multinational issues urgent in this decade. Businesses most able to respond to these challenges needed to have begun tracking and researching the implications of these trends.

2. *Programs of cooperation and participation.* Once general awareness of a public issue is heightened, general agreement on the underlying problems or opportunities characterizes stage two of the ILC. Businesses use programs of participation and cooperation to gain agreement on issue definition in stage two so that policy proposals in later stages can gain legitimacy. For example, programs of advocacy advertising can communicate the views of an organization concerning rising health care costs and company benefits packages. A cogent, effective presentation of a problem definition can establish early acceptance and be used as a preemptive strike against those framing an issue in an undesirable way. Also, groups with different views can be studied to determine which key persons might later prove to be friends or detractors.

3. *Building constituency support.* The focus here is on obtaining agreement from grass roots organizations through constituency building, negotiation, and seeking agreements, co-adaptation, and ultimately litigation. These basic SIM strategies and the ILC stage with which they are congruent are outlined in Table 3–4. A dramatic event like news coverage of diseases related to computers in the workplace or the publication of a scientific report on AIDS might increase general awareness and move an issue closer to the public policy agenda. If an organization became aware that such developments were likely to impact its performance or the workability of its current practice, then some form of education and public affairs release might be appropriate. For example, in ILC stage two, the public issue problem is defined. In stage three, advocacy advertising might help to steer the issue.

4. *Negotiation and agreement with lawmakers and constituency groups.* In stage four of an ILC, the issue is clearly on the public policy agenda and lawmakers and those influencing the public policy

TABLE 3–4
Issue Life Cycle Phase Two of SIM: Developing Strategic Alternatives

Issue Life Cycle Stage	Preferred Strategy	Description of Strategic Activities
1. Sociopolitical changes occur; developments	Education and communication	Support research; Monitor and anticipate
2. Problem becomes defined	Participation and involvement; cooperation	Advocacy advertising ; Define constituency; Neutralize critics; Define issue favorably
3. Organizations are established	Build constituency support	Build coalition; Political action committees; Work toward consensus; Public hearings
4. Policy agenda is set	Negotiation and agreement with policymakers in congress	Lobbying; Negotiate with foes and allies
5. Public policy is formalized	Agency relations, cooperation, pressure, negotiation	Define/redefine agency's jurisdiction; Assist in setting agency's standards; Delay implementation of standards; Influence agency staffing and budget; "Capture" agency
6. Public enforcement becomes routine	Litigation	Lawsuits, out-of-court settlements; Change of venue; bankruptcy (chap. 11); legal delays

process are drafting legislation. Legislative hearings and negotiations with the various interest groups in this pluralistic society are competing for alternative drafts of bills before Congress. If business has been successful in stage three of the ILC, then constituency support for a public policy position may be sufficient to influence the shaping of public policy in a favorable way. Compromises may have to be made, and, of course, business may not be able to obtain the sort of public policy it desires.

5. *Formalization of public policy.* Once a law formally establishes a public policy, the policy needs implementation. At the federal level, such administration involves the creation of an agency, estab-

lishing the public mandate and enforcement power of the agency and its funding and staffing. The strategic objective of achieving a favorable administration of a policy in this stage of the ILC requires a favorable relationship with the appropriate agency.

Business can attempt to influence the regulatory process at each phase of agency activity by attention to (1) establishment of the agency, (2) determination of agency jurisdiction, (3) the budget and staffing process that determines levels of funding and staffing, (4) agency rule and regulation development, and (5) the administrative law proceedings under agency jurisdiction.

ESTABLISHMENT OF THE AGENCY.   Most of the time laws are passed and their enforcement is assigned to already existing agencies. However, occasionally an agency is created to deal with a specific problem. For example, the president, through executive order, established the Equal Employment Opportunity Commission (EEOC) to enforce the Civil Rights Act of 1964 and the Equal Pay Act of 1963, and Congress established the Occupational Safety and Health Administration (OSHA) in 1972 to enforce laws concerning these areas. Industry might want to support the creation of a new agency or seek to expand the mandate of an existing agency with which business has some rapport and familiarity.

Sometimes organizations seek to influence the activities of federal agencies by influencing the definition of jurisdiction. For example, American Cyanamid blocked the action of OSHA concerning its fetal protection policy by arguing that the case was not within its jurisdiction. The administrative judge ruled that the exclusionary policy was under the jurisdiction of the EEOC rather than OSHA. This issue passed through to stage six of the ILC and was resolved by a recent Supreme Court case in which the Court ruled that the fetal protection policies at Johnson Controls were discriminatory and thus illegal.[11]

AGENCY FUNDING AND STAFFING LEVELS.   A major strategy used during the 1980s was to reduce budgets sufficiently to limit the number of field inspectors, auditors, and litigators available to agencies. Most staff members of regulatory agencies are professional employees covered by civil service regulations. However, the top positions are political appointments made by the executive branch with the advice and consent of the Senate. Various interest groups can and do influence this process by filing statements, making public pronouncements, and appearing before Congress.

DEVELOPMENT OF REGULATIONS AND STANDARDS.   Laws are usually written in a vague form, which means the formalization of public policy depends upon numerous regulations developed by the regulatory agency. Because businesses usually have the most technical expertise in an area, they often seek to assist in the development of regulations. The objective is to have regulations that are technically sound in terms of current scientific developments, economically efficient, and administratively workable.

Organizations with a type-three institutional orientation can develop research studies to inform regulators of the consequences and possibilities of regulations along these dimensions. However, if they block or delay standards or lobby for a lesser standard without fixing the problem, the issue can come back to haunt business later. For example, the Ford Motor Company successfully influenced the timing and level of regulations that governed the fuel system on their Pinto model in the 1970s. Passengers of these models experienced often fatal fires when the car was involved in a rear-end collision.

The fact that the car complied with existing federal standards did not convince juries not to award punitive damages when they discovered that the poor standards were the result of Ford's SIM program with the agency. Thus cooperation with agencies in the standard-setting process should be based upon sound engineering practices and done in conjunction with fixing any serious technical problems in safety.

ENFORCEMENT PATTERNS OF REGULATIONS.   Because regulatory agencies have limited resources, they usually try to be strategic in the enforcement of regulations. For example, the Justice Department may have dozens of cases that could be prosecuted in the area of discrimination or employment law. However, it does not have the resources to research and prosecute each case thoroughly. Thus, it seeks cases that will move the law in a direction that will have the greatest impact in realizing public policy objectives. Similarly, some toxic wastes and environmental pollutants are more dangerous and have a wider range of negative effects than others. Thus the Environmental Protection Agency also seeks to establish rational priorities in the enforcement of national policies relating to toxic substances in the workplace. Business seeks to communicate its priorities and concerns to regulatory agencies to influence enforcement patterns.

Implementing SIM Alternatives

The implementation of SIM alternatives is the last phase of the SIM process. In the model presented here, we argue that the relevant resources, the arena of action, primary public, and type of influence most appropriate for SIM varies with the ILC stage. Implementation of SIM requires that actions be taken in each of these areas, as outlined in Table 3–5.

In stage one, changes are underway in society that give rise to problems that are poorly understood. A scientifically based understanding of the issue at this stage is important for establishing credibility for issues management. Technical knowledge will help corporations develop response patterns that will not only be likely to influence public policy later but also be an effective corporate response technically. Thus, technical credibility is the most important resource preceding the definition of an problem created by an emerging issue.

As the issue moves into stage two, the public understanding of it can be strongly influenced by opinion leaders with access to the media. For example, as an issue breaks, talk show hosts on

TABLE 3–5
Issue Life Cycle Phase Three of SIM: Implementing Strategic Action

Issue Life Cycle Stage	Relevant Resources	Arena of Action	Primary Public	Type of Influence
1. Sociopolitical changes occur	Informational technical credibility	Research	Experts	Technical
2. Problem becomes defined	Informational popular support	Public statements; Preemptive strike; Cooperative actions	Media; opinion leaders	Communication expertise: persuasion
3. Organizations are established	Political: interest group	Public statements; Coalition building	Interest groups	Public support; Legitimacy
4. Policy agenda is set	Political: legislative group support	Lobbying; Hearings before lawmakers	Legislature; Congress	Public support; Political power
5. Public policy is formalized	Political: legal and technical expertise	Hearings before agencies; Confirmation hearings; Agency review boards	Executive branch; Agencies	Political power; Technical expertise; Legal competence
6. Public enforcement becomes routine	Legal expertise	Courts; Judicial hearings	Judicial branch; Courts	Legal competence

national radio or television are likely to interview someone who has recently written a book or who has done a major study of the issue. Industrial representatives who have recognized scientific or empirical knowledge and have access to sophisticated monitoring capability are likely to have the best sense of the importance of the issue, and also the best access to opinion leaders.

As an issue moves through the ILC, relevant resources change from informational, to political, and then to legal. The relevant resources outlined in Table 3–5 systematically vary, as do the arena for SIM action, the primary public, and types of influence appropriate to the various stages of the ILC. The use of an inappropriate SIM strategy could have unexpectedly negative consequences. For example, in the Nestlé infant formula controversy, the public was made aware of the issue by the publication of two inflammatory booklets in Europe.[12] The model suggests this would be a stage-two issue, which calls for a strategy of participation and involvement implemented by activities such as advocacy advertising, public statements to neutralize critics, and statements to the media.

Instead, Nestlé chose a stage-six strategy and sued the publishing organization for libel. Nestlé won the lawsuit but suffered defeat in the early development of the issue. The court case did not shed any light on the problems of safe infant nutrition in the Third World nutrition. Nestlé was late in investigating practices within the company and late in making any modification that would alleviate the problem. Furthermore, the court case brought favorable public exposure to their adversaries, who then launched a relatively successful consumer boycott of Nestlé in the United States, where they did not even market that product.

Decycling SIM Strategies

The SIM approaches congruent with the particular circumstances posed by each stage of the ILC are likely to be the most effective. However, there are times when the prognosis of an issue is particularly unfavorable, and thus issues managers seek to recycle or decycle an issue in its ILC development. We would argue that attempts to recycle an issue are ILC-congruent, but that attempts to decycle an issue are not. The Business Roundtable, an association of large businesses, seems to have a recycling approach to defeat the Consumer Protection Act.[13] Bills had been passed several times by the House and Senate separately, but threats of veto by Presidents Nixon and Ford had prevented passage of a bill in both houses of Congress during the same session. President Carter's support of the legislation indicated to supporters that the bill would pass the Democratic Ninety-fifth Congress. The Roundtable, together with the U.S. Department of Commerce, the National Association of Manufacturers (NAM), and the National Federation of Independent Business, adopted a grass roots strategy to convince newly elected members of Congress and those reelected deemed open to persuasion that the proposed bill was not needed. Simultaneously, professional analysis and factual communication in simple language helped change the public perception of the bill. The bill failed to pass the House of Representatives.

In January 1993 the EPA released a study indicating that secondary smoke is carcinogenic and harmful to nonsmokers who breathe it. The ILC seems to be at stage five as the EPA contemplates further restrictions on both cigarette advertising and smoking in public places. A decycling approach seems to have been adopted by the tobacco industry in its attempts to redefine proposed bans on cigarette advertising as a free speech issue rather than one of public health. Members of the industry appear to have used what would normally be a stage-two strategy of defining a public issue in a favorable manner.

The cigarette manufacturers sought to redefine tobacco advertising. The issues management strategy was to move the issue away from public health, which would be unfavorable to the industry, to freedom of speech, where the industry stood a better chance to prevail politically. It remains to be seen if this decycling strategy will prove successful.

TABLE 3–6

The Organization/Administration and Activities of Issues Management Programs

	Group A	Group B
Organization	Separate and distinguishable IM unit	IM is part of Public Affairs/Public Relations or Corporate Communications
Focus	External; well defined	Internal; eclectic
Unit of analysis	The corporation as a whole	A single department or task
Process	Very broad; includes all three phases of the IM process	Tied to particular function (e.g., advertising); only one phase of the IM process is practiced
Emphasis	Advisory; decision-directed	Educational; informational; problem-oriented
Interaction with Top Management	Frequent; routine; helps set issues agenda	Occasional; ad hoc; uses IM as a tool
Type of Interaction	Direct reporting or reporting through a committee of the board	Through department head and "levels of bureaucracy"
Role of issues manager	Leader; coordinator; consensus builder	Information collector and provider; clearinghouse

SOURCE: Copyright 1986 by the Regents of the University of California. Reprinted from the *California Management Review,* Vol. 29, No 1. Permission by the Regents.

Organizing for Strategic Issues Management

Wartick and Rude studied how businesses organize for strategic management and found two distinct approaches.[14] In the framework developed, type A organizations established a separate operating issues management unit. In type B organizations issues management responsibilities were assumed by the Department of Public Affairs, Public Relations, or Corporate Communications, as shown in Table 3–6.

In organizations where SIM was organized into a separate and distinguishable department, the focus of its activity was well defined; it served the issues management needs for the entire corporation, and its activities included all three of the processes outlined above. Though its activities were decision-directed, its recommendations were considered advisory by line management. The management of this department tended to have access to top management and frequent contacts with executives. The manager of the issues management department frequently met with the board of directors and assisted in setting the strategic policy agenda for the organization.

In organizations where issues management was an additional responsibility of the public affairs department, the role and responsibility was very different. The tasks of these departments were fragmented, internal, and eclectic as far as issues management was concerned. Typically concerns were focused at the department level and were only occasionally involved with top management concerns. In the type B configuration, the issues management official's relationship with top management was one of providing information reports through several layers of bureaucracy. Thus, the emphasis in this type of organization was problem-oriented and informational, with the goal of educating managers on the developments concerning issues.

Organizations that are strategically affected by public issues are likely to be organized along the type A organizational arrangement outlined in Table 3-6. In organizations where the impact of public issues is somewhat small and the probabilities are considered low, the emphasis and organizational capability is likely to be reflected in a type B issues management.

Organizational Stakeholders

An organizational stakeholder is "any group or individual who can affect or is affected by the achievement of the firm's objectives."[15] Who are the organizational stakeholders? Managers often consider such primary stakeholders as owners and investors, customers and consumer interest groups, employees and organized labor, the community and significant interest groups within a pluralistic society, and environmentalists. Managers can map the various stakeholders as shown in Figure 3-3. Any given management decision is likely to affect each of these stakeholders differently.

Therefore, the relations between business and some stakeholders may be cordial and warm while hostile and cold with others. Stakeholder relations may vary with time and circumstance. For example, consider a major oil company that has a large number of stakeholders with extremely complex relationships between and among them. Using Figure 3-3 as a guide, we can identify some of these relationships and hint at some of the implications.

Suppliers. An oil company obtains supplies of oil from both domestic and international sources. Some suppliers are members of OPEC, the international oil cartel that seeks to control the international supply and price of crude oil. Other suppliers of oil are domestic and located in such states as Texas, Louisiana, and Oklahoma. The economic well-being of people who live in these states is highly dependent upon the oil industry and their relationships with the major oil companies.

Local community groups and significant interest groups (SIG) have organized to protest against oil companies that obtain oil through offshore drilling and who use single-hull super tankers in dangerous waters because of the danger of oil spills. Obtaining the oil and shipping it to refineries can result in major oil spills such as the Exxon oil spill, which occurred in 1988 off the Alaskan coast. Groups would like to stop or tightly control offshore drilling and the use of super tankers. These groups are concerned with the environmental consequences of pollution due to oil in the oceans, exhaust fumes in the air, and petrochemicals in the water. Some of these groups have market interactions with major oil companies, some own shares of stock, but most are likely to be concerned with the results of oil company decisions and seek to control behavior through political rather than economic processes.

Customers and consumer advocates call for fair prices, high-quality gasoline and petrochemical products, and product labeling about the effects of using products. Some have sought to control price increases in the cost of gasoline.

Employees. Major oil companies, like many large organizations, have thousands of employees in many countries. Some of these employees are members of labor unions. Some are highly trained professional geologists and engineers. Others are oil field workers, crew members on ships, and workers in chemical factories and refineries. Decisions made by managers relating to compensation, plant closing, modernization of facilities, marketing, and distribution can have major effects on employees' lives.

Owners and investors include stockholders, creditors, and other members of the financial commu-

STAKEHOLDER VIEW OF FIRM

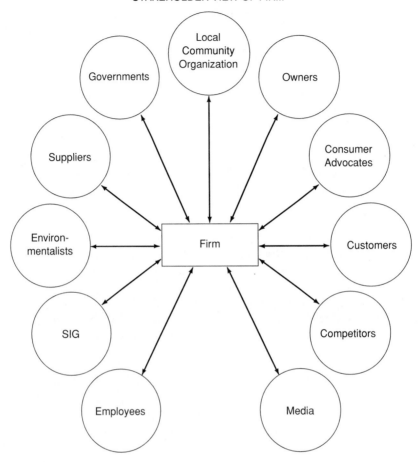

FIGURE 3–3 Stakeholder View of the Firm

SOURCE: R. Edward Freeman, *Strategic Management: A Stakeholder Appproach* (Marshfield, Mass.: Pitman, 1984), p. 25.

nity. During the 1980s there were many takeovers in the oil industry. Getty Oil was acquired by Pennzoil after a costly and hostile court battle with Texaco. USX acquired Marathon Oil in competition with Mobil. Standard Oil acquired Gulf, which sold out to avoid a hostile takeover attempt by Mesa Petroleum. The financial community, with its stockholders, prospective stockholders, financiers attempting hostile takeovers, investment bankers supplying capital in the form of junk bonds, investment analysts, and money managers, forms a complex network of stakeholders for a major oil company.

There are other stakeholder groups than those identified above, but these comments will be suggestive of the realities facing management in large oil companies as well as other companies today. Figure 3–4 shows a general stakeholder map of a major oil company in the 1980s.

STAKEHOLDER CLAIMS AND BUSINESS SOCIAL PERFORMANCE

Organizational stakeholders make claims on business based on their interests and institutionally

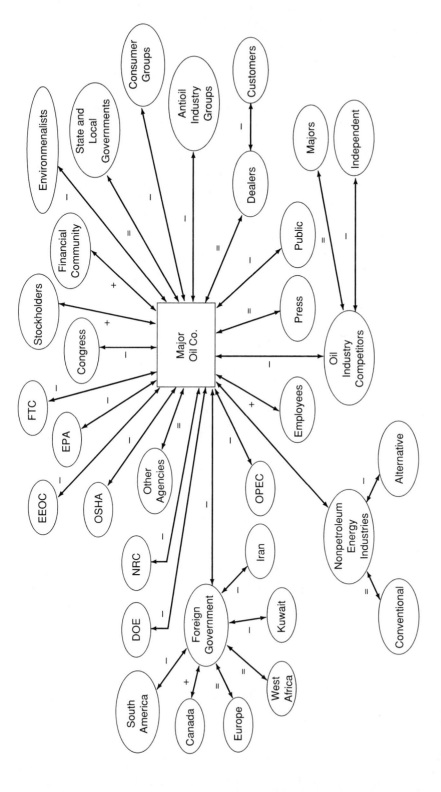

Strategic Issues:
- OPEC policy
- New sources of supply
- U.S. govt. policy on energy
- Managing "regulation"
- Public image

Notes:
+ means generally positive relationship
− means generally negative relationship
= means generally neutral relationship

FIGURE 3–4 Stakeholder Map of Major Oil Co. in 1980s

SOURCE: R. Edward Freeman, *Strategic Management: A Stakeholder Appproach* (Marshfield, Mass.: Pitman, 1984), p. 122.

67

defined roles that stakeholders consider legitimate. What are these concerns and interests? On what basis do stakeholders make claims on business? Are the claims just? What if the claim of one stakeholder conflicts with the claims of another? These important problems face the practicing manager. As is the individual context of ethical decision making discussed in Chapter 6, the context of organizational decisions is fraught with complex situations and competing stakeholder demands. Managers must strike a balance among these competing claims, if they are to be just and to maintain public support while obtaining excellent economic performance.

Sometimes stakeholder claims take the form of demands that legal and moral rights not be violated and that cultural values and ideology be supported. In a threefold society, stakeholder claims can be classified according to the social sphere in which they appear. The government has the role of protecting rights and maintaining justice. The cultural sphere is concerned with social values and ideology. The economic sphere is concerned with the material welfare of the society. Table 3–7 classifies stakeholder claims according to these three social spheres.

Employee concerns for economic justice center around job security, just rewards or compensation, and opportunity for career advancement. However, employees also claim their rights of privacy; freedom of association, which includes union membership; freedom of expression; the right not to be wrongfully discharged; and the right to equal opportunity and nondiscrimination in employment practices.

Investors include both the stockholders or owners and the creditors of the organization. The economic justice concerns center around the return

TABLE 3–7
Stakeholder Claims in a Threefold Society

| Type of Stakeholder | Social Sphere of Stakeholder Claim | | |
	Economic	Political (Rights Sphere)	Cultural
Employees	Job security, fair rewards, career development	Privacy, association, expression, safety, discharge for cause, nondiscrimination	Quality of work life, individual dignity
Investors	Fair returns, debt repayment, reasonable risk, choices	Financial disclosure, sound management, business judgment rule	Ethical investments
Customers	Fair and competitive prices, quality availability	Honest advertising, fulfilled contracts, safety, free choice	Consistency with cultural values, quality of life
Community	Economic development, standard of living, employment tax base	Notice of plant closing, control of externalities, side effects, obey laws, regulations	Quality of life, corporate citizenship, community involvement

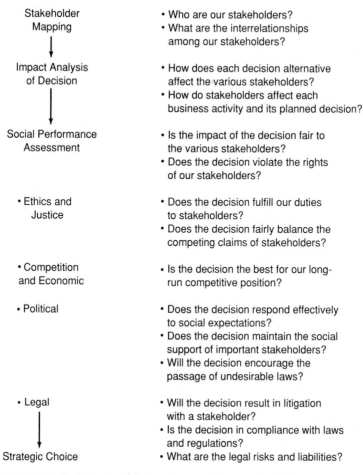

FIGURE 3–5 Stakeholder Analysis and Strategic Choice

on their investment, debt repayment, and sound management, which has implications for the long-term value of their investment. Customers are concerned about prices, quality and availability of goods and services, and product safety. The legal rights claimed by customers include honest and adequate information, fulfilled contracts, safety, and the ability to make economic choices without undue pressure or coercion. The various individuals, governments, and organizations representing the community have economic claims that relate to regional economic development, standard of living, employment, and maintenance of the tax base.

Managers need to weigh the many complex and competing claims of various stakeholders in light of the realities of competitive position, legal requirements, political pressures, and justice. The process of strategic choice includes (1) stakeholder mapping, (2) impact analysis of decision alternatives, (3) social performance assessment, and (4) strategic choice as outlined in Figure 3–5.

Summary

The fourth dimension of business social performance is concerned with legitimacy, that is, with maintaining an acceptable level of social and political support for business activities and interests. Low legitimacy leads to an unfavorable political climate and punitive laws and an unfavorable regulatory environment. High legitimacy leads to cooperation between business and the government and the establishment of a favorable regulatory environment that considers the concerns and interests of business as part of the input for regulations.

A primary tool for developing the response capability to maintain high levels of legitimacy is the strategic issues management (SIM) process. This process includes nine steps: (1) issues identification, (2) assessment of the impact of an issue on corporate interests, (3) priority setting, (4) diagnosis of the broad issue life cycle stage of the focal issue, (5) development of a broad strategy to deal with the public issue, (6) organizing for issues management, (7) development of specific action plans that implement the strategy, (8) implementing the action plans and following through with needed details, and (9) evaluation of the feedback on the results of the SIM process.

Issues identification begins with a mapping of the issues that a business organization faces. It is unlikely that a single manager will be aware of all the issues facing an organization or of the probabilities and size of impacts. Thus the mapping of the issues and a systematic assessment of the probable impacts should be done carefully and systematically. Small businesses can use outside information from the chamber of commerce, industry association newsletters, special reports from trade publications, and newspapers to obtain most of the needed information. The mapping done by larger business organizations is likely to be much more elaborate.

The issue life cycle (ILC) includes six stages that an issue passes through in the course of its development:

1. Social, technological, or political changes over time that lead to
2. Problems that are vaguely experienced at first and later are socially defined as problems as they grow in public awareness.
3. Interest groups and organizations begin to firm around issues and the problem definitions as groups of people in a pluralistic society attempt to do something about the issue.

4. The activities of these organizations move the problem, now a clearly identifiable public issue, on the public policy agenda, where it is the focus of a controversial public debate. Public laws are passed or policies are approved to resolve the problems brought about by the societal and technological changes. These laws usually constrain or guide business behavior in areas that relate to any specific issue.
5. Agencies are formed or changed and charged with the responsibility for implementing the new social policy. They enforce the law through developing regulations, holdings hearings, monitoring business behavior, and engaging in administrative law or quasi-judicial proceedings.
6. Disputes concerning the agency regulation or other controversies concerning the formalized administration of the issue are litigated in the courts.

Business organizations strategically manage public issues by systematically adapting the SIM process within three broadly defined phases that include (1) forming strategic objectives, (2) selecting broad strategic alternatives to achieve the desired objective, and (3) developing more specific action plans that are implemented. The adjustment of these phases of the SIM process are made within the context of the issues life cycle (ILC). Each phase of the SIM process should be congruent with the ILC if it is to be effective. The appropriate strategy for managing a public issue shifts with each change in ILC stage.

Not only do the strategies for the strategic management of public issues shift with the unfolding of the ILC but management action programs, expertise, arenas, and approaches to influence or to interact with the political sphere also vary systematically with each phase of the ILC. Science and education dominate early stages of the ILC, political activities and lobbying dominate the middle stages, and expertise in regulations, administrative law, and litigation dominate its latter stages.

Organizations institutionalize the SIM process by the development of issues managers within the public affairs activities of the firm or by integrating the responsibility for SIM into its managerial operations. In the former, specialized departments are held accountable for coordinating business social performance in the political sphere, while managers focus almost entirely on the economic dimension of business activities. In the latter, a manager is responsible for both the economic and political dimensions of business social performance.

Conclusions

The issue life cycle (ILC) can provide a conceptual framework to guide thinking about the social issues management (SIM) process. This ILC model provides a basis for structuring problems that are inherently unstructured and difficult to manage. The initial strategic issue diagnosis is critical to using the model because a misdiagnosis could trigger organizational decision-making processes that inappropriately define the issue or the appropriate strategy, or misguide corporate responses.

Because public issues of strategic importance are often viewed as threatening to managers within an organization, the SIM process can lead to defensive activities throughout the organization. Defensiveness often distracts from an objective view of the situation and can close off cooperative behaviors and lead to premature litigation that can lower legitimacy. Managers are likely to have greater latitude for flexible responses in the early stages of the ILC. However, defensiveness can lead to biased perceptions that in effect hide many alternatives available to business. Thus managers need to avoid the temptation to become defensive when negative concerns about their activities are expressed in the early ILC stages.

Once the ILC stage has been determined, the strategic management process can be clarified by using the ILC model outlined in this chapter. Though there is a certain amount of momentum for action inherent in any issue as suggested by the ILC model, managers need to carefully consider the implications of momentum. For example, the fact that an issue grows in intensity and continues

to unfold through several stages of the ILC is often a clue that an organization has mismanaged the issue. Competent management should solve the public concern, effectively respond to outcomes of technology or business practices, and thus diffuse the intensity of concern about an issue.

Institutional orientation of a business organization can encourage or discourage its capacity to respond strategically to a public issue. A defensive and reactionary institutional orientation can lead to biased and negative response patterns. Management can build a certain amount of negative momentum with respect to an unfolding issue that can bias its response pattern and render the political performance of the business ineffective. This is particularly the case in the management of product safety. Companies that assume that the environment is hostile—that their products are good but irresponsible elements in the environment are "out to get them"—can make SIM blunders. This was the case for Nestlé in the international controversy over infant formula.[16]

Discussion Questions

1. What is the strategic issues management process? What are the various steps in this process?
2. What is the issue life cycle? Read the first page of a popular newspaper or news magazine. Try to find a copy of a technically oriented trade publication. List the major stories or issues reported in each. At what stage in the life cycle are the issues discussed? Which publication seems to be reporting issues in the earlier stages? Which one seems to be reporting on well-developed or mature issues? What might explain the difference?
3. Select a large company from the *Fortune* 500 list of the largest organizations. Assume you are an executive in this organization. Now take a recent issue of the *Wall Street Journal* or other major newspaper and identify all the major issues reported. Develop a probability-impact

matrix that classifies all the issues you have identified from the point of view of the company you have selected.

4. Using the probability-impact matrix developed for question three above, identify the stage in the ILC for some of the issues. What should be the general strategy for these issues according to the ILC model? Does this make sense to you? Explain why or why not.

5. Review the type three model for institutional orientation outlined in Chapter 1. Select an issue of concern to business that has recently been reported in the popular press. Outline a business response that you would anticipate for three businesses, assuming type-one, type-two, and type-three institutional orientation.

6. What is legitimacy and how does this concept relate to the issue life cycle? How should a business strive to maintain its legitimacy when an issue is in stage five, agency enforcement, of the issue life cycle? Explain your reasoning.

Notes

1. S. L. Wartick and R. E. Rude, "Issues Management: Corporate Fad or Corporate Function," *California Management Review* (1986): 29, 124–40; R. Zentner, "Issues and Strategic Management, in *Competitive Strategic Management*, ed. Robert B. Lamb (Englewood Cliffs, N.J.: Prentice-Hall, 1984), pp. 634–48.

2. I. H. Ansoff, "Strategic Issue Management," *Strategic Management Journal* (1980): 1, 131–48.

3. Joseph F. Coates and Jennifer Jarratt, "Mapping the Issues of an Industry: An Exercise in Issues Identification," in *Strategic Issues Management: How Organizations Influence and Respond to Public Interests and Policies*, ed. Robert L. Heath and Associates (San Francisco: Jossey-Bass, 1988), pp. 122–36.

4. Newman S. Peery, Jr., and Mahmoud Salem, "Strategic Management of Emerging Human Resource Issues," *Human Resource Development Quarterly* 4, no. 1 (Spring 1993): 81–95.

5. G. T. T. Molitor, "Environmental Forecasting: Public Policy Forecasting," in *Business Environment/Public Policy 1979 Conference Papers*, ed. L. E. Preston (St. Louis: American Assembly of Collegiate Schools of Business, 1979).

6. S. P. Sethi amd C. M. Falbe, *Business and Society: Dimensions of Conflict and Cooperation* (Lexington, Mass.: Lexington Books, 1987).

7. J. E. Dutton, L. Fahey, and V. K. Narayanan, "Toward Understanding Strategic Issue Diagnosis," *Strategic Management Journal* 4 (1983): 307–23.

8. J. E. Dutton and S. E. Jackson, "Categorizing Strategic Issues: Links to Organizational Action," *Academy of Management Review* 12 (1987): 76–90.

9. J. E. Post, *Corporate Behavior and Social Change* (Reston, Va.: Reston, 1978).

10. D. J. Wood, *Strategic Uses of Public Policy: Business and Government in the Progressive Era* (Boston: Pitman, 1986).

11. Thomas Brierton and Laurie Lichter-Heath, "Fetal Protection Policies: Balancing the Interests of the Employee, Employer, and the Unborn under Title VII," *Labor Law Journal* (October 1990): 725–35.

12. S. P. Sethi and J. E. Post, "Public Consequences of Private Action: The Marketing of Infant Formula in Less Developed Countries," *California Management Review* 21 (1979): 35–48.

13. E. A. Molander, *Responsive Capitalism: Case Studies in Corporate Social Conduct* (New York: McGraw-Hill, 1980).

14. S. L. Wartick and R. E. Rude, "Issues Management: Corporate Fad or Corporate Function," *California Management Review* 29 (1986): 124–40.

15. R. Edward Freeman, *Strategic Management: A Stakeholder Approach* (Marshfield, Mass.: Pitman, 1984), p. 25.

16. John Dobbing, ed., *Infant Feeding: Anatomy of a Controversy, 1973–1984* (London: Springer-Verlag, 1988).

Case I–1

The Unibody Case

Last fall, a newsman on a local channel in Stockton, California, carried a week-long series of news stories relating to the problems surrounding the new unibody design automobile. During the first day, the news anchorman began by stating:

Unibody vehicles are a relatively new type of vehicle construction. Most unibody vehicles are not being properly repaired. Several major insurance companies are unwilling to pay for safe repairs. Most consumers have been kept in the dark about all of this. The result is that many improperly repaired unibodies are on the highways. Experts call them "death traps, rolling coffins."

Unibody vehicles are the embodiment of high tech manufacturing, automobiles specially designed with lasers, computers, and exotic materials all aimed at creating light weight, aero-dynamic, fuel efficient vehicles. You have all seen the commercials: "smaller and smaller". . ."breathtaking acceleration with handling to match". . . "you are looking at style and technology in total harmony. . ."

If you are driving a Japanese automobile, a European import, or a late-model domestic vehicle, most likely you are behind the wheel of a unibody. Chances are your car dealer, your insurance agent, or your local repair shop never told you that you own a unibody or bothered to explain what that means. It means potential danger, danger in repair owing to their unique construction. Unibody vehicles are extremely dangerous unless repaired properly.

Several local automobile body shop owners were then interviewed who said the following about the new unibody designs:

Bob Koftinow, Delta Body Shop: These cars are designed to absorb crushability to protect drivers and passengers in these vehicles. If you build them back rigid, someone could get killed.

Rob Bebler, Pettinato's Body Shop: It's possible that the pre-stress of the vehicle may be taken out of it and the panels would then fall into the passengers instead of going out away from the passengers.

Al Farner, A & W Body Shop: Most people would not notice the problem in everyday driving, but in a panic situation where they really had to hit the brake, the car wouldn't handle properly and it could kill them.

The newscaster then continued with film clips of factory scenes followed by shots in repair shops that illustrated his narrative. "Just what is a unibody? It is a whole new concept in the structural integrity of an automobile. Traditionally the body of a vehicle was placed on a heavy-duty frame called a standard parameter frame or chassis. With a unibody, the body of the automobile itself is the frame. A series of panels welded together with key structural members like bones in your body add additional support. When unibodies roll off the assembly line, they actually are safer than traditional standard framed vehicles. Convolutions in the structural members are designed to collapse and absorb the impact of the collision. But if they are not repaired properly, that safety feature becomes a danger."

Joe Jenkins, a unibody repairman, then illustrated his point before the camera: "You could have cracks, welds cracking, and when you have an accident, parts that are supposed to give, won't give and end up doing damage or possibly killing a person in the car."

Unibodies are much more costly to repair and it takes additional training and high-tech equipment to do the job properly. Training and equipment necessary for unibodies, which over 90 percent of auto body shops in the United States do not have, cause higher repair bills that many automobile insurance companies are unwilling to pay.

An auto body shop owner was then filmed while saying: "Most major insurance companies are blackballing me." The news narrator then continued, "During this series of reports we will investigate allegations that major insurance companies blackball body shops that do invest in proper training and equipment."

A former AAA insurance adjuster then faced the TV audience and said: "There was never any emphasis on safety or quality of repair. The dollar was the most important. The main thing was the bottom line." The news reporter continued, "We

will investigate allegations that insurance companies are more interested in cutting costs than in quality repair and passenger and vehicle safety."

Film clips were then given of the local offices of four major insurance companies, who said on camera, "I don't know anything about that." Newsman: "Do you want to know about it?" Answer: "No, I don't" said the insurance company employee as he walked away from the camera.

The second company's representative said "No comment."

A third added, "I don't want to say anything with that camera going." And a fourth insurance firm's representative loudly said, "If that's on tape it better not be, I told you not to."

Day two of this news series ended with the newsman saying, "Four major insurance companies were asked to comment about the report.

STAKEHOLDER MAP FOR UNIBODY CASE

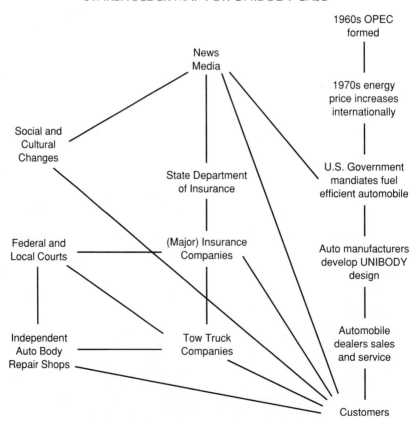

They all referred the reporter to their public relations departments in various parts of the country. All insurance companies ultimately refused to comment on camera. What we have, according to many experts we have heard from, is unibody vehicles rolling out of most body shops improperly repaired, allegedly unsafe death traps, rolling coffins, all to save money instead of saving lives."

Unibody Vehicles—Day Two of the News Series

Year	Number of Unibodies (millions)	Average Price
1979	2.3	$4,900
1982	14.5	$8,500
1985	38.8	$13,000

On day two, the newsman began with statistics showing the growth in numbers of unibody automobiles on the highway. He also pointed out that the average price of a new car was also rising because of the new unibody designs. He then moved to the rising cost of auto repairs due to this new high-tech design. A 10–15 mile per hour accident that used to have a $1,500 price tag for repair now generally costs $4,000 to $5,000. This is due to the nature of the construction of the unibody vehicle. Parts designed to collapse during an accident do collapse and cause damage to travel further throughout the vehicle.

Showing examples on camera, the newsman said that "for example, the apron under the fender of this vehicle is designed to collapse in an accident, causing it to have to be replaced. This part costs $85 but the labor to replace it is over $340." He continued on camera: "This 1983 Mitsubishi with minor damage to the front end cost over $5,000 to repair. This BMW with minor damage to the front end is again $5,000 to repair. Minor rear end damage to this late model BMW cost over $11,000 to repair.

"Major insurance companies are forcing policyholders to pay a large portion of their own repair bill or move their car to a cheaper shop."

Several people were then interviewed: First, a man whose car was stolen and vandalized looked into the camera and said, " I and a lot of other people are being ripped off by insurance companies. I pay over $1,200 per year for insurance for this car alone." While pointing to his repaired automobile, he continued, " Now when I need it repaired, I am out of my pocket a couple of thousand dollars. That is a hell of a lot more than a $250 deductible."

A woman interviewed later said, "The insurance companies don't care about anyone. Their children don't have to drive in an unsafe car. All they care about is profits."

The newsman continued,

[These people], like many, are victims of prevailing rates used by insurance companies to keep costs down. Body shops are surveyed to get the average time and labor costs for repairs. [These average times and labor costs are used to develop standard rates that determine how much an insurance company will pay for a particular type of vehicle damage.] But these time and labor rates do not count the extra schooling and extra equipment costs required to repair unibodies properly and safely.

The bottom line is that if your unibody vehicle is not properly repaired, even after a minor accident, it is most likely out of alignment. That could mean danger on the highway. Your alignment affects your tire wear, your breaking ability, your steering ability, and your acceleration. All of these could mean the difference between life and death in a critical accident.

For body shops across the country it is a crisis. If they spend the money and time to gear up for proper repair of unibody vehicles, they could lose money. If they give up and do substandard work, they could be liable for someone's life in an accident. And if they buck the system, the insurance companies are capable of putting them out of business.

The newsman then interviewed a number of repair shop owners who were having trouble with insurance companies. First one said, "This shop will want to replace certain panels [in a unibody vehicle], and this will make for a higher estimate [than the estimate of a shop not set up to do proper repairs on unibodies]. The insurers are forced to make up the difference [between my price and the prevailing rate table they use to determine allowable damage limits] or go to a less expensive shop." A second added, "It is pretty difficult to be in business when you are trying to do a quality job and the insurance companies are constantly putting you on the defensive by putting you on the low side of the spectrum for what it takes to do that job properly and safely." A third said, "All [the insurance adjusters] do is come in the shop and start cutting you down. I've had them come in and look at the estimate, they are not even looking at the job or the car, and saying this is too high and this is too high." Another said, "People are pretty brainwashed that if they do not go out and help the insurance companies, they may not get their car repaired at all."

It was then reported that an owner of a local automobile body shop was allegedly being blackballed by an insurance company. The insurance company had told tow trucks not to take damaged vehicles to that repair shop and has allegedly had tow trucks even come and remove damaged vehicles from the shop. The owner of the shop said he had won a court judgment but the blackballing was continuing. He said, "They blackball you because they cannot get you to come down to the lower bid price. They tell their insurees not to take their vehicles to my shop for repairs. The person with insurance does not really understand all this. Most insurance companies work based upon the ignorance of the insurees not knowing what to do."

Subsequent installments of the series were devoted to the details of major insurance companies blackballing local repair shops and the lawsuits now in process over the controversy. One insurance adjuster representing a major insurance company specifically identified on camera scolded the newsman saying, "This does not concern you." As he put his hand in front of the camera, he added, "and I do not like this!"

The series ended with a feature on the rights of those insured and the names, addresses, and procedures for filing complaints with the State Department of Insurance. Also, they mentioned that they were sending a video copy of the entire series to a U.S. senator who was investigating the insurance industry with the idea of trying to remove the industry exemption from antitrust laws.

The TV scene then had a sign that read:

YOUR RIGHTS:
    Shop of your choice.

You do not need three estimates.
Get an appraisal of the damages.
Contact your State Department of Insurance.

Case Discussion Questions

1. Is this TV news report objective? Is it biased? Does this make any difference?
2. What institutional orientation do the insurance firms seem to have in this news report? Explain.
3. How are prices for insurance policies set? How do regulated insurance prices differ from prices established by market forces of supply and demand?
4. Assuming that insurance policy prices are regulated, what information is used to justify policy rates? Do you think that insurance regulators put pressure on insurance companies to control costs?
5. What role does "prevailing rates" play in determining coverage limitations? Why is the unibody design a problem when it comes to prevailing rates?
6. Do you think that local managers in insurance companies are authorized to make public statements? If not, where is the media relations function located within an insurance company? How does this influence an insurance company's ability to respond to this news report?
7. If you were an insurance executive, what would you do when you viewed this news broadcast? What would you do immediately? What would you do in the long run?
8. What should the proper role of government be in this case? Explain.
9. Who are the stakeholders, that is, the various persons affected by the unibody controversy? What are the interrelationships among the various stakeholders?
10. Evaluate the business social performance of the insurance industry. The auto repair shops. The automobile industry.
11. How should the management of the insurance companies respond now?
12. What social and/or technological changes contributed to the unibody controversy? What social control mechanisms were present in the case?

Case I–2 _____

Asbestos and Johns-Manville

Awareness of Asbestos As a Workplace Hazard

Asbestos is a gray-white fiber that has been used to make fireproof fabrics and insulation for most of recorded history. The first documented report of asbestos and occupational disease was made by Pliny the Physician in Roman times. He observed that miners in the asbestos mines suffered from respiratory illnesses. Charlemagne, the French king of the ninth century, was reported to have had a tablecloth made of asbestos. He routinely impressed his guests by throwing his tablecloth into a flaming fireplace after a feast. Afterward he would shake it and replace it unharmed on the banquet table.

Because of its unique characteristics, asbestos has been in demand for over two millennia as a heat-resistant substance. Unfortunately, it has caused occupational illnesses for that same period. In the twentieth century, the asbestos issue continued to be in the early stages of the ILC, and thus knowledge of its dangers was limited to a relatively small group of health care professionals and certain managers within the asbestos industry. The first report of asbestos-related diseases among medical workers was published by the U.S. Bureau of Labor Statistics in 1918. This monograph noted that because of increased mortality among asbestos workers, insurance companies had become reluctant to cover workers in this industry.[1] Later during the 1920s a series of articles appeared in British medical journals that discussed asbestosis among textile factory workers.

The major producers of asbestos were Johns-Manville, Inc. and Raybestos-Manhattan Corporation. Johns-Manville, the largest producer, incorporated in New York in 1926 and soon began producing asbestos. When Johns-Manville became aware of the dangers of asbestos during the 1920s, the firm commissioned laboratory studies on animals by the Saranac Laboratory in the state of New York. This action is consistent with the key strategic objective in stage one of the ILC, which should be to conduct or sponsor research on issues before they develop into major public policy issues.

When the results of the sponsored studies began to document the dangers of asbestos, Johns-Manville and the asbestos industry began a major effort to suppress this knowledge from the public that was to continue for over 30 years. Baldwin, the plaintiff's attorney in *Jackson v. Johnsville*, summarized this coverup in the following manner:

> After pointing out that there was overwhelming evidence to show that insulation products made by Johns-Manville and Raybestos-Manhattan had been widely used in the Ingalls shipyard, Baldwin reminded the jury that neither company had placed warning labels on any of those products. At that point, he set a large crayon-drawn chart on the viewing board and told the jury that it listed sixteen acts of gross indifference on the part of Johns-Manville—five of which had been joined in by Raybestos-Manhattan. He then ran through some of the highlights in these acts, and in doing so, delivered a comprehensive summation of wrongdoing by the two companies.
>
> "You know that by 1933 they began to have lawsuits," Baldwin said, referring to the first asbestos lawsuits against Johns-Manville, that had actually been brought in 1929 and 1930. "They settled eleven in the year 1933, but more important, when they settled those eleven lawsuits in 1933, they bought the lawyer. They made him agree not to bring any more lawsuits against Johns-Manville. . . ." Baldwin went on to remind the jury that in 1934 Vandiver Brown, the corporate attorney for Johns-Manville, persuaded Dr. Lanza of Metropolitan Life to delete some unfavorable references to the disease-producing potential of asbestos in a study that was published by the United States Public Health Service; that in 1935 Brown and Sumner Simpson, the president of Raybestos-Manhattan, exchanged letters in which they agreed that it would be beneficial if no articles about asbestos appeared in the asbestos industry's trade journal; that

in 1947 the Industrial Hygiene Foundation, an organization financed in part by the two companies, failed to publish a study showing that about twenty percent of the workers in two of their asbestos-textile factories had developed asbestosis; that in 1949 the medical director of Johns-Manville's Canadian subsidiary advocated a policy of not informing workers of X-ray changes showing that they were developing this incurable lung disease; and that during the nineteen-fifties Johns-Manville made efforts to suppress public knowledge of the link between asbestos exposure and the development of cancer."[2]

Stage Two of the ILC and the Asbestos Industry

Stage two of the ILC is concerned with defining the issue in a favorable way. As noted above, the key strategy followed by the industry was to neutralize the emerging issue of occupational health and safety by suppressing spread of the knowledge of the dangers of asbestos.

Stage Three: The Mobilization of Organized Interest

Labor unions were the primary organizations active in pressuring companies and the government for a safer workplace. Union membership rose to around 30 percent of the nonfarm workforce by the year 1945 and remained at around that level until 1975. It was during this period that major legislation was enacted. Since then union membership has dropped to just over 16 percent.

In addition to the efforts of labor unions concerned about job safety, some key trigger events brought the issue to the public policy agenda. In 1968, a coal mine explosion that killed 78 miners in Farmington, West Virginia, coincided with congressional hearings on black lung disease, a chronic debilitating repiratory disease suffered by miners.

Stage Three ILC: Organizing Around the Asbestos Issue

The major producers of asbestos formed industry associations and held periodic conferences to deal

with the emerging issue of asbestos-related occupational diseases and mortality. For example, a conference held in 1945 was attended by representatives of Johns-Manville to develop approaches to the liability problems posed by lawsuits brought by survivors of victims. Mr. Brown, the head of the legal department at Johns-Manville in January 1935, reported on one such conference in the following terms in a memo sent to management:

> The menace of ambulance-chasing lawyers in combination with unscrupulous doctors. The uncertainties surrounding diagnosis of any of the various forms of pneumoconiosis are so many that a question of fact is presented in every case. Expert testimony can be produced by both plaintiff and defendant, and. . .the jury is not likely to favor the opinion of the experts produced by the employers. . . .
>
> One of the speakers [at an industry conference on lawsuits brought by survivors over deaths from asbestos] stated that "the strongest bulwark against further disaster for industry is the enactment of properly drawn occupational disease legislation." Such legislation would (a) eliminate the jury and empower a medical board to determine the existence of the disease. This power would extend to determining disability; (b) eliminate the shyster lawyer and the quack doctor, since fees would be strictly limited by law.[3]

This memo anticipates the fourth stage of the ILC, public debates over public issues that often end in legislation. The asbestos industry sought to guide the public issue by framing the problem in terms of unscrupulous lawyers and doctors rather than on the issue of occupational health and safety. Thus, its legal remedy was a law that discouraged the legal defense and treatment of victims to asbestos-related diseases.

Organizations opposed to the asbestos industry and its manufacturers did not sponsor new legislation for a safe workplace but for developing litigation of product liability cases. State courts had required that claims relating to asbestos be filed under the state workers' compensation laws. However, in 1973 a state court allowed a case to be tried as a tort case under the doctrine of strict liability (see Chapter 15 for a discussion of this concept).[4]

Once the state courts began to allow this product liability, a coalition of some five hundred lawyers and persons filing suit against Manville formed the Asbestos Litigation Group. Other groups such as the Asbestos Victims of America and the White Lung Association also appeared. A biweekly *Asbestos Litigation Reporter* was published to share information that would be useful for plaintiffs seeking to bring cases against Manville. Unlike the typical ILC, these interest groups did not form to focus public policy on some controversial issue so that litigation would be passed. Rather, they apparently concluded that rather than push for legislation or regulation of occupational safety and health, litigation of product liability would be more effective. Thus, the courts and not the legislation became the arena for action in subsequent stages of the ILC.

Stage Four of the ILC and the Asbestos Industry

The strategy used to manage this public issue *as an occupational safety and health issue* by Johns-Manville was largely successful until after the passage of OSHA in 1970. No specific law was passed that responded to the health threat posed by asbestos. However, the issue was unresolved because the problem was not solved and the risk of cancer and other serious diseases from exposure to asbestos continued. Thus, extensive litigation became all but inevitable.

OSHA AND THE ASBESTOS ISSUE. By the time OSHA was passed, the asbestos issue was in the courts. As noted above, the first lawsuits over asbestos-related injuries and diseases began in the 1930s. Most had been settled out of court in the early years. However, the number of lawsuits filed had grown even though no plaintiff had won an award before the landmark case in 1973.

Stage Six: Litigation and Bankruptcy of Manville

A landmark products liability case in 1973, *Clarence Borel v. Fiberboard Paper Products Corporation et al.,* was the first product-liability lawsuit involving asbestos insulation in which the plaintiff won a jury verdict. Asbestos was determined to be an unsafe product under the doctrine of strict liability. This triggered the greatest avalanche of product safety litigation in the history of American jurisprudence. Nearly a decade later the court ruled against the defense that Manville had successfully used to defend itself against product liability claims, namely, that (1) the illnesses alleged to be due to exposure to asbestos were due to multiple causation, and (2) the long time lags between exposure to a carcinogen like asbestos and the appearance of the disease made it impossible to prove that asbestos caused the disease.[5] By August 1982, more than 17,000 claims were pending against Manville and new lawsuits were being filed at the rate of over 400 per month. The liability from these claims was estimated to be over $2 billion, not considering any punitive damages.

Each of the five largest claims in 1982 had averaged over $600,000 in punitive damages. As discussed in Chapter 15, *punitive damages* are court judgments in excess of economic damages assessed as punishment for persons who are callously neglectful, have malicious intent, or are flagrantly negligent in their behavior. The upward trend in punitive damage awards by juries would have probably increased the total liability of Manville to substantially more than the estimated $2 billion.

BANKRUPTCY. On August 26, 1982, Johns-Manville filed for Chapter 11 bankruptcy protection from the many lawsuits filed against it until it could be reorganized. Chapter 11 of the bankruptcy act allows a firm to self-initiate a bankruptcy action to gain relief from creditors. This legal action allows a firm to continue to exist on a court approved plan to distribute available resources from the operation to repay its debts. The repayment of some creditors has priority over others: (1) Debts backed by assets of the firm used as collateral are normally paid before those liabilities without collateral. (2) Normally unpaid salaries and wages are paid prior to other types of liabilities. (3) Remaining creditors are paid an agreed upon proportion based upon the court-approved percentage. (4) New debts, that is, liabilities that occur after the Chapter 11 filing, have priority over existing debts. Thus, suppliers are often willing to resume shipments to a troubled firm *after* it files for Chapter 11 bankruptcy because payment for new deliveries is made in full while payment for old deliveries is uncertain and depends on the restructuring plan.

Manville management filed for Chapter 11 bankruptcy primarily to avoid the liability, including the mounting punitive damage judgments, resulting from all the lawsuits that had been filed and were in process at the time of the filing. In 1981, the year prior to its bankruptcy, Manville had made a profit of $60.3 million on sales of $2.2 billion and was ranked as the 181st-largest company in the United States by *Fortune*. Shortly after filing for Chapter 11, Manville ran advertisements in the *Wall Street Journal* reassuring the financial community of the financial strength of the firm. Manville was the largest and, perhaps, the most financially healthy firm ever to declare bankruptcy.

THE CONTROVERSY OVER CHAPTER 11. The bankruptcy strategy used by Manville's management to avoid liabilities brought about by litigation was very controversial. It was characterized as follows in the *Wall Street Journal:*

Opinions vary widely on whether Manville even belonged in Chapter 11. Some say it could have survived without such a drastic move. Others say that a Chapter 11 filing wasn't drastic enough and that Manville would have been liquidated if it hadn't evaluated conservatively the epidemiological study, which Manville had itself commissioned and which it used to justify the filing. Manville argues that an accounting rule would have required a $1.9 billion reserve for future liabilities—wiping out its net worth.

In choosing bankruptcy proceedings, most observers now say, Manville made two major miscalculations. first, it underestimated the complexity of using the bankruptcy code to grapple with toxic-torts litigation. That novel strategy required Manville to negotiate with more than double the number of creditor groups common in most such filings—not only commercial creditors and shareholders but also about 20 representatives for plaintiffs, another dozen or so representatives of codefendants, and a representative for future claimants.[6]

In addition to the complexity and controversy over the social justice of a Chapter 11 filing to avoid the court judgments, the management of Manville behaved in a manner that increased the conflict: (1) They took a very acrimonious and somewhat arrogant posture in dealing with plaintiffs presenting Manville, rather than the users of asbestos, as victims in the situation. They considered themselves as victims because the federal government refused to share any liability in cases involving the naval shipyard workers; and they viewed the plaintiffs' lawyers as exploitative. (2) Manville presented their reorganization plans to their bankers and to the court without prior consultation with their commercial creditors. This alienated a significant group in the negotiations that might have otherwise been more sympathetic. (3) Manville was perceived as presenting their initial plan with a "we'll show them" attitude violating the unwritten norm of compromise in bankruptcy proceedings. They seemed to act in terms of ultimatums rather than cooperation.

On November 28, 1988, the renamed Manville corporation's six-year bankruptcy period ended, and a court-approved reorganization plan began. According to this plan, $2.5 billion was to be provided by Manville from several sources: (1) 80 percent of Manville's stock was placed in trust, (2) 20 percent was from company profits, and (3) some came from insurers for a trust fund to be used to pay the more than 200,000 claims against the business. Manville thus became the first company owned by a trust fund established to benefit the people its products had injured.

Case Discussion Questions

1. How would you rank Johns-Manville's business social performance?
2. Do you think the use of bankruptcy to avoid product liability damages was ethical? Explain.
3. What social control mechanisms were present in this case? How did they operate or fail to operate?
4. Were the conditions present for a competitive market? Which conditions were absent or not working? Explain.

5. Evaluate the strategic issues management (SIM) process used by Johns-Manville. Was it effective? Was it ethical?

Case Endnotes

1. U. S. House of Representatives, *Asbestos-related Occupational Diseases: Hearings before the Subcommittee on Compensation, Health, and Safety of the Committee on Education and Labor,* 94th Congress, 2d sess., October 22–23 and November 13–14, 1978.
2. Paul Brodeur, "The Asbestos Industry on Trial," in *Moral Rights in the Workplace,* ed. Gertrude Ezorsky (Albany: State University of New York Press, 1987), pp. 41–42.
3. U.S. House of Representatives, *Asbestos-related Occupational Diseases,* pp. 94–95. Also quoted in Manuel Velasquez, *Business Ethics,* 2d ed. (Englewood Cliffs, N.J.: Prentice-Hall, 1988), p. 50.
4. *Borel v. Fiberboard Paper Products Corporation et al.,* 493 f. 2d 1076 (1976).
5. *Beshada et al. v. Johns-Manville,* New Jersey 447 A. 2d 539 (1983) and 51 U.S.W. 2083 (N.J. Supreme Court, July 7, 1982).
6. Cynthia F. Mitchell, "Manville's Bid to Evade Avalanche of Lawsuits Proves Disappointing," *Wall Street Journal,* July 15, 1986, p. 1.

Case I–3

Note on the Export of Pesticides from the United States to Developing Countries

The sale or distribution of any pesticide within the United States was prohibited by law unless it was registered with the Environmental Protection Agency (EPA). Registration required the submission of toxicity data showing that intended use of the pesticide posed no unreasonable risk to people or the environment. Each year, however, U.S. companies exported to developing countries millions of pounds of unregistered pesticides and pesticides whose registration had been canceled or restricted. In 1976, for example, 25 percent of U.S. exports, or 140 million pounds, were unregistered and another 31 million pounds were pesticides whose registration had been canceled.[1] This practice was legal as long as these pesticides were manufactured only for export.

As concern about the environment increased in the 1970s, the morality of this practice, what to do about it, and who was responsible for changing it became widely debated. In *Circle of Poison,* David Weir and Mark Schapiro claimed that the export of these pesticides resulted in tens of thousands of poisonings and scores of fatalities in developing

countries each year. Referring to the practice as an international scandal, they blamed the pesticide industry for dumping these pesticides in developing countries and argued that Americans were also harmed because imports treated with these pesticides contained toxic residues. The *Christian Science Monitor* called the situation morally indefensible and urged government intervention.[2] A main charge of critics was that the practice was based on a double standard—the lives of people in developing countries were less valuable than the lives of Americans. Philip Leakey, assistant minister of the environment in Kenya, asserted: "There is no question that the industrial nations and the companies which are manufacturing these things are guilty of promoting and sponsoring dangerous chemicals in countries where they think people don't care."[3] "What is at stake here is the integrity of the label *Made in U.S.A.,*" argues Rep. Michael D. Barnes (D.–Md.), who introduced legislation in 1980 to limit the export of dangerous pesticides abroad.[4]

The U.S. pesticide industry was opposed to more government regulation and countered that it, too, was concerned about the harm done by pesticides, but that this was largely a problem of misuse. Spokespeople for the industry argued that they were making significant attempts on their own to

CASE I–3A
Key to Acronyms

ADI	Acceptable daily intake
AID	Agency for International Development
Amvac	American Vanguard Corporation
EPA	Environmental Protection Agency
FAO	Food and Agricultural Organization
FDA	Food and Drug Administration
FFDCA	Federal Food, Drug and Cosmetic Act
FIFRA	Federal Insecticide, Fungicide, and Rodenticide Act
GAO	General Accounting Office
GIFAP	Groupement International des Associations Nationales de Fabricants de Produit Agrochimiques
IPM	Integrated pest management
NACA	National Agricultural Chemicals Association
OSHA	Occupational Safety and Health Administration
OXFAM	Oxford Committee for the Relief of Famine
WHO	World Health Organization

reduce harm through education and by developing safer promotional and advertising methods. A principal argument of the industry was that each country had the right to make up its own mind about the risks and benefits of using a particular pesticide. Dr. Jack Early, president of the National Agricultural Chemicals Association (NACA), accused critics of elitism and asked: "Should we tell other countries on the basis of our affluent standards where the appropriate balance of benefits and risks should lie for them? What does the EPA know—or care, for that matter—about the strength of Brazil's desire to obtain a particular pesticide that has some undesirable ecological effect?"[5]

Some Examples of Manufacturing and Pesticides

VELSICOL AND PHOSVEL
In 1971 Velsicol Chemical Company of Chicago began U.S. production of Phosvel, its trade name for the pesticide leptophos. The WHO classified leptophos as extremely hazardous, owing to its delayed neurotoxic effects—it could cause paralysis for some time after exposure. Phosvel was not approved for sale in the United States by the EPA, although it was granted a temporary registration. Velsicol, however, sold it to developing countries where there were no restrictions on its importation.

There were reports in 1971 that Phosvel was involved in the deaths of water buffalo in Egypt.[6] Velsicol contended, citing the report of the U.S. Pesticide Tolerance Commission, that a conclusive determination of Phosvel's role in the incident could not be made because of incomplete facts. In 1973 and 1974 there were additional accounts of poisonings of animals and people.[7]

In 1976 OSHA revealed that workers at Velsicol's Bayport, Texas, plant, which manufactured Phosvel, had developed serious disorders of the nervous system. They vomited, complained of impotence, were fatigued and disoriented, and became paralyzed. Workers sued Velsicol, the EPA sued for pollution violations, and OSHA leveled fines. The company then withdrew its application for registration of Phosvel and closed the Bayport plant.

From 1971 to 1976, when Velsicol stopped manufacturing Phosvel, estimates were that it exported $10–18 million worth of Phosvel to developing countries. After the Bayport incident, several countries banned the import of Phosvel. Claiming that when used properly, Phosvel was safe, Velsicol tried to sell remaining stocks of Phosvel in developing countries.[8]

In 1978 Velsicol began reforms to change its environmental image. Responding to criticisms of the company, Richard Blewitt, vice president of corporate affairs, stated: "I'm sorry to say we don't have control over worldwide inventories of Phosvel. Velsicol has made an attempt. . .to secure at our cost those inventories and make sure they are properly disposed of. . .which far exceeds our obligation."[9] He observed, however, that some distributors were resisting the efforts to buy back inventories of Phosvel.

As of 1984, Velsicol sold heptaclor, chlordane, and endrin to developing countries. Use of these pesticides had been canceled or restricted in the United States because they were suspected of being carcinogenic or mutagenic, although Velsicol claimed that there was no medical evidence that exposure to these chemicals had caused any case of cancer or birth defects in man.

AMVAC AND DBCP

After workers at an Occidental plant in California were found to be sterile in 1977, the state canceled the use of another pesticide, DBCP. At that time Dow, Occidental, and Shell stopped producing it. In 1979 the EPA canceled all uses of DBCP except for use on Hawaiian pineapples because it was suspected of being carcinogenic.

After the ban the American Vanguard Corporation (Amvac) could no longer sell DBCP directly to American companies, but it did continue exporting it. The company's 1979 10-K report stated: "Management believes that because of extensive publicity and notoriety that has arisen over the sterility of workers and the suspected mutagenic and carcinogenic nature of DBCP, the principal manufacturers and distributors of the product (Dow, Occidental, and Shell Chemical) have, temporarily at least, decided to remove themselves from the domestic marketplace and possibly from the world marketplace." The report continued: "Notwithstanding all the publicity and notoriety surrounding DBCP it was [our] opinion that a vacuum existed in the marketplace that [we] could temporarily occupy. [We] further believed that with the addition of DBCP, sales might be sufficient to reach a profitable level." According to Weir and Schapiro, a former executive had stated: "Quite frankly, without DBCP, Amvac would go bankrupt."[10]

DOW CHEMICAL AND 2,4-D AND 2,4,5-T

2,4-D and 2,4,5-T were herbicides that often contained dioxin as a contaminant. These herbicides were probably best known as components of Agent Orange, one of the herbicides used as a defoliant by the United States during the war in Vietnam. A study done by Dr. Marco Micolta, director of the San Antonio Central Hospital in rural Colombia, claimed that 2,4-D and 2,4,5-T were responsible for many miscarriages and birth defects—usually harelip and cleft palate or both—that occurred in the region.[11] In the United States 2,4-D and 2,4,5-T were manufactured and sold abroad by several companies, including Dow

Chemical Company. All uses of these pesticides containing dioxin were illegal in the United States, and use of them without dioxin was restricted.

"Dioxin Reportedly Worst Cancer Causer" read the headline of an article in the Boston Globe. The article summarized a report by scientists for the EPA that concluded that dioxin was "the most potent cancer-causing substance they have ever studied." It was further stated that dioxin probably caused cancer in humans and presented an unacceptable cancer risk when found in water in parts per quintillion. A trillionth of a gram of dioxin in a cubic meter of air would produce about nine additional cases of cancer for each 100,000 people, it was reported. The article pointed out that the conclusions in the report contrasted sharply with industry claims that "the most serious health effect caused by exposure to dioxin is a serious skin rash called chloracne."[12]

In testimony to Congress, a Dow vice president and toxicologist, Perry Gehring, stated that dioxin had "only mild effects on humans." Consistent with its policy of maintaining that 2,4-D and 2,4,5-T were safe when properly used, Dow had been lobbying to have restrictions of these pesticides eased. Robert Lundeed, chairman, said that Dow was trying to reverse the 1979 suspension of 2,4,5-T because "it was patently unsound and had no scientific merit. If we caved in on this one, we might lose the next one, when it was important." One study of the herbicide followed 121 workers in a Monsanto plant that had produced 2,4,5-T. They had accidentally been exposed to dioxin in 1949 and developed chloracne and other temporary symptoms. After 30 years of observation, the University of Cincinnati's Institute of Environmental Health reported that their death rate was below average and rates of cancer and other chronic disease was at or below normal.[13]

What Is a Pesticide?

Most pesticides were synthetic organic chemicals that were able to kill pests, including insects, weeds, fungi, rodents, and worms. (Clearly, people had different ideas as to what counted as a pest. One survey in the Philippines found that the farmers studied believed that any insect found in their field should be killed by insecticides.) Pesticides were classified either by use or by chemical makeup. The three major kinds of pesticides by use were herbicides, insecticides, and fungicides. Classification by chemical makeup produced four major categories: organochlorines, organophosphates, carbamates, and pyrethroids. In addition to the generic names of the active ingredients (e.g., paraquat) pesticides had also been given brand names by the companies that produced them (e.g., Gramoxone).

In assessing the risks or hazards of using a pesticide, it was common to distinguish between the intrinsic properties of the chemical and aspects of risk that were under human control. Toxicity, persistence, and fat solubility were important innate characteristics to consider. Toxicity was measured in terms of the lethal dose (LD_{50}) required to kill 50 percent of the test animals—usually rats. Acute toxic effects included nausea, dizziness, sweating, salivation, shortness of breath, unconsciousness, and possibly death. Some commonly used pesticides, like parathion, could cause death by swallowing only a few drops or by skin contact with a teaspoon of the chemical. Chronic toxicity was produced by long-term, low-level exposure and was evidenced by infertility, nervous disorders, tumors, blood disorders, or abnormal offspring. A pesticide was considered persistent if it did not break down easily. Since persistent chemicals remained in the environment longer, they were more likely to affect organisms other than the target pest. The persistence of a chemical varied according to its interaction with the environment. For example, DDT had a half-life of 20 years in temperate climates but was reported in some studies to have a half-life of less than a year in the tropics as a result of increased sunlight, warmth, and moisture.[14] If a pesticide was fat soluble, it could bioaccumulate in the body and remain there. This accumulation might result in long-term harm. Although not acutely toxic, DDT was considered hazardous because of its persistence and fat solubility.

Controllable risk factors included the precautions taken in the manufacture, storage, and transport of a pesticide; the nature of the formulation of the active ingredients; the manner of application; the place used; and the amount of chemical applied.

The Pesticide Industry

The first step in producing a pesticide was synthesizing or creating thousands of chemicals and testing them for useful biological activity—in this instance, the ability to kill pests. If the chemical passed this initial screen (and only 1 percent did in the first stages of development) then laboratory tests for acute toxicity began, along with a patent application. In the second stage of development, laboratory and greenhouse tests continued. The chemical was tested for specificity of action—did it kill only a few pests or a wide variety? An experimental permit was also applied for, and final preparations for manufacturing and marketing began. (Figure A shows the process in more detail.) In 1981 it took six to seven years from the time of discovery of a chemical with biological efficacy to final registration with the EPA. A company might have screened 12,000–30,000 chemicals before it brought one to market. It was estimated that the research and development costs for a single pesticide averaged $20 million.

Major pesticide companies synthesized active ingredients and formulated them, or combined active ingredients with inert substances to make them ready for application. U.S. production moved from the pesticide manufacturer to distributor to dealer to the farmer. Production in developing countries was similar, except that dealers in the United States were often trained by pesticide companies and were knowledgeable about pesticide use, whereas in developing countries the user often bought pesticides from a small shopkeeper who was not well informed about pesticide use and toxicity. In addition, some large companies had established plants in developing countries that formulated the basic toxicants, which were then imported by the parent company. This enabled companies to decrease production costs owing to lower labor costs and less government regulation. They were also able to take advantage of tax incentives offered to foreign investors in these countries. (Table A lists the top 10 producers of pesticides in 1980.)

From the 1940s to the late 1970s the pesticide industry, driven by the frequent introduction of new products, experienced rapid growth. Investment of R&D was high to sustain innovation and cheaper

Years

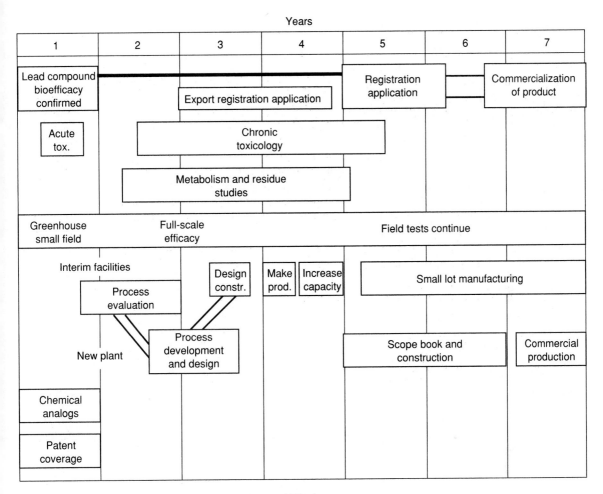

FIGURE A Pesticide R&D Process: Activities and Timing

SOURCE: Data gathered by casewriter.

manufacturing processes. In 1981 R&D budgets were 8 percent of sales. The industry also required high capital investment because of the rapid obsolescence of plant and equipment; thus, capital expenditures were 7.2 percent of sales. The high technology costs, as well as high regulation and marketing costs, posed significant barriers to entry.

Sales of U.S. producers steadily increased from $1.2 billion in 1972 to $5.4 billion in 1982. (Figure B shows the increase in sales and exports of pesticides from 1960 to 1980.) Exports steadily rose from $220 million in 1970 to about $1.2 billion in 1980.

Prices and profits for pesticides depended largely on whether or not patents were involved. Pretax profit margins on proprietary products that had a market niche were about 48 percent. Older products, like DDT and 2,4-D, functioned more like commodities and returned considerably less on investment. Even though a product was patented, competing companies often developed similar products not covered by the original patent. Prices of pesticides tripled between 1970 and 1980; in 1981 herbicides had the highest price and accounted for 60 percent of sales.

The pesticide industry was a mature industry and U.S. markets had become saturated. As demand in the United States slowed, exports increased. In 1978 exports were 621 million pounds and 36 percent of total shipments. In 1990, it was predicted, exports would be 855 million pounds and would be 43 percent of total pesticide shipments. Dollar volume of U.S. exports was projected to reach $2.6 billion by 1990.[15]

Industry analysts agreed that exports would provide the fastest growth for U.S. producers, since the U.S. markets were saturated. Farmers were also using fewer pesticides because of increased costs, declining acreage under cultivation, a slowing of growth in farm income, and increased use of integrated pest management (IPM) techniques, which relied more on cultural and biological controls and less on pesticides.

There were 35 producers of pesticides worldwide with sales of more than $100 million per year. In 1982 total worldwide sales were $13.3 billion, up from $2.8 billion in 1972. Six countries—United States, West Germany, France, Brazil, the USSR, and Japan—accounted for 63 percent of worldwide sales. All of the developing countries combined accounted for 15 percent of the worldwide market in dollar volume. A report by the U.S. General Accounting Office (GAO) estimated that pesticide requirements in dollar value for these

countries were expected to increase fivefold from 1979 to 1985.[16]

The Benefits of Pesticides

The pesticide industry and many agricultural scientists defended the sale of pesticides to developing countries, declaring that pesticides were necessary to feed an ever-increasing world population, most of it poor, and that pesticides were of great value in fighting diseases that primarily affected the poor. They also argued that there were important secondary benefits.

In 1979 the world population reached approximately 4.4 billion. Using a minimum-intake level for survival, with no allowance for physical activity, the Food and Agricultural Organization (FAO) of the United Nations estimated that there were 450 million chronically malnourished people in the world. Using a higher standard, the International Food Policy Research Institute put the figure at 1.3 billion.[17]

World population doubled from A.D. 1 to A.D. 1650; a second doubling occurred after 200 years; the next took 80 years; and the last doubling took place in 1975, requiring only 45 years. Given the 1980 worldwide average birthrate of 2.05 percent, according to Norman Borlaug the next doubling

TABLE A
Top 10 Producers of Pesticides, 1980

Company	Value ($ million)	Production (million lb.)	% market share by value	% cumulative market share
Monsanto	$552–580	169–173	20	20
Ciba-Geigy	354–358	142–147	13	33
Stauffer	330	150–117	12	45
Eli Lilly	285–300	72–82	10	55
DuPont	220	75–99	8	63
Cyanamid	220	82	8	71
Union Carbide	150–160	57–63	6	77
Shell	132–155	40–55	5	82
FMC	135–140	55	5	87
Mobay	125–135	40–45	5	92

SOURCE: *U.S. Pesticides Market* (New York: Frost and Sullivan, 1981), p. 126.

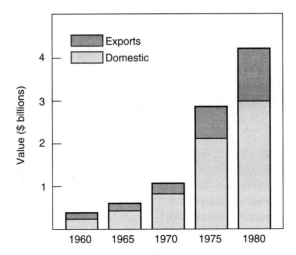

FIGURE B U.S. Sales of Pesticides, 1960–1980

SOURCE: Data gathered by casewriter.

would occur in 2015, when world population would total 8 billion. At that birthrate, 172 people would be born every minute, resulting in an additional 90 million people each year. David Hopper of the World bank stated that developing countries accounted for 90 percent of this increase.[18]

In 1977, Borlaug noted, world food production totaled 3.5 billion tons, 98 percent of which came directly or indirectly from plants. On the basis of rates of population growth and projected income elasticities for food, Hopper emphasized the necessity for an increase in food availability of about 3 percent per year, requiring a doubling of world food production to 6.6 billion tons by 2015. Increasing demand for food by developing countries was reflected in the fact that imports of grain to these countries rose from 10 million tons in 1961 to 52 million tons in 1977, according to Maurice Williams, and food shortages were projected to reach 145 million tons by 1990, of which 80 million tons would be for the low-income countries of Asia and Africa.[19]

A major cause of these shortages was that food production in developing countries had not kept pace with the increased demand for food. While per capita production of food for developed countries had steadily increased since 1970, per capita production in developing countries *decreased* by

an average of 50 percent, with the economies of Africa and Latin America showing the greatest drop.

Although experts agreed that it was important to attack the world food problem by lessening demand, they also concurred that deliberate efforts to slow population growth would not produce any significant decline in demand for food for the next decade or so. It was argued, then, that ameliorating the world food problem depended on increasing the food supply. Norman Borlaug, recipient of the 1971 Nobel Peace Prize for the development of the high-yield seeds that were the basis for the Green Revolution, argued that developed countries would not make significant additional increases in yields per acre and that developing countries had to increase their per capita food production. Owing to the scarcity of easily developed new land, Borlaug concluded that increases in world food supply could come only from increased yields per acre in these countries, and that this required the widespread use of pesticides.[20]

There was little argument, even from critics, that pesticides increased food production. The technology of the Green Revolution, which depended on pesticides, had enabled scientists in the tropics to obtain yields of 440 bushels of corn per acre versus an average yield of 30 bushels per acre by traditional methods.[21] The International Rice

Research Institute in the Philippines had shown that rice plots protected by insecticides yielded an average of 2.7 tons per hectare (2.47 acres) more than unprotected plots, an increase of almost 100 percent. They also found that the use of rodenticides resulted in rice yields up to three times higher than those of untreated plots.[22] (*Only producing more food would not end world hunger. What kinds of food people eat and the quantity are correlated with income. Thus, many experts maintain that economic development is equally important in eliminating world hunger.*)

Even with the use of pesticides, worldwide crop losses because of pests before harvest averaged about 25 percent in developed countries and around 40 percent in undeveloped countries. In 1982, GIFAP estimated that total crop losses due to pests for rice, corn, wheat, sugar cane, and cotton were about $204 billion. Most experts (quoted in Ennis et al.) estimated an additional loss of 20–25 percent of food crops if pesticides were not used.[23]

Pesticides also contributed to reducing losses after harvesting. A National Academy of Sciences study identified most postharvest loss resulting from pests and observed that "conservative estimates indicate that a minimum of 107 million tons of food were lost in 1976; the amounts lost in cereal grains and legumes alone could produce more than the annual minimum caloric requirements of 168 million people." Postharvest losses of crops and perishables through pests were estimated to range from 10 percent to 40 percent. Insects were a major problem, especially in the tropics, because environmental conditions produced rapid breeding. The National Academy of Sciences noted that "50 insects at harvest could multiply to become more than 312 million after four months." In India, in 1963 and 1964, insects and rodents attacked grain in the field and in storage and caused losses of 13 million tons. According to Ennis et al., this amount of wheat would have supplied 77 million families with one loaf of bread per day for a year.[24]

Many developing countries also relied on the sale of agricultural products for foreign exchange that they needed for development to buy the commodities they could not produce. Cotton, for example, was an important cash crop for many of these countries. Several experimental studies in the United States had shown untreated plots produced about 10 pounds of seed cotton per acre, but over 1,000 pounds were produced when insecticides were used.[25] It was estimated that 50 percent of the cotton produced by developing countries would be destroyed if pesticides were not used.

It was also argued that major indirect benefits resulted from the use of an agricultural technology that had pesticide use as an essential component. This "package" was more efficient not only because it increased yields per acre, but also because it decreased the amount of land and labor needed for food production. In 1970 American food production, for example, required 281 million acres. At 1940 yields per acre, which were generally less than half of 1970 yields, it would have taken 573 million acres to produce the 1970 crop. This was a savings of 292 million acres through increased crop yields.[26] The estimated 300 percent increase in per capita agricultural production from 1960 to 1980 also meant that labor resources could be used for other activities. Other experts estimated that without the use of pesticides in the United States, the price of farm products would probably increase by at least 50 percent and we would be forced to spend 25 percent or more of our income on food.[27] It was held that many of these same secondary benefits would accrue to developing countries through the use of pesticides.

Pesticides also contributed both directly and indirectly to combating disease; because of this, their use in developing countries had increased. Pesticides had been highly effective in reducing such diseases as malaria, yellow fever, elephantiasis, dengue, and filariasis. Malaria was a good example. In 1955, WHO initiated a global malaria eradication campaign based on the spraying of DDT. This effort greatly reduced the incidence of malaria. For example, in India there were approximately 75 million cases in the early 1950s. But in 1961 there were only 49,000 cases. David Bull estimated that by 1970 the campaign had prevented 2 billion cases and had saved 15 million lives. In 1979 Freed estimated that one-sixth of the world's population had some kind of pest-borne disease.[28]

Risks to Humans

Reliable estimates of the number of pesticide poisonings worldwide were difficult to obtain because many countries did not gather such statistics. Using figures from WHO, Bull of the Oxford Committee for the Relief of Famine (OXFAM) calculated that in 1981 there were 750,000 cases of pesticide poisoning and about 14,000 deaths worldwide, with over half of the fatalities being children. OXFAM estimated that in developing countries there were 375,000 cases of poisonings with 10,000 deaths a year. Thus, developing countries, with 15 percent of pesticide consumption, suffered half of the accidental poisonings and three-fourths of the deaths. Another survey by Davies et al. estimated that in 1977, the annual worldwide mortality rate was over 20,000.[29]

Experts agreed that these estimates contained large margins for error, and they believed that the actual number of cases was substantially higher. Many countries did not collect statistics on pesticide poisonings. In addition, pesticides were often used in remote areas that lacked easy access to clinics or had physicians who were not trained to recognize the symptoms of pesticide poisoning.

Causes of Pesticide Poisoning in Developing Countries

Pesticide poisoning resulted from many causes in developing countries. Workers would remain in the fields when planes were spraying crops; they might not have left for fear that they would lose their jobs, or they might not have understood the risk. Much of the spray drifted through the area to cover homes, utensils, clothes hanging on lines, children playing, irrigation ditches, and animals. Sometimes workers too quickly entered a newly sprayed field; the pesticide, then still moist on the plant, rubbed off on their skin and clothing. Later, when they washed, they did so with what was available—the pesticide-contaminated water in the irrigation ditches. This may also have been the source of their drinking water. Reports also surfaced of pilots dumping excess pesticide into lakes and rivers that were often vital food and water sources.

Another cause of pesticide misuse was the lack of education—many of the people who used pesticides in developing countries were illiterate. In addition, they knew little or nothing about the dangers of pesticides and how they interacted with the environment. Developing countries did not

have the elaborate agricultural extension services that existed in industrialized countries, especially in the United States. The farmers and laborers often did not know safe or effective methods for transporting, mixing, applying, storing, and disposing of pesticides.

Consider the example of one village on the shore of Lake Volta in Ghana. The fishermen began using Gammalin 20 (lindane) to catch fish. They would pour the pesticide into the lake and wait for the poisoned fish to float to the surface. The village depended on the lake for its food, income, drinking water, and water for cooking and washing. Soon the people around the lake complained of blurred vision, dizziness, and vomiting—all symptoms of lindane poisoning. The number of fish in the lake declined 10–20 percent a year. The villagers initially did not connect their symptoms with the declining fish population. They believed that both were due to natural causes. When they did become aware that the fish were poisoned, they believed the poison remained in the fish's head and that cutting off the head made the fish safe to eat.[30]

Sometimes poisoning resulted because proper safety precautions were not taken when chemicals were mixed and applied. Often workers mixed the pesticides with their hands, or, if in granular form, they sprinkled pesticides on the plants with their hands. The director of the National Biological Control Research Center in Thailand reported: "When mixing the formulation for spraying, the farmer may dip his finger into the mix and taste it by dabbing his finger to his tongue. If it gets numb it indicates the right concentration." Frequently, workers were not supplied with protective clothing, could not afford it, or chose not to wear it because of the heat. They also often had faulty equipment. If sprayers were carried on their backs, leaky valves allowed the pesticide to run down their shoulders. One survey done in the Philippines indicated that none of the farmers studied knew that a leaky valve could be fatal. Another survey in Gujarat, India, showed that none of the farm workers had face masks, only 50 percent covered their noses and mouths with a cloth, and 20 percent did not wash after spraying.[31]

Distribution methods in developing countries also caused problems. Pesticides were shipped in bulk containers and were then repackaged in smaller containers. Local merchants customarily sold the products in unlabeled bottles and kept them on the shelves with other foodstuffs. Farmers relied on the local shop owner, often untrained, to advise them about what pesticide to use and how. For example, paraquat, which was dark in color, caused numerous poisonings because it was mistaken for cola, wine, or coffee.

The large drums in which pesticides were shipped were frequently used to hold drinking water and store food. Few understood that the residues of the pesticides on the walls of a drum might still be toxic. In one case 124 people were poisoned, eight fatally, after eating food prepared in recycled pesticide drums.[32]

Critics contended that labels often failed to give the detailed information necessary for safety precautions and were sometimes not written in the language of the area in which they were to be distributed. Even when they were, however, many of the users could not read them because they were illiterate. According to Dr. Fred Whittemore, pest management specialist for AID, a check in Mexico found that 50 percent of the pesticides sold were incorrectly labeled. Labels usually did not state first-aid recommendations or contained recommendations that were unrealistic. In a remote part of India one pesticide label specified calling a physician and using the substance atropine and 2 PAM as an antidote; however, the local clinic was hours away and when checked, had never heard of 2 PAM.[33]

Critics charged that through promotion and advertising, companies encouraged farmers to view pesticides as panaceas. They emphasized that frequently the advertisements failed to mention the dangers of pesticides and created the impression that pesticides were safe to use. Critics also argued that companies occasionally encouraged overuse by advocating calendar spraying rather than spraying on the basis of the number of pests attacking a crop. They pointed out that many in developing countries trusted the goodwill of American companies. As Dr. Harold Avlo Nuñez, former Colombian Minister of Health, put it: "You know, the label 'Made in U.S.A.' is very powerful here."[34]

Risks to the Environment

Problems with pesticide overuse were particularly severe in developing countries. For example, Weir and Schapiro estimated that pesticide use was 40 percent higher in Central America than necessary to achieve optimal production. In 1975 El Salvador, with a population of 4.5 million, was using 20 percent of the world production of parathion. This averaged out to 2,940 pounds per square mile, according to Wolterding.[35]

In *A Growing Problem,* David Bull described the process by which farmers became hooked on using greater and greater quantities and more and more varieties of pesticides. He called this the *pesticide treadmill.* When an insecticide was used, for example, it killed not only the targeted insect but also other insects that were its natural enemies. These natural controls also kept in check other insects that potentially could become pests. Once the natural controls were killed, there could not only be an increase in the original target pests but also an increase in these secondary pests. Faced with an unexpected increase in pests, the farmer's typical response was to spray even more. Another result of repeated pesticide use was that pests developed a genetic resistance to them. Once this happened, the usual response again was to spray in larger quantities and then to try another pesticide. An additional reason for overuse was that formulation and methods of application for many chemicals had been developed for use in temperate climates. The more rapid breakdown of chemicals in tropical climates, however, required more frequent and larger applications.

The cultivation of cotton in Central America illustrated the pesticide treadmill at work. At the turn of the century, Central American farmers began growing cotton, which was native to the region, on a commercial scale. At that time, the boll weevil was cotton's only major pest and it was controlled by natural enemies and by hand removal from the cotton plants.

In the 1950s, as the amount of acreage under cultivation increased, mechanization and intensive use of pesticides began. Initially, insecticides were applied about eight times a year and resulted in improved yields. By the mid-1950s, three new pests were attacking cotton. During the 1960s insecticide use increased; as many as 50 different pesticides became available for a single pest. The number of applications increased to 28 per season. By 1970 there were eight pests causing serious damage to cotton. As new pests appeared the old ones became more resistant, and farmers applied more and more pesticides. By 1974, Central American growers were spraying up to 40 times a season. An average of 3,380 pounds of pesticide was being applied for every square mile.[36]

Food crops as well as cash crops were affected. Rice was the staple crop for hundreds of millions of people in Southeast Asia. One study reported that 8 rice pests were resistant to at least one insecticide in 1965; 14 pests were resistant to pesticides by 1975.[37]

Pests worldwide have rapidly developed resistances to pesticides. In 1951 there were 6 species of pests of either medical or agricultural importance that were resistant. By 1961 Davies estimated that the number was 137 and in 1980 resistant pests increased to 414 species. An exacerbating factor was that sometimes pests developed multiple resistance to a whole group of chemicals in the same class. An example was the diamondback moth, which attacked cabbage in one region of the Malay peninsula. The moths had become so resistant that farmers often sprayed three times a week, often using a "cocktail" made up of several insecticides. The diamondback moth, in turn, developed some degree of resistance to at least 11 insecticides. Bull estimated that in 1978 insecticides accounted for one-third of the production costs of cabbages. It was believed that soon it would no longer be profitable to grow cabbage in the region.[38]

In the 1970s a resurgence occurred in the incidence of malaria. For example, in India, although the number of cases dropped from 75 million in the 1950s to 49,000 in 1961, the figure rose to 6.5 million in 1976. In Haiti there were 2,500 cases in 1968 but 26,000 in 1972. Worldwide the number of cases increased by 230 percent between 1972 and 1976.[39] This increase was attributed to the disease-carrying mosquito's resistance to pesticides. (As Figure C indicates, the rate of introduction of new pesticides had not kept up with the rate at which pests were developing a resistance.)

Industry Response

The pesticide industry argued that each country had the right to have its own policy based on its individual estimate of the risk/benefit ratio of using a particular pesticide, and that the risk/benefit ratio for developing countries varied with economic and social conditions. A country with widespread malnutrition or insect-borne disease might be more willing to risk using a pesticide whose use had been canceled or restricted in the United States. Dr. William Upholt, consultant to the U.S. National Committee for Man and the Biosphere, stated: "Less industrial countries may consider a few cases of cancer in older people a small price to pay for

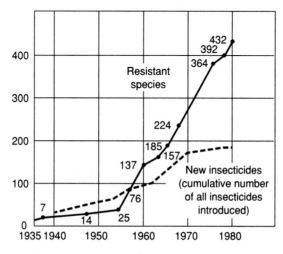

FIGURE C Resistant Species of Arthropods and New Insecticides, 1938–1980

SOURCE: David Bull, *A Growing Problem* (Oxford: OXFAM, 1982), p. 24.

the increased yield of food crops. So it is reasonable to conclude that all nations do not need the same pesticide. There is an old saying that one man's food is another man's poison, and I guess that could be reversed."[40]

DDT was cited as an example of a pesticide whose registration had been canceled for use on food crops but which was still produced in India and used by several developing countries. Robert Oldford, president of Union Carbide's Agricultural Products Division, said:

> How do some of the developing countries consider chemicals that have been banned or restricted here? Burma, for example, has stated that, "In many other countries the use of chlorinated hydrocarbons is being restricted because of their persistent nature. The official position here is that these insecticides are effective, cheap, and, if used properly. . .no more hazardous than other newer and more expensive insecticides."[41]

In developing the risk/benefit argument, Frederick J. Rarig, vice president and associate general council of Rohm and Haas Company, stated:

> Margaret Mead taught us that mortality is a relative, cultural concept. I have learned in 35 years of work in the field of hazard analysis that safety is similarly a relative, cultural concept. Safety is never an absolute. It is *not* an *absence* of hazard. Safety is an *acceptable* level of hazard.
>
> Men will not forgo shelter simply because the only shelter they can build is combustible. Mothers will not leave their children naked and exposed to the elements because the only available cloth with which to clothe them is combustible cotton. . . . Men will not starve while insects and rodents flourish simply because there are risks connected with the poisoning of insects and rodents.[42]

Dr. William Hollis, science coordinator of NACA, also pointed out the toxicological risks from crops damaged by pests. He observed: "In this light, the risk versus benefit concept to evaluate pesticides is inappropriate. The ultimate evaluation to be made must consider risk versus risk. That is, the risk of using the pesticide versus the risk of not

having optimum production and protection of food, thereby not preventing unnecessary human health hazards. Such health hazards include exposure to pest-induced toxins, carcinogens, mutagens, and allergens."[43]

NACA claimed that sometimes the EPA was out of step with other countries in its interpretation of toxicological data. For example, NACA pointed out that whereas the EPA suspended on-food uses of 2,4,5-T on the basis of study of its health effects, other countries—including the United Kingdom, Canada, New Zealand, and Australia—reviewed the same data and concluded it was acceptable to continue using the herbicide for such purposes.[44]

In trying to place the toxicity of certain pesticides in perspective, Dr. Ram Hamsager, chairman of Hindustan Insecticides Limited, compared the LD_{50} of DDT with nicotine. He indicated the LD_{50} for DDT was about 118 mg per kilogram of body weight while the LD_{50} for nicotine was about 60 mg per kilogram of body weight. He asserted: "This proves that nicotine is twice as poisonous as DDT. The toxicity levels of some of the other naturally occurring chemicals which form part of our daily intake, like caffeine found in coffee and thiobromine found in tea, are comparable to safe pesticides like DDT, and BHC."[45]

Defending the export of pesticides that were not approved for use in the United States, Robert Oldford stated: "There are two fundamental reasons why such exports occur. First, products are not usually registered in the United States for an agricultural pest crop use which does not exist here—coffee or bananas, for example. Second, developing countries have approval agencies that typically will require valid evidence of registration in a developed country in addition to other information needed to make a decision in the best interest of their citizens."[46]

The industry was trying to minimize pesticide misuse through education and had cooperated with several international organizations such as FAO, AID, WHO, and the World Bank. Dow Chemical conducted over 400 agricultural meetings in South America in 1981, and Monsanto brought union officials of one developing country to the company's U.S. plants to learn of the safety procedures used there. Since 1978 NACA sponsored a series of international conferences between representatives of importing countries and U.S. manufacturers to harmonize registration requirements and develop safety training programs. As a result of a two-year consultation process with industry, consumer, church, and environmental representatives, NACA had adopted product stewardship code containing voluntary guidelines for its 115 member companies.

It was also argued that 1978 amendments to U.S. law greatly reduced the possibility of inadequate labeling, but that the industry on its own was trying to develop better labeling procedures. For example, Velsicol had developed a "One World Communication System," using pictographs adapted to different cultures to instruct users in safer handling techniques, supplementing the labels required by U.S. law. Manufacturers, however, had little control over how distributors in developing countries repackaged and labeled pesticides after removing them from bulk shipping containers.

The U.S. pesticide industry showed concern over the rise of thousands of small "pirate" manufacturers of chemicals that were imitations or proprietary pesticides produced in the United States. These companies, usually not closely regulated, sold products in developing countries that were less effective and more dangerous because of contaminants. They were often cheaper, however, than pesticides sold by quality-conscious U.S. companies.

Regulating Pesticides

Jacob Scherr of the Natural Resources Defense Council commented at the 1979 U.S. Strategy Conference on Pesticide Management: "Some developing countries have enacted virtually no legislation to govern the importation, domestic use, and disposal of potentially toxic chemicals. Few maintain any facilities for monitoring the effects of the products on health or the environment. Even where decent laws are on the books, many governments lack the technical and administrative capacity to implement them."[47]

REGULATION IN DEVELOPING COUNTRIES

An Agromedical Approach to Pesticide Management asserted that "a number of developing countries already have strong pesticide laws on their books, but in many cases efforts aimed at enforc-

ing the laws are either negligible or nonexistent."[48] Few countries, it was reported, had the necessary regulatory infrastructure for monitoring, testing, setting residue limits, enforcement, and so forth.

The FAO studied the extent of pesticide control among members. Of 144 countries surveyed, 31 had well-developed procedures but the degree of enforcement was unknown; 6 were developing control procedures; and 81 had no control procedures or gave no information.[49]

Many developing countries asked the United States and other industrialized countries to help them develop adequate legislation, monitoring, and enforcement mechanisms. In particular, they requested the United States to share its knowledge of the harmful effects of the many chemicals already tested by the U.S. government or corporations. Many also wanted to be kept informed of changes in the status of pesticides registered in the United States.

The following comments made by Samuel Gitonga, agricultural expert for the National Irrigation Board of Kenya, were typical:

> We do not have the necessary machinery to go through an entire testing program to determine whether a product is safe or not. For these reasons, I believe that the United States and other developed countries have a responsibility to ensure that the information they have painfully gathered is made available to as many people as possible in the developing world. I certainly reject the idea that the developing countries always know what they want or which pesticides are best to use. Information that a product is not allowed for use in a particular country would be a very useful starting point. The less developed countries must be made aware that there is a problem with using a particular product. These very real dangers of incompletely tested or banned products being used in the less developed countries should be strongly condemned by the international community.[50]

REGULATION IN THE UNITED STATES

A 1979 report by the General Accounting Office to Congress, entitled *Better Regulation of Pesticide Exports and Pesticide Residues in Imported Food is Essential,* contained the following passage:

The Food and Drug Administration does not analyze imported food for many potential residues. It allows food to be marketed before testing it for illegal residues. Importers are not penalized if their imports later are determined to contain illegal residues. The safety and appropriateness of some residues allowed on imported food has not been determined.

In 1977 the United States imported $13.4 billion of agricultural products. Most of these imports were from developing countries with less effective regulatory mechanisms than those in the United States—28 percent of U.S. pesticide exports went to Central American countries from which we obtain 38 percent of our imported agricultural commodities. The United States imported approximately 600 different food commodities from over 150 countries in 1979.[51]

U.S. pesticide exports and imports were regulated by the Federal Insecticide, Fungicide, and Rodenticide Act of 1947, as amended, and the Federal Food, Drug, and Cosmetic Act of 1938, as amended.

FIFRA required the EPA to register all pesticides before they were distributed, sold, or used in the United States. The EPA registered a pesticide when it was determined that the pesticide, when used according to commonly recognized practice, could safely and effectively perform its intended function without unreasonable risk to humans or the environment. If a pesticide was produced for export only, however, it was not required to be registered by the EPA and could be exported regardless of its regulatory status or its intended use. FIFRA required that domestic producers maintain records of shipments and purchasers' specifications for packaging. Amendments made in 1978 required that unregistered pesticides produced solely for export be labeled "Not Registered for Use in the United States of America." Foreign purchasers of unregistered chemicals had to sign statements acknowledging their understanding that these pesticides were not allowed for U.S. use. Among those requirements were the display of a skull and crossbones if highly toxic and a statement of practical treatment, warning or caution statements, and no false representations.

FFDCA required that tolerances be established for pesticide residues. Any food was considered adulterated if it contained residues in excess of these tolerances or if it contained a residue for which the EPA had not established a tolerance.

The EPA and the Food and Drug Administration (FDA) administered these laws. The EPA established tolerances on the basis of the nature, amount, and toxicity of the residue of a pesticide. The FDA was responsible for ensuring that all food marketed in the United States, either domestic or imported, met FFDCA residue requirements. The FDA monitored imported food for conformance with these requirements by chemically analyzing samples collected from individual shipments received at various U.S. entry points. Food that was adulterated was required to be denied entry and reexported or destroyed.

In its report, the GAO stated that "pesticide use patterns in foreign countries clearly indicate that a large portion of food imported into the United sates may in fact contain unsafe pesticide residues."[52] For example, a 1978 study of coffee imported to the United States showed that 45 percent (25 out of 55) of the samples contained illegal residues. All of these residues were from pesticides whose use had been canceled or severely restricted in the United States. The cycle of food contaminated by U.S. pesticide exports being imported into the United States was referred to as the *boomerang effect*.

The FDA estimated that approximately one-tenth of the food imported into the United States contained illegal residues. However, the GAO argued that this estimate was probably too low owing to inadequacies in the FDA's analytical and sampling procedures. The two multiresidue tests used by the FDA could detect residues of only 73 of the 268 pesticides that had U.S. tolerances. The GAO studied the pesticides allowed, recommended, or used in developing countries on ten major commodities: bananas, coffee, sugar, tomatoes, tea, cocoa, tapioca, strawberries, peppers, and olives. It found that an additional 130 pesticides used on these foods had no U.S. tolerances and could not be detected by the FDA's tests. Since the FDA did not know which pesticides were used by other countries on food imported into the United States, it did not know which analytical test to use. This was one reason why the FDA used only *two* of the six multiresidue tests available and *no* single residue test. Without this knowledge, use of other tests would be too costly in terms of time and money. The GAO further concluded that the "anomalies" it found "do not inspire confidence in the validity of the FDA's sampling program."[53]

The report also pointed out that "even when the pesticide residues on imported food are identified as being violative, the food will probably be marketed and consumed rather than detained or destroyed." For example, in Dallas, Texas, Department of Agriculture personnel complained of an insecticidelike smell coming from a shipment of imported cabbage. Despite this complaint and the fact that the importer had a history of shipping adulterated products, the cabbage was allowed to be marketed. The GAO found that "half of the imported food that the Food and Drug Administration found to be adulterated during a 15-month period was marketed without penalty to importers and consumed by an unsuspecting American public."[54]

The Department of Health, Education and Welfare criticized the methodology of the GAO report and disagreed with several of its conclusions and recommendations:

We believe this draft report neither accurately nor fairly reflects either the degree to which pesticide residues pose a risk to the U.S. consumer or the Food and Drug Administration's (FDA) program for identifying and detaining violative imported products. We recognize the need for improvements in FDA's coverage of imported food for pesticide residues, and several actions are well under way to accomplish these improvements. However, many of the criticisms of FDA programs and professional competence are based upon unsubstantiated conclusions. GAO has posed hypothetical situations without citing sufficient evidence to substantiate their occurrence and thereby may create unfounded apprehensions about the food supply and those charged with assuring its safety.[55]

NACA argued that the safety factor built into the setting of tolerance levels and the Market Basket Surveys carried out by the FDA since 1965 provided adequate safeguards for the American con-

sumer. Tolerances were established by first determining a no-toxic-effect level for a pesticide on test animals and then increasing that many times over, usually by a factor of 100, to set the legal maximum for humans. As part of its yearly surveillance programs, the FDA examined 30 samples, each composed of 117 food items, from different regions and representing the diets of adults and children to determine the average daily intake of pesticide residues. The results were then compared with acceptable daily intake levels. Several studies had consistently shown that actual daily intake was less than ADI levels. For example, the average daily intake of parathion consumed in 1977 was 1/5,000–1/1,000 of the ADI. In no instance was the actual intake of a pesticide as high as the ADI.[56]

NACA asserted that "we are being indicted in the so-called 'circle of poison issue' in spite of the basic fact that, according to the best experts, no one anywhere in the world has suffered illness from pesticide residues in or on food commodities."[57]

The pesticide industry was not in favor of increased government regulation of pesticide exports to alleviate the risks of pesticide use in developing countries and, indirectly, in the United States. About such a proposed change in 1980, Earl Spurrier, director of government relations for Monsanto, said that "the extra restrictions are unduly stringent and they are going to throw much of the export business to foreign competitors, who are not similarly restricted."[58] Instead, the industry favored voluntary efforts by companies to alter the pattern of pesticide misuse that existed worldwide.

Case Endnotes

1. *Better Regulation of Pesticide Exports and Pesticide Residues in Imported Foods is Essential* (Washington, DC: General Accounting Office, 1979), p. 3.
2. "Exporting Poisons," *Christian Science Monitor*, February 13, 1980, p. 12.
3. "Kenya tries to put cap on imports of hazardous chemicals," *Christian Science Monitor*, May 3, 1983, p. 13.
4. "Hazards for Export," *Newsday*, December 1981, reprint, p. 14R.
5. Ibid., p. 13R.
6. Cited by Jacob Scherr, *Proceedings of the U.S. Strategy Conference on Pesticide Management* (Silver Springs, Md.: Teknekron Research, 1979), p. 33.

7. David Bull, *A Growing Problem* (Oxford, England: OXFAM, 1982), p. 40.
8. David Weir and Mark Schapiro, *Circle of Poison* (San Francisco: Institute for Food and Development Policy, 1981), p. 23.
9. *Newsday*, p. 11R.
10. Weir and Schapiro, *Circle of Poison*, p. 22.
11. *Newsday*, p. 11R.
12. *Boston Globe*, July 24, 1983, p. 19.
13. "Dow vs. the Dioxin Monster," *Fortune*, May 30, 1983, pp. 84–85.
14. Ram S. Hamsagar, "Petrochemicals and the Environment," Paper published by *Groupement International des Associations Nationales de Fabricants de Produit Agrochimiques* (GIFAP), September 23, 1983, p. 4.
15. "Pesticides: $6 Billion by 1990," *Chemical Week*, May 7, 1980, p. 45.
16. *Better Regulation*, p. 1.
17. Maurice J. Williams, "The Nature of the World Food and Population Problem," in *Future Dimensions of World Food and Population*, ed. R. G. Woods (Boulder, Colo.: Westview Press, 1981), p. 20.
18. Norman Borlaug, "Using Plants to Meet World Food Needs," *Future Dimensions*, p. 180: David Hopper, "Recent Trends in World Food and Population," *Future Dimensions*, p. 37.
19. Borlaug, *Future Dimensions*, pp. 118, 128; Hopper, "Recent Trends in World Food and Population," p. 39; and Williams, "Nature of the World Food and Population Problem," p. 11.
20. Borlaug, *Future Dimensions*, pp. 114, 129–34.
21. Hopper, "Recent Trends in World Food and Population," p. 49.
22. Bull, *A Growing Problem*, p. 5.
23. *GIFAP Directory 1982-1983*, p. 19; W. B. Ennis, W. M. Dowler, W. Klassen, "Crop Protection to Increase Food Supplies," in *Food: Politics, Economics, Nutrition, and Research*, ed. P. Abelson (Washington, DC: American Association for the Advancement of Science, 1975), p. 113.
24. E. R. Pariser et al., *Post-Harvest Food Losses in Developing Countries* (Washington, D.C.: National Academy of Sciences, 1978), pp. 7, 53; Ennis et al., "Crop Protection to Increase Food Supplies," p. 110.
25. William Hollis, "The Realism of Integrated Pest Management as a Concept and in Practice—with Social Overtures," paper presented at Annual Meeting of Entomological Society of America, in Washington, DC, December 1, 1977, p. 7.
26. Borlaug, *Future Dimensions*, p. 106.
27. Ennis et al., "Crop Protection to Increase Food Supplies," p. 113.
28. Bull, *A Growing Problem*, p. 30; Freed, *Proceedings*, p. 21.
29. Bull, *A Growing Problem*, p. 38: John Davies et al., *An Agromedical Approach to Pesticide Management* (Miami, Fla.: University of Miami, 1982), p. 9.
30. Ruth Norris, ed., *Pills, Pesticides and Profits* (Croton-on-Hudson, N.Y.: North River Press, 1982), p. 13.
31. Bull, *A Growing Problem*, p. 49.
32. Davies, *An Agromedical Approach*, p. 88.
33. Bull, *A Growing Problem*, p. 89.
34. *Newsday*, p. 11R.
35. Weir and Schapiro, *Circle of Poison*, p. 6; Martin Wolterding, "The Poisoning of Central America," *Sierra* (September–October 1981): 64.
36. Wolterding, "The Poisoning of Central America," p. 64.
37. Bull, *A Growing Problem*, p. 13.
38. Davies, *An Agromedical Approach*, p. 65; Bull, *A Growing Problem*, p. 18.
39. Bull, *A Growing Problem*, p. 30.
40. Upholt, p. 35.
41. Robert Oldford, Statement to the Subcommittee on Department Operations, Research, and Foreign Agriculture of the Committee on Agriculture, U.S. House of Representatives, June 9, 1983, p. 13.
42. *Proceedings*, p. 29.
43. Hollis, "The Realism of Integrated Pest Management," p. 11. See Wendell Kilgore et al., "Toxic Plants as Possible Human Teratogens," *California Agriculture* (November–December 1981): 6; Garnett Wood, "Stress Metabolites of White Potatoes," *Advances in Chemistry* (1976): 149, 369–86; Bruce Ames, "Dietary Carcinogens and Anticarcinogens, *Science*, September 23, 1983, pp. 1256–62.
44. *Food, Health, Agricultural Chemicals and Developing Countries*, published by NACA, May 1983, p. 4.
45. Hamsagar, "Petrochemicals and the Environment," p. 8.
46. Oldford, Statement to the Subcommittee, p. 13.
47. *Proceedings*, p. 32.
48. Davies, *An Agromedical Approach*, p. 238.
49. Bull, *A Growing Problem*, p. 144.
50. *Proceedings*, p. 41.
51. *Better Regulation*, cover page.
52. Ibid., p. 6.
53. Ibid., p. 14.
54. Ibid., pp. 39–40.
55. Ibid., p. 70.
56. See the ongoing study of the dietary intake of pesticides in the United States in *Pesticide Monitoring Journal*, in Vols. 5, 8, and 9. See also J. Frawley and R. Duggan, "Techniques for Deriving Realistic Estimates of Pesticide Intakes," in *Advances in Pesticide Science*, Part 3, ed., H. Geissbuhler (New York: Pergamon Press, 1979).
57. Jack Early, Remarks of the National Agricultural Chemical Association before the Latin American Forum, May 4, 1982, p. 6.
58. "The Unpopular Curbs on Hazardous Exports," *Business Week*, September 1980.

CHAPTER 4

Competitiveness in a Global Marketplace

CHAPTER OBJECTIVES

1. Demonstrate how the U.S. and the world economy have become an internationalized marketplace.
2. Present a model of international competitiveness.
3. Review trends in international competitiveness showing changes in the U.S. position in recent years.
4. Discuss developments of European Integration planned for 1992 and the emerging competition from Pacific Rim countries.
5. Outline some of the current issues and options available under consideration for the government in developing a national competitive strategy.
6. Review some of the practices of high performance companies which serve as models of excellence in international competitiveness.

Introductory Case One _____

The Global Marketplace

Natural gas owned by Indonesia's oil agency, Perta-mina, flows out of a well discovered by Royal Dutch Shell into a liquification plant designed by French engineers and built by a Korean construction company. The liquified gas is loaded onto U.S. flag tankers, built in U.S. yards after a Norwegian design. The ships shuttle to Japan and deliver the liquid gas to a Japanese public utility, which uses it to provide electricity that powers an electronics factory making television sets that are shipped abroad to American farmers in Louisiana who grow rice that is sold to Indonesia and is shipped aboard Greek bulk carriers. All the various facilities, ships, products, and services involved in the complex series of events are financed by U.S., European, and Japanese commercial banks, working in some cases with international and local government agencies. These facilities, ships, products, and services are insured and reinsured by U.S., European, and Japanese insurance companies. Investors in these facilities, products, and services are located throughout the world. This illustration is not only factual but typical of transactions that take place over and over again daily throughout the globe.[1]

Introductory Case Two _____

Cornerstone Eroding for American Chip Industry

Industry and government officials have been increasingly concerned over the erosion of the little-known but crucial American industry that supplies the silicon wafers, etching equipment, and other machinery and materials used in making computer chips. Worldwide sales of such equipment and materials amounted to about $15 billion in 1988. That equipment made $50 billion worth of computer chips, which in turn was used for about $700 billion worth of computers and other electronic equipment.

In a change reminiscent of that in consumer electronics of a decade ago, foreign companies like Nikon and Canon have come to dominate fields once ruled by U.S. companies. Until now, most attention in industry and government has focused on the plight of the nations's semiconductor industry itself as it loses market share to Japanese competitors. But the companies that supply the chip-making companies with sophisticated equipment and materials have also lost ground to Japanese companies. Without a viable equipment and materials industry, officials say attempts to revive the semiconductor will be doomed. This in turn could threaten U.S. leadership in many high-technology fields.

THE MONSANTO EXAMPLE. The concern was highlighted recently by the Monsanto Company's agreement to sell its silicon wafer operation to Huels A.G. of Germany. Because of the sale's possible national security ramifications, it underwent a federal review. The White House approved it on the theory that a sale was better than having the business shut down. The sale, which followed the purchase of several other American silicon wafer producers by Japanese companies, will leave the United States without a major domestic vendor of such wafers, the basic material for computer chips.

REASONS FOR THE DECLINE. Since foreign semiconductor companies have been gaining market share, American suppliers to this industry have lost some of their customer base. Many industry experts say that Japanese suppliers simply provide more reliable equipment and higher-quality materials. Japanese equipment is said to run longer and, once it is down, it is returned to operating condition sooner than American equipment. Others argue that Japan has unfair trade practices and call for government action to open foreign markets or to protect American producers. Also, reduced profitability in recent years has discouraged the investment in American companies. Without investment in future products and technology, the international leadership of American business has been increasingly difficult to maintain.[2]

International Competitiveness

The two short cases opening this chapter highlight two themes developed here.[3] First, markets have become increasingly global, and second, the leadership that the United States has enjoyed since the 1940s is being seriously challenged. During the 1980s, the United States' international trade balance moved from a slightly positive position to a negative balance, exceeding $170 billion in the latter part of the decade.[4] The United States moved from being the largest creditor nation to the largest debtor nation in the world during this period.

The decline in the U.S. relative global economic position has led to widespread concern about global competitiveness. The United States has followed the pattern of the British, who enjoyed a favored position but failed to respond to customers in multinational operations. This decline is reflected by relative changes in U.S. productivity, investment, standard of living, and trade balances since 1980. While still ahead of other countries in stan-

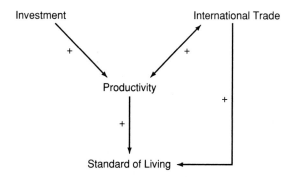

FIGURE 4–1 A Model of International Competitiveness

dard of living and absolute levels of worker productivity, the United States is losing ground overall. A number of reasons for the competitive decline suggest that two factors in competitive renewal are critical. Business needs to renew its competitiveness by developing a distinctive competence that responds to the emerging global consumer.

The issue of U.S. competitiveness has occupied the American mind for much of the last decade. Although pockets of competitive excellence are slowly emerging, there is little disagreement about the fact that the U.S. competitive position is generally deteriorating. Only recently, the 1992 World Competitiveness Report, an authoritative scoreboard of 22 industrialized and 14 newly industrializing economies, has downgraded the United States from second place behind Japan to fifth place, having been overtaken by Germany, Denmark, and Switzerland[5]. The purpose of this chapter is to reflect on the reasons why this is so, how this happened, and what businesses can do to improve their global competitiveness.

This deterioration of the U.S. relative global economic position has led to widespread concern about global competitiveness. Global competitiveness is ultimately important because of its effect on the standard of living. Former President Ronald Reagan's Council on Competitiveness defined *international competitiveness* as:

The degree to which a nation can under free and fair market conditions, produce goods and services that meet the test of international markets while simultaneously maintaining and expanding the real incomes of its citizens.[6]

The President's Council on Competitiveness developed a *four-factor index to measure competitiveness* that included:

1. *The standard of living* was defined in terms of real per capita gross domestic product.
2. *Productivity* was defined as the amount of gross domestic product produced per manufacturing employee in dollars.
3. *Investment* was defined as the percent of gross domestic product spent on plant and equipment.
4. *International trade* index was based on the balance of trade. For example, in 1989 the United States exported a record $364 billion, compared with $492.9 billion spent on imports, for a net negative balance in international trade of $128.9 billion for the year.

These four factors can be connected into a model of international competitiveness as shown in Figure 4–1.

Quality of Life, Standard of Living, and Competitiveness

Because business is the key social institution within the economic sphere of society, one must consider standard of living as an important aspect of life in modern society. However, this measure is limited in that it is an economic measure only. As discussed in Chapter 1, a threefold society includes the economic sphere, the political-governmental, and the spiritual-cultural sphere. The quality of life in society, broadly considered, should include

1. the protection of rights and economic justice as a variable in the performance of the governmental sphere
2. the quality of the intellectual, spiritual, and cultural life within society as a measure of the spiritual-cultural sphere
3. the standard of living, which is a key indicator of the performance of the economic sphere within society.

Our consideration of quality of life within the context of international competitiveness considers primarily the standard of living.

The *standard of living* is defined by the Council on Competitiveness as the gross domestic product plus the balance on current accounts divided by the number of employed persons. In other words, it is the value of the goods and services produced within a society plus the net effects of international trade. The standard of living has declined in the United States since 1972.[7] During the 1970s a combination of things brought a halt to the increase in living standards that had occurred since World War II. The Vietnam War, sharp price increases in oil made by the Oil Producing and Exporting Countries (OPEC), and growing competition from foreign countries that rebuilt and modernized their production facilities that had been destroyed during World War II all interacted to halt the growth of the American standard of living.

Many of the basic industries in the United States were dismantled as many plants were closed in the face of international competition and some facilities were moved to lower-labor-cost countries. While many new jobs were created in lower-skilled areas like data-input clerks, many middle-class manufacturing jobs were lost as American producers moved their production to "offshore" sites in Asia.[8] By 1986, the real wages of the American worker had returned to their 1969 level.

The Council on Competitiveness compared the international competitiveness of the United States with seven other industrialized countries. As shown in Box 4–1, even though the U.S. standard of living has declined since 1972, it is still higher than that of Japan, Canada, France, Italy, and the United Kingdom. By 1987, the gross domestic product per employee in the United States was $28,400, compared with Japan's $23,400 and West Germany's $34,000. While living conditions in the United States have continued to be among the best in the world, living standards have been maintained primarily by smaller families supported by two incomes. Also, the benefits of credit and imported goods from other countries have helped to sustain a high standard of living in the United States.

Productivity and International Competitiveness

Productivity is defined by the Council on Competitiveness as the output in dollars per employee in the manufacturing sector of the economy. The council developed a productivity index to compare U.S. performance with the Summit 7 industrial nations, which include Canada, France, Italy, Japan, the United Kingdom, West Germany, and the United States. Between 1972 and 1986, American manufacturing productivity expanded one-fourth as fast as the average of the other industrialized countries in the sample, one-third as fast as West Germany, and only one-eighth as fast as Japan.

The American worker was still the most productive in the world in 1992, but the gap in productivity has narrowed sharply since 1972. In 1986, the average manufacturing employee produced $32,000 in America, $31,400 in Japan, $26,700 in West Germany, and $29,100 in the other industrialized countries sampled. The lagging productivity increases made by American workers have nearly eliminated the sizable competitive advantage enjoyed by the United States in the early 1970s.

Improved efficiency or productivity increases result from technological advances, the efforts of people, and values and cultural variables that influence behavior. Investments in technology, plant modernization, and new facilities can increase worker productivity. Also, people's skills create large differences among societies and within companies. For example, Japan has the highest per capita incidence of engineers of any industrialized society, while the United States has the highest per capita incidence of lawyers. During the late 1980s, one-half of the engineering students in American universities were international students. Enrollments of American students in engineering programs were down while the numbers of students studying law have sharply increased. For the past 12 years, the number of patents for new inventions granted in Japan has been double the number granted in the United States.[9] It has been said that if a Japanese company has a competitive problem, it tends to redesign the product; a U.S. firm facing a similar problem is much more likely to use a legal strategy like litigation or trying to influence public policy to maintain its competitive position.

Lester Therow has remarked that in international competitiveness with Japan, the "bottom half" of the Japanese workforce is outperforming the "bottom half" of the American workforce. The dropout rate from high school is nearly 50 percent in many areas within the United States. Those graduating from high school are often characterized as poorly prepared for the workplace, causing the United States to be "a nation at risk." This has led to forecasted long-term shortages of highly skilled workers for jobs for systems analysts, engineers, product designers, and computer programmers in many technical fields. In contrast, there is likely to remain an abundance of people in the workforce available for a limited number of unskilled jobs.

Another aspect of people and productivity is demography, or population structures within society. The proportion of the population in various age categories provides an indication of how many entry-level jobs are available and people available to perform them. The U.S. workforce will be growing slower and there will be an increase in the number of workers between 35 and 54 years of age,

and a growing percentage of the workforce will be women and minorities.[10]

When the Social Security system was created in the 1930s, there were between seven and ten workers for each person retired. By the 1970s, there were between five and seven workers for ever person retired within the Unites States. The so-called baby-boom generation born in the 1940s, which accounts for nearly one-third of the U.S. population, are now in their fifties. By the year 2000, there will be only two and one-half workers for every retired worker. The Japanese workforce is demographically significantly older than the workforce of the United States. This is likely to lead to significant productivity problems both for Japan and for the United States by the turn of the century.

Cultural values and motivation also influence productivity. The research of David McClelland during the 1950s is very suggestive.[11] He analyzed the content of the fourth-grade readers and the popular songs of various countries, looking for imagery for achievement. He was assessing the relative role of high standards, ideals of excellence, hard work, and winning prizes because of personal effort across societies. This research found that the motivation to achieve was a core value of culture. McClelland compared the results of the content analysis of need for achievement with the rate of economic growth within the society. The achievements that people sang or thought about and the accomplishments that children were reading about were highly correlated with the growth rate of gross national product of the society five years later.

Cultural values such as work ethic or the ideals of success can be an impetus for productivity. When McClelland did his studies in the 1950s, there was a strong work ethic in the United States and a high presence of achievement symbolism in songs, reading materials, and the thinking of people. In contrast, the themes in the popular songs of today, the reading materials used in elementary education, and the central struggles found in television plots place achievement in a significantly different place as a core cultural value than was found in the United States during the 1950s.

In summary, productivity is influenced by both capital investments in technology and by the workforce. From the perspective of people and productivity, the important factors include (1) the level of skill and areas of expertise available within the workforce, (2) the basic literacy rate of the lower-skilled people within the society and within organizations, (3) the work ethic and motivation found among workers and generally within the culture, and (4) the demographic characteristics of the society.

Investment and International Competitiveness

Investment in plant and equipment modernization increases productivity because the flexibility of responding to changing consumer demands can be increased and the cost per unit produced can be decreased. Businesses seeking to improve their competitive position should consider long-term performance needs for plant modernization, new plant and equipment, and investments in the human capital needed to maintain the quality of their labor force. Investments of business, taken collectively, increase productivity. The result, in more goods and services available to society, can increase the standard of living of its people. When the investment patterns of the United States are compared with other industrialized countries, the United States spends relatively more on education and research and development but less on plant and equipment (see Box 4–1). Investments in military applications have been higher for the United States than for other industrialized countries, as reported by the President's Council on Competitiveness.

NATIONAL SAVINGS AND INVESTMENT

The rate of investment is closely associated with the rate of net national savings. The net savings rate in the United States is under 7 percent of gross domestic product, which is among the lowest of the industrialized countries, as shown in Figure 4–2[12]. Funds are made available for investment in plant and equipment primarily through savings. Thus, it is clear there should be a close relationship between the net national savings rate and growth in productivity, as shown in Figure 4–3. Again, the rate of productivity growth for the United States is the lowest for the industrialized countries shown in this figure. This seems to be largely due to the low savings rate in this country. Countries with higher savings rates also enjoy higher rates of investment and subsequent improvements in productivity growth rates.

INVESTMENTS IN PRODUCT AND PROCESS ENGINEERING

Investments can be targeted toward product engineering that develops new products, new commercial applications for scientific breakthrough, and higher-quality products. Alternatively, investments can be applied to process engineering concerned with the methods of manufacturing products that have been developed. Process engineering can lower production costs and improve product quality. Through reverse engineering used by global MNCs, a new product is routinely dismantled, studied, and redesigned by competing businesses. Thus, the product engineering investments are more subject to technology transfer to other countries and competing businesses than is investment in process engineering. Product engineering tends to have less impact on economic performance than does process engineering. It often takes as much investment to figure out how to build a product in a cost-effective way than it does to develop a new product without some sort of technology sharing.

Japanese-based global companies typically invest two-thirds of their R&D in process engineering and the remainder into new products. German companies regularly split the types of investments equally, whereas U.S. companies are more likely to emphasize new products over process technology. Both Japan and Germany have highly effective programs of on-the-job

BOX 4–1 **Third Annual Index Shows Competitiveness Trend**

The Council on Competitiveness's third annual Competitiveness Index reveals a mixed picture of America's 1989 economic performance relative to the other Summit 7 nations (Canada, France, Great Britain, Italy, Japan, and West Germany). Among the trends noted in the Index—

- The U.S. standard of living continued to exceed that of other Summit 7 countries, except West Germany, but the other nations are catching up.
- Despite record exports, the U.S. continues to rack up $100 billion-plus trade deficits because of high import levels.
- The U.S. continues to lead in manufacturing productivity, but other countries are steadily closing the gap.
- The U.S. continues to outinvest its Summit 7 competitors in absolute dollar amounts only because the U.S. gross domestic product (GDP) is so much higher than those of the competing nations. But, for the first time since World War II, another country—Japan—out-invested the U.S. in plant and equipment.

"After looking at the Index, Satchel Paige would have to tell America, 'Don't look back because everybody's gaining on you,'" said Council President Kent Hughes. "America is looking like an aging athlete—still on top but trying to ignore all the younger talent that is breaking into the line-up."

STANDARD OF LIVING

In 1989, the U.S. standard of living, which is defined as real GDP per capita (in constant 1980 dollars), was $14,180, compared with West Germany's $15,250. The average for the Summit 7 countries was $13,070, giving the U.S. a margin of only 7.8 percent—much narrower than the 17.6 percent gap between the U.S. and the other Summit 7 nations in 1972.

SOURCE: *Challenges* 3, No. 9 (July 1990): 1, 4–5.

To average Americans, a decline in the standard of living measurement means that it is becoming more probable that average citizens of other Summit 7 nations will have higher incomes and more economic choices.

In 1987, for instance (the last year of available data for all countries surveyed), average American manufacturing workers were earning barely $1,000 more in salary and benefits in real terms than they were in 1972, while average West German workers were earning about $7,500 more and average Japanese workers, about $5,000 more.

TRADE

In terms of trade, the U.S. recovered its position as the world's leading exporter in 1989, but its record $364 billion export sales were overshadowed by its $492.9 billion in imports. Continued U.S. reliance on imports—despite a declining dollar that makes imports relatively more expensive—points to some basic problems in U.S. manufacturing competitiveness that go beyond relative prices.

The 1989 U.S. trade deficit of $108.6 billion was markedly lower than the $152.1 billion 1987 deficit. However, because the dollar's decline after 1985 was an important factor in bringing down the trade deficit, the recent upturn in the dollar has sparked fears that a larger trade deficit is in the offing for 1990. Most of the trade imbalances are due to American imports of consumer-related electronics and automobiles.

West Germany and Japan, meanwhile, racked up trade surpluses of $71.4 billion and $63.9 billion, respectively, in 1989.

PRODUCTIVITY

After a period of slow growth between 1974 and 1982, U.S. manufacturing productivity has begun picking up momentum again, increasing 5.7 percent between 1983 and 1987, just slightly less than the 5.9 percent average of the other Summit 7 nations.

Box 4–1 (Cont'd)

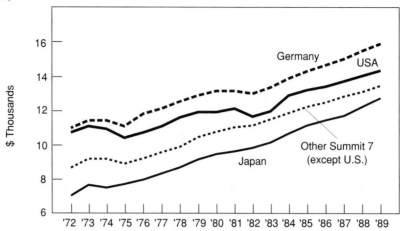

Standard of Living GDP per Capita (constant 1980 dollars)

SOURCE: Council on Competitiveness and OECD National Accounts.

Productivity growth is an excellent indicator of a nation's changing competitiveness, because when a country's productivity increases, it provides more goods and services at a lower cost. Thus, businesses become more profitable, and real wages improve. Moreover, because the bulk of international trade is still in manufactured goods, manufacturing productivity growth is a key indicator of a nation's ability to improve its competitive position in world markets.

In 1987, the most recent year for internationally comparable data, manufacturing productivity grew 4.1 percent in the U.S., 8.4 percent in Japan, and 0.9 percent in West Germany.

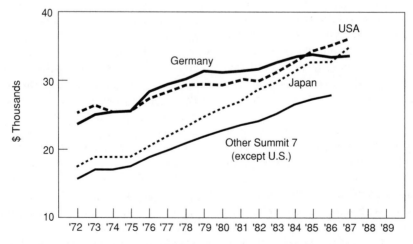

Productivity GDP per Manufacturing Employee (constant 1980 dollars)

SOURCE: Council on Competitiveness and OECD National Accounts.

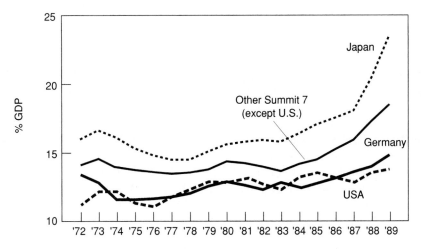

Investment Private Industry Expenditure on Plant and Equipment
SOURCE: Council on Competitiveness and OECD National Accounts.

In dollar terms, the average American employee produced $38,800 worth of goods in 1987; the average West German employee, $35,500; and the average Japanese employee, $36,900.

INVESTMENT

The other Summit 7 countries, on average, allocate a higher percentage of GDP to fixed, nonresidential capital and nondefense R&D than the U.S. does. And although the U.S. continues to allocate more of its GDP to education than other countries, the level of academic performance by American students does not measure up to international standards.

In 1989, the U.S. spent 12.5 percent of GDP on nonresidential fixed investment, slightly more than the previous year but below the 17.3 percent average of the other Summit 7 nations.

The other nations' average was high largely because of Japan's tremendous capital infusions. That nation spent a record 23.6 percent of GDP, or $549 billion, on plant and equipment in 1989, becoming the first country to out-invest the U.S. in that category in absolute terms since World War II.

In terms of nondefense R&D, the U.S. spent 1.9 percent of GDP in 1988, up modestly from the 1.6 percent it spent in 1972. By contrast, West Germany raised its investment from about 2 percent to 2.6 percent in that period and Japan, from about 1.9 percent to 2.9 percent.

As for education, the U.S. spent 4.5 percent of GDP on that area in 1987; Japan, 3.5 percent; and West Germany, 3.2 percent. However, America's higher investment hasn't closed the performance gap between its world-renowned higher education system and its ailing K-12 system, where poor test scores, high dropout rates, and inadequately prepared graduates continue to signal severe problems.

Because net national saving is the domestic source of investment, it is significant that the U.S. savings rate declined from 16.6 percent of GDP in 1972 to 14.9 percent in 1989. Although the other Summit 7 countries' average has also declined, some of those nations still save about 10 percentage points more than the U.S. does—West Germany's 1989 rate was 21.1 percent of GDP, and Japan's 25.8 percent.

Box 4–1 (Cont'd)

Index Numbers

As for the Competitiveness Index itself, the WEFA Group (Wharton Econometrics Forecasting Associates), which provides the council with technical assistance in compiling the index, has modified its methodology over the past year to take into account revisions in OECD data and improvements in data collection.

The four-part index uses 1972 as its base year for measuring the changing relative performance of the U.S. and the other Summit 7 nations. The index for 1972 is set at 100. A rise in the index to more than 100 signifies that the U.S. has out-performed other nations since then; a drop below 100 signifies that other countries have out-performed the U.S.

The latest Competitiveness Index readings:

- The standard of living index dropped from 90.5 in 1988 to 89.4 in 1989.
- The trade index rose for the third consecutive year, reaching 96.1 in 1989.
- The productivity index increased to 70.6 for 1986—the most recent year for internationally comparable data.
- The investment index dropped from 93.8 in 1985 to 91.7 in 1986—again, the most recent complete data available.

"For years, the United States had had the luxury of relying on its big post–World War II lead and strength that came from a continental economy to sustain its competitive advantage," said Hughes. "Now the big lead is gone, and the competition is more intense."

The Competitiveness Index and the data used to construct it can be obtained by contacting the Council.

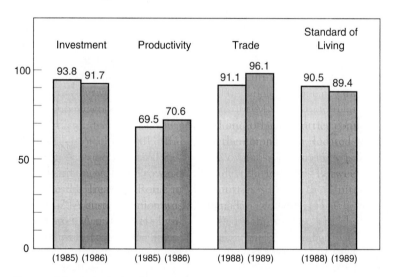

Competitiveness Index Summary
SOURCE: Council on Competitiveness.

training in teaching new processes, while the United States tends to spend more on formal education at the university level.

The United States invests relatively less than other industrialized countries as a percent of gross domestic product but more in absolute terms because of the large size of the U.S. economy. The United States spends relatively more on education and product-oriented R&D but less on plant and equipment and process engineering. The emphasis on product development over process engineering limits the overall effectiveness of R&D when the

Net national investment as a function of net national saving (average annual percentage of gross domestic product, 1962-1985)

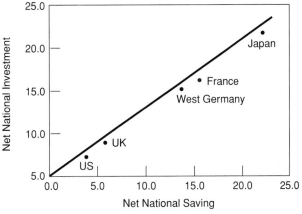

FIGURE 4–2 Net National Investment as a Function of Net National Savings

SOURCE: George N. Hatsopoulos, Paul R. Krugman, and Lawrence H. Summers, "U.S. Competitiveness: Beyond the Trade Deficit," in *International Economics and International Economic Policy*, edited by Philip King (New York: McGraw-Hill Publishing, 1990), p. 116.

Manufacturing productivity growth as a function of net national saving (average annual percent, 1962-1985)

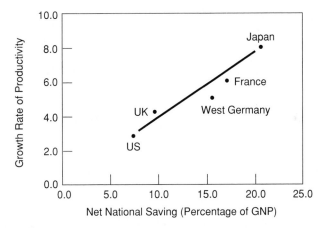

FIGURE 4–3 Manufacturing Productivity Growth as a Function of Net National Savings

SOURCE: George N. Hatsopoulos, Paul R. Krugman, and Lawrence H. Summers, "U.S. Competitiveness: Beyond the Trade Deficit," in *International Economics and International Economic Policy*, edited by Philip King (New York: McGraw-Hill Publishing, 1990), p. 118.

effects of reverse engineering are factored into the equation.

International Trade and Competitiveness

Foreign trade can provide consumers with unique products at favorable prices and thus increase the standard of living within society. According to Ricardo's economic theory of comparative advantage, some countries would benefit from specializing in producing certain products or services. Even when a country has an absolute disadvantage because its costs of production for manufactured products are more than those of other countries, it may have a relative advantage in the production of some products. If it specializes in these areas where relative advantage exists, then all countries can benefit from international trade. The standard of living can be enhanced in all countries because of the net benefits of international trade.[13] Such a theory might explain why the United States has become a leader in manufacturing computers and in making films, why Persian Gulf states produce oil, and why certain European countries may have an advantage in producing luxury automobiles.

The availability of low-cost components from other countries could increase the relative productivity of a business. Also, increases in productivity lead to unique or low-cost products and encourage international trade. Thus international trade can improve the standard of living and the productivity of a country under appropriate circumstances. International trade can be an indicator of competitiveness. If the goods and services meet the test of international competition, then the things produced should be desirable to other countries. Trade flowing between countries, as measured by the balance of payments, should provide valuable information about whether a country is internationally competitive.

The leadership that the United States enjoyed since the 1940s is being seriously challenged. During the 1980s, the United States' international trade balance moved from a slightly positive position early in the decade to a negative balance exceeding $155 billion before improving to the $100 billion negative trade balance experienced in 1990. This trend can be seen in the U.S. Current Account Balances, as shown in Figure 4–4.

GLOBAL MARKET SHARE

The United States, Japan, and Germany have approximately equal shares of world trade. Sales outside the United States by American-based global corporations account for a substantial amount of revenue. The degree of involvement of some major U.S. corporations abroad suggests why an improvement in U.S. competitive posture is paramount for the economic health of the United States. The share of the global market enjoyed by

the United States has declined nearly 1 percent per year over the past five years to 16.5 percent in 1991. This is comparable to the world market share of both Germany and Japan, whose increases have roughly equaled the U.S. decline over the same period.

During the 1980s, U.S. exports increased from $221 billion to $394 billion, an increase of 78 percent. Unfortunately, total U.S. imports increased to a whopping $495 in 1990, from $241 billion in 1980, an increase of 105 percent. Imports have significantly increased from every major region, indicating that serving the domestic market has become a critical part of global competitiveness for American business, as shown in Table 4–1.

Trade Balances in Commodity Groups

When we examine the competitive position of leading industries, we find that surpluses are limited to only a few industries like agriculture, aircraft, computers, professional instruments, and plastics. Sizable trade deficits exist over a large number of other manufacturing industries, with particular difficulties in automobiles, which accounted for one-third of the total trade deficit in 1986. While the balance of trade in aircraft, computers, and professional, scientific, and control instruments was positive, the surpluses in these areas have been declining.

Trade Balances with Trading Partners

What about the countries that the United States is selling to? The United States has surpluses with such countries as Australia, Saudi Arabia, Venezuela, and the Netherlands totaling around $10 billion. Deficits in 1986 included $1.5 billion to Singapore; $1.5 billion to China; $1.7 billion to Brazil; $2 billion to Canada; $2.5 billion to Switzerland; $2.8 billion to Sweden; $2.9 billion to the United Kingdom; $3 billion to France; $7 billion to Italy; $7 billion to Hong Kong; $10 billion to South Korea; $17 billion to West Germany; and $18 billion to Taiwan. Our trade deficit in 1986 to Japan alone was $68 billion.

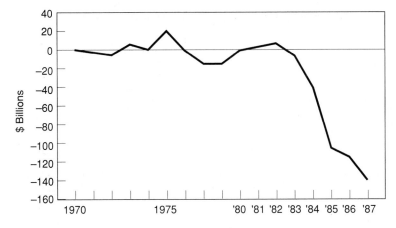

FIGURE 4–4 U.S. Current Account Balances, 1970–1987

Thus, there have been widespread declines in the U.S. international trading position across a wide variety of commodity groups and with most of its trading partners. The international competitiveness in terms of international trade in the United States has deteriorated rapidly during the last five years. The deterioration in the automobile category is catastrophic. It appears that the international competitiveness of American industry is undergoing serious challenges in nearly every industry and by producers from most of the major trading partners of the United States.

Reasons for the U.S. Competitive Decline: What Do the Experts Say?

American manufacturing productivity expanded only one-fourth as fast as the average of the other industrialized countries, one-third as fast as West Germany, and a meager one-eighth as fast as Japan. What are the underlying causes of this?

Productivity is influenced by both capital investments in technology and by the workforce.

In diagnosing the causes for U.S. competitive decline, there is hardly any agreement among the experts. Several writers have attempted to determine the reasons for such decline. Abernathy et al. attributes it to management policies.[14] Similarly, Hays and Wheelwright refer to specific deficiencies in the way that U.S. managers guided their firms.[15] Stalk singled out ineffective management strategies as the major culprit and added to that overall lack of flexibility.[16] Carlisle and Cater suggested that the main reason for the decline is overemphasis on financial results and profitability.[17] To this, Scott added the emphasis on short-term results.[18] Similarly, *The Cambridge Reports* blamed the focus on profits rather than on satisfying customer needs.[19]

Several experts identified the state of the workplace as the overall contributing cause of the U.S. competitive decline. The *Harvard Business Review* and *The Cambridge Reports* referred to the deterioration of the work ethic. Both that report and the Report of the *President's Commission on Industrial Competitiveness* (1985) mentioned increasing conflict and absence of cooperation between labor and management. The President's Commission Report added lack of effective human resource strategies. Scott blamed an unskilled and unmotivated workplace.

For Drucker, the reasons lie in the inability to meet employee expectations and the lack of effective restructuring of jobs.[20] The GSIA suggested a serious lack of managers who could adapt rapidly to changing technologies. On a more macro level, GSIA added that an important reason is that management is not prepared for the new realities of global business.[21] In a similar vein, the *Harvard Business Review* referred to lack of attention to international trade. Furthermore, it ventured to say that American managers are simply unable to respond to the competitive challenge. The real problem may be a lack of commitment to change. Finally, Scott and Lodge represent a large segment of thinkers who see the reason to be a lack of coherent national strategies and industrial policy.[22]

As there are many reasons given by the experts for the decline, there is equally no dearth of proposed solutions for the revival. Among those, two deserve particular attention in the case of the United States: (1) the need to focus on the global consumer, and (2) the need to build a distinctive competence.

Focusing on the Global Consumer

As we have seen earlier, some of the criticism leveled at the U.S. competitive posture is its lack of attention to new global business realities. Among the most compelling of those realities has been the emergence of a global market at the center of which is the global consumer. Naisbitt's *Megatrends* (1982) and its sequel, *Megatrends 2000* (Naisbitt and Aburdene, 1990), using content analysis of more than three hundred publications to detect upcoming trends, document the birth of a global consumer and the emergence of a global lifestyle. One can recognize seven concrete trends:

1. Consumer-driven markets: Groups of consumers in New York, Stockholm, and Milan show more similarities with one another than consumers in Manhattan and the Bronx.
2. Global brands: One need only think of Sony, Coke, IBM, McDonald's, and Nestlé to realize the depth of that trend.

TABLE 4–1
Imports and Exports of the United States, 1980–1990

	Exports (Bil. $)		Imports (Bil. $)	
	1980	1990	1980	1990
Total	221	394	241	495
Americas	74	138	78	155
Canada	34	84	41	91
Latin America	39	54	33	64
W. Europe	71	113	48	109
E. Europe	4	1	1	1
USSR	1	3	.4	1
Asia	60	172	79	284
Near East	12	11	17	19
Japan	21	49	31	90
E & SE Asia	27	60	31	98
Oceania	5	10	3	6
Africa	9	5	32	10

SOURCE: *World Almanac*, 1982, 1989, 1992.

3. Globalized markets: Impacted by the explosive development of information technology and telecommunications, the world of today is essentially a single global economy where trading extends from raw materials to stocks and bonds.

4. Media's massive influence: The influence of the media on the development of a global lifestyle is evident everywhere, from common foods (Kentucky Fried Chicken) to common television programs ("Dallas"), to common fashions (Benetton), to common furniture (IKEA) to common political agendas (the Greens).

5. Rapid rate of lifestyle changes: Aided by media, telecommunications, and the emergence of the travel industry as the number one global business, lifestyle changes occur at a breathtaking pace.

6. Global pricing: In an increasing number of firms, aided by electronics, prices are regulated throughout the world to protect all outlets from currency fluctuations and take account of shifts in currency values that could hurt business.

7. Decreased local options: As greater homogenization takes hold throughout the world, local brands either disappear or become versions of the global products.

The Postindustrial Society

Some observers characterize the United States as a postindustrial society.[23] The theory is that as society advances, its economy and technology move from an agrarian to an industrial base and ultimately to a postindustrial society based on knowledge and service industries.[24] For example, in 1834 during the Jackson administration, agricultural employment was about 70 percent of the population, and manufacturing was little over 20 percent. At the turn of the century, about 30 percent of those employed worked in agriculture, while the percentage employed by manufacturing had increased to around 65 percent. Today, manufacturing employs nearly 18 percent of the workforce, while service industries account for the majority of U.S. employment. The industrial profile of the country has shifted dramatically over the past century. Can modern society maintain a high standard of living and remain internationally competitive if its economy is based upon service and knowledge-based industries?

Naisbitt, in his best selling *Megatrends*, identified ten major trends in the society. The advent of the computer and telecommunications has led to an economy based upon computer-oriented, knowledge-based cottage industries. Similarly, Peter Drucker has noted that today only 6 percent of the U.S. workforce is employed in agriculture, but because of the capital intensity of agriculture, this 6 percent is able to sustain a global competitive advantage in agriculture, providing for both the domestic and export needs for agricultural products internationally. Drucker suggests that with sufficient increases in productivity through advanced technology, manufacturing employment and productivity could follow the same pattern as agriculture. These theories of postindustrial society suggest that a country can prosper even if most of its employment is based upon knowledge and services.

Recent trends in international trade raise questions about whether a service- and knowledge-based society can remain internationally competitive. Can a society prosper without a strong industrial base supported by a strong manufacturing sector? Only 18 percent of the workforce in the United States was employed in manufacturing, while there was a merchandise trade deficit of approximately $100 billion in 1992. Well over 50 percent of the workforce was employed in the service area. Trade surpluses in investment income amounted to $23 billion, and the recent surplus in internationally traded services was only $3 billion.

It appears that although services may employ most of the workforce, productivity increases in service industries have been too small to support large-scale international trade. Competitive advantages in trade continue to be based on goods rather than on traded services. The only way the United States can maintain its position of international competitiveness is to sell more goods, and the only way to increase sales of goods is to have a strong manufacturing base. A knowledge-based society is likely to collapse if a country seeks to use such economic activity as the basis for its international competitiveness in the absence of trade in manufactured goods.

The Role of Business in Global Competitiveness

FOREIGN DIRECT INVESTMENT BY MULTINATIONAL CORPORATIONS

Much of the investment in plant and equipment by U.S.-based business has not been invested in the United States but in offshore facilities for manufacturing goods in other countries. There has been a corresponding investment in American business by multinational corporations based in other countries. For example, Honda is the forth-largest producer of automobiles *in the United States*. A French-based multinational acquired General Electric's consumer electronics division. Investment by American-based multinationals in other countries and investment in plant and equipment by multinationals outside the United States usually consider the economic decisions from the perspective of the business, *not* from the perspective of the United States or of any other country. However, these private decisions can have significant consequences for the international competitiveness of the countries where the investments are made.

Building a Distinctive Competence Through Generic Strategies

If the decline in competitiveness is due to such factors as lack of flexibility, low quality, or the nonacceptance of American products and services, then businesses need to improve their distinctive

competence. Competitiveness can be enhanced by increasing responsiveness to changing market realities, improving quality, developing distinctive products, and improving cost structures so products can be made available at competitive prices.

The basis of competition varies from industry to industry. Not only is the portfolio of industries important to a country but the basis on which businesses within an industry compete is important to international competitiveness[25]. As noted in Chapter 1, competitive advantage can be based upon a superior cost structure that enables a business to compete on the basis of price. In situations where there are undifferentiated products, one must have low costs so as to use *price leadership* as the basis of competitive advantage. For example, Korean steel is probably just as good as Japanese steel that is just about as good as American steel. If a steel company wants to sell steel it must meet the price of its competitors and meet quality and delivery time requirements. Even for such consumer electronic businesses as the VCR, it is getting to the point where most producers offer the same features, making price competition important in this industry too.

Developing Cost Advantages   *Comp Adv.*

Businesses in some industries compete on the basis of controlling cost structure to increase value added for each expenditure. How does one obtain value-added? Find those areas where people are willing to pay more for those products and then specialize in them. Companies with favorable cost structures can use that for a basis of competitiveness. All businesses have a value stream that includes various elements in a total business process. Materials are acquired and parts are designed, manufactured, and packaged and then entered into a distribution system followed by a service function and warranty activity. This whole stream of processes, functions, and activities has to occur in some form in every business. Each one of those things has a cost, and so cost structure means the structure of a business's cost all the way through that process. Thus achieving a cost advantage requires considerable attention to detail throughout the organization.

Differentiation

Also, flexibility, high quality, and a uniquely desirable product or service can provide the basis for differentiation as a competitive tool. Differentiation means that a particular product is different and leads to loyalty or preference. When customers prefer one company's products or service, it can charge a higher price with better margins, margins being the percentage profit out of every dollar sale. Such a business must also then have a basis of differentiation, and to differentiate, it had better know something about quality and consumers' changing tastes and expectations, and be able to adapt to such changes.

Target Marketing and Focus Strategy

Last of all, target marketing or focusing on a propitious niche can be an important competitive approach. This suggests that competitive organizations also need the capacity for renewal, which means they must adapt to changing market spaces or niches. In our rapidly changing society, the basis of competition is changing all the time in new products, ways of making them, new features, and totally new industries. Business competitiveness can be enhanced by increasing responsiveness to changing market realities, improving quality, developing distinctive products, and improving cost structures so that products can be made available at favorable prices.

Competitive Strategies of the Global Firm

Porter has classified the international competitive strategies of the MNC as varying from high to low in coordination of activities and from geographically concentrated to widely dispersed.[26] This classification scheme results in four strategies identified in Figure 4–5 as (1) a complex global strategy with high foreign investment and extensive coordination among subsidiaries, (2) a simple global strategy with centralized R&D, relatively narrow and standardized product line, and extensive coordination of worldwide operations, (3) a multidomestic strategy based on exports to several countries with decentralized marketing, and (4) a nationally responsive strategy by a MNC or a domestic firm operating in only one country.

THE NATIONALLY RESPONSIVE STRATEGY

Doz has classified the major strategies used by the MNC as integrated, nationally responsive, and multifocal.[27] The integrated firm has a complex global strategy characterized by high degrees of coordination of activities that form an efficient network of manufacturing and logistics, marketing, and research and product development in a number of countries. Most activities tend to be centralized for coordination and integration on a worldwide basis. Those integrated MNCs are likely to be efficiency seekers that use networks as do MNCs that operate in the automobile industry.

Research and product development tend to be centralized in the home country of the multinational: Detroit in the case of the U.S.-based General Motors and Tokyo in the case of the Japanese-based Toyota. Sales and distribution channels tend to be more decentralized so that some adaptation can be made to the demands of local markets where the automobiles are sold. However, both firms now have complex global strategies as production facilities have spread throughout the world, with a network of highly integrated suppliers, dealers, and service centers.

A nationally responsive strategy could be used by either an MNC or a domestic firm that operates in only one country. The nationally responsive MNCs studied by Doz chose not to integrate worldwide operations. Rather, they decentralized subsidiaries so they could operate similarly to national companies. They were free to negotiate with host governments and adopt products and services to meet the unique demands of the local market. Here it is the

FIGURE 4–5 Competitive Strategies of the Multinational Corporations

SOURCE: Adapted from Michael E. Porter, ed., *Competitiveness in Global Industries* (Boston: Harvard Business School Press, 1986), p. 28 (Fig. 1.5). Reprinted by permission.

unique characteristics of the local consumer that dominate marketing decisions rather than the concept of the global consumer.

The parent company of the MNC pursuing a nationally responsive strategy can (1) share risks with subsidiaries located in host countries, (2) avoid costly duplications in research and product development by making developments made by one subsidiary available in other parts of the MNC, and (3) support the nationally responsive subsidiary through its wider export network. Such support can involve making channels of distribution available to the semi-autonomous subsidiary in another part of the world.

Since accounting systems, planning and information systems, budgeting systems, and managerial career paths vary from subsidiary to subsidiary in the nationally responsive MNC, coordination and integration of widespread activities in different countries is very difficult. Integration of these activities through standardization of systems throughout the MNC might bring about efficiencies, but at a cost of local market responsiveness.

The nationally responsive MNC opts for national responsiveness to (1) obtain a competi-

tive advantage in a local market, (2) negotiate a protected market position from the host government, or (3) take advantage of some special incentives provided by the host government in return for locating an operation in the country.

Prahalad and Doz observed that even major U.S. firms that primarily used a nationally responsive strategy, like Whirlpool in appliances and RCA in large color televisions, were very vulnerable to foreign-based MNCs with global strategies.[28] Such firms faced profit margin pressures when large MNCs used operations in other parts of the globe to cross-subsidize competitive moves in the United States. These global competitors first moved into related markets within appliances, consumer electronics, and televisions where market positions were easier to establish. Because the United States provides a large, open market, that market is of key significance for global competition. As Table 4–1 shows, rising imports by the United States account for much of the U.S. competitive decline. Even U.S. businesses that do not consider themselves global competitors are engaged in global competition in the U.S. market.

GLOBAL STRATEGIES

The *global strategy* is one where a MNC concentrates as many activities as possible in the country that serves as its home base and seeks to gain a competitive advantage in various countries where its products are marketed. During the 1960s and 1970s, Toyota used this strategy. As protectionist pressures increased in the United States and elsewhere, Toyota began to engage in foreign investment while dispersing some of its activities geographically but continued to maintain a high degree of coordination in the total system of input sourcing, assembling, logistics, and marketing its products, leading to a complex global strategy. Product development and capital allocation decisions continue to be centralized in Japan. These global strategies can be based upon global cost leadership and/or differentiation targeted at the particular needs of the global consumer.

Another example of a simple global strategy seems evident in the film industry. The film capital of the world seems to be Hollywood. U.S. filmmakers have come to rely increasingly on foreign distribution of their products to achieve necessary levels of economic performance. With minor changes like using subtitles or dubbing, U.S.-made films are marketed throughout the world. Recently, Japanese companies have acquired major American film companies to take advantage of this global opportunity.

THE MULTIDOMESTIC STRATEGY *All*

The multifocal MNC studied by Doz often seeks some degree of standardization of products but locates manufacturing, product development, and marketing operations in the host countries where its products are sold. Sometimes, it can obtain a protected market or some other economic incentives from the host country in return for locating its facilities there.

The MNC utilizing the multidomestic strategy often takes such strategic actions as (1) negotiating with host country governments to obtain some pro-

tected market or government-sponsored basis for competitive advantage; (2) decentralizing subsidiary operations managed by citizens of the target market countries; (3) using a nationally responsive strategy that requires the tailoring of products, distribution, and marketing efforts to fit the cultural requirements of the target country. This requires that global marketing be developed with the local consumer in mind to achieve differentiation, while taking advantage of systemwide efficiencies to achieve price competitiveness.

The multidomestic strategy of MNCs is often combined with the focus or niche strategy. Because domestic markets often have unique demands reinforced by the culture and regional lifestyles found locally, niches can be identified and serviced by firms willing to cater to local demand patterns. This approach uses the concept of the global consumer only to a limited extent.

U.S. domestic firms like RCA were apparently willing to ignore moves in the black-and-white and smaller television set segments because they did not see the long-run implications. Once foreign-based competitors using a global strategy developed a peripheral position in minor market segments, it served as a staging platform for more direct competition with U.S. firms that had stronger initial competitive positions in their core businesses. This is an example of declining U.S. global competitiveness manifested by imports into the U.S. market.

Keys to Improving International Competitiveness: The Role of Government

INDUSTRIAL POLICY, NATIONAL INDUSTRIAL STRUCTURE, AND DYNAMIC COMPARATIVE ADVANTAGE

The *national industrial structure profile* can be used to describe the kinds of industries that make up the economy and define the productive capacity of a nation. Variables included in the industrial structure include natural resources, low-skilled and low-cost labor, advanced knowledge and technology, and capital-intensive industries, as shown in Figure 4–6.

According to Figure 4–6, the industrial structure of a country can be defined in two dimensions. Dimension one includes knowledge-intensive industries like computers, electronic instruments, and heavy machinery on one end of a spectrum and industries requiring intensive unskilled labor such as the clothing, shoes, and toy industries at the opposite end of the spectrum. On the other dimension, capital- and machine-intensive industries, like consumer electronics and appliances, are at one end of the second spectrum, and capital and

raw materials–intensive items like steel, plastics, and fibers form the opposite end of the spectrum.

The national industrial structure profile of Japan has changed dramatically during the last three decades. Figure 4–6 suggests that in 1959, the Japanese economy was based on unskilled, labor-intensive businesses like toys. Very few businesses produced computers, industrial measurement instruments, and heavy machinery, and there was only moderate manufacturing of appliances and consumer electronics. Between 1959 and 1974, the profile of Japanese industry had changed by upgrading the quality of the labor force and the technological capability of the country. The Japanese were exporting a smaller proportion of products requiring unskilled labor and

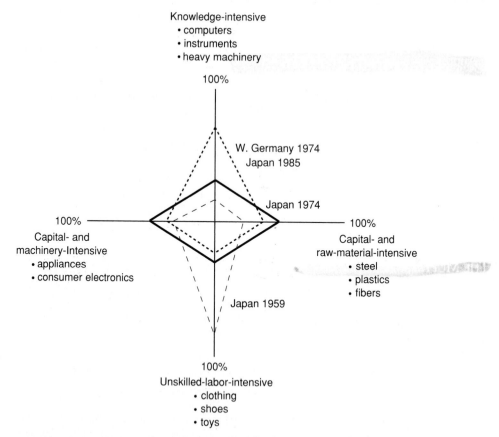

FIGURE 4–6 Evolution of Industrial Structure

SOURCE: Japanese Economic Planning Agency.

exporting a larger proportion of knowledge-intensive products. By 1985, Japanese industry was much more involved in the production of such goods as computers, specialty instruments, and heavy machinery, and it was also exporting steel and other capital- and raw materials–intensive products.

The national industrial structure profile characterizes the kind of portfolio of industries operating in Japan. The dimensions that underlie this portfolio define the basis upon which a country engages in international competition. Japan has systematically shifted investments and resources from one industrial base to another. This has upgraded its economy and its competitive position to enhance its standard of living.

Central to the competitive strategy of Japan has been the concept of *dynamic competitive advantage*. The idea developed by Ricardo in the eighteenth century conceived of comparative advantage as static, so that a country specialized in the production of a particular good over the long run. One of the lessons to be learned from Japan's successful international competitive strategy is that countries, like companies, need to change over time. Dynamic comparative advantage can be used strategically to modify systematically the basis of competitive advantage over time. It is very important for the shifts to occur.[29]

These shifts in the industrial profiles of a country can be encouraged or coordinated by a government-sponsored industrial policy administered by a government agency like MITI, as is the case with Japan. MITI ponders the strategically best competitive position for the country in terms of the potential for dynamic comparative advantage. The agency cooperates with banks and private industry to channel investments and industrial development into those business areas that have the most potential for global competitiveness. However, individual business leaders reserve the decision-making power. For example, MITI recommended against the launching of another automobile company, but the top management of Honda decided to launch an automobile manufacturing business anyway. Honda has gone on to become a highly competitive global automobile maker and has been especially successful in the U.S. market.

Alternatively, some argue that such shifts in the industrial profile of a nation should be left to market forces guided by the "invisible hand" operating in the private sector. In the United States, both the Reagan and Bush administrations (1980–92) opposed an industrial policy directed by the "visible hand" of an activist government. These two administrations favored reliance on free market forces. More recently, the Clinton administration has favored government support of a national competitive strategy that calls for a partnership between government and business.

TWIN DEFICITS: TRADE AND GOVERNMENT SPENDING

There are essentially two twin deficits: the deficit in international trade and the growing federal government deficit. Since the interest rate has been favorable in the United States and there has been relative stability in the foreign exchange rate, foreign investors have been willing to invest some $200 billion in U.S. Treasury bills for most of the past decade. These loans from foreign countries have financed a substantial part of the U.S. federal government debt during this period. If such foreign sources of debt capital were to become unavailable, the federal debt would have to be financed by capital within the United States. Alternatively the federal government, through its ability to control interest rates, could lower the rates to encourage business growth and to simultaneously cut the government interest expense on the national debt.

The U.S. trade deficit continues to be nearly $100 billion annually. One may wonder what a country that has a trade surplus with the United States can do with its U.S. dollars. Foreign holders of dollars received from international trade have a limited number of ways to spend them. They can (1) loan money to the U.S. government or other borrowers in the United States, (2) purchase goods or services from American producers, or (3) purchase business operations, real estate, or other assets in the United States.

Japanese and German holders of U.S. currency obtained as a result of the U.S. trade deficit have, until recently, used these funds to finance the huge American federal budget deficit. U.S.-based competitors have had some difficulty selling goods in Japanese markets because of the high quality requirements of Japanese consumers and because of bureaucratic government trade barriers. To avoid the negative consequences of rising American protectionist sentiments, many Japanese-based global businesses have located their facilities in the United States. Also, they have bought such companies as MCA, Firestone Tires, and other American businesses. This foreign domestic investment (FDI) by the Japanese has been an important source of investment capital, creating employment in the United States.

If a large part of the available savings that make investment capital available were diverted from private investments to government use, the national debt would discourage private investment in the things that improve international competitiveness. Thus an increase in the national savings rate could only increase productivity if the money saved is invested in ways that encourage competitiveness. This suggests the government may be able to contribute to global competitiveness by practicing sound fiscal and monetary policy. This would imply reducing the federal deficit to free capital for more productive investments.

REMOVING TRADE BARRIERS AND UNFAIR COMPETITION

If foreign markets are closed owing to unfair competition or if American producers are not competitive in foreign markets, consumers and businesses in other countries will not purchase American products. It is a key task of the U.S. government to insure that trade with other countries is fair. This requires prohibiting foreign countries from "dumping" their products in the United States by selling them at below production costs and the elimination of unfair trade barriers. Also, countries that have access to U.S. markets should make their own domestic markets available to U.S.-based businesses.

There has been a growing protectionist sentiment in the United States because of declines in international competitiveness, perceived and actual trade barriers and unfair foreign competition, and economic hardships endured by many as a result. Those involved in manufacturing are more likely to be eager to stop goods from coming into this country because they have been adversely affected. In contrast, retailers buying low-cost clothing and footwear overseas have been more likely to lobby for free trade. This issue is complex because different areas, businesses, and people are affected in different ways by the growing internationalization of the American market.

It is one thing to try to be fair but quite another to be protectionist. There was a worldwide protectionist movement in the early 1930s, when most countries in Europe and the United States used high tariffs to protect their markets. The net effect was to amplify a worldwide depression. Every country followed the example of the United States, and most other countries became protectionist as the worldwide economy came to a halt. What has happened since World War II is that the world economy has become global. The level of interdependence among nations is exceedingly high, and if protectionism occurs and is reciprocated, it will have even more devastating consequences than was the case during the Depression of the 1930s.

INTERNATIONAL CURRENCY EXCHANGE RATE POLICY

The rate of international exchange is the price at which the U.S. dollar is exchanged for foreign currency. Prior to 1985, the U.S. government followed a policy of maintaining the dollar's value at an artificially high level. This made prices that Americans had to pay for foreign goods relatively low and thus more desirable. Unfortunately, the obverse of this national policy was to make U.S. goods more expensive overseas. This was a key element in the eroding of American competitiveness.[30] The currency exchange rate policy has been altered since 1985 and the value of the dollar has declined sharply relative to other key international currencies. However, prices of imported goods have risen far less than the amount accounted for by the drop in the value of the dollar. Foreign producers have been willing to allow the profitability of goods sold in the United States to shrink rather than give up market share to American competitors.

POLICIES THAT INFLUENCE RATES OF SAVING AND INVESTMENT

As shown in Figure 4–2, the United States has a relatively low national savings rate when compared with other countries.[31] A strong capital formation rate requires investments in technology, research and development, plant and equipment, modernized facilities, and people. Savings of an equal amount are needed to support the investments necessary to maintain international competitiveness. Rates of saving and investment can be influenced by monetary policy, tax policy, investment opportunity, interest rates, and a variety of public policies.

There are arguments that a lot of wealthy people and business corporations do not pay their fair share of income tax. The stated goal of the tax reform act of 1986 was to remove unfair tax loopholes in the spirit of economic justice. It was believed that it would be more just if certain tax rules related to accelerated depreciation on factory equipment and capital gains were modified. Recent tax policy in the Unites States has been not to use tax policy to encourage capital formation rates. This is an area where the trade-offs among social justice, international competitiveness, and economic growth leading to an increased standard of living are complex and controversial.

Summary

Both the U.S. and the world economies have become increasingly global. Interdependence and international trade have increased the importance of international competitiveness. International competitiveness requires that a company or a country produce goods and services that meet the test of the marketplace and improve the standard of living within the society under conditions of fair and free competitive markets.

The decline in the U.S. relative global economic position has led to widespread concern about global competitiveness. The United States has followed the pattern of Great Britain, which enjoyed a favored position but failed to respond to customers in multinational operations. This decline is reflected in relative changes in U.S. productivity, investment, standard of living, and trade balances since 1980. While still ahead of other countries in standard of living and absolute levels of worker productivity, the United States is losing ground overall. A number of reasons for the competitive decline suggest that two factors in competitive renewal are critical. Business needs to renew its competitiveness by developing a distinctive competence that responds to the emerging global consumer.

International competitiveness is measured by including such factors as (1) the standard of living, (2) productivity, (3) investment, and (4) international trade. The U.S. international competitive position has been declining in recent years. This decline was reflected in a sharp decline in the balance of payments since the early 1980s. Moreover, the standard of living has been declining since 1972 and family living standards have been maintained primarily by two-family incomes. A relatively low level of investment in plant and equipment in the United States relative to other industrialized countries has occurred, and the competitive decline is also reflected in the narrowing gap in productivity. However, the American worker is still the most productive worker in the world.

Business can influence national competitiveness by developing its distinctive competence through the generic strategies of cost leadership, differentiation, and focus. These strategies can systematically strengthen global business in its various configurations. The strategic approaches of the multinational corporation include global strategies, nationally responsive strategies, and multidomestic strategies. Each of these offers a very different approach for dealing with the global environment.

Businesses seeking to improve their competitive position also need to consider long-term performance outcomes of trade-offs between process and product engineering, the emphasis on investments directed toward commercial applications, and the investments in human capital through on-the-job training and total quality management programs. Both Japan and Germany currently enjoy a higher competitive impact from their investments than does the United States because of their decisions concerning these trade-offs. Process engineering is especially critical for quality improvement and for lowering overall costs. These factors are of key importance to discriminating global consumers, who now select on the basis of competitive prices, quality, and differentiation bases upon global product awareness.

In considering what can be done about international competitiveness, we note that the government can do certain things and there are areas in which management can take action. The government can develop competitive policies in the areas of taxes, interest rates, and foreign exchange rates; implement sound monetary policy; encourage fair trade policies; and encourage business investments in research and development of new technology and products, and seek to stimulate new business startups.

Conclusion

American competitiveness is declining and is being severely challenged in international markets, as reflected by the information discussed above. The government through its actions can do only a part, albeit an important part, of what is needed to build American international competitiveness. Many of the problems and much of the responsibility belongs with managers, who need to manage much better than they have in the last 20 years in this country.

This suggests that competitive organizations need to have the capacity for renewal, which means they have to adapt to changing market spaces or niches. The basis of competition is changing continuously in new products, new features, even totally new industries. Learning how to adapt to the changes so that one's products continue to be superior requires an organizational capacity for renewal. Competitive positions based upon a domestically responsive strategy must be especially adept at adapting to selective high value-added niches.

Businesses can develop unique strategies suitable to the specific industries in which they operate. Global businesses need to integrate their strategies and consider the emerging global consumer. The unique demands of the global consumer are especially relevant to businesses using the multidomestic and both types of global strategies. Multidomestic strategies and global strategies are especially dependent upon the trends that will continue to create the global consumer.

There is nothing deterministic about the decline of American competitiveness. There is no reason why we have to preside over an inevitable decline in productivity and international competitiveness. Managers need to make really significant changes in their management systems. They need to respond to the global consumer and design strategies for the global marketplace. Otherwise, American business will face increasingly difficult challenges to competitiveness in the marketplace. If U.S. global competitiveness continues to decline, a continuing long-term slide in the standard of living in this country will be the result. If a country wants to continue to live well, it will have to produce well and respond to customer needs in an increasingly dynamic marketplace. This is a key responsibility of business leaders.

Discussion Questions

1. Why is global competitiveness important for a country like the United States?
2. What is U.S. global competitiveness and how is it measured?
3. In a postindustrial society most of the workforce is employed in knowledge or service

industries. What problems does this pose for global competitiveness?

4. What strategic opportunities have developed with the emergence of the global consumer? Which strategies are the best equipped to take advantage of this opportunity?

5. How do the generic strategies of cost, differentiation, and focus relate to the strategy configurations used by the global firm?

6. What are the competitive implications for process and product engineering? How do the general patterns for the United States, Japan, and Germany compare?

7. How is the large U.S. budget deficit likely to influence the country's long-term global competitiveness?

8. How do artificially high foreign currency exchange rates affect the ability of U.S.-based businesses to compete in global markets?

9. Explain the concept of dynamic comparative advantage. How is it influenced by the industrial structure of a nation?

10. Discuss the key government policy areas that can influence global competitiveness.

Notes

1. Walter Wriston, *Risk and Other Four Letter Words* (New York: Harper and Row, 1986), p. 152. Quoted in Tom Peters, *Thriving on Chaos* (New York: Harper and Row, 1988), pp. 151–52.

2. Based on the report of Andrew Pollack, "Pillar of Chip Industry Eroding," *New York Times*, March 3, 1989, pp. C1, C6.

3. Much of this section is based on Mahmoud Salem and Newman S. Peery, Jr., "The Decline and Renewal of U.S. Competitiveness," *Proceedings of the 1993 National Conference, Academy of Business Administration*, Las Vegas, February 24–28, 1993, pp. 694–701.

4. Allen J. Lenz, "U.S. Trade Deficits and International Competitiveness," paper presented at the Stanford Manufacturing Conference, Success on the Line—Manufacturing in the '90s, Stanford University, April 16, 1988; also see Karen Elliot House, "The '90s and Beyond: For all Its Difficulties, U.S. Stands to Retain Its Global Leadership," *Wall Street Journal*, January 23, 1989, p. A8.

5. H. Enchin, "Canada Downgraded in Competitive Report," *Globe and Mail*, Toronto, Canada, June 22, 1992, p. B1.

6. Council of U.S. Competitiveness Report, 1988.

7. See "Can America Compete?" *Business Week*, April 30, 1987, pp. 45–69.

8. Robert B. Reich, *The Next American Frontier* (New York: Times Books, 1983); and Barry Bluestone and Bennett Harrison, *The Deindustrialization of America: Plant Closings, Community Abandonment, and the Dismantling of Basic Industry* (New York: Basic Books, 1982).

9. Graham T. T. Molitor, "Why Issues Emerge," Presentation at the Electric Power Research Institute, Research Results Seminar: Issues Identification and Management, May 17, 1989, San Francisco.

10. "Census '90," *Wall Street Journal*, March 9, 1990, p. R1.

11. David C. McClelland, *The Achieving Society* (Princeton, N.J.: Van Nostrand, 1961); and David C. McClelland, "Business Drive and National Achievement," *Harvard Business Review* 40 (July-August 1962): 99–112.

12. George N. Hatsopoulos, Paul R. Kurgman, and Lawrence H. Summers, "U.S. Competitiveness: Beyond the Trade Deficit," in Philip King, ed., *International Economics and International Economic Policy: A Reader* (New York: McGraw-Hill, 1990), pp. 108–37.

13. Donald A. Ball and Wendell H. McCulloch, Jr., *International Business* (Plano, Texas: Business Publications, 1982), pp. 51–57.

14. W. Abernathy, C. Kim, and A. Kantrow, "The New Industrial Competition," *Harvard Business Review* (January-February 1989).

15. R. Hays and S. Wheelwright, *Restoring Our Competitive Edge* (New York: Wiley, 1984).

16. G. Stalk, "Time—The Next Source of Competitive Advantage," *Harvard Business Review* (July-August 1988): 41–51.

17. E. Carlisle and K. Cater, "Fortune Service and Industrial 500 Presidents: Priorities and Perceptions" *Business Horizons* 31, no. 2 (1988): 77–83.

18. B. Scott, "Competitiveness: 23 Leaders Speak Out," *Harvard Business Review* (July-August 1987): 106–9.

19. *Cambridge Reports: A 1986 Survey of 1,500 People* (Cambridge, Mass.: Cambridge Reports, 1988).

20. Peter Drucker, "Keeping U.S. Companies Productive," *Journal of Business Strategy* 7, no. 3 (1986): 12–15.

21. GSIA, *Are U.S. Managers Prepared for the 1990s Global Challenge?* Vol. 1 (Pittsburgh: Carnegie Mellon Univ., 1989).

22. B. Scott and George Cabot Lodge, *U.S. Competitiveness in the World Economy* (Cambridge, Mass.: Harvard Univ. Press, 1984).

23. Daniel Bell, *The Coming Post Industrial Society* (New York: Basic Books, 1973), chap. 2; and Alvin Toffler, *The Third Wave* (New York: Bantam, 1981).

24. Daniel Bell, "The Third Technological Revolution," *Business Quarterly* (August 1982): 33–37; and John Naisbitt, *Megatrends* (New York: Warner Books, 1982).

25. Michael E. Porter, *Competitive Strategy: Techniques for Analyzing Industries and Companies* (New York: Free Press, 1980); Michael E. Porter, *Competitive Advantage: Creating*

and Sustaining Superior Performance (New York: Free Press, 1985); and Michael E. Porter, *Competition in Global Industries* (Boston: Harvard Business School Press, 1986).

26. Michael Porter, *Competitiveness in Global Industries* (Cambridge, Mass.: Harvard University Press, 1986).

27. Yves Doz, *Strategic Management in Multinational Companies* (New York: Pergamon Press, 1986).

28. C. K. Prahalad and Yves Doz, *The Multinational Mission: Balancing Local Demands and Global Vision* (New York: Free Press, 1987).

29. For example, see Ira Magaziner and Robert Reich, *Minding America's Business* (New York: Vintage, 1984). Both these authors have key positions in the Clinton administration, and their support of an industrial strategy sponsored by the government is expected to have a receptive audience in the new administration.

30. "Trade: Will We Ever Close the Gap?" *Business Week*, February 27, 1989, pp. 86–92.

31. "Can America Compete?" *Business Week*, April 20, 1987, pp. 45–69.

CHAPTER 5

Multinational Business-Government Relations

CHAPTER OBJECTIVES

1. Illustrate how the internationalization of the world economy alters the nature of the business-government relationship.
2. Discuss the development of the multinational corporation (MNC) and outline the types of strategies used by the MNC.
3. Review the objectives and competitive strategies of host governments in their interactions with the MNC.
4. Discuss the developmental pattern of national competitive strategies.
5. Discuss the negotiation process between the MNC and host governments.
6. Show how regional cooperation influences interaction patterns and competitive approaches used by MNCs and national governments.

Introductory Case

IBM in Mexico

IBM has operated in Mexico as an importer of mainframe and minicomputers since the 1950s. Manufacture of minicomputers was begun near Guadalajara in 1981; at the time, all IBM facilities abroad were wholly owned by the company. Mexico is a relatively small market for IBM, accounting for annual sales of only 90,000 PCs in 1986, valued at approximately U.S.$200 million. On the other hand, Mexico's proximity to the United

SOURCE: Jack N. Behrman and Robert E. Grosse, *International Business and Governments: Issues and Institutions* (Columbia: University of South Carolina Press, 1990), pp. 170–71.

States and the availability of low-cost labor presented an important opportunity to IBM for reducing production costs of its computers that are sold elsewhere.

Since 1973, Mexico has required all foreign domestic investment (FDI) projects to accept a minimum of 51 percent local ownership. But, as with IBM in Guadalajara, this rule has been broken when the government found compelling reasons to permit greater foreign ownership (typically owing to the investment's introduction of new technology, creation of many jobs, and/or generation of significant exports). Nonetheless, the Mexican government has largely held to the minority joint-venture law, even during the 1980s foreign debt crisis.

Mexico passed legislation in 1981 to require foreign computer manufacturers to meet the 1973 rule on 51 percent minimum local ownership and to increase their Mexican local content beyond rules established for most other industries. The stated goal was to achieve 70 percent local supply of the nation's computer needs by 1986. In addition, computer manufacturers were required to meet minimum export requirements to generate foreign exchange in Mexico.

In 1984, IBM proposed to construct a PC (personal computer) plant at the site of its existing minicomputer facility near Guadalajara, to invest about U.S.$40 million, and to produce about 100,000 personal computers per year, 75 percent of which would be exported. The firm sought 100 percent ownership of the plant, stating that the project would create many major benefits for Mexico (namely, about 80 direct new jobs and over 800 indirect ones; transfer of high-tech job skills into Mexico; new direct investment of U.S.$7 million, and exports of 75,000 personal computers per year). The government initially rejected the proposal, on the grounds that IBM did not propose to use sufficient local content in the plant, and thus would be importing too much in parts and materials. It appears as well that the other foreign firms producing PCs locally successfully lobbied the government to refuse 100 percent ownership to IBM, because they all had accepted minority positions.

A year later, with Mexico increasingly hobbled by its more than U.S.$100 billion indebtedness to foreign banks and other foreign lenders, IBM twice more resubmitted the proposal, each time increasing its commitment to purchase local inputs, to increase investment more than tenfold, and to raise the level of exports, but to retain 100 percent ownership. On the third occasion, with the enhanced offer and the promise of more technology and the establishment of secondary and tertiary corporations, the Mexican government found itself much less able to resist the clear balance-of-payments and employment benefits to be produced by the project, and agreement was reached.

The final agreement called for IBM to invest a total of U.S.$91 million. This money was distributed to expansion of the Guadalajara plant ($7 million), investment in local research and development ($5 million), development of local suppliers ($20 million), expansion of purchasing and distribution network ($13 million), contribution to a government-sponsored semiconductor technology center ($12 million), and the remainder to begin local university partnerships and other linkages to local computer-related activities. Also, IBM agreed to achieve 82 percent local content by the fourth year of operation and to export 92 percent of the PCs produced in Mexico. The firm retains 100 percent ownership of the plant.

The Threefold Society and the World Economy

The threefold society includes the economic sphere, which is concerned with producing goods and services; the political sphere, which establishes laws and protects the rights of citizens; and the cultural sphere, which sustains the intellectual and spiritual life of a nation and maintains its values. Rudolf Steiner, shortly after World War I, argued that European society should separate these three spheres if it was to be released from the ravages of the world war. Furthermore, the pattern of relationships between the spheres would be crucial for the social renewal that was so badly needed at that time.[1] He suggested that the war had been caused primarily by those involved in economic pursuits who sought to promote their interests by political means. Also, he anticipated that the development of a world economy would complicate the interactions among the spheres, requiring a new science of global economics.[2]

The key to success in the economic sphere is meeting human needs, and this task is closely associated with competitiveness, sustaining market share, and profitability. Meeting those needs in a market context usually involves voluntary processes between two parties who both benefit from the exchange. However, meeting human needs in market exchanges can lose its focus when a business has worldwide operations. In the IBM case, whose needs are to be met? The customers in each country? The employees in production operations in Mexico? The sales and distribution employees throughout Central and South America? Or the product development engineers in California?

Business has become global in scope to maintain competitiveness, as suggested in Chapter 4. To do this, the multinational corporation (MNC) has evolved and adapted competitive strategies using global networks of operations including research and development, production, marketing, and distribution. In designing these networks, the MNC can adopt a decentralized mode of operations with little centralized coordination or can have a high degree of centralized coordination over its diverse activities. Also, it can focus on a single market, with its relationships with other host countries limited to supplying low-cost labor or resource inputs. Activities of the multinational enterprise affect the welfare of people in many parts of the globe.

The key task of the governmental sphere is to provide for the safety and security of citizens and to protect individual rights. In an international context, each government focuses on the interests and rights of its citizens first and may not consider the rights of citizens of other countries. What rights was the Mexican government trying to protect in its negotiations with IBM? Why did Mexico have a policy that required majority ownership by Mexican citizens of all businesses in Mexico? Why did it want to insure that much of the content of computers assembled in Mexico be sub-assemblies and parts that were also manufactured in Mexico?

Should the home governments of multinational corporations play a role in the policy of business activities conducted in other countries? Consider the use of products and technologies of industrialized democracies in the Third World. During the 1980s, the Iraqi government used chemical weapons against the Kurds, a minority group in

Iraq. It manufactured these weapons using technology illegally purchased from a West German–based MNC. Did the German government have a responsibility to the people of Iraq in this case? A German law prohibited the transaction, but it appeared that the government was very reluctant to enforce it. Only after widespread public exposure in the popular press did the government appear to take any action to investigate the matter and constrain the activities of its multinational businesses.

American-based multinationals export dangerous pesticides to Third World countries that are banned in the United States (see Case I–3). Should the U.S. government take action to protect the citizens of other countries? Third World countries rarely have the infrastructure or the financial and administrative resources to establish standards and monitor and regulate business activities. Thus, the export of these pesticides from industrialized countries places the residents of Third World countries at greater risk than would be the case in industrialized countries. Who should be responsible for protecting the safety of the citizens of these countries? The development of an internationalized marketplace requires us to rethink what is meant by business social performance, and the responsibilities of government and business when international interdependencies and exchange exists.

The cultural sphere is the custodian of the customs and values within the society. Cultural institutions of education and science also generate the intellectual property and technology needed for economic development. However, the institutions, customs, and values vary from society to society. In China it would be a major social error not to toast the host at a formal dinner. In Saudi Arabia it would be considered immoral to toast anyone at a banquet if alcohol were used.

In many non–Western countries, petty civil servants are not paid enough by the government to meet their subsistence needs and thus have to rely on gratuities to supplement their income. In the West, such gratuities are considered bribery. Thus managers of global enterprises have to adjust their

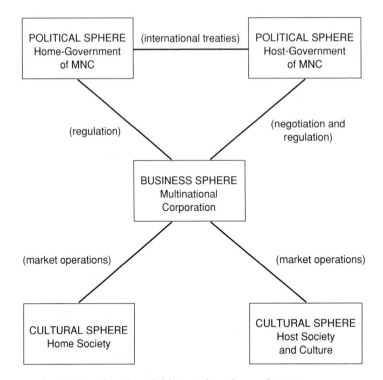

FIGURE 5–1 The Threefold Social Order and Business-Government Relations

behavior to the local cultural expectations if they are to adapt to the global environment.

The multinational enterprise is a key institution of the world economy in the threefold social order that overlaps national boundaries. Figure 5–1 suggests that the MNC must have relationships with both its home government where its headquarters is located and with host governments where its marketing, engineering, manufacturing, or logistics operations might be located.

The world economy now has global capital markets, regional economic agreements, and domestic and multinational corporations competing in a globalized marketplace. Stocks can be purchased on exchanges in New York, London, Hong Kong, and Tokyo. The major capital markets throughout the world are closed only about four hours out of every twenty-four.

There are regional economic associations in most parts of the world. The European Union

(EU) will become the largest integrated market in the world in 1992. Recently the North American Free Trade Agreement (NAFTA) has been established by treaty to include Canada, the United States, and Mexico. Other regional markets have been developed in South America and Asia.[3] The MNC can obtain capital, labor, and other resources from many places throughout the world. Also, the MNC often operates in diverse markets with different cultural settings and must interact with the various governments that have sovereignty over the lands where markets, economic activities, and exchanges are located.

Furthermore, there is more than one level of government with which a multinational corporation must deal. Typically there are government regulations at the national, regional, and local levels. In regions of economic cooperation and integration like the EU, international agreements will regulate business.

The Multinational Corporation

International trade began in silk, jewelry, and spices between Europe and the East before the Renaissance. By the eighteenth century countries like England used national monopolies to exploit the resources of their newly established colonies.[4] The American colonies were intended to export raw materials and provide markets for goods manufactured in England. After the American Revolutionary War, international trade between the United States and Europe increased as the U.S. economy developed. The first American company to move beyond exports to have operations in several European countries was I. M. Singer, which developed an international network of affiliates for the sewing machine industry during the 1870s.[5]

The worldwide depression of the 1930s produced a round of protectionism by most major countries that served to sharply reduce international trade. Most countries closed their markets in an effort to protect local producers in hopes of stimulating their economies and regaining economic health. Unfortunately, the opposite results occurred. Europe saw the rise of fascism and a second world war followed the rise of Hitler in Germany.

After World War II, The U.S.-financed Marshall Plan helped to finance the rebuilding of wartorn Europe. Also, Japan needed much foreign investment to rebuild its economy. Thus, the half century since World War II has witnessed the building of global capital markets, the rise of the multinational corporation, the internationalization of major world markets, regional economic agreements, and a global economy.

Types of Multinational Corporations

A *multinational corporation* (MNC) is a business organization that has activities in more than one nation. It might obtain natural resources in one country, perform manufacturing operations in another country, and license the sale of its products or have its marketing operations in yet another country. Behrman and Grosse have suggested that as MNCs expand operations internationally, they can be characterized by their objectives. The types of MNCs include the following:

1. natural resource seekers
2. human resource seekers
3. market seekers
4. efficiency seekers
5. network seekers.[6]

Resource seekers include multinational corporations that invest in other countries to obtain low-cost labor, some specialized technology, or raw materials that are either not available at home or are less expensive in other countries. The use of offshore production facilities or assembly operations along the border of Mexico as described in the opening case are examples of resource-seeking activities.

Often critical materials can be found primarily in other countries. For example, Japan is a major producer of steel and steel products but has neither iron ore nor the fossil fuel to heat steel smelters domestically. Coal is imported from Australia and iron ore is obtained from Brazil by Japanese multinationals so that steel refineries in Japan can have the needed raw materials. This enables Japanese steel producers to be among the lowest-cost producers in the world, and they have been formidable competitors in the U.S. market.

Market seekers are multinational corporations that want to gain access to the markets of another country. For example, the growth in the fast-food business in the United States has declined and McDonald's, the leading producer of fast foods, sought overseas markets for its products. Currently McDonald's has 6,000 restaurants in the United States and about 1,500 in other countries. Most recently, McDonald's has begun expanding its restaurant chain into India with a version of tofu burgers. The cow is considered holy by many in India and McDonald's adapted to local values and religion by switching from a beef-based menu to one more consistent with local cultural standards.

Soft drinks like Coca-Cola and Pepsi are found throughout the world. As the market growth rates for such products have dropped below 5 percent per year, companies in the soft drink business have emphasized international operations, where market growth rates are well over 10 percent. During the 1960s many countries of South America invited U.S.-based MNCs to develop the soft drink industry locally where public water systems were considered unsafe.

Efficiency seekers are often larger multinationals that seek to optimize a large-scale system that includes activities throughout the value chain.[7] The activity chain includes the sequence of operations from research and product development through purchasing resource inputs, manufacturing, outbound logistics, marketing, and postsale customer service systems. Such MNCs are likely to centralize decisions relating to capital investments, logistics, and overall manufacturing. To gain efficiencies, these MNCs use a high degree of coordination across diverse organizational units along the value chain located in numerous countries around the world.

Network seekers include MNCs that engage in joint ventures, consortia, and less permanent cooperative arrangements to complement their strategic capabilities. For example, GM-Allison Japan was a joint venture between Isuzu—a Japanese manufacturing firm—and General Motors of the United States. General Motors sought to market its automatic diesel transmissions in Japanese-made vehicles through this strategic alliance.

Behrman and Grosse suggest that the United States was the major source of technology transfers for international organizations until the 1980s.[8] Much international technology is now being developed by MNCs that are forming joint ventures or consortia among various other countries to develop capabilities in aerospace, telecommunications, and computers. For example, Airbus Industrie is a consortium of four European firms that have developed wide-body aircraft for short hauls

that now compete directly with the U.S.-based Boeing Corporation.[9]

Types of Multinational Business and Global Strategies

As suggested by the last chapter, multinational corporations seeking new markets can do so with a variety of strategies, including the sale of a standardized product globally, adapting of a differentiated product for the local needs or tastes of a foreign market, or responding to some specialized niche in another country. Market seekers responding to local needs are more likely to decentralize their operations and use nationals from local markets as managers. Such firms have been characterized as having *multidomestic* strategies because they have a number of semi-autonomous operations in the various countries where they do business.

Firms that have efficient and highly coordinated activities including manufacturing, distribution, logistics, research and development, as well as marketing operations in numerous countries, are often called *global industries*. Examples of industries that tend to be global include computers, automobiles, and consumer electronics.

LOW-COST STRUCTURES AND EFFICIENCY SEEKERS

Businesses that seek to compete on the basis of lower costs must be efficient and strive to maintain a competitive advantage in their cost structures. Costs are incurred along the value chain of operations from raw materials sourcing and inbound logistics, in research and product development, in manufacturing and assembly operations, and in the marketing and distribution of their products and services in outbound operations.[10] Thus domestic American firms facing pressures to lower overall costs will sometimes be labor resource seekers that develop international operations to assemble products offshore or in Mexico to take advantage of low labor costs as the introductory case suggests.

Global firms can be efficiency seekers that maintain lower overall costs by finding favorable prices for parts and factor inputs, by manufacturing subassemblies at foreign locations, by obtaining less expensive raw materials, and by exercising a high degree of coordination from their diverse operations. However, fluctuating foreign exchange rates can change the relative costs of labor, components, and natural resources among alternative countries where such factor inputs are available. Thus the coordination of the system must include manufacturing, distribution, and international financial operations.

Sometimes a smaller company can design products in the United States and manufacture them offshore to take advantage of lower-cost labor. For example, few warm-up jackets with professional sports logos are actually manufactured in the United States because of cost advantages available in South Korea and other Pacific Rim countries. Companies primarily interested in the sports enthusiasts market design sports jackets, sweat suits, and novelty items to cater to the taste of loyal fans. They get permission to use the copyrighted logo from the professional sports associations and incorporate them into NBA or NFL team logos into the product designs.

Then foreign-based manufacturing firms are contracted to produce the finished product that is eventually marketed in the United States. Thus, even relatively small nationally responsive firms can be efficiency seekers in a global context. These businesses utilize a mix of generic strategies: they produce a highly differentiated product at low cost for a market focused on sports fans. However, the differentiation allows them to charge premium prices, even though production costs might be relatively low.

DIFFERENTIATION AND MARKET SEEKERS

Firms that seek to compete on the basis of differentiation are global in their orientation if the basis for differentiation can be generalized. Such firms seek to expand the scope of their opportunities through exports and thus must seek markets in other countries. For example, high-quality automobiles that have unique features like special engineering capabilities might be sought by the global consumer throughout many parts of the world. Drugs that can treat ailments common in many countries and high-technology products of interest to all industrializing countries are generalizable forms of differentiation for market seekers. Firms in these industries

FIGURE 5–2 Multinational Strategies and Types of Global Firms

can use either simple or complex global strategies, because they are likely to have highly coordinated activities in the value chain with marketing operations in either few or many countries.

FOCUS, NATIONAL RESPONSIVENESS STRATEGIES, AND MARKET SEEKERS

If a local market within another country is large enough to yield profitable operations, then it is economically feasible for an MNC to focus on the unique needs defined by that market niche. Multinational corporations that can make foreign domestic investments (FDI) that could in turn provide jobs, transfer needed technology, and make products available are of particular interest to host governments.

Firms that can offer something of special interest to the host country often can negotiate a protected market with the host government. This might involve favorable treatment not available to other MNCs, like tax incentives, special regulatory status, or access to government contracts. This depends upon the unique needs and objectives of host governments as they relate to the strategic objectives of the MNC.

National Government Economic and Competitive Objectives

As suggested earlier, society can be viewed as a threefold social order. The political-governmental sphere is concerned with security and the protection of citizens' rights. Governments interact with the economic sphere by regulating business, providing macroeconomic policies that affect the economic climate for business, and serving as a major customer. Businesses in the economic sphere have the task of providing needed goods and services for the material welfare of society through competition. Culture has the task of maintaining values and providing for the intellectual and spiritual life of society. Markets occur within a cultural context because goods and services are demanded according to lifestyle preferences that are defined culturally.

In Chapter 2 and subsequent chapters in Part 4, the discussion of the role of government was expanded to include regulation of business. Such regulation is meant to assure that citizens receive the benefits of competitive markets without suffering unduly from their shortcomings. Market failures include lack of competition because markets are dominated by too few firms, unstable competition or natural monopolies, imperfections in knowledge that constrain buyers' or sellers' choices, externalities or side effects like pollution, and maldistribution of factor inputs owing to employment discrimination. These market failures take special forms and cause unique problems in a global context, where government jurisdictions overlap and competitors are based in different countries.

Also, governments provide for the infrastructures in transportation, education, and other public facilities to support the economic activities necessary for industrialized society. As the world economic system globalizes, a government's role must adapt to the special problems and opportunities provided by the MNC. The relationship between the MNC and the government of a host country for its multinational operations depends upon the objectives and strategies of both the MNC and the host government. As outlined above, multinational corporations operate in various countries to seek resources, efficiency, markets, technology, or access to networks.

Host government goals include the following:

1. Maintaining national sovereignty
2. Adopting policies that bring about favorable standards of living for citizens through encouraging economic development, controlling inflation, and maintaining high levels of employment
3. Developing the competitiveness of its domestic industry by implementing an industrial policy or national competitive strategy
4. Maintaining national security
5. Protecting the rights of its citizens

Because many countries lack the financial resources, technology, and infrastructure to accomplish their goals by themselves, they often seek cooperative arrangements. In a global environment where capital can move from any market to another on short notice, the MNC can play a special role. It not only has financial resources in the form of foreign direct investments (FDI) but may also have key technological or other capabilities of importance to host countries.

NATIONAL SOVEREIGNTY

Many small countries need technology, job creation, and high-technology products that the MNC can make available. However, the FDI and the subsequent MNC activities can often threaten the sovereignty of a nation.[11] This was particularly true during the 1970s as the negotiations between IBM and Mexico in the case at the beginning of the chapter suggest. More recently, many host country governments have discovered that protecting their sovereignty by constraining the behavior of MNCs may not be in their best interest.

Protecting sovereignty through asserting independence may be less productive than recognizing interdependence in a global economy. Economic development can be improved by entering into a more collaborative relationship between the host country and the MNC. Thus, most countries at all levels of government are aggressively seeking FDI and the economic activities of the MNC, as the recent policy changes of the Mexican government suggest.

The issue of sovereignty sometimes takes the form of a conflict over foreign policy of governments. The U.S. government sometimes attempts to get U.S.-based MNCs to act in a manner consistent with its foreign policy. The home government of the MNC may ask the MNC to influence the behavior of a foreign affiliate or a subsidiary to comply with U.S. foreign policy. A conflict can exist when the government of the host country has a different goal and thus an incompatible foreign policy. For example, the USSR attempted to build a pipeline from Russia to France during the early 1980s to reduce its dependence on OPEC oil.

The U.S. government considered the USSR its enemy and ordered a boycott of the project by all U.S.-based companies. A European subsidiary of the U.S.-based MNC, Dresser Industries, received contradictory orders from its U.S. parent organiza-tion and various European governments of the countries where its operations were located. The French government insisted on its sovereign right to trade with any country. At the time, they were seeking to increase their trade with the Soviet Union to reduce their dependence on Persian Gulf oil. The MNC in this case was cast in the role of being an extension of U.S. foreign policy and thus threatened the sovereignty of another country.

Because governments can control domestic firms more easily than MNCs and are considered to be more concerned with the needs of their country than is the MNC, host governments often try to encourage the development of domestic businesses. This might lead them to conclude that their markets should be protected from the MNC. Governments also want to maintain control, or similarly prevent the foreign dominance, over their defense, communications media, and transportation systems. Thus any MNC activities that affect these areas are of special concern to host governments. Thus the government might seek to protect domestic firms from international competition, encourage economic growth, particularly in strategically important industries, and eventually encourage exports to other countries.

STANDARD OF LIVING

Government economic policy is usually concerned with the overall economic prosperity of the nation. The policy areas of central concern in the United States have historically been inflation, economic growth, productivity, and employment. These variables are all related to the country's standard of living. Multinational corporation-government relations often focus on the effects on the standard of living that might result from MNC activities within the host country.

The standard of living, as suggested in the previous chapter, can be affected by international competitiveness in the global economies of the 1990s. The components of international competitiveness including productivity, international trade, and investment patterns are all areas for government policy objectives. Thus, issues of concern to a host government in its relationships with the MNC include the following:

1. Improvements in the standard of living that may be afforded by the activities of the MNC
2. Employment and job creation by the MNC in exchange for
3. Access to a low-cost or an educated workforce
4. Productivity
5. Technology transfer
6. Foreign direct investment (FDI)
7. Developing local industries
8. Maintenance of national sovereignty through the ownership and control of local businesses
9. Development of favorable international trade balances.

Host countries are interested in the exports generated for their country by the presence of the multinational business.

These factors are often central in negotiations between the MNC and host governments, as with the case concerning IBM and Mexico. That country has sanctioned the use of assembly operations, called *maquiladora* plants, in which the MNC takes advantage of low-cost labor and Mexicans benefit by increased employment and the transfer of technology to their country. President Salinas of Mexico had the goal of expanding such programs over the next decade to ultimately achieve a North American Free Trade Agreement (NAFTA).[12] Mexico hopes to gain a higher standard of living through the initial creation of low-skilled, low-cost jobs followed by formation of higher-skilled, higher-wage jobs. Also, foreign investment will help to finance industrialization that will increase availability of industrialized products within Mexico and foreign exchange through increased exports from Mexico to other countries.

National Competitive Strategies

DEVELOPMENT OF DOMESTIC INDUSTRY COMPETITIVENESS

Because governments value their sovereignty, they often prefer industrial development based upon

domestic competitors. However, sometimes domestic companies are not strong enough to compete against MNCs in domestic markets. This could be the result of any number of factors, as follows:

1. A country may not have sufficient resources or technology for industrialization and international competitiveness.
2. It may be well endowed with natural resources but have insufficient technological knowledge or industrialization to make this a competitive advantage.
3. A developing country may have a small market that cannot support efficient economy-of-scale business operations. Thus it may choose a protectionist policy until its industry can compete effectively against the MNC based in other countries. This was the pattern initially followed by Japan during the postwar era.
4. Skill levels and infrastructure within a country may be insufficient for certain industries.

Thus, most countries find they need to be part of the internationalized global economy and cooperate with MNCs if they are to develop a competitive national position. However, their strategy of cooperation and their strategy of national competitiveness may depend upon their economic stage of development, as discussed in a subsequent section of the chapter.

Doz has suggested that host governments seek to accelerate the development of a competitive national position of domestic firms through the sequential application of different national competitive strategies, as shown in Figure 5–3. He has described this process as follows:

First, the domestic market is closed to imports, to create a large repressed domestic demand, then an "infant industry" is promoted and protected. In some cases, the state administers the acquisition and diffusion of foreign technology, and several domestic competitors may be supported. Rapid growth of the domestic market allows national firms the opportunity to achieve competitiveness. Competition among them selects winners and weeds out losers. Protection of domestic producers is then decreased, and successful ones are poised to

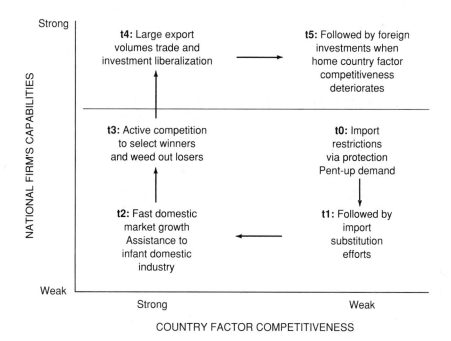

FIGURE 5–3 Accelerating the Development of a Competitive National Position in a Global Industry

SOURCE: Yves Dos, "Governmental Policies and Global Industries," *in Competition in Global Industries*, ed. Michael Porter (Boston: Harvard Business School Press, 1986), p. 240. Reprinted by permission.

achieve international competitiveness. The development of the Japanese automobile or computer industries are good examples of this scenario.[13]

A country's national competitiveness depends upon its unique circumstances, including the competitiveness of factor inputs like labor and natural resources, the capabilities of national firms within the country, and the size and other characteristics of domestic markets.[14] The first dimension of international competitive strategy is the basic orientation of a country's policies, ranging from open to restrictive with respect to FDI by MNCs and other MNC activities.[15] A second dimension is the degree to which a country has an industrial policy to orchestrate international competitiveness or whether it relies primarily on market mechanisms to shape its national competitive profile.

HOST GOVERNMENT POLICIES

Behrman and Grosse suggested that the international orientation of host governments can be characterized as open, mixed, and restrictive.[16] Policymakers for countries adapt policies they feel will best increase the standard of living while producing economic growth and development. Because sovereignty is also an objective, some countries prefer an economy dominated by domestic- rather than foreign-based MNCs. However, frequently investment capital for economic development is available only from foreign sources made by MNCs. Furthermore, even the most advanced countries need technology that has been developed in other countries. Thus, countries find themselves in need of resources, technology, and skills available from the MNC if they are to have healthy economies and be competitive.

Open Policies

Countries with policies open to the MNC include the United States, Canada, Germany, the United Kingdom, Sweden, and Chile.[17] These countries tend to favor a free-market approach to international trade and allow the MNC to make investments, withdraw capital, and freely engage in economic activities on much the same basis as domestic firms. Open countries attempt to use standard policies often codified in international agreements in their relationships with domestic and multinational enterprises.

Thus, the negotiations between host governments and the MNC are very selective and are an exception to the rule. For example, the United States allows capital from foreign-based MNCs to be withdrawn except for cash flows to Cuba, Vietnam, North Korea, and Cambodia. These restrictions are due to U.S. foreign policy. The United States does not require that a minimum percent of production be local content. However, it does levy a tariff on goods brought into the country, but as Levi-Strauss, Case II–2, illustrates, such tariffs are limited to labor costs in the offshore facilities if the fabrics are manufactured in the United States.

Mixed Policies

Countries with mixed policies with respect to the MNC recognize the need for foreign investment capital, technology, products, and valued capabilities available from the MNC. However, these countries are inclined to restrict the MNC and to protect the competitive positions of domestic industries. Behrman and Grosse suggest examples of countries using mixed policies as including France, Italy, Japan, Mexico, and South Korea.

In South Korea, the MNC is precluded from making FDI in many agricultural activities, financial institutions, transportation, and communication. These industries are considered vital to the national interest and thus Korean policymakers insure that these activities are under the control of Korean businesses. For those businesses in which FDI is allowed, there is an implicit limitation of 50 percent ownership by the MNC.

The Korean government requires MNCs that invest in certain industries like heavy transportation equipment to produce a certain percent of the content in Korea or to use parts and subassemblies manufactured in Korea. An exception to this policy is negotiable in certain industries if the MNC agrees to export the output from the Korean affiliate, as in the case of high technology.

Through its mixed national policies that allow a degree of openness to MNC activities while restricting others, the government strives to balance its economic and political interests against the interests of the MNC. The government seeks to generate foreign exchange, acquire advanced technology, and increase employment and the standard of living through such restrictive practices. However, Korea, one of the four newly industrialized countries (NICs) on the Pacific Rim is competing aggressively in international markets and thus is relatively open to MNC activities if such relationships further national objectives. The other NICs include Hong Kong, Singapore, and Taiwan.

Countries with Restrictive Policies

Countries with restrictive policies toward MNC activities and FDI include China, India, and most eastern European nations. However, the collapse of the eastern European governments in 1989, the move toward market economies, the reunification of Germany, and the crackdown in China on students and other dissidents all suggest that things can change quickly. Sometimes there is a move toward more economic openness and at other times relationships with the MNC become more restrictive.

India limits foreign ownership of businesses within India to 40 percent. Exceptions to this rule have been negotiated in high-technology businesses when a significant portion of the output is exported. India also requires special licensing for foreign-based MNCs, charges high tariffs on all goods exported to India, and has a high corporate income tax on MNC profits. However, MNC profits can be withdrawn from the country by special permission of the Reserve Bank, and such cash withdrawals are often delayed. Tax rates can be altered through negotiation as a special incentive to attract FDI and critical technology made available by the MNC.

Host Government–Multinational Corporation Negotiations

Host governments often need the MNC to obtain the advantages of foreign investment, critical tech-nologies, and foreign exchange to purchase goods and services not locally available. The MNC seeks low-cost labor, natural resources, markets, efficiencies in production and distribution, and opportunities to participate in international networks. These can be obtained in a number of countries.

BARGAINING RESOURCES OF MNCs AND HOST GOVERNMENTS

The MNC can offer the host country assistance in improving both the internal balance within its economy and in enhancing the international competitiveness of the country, as shown in Table 5–1.

TABLE 5–1
Bargaining Resources of MNCs and Host Governments

Basis of Bargaining Power	
Strengths of MNCs	Strengths of Host Governments
1. Assistance in improving host country internal balance (e.g., income, employment)	1. Control over access to the host country market
a. Proprietary technology including product, process, and managerial	a. control over access to the market in general
b. access to funds for investment in the host country	b. ability to offer an important market to MNCs when the government itself is a customer
c. managerial/marketing skills	
d. access to information	
2. Assistance in improving host country external balance	2. Control over access to factors of production
a. access to low-cost inputs	a. natural resources like minerals and metals, farmlands, forests, fisheries
b. access to foreign markets for exports	b. low-cost production inputs like labor

SOURCE: Adapted from Jack N. Behrman and Robert E. Grosse, *International Business and Governments: Issues and Institutions* (Columbia, S.C.: University of South Carolina Press, 1990), Chart 1.2, p. 8. Reprinted with permission.

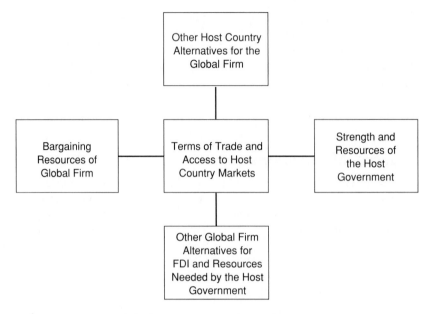

FIGURE 5–4 A Model of Negotiating Relationships Between Host Governments and the Global Firm

Internally, the MNC can often supply its proprietary technology, including designs for high-technology products, advanced production processes, and management skills. Also, the MNC often plans to locate facilities in the host country and make other investments that contribute to the economic development of the country. Externally, the MNC can provide needed supplies, parts, or other inputs at a lower cost than would otherwise be available in the host country. The MNC may have a developed distribution system by which the host country can gain greater access to export markets.

The host country government can often offer favored access to its markets. This is particularly true when the government itself is a major customer, as in the case of telecommunications, heavy equipment for infrastructure construction, or high-technology. The government may be able to offer a young and able workforce at relatively low cost, as is the case in Mexico, or it might be able to offer a well-educated and highly skill workforce, as would be the case of Singapore.

Table 5–1 outlines the bargaining resources of MNCs and host governments, both of which need

something that the other has to offer. The ultimate agreement is often the result of protracted negotiation, as the case of IBM and Mexico at the beginning of this chapter suggests.

HOST COUNTRY-MNC NEGOTIATIONS

Both the multinational corporation and the host country have things to offer the other that are very valuable. The possibility of an exchange relationship in which both parties have something to gain is the basis of all successful market relationships. However, the terms of the negotiation may be influenced by the overall pattern of interdependence between the MNC and the host government, as shown in Figure 5–4.

Some MNCs have much more to offer a country than others, depending upon its unique set of resources as they correspond to the needs of the host country. The greater the resources a MNC can offer a potential host country, the more that host country will seek out the multinational. Also, if only one or a very small number of global firms is trying to locate in a particular country, each of these MNCs will become relatively more important to the host country. If many multinationals are trying to expand operations into a given country, then that country can become more selective in its requirements and in what it offers the MNC.

Some countries are blessed with opportunities like abundant resources, lucrative markets, skills, and needed technology. Those that have abundant resources are sought out by MNCs with strategies for globalization. Each country seeks certain types of MNCs that can respond to its particular needs. For example, Singapore no longer offers a low-cost, low-skilled workforce. It has also adopted stringent environmental control regulations. Thus it seeks MNCs that wish to take advantage of its highly educated workforce and skills in high-technology areas that are unlikely to degrade the environment. Multinationals with high value-added products and whose operations are friendly with respect to environmental impact are sought by Singapore. In contrast, other developing countries on the Pacific Rim may seek FDI from MNCs that can take advantage of a low-cost labor supply.

The incentives offered to the MNC by the host country are a function of its need for particular MNC resources relative to alternative MNCs that are also planning to expand internationally. Similarly, the MNC seeks a host country where its resources can be put to the best economic use and offer the best economic arrangements. Because many firms are in the process of globalization and many host countries are trying to use their relationship with the MNC as an instrument for economic development, the MNC-host country relationship is very dynamic. The terms of exchange between the MNC and host country can also be influenced by the trend toward regional cooperation.

Regional Economic Cooperation

The past decade has witnessed growing interest in regional economic cooperation. Countries are banding together in efforts to create large, unified markets in Asia, South America, North America, and Europe. In addition, many countries have signed the General Agreement on Tariffs and Trade (GATT) with the long-term goal of eliminating all tariffs and trade barriers This will encourage free trade and the increasing globalization of world markets.

NORTH AMERICAN FREE TRADE AGREEMENT

The North American Free Trade Agreement (NAFTA) includes the United States, Canada, and Mexico. This treaty was signed by the heads of state of each country near the end of the Bush administration and was ratified by the United States Congress in 1993. This agreement phases out barriers to trade in North America, eliminates tariffs and barriers to investment, and would strengthen the protection of intellectual property rights like patents and copyrights. NAFTA could result in a market of over 360 million people with a gross economic output of over $6 trillion.

Mexico reversed its protectionist trade policies in 1982 when it experienced high foreign debt exceeding $80 billion and the worst depression in its history. Discussions of economic and trade reform were begun with the United States and with MNCs. President Salinas renegotiated the debt, reduced the level of inflation, and sought long-term investments by MNCs. He also sought to expand the US-Canadian Free Trade Agreement to include Mexico, thus creating NAFTA.

Many Americans opposed the creation of NAFTA, fearing that even larger numbers of jobs would be exported to Mexico than was the case under the *maquiladora* program since the 1960s. Others argued that NAFTA would lead to a healthier economy in Mexico, eventually causing markets to develop and affording opportunities both to Canadian and US-based businesses that wished to export to Mexico. Currently Mexico has little market potential not only because of its history of protectionism but also because the low level of economic development. NAFTA could lead to economic development, to the growth of the middle class, and to the development of attractive markets for global firms. As Mexican citizens enjoy increases in income, they will be more likely to purchase consumer products sold by Canadian and U.S.-based businesses.

Another objection to NAFTA is the difference in enforcement of environmental standards between Mexico and the United States. The U.S. Environmental Protection Agency (EPA) regulates pollution and toxic waste disposal practices by business much more stringently than does Mexico. Many feared that the passage of the NAFTA treaty would lead to the location to Mexico of more businesses with environmentally unsound practices because of the lax enforcement there. However, part of NAFTA's goal is to reduce the disparity between the environmental protection standards and regulations of member countries.

Another argument given for the ratification of NAFTA is that it will help to offset the market developments of the single European Union that was planned for 1992. Many feared a "fortress Europe" that would favor EU members and discriminate against global firms based outside Europe. NAFTA would provide a better base for reciprocal trade agreements between these two major areas of regional economic cooperation.

EUROPEAN INTEGRATION

There has been a constant movement toward European integration since the Treaty of Rome in 1957, as shown in Table 5–2. A customs union was established for a single market. A number of physical, technical, and administrative barriers remained that prevented the creation of a true European market. In 1985, the Commission of the EU sought to remedy these problems and published a set of 300 proposals for regulatory changes. Titled "White Paper on Completing the Internal Market," the plan called for the complete elimination of trade barriers and the free movement of goods, services, capital, and people throughout the EU.

The EU member countries reviewed the white paper and unanimously committed themselves to the single market through several treaty reforms known as the Single European Act (SEA). The target date for establishing the integrated European market was 1992. To achieve unification, the commission identified three general barriers to be eliminated:

1. Physical barriers like customs controls and border formalities
2. Technical barriers like different health and safety standards for products
3. Fiscal barriers including differences in value-added taxes and excise duties

Many of these barriers were interdependent and required related changes in other laws. For example, eliminating customs controls among EU members required modifications of the value-added tax (VAT) mechanisms used within individual countries. Creating the single European Union also required changing national safety standards so that European market standards would be consistent across country borders. The same was the case for national laws concerned with employment practices, security laws, and consumer laws.

The single European Union has wide implications for MNCs. Trade relationships between the EU and other countries continue to be negotiated by the commission, located in Brussels. Currently the commission's strategy is to develop reciprocal trade relationships between the EU and other countries such as the United States, Japan, and Canada.

With the internal EU barriers removed, it is hoped that EU members will take full advantage of the large size of the market, available human resources, and other resources. The final agreement must be approved by elections in individual member states. The initial election was held in Belgium and was narrowly defeated. Opponents felt that Belgium would have to give up too much of its sovereignty for the benefits of the single European Union. Although a major setback, the negative results of this election are likely to slow down rather than stop the process of moving toward a single market.

TABLE 5–2
European Union Milestones

1957	Treaty of Tome establishing the European Economic Community (EEC), or Common Market. Original members were Belgium, France, Italy, Luxembourg, the Netherlands, and West Germany.
1959	First reduction of EEC of internal tariffs.
1962	Common Agricultural policy established.
1967	Agreement reached on value-added tax (VAT) system.
1968	All internal tariffs eliminated and a common external tariff imposed.
1973	United Kingdom, Denmark, and Ireland become members.
1979	European Parliament directly elected for the first time.
1979	European monetary system comes into effect.
1981	Greece becomes a member.
1985	Lord Cockfield presents a White Paper to the European Commission outlining 300 steps to eliminate remaining barriers to internal trade in goods and services. The is endorsed by the member states and becomes Community policy.
1986	Spain and Portugal become members.
1987	Single European Act (SEA) comes into effect, improving decision-making procedures and increasing the role of the European Parliament.
1992	Elimination of all trade barriers within the EU. The single market becomes a reality.

Summary

The multinational corporation can be classified according to what it hopes to obtain from an activity in a host country. The types of MNCs based upon this viewpoint include (1) labor and natural resource seekers, (2) market seekers, (3) efficiency seekers, and (4) network seekers. The strategies of global business include simple and complex global strategies, nationally responsive strategies, and multidomestic strategies. Each of these strategies requires seeking markets or more efficient operations in global operations. These global operations can be highly coordinated or operated in a more decentralized manner.

Firms can also use global networks of operations to market a highly differentiated product or service to the global consumer. Such networks may also have the advantage of low-cost labor or technological efficiencies that allow business to compete on the basis of price through low-cost structures and quality. Also, the businesses who use either a multidomestic or a nationally responsive strategy might benefit by the use of a focus strategy.

The governments of potential host countries of the global firm have certain roles or objectives that include (1) maintaining national sovereignty, (2) enhancing the economic welfare or development of the country, (3) assuring national security, and (4) protecting the rights of citizens. Their relationships with global business can help host country governments to accomplish their national objectives. The foreign domestic investment (FDI) of global business can increase industrialization, provide jobs and technology, and improve the level of economic development. However, in return for this, a country may become interdependent with the MNC. This raises questions about the independence or sovereignty of the country and may even raise fears concerning the erosion of its national security. Thus, host government relationships with global business may involve trade-offs that have to be considered when embarking on a negotiation.

The terms of interaction between the MNC and the host government depend on (1) the bargaining resources of both the MNC and the host country, (2) alternative sites for global operations that work strategically for the MNC, and (3) the relative need of the host country for the MNC to have a role in the accomplishment of national objectives. In addition, recent trends toward regional cooperation like the EU and NAFTA may significantly influence MNC-host government relationships in the future.

Conclusions

The threefold nature of society is made significantly more complex by the globalization of markets and the advent of the MNC. Business now must interact with the home government where it is based but also with the host governments of the various countries where its operations are located. Also, the cultures, lifestyles, and expectations of society vary from country to country. Different countries provide different regulatory and legal environments within various jurisdictions. Also, each country has its own concept of what is acceptable cultural behavior for business operating within its boundaries.

Relationships between the host country and the MNC are inevitably influenced by the nature of the interdependence and relative power of each party in a negotiation. However, each side would do well not to abuse a temporary advantage, because the global marketplace is dynamic and the relative position of both countries and business can quickly change. Thus relationships based upon trust and responsibility need to be cultivated even though certain political realities underlie these relationships.

Business needs to be aware of what is strategically needed if its global system is to be competitive. This includes what can be provided by each host country as well as what the MNC can offer in exchange for the privilege of doing business in a particular country. Countries often have long-term competitive objectives based upon some concept of dynamic comparative advantage. The national competitive strategy and industrial policy of host countries guide the competitive position of the country in a global market. Similarly, the MNC must consider its long-term competitive position in the context of a global market. The long-term needs of the MNC, the home country, and the host country should be considered in multinational business–government relationships.

Discussion Questions

1. Multinational corporations can be classified according to what they hope to gain from their relationship with a host government. Discuss the types of multinationals from this perspective.
2. How do the types of multinationals relate to the global strategies used by the MNC?

3. What are the primary objectives of host governments? How can the MNC help to achieve them?

4. What are the major bargaining resources of the MNC?

5. What are the major bargaining resources of the host government?

6. Discuss how the foreign policy of the home country government influences the relationship between the MNC and the host government. Is this appropriate? Explain.

7. What factors determine the negotiations between the MNC and the host government? Apply this model to an actual situation like the Levi-Strauss case at the end of this part.

8. What problems does the marketing of products and technologies by global businesses from industrialized countries create in the Third World? What should the governments of the home country do in this situation?

9. What are some of the likely results of growing patterns of regional cooperation like the North American Free Trade Agreement or the EU have on the relationship between the global firm and host governments?

10. Discuss the trade-offs between the concerns of host country governments about national sovereignty and economic development.

11. What strategies can a host government use to accelerate economic development?

Notes

1. Rudolf Steiner, *The Renewal of the Social Organism* (Spring Valley, N.Y.: Anthroposophic Press, 1985).

2. Rudolf Steiner, *World Economy: The Formation of a Science of World Economics* (London: Rudolf Steiner Press, 1972).

This lecture series was given from July 24 to August 6, 1922, in Dornach, Switzerland.

3. See Alan M. Rugman, *Multinationals and Canada–United States Free Trade* (Columbia: University of South Carolina Press, 1990).

4. See Adam Smith, *Wealth of Nations* (New York: Modern Library, 1937). First published in 1776, it provides an extensive analysis and criticism of these first multinational enterprises.

5. Mira Wilkins, *The Emergence of Multinational Enterprise: American Business Abroad from the Colonial Era to 1914* (Cambridge, Mass.: Harvard University Press), pp. 37, 45.

6. This section is based on Jack N. Behrman and Robert E. Grosse, *International Business and Governments: Issues and Institutions* (Columbia: University of South Carolina Press, 1990), chap. 3. For other excellent discussions of multinational strategy, see C. K. Prahalad and Yves L. Doz, *The Multinational Mission: Balancing Local Demands and Global Vision* (New York: Free Press, 1987); and Michael E. Porter, ed., *Competition in Global Industries* (Boston: Harvard Business School Press, 1986).

7. Michael Porter, *Competitive Advantage* (New York: Free Press, 1985).

8. Behrman and Grosse, *International Business and Governments*, pp. 47–48.

9. Michael E. Porter, *The Competitive Advantage of Nations* (New York: Free Press, 1990), p. 88.

10. Michael Porter, *Competitive Advantage* (New York: Free Press, 1985). Also see Michael Porter, "Changing Patterns of International Competition," in David J. Teece, ed., *The Competitive Challenge: Strategies for Industrial Innovation and Renewal* (Cambridge, Mass.: Ballinger, 1987), pp. 28–57.

11. See Raymond Vernon, *Sovereignty at Bay* (New York: Basic Books, 1971), and *Storm over the Multinationals* (Cambridge, Mass.: Harvard University Press, 1977).

12. "Mexico: A New Economic Era," *Business Week*, November 12, 1990, pp. 102–110.

13. Yves Doz, "Government Policies and Global Industries," in *Competitiveness in Global Industries* (Boston: Harvard Business School Press, 1986), p. 238.

14. Ibid., chap. 7.

15. Behrman and Grosse, *International Business. and Governments*.

16. Ibid., chaps. 7, 8, and 9.

17. Ibid.

PART II CASES

Case II–1 _____

Mastering the Market: Japanese Government Targeting of the Computer Industry

To explore how government policies influence corporate decisions in an industry, I have analyzed the effects of Japan's persistent efforts to nurture a computer industry. Computers is a useful case for several reasons. Since the government viewed it as strategic to long-term economic growth, intervention has been extensive, providing ample opportunity to evaluate the ways that the Ministry of International Trade and Industry (MITI), which creates and implements Japan's industrial policies, has influenced private sector decisions in the computer industry.

The Japanese computer industry's development has been remarkable by any measure. Enormous capital requirements and the rapid obsolescence of products make the computer industry among the most difficult industries to enter. With IBM holding a 70 percent share of the world computer market in the early 1960s, any firm interested in moving into the computer field faced tremendous odds. General Electric and RCA both gave up in the early 1970s. Honeywell recently broke off its computer division and merged it into Honeywell Bull, a joint venture with NEC of Japan and Machine Bull of France; Sperry and Borroughs have merged in an effort to survive in the competitive market. European companies, despite an early lead, have also struggled to stay competitive.

The United States, with the world's largest computer market, the most advanced computer scientists, and heavy aid from the Defense Department,

SOURCE: Excerpted from an article with the same title by Marie Anchordoguy, Research Fellow, Harvard Business School. *International Organization* 43, no. 3 (Summer 1988). © 1988 by the World Peace Foundation and the Massachusetts Institute of Technology. Reprinted with permission from MIT Press.

has always maintained a large lead over the rest of the world in the computer field. Yet Japan, with little defense spending and far behind the United States in technical computer training, has managed to sustain three major computer companies and several small ones. Only in Japan have local firms been able to roll back IBM's market share to below 30 percent. Six years ago, Fujitsu became the first firm to overtake IBM in a national market. While there is no danger that Japanese firms will take over the world mainframe computer market in the foreseeable future, they have steadily increased their share. Fujitsu, once a tiny communications maker, supplies mainframes and supercomputers to ICL of Britain, Siemens of Germany, and Amdahl of the United States; Hitachi exports mainframes to BASF of Germany and National Advanced Systems of the United States; NEC, once an importer of Honeywell technology, has been supplying technology and mainframes to Honeywell for the past five years and is the primary supplier of technology for the recently established joint venture between Honeywell, NEC, and France's Machine Bull.

What were the key elements in the development of Japan's computer industry? I suggest that the government, through various microeconomic policies, created a market environment conducive to the industry's development. More specifically, by using protection and promotion policies to reduce costs and risks of operating in the computer market and to limit the number of players in each market segment, the government altered profit expectations in ways that provided firms with market incentives to enter the industry, increase investment, improve quality and technology, and reduce costs. They primarily used heavy protectionism, a quasi-governmental computer rental company, substantial financial assistance, and consolidation of the industry in government-sponsored cooperative R&D projects.

Protectionism

MITI had its heaviest hand in the computer market in the 1960s, when it used powerful protectionist policies to keep out foreign firms and computers. In 1960, when the government and businesses agreed to nurture a domestic industry, the government raised the tariff on computers from 15 to 25 percent.[1] Even more effective than tariffs were import quotas, which were easy to enforce because importing a computer required an import license from MITI. "Why do you have to use a foreign computer?" was the greeting users faced when they came from MITI to apply for a computer import. Pressure tactics were not uncommon. "There were even cases when we had to make it compulsory for them to change their minds from a foreign to a domestic computer," recalls MITI's Hiramatsu Morihiko, who became known as the "Devil Hiramatsu."[2]

Some firms complained bitterly about policies that forced them to use low-quality, unreliable domestic computers. MITI's pressure was particularly resented in the 1960s, when domestic machines were substantially inferior to their foreign counterparts. In 1961, responding to MITI pressure to buy domestic machines, a group of firms explained that they were sorry to apply for imports but they did not want to be the guinea pigs for domestic computer makers.[3] Other firms criticized MITI policy, saying that domestic computers were "obstructions to the promotion of rationalization efficiency."[4]

Government institutions were also expected to buy domestic machines, although exceptions were made, such as for Japan Telegraph and Telephone Company (NTT), when inferior domestic machines would have hindered the nation's communications system. Dependence on the Ministry of Finance for funds and interdependence with other government agencies also made it very difficult for MITI to reject all government import requests. Still, such approvals were exceptions; the government clearly favored domestic machines. In 1982, 91 percent of the computers used by the government were domestic machines, 9 percent foreign; in comparison 56 percent of all the computers in use in Japan at the time were domestic machines, 44 percent were foreign.[5] Favoritism toward domestic machines is all the more dramatic because the government primarily used very large computers, a market that even today is dominated by IBM. The government provided a huge market for domestic makers: the government purchased or rented 25 percent of all domestic computers during the 1960s and 1970s; by the early 1980s, this share had increased to 30 percent.[6]

In addition to limiting imports, several laws gave the Japanese government tight control over foreign investment in the Japanese market. These laws allowed the government to use access to the Japanese market as leverage for acquiring foreign technology cheaply and for pressuring foreign companies to make joint ventures with Japanese companies.

The most dramatic example of government control over a foreign computer company was MITI's web of regulations over IBM, which first entered Japan in 1937 as the Japan Watson Tokei Kikai Company. In 1949, the company was reestablished as Nihon (Japan) International Business machines. This was just one year before the Foreign Capital Law was enacted, enabling IBM Japan to avoid being forced by Japanese law to join hands with a Japanese firm.[7] Still, however, laws prevented IBM from producing in Japan or repatriating earnings. MITI used these laws in the late 1950s to obstruct IBM's attempts to supply the capital and technology IBM Japan needed to produce in Japan.[8] But blocking IBM Japan from producing in Japan did not stop Japanese firms from flooding MITI with import applications for IBM's very popular 1401 computer. Heavy demand for the foreign machine made the Japanese makers and the government keenly aware of the giant gap between domestic and IBM machines.

The Japanese government faced a dilemma: Japan could not develop a computer industry without IBM's basic patents, but IBM would not license its patents unless it was given the right to produce in Japan. While Japan needed the patents, it did not want to allow IBM to produce in Japan because it would reduce its control of IBM's sales. To acquire the patents while giving in as little as possible to IBM's demands for local production, long and sometimes bitter negotiations took place between IBM and MITI, which represented the firms.

In 1960, when J. W. Birkenstock of IBM requested permission to produce in Japan and remit profits to its U.S. parent in exchange for giving the Japanese companies access to IBM patents, Hiramatsu Morihiko of MITI demanded that IBM, in addition, make a joint venture with a Japanese firm.[9] But Birkenstock did not budge; in fact, he got tougher, announcing that IBM would not give access to its patents unless MITI allowed IBM Japan to manufacture its popular 1401 small computer in Japan. Angry about the introduction of a new condition, MITI abruptly broke off the negotiations. MITI knew, however, that without IBM's patents, domestic firms could not produce computers. Sabashi Shigeru, head of MITI's Heavy Industries Bureau, finally agreed to allow IBM to produce in Japan but politely warned IBM not to go too far: "Japanese makers are mosquitoes, IBM is an elephant. I would appreciate it if IBM does not do anything to crush the mosquito under its feet."[10]

Sabashi not only got the patents; IBM also reduced the royalty cost by 20 percent from what had originally been negotiated.[11] The makers paid IBM a 5 percent royalty of sales on systems and machines and 1 percent on parts. MITI let IBM Japan pay its parent 10 percent of sales in royalties despite strict foreign exchange regulations that restricted such large transfers.[12] MITI made sure IBM's technology was spread widely; 15 firms signed a five-year contract. Although the contract went into effect January 1, 1961, the government did not allow IBM Japan to start production until 1963. Moreover, MITI kept its strings tightly wrapped around IBM by placing conditions on the volume it exported and the type of machine it sold in Japan.[13] MITI was particularly concerned that IBM Japan not produce small- and medium-scale machines that would, free from the high tariff on imports, threaten the sale of domestic ones.[14] IBM generally cooperated. MITI's Hiramatsu praised IBM's cooperation with the Japanese government: "Without using any political power, it [IBM] is trying to tie a loyal relationship with MITI."[15]

Because they needed IBM patents, the Japanese government could not force IBM to make a joint venture with a local firm, but it succeeded in doing so with other U.S. makers. Sperry Rand, which makes UNIVAC computers, was forced to make a joint venture with Oki to gain access to the Japanese computer market. In this way, Japanese firms gained relatively easy and cheap access to foreign technology, machinery, and R&D. By the mid-1960s, all the Japanese computer firms except Fujitsu had made technological licensing agreements with foreign firms: Hitachi with RCA, Toshiba with General Electric, Mitsubishi with TRW, and NEC with Honeywell.

Limiting imports and foreign investment shifted demand to domestic machines, which in turn stimulated supply. By raising the prices of foreign machines, protectionism helped the firms price lower than their foreign counterparts. Indeed, despite inferior computers, dependence on imports dropped from 80 percent in 1959 to 20 percent by 1968[16]; sales of foreign computers declined from 93 percent in 1958 to 42.5 percent by 1969.[17] By the late 1960s, foreign firms dominated only the large-scale computer market. The foreign share increased in the early 1970s when IBM introduced a new, far more advanced series of computers, but by late 1975, when the market was officially liberalized and the Japanese started to bring out machines competitive with IBM's, the foreign share was whittled down to about 44 percent of the market; the foreign share has decreased gradually up to the present to about 40 percent (see Table 1).

One might expect that this heavy government protection would lead to gross inefficiencies, and Japanese users sometimes complained in the 1960s about being forced to use inferior domestic computers. But protectionism did not lead to sluggish growth in the long run. A key reason is because, while domestic companies were buffered from foreign firms, they were not protected from one another; indeed, the government promoted competition among several domestic firms. Moreover, the government constantly compared Japanese machines to those of IBM. With the government using IBM as a threat to domestic firms, coupled with foreign pressure for Japan to open up its high-technology markets, the companies real-

TABLE 1

Japanese and Foreign Shares of the Japanese Computer Market, 1958 and 1982 (billions of yen, %)

	Year*	1958	1959	1960	1961	1962	1963	1964	1965	1966	1967	1968
Japanese	Amount	0.07	0.52	1.83	2.42	7.35	12.87	17.85	26.89	35.81	51.25	91.23
	Growth (%)	—	619.3	250.6	32.6	203.3	75.1	38.7	50.7	33.2	43.1	78.0
	Market share (%)	7	21.5	27.3	18.3	33.2	29.7	42.8	52.2	53.6	47.2	56.5
Foreign (primarily IBM)	Amount	0.94	1.9	4.87	10.85	14.76	30.44	23.82	24.63	31.01	57.4	70.14
	Growth (%)	—	102.6	156	122.7	36	106	(-21.9)	3.4	25.9	85.1	21.8
	Market share (%)	93	78.5	72.7	81.7	66.8	70.3	57.2	47.8	46.4	52.8	43.5
Total	Amount	1.01	2.42	6.7	13.27	22.11	43.31	41.6	51.52	66.82	108.7	161.4
	Growth (%)	—	139.5	176.3	98.1	66.6	95.9	(-3.9)	23.7	29.7	62.6	48.3
	Market share (%)	100	100	100	100	100	100	100	100	100	100	100

	Year*	1969	1970	1971	1972	1973	1974	1975	1976	1977	1978	1979	1980	1981	1982
Japanese	Amount	122.0	197.4	206	222.7	271.4	310.3	342.7	415.1	882.8	970	1,076.8	1,211.5	1,372	1,563.4
	Growth (%)	33.7	61.8	4.3	8.1	21.9	14.3	10.4	21.1	—	9.9	11	12.5	13.3	14
	Market share (%)	57.5	60	59	53	51	48	56	57	54.2	52.1	53	32.5	54.8	55.9
Foreign (primarily IBM)	Amount	90.4	133.5	144.1	196	256.9	330.6	271.3	316.4	745.1	890	953.2	1,099.2	1,134.1	1,233.4
	Growth (%)	28.8	47.8	7.9	36	31	28.6	(-17.9)	16.6	—	19.5	7.1	15.3	3.2	8.8
	Market share (%)	42.5	40	41	47	49	52	44	43	45.8	47.9	47	47.5	45.2	44.1
Total	Amount	212.4	330.9	350.1	418.7	528.3	640.9	614	731.5	1,628	1,860	2,030	2,310.3	2,506.1	2,796.8
	Growth (%)	31.6	55.8	5.8	19.6	26.2	21.3	(-4.2)	19.1	—	14.3	9.1	13.8	8.5	11.6
	Market share (%)	100	100	100	100	100	100	100	100	100	100	100	100	100	100

*1958–1976: Share of annual deliveries (rental/purchase) of general purpose computers; 1977–1982; share of installed base.

SOURCE: JECC Computer Notes, 1979, pp. 10–11; Computopia, January 1981, 1983, and other January issues.

Note: Some discrepancies may occur due to rounding.

ized that without competitive machines, they would not be able to survive in the long run.

The Japan Electronic Computer Company

Despite the importance of protectionism in allowing MITI to bargain for the necessary patents and to control foreign imports and investment, these policies alone would not nurture a domestic industry. A key problem was that to compete with IBM, which was renting its machines, the Japanese also needed to offer rentals; to rent, they needed capital. Japanese users could not afford to buy Japanese computers, yet Japanese computer firms could not afford to rent them.

Renting computers is costly and risky. It not only involves huge amounts of capital to finance rentals but also the risk that users may trade in a computer after a short time for a newer model. Indeed, the huge sum of capital needed to rent computers and invest heavily in R&D is a major barrier to entering the computer industry. To reduce this barrier, MITI helped establish the Japan Electronic Computer Company (JECC) in 1961. With no sales division, only a couple of hundred employees, and profits of, at best, $1–2 million a year, it is not surprising that few Japanese have ever heard of JECC. Yet this quasi-private computer rental company played a critical role in nurturing the industry's development. To the all-star team of Japanese computer makers that jointly owned JECC—Hitachi, Fujitsu, NEC, Mitsubishi, Toshiba, and Oki—the company served as a funnel for a generous flow of government low-interest loans. Between 1961 and 1981, the government channeled about $2 billion in loans into JECC to help the company buy computers from member firms and rent them to the public for low monthly fees.[18] Through JECC, the makers were able to borrow funds from banks to which they would not otherwise have had access.[19] For MITI, which placed its retired officials into top management positions at JECC, the rental company provided an institution through which to guide the industry. Through JECC, MITI quelled price wars and stimulated the demand and supply of domestic computers.

Only seven companies joined JECC even though 15 had made contracts to use IBM's basic patents. A MITI committee of people from government, industry, and academia decided that success in the computer industry would require huge sums of money—amounts that only the seven large and experienced electric and telecommunications firms could generate.[20] The JECC system was set up to work as follows: when a user asked to rent a computer, JECC purchased it from the maker and rented it to the user at a monthly rate decided by JECC; the rental rate could not be changed.[21] Users were required to keep a computer at least 15 months. Afterward they could trade it in for a new one without penalty. When a computer was returned, the maker had to buy it back from JECC at the remaining book value.

One of JECC's major functions was to enlarge the market for domestic computers by offering them at low monthly rental fees. In 1960, the year before JECC's establishment, only 4 percent of Japanese computers were rented; within two years, this had jumped to 46 percent and by 1965, to 78 percent.[22] The market for domestic machines grew much faster than that for foreign machines, even though foreign computers were considered far better than Japanese ones until the mid-1970s.[23] With overall growth of 67 percent in computer sales from 1961 to 1962, domestic makers enjoyed a 203 percent increase, while foreign firms increased only 36 percent. By 1965, the Japanese firms overtook foreign firms, increasing sales 51 percent to gain a 52.2 percent share of the domestic market. That same year, foreign firms' sales grew by a mere 3.4 percent to 24.6 billion yen; they watched their share slide under the 50 percent mark for the first time (see Table 1).

JECC not only stimulated the demand and supply of domestic computers, it also funneled hugh amounts of relatively invisible government funds to the firms. Since JECC carried the burden of financing rentals, the computer firms did not need to acquire large loans to provide rentals themselves. JECC also gave them an immediate return on investment; if the firms had had to finance their own rentals, they would have received their return in small monthly payments spread over 3.7 years per machine.[24] In the meantime, they would have had to provide financing for the user. Receiving their return immediately through JECC not only provided the companies with vital up-front cash, it also enabled them to focus their scarce resources on production, technology, quality, and cost. JECC accelerated the market forces driving the development of low-cost, technologically sophisticated computers.

While it is impossible to calculate definitively the importance of JECC to the firms, an estimate suggests that they received substantial benefits. By receiving their return in advance through JECC, the firms got the benefit of $269.44 million in up-front cash in the period 1961–1969 and $495 million from 1970 to 1981.[25] This up-front cash—an interest-free loan—represented a subsidy of $22.5 million in the 1961–1969 period and $45.12 million from 1970 to 1981.[26] Low-interest JDB loans to JECC also provided the computer makers with a subsidy of $178.2 million during the 1961–1981 period.[27]

While absolute numbers are important, it is the amount relative to the firms' other resources that helps us more critically evaluate their importance to the firms. From 1961 to 1969, the firms would have had a cash flow of 120.3 billion yen if they had run their own rental systems, compared to the flow of 217.3 billion yen they received under the JECC system.[28] With only 120.3 billion yen, they would have had difficulty renting their own computers in addition to investing 103.9 billion yen in R&D and plant and equipment during the 1960s. A mere 16.4 billion yen would have remained to cover production and overhead cost.

The real question, however, is whether the firms could have acquired enough loans from private sources to finance their own rentals, and, if they could have, whether they would have been willing to invest heavily in computers. While it cannot be proved, the evidence suggests that it would have been very difficult, if not impossible, for the firms to have gotten enough loans, with the possible exception of Hitachi. Indeed, even the government-backed JECC found it difficult to attract enough funds from private banks. In the early 1960s, private banks were only willing to match JDB loans to JECC; later, the JDB supplied about 40 percent of the loans, private banks 60 percent. But each bank only lent a small amount to JECC. A high-ranking JDB official explained that, in order to get private banks to lend to JECC in the 1960s, the JDB had to guarantee the loans.[29]

Since banks required a JDB guarantee to induce them to lend to the government-backed JECC in the 1960s, it is highly unlikely that they would have made the necessary loans to the computer firms, especially since such loans would have tightly pinched the firms' finances. JECC borrowed a total of 140.4 billion yen from 1961 to 1969[30]; in comparison, the industry as a whole only invested a total of 103.9 billion yen in plant and equipment and R&D during this period. Thus, to rent their computers during the 1960s, the firms would have needed a sum of money more than the amount they were already investing in R&D and plant and equipment. It is highly improbable that they could have borrowed that much money, and even if they could, that they would have been willing to invest that much in a computer rental system. Indeed, one of JECC's major functions was to manipulate the market so that firms would view entry as profitable in the long run. Without JECC and its government backing, it is highly unlikely that they would have entered; if they had, they, like RCA and GE, would have been under heavy pressure to withdraw from the market.

JECC's financial backing was undoubtedly critical to the firms. But direct financial benefits were not the only way that JECC assisted the firms. By acting as the manager of a price cartel, JECC assured the firms a reasonable return on their machines. This price cartel was particularly important in the early years when the firms were already selling at a loss to compete with IBM and to promote the diffusion of domestic machines. As the computer makers became more competitive, JECC gradually reduced, in relative terms, its support of the industry and shifted the burden to the private sector's shoulders. In the 1960s, 65 percent of the domestic computers were rented through JECC; this dipped to about 30 percent of the machines in the 1970s and only 11 percent by the early 1980s.[31]

One might suspect that the computer companies used JECC as a dumping ground for computers they could not sell on the open market. But the government only allowed JECC to buy computers that users wanted to rent. There was a direct link to the market; if no one applied to rent a computer JECC did not buy it. Those with the best machines got the most benefit from JECC.

Governmental Financial Assistance

Protectionism and JECC were key ingredients to nurturing a domestic computer industry. But the firms needed funds so that they could invest heavily to make better computers. A variety of subsidies, low-interest loans, tax benefits, and loan guarantees lowered costs and risks and raised profit expectations in the computer industry, thereby inducing increased investment in R&D and plant and equipment.

Contrary to the conclusions of some studies of Japan's industrial policy,[32] I found that government financial aid to the computer industry was relatively large in proportion to what the firms were investing. From 1961 through 1969, estimated subsidies and tax benefits ($132.6 million) were equivalent to 46 percent of what the private sector was investing in R&D and plant and equipment; if we include government loans, total aid ($542.8 million) was equal to 188 percent of what the firms were investing; indeed, the government was also giving loans for use as working capital. From 1970 to 1975, subsidies and tax benefits ($636.55 million) were equivalent to 57 percent of what the firms were investing, and with government loans, total aid ($1.8 billion) was 169 percent the firms investment. From 1976 to 1981, subsidies and tax benefits ($10.3 billion) declined to 25.2 percent of what the firms were investing, but with government loans, aid ($3.74 billion) was still equal to 91.6 percent of what the firms were investing.

In addition to analyzing the absolute and relative amount of aid, we must also look at the context in which the aid was given. Aid was particularly critical in periods following an IBM announcement of a new computer. During these periods, MITI would group firms together in cooperative R&D projects to develop machines to compete with IBM's new models. In the early 1970s, for example, IBM came out with its 370 series, which had several times the power of Japanese computers at the time. The IBM 370 shocked the world computer market and led to the withdrawal of RCA and GE from the industry. The Japanese were particularly shocked because the 370 was introduced before they had even finished an R&D project to develop a machine to match IBM's earlier computer series. Moreover, the oil shock and sharp

reevaluations of the yen in the early 1970s had plunged the Japanese economy into a recession, and the United States was pressuring Japan to open up its computer market. The introduction of the 370 at the time threatened to destroy Japan's computer industry once and for all.

The firms knew this and would not have continued to pour resources into such a risky venture without some assurance of support and protection. MITI stepped in with $213 million for the "New Series" project to build machines that would counter IBM's 370 series. The money was contingent on the six computer firms consolidating into three groups. The government hoped that with groups focusing on different sizes of computers, the industry would be able to compete with IBM's full line of computers, even though no single firm could have done so.

Some would argue that, by U.S. standards, $213 million was a small amount. But it was a relatively large amount for the Japanese companies—equivalent to 30 percent of what they invested in R&D for computers themselves during that same period.[33] Moreover, it was concentrated on a high-risk research project that the firms were unlikely, and perhaps unable, to undertake on their own, although it was nonetheless critical to their survival. As one former high-level MITI official explained: "Government financial aid in the seventies was critical to the firms' survival. . .the firms cooperated in the New Series Project because of the fear of bankruptcy."[34] Kobayashi Taiyu, Fujitsu's chairman, also attributed the survival of the Japanese industry at this critical juncture to government subsidies for cooperative R&D.[35] Indeed, the infusion of government aid helped the industry develop machines to counter the IBM 370 series, bringing them neck-to-neck with IBM in computer hardware. When the IBM 370 was introduced in 1970–1971, the foreign share of the Japanese market increased until the results of the "New Series" project started coming out in 1975; then the Japanese share rose (see Table 1).

The impact of government aid on a firm during this risky period is shown by comparing government aid to Fujitsu in 1975 with its profits and investment that year. A conservative estimate is that Fujitsu received $32.59 million in government subsidies and tax benefits in 1975, equivalent to 36 percent of what Fujitsu invested in R&D and plant and equipment in the computer industry that year. Including low-interest government loans of $75.25 million to Fujitsu that year, total government benefits were equal to the total of Fujitsu's investment in plant and equipment and R&D that year and half of its profits. This tremendous amount of aid helped Fujitsu maintain its computer operations during this very risky period.

NTT, a government monopoly until April 1985 and still under government control, also funneled large, but relatively invisible, sums of money into the computer industry. Its huge R&D and procurement budgets provide heavy support to Hitachi, NEC, Fujitsu, and Oki. As the fields of computers and data communications started to blur in the late 1960s and early 1970s, NTT channeled profits from its telephone operations into data communications R&D. Most of the funds were consigned to Fujitsu, Hitachi, and NEC—the same firms that MITI consistently promoted. By favoring these firms, NTT lowered the barriers for their entry into the field and substantially reduced their costs and risks of operating in the industry.

Honoki Minoru, director of NTT's data communications division, explained why NTT got into the field of computers and data communication:

Behind NTT's aggressive entry into data communication was, frankly, a view of it as a policy to counter IBM. If our computer makers had only been a bit stronger, it would have been okay for NTT not to do the DIPS Project (a cooperative project among NTT, Fujitsu, Hitachi, and NEC to develop computers for data communications use.) But five or six years ago, our national (computer) technology and IBM's were on different levels. Because of this, NTT had to take the lead and do it [develop computers for use in data communications]. Also, with regard to liberalization of communications circuits, the reason was the same. The reason we hesitated for many years was because we were waiting until domestic technology got up to that ([BM's] level.[36]

Despite its archrivalry with the Ministry of Post and Telecommunications (MPT), which supervises NTT, MITI cooperated with the MPT to gain more

aid for the computer industry.[37] Indeed, while MITI could not get as much money from the Ministry of Finance (MOF) as it wanted for the industry, NTT was a gold mine, flush with funds from high-priced telephone services. As an "independent" entity, NTT was relatively free to subsidize data communications with profits from telephones. NTT also received other government funds annually. For example, from 1964 to 1971 NTT received $436.1 million in low-interest loans from the FILP budget—largely composed of citizens' savings in post office accounts—and $1.4 billion in grants from the general budget.[38]

NTT's dependence on private firms for all of its equipment and much of its R&D gave those firms in the "NTT family" a guarantee of substantial R&D grants and heavy procurement of their products. NEC's president Kobayashi Koji said:

. . .if we are to start doing an on-line information service, it will take a substantial amount of money, so if a large firm like NTT doesn't start it for us. . .it cannot be done. . .so I want NTT to put all its power into it for us and invest in it. I look forward to NTT doing it the same as America's Department of Defence.[39]

Indeed, firms in the so-called "NTT family" not only got NTT to finance a substantial part of their research, they also, by producing what NTT wanted, were essentially guaranteed a large part of the NTT market, which totaled approximately $13.3 billion from 1965 to 1975.[40] As of 1968, 70 percent of all NTT purchases were from Fujitsu, NEC, Oki, and Hitachi: NTT bought 60 percent of each of these firms' telecommunications production.[41] NTT spent 170 billion yen ($472.2 million) on data communications over the five-year period starting in 1968.[42]

One might suspect that the funds the firms received through NTT, JECC, and MITI were used to support inefficient operations. While the firms' operations were clearly inefficient in the early years, aid was generally given in ways that encouraged efficiency over the long run. Firms often had to match subsidies. Tax benefits increased with marginal increases in investment. Strings were tightly attached to subsidies and loans; they had to be used for specific R&D or machinery. Most important, aid was closely tied to results. A firm that was not competitive could expect to be cut off from future subsidized R&D.

Cooperative Research Projects

Protectionism, JECC, and financial aid were all critical to creating an environment for computer industry growth, but the firms were far behind IBM when they launched their computer efforts and would never catch up without rapidly improving their technology. The government helped narrow the technology gap by using cooperative projects to reduce redundant research, to accelerate technological advancement, and to encourage the firms to specialize so that they could achieve the economies of scale necessary to compete with IBM. "Cooperation" usually meant that labor was divided, with resulting patents open to all participants at low cost. In some cases, firms took different approaches to the same problem; in a few cases, firms researched the same topic together.

In the first major government–private sector computer research project, called "1966 Super High-Performance Computer Project," the government concentrated the entire computer industry on the development of one system: the prototype of a machine to counter IBM's 360 series, which was the world's first third-generation computer, characterized by integrated circuits, a series of compatible machines ranging from small to large, and a buffer memory. A 12 billion yen ($33.33 million) grant supported the project, which continued until 1972. While 12 billion yen may seem like a small amount today, it was relatively large then. Indeed, the firms had only invested 11.2 billion yen ($31.11 million) of their own funds on R&D related to computers between 1961 and 1965.[43]

Hitachi, Fujitsu, and NEC researched mainframe architecture and integrated circuits; Mitsubishi, Toshiba, and Oki were to work on peripheral equipment. Each firm worked separately. Hitachi, by submitting the best design proposal, was made the leader of the project and given responsibility for creating the final prototype computer. The government, by fully funding the project, owned the resulting patents, which it offered at low cost to participating firms.

While the project fell short of its goals (the resulting prototype did not match IBM's most advanced 360 series models, let alone the advanced 370 series of computers IBM announced in the early 1970s), the effort nonetheless helped the industry make critical technological advances in integrated circuits, buffer memories, and mainframe architecture. It also established a standard for the interface between peripherals and mainframes.[44] Hitachi, NEC, and Fujitsu incorporated these advances in their subsequent mainframe computers,[45] which, while not competitive with IBM, sold well because of important restrictions and government procurement; the results were also used in a subsequent NTT project to develop computers for use in data communications.[46]

In the early 1970s, when IBM introduced its revolutionary 370 series, the Japanese government and industry panicked. IBM was pulling even further ahead of the Japanese. While RCA and GE withdrew from the computer industry after the IBM announcement, the Japanese took drastic measures to survive. MITI tried to persuade the six firms to merge into two or three. The Ministry of Finance also pushed for mergers. According to one MOF official, "If we are going to promote the computer industry, six firms should not be selfishly competing; we should reduce the industry to about three firms in order to gain international competitiveness."[47] But the firms were not willing to merge. In the end, they compromised and reorganized into three groups for the "New Series" project to develop computers to counter IBM's new series.

Fujitsu vice president Kiyomiya Hiro explained the importance of cooperation between Fujitsu and Hitachi in the "New Series" project to his employees:

> To explain our cooperation with Hitachi, the important thing is "cooperation and competition." Frankly speaking, if we do not do this, we cannot confront our American competitors. For example, if Japanese makers in the domestic market did not cooperate and only competed, before we knew it, we would be taken over by the American firms; there is a danger that every maker would be dealt a fatal blow. On the other hand, if we only cooperate and do not compete at all, we will slide into stagnant waters, which would also be bad. The British and French computer industries are examples of this. Thus, using cooperative relations

during the early stages of development as a case, we will then compete on commercializing the product; as a whole we must oppose the threat posed by foreign capital. Thus we will cooperate on R&D but in sales and production we will compete fiercely as we have in the past. . .Finally, I would like to add that in the background of this move is the earnest guidance of MITI and the deep understanding of NTT. In regards to the big problem created by the decision to liberalize the computer industry in three years, both NTT and MITI have been serious and forward-looking in considering what form our computer industry should take in order to oppose the giant power of American capital.[48]

The "New Series" project was different in type and degree from earlier cooperative efforts. First, financial backing was greater; the government gave $213 million for the five-year "New Series" project compared to $33.33 million in subsidies given for the six-year "1966 project." Second, the firms were expected to cooperate more closely; Fujitsu and Hitachi developed large IBM-compatible computers, NEC and Toshiba medium and small Honeywell-compatible computers, and Oki and Mitsubishi small, specialized computers. By having each group focus on certain technologies and models, the project produced competition and redundant research and helped the industry to develop a full series of computers to compete with IBM's 370 series, even though no single firm had the resources to do so.

The computers developed in this project made the Japanese computer makers competitive with their foreign counterparts in hardware. Indeed, according to Fujitsu chairman Kobayashi Taiyu, the reason the Japanese makers were able to survive when IBM brought out the 370 series, even though RCA and General Electric left the industry, was "because MITI started providing research grants and made different companies get together for cooperative development of new machines: for the first time, Japanese makers were ready for battle."[49]

In the "1966" and "New Series" R&D projects, it was easy to determine the research goal—to match existing IBM computers. But as the firms caught up with IBM in hardware in the mid-1970s and became stronger and more independent, cooperation among competitors became increasingly difficult. It became necessary to focus cooperation on

basic or production technology that was one step removed from product development. "If R&D content is too close to commercialization, cooperation will not go far," explained Shimizu Sakae, senior managing director of Toshiba.[50]

The next challenge fit the bill. IBM was expected to use very large integrated circuits (VLSI) in its next generation of computers. If Japan were to remain competitive, it needed the capability to produce those advanced integrated circuits. To receive subsidies to study VLSI production technology, MITI required that the firms reorganize into two groups. Mitsubishi, Fujitsu, and Hitachi set up one group lab; Toshiba and NEC formed another. NTT, which had its own VLSI project involving Fujitsu, Hitachi, and NEC, had a separate lab but exchanged information with the MITI project labs. The four-year project started in 1976 and cost 72 billion yen ($360 million), 30 billion yen of which was funded by the government. The firms each contributed an equal amount to cover the remaining 42 billion yen.[51]

The division of labor varied according to the research theme. The most important research topic—the electron beam and X-ray beam exposure devices for drawing narrower lines on wafers—were studied in three parallel research groups. Each took a different approach in hopes that at least one would succeed. The project members tried a total of seven different ways to get the electron beam to draw narrower patterns on the wafer. Each of the three groups was led by one firm but included members from other firms. Tarui Yasuo, head of the project, said that it would have been difficult to mix equal numbers of people from rival firms for R&D on the most important devices.[52] In contrast, the different research groups worked together to develop ways to reduce defects in silicon crystals.

The project helped the firms in several key ways. It induced them to take the risky step of committing themselves to VLSI. According to Nishimura Taizo, general manager of Toshiba's International Operations: "That a project is assigned by the government is a clear sign that if you are not on the bandwagon, you will miss something important."[53] Another was to reduce the cost of R&D: "Because of the limited R&D resources of a private firm, we cannot allow a failure; we cannot deny that this participation in MITI's VLSI project is a big hedge against risk."[54]

The project achieved most of its technical goals. They developed technologies to draw narrower patterns on silicon wafers and found ways to decrease defects in silicon crystals.[55] Shimizu of Toshiba said the project was very important in helping the firms produce 64K RAM and ultimately the one megabyte chip. Toshiba and NEC jointly developed an electron beam device in the project and are using it today in their VLSI efforts. Shimizu noted that "the timing of the project was critical; there was no electron beam and we needed a breakthrough to get ahead. The firms did not have any of the equipment for producing VLSIs, such as the electron beam or testing equipment."[56] The program resulted in about a thousand patents; 59 percent were held by one person, 25 percent by one company with a few members from other companies, and 16 percent by groups consisting of several members of various firms.[57] The different groups also exchanged information, and patents were open to all the members.

The VLSI project helped the makers produce low-cost, high-quality VLSI, thereby boosting their computer sales at home and abroad. Indeed, advances in VLSI, which helped increase the processing speed and memory capacity of Japanese machines, were key in the Japanese makers' ability to keep up with IBM hardware in the late 1970s. More recently, they have helped the Japanese come out with mainframes that exceed IBM's top machines in performance but that are lower in price.[58] Today, eight years after the project has ended, the technology from this project is playing an important role in the mass production of one megabyte chips.[59]

R&D in new areas is risky, inevitably involving some failures. Joint research projects reduced costs and risks by dividing firms into teams to take different approaches to a problem, to focus on different parts of a computer system, or to work on completely different systems. To encourage specialization, the firms were generally assigned research in specific market segments. NEC, Fujitsu, and Hitachi have always been assigned the mainframe and integrated circuits, and Mitsubishi, Oki, and Toshiba the less sophisticated peripheral equipment. Not surprisingly, Fujitsu, Hitachi, and NEC are Japan's primary mainframe producers today and the other three its major producers of peripherals.

Indeed, the ability of government to influence the actions of private companies was far greater than one might suppose from the subsidies. First, in most cases, the government required that the firms match R&D subsidies and commit engineers to the projects. The government used subsidies as leverage to get the firms to invest more. Second, the threat of being dropped from future government-sponsored projects, as Oki was when it did not commercialize the results of the "New Series" project, also pushed the companies to work hard, advance technologically in the projects, and commercialize their results.

Cases of Ineffective Policies

Discussion thus far has focused on the successful cases of governmental intervention, but policies have not always been effective. In general, failures occurred when the government did not incorporate market incentives into its policies. For example, the government sponsored the creation of a special software company—the Japan Software Company—in the mid 1960s to develop software for a government–private sector cooperative R&D project. The company, a joint venture among Fujitsu, Hitachi, NEC, and the Industrial Bank of Japan, was also expected to take orders from private companies for software development.

The software goals for the project were far too ambitious: to make a "common language" software that could run on Fujitsu, Hitachi, and NEC mainframes. Lagging far behind IBM, and with scant experience in developing software, the company was not able to even come close to meeting the goals. Soon after the project ended, the firm went bankrupt; it had not developed enough outside orders to support its existence once the project subsidies ended. It had become an organization with all the characteristics of a bureaucracy—slow, clumsy, and inefficient.

The primary factor involved in the downfall of Japan Software was its insulation from the market. Once they were guaranteed financing for the project, managers of the company had little incentive to compete in the market or attract outside orders.[60] Confident that the government would not allow the company to go bankrupt, the managers ignored the financial health of the company. This contrasts sharply with JECC, the computer rental company: computer makers were required to buy back from JECC the machines that had been traded in; JECC was prohibited from losing money by a requirement that the computer makers bear any losses: and JECC was never guaranteed any money—it had to negotiate annually for new loans. With software that was inferior and more expensive than that of its competitors, it was not surprising that Japan Software received few outside orders.[61] When the project ended, the subsidies stopped, leaving the firm with no option but to fold.

Another case of ineffective targeting policies is the Information Processing Promotion Association (IPA), established in 1970 to promote the diffusion of general-purpose software programs. The idea was perfectly reasonable: by having the IPA fund the development of software packages and rent them for low monthly rental fees, the government hoped to change the Japanese habit of using custom-made software, which was draining the productivity of the nation's small pool of software engineers. Firms applied to the IPA for funds to develop software packages. The IPA, after approving an application, funded the software package development. Once again, the problem was that the institution operated without the constraints of market competition; there was no effort to match the software developed with market needs. Not surprisingly, few of the packages have ever been rented.[62] In contrast to JECC, which only bought a computer when a user specifically asked for it, the IPA bought software and then tried to persuade firms to use it.

The fundamental flaws in Japan Software and IPA were partly because of deeper problems in Japan's software industry. First, Japan Software's products were the nation's first major efforts to develop advanced software. The government and the firms had little experience to draw from and the reverse engineering that worked so well in hardware was ineffective in software, which must be tailored to differences in language and business practices. The IPA was also given a formidable task: to change the Japanese preference for custom-made software, a preference deeply rooted to the belief that custom-made programs give the user an edge over competitors who use mass-produced packaged software. The key defects of these two institutions—the lack of ties to the marketplace and the existence of

only vague, overly ambitious goals—thus in part resulted from the government and businesses failing to understand the software market. With reverse engineering impossible, and few trained software engineers, the tasks that were given to these institutions were completely unrealistic.

Case Endnotes

1. *Denshi Kogyo nenkan* (Electronic Industry Yearbook). (Tokyo: Dempa Shimbunsha, 1962), p. 161. Rate was reduced to 15 percent for GATT members in 1964, when Japan changed its status in GATT and joined the OECD. *Genku Yunyu Seido Ichtran* (A Summary of the Current Import System) (Tokyo: MITI Chosa Kai, annual).

2. "JECC Monogatari" (The JECC Story), segment 19 in *Kokusan Denshi Kezsanki Nyuzu* (Domestic Computer news), no. 135. (Tokyo: JECC). April 1, 1981, p. 8.

3. *Asahi Shimbun* (Asahi News), June 6, 1961.

4. *Yomiuri Shimbun* (Yomiuri News), September 14, 1961.

5. Percent and monetary value. *Kompyutopia* (Computopia), (Tokyo: Kompyuta Eiji Sha, January 1983), pp. 92, 95.

6. Estimated using data on computers in general at government institutions. In the 1960s, about 25 percent of domestic computers were used in government offices, thus the assumption that the government bought or rented about 25 percent of Japanese computers annually. *Kompyutaa Jutsudo Tokyo Chosa* (Survey of Computers Currently in Use) (Tokyo: JECC, annual); *Kompyutopa*. January issues.

7. *Denshi Kogyo Nenkan*, 1976, p. 683. The Foreign Capital Law is sometimes translated as the Foreign Investment Law.

8. "JECC Monogatari," segment 3, no. 119, December 1, 1979: Matsuo Hiroshi, *IBM Okoku o Obiyakasu Fujitsu* (Fujitsu Threatening the *IBM Okoku o Obiyakasu* Monarchy) (Tokyo: Asahi Somorama, 1980), p. 152.

9. "JECC Monnogatari," segment 3, no. 119, December 1, 1979.

10. Ibid., segment 4, no. 120, January 1, 1980, p. 6.

11. Kompyutopic, December 1973, p. 24.

12. "JECC Monogatari," segment 5, February 1, 1980, p. 3.

13. Ekonomisuto Board, ed., *Sengo Sangyo Shi e no Shogen* (Interviews for a History of postwar Industry), Vol. 1 (Tokyo: Mainichi Shimbunsha, 1977), pp. 142–43.

14. "JECC Monogatari," segment 5, February 1, 1980, p. 3.

15. "JECC Monogatari," segment 4, no. 120, January 1, 1980.

16. *Denshi Kogyo Nenkan*, 1971–1972, p. 172.

17. *JECC Kompyuta Noto* (JECC Computer Notes), (Tokyo: JECC, 1979), p. 10.

18. *JECC 10 Nenshi* (Ten-Year History of JECC), (Tokyo: JECC, 1973), pp. 50–51, 59; *JECC Kompyuta Noto*, annual.

19. Interview with Ishiguro Ryuji, director of the JDB's Center for Research on Investment in Plant and Equipment, November 12, 1984.

20. "JECC Monogatari," segment 9, June 1, 1980, p. 2.
21. Interview with Ishii Yoshiaki, general manager, JECC Research Division, July 19, 1984; various discussions with Hirose Koichi of JECC in 1984.
22. *Denshi Kogyo Nenkan*, 1970–1971, p. 180.
23. Interview with Hirose Koichi of JECC.
24. JECC's monthly fee is one-forty-fourth of the sales price; 44 months equal 3.7 years.
25. Marie Anchordoguy, "The Role of Public Cooperations in Japan's Industrial Development: Japan Electronic Computer Company," *Political Science Quarterly* (Winter 1988–1989).
26. Ibid.
27. Marie Anchordoguy, "The State and the Market: Industrial Policy Towards Japan's Computer Industry," Ph.D. dissertation, University of California, Berkeley, pp. 382–83. Subsidy is the difference between interests JECC paid on JDB loans and the estimate of what firms would have to pay if they had borrowed the money at the prime rate from private banks.
28. Anchordoguy; "The Role of Public Cooperations."
29. Interview with Ishiguro Ryuji, November 12, 1984.
30. *JECC 10 Nenshi*, pp. 50–51, 59.
31. Calculated using data from *JECC Kompyuta Noto*, 1979, pp. 10–11, 377: *Denshi Kogyo Nenkan*, 1979, p. 447; Dokusen Bunsek Kenkyukai, ed., *Nihon no Dokusen Kogyo* (Japan's Monopolistic Enterprises), Vol. 1 (Tokyo: Shin Nihon Shuppankai, 1969), p. 292; *Kompyuta Warudo* (Computer World), May 31, 1982, p. 21.
32. See Jimmy Wheeler, Merit E. Janow, and Thomas Pepper, *Japanese Industrial Development Policies in the 1980s* (New York: Hudson Institute, 1982).
33. They invested $708.8 million.
34. Interview with Maeda Norihiko, February 28, 1986.
35. Interview with *Bungeishunju*, September 1982, p. 101.
36. Cited in *Kompyutopia*, October 1973, p. 43.
37. See Anchordoguy, "The State of the Market," pp. 120–21.
38. Calculated at 360 yen to the dollar. *Nihon Kaihatsu Ginko Tokei Yoran* (JDB Summary of Satistics) (Tokyo: JDB, annual); *Hojokin Benran* (Handbook of Subsidies) (Tokyo: Ninon Densan Kikaku Kabushiki Gaisha, annual).
39. *Kompyutopia*, April 1969, p. 30.
40. Nihon Denshin Denwa Kosha 25 Neshi Iinkai, ed., *Nihon Denshin Denwa Kosha 25 nenshi* (25 Year History of NTT), Vol. 3 (Tokyo Denki Tsushin Kyokai, 1978), p. 249.
41. Nihon Choki Shinyo Ginko Sangyo Kenkyukai, *Shin Jidai ni Chosen suru Nihon no Sangyo* (Japan's Industries: Challenging the New Era) (Tokyo: Mainichi Shimbun Sha, 1968), pp. 230–33.
42. Ibid., p. 10.
43. *Denshi Kogyo 30 Nenshi* (Thirty Year History of the Electronics Industry) (Tokyo: Nihon Denshi Kikai Kogyo Kai, 1979), pp. 82, 108.
44. *Kogyo Gijutsu In. Ogata Purojekotu ni yoru Choko Seino Denshi Keisanki* (The Super High-Performance Computer Project of the Large-Scale Program) (Tokyo: Nihon Sangyo Gijutsu Shinko Kyokai), July 1972, pp. 9–10, 17: Kompyutopia, June 1973, pp. 15–17; *Electronics*, May 24, 1971, pp. 42–49; April 24, 1971, pp. 42–43; *Denshi Kogyo Nenkan*, 1973, pp. 312–15.
45. *Kompyutopia*, June 1973, p. 15.
46. *Ogata Purojekuto ni yoru Choko Seino Denshi Keisanki*, p. 202.
47. *Toyo Keizai Shukan* (Oriental Economist Weekly), January 24, 1970, p. 42.
48. Letter from 1971 reprinted in *Fujitsu Shashi*, Vol. 2 (Tokyo: Jyoban Shoin, 1977), pp. 134–36 (A History of Fujitsu).
49. Interview with Kobyashi in *Bungeishunju*, September 1982, p. 101.
50. Interview with Shimizu Sakae, February 3, 1986.
51. *Denshi* (Electronics) (Tokyo: Nihon Denshi Kikai Kogyokai, July 1976), pp. 9, 14.
52. Tarui Yasuo, *IC no Hanashi, Toranjisuta kara Cho LSI made* (The Story of IC, from Transistors to LSI) (Tokyo: Nihon Hoso Shuppan Kyokai, 1984), pp. 147, 156.
53. Interview with Nishimura Taizo, general manager of Toshiba's International Operations Electronic Components Division, February 3, 1986.
54. Quotation from a participant in VLSI project, cited in Uozumi Toru, *Komptuta Senso* (The Computer War) (Tokyo: Aoya Shoten, 1979), p. 156.
55. Tarui, *IC no Hanashi, Toranjisuta kara Cho LSI made*, pp. 168–70; *Japan Computer News*, September 1977, p. 7; *EDP in Japan* (Tokyo: JECC, 1977), pp. 53–54; *JECC Kompyuta Noto*, 1981, p. 183.
56. Interview with Shimizu, February 3, 1986.
57. Tarui, p. 149.
58. *Electronics*, November 25, 1985, pp. 20–21.
59. Discussions with Todoriki Itaru, director general of MITI's Agency for Industrial Science and Technology; January 23, 1986.
60. Interview the Yamamoto Kinko, managing director of Japan Information Processing Development Center, February 28, 1986.
61. *Kompyutopia*, February 1973, pp. 27–30.
62. Minamisawa Noburo, *Nihon Kompyuta Hattan Shi* (The History of the Development of Japanese Computers), (Tokyo: Nihon Keizai Shimbonsha, 1978), pp. 173–74.

Case II–2_____

Levi Strauss and Company Exports Production to Third World[1]

U.S. Trade Policy Gives Away Garment Industry to Third World

When Levi Strauss and Co. moved its Dockers production from San Antonio to Costa Rica and the Dominican Republic in January 1990, it was following a growing trend in the garment industry. Nearly 60 percent of the clothes sold in the United States were sewn in other countries and the percentage was increasing. This is a significant change from 30 years ago, when Japanese-made clothing was first introduced into the U.S. market. By the early 1980s, national trade policy made it financially worthwhile for U.S. garment companies to manufacture clothes overseas and import the finished product for domestic sales.

While the average wage for garment workers in the United States was about $4.50, it was less than one dollar per hour in many Third World countries, according to Roy Maynard, manager of Colt Enterprises, which was formed when workers bought a plant in Tyler, Texas, after it was closed by Levi in 1986. Many U.S.-based companies close plants located in the United States and move to more cost-effective locations; other who try to stay in the United States later close because they cannot compete with the lower-cost garments assembled overseas.

Apparel imports are governed by the Multi-Fiber Arrangement, established in 1974 and periodically updated. It sets quotas in various categories for each foreign country and then exports clothing to the United States. Critics argue that the agreement is hard to enforce, partly because countries are allowed to borrow from future quotas and to exceed their quota in one category if they fall below it in another.

The Reagan administration boosted apparel imports by creating the Caribbean Basin Initiative,

a series of trade incentives designed to help countries in the Caribbean and Central America develop their own garment industries. The theory was that those countries would be more stable politically if they had a steady economic base, That, in turn, was supposed to help them repay foreign debts, many of which were held by U.S. banks. The United States can also benefit from a global marketplace because new markets are being sought abroad for U.S. products.

GARMENTS ASSEMBLED ABROAD. A crucial step in making the Caribbean Basin Initiative work is Item 807 of the U.S. Tariff Code, which permits U.S. firms to send cut pieces of fabric to be assembled offshore and then pay tariffs only on the value added, basically the wages of the people who did the sewing. Another provision allows an unlimited quota for apparel assembled in certain Caribbean and Central American countries, as long as U.S.-made fabric is used. Item 807 could be applied to imports from any country, but the time and cost involved is double the long-distance shipping. This makes it practical mainly for use in Mexico and the Caribbean. Because foreign companies export lower-priced clothing to the United States, U.S. companies say they are forced to manufacture overseas to keep their prices competitive.

One line of reasoning behind U.S. policies is the economic theory known as comparative advantage, the idea that in a global economy, each country should produce what it can produce best and most cheaply. According to the theory of comparative advantage, Third World nations are better suited for the garment industry, while workers in the more developed nations handle more technologically advanced jobs.

Joan Suarez, a St. Louis–based vice president for the Amalgamated Clothing and Textile Workers Union, says the United States still needs jobs for semiskilled workers. "If the garment industry doesn't survive [in the United States], then we've made a

SOURCE: From Jeannie Kever, "A Thousand Lives," *San Antonio Light.* A three-part special report. November 11, 12, and 13, 1990. Reprinted by permission.

serious miscalculation in public policy in this country." Suarez added further:

> If we don't preserve entry-level manufacturing jobs in a country that continues to grow mostly by immigration, there won't be jobs for the folks who need to enter the labor market at the entry level. . .And we've got plenty of folks like that in our society. Not everybody is going to go to college. Not everybody is going to become a computer technician. And not everybody can go to work at McDonald's or wants to. What we will have done is created a permanent underclass. That is a problem politicians and corporate moguls cannot afford to ignore. Yet San Antonio and other cities have done little to deal with it.
>
> I think the Bush and Reagan administrations made a decision that somehow, this was an industry we could give away. That we could trade it off to keep [friendly governments] in place in the Third World Countries. . .On Levi Strauss' part, they miscalculate when they think they won't end up paying the price. They live here. Unless they're prepared to relocate someplace, then [company officials] are going to live in a society that isn't a very nice place to live, a very large split between rich and poor.

Costa Rica: Economic Growth Tied to Wooing Foreign Investment

Costa Rica is a tropical paradise with a stable, democratic government and one of the Third World's most literate and healthiest workforces. Daily wages are much lower than they are in the United States, while national health care and other government benefits allow workers to enjoy a good standard of living. These are all appealing incentives for Levi Strauss and Co. and other U.S. corporations shopping for new places to make their products. Costa Rica has become a competitor for semiskilled jobs, including those in the garment industry.

TOOL FOR ECONOMIC GROWTH. Roberto Rojas, Costa Rica's minister of foreign trade, has said, "Foreign investment for Costa Rica is urgently needed. It is the tool we are trying to use for economic growth." Costa Rica exports $1.7 billion in

goods but imports $2.1 billion. Agricultural products, mainly coffee and bananas, make up about half of the country's exports. But economic planners hope apparel and electronic exports eventually will help shrink the trade deficit. More than 100 U.S. firms do business in Costa Rica as well as a smaller number of Japanese, Canadian, and European companies. That is one step toward Costa Rica's goal of higher-technology and higher-paying garment industry jobs, including those in sales, distribution, textile mills, and design houses.

GARMENT INDUSTRY IS KEY. The export garment industry plays a crucial role in Costa Rica's economic development. It has grown about 30 percent per year for the past eight years and provides about 40,000 jobs. The garment industry accounts for about $100 million in exports, which is greater than 5 percent of Costa Rica's total exports. But nearly all these exports are generated by assembling clothing, often from cloth woven and cut in the United States.

Levi Strauss was one of the first big garment companies to use Costa Rican contractors. The company has 11 production plants overseas, but contractors handle most foreign production, according to Bob Dunn, Levi's vice president for community affairs and corporate communications. Most jeans are still made in the United States, but labor-intensive items—shirts, sweaters, many styles of slacks—can be made more cheaply overseas.

CHANGING INDUSTRY PATTERNS. Despite Costa Rica's interest in the garment industry, the nature of that business is changing. Rojas has suggested that Costa Rica is no longer competing with cheap labor because wages for unskilled jobs are even lower in other Caribbean and Central American countries. Some have suggested that the trend for Costa Rica during the next five years for industries with the low-end technology like the apparel industry will become less attractive. Wages in Costa Rica are becoming relatively high and its labor force less competitive by Third World standards.

The lower-skilled jobs within the garment industry may find their way to Panama and Nicaragua as multinational enterprises begin to consider those governments more stable. Costa Rica will have to cope with this competitive challenge by attracting the higher-technology garment industry jobs and by diversifying its export products.

Rojos expects Costa Rica to remain attractive to foreign investors because

You see all the Latin countries, so many problems, turmoil, guerrillas, wars. We don't have any of that. We have a very peaceful country. We have been a democracy for over 100 years. The country is very open to foreigners. The investor feels very much at home. We have good telephone services, good living conditions, cheaper staffs. Communication with the world is pretty easy from Costa Rica. You can dial direct anywhere. You can fax anywhere.

The Controversy over the Plant Closure in San Antonio

Levi Strauss and Company closed 58 plants from 1981 until January 1990, putting some 10,400 people out of work. Management did not anticipate that their decision to shut down their San Antonio Dockers plant and move production to the Third World would create a *cause célèbre*. But when Peter Thigpen, Levi's senior vice president of operations, arrived from San Francisco to make the announcement in January, he set into motion a series of events that continues to unfold.

Prior to Thigpen's announcement, Levi employed more than 2,400 workers at three plants in San Antonio. By November 1990 there were 1,300 workers remaining at two plants. Local labor activists helped workers organize to fight the closing, leading to an $11.6 billion class-action lawsuit and a boycott of Levi products. By September 1990, a group based in Albuquerque, New Mexico, had begun to push the protest across the Southwest.

The boycott generated little visible effect, but the resulting publicity was painful for the company that had spent more than a century building a reputation as benevolent employer and enlightened corporate citizen. Levi found itself practicing damage control, donating nearly $100,000 to help local agencies cope with the influx of 1,115 suddenly unemployed workers, giving the city an

additional $340,000 to provide extra services for its former employees and hiring two consultants experienced in Hispanic employment and job training issues.

The company promised to keep the local office open through March to ease the transition for its former workers. Despite these efforts, the transition has been painful. The city had coped with layoffs before, but Levi's layoff in January 1990 was the largest in the city's history. As much as $10 million will be spent on unemployment benefits and to educate, retrain, and find jobs for former Levi workers. But ten months after the plant closing was announced, the tax-funded retraining system had found jobs for just 14 workers.

Hundreds of Levi workers, most of them women with families to support, enrolled in English and basic academic classes, months or years away from finding work. Others simply dropped out of sight. Some of the workers—older poorly educated, unable to speak English—may never find work. The loss of garment industry jobs may turn these people into permanently unemployed citizens.

Bob Dunn, Levi's vice president for community affairs and corporate communications, said:

We didn't do anything we shouldn't have done. But we're working very hard to mitigate the harm [caused by the plant closing]. If I had lost my job, I'd be angry, and I understand their being angry. My hope is that as time passes and people have a chance to reflect on what we've done, they will judge us to have been responsible and fair.

For many workers, the plant on South Zarzamora Street had been home long before Levi bought the business for $10 million in 1981. The company was founded as Juvenile Manufacturing in 1923, and some employees had been there through most of its subsequent incarnations. Juana Marcias had spent 50 of her 70 years sewing and pressing garments.

Fabric cutter Ruben Acosta and finisher Emilia Cervantes had been there for 42 years. Marion Hardin had been there for 40 years, Frank Rodriguez, Jr., for 38 years, and Esperanza Max for 37. Hundreds had been there for more than a dozen years, and hundreds more had joined the workforce within the past two years. Those who worked at the factory witnessed the changes that have shaped the garment industry in the United States.

When Juvenile Manufacturing opened, workers made infants' and children's clothing in their homes. But home work was declared a social evil after the national minimum wage and hour law was passed in 1933, and a small factory was opened on Pecan Street. The name was changed to Santone Industries, Inc., in the 1930s, when production switched to boys' and men's clothing.

By the mid-1970s, workers were making suit jackets and sports jackets under a contract with Levi. By January most people at the plant were working on Dockers, the trousers that Levi successfully promoted to symbolize a lifestyle for aging baby boomers. When Levi acquired the plant, workers had been optimistic. The garment industry was struggling elsewhere in the United States, but it seemed strong in San Antonio, where there was a steady supply of semiskilled workers.

Despite the garment industry's sweatshop image, many found Levi a good place to work. The $12.8 million payroll with an average of $11,480 per worker paid bills and fed the children of the workers. The plant closed for ten days at Christmas and another ten days during the summer and paid vacations for everyone. Workers were given a turkey at Thanksgiving and a modest gift at Christmas. Jobs were guaranteed while women were on maternity leave; most qualified for paid maternity leave. The company paid for health insurance, and nearly everyone received a small pension when the company closed.

By the time the plant closed, workers were producing an average of 16,000 pairs of trousers every day, along with about 500 sports jackets. More work meant more money. Less work meant less money. Average pay at the plant was $6 an hour.

According to Dunn, about 75 percent of all Levi products sold in the United States are still made in the United States but increasingly, Levi and other firms within the industry are sending jobs overseas.

Peter Thigpen, the Levi executive who broke the news to workers about the plant's closing, made the final decision to shut down the facility. Because he is a principal figure in the lawsuit filed by the former workers, company lawyers recommended he not be interviewed. He later announced plans to leave the company at an unspecified date.

Ironically, sales of Dockers had never been better than when the plant closing was announced. In the second quarter of this fiscal year, the line surpassed sales of 501 jeans, traditionally the company's best seller. For the full year, Dockers were expected to bring in at least $500 million.

The South Zarzamora Street plant was one of three U.S. plants making Dockers trousers. With more than 1,100 people working two shifts, it was one of the company's largest factories. Its size, at least in part, turned out to be its downfall. The plant had been making suit jackets and sports jackets, but demand for sports jackets dropped during the mid-1980s. By 1987, the company was faced with a decision. Rather than close the facility, Levi officials converted it to a trousers factory, manufacturing Dockers and a small number of Officers Corps trousers, a style similar to but less expensive than Dockers.

Dunn said, "It may sound like an easy change to people who aren't in the industry. But in fact it's very difficult [to convert from making jackets to trousers.] That would be like saying. . .a good football player would be a good baseball player." The 1987 conversion cost several million dollars and was difficult for many workers. Dockers trousers require more steps to make than a pair of standard jeans, making them more labor-intensive and, therefore, more expensive to manufacture here than in the Third World, where labor costs are minimal.

In a November 30, 1989, memo, Bruce Stallworth, Levi's operations controller, recommended closing the plant, at a cost of $13.5 million, and transferring the production overseas "to achieve significant cost savings. In 1989, it cost $6.70 to make a pair of Dockers trousers at the South Zarzamora plant," Stallworth said in a deposition taken for the lawsuit by workers. Plant management hoped to reduce that to $6.39 per unit in 1990. But it still would have compared with a $5.88 per unit cost at the Dockers plant in Powell, Tennessee, and a $3.76 per unit cost using Third World contractors.

Stallworth attributed the San Antonio plant's high cost to workers' compensation expenses and operating the plant at less than full capacity; he added that "conversion from sport coats to Dockers has not been totally successful."

Dunn declined to say whether the plant was profitable. "The issue is not whether or not in 1990 we were able to make pants in that [plant] profitably. The issue was when we looked at 1991 and 1992," he said. The main problem, Dunn insisted, was one of size. The other two U.S. Dockers plants were substantially smaller. One in Texas had 366 workers; the Tennessee plant had 746. Running the San Antonio plant efficiently meant running it at full production. And with 1,115 workers, full production meant 80,000 pairs of trousers each week and more as sports jackets were phased out. That simply was too many pairs of trousers produced by high-priced U.S. labor. Local workers averaged $6 per hour, about a day's wages for workers with the same skill levels in the Caribbean and Central America.

Another problem, Dunn said, was that many workers had spent years sewing jackets, and retraining them to sew trousers was difficult. Those workers "didn't have much experience with relearning," he said. "We're not in the business of education and training people, and we don't claim to do it well. . .We simply didn't see any way to bring cost in line."

Competing companies can produce similar styles at lower cost, Dunn said, denting Dockers' growing share of the market. "As much as people like Dockers, our research shows people are not willing to pay $5 or $10 more for a pair of pants just because the label says 'Made in the USA.'"

U.S. trade policies allow goods assembled in certain countries, including those in the Caribbean and in Central America, to be brought back into the United States at reduced tariffs if the fabric used is woven and cut domestically. The company has 11 foreign production plants, but most overseas production is done by contractors. That saves on labor costs—in addition to lower wages, the company avoids paying directly for benefits like health insurance and workers' compensation—and allows the company more flexibility to shift production to reflect changing fashions

Dunn declined to say how much money was saved by moving Dockers production from San Antonio to contractors in Costa Rica and the Dominican Republic. However, Stallworth estimated in his recommendation that the company

could recoup the $13.5 million closing costs within two years by moving production overseas. Still, the decision cost the company, both in legal fees and goodwill.

The $11.6 billion lawsuit filed on behalf of Levi workers may drag on for years—lawyers from the Mexican American Legal Defense and Educational Fund have joined forces with the small local firm that filed the lawsuit last spring, injecting money and legal energy into the fight.

In November 1990, 80 protesters gathered in San Antonio and three at Levi headquarters in San Francisco, saying they were launching a 72-hour hunger strike to push the company to settle the lawsuit.

The company also has been forced to acknowledge a boycott called by disgruntled former employees who formed a group known as *Fuerza Unida*, or United Force. Labor activists and a few student groups have joined *Fuerza Unida* in picketing local shopping malls. Image, Inc., a national Hispanic group, and the Progressive Democrats of San Antonio both endorsed a boycott at different times after the plant closing.

So far, it has yet to generate much publicity, especially beyond San Antonio's Spanish-language media and small regional publications by labor and political groups.

Most politicians kept a low profile on the issue, praising Levi for offering laid-off workers more than it legally was required to offer and issuing vague pledges to recruit a new company to use the empty factory.

U.S. Representative Henry B. Gonzales (D.-Texas) was not so reticent: "When a company is so irresponsible—a company that has been making money and then willy-nilly removes a plant to get further profit based on greed and on cheaper labor cost in the Caribbean—I say you have a bad citizen for a company."

The company's response to criticism such as that from Representative Gonzales as reported in the media was as follows:

> We have the sense that people feel we're the most irresponsible employer in San Antonio. Our sense is that we do more than anyone in our industry and more than almost anyone in American Industry. Pressure over the decision to close the plant continues and the company is trying to balance business with

compassion and good public relations. We try to stress the right values. It's not easy. There isn't always one right answer. I feel proud of what this company has done to take a leadership role. . .in the way it treats people when it closes plants.

This is not a reassurance that Levi will continue to employ the remaining 1,300 workers in San Antonio. Garment industry jobs that remain in the United States will require more skill than is needed for assembly line jobs such as those lost by the South Zarzamora Street Workers. And San Antonio won't get those jobs of the future if our work force does not become more highly skilled. Public policy decisions made now will determine whether the garment industry remains in San Antonio or moves elsewhere. By the time a plant shuts down, it's too late to start retraining.

EXHIBIT 1
Levi Strauss & Company Sales and Income, 1980–1989, and Plant Closings

	Sales (US$ millions)	Net Income	Last Ten Plant Closings	
			Location	Month
1980	$2,800	$223.7		
1981	2,800	172.3		
1982	2,500	126.6		
1983	2,700	194.5		
1984	2,500	41.4		
1985*	2,600	32.8	Amarillo, Tex.	Dec.
1986	2,800	49.0	Byrdstown, Tenn.	July
			Blackstone, Va.	August
			Tyler, Tex.	August
			Corpus Christi, Tex.	October
			Wynne, Ark.	Nov.
1987	2,900	135.4		
1988	3,100	111.9	Muryville, Tenn.	Sept.
			Little Rock, Ark.	Nov.
1989	3,600	272.3	Elizabethton, Tenn.	May
1990			San Antonio, Tex.	Jan.

*Levi restructured, going private in a leveraged buyout in 1985.
SOURCE: Information taken from the *San Francisco Examiner*, November 18, 1990, Section D.

EXHIBIT 2
Profile of Former Employees in the Closed Plant

Marital Status	
Single	29.6%
Married	70.4
Sex	
Male	13.9
Female	86.1
Race	
Hispanic	92.4
Anglo	3.7
Asian	2.4
Black	1.3
Total Number Laid Off	1,115 workers

SOURCE: Adapted from Jeannie Kever, "U.S. Gives Away
Garment Industry," *San Francisco Examiner,* November 18,
1990, Section D.

Case II-3

TDK de Mexico

"I want to be the main supplier base of magnets for South and North America," proclaimed Fumio Onouye, general manager of TDK de Mexico, located in Cd. Juarez, a border city of millions close to El Paso, Texas. He continued:

To help gain this status, our operating targets need to be met, and that might include expansion of present plant facilities and more automation. Increasingly I feel, though, that people here don't want to see expansion. . .They seem to enjoy excuses! Whether you call it Japanese or American management, I cannot accept delays, wastes, and excuses! Culture to me is important only when the process of production

and the importance of work are clearly understood. Make no mistake, my parent company (TDK of Japan) wouldn't stand for anything other than making acceptable margins. I am having difficulty in putting reasons for all problems on culture. . .I refuse to take it as a dumping ground.

Production Methods and Technology

TDK de Mexico produced ceramic ferrite magnets of various shapes and sizes that were used for speakers, generators, and motors. It was one of the few plants in its area that produced a final product from the raw material. Production was based on job orders—in other words, production was scheduled as TDK de Mexico received orders for a given number of a given type of magnet. Exhibit 1 shows TDK's plant layout and production process. The

SOURCE: Manab Thakur, California State University-Fresno. Reprinted with permission.

raw material used to make the final product was a black powder called ferrite powder. The ferrite powder, a critical raw material, was imported, although it was available in the Mexican market. But to ensure quality, TDK of Japan insisted on using ferrite powder from Japan. The manufacturing process started by wetting and mixing the powder in large containers. The mixture was dried and then was fed into the press machine that gave the shape to the magnets. The shape was determined by the mold inserted into the press machine (Exhibit 2). All of the molds used also came from Japan. The various molds for the different shapes

and sizes were stored at the plant and used as needed.

Two distinct methods were used during the press stage of the production process, the dry method and the wet method. The basic difference between the two was that the wet method, installed at TDK de Mexico in 1983 after Fumio Inouye took charge, utilized water during the pressing of raw material. It made stronger magnets, but it took more time. With the wet method, the worker collected the magnets just pressed and placed them in a temporary drying area before they were baked in the ovens. With the dry

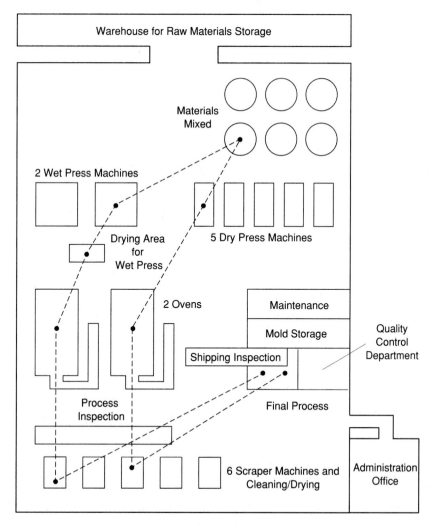

Exhibit 1 Plant Layout and Production Process

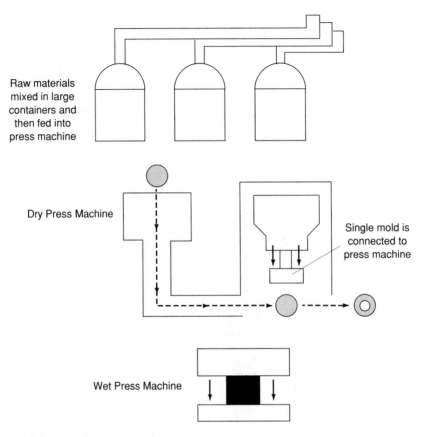

Raw materials
mixed in large
containers and
then fed into
press machine

Dry Press Machine

Single mold is
connected to
press machine

Wet Press Machine

Exhibit 2 Production Technology

method, the worker visually checked each magnet for cracks and other defects. Defective ones were thrown out for scrap. It was important to spot defective magnets at this stage because it was much harder to convert them into scrap after they were baked. All scrap materials were broken down and used again in the raw material mixture.

After pressing, the magnets were mechanically moved through a series of ovens (Exhibit 3). One set of pressed magnets was placed in the oven every 12 hours. The magnets were baked at progressively higher temperatures from entrance to exit. After their exit from the ovens, the magnets continued moving to a temporary storage area to cool. The ovens presently in use were electrically powered, but there was a plan to convert them to gas ovens to take advantage of the lower cost of gas. Once cooled, each magnet was subject to

process inspection by workers. This was one of two main quality checkpoints in the production process.

Cooled magnets were taken to the scraper machine. The scraper machine smoothed the rough edges and surface of the magnets. The scrapings were collected and used again in the raw material mixture. From the scraper machine, the workers placed the magnets in water to be cleaned. After cleaning, the magnets were sent through the drying machine. At the exit point of the drying machine, the magnets were collected by workers and placed in boxes. The boxes of magnets were taken to the final process department where each magnet was given a final check.

This stage was called shipping inspection, and it represented the second main quality control checkpoint. Quality control and specification requirements adhered to at this stage included measurement of weight, length, and appearance of magnets.

About 85 percent of production was exported to the United States—to TDK of America facilities in Chicago, Los Angeles, New York, and Indiana. The remaining 15 percent was exported to Hong Kong. The sales offices and warehouse facilities in these cities were in charge of all selling, shipping, and billing functions. TDK of America sold most of its products to Briggs and Stratton of Milwaukee, Wisconsin, and to Buehler products of Kingston, North Carolina.

TDK de Mexico had encountered no bureaucratic delays or customs problems in shipping out final products, even though other companies in the area were having difficulties arranging for timely shipment of their merchandise out of Mexico. Inouye was proud that he had been able to secure the necessary clearances and paperwork for getting the product out of the country without much hassle. His explanation was, "You don't create a system when you simply need some people who can do things for you. You need to get out and find them. You create systems where systems are accepted. . .It is not here!"

Hiratzuka, TDK's production manager, commented: "We hear that the Mexican government may change the rules of the game. There are rumors that we may have to buy 20 to 25 percent of our raw materials from Mexican suppliers." He went on, "Other than what the government will and will not do, I think you also need to understand that our primary concern is to attract quality labor, since our production process demands it. . .We can't just hire anybody that walks in."

TDK de Mexico had not looked into possible changes in the Mexican government's local procurement rules to any extent, but had expressed its apprehension to Mexican officials if the firm was forced to buy ferrite powder locally. On another issue, Hiratzuka stated, "As you know, border plants in Mexico like ours have a 'no sale' rule where all goods produced must be exported. But the government is considering a compulsory selling rule whereby 20 percent of a border plant's goods must be sold locally." Such a rule was potentially

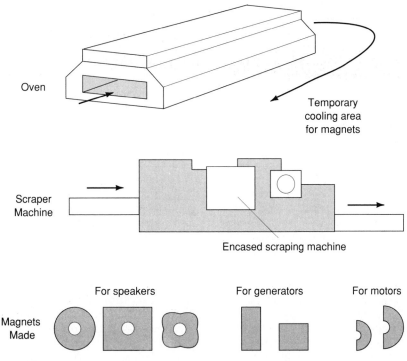

Exhibit 3 Production Technology and Magnets Made

more troublesome to TDK de Mexico because it was not clear that there was much of a market in Mexico for TDK's products.

The Mexican Maquiladoras

In 1965 the United States, working in conjunction with the Mexican government, set up the *maquiladora* program to create jobs for unemployed and underemployed Mexican workers. The idea was to get U.S. companies to open light assembly plants just across the Mexican border and to use cheap Mexican labor to assemble American-made parts into finished goods. In many cases, the components were manufactured in plants located on the U.S. side of the border; this allowed the components to be easily and quickly transported to the Mexican side for final assembly. The effect was to create twin plants a few miles apart—the U.S. plant being used for capital-intensive/skilled-labor operations and the Mexican plant being used for labor-intensive, assembly operations.

When the finished products were shipped back into the United States, U.S. companies were taxed only on the value added in Mexico (mostly labor costs) rather than on the total value of the goods being imported. When the Mexican government experienced a debt crisis in 1982 and the value of the Mexican peso collapsed against the dollar, cheap Mexican wages triggered a *maquiladoras* explosion. By early 1987, there were over 630 plants employing over 178,000 people along the Mexican side of the U.S. border. These plants, known as *maquiladoras* (Or "in-bond" or twin plants), were all engaged in assembling components in Mexico for reexport in the United States and elsewhere and had become an important economic force along the U.S.-Mexican border. Juarez, where TDK de Mexico's plant was located, had a big concentration of *maquiladoras*, Exhibit 4 presents some of the features of the *maquiladoras* program.

Maquiladoras operated within a highly volatile political environment, one that affected every aspect of their existence. They were dependent upon the Mexican government continuing to permit raw materials and components to enter duty free and the U.S. government simultaneously permitting finished products to return with duty paid only on the value added in Mexico. Any major

change in these policies by either company could shut down most *maquiladoras* overnight by making assembly operations on the Mexican side of the border uneconomical. Both countries had strong political groups opposed to the *maquiladora* concept. Opponents labeled such operations as sweatshops and claimed that workers were being exploited by capitalistic interests.

The average age of the *maquiladora* worker was 24, with a relative dearth of workers over 30. Seventy percent were young women and teenage girls. Workers lived under crowded conditions—the mean household size of *maquiladora* workers was 7.8 persons. Their wages averaged about $0.80 per hour, barely more than half the 1987 Mexican manufacturing wage of $1.57 an hour (including benefits). The low wages made it very attractive for mass-assembly operations requiring low-skill labor to be located on the Mexican side of the U.S. border. Managers of *maquiladoras* expressed a preference for hiring "fresh or unspoiled" workers that had not acquired "bad habits" in other organizations. The work was so low-skilled that workers received very little training. The turnover rate ran 50 percent to 100 percent a year in many plants.

However, many of the large multinational companies with *maquiladoras* paid more than the wage minimums, and their overall compensation package was more attractive than the lowest-paying operations. Some of the multinationals also spent substantial amounts in training and employee development.

The location of twin (or *maquiladora*) plants along the northern border of Mexico was increasing at a phenomenal speed, and unemployed Mexicans were flocking to the northern border towns to fill the rapidly expanding number of job openings. By the end of 1988, it was predicted that *maquiladoras* would employ 350,000 workers, one-tenth of Mexico's industrial workforce, and that the plants would import $8 billion in U.S. components, add $2 billion in value (mostly labor), and ship $10 billion in finished goods back to the United States for sale in the United States and other world markets. A number of Japanese-based companies had begun to set up *maquila* operations to handle the production and sale of their products in U.S. markets—TDK de Mexico was one of these companies.

EXHIBIT 4

The *Maquiladora* Program: Legal and Regulatory Requirements Imposed by the Mexican Government

A. *Foreign Investment*

As a rule, a foreign company may subscribe and own only up to 49% of the stock in Mexican corporations with the exception of *maquilas,* which may be totally owned by foreigners. Except wearing apparel, all items may be produced by in-bond assembly enterprises. Wearing apparel, due to the restriction of textile imports into the United States, is subject to a quota.

B. *Import Duties*

In-bond plants are not required to pay import duties, but the product assembled or manufactured may not be sold in Mexico. Bonds are generally posted by bonding companies and are renewed yearly.

C. *Taxes*

The maximum income tax on corporate profits is 42% on taxable income of P$$500,000 or more in a fiscal year, and employees' share in profits before taxes is at the rate of 8%. There are other taxes such as the Social Security Tax based on salaries earned and state taxes.

D. *Maquiladora versus Joint Venture*

A comparison of the different rules and practices for joint ventures between Mexican and foreign companies is summarized below:

Concept	Maquiladora	Joint Venture
1. Doing business in Mexico	To operate in Mexico under a *maquila* program, a company must be incorporated under Mexican laws.	To carry out industrial or commercial activities for the Mexican market, a corporation or other recognized corporate entity must be organized.
2. Equity ownership	100% foreign ownership is allowed.	The general rule is that foreigners may not hold more than 49% of the stock of a corporation doing business in the Mexican market. Exceptions to allow higher percentages of foreign ownership, up to 100%, may be authorized by the Mexican government under special circumstances.
3. Special operating authorizations	To operate under *maquila* (in-bond) status, the Ministry of Commerce must authorize a *maquila* program, setting forth the products or activities the company may manufacture/assemble or carry out. Certain committments must be made, the compliance with which shall be reviewed periodically.	Unless the company intends to work within a branch of regulated industry, a joint-venture company may freely operate without the need to obtain any special operating permits.
4. Importation of equipment	All production equipment may be imported free of duties, under bond, subject to its being exported once the company ceases to operate under the *maquila* program.	The importation of equipment for the production of items that are to be sold in the Mexican market requires an import permit to be obtained and normal duties to be paid thereon.
5. Importation of raw materials	All raw materials and supplies may be imported free of duties under bond, subject to its being exported within an extendable six-month period, shrinkage and wastage excepted. Under special circumstances, *maquiladoras* may be authorized to sell up to 20% of a specific product within the Mexican market.	The importation of raw materials and supplies for the production of items that are to be sold in the Mexican market requires an import permit to be obtained and normal duties to be paid thereon. In all cases, import permits are granted on an absolutely discretionary basis. Currently such permits are quite restricted. Under certain conditions, the negotiation of a manufacturing or integration program with the government may be required.

EXHIBIT 4

Concept	*Maquiladora*	Joint Venture
6. Currency exchange controls	Any operating expense, including rent, payroll, taxes, etc., must be obtained from a Mexican bank by selling dollars thereto at the controlled rate of exchange. Fixed assets may be paid for in dollars at the free rate of exchange.	There are no specific exchange controls on domestic transactions. If the company exports, it will, in general, be required to sell foreign currencies received to a Mexican bank at the controlled rate of exchange.
7. Labor law requirements	Subject to the Federal Labor Law.	Equally subject to the Federal Labor Law.
8. Acquisition of real estate	Real estate to establish a production facility may be freely bought in the interior of the country. In the border areas or coasts, it may be acquired through a trust.	Same as *maquiladora*.
9. Leasing of real estate	Real estate may be leased under freely negotiated terms, up to a maximum of 10 years.	Same as *maquiladora*, although the term may be longer.
10. Immigration requirements	Foreign technical or management personnel are readily granted work visas, subject to very lenient requirements.	Work visas for foreign technical or management personnel are granted on a very limited basis. Requirements for the obtainment thereof are significantly more stringent.
11. Transfer of technology	For tax purposes it is advisable that a Technical and/or Management Assistance Agreement be executed between the *maquiladora* and its parent. Such agreement would need to be registered with the National Transfer of Technology Registry (NTTR).	If technical or management assistance is granted to a domestic company from a foreign source and royalties or fees are to be paid, an agreement must be registered with the NTTR. To obtain such registration the agreement must meet certain criteria and the amounts that may be charged are limited.
12. Taxes	A *maquiladora* is in principle subject to the payment of all Mexican taxes. However, since such operations are intended to be cost centers rather than profit centers, the income taxes to be paid are limited. Also, any value added tax paid by the *maquiladora* shall be refunded to it upon its request.	A domestic company is subject to all normal taxes such as income tax and value added tax (maximum corporate income tax rate equals 42%).

Despite concerns over the *maquiladoras*, the program was central to the Mexican government's economic revival plans. Mexican leaders were most enthusiastic about a new kind of *maquiladora*. These were plants built in the interior of Mexico that were geared to exports, like the border plants, but unlike the border operations, they undertook in-house manufacturing of many of the components used in the final assembly process. These plants used higher-skilled employees and paid wages much closer to the average manufacturing wage in Mexico, and they did not rely so heavily on female labor. They also relied more heavily on Mexican companies for raw material supplies and services.

TDK's Internal Management

TDK de Mexico had 183 employees (158 women and 25 men). Inouye, before he came to TDK de Mexico, operated machines in a Taiwan plant to help gain a better understanding of workers at that level. After his move to Mexico in 1983, Inouye organized the workforce into teams consisting of workers, subleaders, and leaders. Leaders were not entrusted with the job of supervision: all supervisory responsibilities remained with individuals having a title of supervisor. It took an average of two years for a worker to become a subleader. All subleaders at TDK de Mexico were Mexican; they had a median age of 28.2 years. Only three were women.

There were 11 leaders. The specifics of their job were dependent upon their department. Generally, they oversaw workers and machines in their respective departments but were given little authority and were not accountable for achieving set objectives. They were also in charge of training new workers. The leaders at TDK de Mexico had been at the company for an average of 6.4 years. The average time it took to become a leader was about three years. All of the leaders at TDK de Mexico were Mexican. Very few had ever been promoted to the supervisory level.

Five Japanese filled the 12 positions of supervisors and assistant supervisors (Exhibit 5). Like the leaders, their jobs varied based on the department they supervised. Primarily their duties included supervision of the leaders as well as the teams under the leaders. They determined production plans for their respective departments. Although there were Mexican nationals in higher positions, all Japanese employees, irrespective of their job titles, reported directly to Inouye. Because most of the Japanese could not speak Spanish, Inouye thought it was wise to have this direct reporting relationship. However, some of the managers of Mexican origin did not accept this line of reasoning (one manager called it "clannish behavior"); their protest to Inouye had not met with much success.

Wage Policies

TDK de Mexico paid higher wages than most other companies located in the Juarez industrial park plants. TDK de Mexico had several pay incentives available to the workers. They received a bonus after 30 days on the job. There was extra pay for overtime, night shifts, weekend work, and also generous incentives for attendance. Yet, Alfred Gomez, personnel manager of TDK de Mexico,

stated, "Absenteeism and lateness are becoming problems. In some cases, when a worker decides to leave her job, she just stops coming to work without any notice. One reason for this problem is that Juarez public health hospital gives out medical excuses to workers to miss work for the slightest illness. . .There is very little we can do about it."

Training

TDK had invested a lot of resources in training its employees; most of its training, however, had been confined to leaders and subleaders. Gomez, the head of personnel, did not go through any systematic training need analysis but professed to know "who needed training and who did not by sight." Inouye's position was, "We will spend money on training, of course, but only with those who show promise." Asked how he saw promise, he replied, "I have been working for 25 years. . .I know!" A leader who had just finished an in-house training program on motivation commented, "Whenever we face a major crisis, the six Japanese managers get together with Mr. Inouye and decide what course of action to take. It seems the only decisions I am allowed to participate in are of routine nature that are easily solved. What do I do with what I learned from the training sessions?"

Fumio Inouye's Concerns

In March 1988, Inouye met with all the managers (Mexican and Japanese) and presented the plant's most recent operating statistics (Exhibit 6). He was clearly unhappy with the data. A senior manager from Japanese headquarters also attended the meeting, along with two other managers from TDK of America. Inouye laid out several options that could be pursued:

1. Downsize the labor force, to correct for the decline in sales and the increase in expenses.
2. Try to avoid downsizing and try to reduce operating costs by buying ferrite powder locally. Since it was not known where and how ferrite powder could be obtained from Mexican sources, Inouye suggested that immediate consideration be given to making the material locally or acquiring a native company.

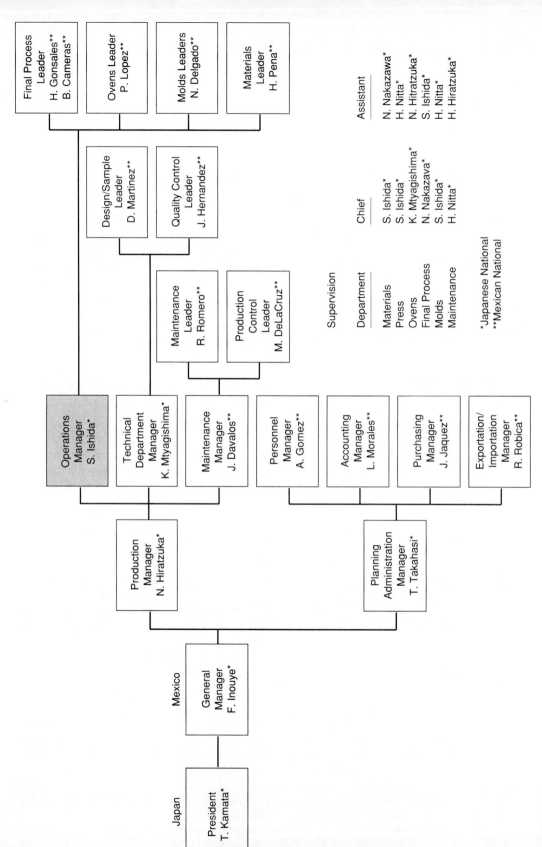

Exhibit 5 Organization Chart

Exhibit 6
Statistics of TDK de Mexico, 1984–87

	1984	1985	1986	1987
Total sales (U.S. Dollars)	$4,168,000	$3,774,000	$3,837,000	$3,168,000*
Employees	112	128	140	183
Sales per person	$29,000	$22,000	$20,000	$23,000
Efficiency rate	82%	81%	80%	80%
Labor turnover rate	16%	47%	46%	39%†
Selling/administrative expenses	$1,623,000	$1,529,000	$1,698,000	$1,878,000
Cost of raw materials	$1,052,000	$1,071,000	$1,099,000	$1,181,000

Shipping cost equals .01¢ per gram or 2–10% of total costs.
Price of magnets equals .05¢ per gram.
Average production for a year equals 5,100,000 grams.
Production figure for 1987 equals 6,900,000 grams.
Plant is presently at full capacity.

*Based on the then exchange rate.
†Other *maquilas* in the park ranged from 35 to 170% per year.

3. Send some senior managers (Inouye emphasized Mexican nationals) to Japan for further training.

The Mexican managers thought the concerns expressed in the meeting were addressed specifically to them. One Mexican manger said after the meeting, "If these people would live in Mexico and not run to their comfortable homes on the other side of the border after 5:00 o'clock, maybe they would understand us a little better!"

Several Mexican managers again suggested to Inouye that the Japanese managers learn the language and work closely with the workers. Inouye was sympathetic to the suggestion but questioned whether learning the language was essential. He advised them to examine "the pockets of inefficiency" and lectured them about the value of hard work.

The manager from TDK Japan left with a stern warning for imminent improvement or else. He explained to the casewriter:

> You see, I came over here in late 1983, after spending years in Singapore, Taiwan, and Hong Kong. I don't know how useful it is to have a grand strategy or any plan per se for an operation like this. . .What it boils down to is *shooten* (focus), *shitsu* (quality), and *bunai* (distribution). . . .I'm not about to give up because of cultural differences here; you do what you have to do to earn more money! And if the answer is anything but work harder, I have a problem!

Inouye began to contemplate what actions he should take.

Ethical and Moral Dimensions of Business

CHAPTER 6

Moral Reasoning and Organizational Culture

CHAPTER OBJECTIVES

1. Understand the context of moral dilemmas within business.
2. Discuss factual situations concerning ethical behavior.
3. Analyze how scientific knowledge about technology, risks, and cause-effect relationships is important for making ethical decisions.
4. Describe how moral standards influence ethical judgments.
5. Review the model of developmental psychology of moral reasoning.
6. Explain why individuals sometimes behave unethically even when they know better.
7. Question whether organizations can be morally accountable.
8. Outline the criteria for establishing moral responsibility.

Introductory Case _____

American Cyanamid

American Cyanamid had nearly 45,000 employees, of whom one-half were unionized hourly wage earners. The Willow Island plant in West Virginia was used to manufacture pigments, dyestuffs, melamine, platinum catalysts, plastic antioxidants, and animal feed supplements. These manufacturing activities required using five toxic substances, some

SOURCE: This case was developed from news articles found in *Washington Post,* January 1, 1979; *New York Times,* January 4, 1979; February 3, 1980; *Wall Street Journal,* February 9, 1979; December 9, 1980; and "Controversy over Fetal Safety," *Chemical Week,* January 10, 1979.

of which were mutants that damaged reproductive systems and caused birth defects; others were toxic to embryos, leading to miscarriages or stillbirths. The substances of concern at the Willow Island plant included lead, hydrazide hydrate, hydrazide sulfate, and the pharmaceuticals Thiopeta and Methotrexate.

The lead chromate pigment unit at the Willow Island plant used lead, a toxic substance, widely regarded as a mutant by public health officials. According to the Occupational Health and Safety Administration (OSHA), if sufficient quantities of lead are accumulated in the body, male workers may be rendered infertile or impotent and both men and women are subject to genetic damage that may affect both the course and outcome of pregnancy. During April 1979, OSHA established a standard of 50 micrograms per cubic meter, but 200 micrograms were temporarily allowed for pigment plants.

After much deliberation, American Cyanamid announced a policy on January 30, 1978, designed to "protect the unborn children of working employees from any possible harm." American Cyanamid pledged not to assign women of child-bearing age to jobs that might expose them to chemicals that might be harmful to fetal life. Women between the ages of 16 and 50 were prohibited from working in those parts of the plant where toxic chemicals were used that might interfere with the normal development of the fetus. When the policy was announced, the company offered alternative work assignments to women where possible. When the alternative assignment offered lower pay and status, as did some of the available custodian positions, the woman were paid the higher rate of their former jobs for 90 days. The company's doctor met with those affected by the new policy and explained the danger to women. During the meeting, the doctor also tried to discourage sterilization.

Men were not affected by the new policy and were allowed to continue working in the areas with toxic substances because these chemicals were viewed by the company as embryotoxic and not mutagens. An embryotoxic substance can cause birth defects after a fetus has been exposed, whereas a mutagen causes birth defects before conception by altering the biological traits encoded in chromosomes. The risk of legal liability was considered much higher for women than men because of the relative difficulty of establishing proof in cases involving men.

Alternative job assignments available to women within the plant were scarce and economic opportunities in the area were quite limited. Because of this, several women tried to maintain their jobs in the lead chromate pigment unit. They discussed the situation with management: one expressed willingness to use birth control pills; a second indicated a willingness to sign a release agreeing not to hold the company liable for any harm that might result from her employment; a third argued that her husband had had a vasectomy and there would be no danger of pregnancy because they planned to have no more children. These proposals were considered inadequate by the company.

Each alternative was seen to contain unacceptable risk owing to an unexpected pregnancy leading to birth defects. A signed release would apply only to the legal rights of the person who signed the release form, not to the rights of the child, who would have the right to sue later for damages. Lawsuits filed on behalf of children who had survived birth but were deformed would be a sizable legal liability.

Several women ranging in age from 26 to 43 were sterilized so they could keep their jobs. In October 1979, OSHA cited the company for willfully exceeding the OSHA standard for lead and ordered it to cancel the policy and pay a fine of $10,000. In July 1980 an administrative judge threw out the case on the grounds that OSHA regulations that applied to job safety did not apply to this situation. He indicated that other federal regulations relating to discrimination, civil rights, or labor-management relations might apply to this case but not OSHA job safety standards.

The Oil, Chemical and Atomic Workers Union agreed with the judge that OSHA regulations should not apply. The union felt that a consideration of an exclusionary rule on the basis of sex would be a bad precedent. A policy to remove women from the workplace "would have established the principle of altering the worker to the configuration of the work place instead of altering the configuration of the work place to protect the worker." OSHA appealed the case and it was again thrown out by administrative judges at the next level, and the fine was dismissed.

Meanwhile, several women sued the company because lead was harmful to the reproductive systems of men as well as women. Some argued that the company had forced them to have themselves sterilized. In 1983, American Cyanamid ended the controversy by paying some $200,000 in damages in a settlement with the women and accepted an "offer of judgment," meaning that it admitted no wrongdoing but did not wish to pursue the case in court. Also, the lead chromate pigment unit had been closed because of falling profitability due to a declining market for lead pigment paints and the increased government regulation of lead-based paints. Less hazardous materials became available and substitutes for lead pigments had been developed.

The Context of Ethical Behavior

Ethical dilemmas concerning business usually occur within the context of organizational life. Our introductory case is an example of such a context. This context includes such dimensions as the facts in the situation, the ethical and moral standards of the individuals involved, moral reasoning and ethical analysis leading to a judgment, and the subsequent behavior that followed a decision. Moral judgments are concerned about whether a person considers a particular action right or wrong and whether the consequences of that action are good or bad, as illustrated in Figure 6–1.

SITUATIONAL FACTORS

Ethical and moral judgments begin by considering the fact patterns that define a moral dilemma or situation. The American Cyanamid case illustrates a number of factual dimensions including scientific and technological knowledge, legal constraints, role relationships, and the perceptions of those involved in the moral dilemma or controversy. There was a disagreement over whether lead was embryotoxic or a mutagen. The company's scientists argued for the former and thus believed that the job sites with lead pigments would be harmful only to an unborn child after the mother became pregnant. Other scientists within OSHA presented evidence indicating that the substance was a mutagen and thus equally harmful to the reproductive organs of men and women.

The situation surrounding a moral dilemma has a number of important dimensions including the following:

1. serious results in which actions or policies affect human beings
2. the possible consequences of something serious varies in risks and uncertainty

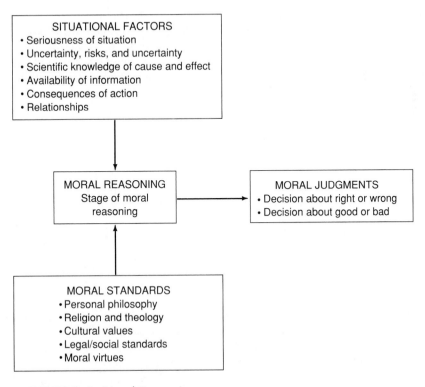

FIGURE 6–1 Moral Reasoning

3. the knowledge of the cause-effect relationships among the individuals and things related to a decision. Uncertainty exists when the probability of consequences that are potentially harmful are unknown.

Risks exist when there is some probability that some result is likely to occur. Certainty exists in situations when the cause-effect relations are perfectly known and thus the consequences of a decision can be accurately predicted. In the American Cyanamid case, the consequences of the policy were serious for those involved and for unborn children. There was a probability that exposure to a toxic substance would have a harmful effect, but the knowledge of cause-effect relationships was in dispute.

Because the exact cause-effect relationship was only partially known, the choice of a policy by American Cyanamid was controversial. Management seemed to feel that lead was embryotoxic in that it would harm an unborn child, but it was not believed to be a mutant. However, management's apparent overriding concern for legal liability based upon the difficulty of proof concerning men raises questions about their sincerity. The company developed a policy designed to prevent exposure to embryos during pregnancy by not allowing women of childbearing ages to work in dangerous areas.

In contrast, OSHA argued that lead was a mutant that could cause birth defects if either men or women were exposed and thus OSHA considered the American Cyanamid policy seriously flawed because OSHA felt that management did not properly consider the problem from a medical and scientific perspective. The OSHA regarded the work sites as unsafe for both women and men because OSHA exposure standards were exceeded.

In Chapter 7, we argue that sometimes overwhelming reasons justify behavior that is inconsistent with the ethical standards. American Cyanamid seemed willing to violate the right of privacy concerning health and off-the-job behavior because it felt the situation concerning embryotoxic substances justified it. One of the most diffi-cult management tasks is to review carefully the facts of complex situations and make moral judgments concerning them.

Legal standards. A second dimension of an ethical dilemma concerns legal standards and regulations. Compliance with legal and regulatory standards is often considered a "moral minimum" when guiding or evaluating ethical behavior. Culturally and politically supported behavior is codified and sanctioned by law. As scientific, medical, and technological information is made available, it is used to guide the writing of legal and regulatory standards for workplace safety and the environment.

However, standards change as more is known about the scientific and technological relationships. What is considered safe at one time may be later found to be unsafe, as the history of asbestos and many other toxic substances suggests. Rapid changes in science and technology greatly increase the complexity of understanding ethical controversies and also increase the perplexities of conflicting laws and regulations. Changes in standards are influenced by technological capacity to measure the presence of harmful substances and the feasibility of control, the magnitude and likeliness of dangerous consequences, and the availability of substitutes for a dangerous substance or process. Standards are also influenced by economic and political considerations that unfold during the public policy process.

For example, in the American Cyanamid case the standard was 50 parts of lead per cubic meter, though companies in the process of changing systems could temporarily use a standard of 200 parts per cubic meter. It was argued by some that the company's policy, which applied only to women, was designed to minimize legal liability by taking advantage of limited scientific knowledge of cause-effect relationships in cases concerning men. Such an argument would be supported if the company thought lead was a mutant. Management would have to develop an approach to the policy that applied equally to men and women employees. However, if lead were not a mutant, the policy of prohibiting women of childbearing age would be sound on both medical and legal liability grounds.

Relationships. Role relationships include professional, employment, agency, and personal relationships between people. Professional relationships like those between lawyer and client, doctor and patient, priest and layperson, certified public accountant and client are special because confidentiality is expected. Employment and agency relationships typically involve the requirement that a person follow the policies of the employing organization and work to achieve company objectives. In return it is expected that an agent will not be asked to do anything illegal or unsafe and that an employee will not be endangered while working on behalf of the company. Employment relationships are often defined by federal and state law. Policies involving employees should be nondiscriminatory and consistent with state law relating to wrongful discharges.

The administrative judges in the American Cyanamid case seemed to rule that the scientific and medical facts concerning job safety were less important than facts concerning relationships. The ruling seemed to indicate that the sexual discrimination issue was more critical than what type of toxic substance lead proved to be.

Exposing a person to a hazardous substance without his or her knowledge or consent is inherently unethical. Thus, American Cyanamid held a meeting conducted by a company doctor to explain the new policy and the hazards involved with employees. Personal relationships often define moral dilemmas in important ways. People often have expectations concerning the inherent quality of relationships, and facts in a situation concerning keeping secrets, truthfulness, promise keeping, and fair dealing can all have important ethical implications.

In the introductory case, the managers facing the moral dilemma needed to develop a workable and an ethical policy. The regulators working for OSHA sought to control the relationship between managers and employees to prevent unsafe conditions. The women working for American Cyanamid needed the employment in an area where jobs were scarce and economic conditions poor. The responsibility of those in various roles and their relationship to others in the case defined the situation and how each perceived the moral or ethical dilemma.

Top management, concerned with key strategic decisions, seeks to make the organization adaptive within a competitive environment. Midlevel managers, responsible for the implementation of those strategies, influence the lives of both employees and customers. Employees are concerned with their livelihoods and career objectives, serving organizational purposes, and a safe working environment.

Individuals involved in the situation approach it with the perspectives of their culture and unique life situation. These individuals have personal values, ideals, needs, and motivations that influence the moral and ethical standards they apply to situations at hand. The characteristics of the situation and ethical standards serve as inputs to the decision processes by which moral judgments are made. However, once a moral or ethical judgment is made, it does not necessarily follow that the behavior that results is ethical.

Many things other than knowledge and judgment influence behavior. Individual integrity is needed to supplement understanding so that behavior is consistent with ethical judgment. Sometimes an individual must exert strong will or courage to do what he or she believes to be ethical. For example, the women in American Cyanamid had themselves sterilized when threatened with the loss of their livelihood. Organizational variables like corporate culture, information systems, and reward structures also influence behavior, as shown in Figure 6–1, the context of ethical behavior.

INDIVIDUAL VIRTUES AND MORAL STANDARDS

According to Valesquez, individual moral standards should

1. deal with serious matters of importance to human beings
2. be held by personal conviction and not be changed by policy and rules made by authoritative bodies

3. override self interest
4. be objective and impartial
5. result in special emotions like pleasure or satisfaction when a person behaves morally or guilt
or disappointment when a person violates his or
her moral standards.

Moral standards of behavior are used to interpret
the factual patterns found in a moral dilemma, as
suggested in Figure 6–1. Personal values,[2] religion,[3]
cultural values,[4] ideology,[5] and individual virtues all
influence the development of moral and ethical
standards used to make judgments. With all the
possible sources of moral standards within the value
diversity of a pluralistic society like the United
States, moral standards are also likely to vary widely.
However, some themes recur in the moral standards
of various religions, philosophies, and cultures.

Standards of Moral Behavior

Examples of standards of behavior often include
the following:

1. *Truth telling:* This standard is usually an admonition against lying or saying something that you
know to be untrue when you say it.[6]
2. *Promise keeping:* The standard of fulfilling agreements is the basis for *contract law.* If people could
not be depended upon to keep promises, then contracts and trustworthy interactions would be
fraught with uncertainty.
3. *Confidence keeping:* Keeping secrets forms the
basis of many personal, professional, and business
relationships.[7] Some interactions are considered
privileged under law, such as the confidences
between lawyer and client or doctor and patient.
Also, in an age when proprietary technology is of
key importance, companies seek to establish standards concerning trade secrets.
4. *Avoiding harm to others:* The moral standard of
not harming others is the basis of *tort law.* Though
there are exceptions, societies generally try to cul-
tivate this moral standard so that safety can be
enjoyed. Ethical principles of rights to safety and
an entitlement to damages from those who cause
harm are derived from this moral standard. In its

extreme form, this moral standard changes from
the negative standard of not harming others to a
positive standard of caring for the welfare of others. In its positive expression, this is the moral
standard of *beneficence.*
5. *A sense of fair dealing:* Almost all persons and
societies have some standard relating to what is
fair dealing or fair business practices. However, of
all the moral standards listed here, this one is likely
to have the most diversity because views of what
constitutes fair dealing varies from industry to
industry and from culture to culture.

Virtues Basic to a Good Society

Chapter 2 suggested that market competition was
the primary source of social control of business
behavior. The model of competition was based on
Adam Smith's *Wealth of Nations,* published in 1776.
This model of a market-oriented society identified
prudent behavior and several other conditions necessary for its proper operation. However, prudence
is only one of three virtues identified by Smith as
important for a good society. In an earlier work,
The Theory of Moral Sentiments, first published in
1753, Smith argued that a good society requires
three social virtues: *prudence, justice, and beneficence.*[8] He suggested that as a person matures, these
virtues develop out of life experience beginning
with prudence and ending with beneficence.

Smith believed that virtuous actions required
more than those that are self-seeking in orientation and obedient to the minimum legal requirements. He argued for the balance of three virtues:
prudence, justice, and beneficence, as summarized
in Table 6–1. *Prudence* is the self-interested behavior necessary for existence and competitive success. *Justice* is obeying laws enforced by the government and is needed so that legal rights are
respected. *Beneficence* is the voluntary caring for
the needs of others out of love or concern for their
dignity. These virtues closely parallel the work of
motivational psychologists who have investigated
such needs as existence, relatedness, and growth.
These virtues are also consistent with what behav-

TABLE 6–1
Summary of Adam Smith's Theory of Moral Sentiments

Key Dimension/ Virtue	Prudence	Justice	Beneficence
Dominant Moral Sentiment	Fear and greed	Respect for others' rights defined by law	Love and affection for others
Ethical Behavior	Self-interested behavior and self-preservation	Avoiding harming others; obeying the law	Concern for the welfare of others
Social Maintenance	To maintain the individual	To maintain the society	To embellish the society
Pattern of Interaction	Mercenary exchange	Exchange without fear of harm	Mutual admiration and gratitude
Quality of Virtue	Low	Medium	High
Quality of Life in Society	Negative	Neutral or minimal	Positive
Role of Government for Implementation	Force not needed	Compliance must be commanded by government	Cannot be commanded by government, must be willingly given

ioral science tells us about developing the capacity for moral judgment discussed below.

The relative emphasis of these virtues forms the basis for moral standards used by individuals in making ethical or moral judgments. Each of these virtues is important for society, but their relative dominance in managers could lead them in different directions. Below we discuss the ethical virtues first promulgated by Adam Smith in terms of how they might have guided management action differently in the American Cyanamid case that introduced this chapter.

PRUDENCE AS SELF-INTERESTED BEHAVIOR

Prudence is the virtue of self-interest. Smith characterized the prudent person as always sincere but not always frank and open. Such a person tells the truth but not the whole truth and is cautious in actions and reserved in speech. "The prudent man is not willing to subject himself to any responsibility that his duty does not impose upon him."[9] The virtue of prudence may encourage self-preservation and the creation of individual wealth and social status. It is needed for the growth of the economic system and the stability of society. However, prudence is not the only virtue needed for a good society; Smith also argued for justice and beneficence.

The managers of American Cyanamid thought they were acting prudently by formulating a policy that prevented women of childbearing age to work in the lead chromate pigments unit. They appeared to be concerned with the economic performance of the company and seemed to be especially concerned with the possibility of legal liability associated with risks inherent in women working in those jobs. Though it was possible that men might also experience the adverse effects of birth defects suffered by their offspring, the likeliness of losing a lawsuit involving a man was considered to be less. Thus the most prudent policy seemed to be directed exclusively at women employees.

JUSTICE AS OBEYING THE LAW

Justice, according to Smith, was obeying the laws that protect the rights of others and are enforced by the government. As noted in Chapter 2, the government regulates business to protect the rights of people to safe jobs and safe products and to respond to market failures when the conditions of competition are lacking. Managers at American Cyanamid were seeking to form a policy that took into account the legal rights of American Cyanamid to hire employees, assign specific task assignments, and assume the responsibility of insuring safe working conditions. Also, the legal rights of employees, especially women, were the major consideration in drafting the policy that they thought would protect both sets of rights and responsibilities. Managers activated by prudence and justice, as defined by Adam Smith, might be expected to formulate a policy consistent with the one found in the introductory case.

BENEFICENCE AS VOLUNTARILY DOING WHAT IS RIGHT

Beneficence was considered by Adam Smith to be a positive virtue of doing good by voluntarily caring for the needs of others out of love or regard for their personal dignity. Beneficent actions were considered by Smith to be

> the most graceful and agreeable of all the affections;. . .it is the proper object of gratitude and reward; and that upon all these accounts, it appears to be our natural sentiment to possess a merit superior to any other.[10]
>
> Those actions which aimed at the happiness of a great community. . .they were likewise proportionally the more virtuous."[11]

Justice is more important for stable societal interaction than is beneficence, though the latter might be critical to a high quality of life both on and off the job. The virtue of beneficence requires the *moral imagination* of managers so they can find ways to honor the dignity of others. Managers could develop alternatives that may not be strictly required by law. For example, in the American Cyanamid case, the managers could have sought ways to redesign the jobs or change technologies used to make them safer for everyone. They might have invested in research and development of alternative ingredients that would be less toxic. They might have weighed the potential health effects of the chemicals on men more evenly, though the legal pressures to do so seemed small. They might have sought to provide a greater measure of employment security through transfers to other parts of the organization or through an outplacement program to find jobs in other companies for those displaced by the new policy.

Moral Reasoning: Psychological Perspectives

The psychological dimension of decision making is influenced by the individual's motivation and by the capacity for moral judgment.[12] Maslow has suggested that unfulfilled needs motivate and those needs follow a developmental hierarchical pattern. Individuals must first fulfill lower-level needs before needs in the next level of the hierarchy become active. Individuals must first satisfy physical needs; next, needs for safety become active, followed by social needs, esteem needs, and lastly self-actualization needs.[13]

Alderfer used the needs hierarchy as his basic framework for motivation but reduced the number of categories to three that included existence needs, relatedness needs, and growth needs to make up his ERG Model of motivation.[14] In the beginning of psychological development individuals need to satisfy basic physical needs first. Once the need for food, shelter, and safety is relatively well satisfied, the healthy individual then seeks out social interactions with others. Later, as social relationships are developed and psychological development continues, the individual seeks to satisfy growth needs. These growth needs are satisfied by recognition and by experiencing self-esteem. The satisfaction of these needs in an organization can be used to evaluate corporate social responsibility.[15]

STAGES OF MORAL REASONING

The psychological research in the area of moral judgments parallels the work in motivation. In work similar to Alderfer's ERG model of motivation, Lawrence Kohlberg has found that an individual's capacity to make moral judgments follows a hierarchical development pattern that first focuses on the self, then on relationships with others, and last on some internalized standards of behavior.[16] These three levels parallel prudence, justice in relationships, and the beneficence of Adam Smith. Kohlberg subdivides the three basic levels into six stages of moral reasoning as follows.

Moral reasoning in organizations can be strongly influenced by early childhood experiences as well as by management leadership and organizational policies experienced later in life. In an argument similar to Smith's *Theory of Moral Sentiments*, Kohlberg argues that as children grow up, they begin at level one, where their concerns center on self-interest. Children develop their capacity in level two, where decisions combine the self-interest of level one with level-two justice concepts. Initially justice is defined as following group norms and later as obeying laws and regulations. Some persons develop into level three, where moral judgments are based upon integrity, personal convictions, and voluntary behavior.

Kohlberg argues that everyone begins at stage one and progresses to higher stages of moral judgment as personality develops normally in response to experiences. It is impossible to skip any of the stages, though all people do not progress to stage six. Stage four, moral reasoning—morality based on obeying government laws and following company

policies—is the type of moral judgment found to be the most common in the United States among men. Women seem to develop moral reasoning in a manner that places more emphasis on commitment to personal relationships based on individual integrity than to a law and order orientation.[17]

LEVEL ONE: SELF-INTEREST AS MORAL REASONING

Stage one: moral reasoning of fear and punishment is based upon fear and obedience to authority to avoid punishment. This is normal judgment for children of about four to nine or ten years old. Young children copy role models or authority figures. The capacity for abstract reasoning doesn't really develop until about age nine or ten. If a child is fearful of being punished and that fear influences behavior strongly, the result can be an abused child with a distorted pattern of moral development.

Alternatively, a child's behavior can focus on models to copy rather than on his or her judgments concerning punishment and fear to shape behavior. The result of healthy role models is likely to be healthy developmental patterns. A parallel exists when companies operate with autocratic, punitive cultures that motivate employees to protect themselves and to avoid punishment rather than to use creative energies to solve problems.

Stage two: moral reasoning of exchange is characterized by morality-based achieving self-interested goals through exchange; the central idea is "let's make a deal." Any exchange that satisfies one's desires is considered to be morally justified at this stage. For example, different children will like different toys and will trade their toys, then they begin to understand the whole concept of what's involved with making a deal. At this stage the realization that what I value may not be so highly valued by others becomes possible. In adults, stage-two behavior can also include patterns of manipulation to gain one's goals.

Subjective relativity has to do with understanding that what is valued by an individual is unique from what is valued by others. This psychological capac-

TABLE 6–2
Levels of Moral Reasoning

Level One: The Morality of Self-interested Behavior

1. *Fear and obedience to avoid punishement*—"It is moral to do anything that you can get away with."

2. *Self-oriented exchange*—"Let's make a deal; any agreed upon exchange is moral."

Level Two: Morality of Relationships as Defined by Rules

3. *Peer group norms*—"It is moral to do what friends do."

4. *Law and order*—"Morality requires obeying the law."

Level Three: Personal Integrity and the Morality of Individual Decisions

5. *Psychological contract*—"I keep my personal commitments; but it is not moral to obey illegitimate laws."

6. *Principled reasoning based on internalized values*—"I follow my inner guidance based on what I understand to be moral."

SOURCE: Adapted from Lawrence Kohlberg, "Stage and Sequence: The Cognitive Developmental Approach to Socialization." In *Handbook of Socialization*. Ed. by D. Golin. Chicago: Rand-McNally, 1969, pp. 437–480.

ity enables a person to identify with another enough to understand that values can be relative, and that one's value weighing of something is different from another's, and that can form the basis for an exchange. This realization is the basis for all market exchange. Market exchanges consistent with high moral standards along the dimensions outlined above are likely to yield desirable social performance. However, stage-two moral reasoning in the absence of moral standards leads to undesirable social outcomes such as the illegal drug trade and organized crime.

The focus of stage two is on self, and behavior is self-orientated, but some appreciation of how other people view things appears in latent form as the capacity to exchange is developed. In level one of moral reasoning, the individual is totally focused on self, but the stage-two experience of exchanges and deal making leads to an awareness of differences in how others value things available for exchange. This capacity is further developed as a person moves to level two.

LEVEL TWO: NORMS, LAWS, AND SOCIAL ORDER

Stage three: morality of norms. The third stage is the "good boy/nice girl" stage. The idea here is what my friends do is all right and what my friends do not do is not all right. Informal group norms become the basis for making moral judgments at this stage. Most undergraduate students and many adults are at this stage of moral reasoning. For example, if a salesperson who "pads an expense account" is asked for a justification, a common answer might be, "All the other salesmen show more expenses on their reports than they actually have, so I do it, too," or "That's the way it is done in this company."

Managers should recognize that the informal norms of behavior can be very important in explaining behavior. Group norms can reinforce either low or high standards of moral behavior. Companies that have informal norms whereby sales personnel pad expense accounts, purchasing agents accept "gifts" from suppliers, and warehouse personnel help themselves to merchandise have climates that encourage unethical behavior.

In contrast, the managers involved in the development of the "Beliefs at Borg-Warner" outlined in Chapter 14 encourage high moral standards, self-development, and respect for the dignity of others. Managers at Borg-Warner were careful to obtain the support of top and middle levels of management before adopting the beliefs companywide. The informal norms, values, and beliefs found in organizations define much of the corporate culture and set the tone for moral reasoning within the corporation.

Stage four: moral reasoning as law and order is characterized by the response "we obey the law to bring about social order" and if we don't obey the law probably chaos and pandemonium would ensue. At this level a person recognizes that unless a companywide system of cooperation is established and stabilized, no person can make plans. Each person should obey company rules and policies and do his or her job so that everyone obtains reliable performance. Also, it is expected that others will also obey the rules of the organization. Obedience to the law is the key moral virtue, and individuals at this level feel a duty to do so. This level of moral reasoning closely parallels the virtue of justice described by Adam Smith. However, the basis of legitimacy behind the laws is not questioned at this level; the laws simply exist and must be obeyed if society is to be stable, predictable, and safe.

LEVEL THREE—MORAL REASONING AS LEGITIMACY AND PRINCIPLES

Stage five of moral reasoning as integrity and legitimacy is concerned with inner-directed behavior. The individual begins to question the legitimacy of the law. In Chapter 1 we defined *legitimacy* as relevant political support within the society. The person at stage five of moral reasoning begins to consider the processes whereby laws are established and enforced. Are they reasonable? Do they reflect democratic processes? Do the laws have an appropriate level of social support?

At stage five of moral reasoning, the possibility of *disobedience becomes possible as an individual moral*

act if a rule or law is perceived as arbitrary and not legitimate. This is particularly important for managers who wish employees to be able to cope effectively with ethical dilemmas. If rules or inflexibility in organizational structures are perceived as arbitrary and unfair, employees at stage five will reject the management system as illegitimate and will not be inclined to obey the rules, even in the face of punitive measures. Systems based upon objective criteria that are generally acceptable will lead to positive control. Systems perceived as inflexible, unfair, and/or with elements of subjective favoritism in the rewards are likely to cause more capable employees to leave the organization.

The subjective concepts of personal integrity, psychological contract, honor, and commitment also become important aspects of moral reasoning for the individual at stage five. At this stage one is more likely to say, "I will do it because I said I would; it is a matter of personal integrity" to explain why an action is taken. One agrees to obey company policies because they are considered fair and legitimate generally and because of an individual psychological contract with the organization that serves as a moral standard for behavior by the individual. Also, personal commitments to other individuals can be very important at this stage.

Stage six: moral reasoning as internalized principles. The central characteristic of this stage is the internalization of certain personally held values and ways of thinking that influences a person to become an independent moral agent. Such an individual is sometimes perceived as putting him- or herself above the law.

CASE EXAMPLE: MARTIN LUTHER KING, JR.

Stage-six moral reasoning was used by Martin Luther King, Jr., a civil rights leader during the 1950s and 1960s. Rosa Parks, an African-American, refused to go to the back of the bus as the law required. She was arrested and jailed. Martin Luther King, Jr., then a minister at a local church, recognized that the law was unjust even if it might have been the result of a democratic process. King viewed laws that sanctioned discrimination against

African Americans as inherently immoral. African Americans deserved to be treated with dignity, as did other human beings.

King organized a boycott of local buses and the civil rights movement in the United States was launched. He was put in jail, where he received many letters, some criticizing him for disobeying the law and for being in jail. His answer was his now famous "letter from the Birmingham Jail," which asked his detractors why they were not in jail with him. He asked why they could stand by and allow a society with great promise to remain unjust and to discriminate against minorities. He said he was guided by a higher law that he must follow if he was to be moral.

Moral Reasoning and Organization Culture

Managers try to achieve organizational goals through various management and behavioral processes that lead to systems of cooperation. Etzioni has studied the relationship between types of control systems that predominate in organizations.[18] According to his typology, organizational controls can be coercive, remunerative, or normative, that is, they can emphasize fear of punishment, exchange of valued rewards for desired behavior, or some ideal or ethical code. These types of controls correspond, respectively, to the types of organizational commitment by members that are alienated, calculated, or moral. Etzioni's key insight is that organizations work best when control systems coincide with the type of commitment of persons and that incongruence leads to malfunctions.

Coercive controls are based upon fear and threats of punishment to achieve compliance with rules. The most common forms of this type of organization are prisons and some school systems. The second type of control system is found in the remunerative organization that rewards members as incentives to obey rules and to achieve organizational objectives. Such organizations can be viewed as exchange processes in which employees calculate rewards available and exchange desired behavior for those rewards. According to Etzioni, many if not most business organizations are examples of this second type.

Normative controls work best when members have an idealistic or moral commitment to the organization or the profession. Examples of this would be organizations of health care professionals, lawyers, certified public accountants, and possibly research laboratories where the objective standards of scientific inquiry guide behavior. Etzioni suggests that the use of an idealistic normative climate to encourage ethical behavior is not likely to work in a prison. Also, threats of punishment as the central dimension of control is not likely to work well in a hospital. Excellent organizations attempt to develop a culture of commitment based upon the ideals of excellence, respect for the dignity of individuals, and concern for the needs of customers.[19]

Etzioni's key conclusion is that the control system used within the organization should be congruent with the type of commitment that members have to the organization. Similarly, we also suggest that the organizational culture needs to be congruent with the level of moral reasoning within the organization. Organizational culture, control systems, and managerial and behavioral processes in the organization provide key aspects of the context within which ethical judgments are made.

CORPORATE CULTURES BASED ON FEAR, PUNISHMENT, AND EXCHANGE

Stage-one business organizations that rely primarily on fear and punishment are unlikely to exist except perhaps for prison industries. However, organizations characterized by the second stage of preconventional moral reasoning do seem to exist. Such organizations would emphasize punishment, self-interested behavior, and manipulation, as shown in

Table 6–3. Such companies would seek to block regulatory attempts to protect customers. For example, Beech Nut sold fake apple juice for use as baby food to save $250,000 in expenses per year (see Case III–2). When the Food and Drug Administration tried to intervene, company executives stalled the regulators until the unused supplies of fake juice could be sold in markets where customers were not suspicious of the adulterated product. Organizations with cultures characterized by level-two moral reasoning are likely to have little commitment to either employees or customers. Little loyalty is expected and the behavior that is desired is due to compliance from fear or careful calculations of available rewards based upon self-interest.

INFORMAL GROUP NORMS, ORGANIZATION POLICY, AND COMMITMENT

Organizations characterized by stage-three moral reasoning are likely to have cultures based upon informal groups held together by friendship, as suggested in Table 6–3. Stage-four cultures are reinforced by organizational structures with clear rules and policies to guide behavior. Consistent with the insight of Adam Smith, friendships are likely to lead to organizational loyalty and can increase commitment to serving customer needs. Virtue is likely to be defined in terms of compliance with informal group norms and by following company policies.

Stage-three persons are managed through knowledge of group dynamics and informal groups. It is crucial that organizations encourage appropriate informal group norms compatible with organizational goals. Management can work with the group to develop rapport so that group norms are compatible with organizational interests. Punishing or trying to discourage group behavior is likely to lead to highly cohesive groups whose loyalty is to other group members and not to organizational objectives.[20]

From the point of view of conventional management, most management thought is geared to stage-four people who are relatively easy to manage

because they obey authority figures. If employees are at stage four, their behavior can transcend group norms. Such employees may have the strength to oppose groups norms and peer pressure when they are not consistent with organizational goals and values. Formal roles, organizational standards of performance, objectives, and rules need to be made clear enough to meet the needs of employees at this stage of moral reasoning. Procedures should be relatively stable, consistent, and rational if they are to be attractive to this level of moral reasoning.

THE MILGRAM EXPERIMENTS ON OBEDIENCE TO AUTHORITY

Group norms and formal management authority and rules can lead to immoral as well as moral behavior, as the research of Stanley Milgram suggests.[21] Milgram performed a series of experiments designed to test the limits of authority. Under what conditions would people obey authority and commit clearly immoral acts? Subjects were recruited from Yale University and later from the streets of New Haven, Connecticut, for the series of experiments. Subjects were asked to administer electric shocks to other "subjects" (who were actually professional actors) under a variety of conditions. Professional actors, pretending to be the subjects of the experiment, simulated learners in the experiment and made "mistakes" based upon the design of the experiment.

The electric shocks were believed by the subjects to range from a mild 15 volts to a severe 450 volts. The "learner" (that is, the professional actor) was subjected to electric shocks when a mistake was made in the supposed learning attempt. Upon experiencing the shock, the "learner" made a series of protests from "Ugh!" to an agonized scream when the voltage reached 270, although a maximum of 450 volts was eventually to be administered by the experimental subjects.

In experiment 17 in the series, when "two peers" rebelled against the experiment, only 10 percent of the subjects obediently administered the maximum

TABLE 6–3
Models of Personal and Organizational Moral Development

Personal Moral Development	Organizational Moral Development	Examples of Moral Reasoning
Stage One. Physical consequences determine behavior. Avoidance of punishment and deference to power are typical at this stage.	**Social Darwinism.** Fear of extinction and the urgency of financial survival dictate moral conduct. The direct use of force is the accepted norm.	"I won't hit him, because he may hit me back."
Stage Two. Individual pleasure needs are the primary concern and dictate the rightness or wrongness of behavior.	**Machiavellianism.** Organizations' gain guides actions. Successfully attaining goals justifies the use of any effective means, including individual manipulation.	"I will help her, because she may help me in return."
Stage Three. The approval of others determines behavior. The good person is one who satisfies family, friends, and associates.	**Popular Conformity.** There is a tradition of standard operating procedures. Peer pressure to adhere to social norms dictates right or wrong behavior.	"I will go along with him, because I want him to like me."
Stage Four. Compliance with authority, upholding the social order, and *doing one's duty* are primary ethical concerns.	**Allegiance to Authority.** Directions from legitimate authority determine organizational moral standards. Right and wrong are based on the decisions of those with hierarchical power.	"I will comply with her order, because it is wrong to disobey her."
Stage Five. Tolerance for rational dissent and acceptance of majority rule become primary ethical concerns.	**Democratic Participation.** Participation in decision making and reliance on majority rule become organizational moral standards.	"Although I disagree with his views, I will uphold his right to have them."
Stage Six. What is right and good is a matter of individual conscience and responsibly chosen commitments. Morality is based on principled personal conviction.	**Organizational Integrity.** Justice and individual rights are the moral ideals. Balanced judgment among competing interests forms organizational character, which in turn determines the rightness or wrongness of behavior.	"There is no external force that can compel me to perform an act I consider morally wrong."

SOURCE: Joseph A. Petrick and George E. Manning, "Ethics for Total Quality and Participation: Developing an Ethical Climate for Excellence," *Journal of Quality and Participation* (March 1990): 85. Copyright Association for Quality and Participation, Cincinnati, Ohio. Reprinted with permission.

level shocks that were believed to be very danger-ous to the simulated learner. In contrast, when "peers" cooperated with the administration of shocks in experiment 18, over 92 percent of sub-jects obediently administered maximum voltage. This suggests that peer group norms can have a significant effect on behavior.

Also, in the experiment in which an authority fig-ure was present—Milgram dressed in a white smock—over 60 percent of participants admin-istered maximum voltage to the subjects. This sug-gests that organizational cultures can sanction immoral behavior through informal group norms or formal organizational authority. The resulting behavior is likely to be consistent with such cultures.

PERSONAL COMMITMENT, LEGITIMACY, AND EMPOWERMENT

Employees at level three, which includes stages five and six of moral reasoning, are likely to be harder to control by traditional management but may be excellent for the competitiveness in environments that require independent action. In stage-five orga-nizations, governance issues become more impor-tant and employees are sensitive to participative approaches to management. Management decisions must be perceived as reasonable and fair. Thus it is important to give procedural and substantive due process in the governance of employees at level three in their moral reasoning. Management by objectives (MBO) or other management systems that facilitate clear communication and personal commitment to objectives should work well for employees at this level of moral reasoning.

Excellent organizations empower people in ways that encourage them to take personal responsibility for their decisions. Such empower-ment leads to a willingness to take risks, to be cre-ative, and to initiate changes and actions on behalf of the organization. Note that organiza-tions with cultures consistent with level three would be ineffective if employees were at level one, the level of obedience to avoid punishment. A work group operating at level-one moral rea-soning would take advantage of an empowering

organizational culture by actions that were self-serving and abusive. The absence of punishments or controls would be taken advantage of by a per-son at level-one moral reasoning.

People at stage five might ask, "What does man-agement say here, and do we have some consensus or support for a particular policy?" From a motiva-tional point of view, management needs to develop support for a particular policy or people will not enthusiastically implement it. For example, a worker at stage-six moral reasoning in the Ameri-can Cyanamid case might believe it is unethical to have a work environment that endangered employees. A stage-six manager might conclude that the only viable alternatives would be to change the design of work to make it safe or with-draw from business. This would be inconsistent with the policy developed by American Cyanamid, and both worker and manager might experience a moral dilemma in which the policy was inconsis-tent with their ethical judgment.

Moral Reasoning and Moral Judgments

The theory of moral stages is concerned more with the justifications used for making moral judgments than the content of the judgments themselves. Thus persons at different stages of moral judgments might make the same decisions but will explain their reasoning very differently. Also, persons at the same stage of moral reasoning may make different decisions when faced with similar situations because (1) they perceive the facts differently, (2) they have different moral standards, or (3) key ele-ments of the situation are different. For example, persons at stage three are very sensitive to group norms, and thus persons at this stage will respond differently as group composition and norms vary.

MORAL REASONING AND JUSTIFYING DECISIONS

When asked, "Why did you fulfill the contract that you signed?" a person at stage one might explain, "I fulfilled the contract that I signed because I would have been sued if I hadn't." A person at stage two might argue, "I fulfilled the contract because it was worth my while to fulfill it." At stage three the answer might be, "I obey the contract because that's the way we do it in our business." At stage four the justification might become, "I obey the contract because if people didn't obey the contract you couldn't predict people's behaviors, you couldn't plan, and it would be just chaos." Or a person at this stage may simply explain, "It is the law to fulfill contracts; it is our company's policy."

The person primarily operating in stage five of moral reasoning might explain, "I obeyed the contract because I signed it, it was a reasonable contract, and my honor was at stake." The idea of personal integrity, honor, individual commitment, or fulfilling those obligations to which one commits oneself become important. And finally the stage-six person might explain that he or she fulfilled the contract because it was consistent with some principle of justice he or she felt to be especially important.

DEVELOPING CAPACITY FOR MORAL JUDGMENTS

Kohlberg has found that facing moral dilemmas, making judgments, and defending decisions in a generally supportive environment is the most effective way to develop the capacity for making moral judgments. If a person is in a hostile environment and must defend a judgment, the reaction is likely to be one of defensiveness rather than growth. If a person is faced with a highly critical judgment, he or she is likely to digress to a lower level of moral reasoning rather than to accept the argument. Similarly, Alderfer argues that if higher-order needs are frustrated, a person is likely to behave in a frustrated manner by emphasizing lower-level needs that had previously been inactive as motivators.

On the other hand, if a person is in a nonpunitive environment of mutual respect and sharing, the very act of defending or explaining oneself can lead

to changes in the structure of cognition. Experience is an effective way of developing the capacity for dealing with complex moral dilemmas. If one wants to learn how to swim, one practices swimming. If one wants to play the violin, one practices playing the violin. If one wants to develop the capacity for moral reasoning, one has to think about what one is doing in a moral or ethical way. The very act of thinking about values and ethical situations will cause one to increase one's capacity to do so.

According to the psychological theory of moral reasoning, each person begins at stage one and moves to higher stages with experience. Kohlberg would argue that as one increases the capacity of moral reasoning, one goes from level one to as high as level six. The cognitive structure of people qualitatively changes in ways that enable higher levels of reasoning to subsume lower levels, except that a higher-level response is likely to be more sophisticated than a lower-level response. For example, a person with a purely level-two moral reasoning is driven only by self-interest. A person using level-four moral reasoning would include self-interest bounded by obeying the laws and regulations. A person at levels five or six would be more likely to find solutions consistent with self-interest and legal constraints, but would probably go on in the use of moral imagination as briefly discussed above. However, if self-interest was in conflict with morality, morality would prevail.

In general, individuals can understand and often can be persuaded by moral arguments one stage above where they presently are. Behavioral science suggests that people do not understand nor are they persuaded by arguments with moral reasoning two or more stages above where they presently are. Persuasion must be one step at a time when development of moral reasoning is concerned.

MORAL JUDGMENTS AND BEHAVIOR

Knowing what you believe to be moral or ethical does not necessarily mean your behavior is consistent with your knowledge. As shown in Figure 6–2, ethical behavior is a function of the judgments resulting from ethical reasoning, as well as a number of individual and organizational factors.

Individual factors include personal courage, integrity, strength of will, and the degree to which one allows outside forces to influence behavior. For example, several of the women employees in the American Cyanamid case had themselves sterilized even though they believed this to be wrong. They said they wanted to maintain their employment, perceived that the company was pressuring them to sterilize themselves, and could not resist this pressure.

Executives occasionally indicate they complied with a practice they felt to be improper because of company pressure. For example, the price-fixing scandal in the electric generator manufacturing business during the 1950s seemed to be the result of such a situation. Companies like General Electric had very high financial performance standards, and the consequences of not achieving the targeted level of performance were threatening to the executives in the divisions that manufactured electric generators. When the market conditions became unfavorable, these executives conspired with executives in other companies to fix prices at artificially high levels to achieve company-mandated profit objectives. Pressure from above to achieve high profits under poor economic conditions combined with an industry group norm to bring about unethical behavior. Executives knew that the practice was illegal and unethical, but their behavior was not consistent with their knowledge of appropriate behavior. Such inconsistent behavior shows a lack of personal integrity.

As discussed above, people at stage three in their moral reasoning adopt the group norms as their moral standards. Thus it might be argued that their behavior is "consistent with their knowledge" because such people are very susceptible to the values and concerns of others. For example, a warehouse worker might indicate that it is proper to take supplies from the warehouse because "everyone does it." A consulting organization may have an informal norm against hiring minority group members. Salespeople may pad their expense accounts for reimbursement. These practices could be followed despite a company policy forbidding such practices.

Organizational factors include corporate culture, reward systems, information systems, executive leadership, and pressure. Individuals can experience either direct pressure, as was the case of the women employees at American Cyanamid in 1979, or indirect pressure, as was the case at General

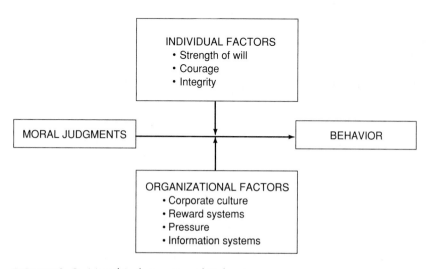

FIGURE 6–2 Moral Judgments and Behavior

Electric in the 1950s. Sometimes management is unaware of the various pressures experienced by employees. A cultural value of "come to me with solutions, don't come to me with problems" is a key source of pressure that can lead to unethical behavior. Often an objective attempt to solve problems can lead to good results because, once informed, top management can bring more resources and information to the solution. However, if management will not listen to problems, then individuals, left to their own devices, can take "short cuts" that prove unethical. This is particularly true in cases involving job and product safety. Management systems also influence the way people behave in organizations. Reward systems communicate what kind of behavior is rewarded and what is subject to negative sanctions. Also, management information systems that help management to monitor results provide employees with cues about what top management pays attention to and thus what is important and what is less important. People who generally strive to be good employees try to accomplish organizational objectives and other things valued by top management and fellow employees. Thus, a reward system, the type of results that get reported, and the routing of management reports all influence employee behavior.

Though few managers may reflect on the moral messages embodied in these systems, they guide the moral and ethical behavior of employees. These systems can yield perceptions consistent or inconsistent with the independent moral judgments of employees. Sometimes one system communicates a different set of values than others. For example, a formal product-testing system may exist to assure safe products, while the informal organizational culture can encourage taking short cuts to get a product out on time.

Management Implications of Moral Reasoning

The management implication of our knowledge of moral reasoning is as follows:

1. Encouraging employees to explicitly consider and explain their reasons when making decisions will in itself lead to increasing their capacity for moral reasoning.

2. Ethical systems that are developed more than one level above the level of employees' reasoning are likely to be viewed as vague and confusing. Because most employees are likely to be at stages three or four, careful attention should be given to the informal organization and the norms and practices at the group level.

3. Organizational policies and rules should be clear, consistent, and well communicated. It is best to ask employees to use their own judgment and not do anything that violates their personal ethics when making a decision.

4. Trying to force people to be ethical within an organizational culture that is judgmental and punitive is not likely to work. In their efforts to avoid punishments and social criticisms, most employees focus on defending themselves in psychological safety and do not entertain new ideas. Thus changes in moral reasoning are unlikely except for possible regressive responses to the corporate culture.

5. The level of moral judgment of most adults is relatively stable and occurs normally about every ten years. Thus management should not expect rapid changes in the capacity for moral judgment. Organizational climates should be compatible with the judgment levels of organizational members, or perhaps have features that do not go beyond one level above the average for the organizations if the climate is to be used as a management tool to encourage ethical decision making.

6. Organizational culture, executive leadership, and the design and administration of various management systems can encourage or discourage the inherent capacity for moral reasoning of individuals.

Moral Responsibility and Accountability

Moral responsibility requires *informed consent*. Such an idea assumes that a person must willingly and knowingly perform an action if he or she is to be considered morally responsible. For example, central to medical ethics is the question of who is responsible for treatment when the treatment has side effects or inherent risks, as in the case of surgery. It is the responsibility of the physician to diagnose the illness and to develop a plan for treatment. However, patients need to share responsibility for the treatment if the doctor is not to be held accountable for anything that may go wrong in the course of the treatment. Thus in medical ethics, a physician is required to inform patients about the possible consequences of a particular medicine or surgical procedure. If the patient understands the information provided by the physician and willingly agrees to the prescribed treatment, then from an ethical point of view, the responsibility for the treatment transfers from the physician to the patient.

In business ethics, informed consent also provides the criteria for establishing moral responsibility, as shown in Table 6–4. A person is morally responsible and can be held accountable for any action that is knowingly and willingly done. These two criteria need to be considered within the broader context of ethical behavior outlined above in this chapter.

WAS THE ACT KNOWINGLY DONE?

The problem of ignorance. A person cannot normally be held accountable for an action if he or she is ignorant of the consequences of the moral dilemma. There are two degrees of ignorance: first ignorance exists if it is scientifically impossible to understand something, and second ignorance exists if one is unaware of some knowledge that could have been known.

Limits of scientific knowledge often exists in areas of science and technology. For example, a toxic waste created as part of manufacturing computer disks has been found to possibly destroy ozone in the earth's atmosphere. How does this happen? How much of this waste must be discharged into the atmosphere to have a significant effect on the ozone layer? Does it interact with any other substances to form a third substance that forms

another pollutant? Can it be mixed with anything to render it harmless? A virtually endless list of questions need to be answered before the scientific aspect of this situation can be completely known. The question is, how completely must something be known before action should be taken? If the cause-effect relationships are unknown and experts are not even able to establish probability relationships, then the issue is uncertain. If probabilities can be statistically established, then we can determine risk levels. Certainty exists if we can predict with complete accuracy that if X occurs then Y will follow.

CASE EXAMPLE: THE CONTROVERSY OVER SMOKING AND CANCER

There is a clearly established correlation between exposure to tobacco smoke and cancer. Does tobacco smoking cause cancer? The tobacco industry argues that correlations do not constitute a proof and the uncertainty is too great to establish a scientific relationship. Thus it would say that if harm results from the use of its product, it is *not knowingly involved* and cannot be held responsible. Also the tobacco industry would argue that the choice to smoke was not its and therefore it is *not willingly involved* and thus cannot be considered morally responsible for cancer that may or may not result from the use of its products. Also, the tobacco industry has argued that smoking is a matter of individual choice, not an addiction.

In contrast, the medical community and the surgeon general of the United States point to a vast collection of statistics showing strong correlations between exposure to tobacco smoke and the incidence of cancer. They argue that the risk can be established and that the knowledge of cause-effect relationships between exposure to tobacco and the incidence of cancer is sufficient to establish the existence of a major health hazard. They also argue that tobacco is highly addictive and thus smokers really do not willingly smoke. Such an argument suggests that the tobacco industry knowingly and willingly exposes its customers to

TABLE 6–4
Criteria for Ethical and Moral Responsibility

The Principles of Informed Consent

KNOWLEDGE: Was the action knowingly done?
  • Was there technological and **scientific uncertainty** or knowledge of cause-effect relationships?
  • Did the **problem of ignorance** exist. Is the excuse "I did not know" acceptable?
  • Did the person fulfill the **duty to know** through use of appropriate testing and information systems?

FREEDOM: Was the action willingly done?
  • Was there a **problem of coercion or outside pressure?** Is the excuse "I had to do it or be subject to punishment or be fired" acceptable?
  • Was the person **proximate to the action?** Is the excuse "It was not done in my department and I had nothing to do with it" acceptable?
  • Was there a **problem of the loyal agent?** Is the excuse "I was only following orders" acceptable?

Should the moral responsibility and accountability be shared?

Can the organization be held morally responsible or can we consider only individuals as moral agents?

---

great health risks and thus is morally responsible. Therefore the industry should be held accountable for its actions.

Unfortunately, knowledge is limited in many moral controversies surrounding the scientific, technological, and medical aspects of business activity. Moral standards concerning whether action should or should not be taken given a certain level of scientific knowledge vary. Some are willing to tolerate a high level of risk in the name of limited knowledge and individual freedom in the sale and use of questionable products. Others would have society accept very low levels of risk, even if it comes at the cost of individual freedom and a lower availability of products that cannot be proven to be safe.

The duty to know and to test. Companies are ethically and legally required to test their products before they are offered for sale. According to this criterion of moral responsibility, a person is required to become aware of the consequences of his or her actions. It is unethical to practice "strategic ignorance," that is, consciously not finding out about what your organization is doing so that you cannot be considered responsible for its actions. In other words, it is a duty for managers to test and to find out about the factual situation concerning their business activities. This involves the use of reasonable testing procedures and the development of information systems that make the responsible parties aware of the factual information concerning the outcomes of their activities.

WAS THE ACT WILLINGLY DONE?

A patient shares responsibility for the outcome of surgery if after becoming aware of the possible adverse effects, he or she agrees to the operation. Similarly, managers would be considered responsible when they willingly engage in an activity. Unfortunately, organizations are often the setting of competing pressures, conflicting objectives, and diverse interests. A young manager strives to become established and accepted in the company early in his or her career. This junior manager often has competing demands from a family that justifiably seeks stability and financial security. The senior manager may be especially concerned about the success of a particular project, even if it means that the junior manager is pressured into "cutting a few corners."

The problems of coercion and outside pressure. Coercion and outside pressure are very real problems experienced by managers seeking to behave morally and ethically. In the introductory case about American Cyanamid, women experienced pressure from managers and subsequently had themselves sterilized. Who was responsible for this? Was the act of sterilization knowingly and willingly done? By whom? The women argued that they were pressured by (1) the threat of the loss of their jobs, (2) the lack of alternative jobs within the organization, (3) the poor economic conditions and low job availability in the community, and (4) their need for a job and an income. Because they were pressured to take such an action, the managers, not the women employees, were responsible and should be held accountable.

In contrast, the managers argued that (1) the women were urged not to have themselves sterilized, (2) the women were provided alternatives and wage guarantees for 90 days, and (3) the company had nothing to do with the private actions taken by employees. Thus the company argued that the burden of responsibility should be assigned solely to the women.

Proximity to the action. Another aspect of moral responsibility is the extent to which a person is involved in a moral dilemma. This often involves the question of role assignments within an organization. In the Beech Nut case at the end of Part 3, the various individuals in the case included (1) managers of organizations supplying fraudulent materials to Beech Nut, (2) a manager of the research and development department of Beech Nut who sought to correct the situation, (3) the vice president and president of Beech Nut who wanted to cut costs to meet the budget, (4) a private investigator hired by another organization, (5) a person overhearing management bragging about wrongdoing at a cocktail party, and (6) government regulators. Each of these parties had different knowledge of the situation. Managers who have direct authority over an operation are more proximate to the situation than would be a manager in a distantly related staff unit like research and development. A top manager with access to the management reports is more proximate than an employee who overhears gossip at a cocktail party. Those who are more proximate also bear more responsibility for an unethical practice.

Once a person becomes aware of a moral dilemma or potential irregularity with respect to moral standards, a number of questions appear: Is it true? Should one try to find out? Is it idle gossip? Should it be reported? Am I responsible for this? To what degree? Those who are the most proximate to the situation who have authority and responsibility for decision making are normally considered the most responsible for doing something about a situation once it becomes known. However, anyone who knows about a crime has a legal responsibility to report it and thus a moral responsibility also.

CAN ORGANIZATIONS BE HELD MORALLY RESPONSIBLE?

Responsibility can be viewed from a moral and a legal perspective. *Moral responsibility* is sometimes to be reserved for humans because only humans are thought to have souls. Because business organizations do not have souls and thus cannot be judged by God nor can they be jailed, they cannot be held morally responsible. Following this line of reasoning, only individuals can be considered to have moral responsibility because only individuals as humans can be judged by the Creator.[22]

If we apply the criteria of moral responsibility to business organizations, we would explore the dimensions of knowledge and will. If information is known by managers at more than one level of authority, then it might be argued that the organization "knows" about something. The information becomes a part of the shared body of knowledge held within the organization, although the "sharing" may be limited. Also, it might be argued that once managers become knowledgeable about something, a responsibility exists. If appropriate action is not taken, there is a presumption that management willingly allowed a practice to continue. For example, if a woman is sexually harassed in the workplace and this comes to the attention of management, a legal and moral responsibility exists to take corrective action.

Legal responsibility has to do with whether a person could be held accountable for something in court. Both managers as individuals and organizations as legal persons can be held legally responsible and thus accountable for something. For example, in the insider trading scandal of Michael Milkin, a top executive of the investment banking firm Drexel, Burnham, and Lambert, the organization was held legally responsible and fined $600,000 in the case. Later Milkin was found guilty and imprisoned for the offense. Thus it is clear that organizations as legal persons and individuals can both be held legally responsible.

Can corporations have a conscience? This question was asked and answered in the affirmative by Goodpaster and Matthews.[23] They reasoned that organizations have cultures, value systems, reporting systems with collectively held information, institutional orientations that are relatively stable over time, and also codes of ethics, rules, and policies that guide behavior. Thus, they can knowingly and willingly act. The organization may not have a soul, but if its culture can preserve a collective conscience that guides behavior, then it could also be argued that moral responsibility also exists. Thus, the issue of corporate social responsibility becomes an ethical and not merely a legal concern of managers. Social responsibility is addressed in Chapter 8.

Summary

This chapter is concerned with the context of ethical behavior. Behavior is a function of moral judgments, individual integrity, courage, and organizational factors. Factual situations are interpreted according to the seriousness of the situation in terms of consequences and the inherent actions or behaviors involved. Results are predicted according to the scientific knowledge of cause-effect relationships, availability of information, and the risks and uncertainties of the situation.

Situations are also interpreted by an individual's filter of moral standards. These moral standards can be based upon individual values, religion, cultural norms, legal and social standards of behavior, and moral virtues. Moral standards are generally developed for things important to human beings; they are held independently by individuals and are not necessarily altered by changes in policies of organizations. These standards can transcend self-interest and be objective. Such moral standards in the context of business organizations are formed in areas like truthfulness, confidentiality and secrets, promise keeping and contracts, avoidance of harming others, property ownership, and fairness.

Moral standards are also influenced by the individual virtues of prudence, obedience to the law, and beneficence. Prudence encourages self-interest but not recklessness. Prudence is curbed by law and regulations and by the beneficence of caring for the dignity and welfare of other individuals.

Individuals can develop the capacity for moral reasoning by passing through six stages. Stage one of moral reasoning is based upon fear and avoiding punishment; stage two focuses on exchange driven by unbridled self-interest. In the conventional level of moral reasoning including stages three and four concerns shift to the norms of the group and then to accepting the laws of society as moral standards of behavior. In the third and highest level of moral reasoning, the individual again becomes the initiator of moral judgments but in a qualitatively different manner than is found in earlier stages. In level five, legitimacy and personal integrity and commitment are key to reasoning. In level six, internalized values and principled ethical reasoning become more important.

Organizational culture and management actions can either encourage or discourage the capacity for moral judgments of individuals. Some organizations have cultures that are characterized by authoritarians and reliance on fear and punishment to influence behavior. Some organizations emphasize external rewards and allow varying amounts of independent judgment or participation by individual employees. Other organizations have cultures characterized by decentralization, productivity through people, caring for the customer, respect for individual dignity, and empowerment.

It is important that organizational cultures, control systems, and management practices be congruent with the type of commitment employees have to the company and to the general level of moral reasoning. Incongruence can lead to overcontrol and frustration at one extreme; at the other extreme, people at lower levels of moral reasoning may be taking advantage of loosely controlled organizations.

When actions are immoral or irresponsible, the question of moral responsibility arises. The central concept of informed consent based on the dual criteria of knowledge and freedom is offered as a guide to determine moral responsibility. Knowledge is not always clear-cut because situations have risks and uncertainties and needed information is not always available. However, ignorance, particularly strategic ignorance, is not an appropriate reason to avoid responsibility. Individuals, managers, and organizations have a duty to know through testing, collecting, and distributing relevant information in a reasonable manner.

Freedom is important for establishing responsibility because a person must willingly do something to be held responsible. Organizational factors, particularly pressure and perceived coercion, moderate the degree of responsibility. Also, responsibility can be shared because of pressure, knowledge, and proximity to moral dilemmas.

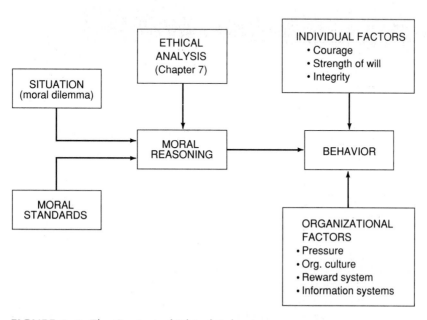

FIGURE 6–3 The Context of Ethical Behavior

Conclusions

Ethical decision making occurs within the context of factual situations, is based upon moral standards and moral reasoning, and is influenced by an individual's strength of will and by various organizational factors. Managers can improve the ethical behavior and the social responsibility of their organizations by paying close attention to the context of ethical decision making and behavior. Particular attention needs to be placed on the dominant values held by individual work groups and by the corporate culture in general. We hope this chapter provides some valuable clues about what managers might do to encourage high moral standards and how management processes and cultures can encourage rather than punish those striving to act with integrity.

The context of moral and ethical behavior is important because it influences the quality of life within organizations and within society. Also, we argue that it is basic to the corporate social performance of business and should be related to other dimensions like long-range legitimacy within society, international competitiveness, and the regulatory environment facing managers. We feel that the context of ethical behavior is a "blind spot" for most managers. Attempts to make more ethical decisions, to be more just, and to be socially responsive and responsible are likely to be ineffective without systematic consideration of the broader moral context as outlined in this chapter.

Discussion Questions

1. Briefly discuss the situational factors that influence ethical reasoning.
2. What is the source of your moral standards? Can you identify areas of conduct within which you have developed standards? Which areas are the most important? Explain.
3. What are the three levels of moral reasoning? What are the key differences between level one and level two? between level one and level three? between level two and level three?

4. Discuss the relationship between levels of moral reasoning and organizational cultures of organizations that are dominated by each of the levels.
5. Can you see any relationship between the institutional orientations discussed earlier in Chapter 1 and organizational climates characterized by the levels of moral reasoning? Explain.
6. What are the criteria for establishing moral responsibility? Apply these criteria to the American Cyanamide case at the beginning of the chapter.
7. Why do people behave in ways that are not consistent with their moral judgments about what they believe to be correct? What can or should a manager do to encourage consistent behavior?
8. How might a manager use information about the level of moral reasoning among employees to encourage ethical behavior within the organization?

Notes

1. Manuel G. Valesquez, *Business Ethics: Concepts and Cases,* 2d ed. (Englewood Cliffs, N.J.: Prentice-Hall, 1988), pp. 13–15.
2. Richard DeMaria, "Values, Decision-making, and the Rich Life," *International Journal of Value Based Management* 1, no. 2 (1988): 33–37.
3. For papers that use theology as a basis for moral standards in making business decisions, see Geoffrey P. Lantos, "An Ethical Base for Marketing Decision Making," *Journal of Business and Industrial Marketing* 2, no. 2 (Spring 1987): 11–16; Thomas F. McMahon, "The Contributions of Religious Traditions to Business Ethics," *Journal of Business Ethics* 4 (1985): 341–49; and Thomas C. Campbell, Jr., "Capitalism and Christianity," *Harvard Business Review* 35, no. 4 (July-August 1957): 37–44.
4. William C. Frederick, "Embedded Values: Prelude to Ethical Analysis," Working Paper number 446, Graduate School of Business, University of Pittsburgh, February 1981; Gerald F. Cavanagh, *American Business Values,* 2d ed. (Englewood Cliffs, N.J.: Prentice-Hall, 1984).
5. Donelson R. Forsyth, "A Taxonomy of Ethical Ideologies," *Journal of Personality and Social Psychology* 39, no. 1 (1980): 175–84, and "Individual Differences in Information Integration During Moral Judgments," *Journal of Personality and Social Psychology* 49, no. 1 (1985): 264—72.
6. Sissela Bok, *Lying: Moral Choice in Public and Private Life* (New York: Pantheon, 1978).
7. Sissela Bok, *Secrets: On the Ethics of Concealment and Revelation* (New York: Random House, 1983).

8. This section is based in part on Bong-Gon P. Shin, Larry C. Wall, and Newman S. Peery, "Adam Smith Revisited: Ethical Implications for Managerial Decision Making," *Western Illinois University Journal of Business* 1, no. 2 (Summer 1989): 73–85.

9. Adam Smith, *Theory of Moral Sentiments* (Indianapolis: Liberty Classics, 1976 [originally published in 1753]), p. 353.

10. Ibid., p. 477.

11. Ibid., p. 479.

12. Shin, Wall, and Peery, "Adam Smith Revisited," pp. 73–85.

13. Abraham H. Maslow, *Motivation and Personality* (New York: Harper and Row), 1954.

14. Clayton P. Alderfer, *Existence, Relatedness, and Growth: Human Needs in Organizational Settings* (New York: Free Press, 1972).

15. Frank Tuzzolino and Barry R. Armandi, "A Need-Hierarchy Framework for Assessing Corporate Social Responsibility," *Academy of Management Review* 6, no. 1 (January 1981): 21–28.

16. Lawrence Kohlberg, *Essays on Moral Development*, Vol. 1, *The Philosophy of Moral Development: Moral Stages and the Idea of Justice* (San Francisco: Harper and Row, 1981);

Lawrence Kohlberg, "Stage and Sequence: The Cognitive-Developmental Approach to Socialization, in D. A. Goslin, ed., *Handbook of Socialization: Theory and Research* (Chicago: Rand-McNally, 1969), pp. 347–480.

17. Gilligan, Carol, *In a Different Voice* (Cambridge, MA: Harvard University Press, 1982).

18. Amitai Etzioni, *A Comparative Analysis of Complex Organizations*, rev. ed. (New York: Free Press, 1975).

19. See Thomas Peters and Robert Waterman, *In Search of Excellence* (New York: Harper and Row, 1983); Thomas Peters, *Thriving on Chaos* (New York: Harper and Row, 1988).

20. Stephen P. Robbins, *Organizational Behavior*, 4th ed. (Englewood Cliffs, N.J.: Prentice-Hall, 1989), chap. 8.

21. Stanley Milgram, *Obedience to Authority: An Experimental View* (New York: Harper Colophon Books, 1974).

22. See Manuel G. Valesquez, "Why Corporations Are Not Morally Responsible for Anything They Do," *Business and Professional Ethics Journal* 2, no. 3 (Spring 1983): 1–18, and the opposing commentaries in the same journal.

23. Kenneth E. Goodpaster and John B. Matthews, Jr., "Can a Corporation Have a Conscience?" *Harvard Business Review* 60, no. 1 (January/February 1982: 132–41.

Discussion Case

Pizza Delivery in Less Than Half an Hour

A regional pizza chain in northern California wanted to directly compete with the Domino's Pizza chain that dominated the home delivery market in Sacramento during the 1980s. This challenging chain guaranteed in its advertisements that it would deliver any pizza in less than half an hour. To launch this growth campaign, they hired inexperienced high school students and required them to use their own cars. Many students were hired to open a number of new pizza outlets. These students took telephone orders and cooked the pizzas, while others were to deliver the pizzas. The order taking and cooking averaged approximately 20 minutes. Also, each order was mechanically clocked to maintain tight control over the 30-minute company standard.

The students were told not to speed and that they were personally responsible for the maintenance of their automobiles, for insurance, and for any traffic citations or accidents that they might experience while at work. Students were paid $.15 per mile for the use of their automobile. They were not told to notify their automobile insurance companies about their delivery activities. Thus, insurance companies were probably bearing a much higher risk than was reflected in the insurance premiums paid by the students.

If the students used their own cars, the company fleet would not have to be enlarged and thus the campaign could be immediately launched. Also, insurance expenses would be lower for the company, and if the campaign failed, it would not have an unneeded delivery fleet to dispose of.

Those responsible for delivery had ten minutes and often would drive at rates of over 50 miles per hour in residential areas. Many accidents resulted from the 30-minute guaranteed home delivery campaign. As turns were missed at high speeds, some parked cars were damaged. Some injuries occurred when neighborhood children were hit, but fortunately no deaths were attributed to student drivers. Several lawsuits were brought against the company and the student drivers. The regional pizza chain decided to abandon deliveries.

Case Discussion Questions

1. Would you take a part-time job with this company?

2. What are the moral problems in this case?
3. Who was responsible for the student driving and its consequences? Explain.
4. What should management do?

CHAPTER 7

Ethical Decision Making

CHAPTER OBJECTIVES

1. Show how considering goal accomplishment and results is used in ethical analysis.
2. Identify the various approaches to ethical decision making.
3. Develop an awareness of how moral principles can guide ethical analysis.
4. Discuss moral and legal rights and duties as an essential concern for managers striving to be ethical.
5. Offer some practical guidelines for ethical decision making.
6. Provide a conceptual framework for ethical decision making that integrates various approaches of ethical analysis into a decision-making approach.

Introduction

Executives of the Beech Nut subsidiary of Nestlé, Inc., were found guilty of selling as "100 percent pure juice" what was little more than sugared water.[1] E.F. Hutton's managers systematically wrote overdrafts that cost banks millions of dollars.[2] Drexel, Burnham, and Lambert, an investment banking firm, pleaded guilty to insider trading in the context of corporate takeovers and was fined $600 million and later declared bankruptcy. Fraudulent behavior was responsible for much of the financial disaster currently befalling the savings and loan industry. Examples abound in which executives are found to act in illegal and unethical ways.

Business ethics is concerned with trying to do the right thing in the economic sphere. Managers are trained primarily to make sound economic judgments, that is, to make those decisions that will be best for the profitability or the long-term competitiveness of the business. However, a brief review of recent news stories mentioned above quickly indicates that managers need to go beyond purely economic concerns if they are to achieve an acceptable level of business social performance. Accepting responsibility for the ethical dimension of decisions is of key importance for management decision makers. Failure to strive to be ethical can lead to a corporate culture of mistrust, fear, and low levels of commitment within the organization. Also, unethical behavior undermines the quality of society and can eventually lead to declining legitimacy of business.

Unfortunately these highly publicized examples of unethical behavior often overshadow the many times executives strive to do what they believe to be correct. Even when executives see nothing unethical in their behavior, their decisions can be questioned later on ethical and legal grounds. Decisions are often complex and have dimensions that require special analytical skills and sensitivity in identifying ethical issues. The concepts and models in this chapter are intended to introduce the basic principles of business ethics.

An example of a businessman believing that he has acted appropriately and ending up in ethical difficulties is the case of John Zaccaro, the husband of former congresswoman Geraldine Ferraro. Zaccaro, a real estate developer, was also the manager of a trust account for a retired widow. He became aware of a lucrative real estate development opportunity in which he invested much of his own money. He considered the risks to be minimal and believed the returns on this investment would far exceed any other opportunities, so he borrowed $175,000 from the widow's trust account at 12 percent interest. He then invested the borrowed funds in the real estate. He was subsequently charged with an ethical violation based upon a conflict of interest.

In his defense, Zaccaro indicated that the widow did not lose any money; on the contrary, she profited handsomely from his investment decision made on her behalf. The investment was superior than others available at the time. Following this reasoning, the decision could be judged as ethical based upon *act utilitarianism,* because the results of the action in this one-time investment decision were best for all concerned. However, he was found guilty of an unethical practice. The judge reasoned that borrowing from trust accounts for projects in which the trustee had a proprietary interest could be a temptation for the trustee to place his own financial needs above those of clients like the widow. Thus this constituted an unethical and illegal conflict of interest.

Laws are standards of conduct promulgated by legitimate authority such as legislatures, Congress, the courts, and administrative agencies. These legal standards of behavior are often based upon a type of ethical analysis called utilitarianism. *Utilitarian analysis* is ethical reasoning that seeks the greatest good for the greatest number within the society based upon the *consequences or results* of the policy. In the public sector, ethics deals largely with the issue of conflict of interest like the Zaccaro case. *Rule utilitarianism* is an approach that considers the *outcome of a rule or policy* rather than the results of a specific decision that is made once. Thus, the ethics of managing a trust fund in the Zaccaro case was based upon the likely consequences of a rule or policy rather than upon the consequences of a particular decision considered by itself.

The principle based upon rule utilitarianism relating to managing trust accounts requires that the financial interest of the manager be kept separate from those of the clients. Such a rule tends to remove the temptation of a trust account manager to place self-interests above those of clients whose interests have been entrusted to him or her. In the Zaccaro case, the investment of the widow's retirement funds would have been ethical if the widow's funds rather than those borrowed by Zaccaro himself had been invested. In this way Zaccaro would not have had a financial interest in the project.

What Is Business Ethics?

Ethics is concerned with decisions or actions of importance to human beings, specifically, with those value judgments concerning the problems of life. It is concerned with determining whether behavior is right or wrong and with whether the results of a decision are good or bad from a moral point of view. *Morality* is an organized set of value judgments about what is right and wrong in general. *Moral reasoning* is the cognitive processes by which a person makes a value judgment about right and wrong or about good and bad; this was discussed in Chapter 6.

THE MORAL IMAGINATION

Moral imagination is the thoughtful consideration that identifies areas of discretion where a manager can improve a situation by trying to do the right or ethical thing. However, use of a moral imagination does require an understanding of business ethics, high standards of behavior, and a developed consciousness within the context of economic decisions in a competitive market environment.[3]

Etzioni has suggested that the arguments in favor of moral decision making in a competitive market are as necessary and as persuasive as the theory that assumes that managers will be self-interested, shortsighted, profit maximizing, and exploitative in their behavior.[4] He provides evidence suggesting that people will sometimes act unselfishly in economic activity and are capable of moral acts. A *moral act*, according to Etzioni, is characterized by

1. An *imperative feeling* by a person that he or she must act in a certain way.
2. *Symmetry in behavior and expectations* that causes individuals to expect others to behave in a similar moral way. Symmetry involves the capacity to generalize that results in "a willingness to accord other comparable people, under comparable circumstances, the same standing or right."
3. *Intrinsic motivation* whereby a person feels good when he or she feels that the morally correct thing has been done. Intrinsic motivation involves an inner commitment that is affirmed or expressed that may be stronger than the impulse to achieve pleasure by consuming an externally available good or service. Although managers do respond to the competitive forces of the marketplace, there are many situations in which moral acts form the basis of self-control of business behavior.

Managers can feel strongly about certain standards of conduct, expect others to follow similar standards, and experience satisfaction when they have done what they consider to be the right thing. For example, Borg-Warner strives to follow the beliefs outlined in Chapter 14 so it can be a moral company. Following such beliefs might mean honoring a commitment to a customer by making an especially difficult delivery. It could mean providing fair rewards to employees when an opportunity to be exploitative exists. It could be in the construction of a tasteful corporate headquarters rather than an unsightly but less expensive structure. Also, a moral act is apparent in the way Johnson and Johnson recalled its product, Tylenol, when product tampering endangered its customers.

The professional manager is trained to achieve economic performance in business organizations. Analytical tools like market research surveys identify market opportunities, financial modeling identifies the most profitable decision alternative, and other analytical tools all seek to guide decisions to obtain the highest possible long-term economic performance. Managers are usually less prepared for considering business ethics that deal with the moral dimension of activities within organizations. Because economic performance is the key responsibility of the economic sphere, business ethics begins with the consideration of the economic and other consequences of a decision or policy. Utilitarian reasoning parallels the economic and financial decision-making practices by managers. Once the economic aspects are clearly established, business ethics should then go on to several other important questions.

Ethical analysis can be broadly divided into two ways of thinking. First, what moral *principle or rule* is the most appropriate in this case? Second, what are the *consequences* of the decisions? Those who emphasize principles and rules tend to focus on the inherent quality or principle underlying the decision. This reasoning usually leads to consideration of the rights and duties of those involved in and affected by the decision. Those who emphasize consequences are results-oriented and judge the ethics of a decision according to whether or not it accomplishes some desirable goal. This form of ethical thinking is more attuned to the concerns of utilitarian analysis. Analyses that use these two questions focus attention on very different considerations and can come to different ethical judgments.

For example, when making a promotion decision a manager could consider candidates in terms of what is likely to happen if a particular candidate is selected. Alternatively, some principle like seniority or equality could be used. To illustrate this point, Box 7–1 shows some of the distinctions and implications of these two aspects when making a promotion decision. We first consider the decision by carefully reviewing some of its consequences. Next we review a number of principles managers commonly use to guide promotion decisions.

ETHICAL ANALYSIS BASED ON RESULTS

In Box 7–1, three candidates are all well qualified for the job. This is a fairly typical decision faced by a manager, and such decisions have important ethical dimensions because they are important to the persons involved. We can use such a situation here for a preliminary analysis before introducing the more formal logic of ethics that appears later in the chapter. The two major questions are concerned with *consequences* of the promotion decision in contrast to the *moral principles* used in making the decision. The first approach to ethics focuses on results: What will happen if I do something? If what happens is good, it is considered moral or ethical to do it. If it is not good, then it is not ethical.

The other approach has to do with the *inherent act of doing.* Is it consistent with a valued moral principle? Do we follow moral principles that we believe to be important? If this is our inclination, what would be appropriate principles for guiding our promotion decision in this exercise?

The first step involves determining the answers to the promotion question: What will happen if each candidate is promoted? Which consequences should be considered? For any decision, outcomes occur along a number of different dimensions; and

---

BOX 7–1   Selection of a New Manager

Your firm is in the computer peripheral equipment business. This is a highly competitive business that requires flexibility and rapid change in new product development, high quality, and cost control. You make specialized equipment compatible with the major computer manufacturers. You have a management opening in the area of applications engineering: a department that modifies existing products either to suit the specialized interests of customers or to maintain compatibility as major vendors change their product line. This section has a history of high performance under highly competitive conditions. You have three good candidates for a job as a manager in your section. Two are from your section, and one is from a similar group in another division of the corporation.

The three candidates from which to choose are as follows:

1.   John Kragen is 62, a white male with 28 years of experience in the area, though he has the equivalent of only two years of education as an electronics technician earned through evening classes. He is well qualified for the position and is from your section. He has been loyal to the company for the last 23 years. During that period he has frequently filled the job of section manager on a temporary basis with good results and with good cooperation from the other members of the group.

It would mean much to him to have the added compensation for the next three years, because it would affect his retirement benefits significantly.

2.   Patricia Zink , age 31, is a white female with a master's in business administration from a top-ranked university. She has been a supervisor in another division for the past two years with above average results and is considered by top management to have great potential for further development. She is from another division but is known by your people as aggressive and highly ambitious. Executive management is eager to see her given new opportunities to widen her experience in career development in preparation for higher-level management responsibilities.

3.   David Bond is a black male, age 44, with a bachelor's in business administration from Middlestate University. He has been working in the section for six years. During this time he has successfully managed a number of temporary task forces involving the introduction of new product. He is well liked by his colleagues and generally regarded as a good performer. His performance appraisals have been slightly better than Patricia's evaluations. There are two other blacks in the group of twelve, one male and one female. The company is eager to show progress in its equal employment opportunity program.

sometimes there are second- and third-order outcomes resulting from the indirect consequences.

In *utilitarian analysis*, the choice that results in maximizing the happiness of the social system is the most ethical choice. In using this approach, managers have to wrestle with measurement problems and with defining what happiness is. The key idea is that ethical selections should be based upon an assessment of the best consequences resulting from the decision.

The criterion in utilitarian analysis is happiness; but as used in business, it is most often expressed in economic terms. How can the economic outcomes of a promotion decision be determined? Consequences could include (1) group morale, (2) acceptance of the new manager by the group, (3) motivation and organizational commitment by employees, (4) stability versus change in work processes, (5) the expected tenure of the new manager before having to make the decision again, (6) acceptance of the decision by top management that might indirectly lead to availability of budget and resources for special projects, and (7) group performance in terms of the overall competitive outcomes for the company.

How can these outcomes be reduced to some measure on a scale of economic or competitive performance? A major limitation of utilitarian analysis is the problem of "comparing apples and oranges," that is, measuring and comparing outcomes to determine the outcome with the most desirable consequences.

Group Morale and Acceptance of the Manager

What about group "happiness"? How happy will the group be with the decision? John is an older man aged 62, and he's taken the job before and has good rapport with the group, so his promotion should lead to high group morale and high acceptance. Patricia has been designated by upper management as on the fast track, a comer expected to develop into a future leader of the company. However, promoting her could be perceived as threatening to the group, resulting in reduced group morale and low acceptance. David is a candidate known and respected by the group, and his promotion should result in moderate to high levels of acceptance and group morale.

Top Management Support

How would top management's "happiness" be considered in this decision? Top management support would be very high for Patricia Zink. They are interested in the career of this young woman and want her to develop her general management skills quickly. On the other hand, affirmative action and correcting the injustice of discrimination is also a priority of top management. They are very interested in their affirmative action record and so top management support is high for David Bond. Support would be moderate for John Kragen because his long-term usefulness to the organization is limited to his remaining three years before retirement.

Motivation

One key result of promotion decisions is motivation. Highly motivated employees tend also to be more productive. If work group members have an opportunity to be promoted as a reward for performance, they are likely to be more highly motivated. In this case, the person with the lowest performance record is Zink, who is considered to have a lot of future potential but has not developed the skills to be a top performer in any of the positions she has previously filled. Selecting her over a person with a better performance record may have a negative impact on motivation within the work group. Also, her appointment may threaten and demoralize the work group and also reduce its motivation.

Capacity for Change

In market environments with high rates of technological change, flexibility and adaptability are key to competitive success. Organizations in these market environments need to develop the capacity for renewal. This renewal requires employees who (1) strive for self-development, (2) take risks with new ideas, technologies, and products, and (3) adapt to changing tastes expressed by customers in the market.

Suppose that this company has a successful record in a market environment where change and competitive intensity is increasing. There does not seem to be an urgency to change any of the existing practices. However, top management support for an external candidate may signal more than merely an interest in the career development of a particular individual. It may also signal the work group that the tempo for change needs to be increased. The promotion of Patricia Zink may include an expectation of change in work processes and in other things. However, if she comes in without work group support, resistance to change is more likely.

If John Kragen is promoted, he isn't likely to change anything for three years. His past performance has been successful and his promotion would sanction a continuation of those past approaches. David Bond is a respected employee in midcareer who has a successful record in new product development. Thus he has experience in managing change, would probably not be resisted by the work group, and would probably introduce a moderate amount of change.

Need to Make the Promotion Decision Again Soon

The need to make this decision again soon is a two-edged sword. If a decision is unclear, it is fortunate to have the opportunity to make it again later. If selection processes are costly and disruptive, then management may wish to avoid filling a position for a relatively short time. In this case, Zink is being rotated through several functional areas to increase her overall knowledge of the business. She is unlikely to remain for a period exceeding two years. Kragen is due to retire in three years. Bond is in midcareer and is likely at the point in his career where more stability is needed.

Decision Based on Results

Who should be promoted to the management position according to the results summarized in Table 7–1? The point of this exercise is to suggest how complicated and involved it is to systematically consider the results of a relatively routine management decision. In the last chapter on the

context of moral decision making, we began with a consideration of the situation. Understanding the situation will help us better predict the consequences of a decision. However, cause-effect relationships are not known with certainty. Also, indirect consequences of a decision, like resistance to change or perceived unfairness, can have third-order results on economic performance. Though it is difficult, we argue here that a systematic and careful analysis of the likely consequences of a decision weighed in terms of desirability is an important first step in ethical analysis. This is the key requirement of utilitarian analysis.

ETHICAL ANALYSIS BASED ON PRINCIPLES

A second approach to the promotion exercise is to try to formulate moral principles to guide the decision. Principles might include the duty (1) to reward loyalty and dedication to the organization, (2) to reward and to promote those with good performance records, (3) to promote those with seniority, (4) to promote those with the highest perceived development potential, and (5) to promote based on some concept of equal opportunity to avoid discrimination based on age, sex, race, or religion.

Table 7–1 shows a possible ranking based upon principles that are designed to be fair or consistent with some idea of duty to employees and the organization, and responsiveness to the demands of the market. In contrast to considering consequences that are not always measurable or comparable, the problem with principles is that sometimes rights and duties contradict one another.

For example, in the exercise above promotion choices based upon immediate past performance often contradict choices based upon perceptions of long-run growth and development potential. Long-term loyalty to the organization may contradict fairness if the company has an established pattern of discriminating against minority group members. Thus managers must strive to find those decision alternatives that are consistent with the most principles or are consistent with the higher or stronger duty. Unfortunately, principles do not inherently

TABLE 7–1
Using Results and Principles in Ethical Analysis of the Promotion Decision

Hypothetical Results of a Promotion Decision

Consequences	John Kragen	Patricia Zink	David Bond
Group Acceptance	High	Low	Medium
Group Morale	High	Low	High
Top Management Support	Low	High	Medium
Stability	High	Low	High
Change and Adaptability	Low	High	Medium
Need to Redo Process Soon	3 years	2–3 years	Indefinite
Competitive Capability		Indefinite for dept; high for organization	
• Short-term	High		Medium
• Long-term	Low		High

Ranking Based on Moral Principles

Principles	John Kragen	Patricia Zink	David Bond
Loyalty and Dedication	High	Unknown	High
Seniority	High	Low	Medium
Growth Potential	Low	High	High
Equal Opportunity	High (age)	High (sex)	High (race)
Previous Performance	High	Medium	High

indicate how a manager should make such a ranking or a determination.

Again, we argue here that a careful and systematic consideration of principles will increase our sensitivity and improve the ethical quality of our decisions. However, a careful ethical analysis is not likely to facilitate our decision making. On the contrary, informed choice needed for ethical responsibility is likely to always be difficult. Ethical decisions are important because they often have significant consequences for human beings and thus should not be taken lightly. They are difficult because these decisions must be made in the context of competing value systems and sometimes contradictory duties, rights, and moral principles. Last of all, ethical dilemmas pose difficulties because our understanding of their consequences are limited. In spite of the difficulties, ethical decision making is a uniquely human activity and is of the utmost importance for business social performance.

Four Dimensions of Ethical Decision Making

Business ethics is concerned with the answers to the following questions:

1. Are the *consequences* of an action or policy good or bad?
2. Does it *honor the rights* of those affected by the decision?
3. Does this decision *fulfill our duties?*

4. Are the results of the *decision fair and just* to those concerned?

Each of these questions represents a different type of ethical analysis, and has its unique analytical focus and central managerial question, as shown in Table 7–2.

The first and last questions consider the consequences of decisions, while the other two are concerned with the inherent nature of the activity or decision made by managers. The remainder of this chapter is concerned with dimensions one through three; the next chapter considers the question of fairness or justice.

Various philosophical theories of ethics have been developed over the years, and debates over the best ethical theory have gone on for centuries. Rather than review these philosophical arguments, we will selectively choose from those theories available to present what concepts seem to be the most useful for improving the ethical quality of manager-

TABLE 7–2
Dimensions of Ethical Analysis

Dimension of Ethical Analysis	Analytical Focus	Management Questions
Utilitarian	**Goal-oriented** • Social goals • Economic goals • Business goals	Which action or policy best accomplishes our goals? Which is the most profitable?
Deontological	**Rights-oriented** • Legal rights • Moral rights	Which action or policy respects the rights of those concerned?
	Duty-oriented • Contractual Duties • Obey laws • Moral duties	Which action or policy best fulfills our duties?
Economic (Distributive) Justice	**Fairness-oriented** • Market returns • Externalities	Which action or policy most fairly allocates the benefits and burdens among stakeholders?

ial decisions and practices. Our position here is that the question of ethical analysis is not an either-or proposition but rather a number of questions must be considered in a thorough ethical analysis.

There are several distinct approaches to ethics that parallel the four basic questions. Utilitarian analysis, introduced earlier in the chapter, is concerned with the first question: what is the desirability of outcomes of a management decision? Deontological analysis is concerned with the next two questions concerning rights and duties. Concepts of economic justice are concerned with the question of fairness. These dimensions of ethical analysis are outlined in Table 7–2, and subsequent sections of this chapter discuss each of these basic dimensions. After discussing each of these dimensions, an integrative model of ethical decision making for managers is presented.

Utilitarian Approaches: It's Ethical If the Results Are Good

Typically, the first question asked by a manager is about the economic consequences and/or manageability of a decision. Does it accomplish our goals? Is the action administratively workable? Can we really do it successfully? These questions are derived from the utilitarian analysis shown in Figure 7–1. As originally formulated, utilitarian approaches to ethics were concerned with the consequence that would maximize the total happiness within society. Within business, the level of analysis is usually the business, and often only those consequences experienced by the organization are considered.

Happiness is expressed in terms of the monetary or economic value of the outcomes associated with a decision or policy. As the exercise discussed earlier in the chapter shows, managers may often have an idea of the likely consequence and whether the value is positive or negative. However, managers may not be able to predict the consequences or the specific monetary value of the consequences with accuracy. If this is the case,

then utilitarian analysis may not reveal the most ethical decision with clarity.

Another example of an ethical dilemma commonly faced by some managers is a situation experienced by many electronics firms in Silicon Valley, California. The waste materials from making certain computer components are extremely toxic liquid solvents. What should the manufacturer do with these wastes? Alternatives may include (1) complying with the toxic waste disposal laws by packaging and transporting the wastes to sites approved by the Environmental Protection Agency, (2) illegally dumping the liquid waste into the sink, and/or (3) redesigning the product and/or manufacturing processes to use alternative substances.

Figure 7–1 outlines the utilitarian analysis that might be involved in the second alternative, *illegal dumping*. A complete utilitarian analysis requires a consideration of all alternatives. We are discussing only the second alternative to reveal the limitations of this form of ethical analysis considered in isolation from other approaches to ethics. The consequences of illegal dumping would be to keep production and waste management costs low. This would enable the manufacturer to charge lower prices that would moderately improve customer acceptance and might greatly improve the willingness of dealers to carry the firm's product. Because the authorities normally do not closely monitor sewage, it was perceived that the regulatory constraints were low and the likeliness of being prosecuted was also low.

A number of firms apparently used this logic in Santa Clara County, California, and decided to dump the waste down their drains. When traces of toxic wastes were detected in the water supply, county officials initiated a program of intensified surveillance and enforcement of environmental laws in 1988. The result was that several small businessmen were found to have acted illegally and were convicted of violating environmental laws. Two small businessmen in Santa Clara County were fined and sentenced to one year in jail. The possibility of these consequences were apparently not accurately considered when they made the decision.

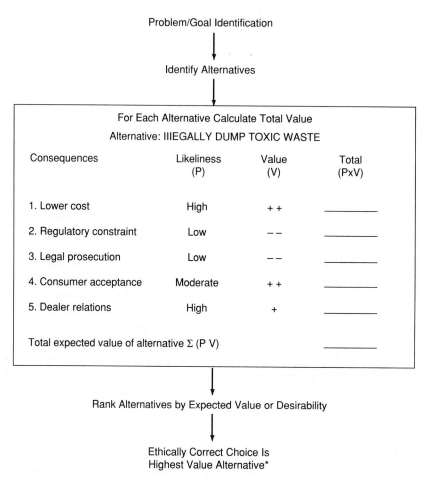

FIGURE 7–1 Utilitarian Ethical Analysis of Illegal Dumping of Toxic Waste

*Method fails if (1) unable to predict consequences accurately.
(2) unable to estimate values accurately.

Limitations of Utilitarian Analysis

This incident highlights some of the limitations of utilitarian analysis: (1) level of analysis, (2) problems of measurement and prediction, (3) violation of duties, (4) violations of rights, and (5) problems of justice. Utilitarian analysis is sometimes criticized as being the ethical approach in which the *ends justify the means.* In other words, to accomplish the worthy end of social or business goals, means are justified that disregard duties, rights, and justice.

LEVEL OF ANALYSIS

The utilitarian method outlined in Figure 7–1 considered only the consequences to the business. Originally utilitarian analysis discussed social policy using a nation, region, or community as the unit of analysis. In such an analysis, the goal was to find the social policy that would yield the greatest amount of happiness for one of those levels of analysis. Managers normally use the business itself as the level of analysis in considering decisions or policies from a utilitarian perspective. Thus the illegal dumping would be ethical from a strictly utilitarian analysis if the business was the unit of analysis. Using the community or society as the level of analysis would yield a different result. Dumping the waste into the sewer system could have resulted in the contamination of the community's water system, leading to such secondary consequences as illness and injury to the local inhabitants.

The dilemma facing a manager is to choose which consequences to include and which ones to exclude from the analysis. Typically, costs that are external to the firm are not considered. As noted in Chapter 2, an externality is a side effect of market exchange that is a type of market failure. The result of this failure is a search for alternatives to market controls that normally lead to the formation of such agencies as the EPA and the passing of laws and regulations to constrain business behavior. Another alternative would be to rely on the ethical behavior of managers. However, this would require that managers consider the external effects of their decisions when making them. Unfortunately, utilitarian analysis most frequently considers the direct consequences for the firm but often excludes consequences for the local community or others outside the business. Therefore, utilitarian analysis is a useful *beginning point* for business ethics but can easily lead to unethical decisions if used without consideration of levels of analysis beyond the business and without consideration of other questions needed for a complete ethical analysis.

PROBLEMS OF PREDICTING THE FUTURE AND MEASUREMENT

A second category of difficulties with utilitarian analysis is the issues of measurement and prediction. As the promotion example in Box 7–1 pointed out, it is not always possible to measure outcomes with precision, nor is it possible to describe such outcomes in terms of a common unit of measure. Also, in Figure 7–1, the predictions are based upon classifications of unlikely, moderately likely, and highly likely to occur. These classifications of probability are often based upon a manager's subjective assessment of the situation. In the

Santa Clara County case, the subjective assessment of several managers was inaccurate in terms of both the likeliness of detection and the severity of the fines and jail sentences that were, in fact, the consequences.

VIOLATION OF DUTIES

Utilitarian analysis does not consider the rights of those affected by decisions or policies, nor does it consider the duties of those making decisions. Utilitarian analysis could lead to an "ethical" decision not to comply with the legal duty to obey toxic waste laws if the expected financial consequences were greater if the laws were ignored. For example, some companies have actually violated environmental regulations because the assessed fines were less than the increased cost to the business if it had complied.

Defenders of utilitarian approaches usually say the problem of violation of legal duties can be solved merely by increasing the penalties or fines and/or increasing the budgets of enforcement agencies so that it is unlikely that a violation can go undetected. Thus, changing the law and/or increasing the resources devoted to enforcement could cause the expected negative consequences of violating the law to be greater than the costs of complying with the law. Such a change in public policy would make the violation unethical by utilitarian standards. The ethical decision resulting from utilitarian analysis would be to violate the law when the consequences are minimal and to comply with the law when the penalties are severe enough.

VIOLATIONS OF RIGHTS

Do citizens of a community have the right to safe drinking water? Most people would believe that safety is an inherent right. Is it always ethical to honor another person's rights or to avoid harming another person? Utilitarian analysis would argue that it depends upon the value of the costs versus the costs of the benefits of the action. Thus, utilitarian analysis might conclude that behavior that results in impure or toxic water could be ethical. If the damages or costs of health care for a few citizens who suffer from toxic water are less than the overall benefits resulting to the community from the competitive business operations leading to the dumping, then the dumping of toxic wastes into the water supply would be ethical.

The *law of torts* is concerned with the recovery of damages by those who are harmed by the unreasonable or negligent actions of others. Damages awarded by the court often have two components: (1) payment for the economic value of the harm experienced, and (2) *punitive damages* designed to punish and to discourage socially undesirable behavior. A utilitarian approach would increase the punitive damages, that is, the negative consequences for undesirable behavior so that it is high enough to discourage actions that undermine the total happiness of society.

As in the case of duties, there is no inherent ethical reason for honoring the rights of others in utilitarian analysis. If the consequences of violating a persons rights or of harming another person are economically beneficial relative to the costs incurred if another person's rights were honored, then utilitarian analysis would conclude that it is ethical to violate another person's rights. If such behavior is to be considered unethical within the context of utilitarian ethical analysis, the punitive damages for violating a person's rights or for harm would have to be sufficiently high to exceed the costs of avoiding harm to others.

UTILITARIAN ANALYSIS CAN LEAD TO UNFAIR RESULTS

Another limitation of utilitarian analysis is that it is concerned only with the total or average consequences within a social system of an act or a rule. Utilitarian analysis usually involves (1) selecting a level of analysis, (2) measuring the total value of the costs and benefits associated with each decision alternative, and (3) concluding that the alternative whose benefits most exceed the costs is ethical. Justice or fairness of the distribution of the various costs and benefits among the population is not considered. The next chapter considers the

question of economic justice or fairness concerned with patterns of distribution of the benefits and burdens of a decision. Under what circumstances is inequality justified? Under what circumstances is inequality fair?

In the toxic waste dumping illustration, some members of the community may use bottled water and thus not be affected by the toxic residues in the water supply. Others may have to rely on the impure water for drinking and suffer adverse health effects. Those doing the dumping are likely to benefit from the dumping more than the population in general. Is this fair? Again, this question of justice is beyond the scope of utilitarian analysis.

Deontological Ethical Analysis: It Is Right If the Decision Is Consistent with Ethical Principles

The second major form of ethical analysis is deontological analysis. Deontology is concerned with the study of moral obligation; in Greek, its root word is "duty." However, duties are more often than not connected with the concept of rights; a person has a duty not to harm another and the other person has a corresponding right not to be harmed. A person has a right to an education and someone else is responsible for providing that education. Thus, *deontological ethical analysis* is concerned with correct behavior in terms of fulfilling one's duties, honoring the rights of others, or following some higher moral principle thought to be important. Some theories of social and economic justice are based on some moral principle that has been derived from the notion that persons within a society have an inherent right to some share of the available benefits.

Figure 7–2 shows how the process of deontological ethical analysis is done. It usually begins with an ethical problem or moral dilemma constraining one's accomplishing a goal. However, the basis for determining whether something is ethical or not using deontological ethical analysis is quite different from utilitarian analysis. In deontological analysis, something is ethical if it is consistent with some moral principle; it does not consider the consequences of an act as the basis for determining whether or not it is ethical. If the action is consistent with the moral principle, then it is considered ethical. If not, then the action is unethical.

Most ethical principles used in deontological analysis relate to the fulfillment of duties or to not violating the rights of another person. In this approach, if a manager has only one decision alternative, action, or policy and it is consistent with all duties and rights, it is clearly ethical. If several alternatives exist that are all consistent with duties

and rights, then all could be considered ethical. In this situation the "tie breaker" in the decision could be based upon some other criterion relating to the consequences of the action or some aesthetic preference of the manager.

Sometimes a manager has a multiple and internally inconsistent set of duties, as the promotion decision in Box 7–1 illustrates. Also, sometimes the same decision will affect the rights of different people differently, or the honoring of one right often makes it difficult or impossible to honor another right. In this case, the manager facing the moral dilemma is forced to place one duty or right in a position of more importance than another. For

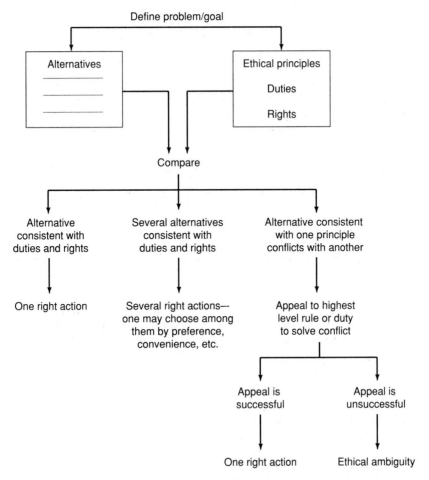

FIGURE 7–2 Deontological Ethical Analysis

BOX 7-2   The Case of the Surprise Bid

Nancy Alright was working for a developer who specialized in building shopping malls. A large project in Boston involved collecting a number of sealed bids from competing construction firms for a new mall development. The construction companies were to submit their sealed bids that included their offer to construct the mall for a stated price within a prescribed period. The bids were due at the developer's office by 3:00 P.M. on the scheduled day. It was the stated policy that the project would go to the eligible contractor submitting the lowest bid. At 3:00 P.M. she collected all the sealed bids that had been submitted, tabulated the results on a note pad, and showed them to the manager.

Nancy Alright's manager, who was not the owner of the development firm, took the bids and

the note, quickly scanned the list. He expressed surprise when he saw that the New Boston Construction Company had offered a bid that was significantly higher than the lowest bidder. He then took the package of bids whose seals had now been broken and the note pad with the rankings to his office. A moment later he returned with a sealed manilla envelope and asked Nancy to deliver the envelope personally to the office manager at New Boston, who was a friend of his. Also, he said not to announce the results of the bid and to keep the delivery a secret.

Two weeks later the project was awarded to the New Boston Construction Company at a bid price that was slightly lower than the bid that had been lowest at the official bid opening.

example, consider the disguised situation (in which all names have been changed) shown in Box 7–2.

What should Alright have done? Her supervisor's request was consistent with a number of her duties. He supervisor often asked her to make deliveries of plans and technical specifications to potential project bidders at his request as part of her normal duties. She was also required to keep the company's private business matters confidential. However, the manager's request was not consistent with a number of other duties. The company policy was to award projects to the lowest acceptable bidder. Also, the sealed bids were confidential and were not to be disclosed to competing construction companies before the awarding of the project. There was a rule against allowing any contractor to change the company bid without affording a similar opportunity to all other bidders. Postbid negotiation was inconsistent with the policy and philosophy of sealed bidding and should be done only if extenuating circumstances warranted. No such circumstances were apparent in this case.

From the deontological analysis outlined in Figure 7–2, it appears that the alternative of delivering the bid to a competitor and keeping the matter secret was consistent with the first set of duties and inconsistent with the second set of duties outlined above. Thus, Alright needs to appeal to the highest-level rule or duty to resolve her ethical dilemma. Which principle or duty should be considered the highest priority? Is the appeal successful? In this situation, such an appeal would probably be intellectually successful in that it should be clear that it is unethical for her boss to make such a request. Is it also unethical for her to obey him?

Chapter 6 suggests that moral and ethical responsibility should be determined from informed consent, that is, from whether a person knowingly and willingly performed some action. Nancy Alright may have a personal loyalty to her manager that makes the dilemma personally ambiguous. Also, the negative consequences of not following his order could lead to her dismissal. She was asked to deliver a sealed package; she may have suspected what its contents were, but she was not sure.

What is the culture within the organization? Should she report this incident to higher management? Is the procedural due process of the organization fair? Does the corporate culture of the development business encourage honesty and fair play? Does the organization value obedience of supervisors above following company policy? What is the culture of ethical behavior within this company? These questions, introduced in Chapter 6, increase the difficulty of doing what one feels to be ethical and may also cause the correct ethical decision to seem unclear. Managers must rely on their own understanding, personal integrity, and strength of purpose to guide their behavior. Organizational culture and the level of moral reasoning that a manager uses are also factors in influencing ethical behavior.

Duties

LEGAL DUTIES

Duties are legal or moral obligations. *Legal duties* of concern to managers generally include complying with existing laws and regulations and with fulfilling obligations set forth in contracts. Legal requirements are often well defined and compliance is enforced by the regulatory agencies within the government and by the court system. Thus, from an ethical perspective, it can be argued that it is ethical to obey the law and unethical to disobey it. Also, it is a moral and ethical responsibility to fulfill one's duties as set forth in legally binding contracts. It is presumed that both parties voluntarily entered into a contract with full knowledge and thus have agreed upon their respective duties outlined in the agreement.

Can a Law Ever Be Immoral?

Could it ever be one's duty to disobey the law? Chapter 6 discussed the six stages of moral reasoning. In stage five, the concept of legitimacy becomes important for one's self-definition of morality. At stage six, a person's personal philosophy and internalized moral principles define his or

her conceptions of both duty and right. Thus the possibility of civil disobedience as a moral duty becomes evident in stages five and six of moral reasoning.

For example, in Nazi Germany the law required the reporting of Jews so their property could be confiscated, and it was known that once reported, the person "disappeared." In South Africa, it was unlawful for a black person to supervise a white person. Before 1955, it was unlawful in many areas within the United States for black persons to sit in the front of a bus, to use public rest rooms, or to eat in many restaurants.

Such examples raise the question concerning the priority of legal and moral duties. Some argue that it is an inviolable ethical duty to obey the laws. A person at stage five or six of moral reasoning would question this duty if laws were clearly unjust or immoral. Similarly, a person may have an employment contract with a firm and thus have a legal duty to obey company policies and the directives from his or her supervisor. Sometimes policies and directives are unfair or perceived as immoral.

The Philosophy of John Locke

A stable society and reliable business practices depend upon the behavior that follows the law. Thus, if one does not like the law or feels it is wrong or immoral, there is another duty to get involved in the political process to change or correct that law. However, such a derivative duty is normally legal only in a democracy. What is one's obligation to obey the law in an unjust or immoral society?

One answer to this question is found in the U.S. Declaration of Independence, signed in 1776. This document was based upon the philosophy of John Locke, who argued that citizens have a moral duty to rebel against a king who violates the property rights of the people.[5] According to Locke, property was created by persons before government appeared. To protect property rights, a social contract was formed that established government. Thus, it was a duty to rebel against a king who violated property rights because property rights were considered to precede and to have priority over government. A careful reading of the U.S. Declaration of Independence reveals a list of wrongful disregard of property rights by King George of England that were used to justify civil disobedience and the Revolutionary War in 1776. Thus, the questioning of the legitimacy of both law and government has a long history in the United States, and this tradition has continued.

The civil rights movement of the 1950s and 1960s challenged racial discrimination in public facilities, transportation, education, and employment. Opponents argued that because business was privately owned, the right of private property could be used as a justification for discrimination. However, civil rights advocates argued that human rights had precedence over property rights, and thus they had a moral duty to passively resist laws believed to be illegitimate.

Normally it is a legal and moral duty to obey the laws. Public policy processes in a just society should strive to insure that laws are moral and based upon the inspiration of the cultural sphere that is the custodian of values and ideals within society. It is no accident that many of the leaders of the civil rights movement in the United States were members of the clergy. These leaders in the cultural sphere of society uphold values and seek to inspire and to guide the political sphere that was, in turn, responsible for validating and protecting the rights of citizens. Civil and human rights were first asserted as moral rights within the cultural sphere. Such assertions found their way into the political process, and after considerable debate and controversy are ultimately sanctioned into law within the political sphere.

In just societies with relatively open political processes, unjust laws can be removed and legitimate laws developed. In unjust societies with institutionalized immoralities, it can be argued that moral duties have priority over laws found to be unjust where social reform is not possible. One dilemma facing managers of international organizations is that cultural norms vary, as do political processes from country to country. Thus, standards of employee rights, use of public accommodations like transportation and lodging, and standards with respect to payments of public officials vary.

The questioning of the moral legitimacy of laws can lead to political and social instability, and action based upon such questioning cannot be taken lightly. Such questioning may be based upon higher levels of moral reasoning or upon lower-level impulses. Questioning society's laws is always likely to be controversial. However, as noted above, it has occurred historically in the American Revolutionary War, in the civil rights movement in the United States of the 1960s, and in the democracy movement in eastern Europe during the 1980s. These movements brought radical changes to business practices and raised many legal and ethical questions. In these cases, a manager's concept of moral duty and respect for morally based rights may serve as a steadier compass to guide behavior than the current status of the law within countries undergoing rapid and controversial change.

SOURCES OF MORAL DUTIES

Moral duties are obligations based upon some philosophical concept or theological principle. For example, a precept of Islam is to give alms to the poor; thus it is a religious duty to contribute to the poor. Also, usury is forbidden by Islam; thus there is a duty not to charge interest on loans. In the Judeo-Christian tradition, keeping the sabbath is a religious duty. Thus, some believe there is a duty not to operate a business on Sunday. Such moral duties parallel legal duties in that religions often have well-established rules of behavior. Because there is a duty to follow the rules of the religion, the duties that follow from this are explicit, identifiable, and may not be as subject to debate as duties based upon personal philosophy.

However, rules vary in different cultures and with different religious traditions. Thus, managers need to develop some "inner guidance" based upon personal philosophy or religious values that can provide a stable basis for moral and ethical behavior and yet accommodate the increasing diversity with which managers in internationalized, highly competitive markets must deal. As noted above, a *moral act* is normally based on an inner commitment to what one personally believes to be proper.

Personal integrity requires that people live in a manner consistent with their inner beliefs. A person without integrity is usually labeled as such when it is believed that he or she is violating his or her inner value system that leads to ethically inconsistent and opportunistic behavior. Thus it could be argued that one has a moral duty to maintain integrity by doing what one believes to be right. Unfortunately, such an admonition may not always help managers identify their duty because inner convictions among people are often inconsistent, just as religious practices vary.

KANT'S CATEGORICAL IMPERATIVE

Philosophers have sought to use intellectual inquiry to discover an ethical basis for duties and rights. The most commonly accepted philosophical formulation of ethics is found in the work of Immanuel Kant.[6] The point of departure of such inquiry is usually the principle of the commonality of the human condition. Kant begins by considering that human beings are capable of rationality and are entitled to dignity. Because of this rationality it is possible to construct moral principles consistent with the shared human condition and thus the possibility of universal and reasonable agreement over moral principles.

These moral or ethical principles would have an a priori logic much like mathematics. Moral principles should be the same for all people, just as a law of mathematics or science equally applies to all. Because of human rationality, human beings are capable of independent judgment and thus are initiators of their own morality and deserving of a measure of dignity. Also, as rational human beings capable of independent thought guided by understanding, obedience to the principles of morality come from self-imposed acceptance.

These ideas that Kant derived from the consideration of the human condition of rationality were formulated into a *categorical imperative* that, he argued, was a law that served as a supreme principle of morality. He had three formulations of the categorical imperative that were internally consistent but focused on different implications derived from considering the rationality of humanity. These three formulations of the categorical imperative were as follows:

1. *Universality.* "Act only according to that maxim by which you can at the same time will that it should become a universal law."
2. *Consider persons as ends and not means.* "Act so that you treat humanity, whether in your own person or in that of another, always as an end and never as a means only."
3. *Autonomy or freedom of the will.* "Act only so that the will through its maxims could regard itself at the same time as universally law giving."

Lying and the Categorical Imperative

These three formulations of the categorical imperative suggest that an act is ethical if and only if it (1) can be applied universally to all, (2) considers persons as ends, and (3) supports or encourages autonomy and freedom of the individual. For example, consider the practice of lying. It would be ethical for me to lie if I were willing for the practice to be universal. Because the consequences of universal lying would be destructive to society and it would not be reasonable for me to allow others to lie to me, it would not be rational to condone it. Similarly, the practice of manipulating another person through lying would serve the purposes of the liar, but would not be consistent with the interest of the person to whom the lie was told. The person would be considered as an object to be manipulated, as a means to a personal end, rather than as an end in him- or herself.

Similarly, because truthful information is important for the exercise of sound judgment, lying would likely not be conducive to the development of independence and freedom. Thus, the three formulations of the categorical imperative drawing from the criteria of universality, human dignity, and freedom based upon the rationality of humanity could be used to derive the moral principle of truthfulness.

In summary, intellectual inquiry such as the philosophy of Immanuel Kant has been used to derive moral principles. The categorical imperative appeals to the common rationality of humanity to adopt a supreme moral principle to define ethical principles, duties, and rights to guide behavior. Once such moral principles are adopted, then a behavior or policy is considered ethical based upon its consistency with the formal rule rather than on the basis of its consequences. This is the key distinction between utilitarian ethical analysis and deontological approaches.

MORAL DUTIES, RIGHTS, AND THE LAW

The moral principles developed in the cultural sphere of society by theologians and philosophers often are legitimized through the public policy process and institutionalized into law. Because the key role of the political sphere is to protect the rights of people and to insure justice, the development of law often focuses on generally accepted duties and rights. Table 7–3 provides a list of duties and rights that most religions and societies have adopted. They embody values that are also consistent with the formulations of the categorical imperative outlined above. They assume that as rational beings, we all have a certain human dignity and deserve respect that is facilitated by duties and rights that reflect certain moral values.

These moral values include the positive duties of (1) self-development, (2) truthfulness, (3) promise keeping, and (4) confidence keeping, and the negative duties of (5) not harming others, (6) not coercing others, and (7) some concept of fair play.

TABLE 7–3
Duties, Rights, and the Law

Duties	Rights	Law
Self-development	Self-development and self-expression	Bill of Rights Civil Rights Geneva Convention
Truth Telling (not lying)	To be truthfully informed	Laws against fraud and deceptive advertising
Promise Keeping	Fulfilled agreements	Contract law
Confidence Keeping	Confidentiality of Secrets Right to privacy	Laws covering professional–client relationships and privacy
Not Harming Others	Not to be harmed	Tort law
Not to Coerce	Freedom of choice	Laws against extortion "Cooling off" laws
Fair Play	Fair and open competition	Civil rights law Antitrust law

Self-development

This duty suggests it is necessary to be personally responsible for one's career and for developing one's capacity for rationality, independent judgment, and freedom. This implies that a manager should take personal responsibility for his or her own career, for relationships with other persons, and for developing the capacities required for mental and physical health, and for the personal values that guide his or her ethical behavior.

The first virtue discussed by Adam Smith in his *Theory of Moral Sentiments* was prudence based upon self-interested behavior. Universally applied, this virtue is one of the assumptions needed for market competition. In the Christian tradition, believers were admonished to "Love one another as you love yourself." The key idea is that it is first necessary to be concerned for oneself before community relationships based upon mutual love and respect can be a reality. In psychology, it is generally considered that self-acceptance is a prerequisite for healthy relationships with others.

Truthfulness

Because of our shared human condition, we also should respect the other person as we respect ourself. According to the idea of self-development, it is a duty to consider self-interests by learning about agreements before one enters into them. Also, one expects others to consider their interests when interacting with us in an interpersonal relationship or in an economic exchange. Because it is difficult for either party to consider self-interest without being knowledgeable, access to truthful information is needed. Thus it is argued that people have a duty not to misinform or not to misrepresent. This moral principle is institutionalized in laws against fraud and deceptive advertising.

The counterpoint to the duty of truthfulness is a right to be informed. If there is equally available knowledge, then the right to be informed is balanced by a duty not to misinform. However, if there is an imbalance such as the market failure of asymmetrical information discussed in Chapter 2, there could be a duty not only not to misinform but an extension of this duty to provide information not readily available to the other party. For example, the duty to provide information is reflected in laws that require corporations to publish financial statements that inform potential investors about their financial situation. Such financial reporting of information is considered necessary so that investors who buy stocks can exercise informed choices, even though they may not have personal knowledge of a company that is issuing stock for sale.

Promise Keeping

The duty to keep promises suggests that once a person has made an agreement, there is a moral responsibility to fulfill it. Also, there is a corresponding right to have the agreement fulfilled. The *law of contracts* has developed within every society to define and to institutionalize the principle of promise keeping. Also, one informal measure of a person's integrity is the degree to which he or she keeps commitments and fulfills agreements.

Confidence Keeping

Confidence keeping is concerned with the keeping of secrets and with the issue of privacy. Some professional-client relationships are considered privileged such as the communications between lawyers, CPAs, doctors, priests, or therapists and their clients. Because it is important for a patient, a client, or a church member to be open and honest if he or she is to obtain useful and needed help, such relationships are privileged. Otherwise, mistrust or fear that disclosed secrets would lead to harm rather than aid would exist.

Trade secrets are also sanctioned by the law. Secrets are important for interpersonal relationships in general because keeping confidences builds trust. However, some secrets are more important than others, as the incident concerning Nancy Alright implied in Box 7–2.

Not Harming Others

Respect for the dignity of others implies caring for their well-being. The minimum for caring is avoiding harm to them. This moral principle is institutionalized in *tort law*. As discussed in Chapter 6,

Adam Smith's *Theory of Moral Sentiments* suggested that the second virtue needed for society was justice and the third beneficence. In his framework, the justification for the government's protection of the rights of individuals is to prevent one person from harming another. The obedience to laws served to secure the public safety from unfettered self-interest.

However, Smith also argued that as a person matures, the virtue of beneficence is developed. Beneficence, or the positive virtue of caring for the needs of another out of love or respect, was not a legally enforceable duty. Rather caring for another's needs out of beneficence is voluntarily done out of inner conviction as a moral act.

Not to Coerce

This duty is based upon the respect for the autonomy and freedom of persons. Rationality requires informed free choice. Market competition is based upon voluntary and rational exchange. Coercion, or pressure that interferes with the exercise of free choice, thus violates the categorical imperative and a basic principle of market competition. Unfortunately, the distinction between effective sales effort and unfair pressure is not always clear. Thus, many states have laws that allow for a three-day "cooling off" period for such purchases as an automobile or a home. These laws allow either party to change his or her mind any time during some established period without penalty. Also, laws making extortion a criminal offense serve to sanction the legal duty not to coerce.

Fair Play

Some concept of fair play is found in virtually every society and every legal system. Though cynics have often said that everything is fair in love and war, expressions of fair play are found in sports, economic activity, and most human relationships. Discrimination on the basis of race is unfair because it arbitrarily excludes certain people from participating in economic activities. Thus, civil rights laws enforce fair play by prohibiting discrimination. Similarly, antitrust laws make certain anticompetitive behavior illegal because they violate the moral principle of fair play.

Rights

A right is an entitlement or a claim to something. Rights often parallel the concept of duties and can also be based upon legal sanctions or moral claims, as outlined in Table 7–2. Legal rights are entitlements that have been sanctioned by public policy and are protected by the government through actions of regulatory agencies and the courts. Like moral duties, moral rights are also based upon some intuitive understanding of the shared condition or experience of humanity.

Moral rights are claims to entitlements rising out of shared experience of a problem and are often expressed as a philosophical or theological statement. The shared values and understanding of moral rights become assertions that find their way into the political sphere as claims for entitlements by individuals or groups within society. Some claims are sanctioned by a public policy process and find their way into law; other claims remain controversial and can be debated for decades before any resolution in law occurs. For example, the freedom of religion was a moral right asserted early in the history of the United States. It is sanctioned in law by the Constitution. In contrast, the rights to medical care and minimal housing, seen by many as moral rights, have been the subject of much public debate for the past several decades.

LEGAL RIGHTS

In the United States, the first ten amendments to the Constitution is the Bill of Rights. Constitutional law defines these rights and how they apply in practice. The public policy debate over rights results in continual changes in the legal limits, interpretations, and applications of the extent to which various rights are sanctioned by the law. For example, the Constitution protects the individual from undo search and seizure that forms the basis for the legal right to privacy. The right of privacy has undergone much redefinition with the advent of electronic technology and telecommunications.

People are concerned about information regarding their private lives that might be damaging if it were in the wrong hands or were used inappropriately. Thus, businesses that have personnel files, credit information, and/or information about purchasing patterns are regulated by privacy laws.

STAKEHOLDER RIGHTS

A stakeholder is any person affected by a decision made by a business. Stakeholders are protected by the laws governing contracts that legally enforce agreements and by tort law, which protects their right not to be harmed or damaged by business activity. Customers also have a legal right to a safe product, to truthful advertising, and to be informed about the potential dangers of products or services. Employees have a right not to suffer from discrimination, a right to a safe work environment, to fair play in employment decisions, and to a measure of privacy. Stockholders and investors have a right to a fair return on their investment, a right to management who serves as responsible agents on their behalf, and a right to be accurately informed about the financial results achieved by companies offering securities for sale. Community members may have a right not to have their water supply polluted through the dumping of toxic waste. These legal and moral rights are discussed in Part 5.

Our purpose here is not to review comprehensively all rights established by law, which is beyond the scope of this chapter. Our point is merely that legal rights are legally and constitutionally based, the scope and interpretation of rights change over time, and it is a responsibility of business to be aware of the rights of those affected by a decision. It is both a legal and a moral duty to honor rights, and thus an analysis of rights is a critical stage in ethical analysis.

POSITIVE AND NEGATIVE RIGHTS

A *negative right* is the right not to be interfered with. Such rights have historically been political or civil and have been constitutionally based. Negative rights were based upon concepts of individual freedom and human dignity, and were designed to curb the arbitrary use of political power. People claimed the right to free expression to speak out against government policies or social injustices. Freedom of speech is a negative right in the sense that one has the duty not to interfere with the free expression of another. Other negative rights are concerned with freedom of religion, association, and privacy. These rights are protection by negative proscriptions against interference by others. Americans value such rights as civil or human rights, and there is general agreement that such rights should be legally protected by the government.

Positive rights are entitlements to receive some good or service or to share in the use of something. Unlike negative rights that tend to be political in their origins, the concern of positive rights tends to be more economic in nature. For example, such moral rights as the rights of the homeless to public housing, the right to medical care, the right to education, and the right to a job or at least the right not to be wrongfully discharged are all examples of positive rights. Consensus concerning these rights does not yet exist, and the controversial public policy debate is continuing.

Every right has a corollary duty, as Table 7–3 suggested. The right not to interfere with someone's negative right has social consensus and normally does not cost the person with the duty very much. Positive rights are more troublesome. If someone asserts that he or she has a right to a shelter, who has the duty or responsibility to provide it? If someone has a right to a job, who has the duty to provide the job? Positive rights as a social issue are relatively new historically, and the legal sanctioning of such rights calls for major redefinitions of the role of government as well as the responsibility of business.

Justice

Justice is concerned with the fairness with which the benefits and burdens resulting from a decision, activity, or policy made by managers are distributed. Often those who benefit from a business activity do not pay for all of the costs involved. For example, Chapter 2 indicated that one of the market failures involved side-effects or outcomes that were external to a particular transaction. An airport located in a particular area may benefit travelers and airlines, while the property owners nearby may suffer devaluation of their homes because of the proximity of the airport.

Consumers may benefit from low prices from offshore production, while factory employees lose their jobs when the plant is closed. It may have been closed because management failed to make investments to modernize the plant, forced wage concessions to reduce labor costs when the plant became noncompetitive, and eventually relocated the plant overseas despite the hard work of employees and the wage concessions granted.

Justifications made for the distribution of economic goods and services have been based upon property rights, relative merit, the effect of a decision on the poor and needy, upon equality, and upon the needs of those affected by the decision. Different stakeholders of an organization such as suppliers, customers, employees, owners, and community members make different claims based upon different justifications. It is an ethical task of managers to consider their decisions in light of the consequences experienced by the various parties who have a justifiable interest. Concepts of economic justice within this perspective are discussed in Chapter 8.

An Integrative Model of Ethical Decision-making

As discussed above, the key dimensions of ethical analysis include (1) the desirability of consequences, (2) honoring the legal and moral rights of those affected by a decision, (3) fulfilling duties, and (4) the fairness of the distribution of the benefits and burdens of a decision outcome. These four dimensions are the concern of utilitarian analysis, deontological analysis, and justice. Rather than

debate which of these approaches are the most appropriate for business ethics, we offer the integrative model of ethical decision making outlined in Figure 7–3. This model incorporates each of the major dimensions of ethical analysis that have been discussed previously in this chapter. Clearly ethical decisions accomplish the economic goals of the business, fulfill its moral and legal duties, honor the rights of stakeholders, and are fair in terms of the distribution of the benefits and burdens of the decision.

Consider the Poletown case at the beginning of Chapter 1. Was it ethical for the City of Detroit to condemn the property of the residents of Poletown to make room for a new "greenfield" plant for General Motors? The ethics of this decision could be analyzed using the integrative model outlined in Figure 7–3. First, was the decision economic? Did the consequences contribute to the greater happiness of Detroit? The City of Detroit weighed the economic benefits of employment, maintaining the tax base of the city, and overall benefits to the standard of living within the city against the loss of homes by Detroit. Assuming the plant would be economically successful, the Poletown decision would be ethical in terms of utilitarian analysis.

Did the Poletown decision violate the rights of the residents of Poletown? The city used the legally established due process for condemning land for public purpose. They were the elected officials of the citizens of the city and had the responsibility for governing the city on behalf of residents. The property rights of the residents of Poletown were honored in that residents were paid the appraised value for their property. Thus it was found by the supreme court of the state that the legal rights of the residents of Poletown were not violated.

Did the residents of Poletown have moral rights not protected by the law? Many of the residents objected to the destruction of their church. They objected to having to leave the homes their families had occupied for generations. They objected to being deprived of their neighborhood, which was the basis for their cultural experience. Although the supreme court of the state resolved the issue of legal rights, the matter of moral rights of the for-

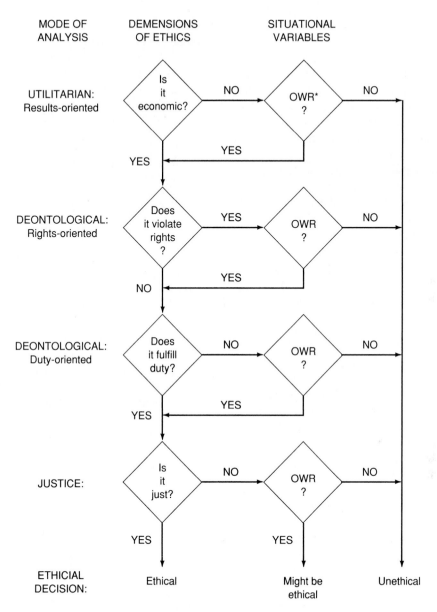

MODE OF ANALYSIS — DEMENSIONS OF ETHICS — SITUATIONAL VARIABLES

UTILITARIAN: Results-oriented
Is it economic? — NO → OWR*? — NO
YES
YES

DEONTOLOGICAL: Rights-oriented
Does it violate rights? — YES → OWR? — NO
NO
YES

DEONTOLOGICAL: Duty-oriented
Does it fulfill duty? — NO → OWR? — NO
YES
YES

JUSTICE:
Is it just? — NO → OWR? — NO
YES
YES

ETHICIAL DECISION:
Ethical — Might be ethical — Unethical

*OWR = overwhelming reason in situation

FIGURE 7–3 Integrative Model for Ethical Analysis

SOURCE: Adapted from Gerald F. Cavanaugh, Dennis I. Moberg, and Manuel Velasquez, "The Ethics of Organizational Politics," *Academy of Management Review*, 6, no. 3 (1981): 368.

mer residents of Poletown continues to be seen as ambiguous by many.

General Motors was able to give a concession that allowed an historical cemetery to remain; everything else had to be cleared. Did GM really need the room for expansion and parking? Did it have to have the standardized "greenfield" design for an efficient production facility? Could or should it have been more flexible? Did its inflexibility amount to a violation of the moral rights of the former residents? Or was this just a matter between the elected officials of the City of Detroit and the residents of Poletown?

What duties were involved? City officials considered their duties to the citizens of Detroit to be greater or more important than duties to a particular neighborhood. General Motors considered its duty to be competitive and stated its conditions to the city government. It was fulfilling duties to its stockholders and customers. Did it also have duties to the residents of Poletown? Legally, the answer is no. Morally, the question of duty is debatable.

Was the removal of the residents of Poletown fair so that a new General Motors production plant could be located in Detroit? Citizens of Detroit were provided employment, the city maintained its tax base so that public services could be paid for, General Motors was able to obtain economic efficiency with a model plant, and the residents of Poletown lost their neighborhood but did receive the appraised value for their homes. Residents, as property owners, were compensated with the appraised value of their property plus a relocation allowance. Many considered the results of the Poletown decision fair or just. Some residents considered it unfair.

Conclusions about the Poletown decision from the perspective of the decision makers in city government using the integrative model of ethical analysis might be

1. had positive economic consequences
2. respected the legal rights of the residents of Poletown and the city of Detroit
3. was consistent with the duties implicit in the role of city government trying to achieve a

favorable economic climate so that the culture of the city could prosper
4. the residents of Poletown were fairly compensated for the loss of their property.

The Poletown case could also be analyzed from the perspective of decision makers within General Motors. Here the area of most intense controversy was the relative inflexibility of GM in obtaining its locations requirements, as suggested above. The decision appeared to be economically beneficial to the firm; it was dealing with city officials and was not directly involved with Poletown residents, and GM was acting within its legal rights. It did not have a legal duty to be more flexible; but many feel it had a moral duty to use its imagination to be more responsive to the divergent needs of everyone involved. The results may have been unfair to some. Thus, the actions of General Motors may not have been clearly unethical, nor were they clearly ethical. This was a very difficult decision with some ethically ambiguous dimensions. It was argued by some that the moral rights of the people of Poletown were violated and city officials and the managers within General Motors had a greater duty to the residents of Poletown.

Conclusions

The Poletown case illustrates how the integrative model outlined in Figure 7–3 should help the decision maker make better ethical decisions. However, many important ethical decisions will continue to be difficult and ambiguities will remain. This comes with the territory of being a responsible decision maker. The use of this model should help sensitize managers to ethical considerations, provide some criteria for making more ethical decisions, and help to resolve some, but not all, ethical dilemmas. Considerable individual judgment will always be required in ethical decision making.

Ethical decision making requires careful consideration of several dimensions. The age-old debates between those in competing philosophical schools will not serve the practicing managers well. The key is not to consider only the economic and social consequences or to consider only one's legal duties when making a decision. Though most managers have an inclination to consider some dimensions or one type of reasoning process more than another, moral imagination requires broadening perspectives. Sound arguments are available for considering all of the four dimensions outlined above: (1) economic and social consequences, (2) legal and moral rights of those affected by a decision, (3) striving to fulfill one's legal and moral duties, and (4) trying to develop alternatives that are fair to those affected.

Discussion Questions

1. What is the difference between act utilitarianism and rule utilitarianism in ethical analysis? Why was Mr. Zaccaro's decision considered ethical by one standard and a conflict of interest by another?

2. In the promotion decision (Box 7–1), which person would you promote? What reasons were the most persuasive to you? What dimensions of ethical analysis did you find to be the most important in this decision?

3. Analyze the case of the surprise bid (Box 7–2). What should Nancy Alright do? Why? What type of ethical reasoning did you use to make your decision? Did you consider the consequences or the principles involved, or both? Explain.

4. What is Kant's categorical imperative? How is it used as a basis for evaluating ethical judgments? Apply it to the Poletown decision. What insights might the use of this concept provide?

5. What is the difference between positive and negative rights? Apply these concepts to employee rights. Give an example of each. Which type of employee rights are sanctioned by law? Which ones are more controversial?

6. Is it ever moral not to obey the law? What guidelines could you develop to help resolve this dilemma for yourself? What are the negative consequences of a person's placing his or her judgment above the law?

7. What types of moral duties are appropriate in your relationships with others? What types of laws have been developed around the moral duties that are generally accepted?

8. What are the problems or limitations of utilitarian approaches to ethical analysis? Apply this approach to a specific situation to illustrate your points.

9. Is it ever proper not to keep secrets? Develop some guidelines for professional confidentiality that might apply to a CPA. To the corporate attorney.

10. Do managers have an ethical responsibility to engage in self-development? Explain your answer.

Notes

1. See Case III–2, "Beech Nut Company and the Fake Apple Juice" at the end of part III.
2. Scott McMurray, "Battered Broker: E.F. Hutton Appears Headed for Long Siege in Bank-Draft Scheme," *Wall Street Journal*, July 12, 1985, p. 1.
3. Amitai Etzioni, *The Moral Dimension: Toward a New Economics* (New York: Free Press, 1988).
4. Ibid.
5. John Locke, *Two Treatises on Government*, Peter Laslett, ed. 2d ed. (Cambridge: Cambridge University Press, 1967).
6. Immanuel Kant, *Foundations of the Metaphysics of Morals*, text and critical essays edited by Robert Paul Wolff (New York: Bobbs-Merril, 1969), pp. 35–59. For discussions of Kant's philosophy, see Richard T. De George, *Business Ethics* (New York: Macmillan, 1982), chap. 4; F. Neil Brady, *Ethical Managing: Rules and Results* (New York: Macmillan, 1990), chap. 6.

Discussion Case _____

The Salem Consulting Group

John Morgan recently graduated with an MBA and joined the Salem Consulting Group. Salem has been very successful but the temporary downturn in the economy has reduced business by nearly 30 percent this year. Although consulting projects were typically bid on a fixed-fee basis, the company kept careful records of the consulting time and other resources expended on each project. There was a policy that consulting time was to be allocated to individual projects, and Salem's management discouraged consulting time that did not represent billable hours. The time assignment sheet was a factor in evaluating individual consulting performance and for developing a database that could be used in bidding and planning other projects.

One of the projects John Morgan has been working on is for the Capital Investment Company, a reputable firm involved in developing resorts on a global basis. The estimated costs of the consulting project is $450,000. This is the first of several projects expected to develop in the next few years. This project is ahead of schedule and under the budgeted amount. The president of the company recently praised Morgan for his contribution.

The Capital Investment project was temporarily slowed down because of construction delays due to obtaining a zoning variance from a local government. During this delay, Morgan and his project team were assigned to another project with the Broadcroff Corporation, a firm that specializes in the development of shopping malls. This new project has been in process for several months. The original project manager took a leave of absence after undergoing an acrimonious divorce. During this period little progress was made, but a lot of consulting time had been charged to the project. Although the deadline for the Broadcroff project was more than a year away, it was estimated that at least twice as many resources would be needed to finish it than actually remain in the budget.

Frank Daniels, vice president for operations of the Salem Consulting Group, called Morgan into his office and asked him to spend most of his time on the Broadcroff project but charge his consulting time to the Capital Investment project, because the cost accounting reports indicated that sufficient time would be available in that project to absorb more consulting time and still remain within budget. Daniels said he would take responsibility for the decision. What should Morgan do?

CHAPTER 8

Social Justice

CHAPTER OBJECTIVES

1. Review the major theories of economic justice.
2. Examine questions about the fairness of organizational rewards including bonuses, stock options, salaries, and fringe benefits.
3. Consider the broad categories of business stakeholders including customers, employees, investors, community, and physical environment in terms of their sometimes conflicting interests and concerns.
4. Review these different stakeholder interests and the justifications used to assert stakeholder claims.
5. Discuss the concept of corporate stakeholders within the context of a threefold society.
6. Show how mapping stakeholder interests can help clarify the problems and issues facing managers in a threefold society.
7. Provide a framework and concepts that help managers to make just decisions in complex situations characterized by conflicting, yet justifiable, stakeholder claims.

Introductory Case _____

Executive Pay: Who Made the Most and Are They Worth It?

Is the average income received by certain top executives relative to other occupations fair? Why

SOURCE: This case is based upon "Executive Pay: Who Made the Most and Are They Worth It?" *Business Week,* May 1, 1989, pp. 46-52. Copyright 1989. McGraw-Hill, Inc. Reprinted by special permission.

do some occupations earn more than others? Do the top executives in large business organizations deserve what they receive? The concept of economic or distributive justice is concerned with these questions. For example, the average earnings of the chief executive officer in U.S. business organizations in 1960 earned 41 times more than the average factory worker. Table 8–1 shows that the average CEO compensation in 1960 was just over $190,000, while the average factory worker earned under $5,000. By 1988, the average CEO received over $2 million, while the factory worker's wage increased to $22,000. Over the 28-year period from 1960 to 1988, the earnings of chief executive officers has increased from a level of 41 times the amount of factory workers to 93 times. The relative earnings positions of engineers, school teachers, and factory workers remained fairly stable during that same period.

There have been major changes in individual tax laws over the last 30 years. The maximum tax rate of 91 percent in 1960 for those with very large incomes had been reduced to 28 percent by 1988. Thus, the income differences after taxes between the highest- and lowest-paying positions are actually much greater than the figures listed in Table 8–1 indicate. Why have the earnings of top managers increased significantly more than other occupations?

Some argue that the risks and responsibilities of top management were much greater in 1988 than in 1960. The increase in global competition, the prospect of hostile takeovers, and the increased threat of being dismissed by the board of directors all increase the challenges of the top management position and also increase compensation. Also, corporate profits were up by 32 percent in 1988, and it could be argued that executive leadership was a key factor in improving corporate perfor-

mance that year. The value stock options and annual bonuses of executive compensation are often tied to economic performance.

The amounts paid to the 25 highest-paid executives in 1988 ranged from $5.8 million to over $40 million and were considerably over the $2 million average that year, as shown in Table 8–2. At the top of the list were two Disney executives credited with the successful turnaround of the firm that resulted in significant increases in the business's profitability. Next were two executives who benefited from golden parachutes when they left RJR Nabisco after a company takeover through the largest leveraged buyout in history. The two executives from Pennzoil were each awarded a $10 million bonus for the successful lawsuit against Texaco that resulted in an award of $3 billion; this amounts to a bonus of .3 percent of the settlement for which they were credited.

TABLE 8–1
Relative Pay Levels from 1960 to 1988

		1960	1970	1980	1988
CEO	($1000)	$190.4	$548.8	$625.0	$2,025.5
	CEO ratio	1	1	1	1
Engineer	($1000)	9.8	14.7	28.5	45.7
	CEO ratio	19.4	37.3	21.9	44.3
School Teacher	($1000)	5.0	8.6	16.0	28.0
	CEO ratio	38.1	63.8	39.1	72.3
Factory Worker	($1000)	4.7	6.9	15.0	21.7
	CEO ratio	40.5	79.5	41.7	93.3

SOURCE: Developed from "Executive Pay," *Business Week*, May 1, 1989, p. 52.

Table 8–2
The 25 Highest-paid Executives in 1988 ($000)

No.	Name	Company	Salary & Bonus	Long-term Comp.	Total Pay
1	Michael D. Eisner, Chmn.	Walt Disney	7,506	32,588	40,094
2	Frand G. Wells, Pres.	Walt Disney	3,778	28,357	32,135
3	E. A. Horrigan, Vice Chmn.	RJR Nabisco	1,280	20,450	21,730
4	E. Ross Johnson, Former CEO	RJR Nabisco	1,836	19,235	21,071
5	Martin S. Davis, Chmn.	Gulf & Western	3,673	12,577	16,250
6	Richard L. Gelb, Chmn.	Bristol-Myers	1,475	12,578	14,053
7	William P. Stiritz, Chmn.	Ralston Purina	1,029	11,919	12,948
8	Baine P. Kerr, Chmn., Exec. Comm.	Pennzoil	10,706	839	11,545
9	J. Hugh Liedtke, Chmn.	Pennzoil	10,872	655	11,536
10	Paul Fireman, Chmn.	Reebok Intl.	11,439	—	11,439
11	James D. Robinson, III, Chmn.	American Express	2,764	8,169	10,933
12	Kenneth H. Olsen, Pres.	Digital Equipment	932	9,052	9,984
13	Donald E. Petersen, Chmn.	Ford Motor	3,340	6,579	9,919
14	John Scully, Chmn.	Apple Computer	2,479	7,013	9,492
15	Dean L. Buktrock, Chmn.	Waste Mgt.	1,400	7,002	8,402
16	Paul B. Rooney, Pres.	Waste Mgt.	1,060	6,425	7,485
17	P. Roy Vagelos, Chmn.	Merck	1,608	5,286	6,894
18	John H. Bryan, Jr., Chmn.	Sara Lee	1,367	5,396	6,763
19	Andrew S. Grove, CEO	Intel	684	5,746	6,430
20	Stephen M. Wolf, Chmn.	UAL	575	5,790	6,365
21	John B. Lyons, Vice Chmn.	Merck	908	5,414	6,322
22	Joseph D. Williams, Chmn.	Warner-Lambert	1,310	4,814	6,124
23	Louis V. Gerstner, Jr., Former Pres.	American Express	2,394	3,564	5,958
24	John H. Stodkey, Chmn.	Quantum Chemical	1,429	4,454	5,883
25	Stantor R. Cook, CEO	Tribune	1,064	4,789	5,853

SOURCE: "Executive Pay: Who Made the Most and Are They Worth It?" *Business Week*, May 1, 1989, pp. 46–52. Copyright 1989. McGraw-Hill, Inc. Reprinted by special permission.

Ford workers called the large compensations for top Ford executives, including Chairman Peterson, the "annual executive pig-out." Some workers see such large compensation increases as selfish and unfair despite the fact that Ford workers averaged $12,200 each in profit-sharing bonuses, owing to the increased competitiveness of Ford. Whose interests are served by such compensation patterns? Should such pay correspond to increased economic performance, judgments received through lawsuits, corporate turnarounds, and takeovers?

Among the highest-paid executives was junk bond dealer Michael Milken, who made $200 million in 1988. He had been charged with securities trading violations such as illegally parking stock and dealing with insider information. His employer, the investment banking firm Drexel, Burnham, and Lambert, had previously pleaded guilty to numerous SEC securities violations and had agreed to pay $600 million in fines. In 1990 after plea bargaining, Milken pleaded guilty to five counts of security law violations and agreed to pay a $600 million fine and serve some time in prison.

While defending himself in this case, Milken allegedly earned some $200 million in trading fees on junk bonds used to finance corporate takeovers. Is income received by those trading on insider information justifiable?

Some executives attempt to protect themselves from the risks of hostile takeovers by approving employment contracts with clauses that pay sizable amounts—called golden parachutes—if the contract is terminated. The ten largest golden parachutes in 1988 ranged from $7.5 million to $53.8 million, as shown in Table 8–3. Most of these large golden parachutes were due to takeover activity. Are the large fees for corporate restructuring through takeovers and related golden parachutes justifiable?

Superstar boxer Mike Tyson made $54 million; movie producer Steven Spielberg made $50 million; and Teamster Union president William McCarthy made $350,000 in 1988. Mary Bicouvaris, selected as Teacher of the Year for 1988, received $34,000. Are these salaries socially justi-

fiable? How should they compare with the $2 million annual earnings of top executives? These are some of the questions raised by theories of economic justice. Such theories often form part of a system of ideology that seeks to justify particular systems of political economy and social institutions.

The Role of Ideology

Ideology is a system of ideals and values that justifies and supports a way of life or the institutional arrangement of society. Ideology often provides assumptions about how wealth should be distributed and can be a part of a theory of economic justice. For example, if individual responsibility is a central value, then rewards are based upon individual initiative. If community or brotherhood is the highest value, then rewards based upon community membership are likely to be a part of society's conception of justice. The traditional ideol-

TABLE 8–3
The Ten Largest Golden Parachutes

No.	Name	Company	Reason for Payment	Total Pkg. ($000)
1	F. Ross Johnson, CEO	RJR Nabisco	Leveraged buyout	53,800
2	E. A. Horrigan, Vice-Chmn.	RJR Nabisco	Leveraged buyout	45,700
3	Gerald Tsai, Jr., Chmn.	Primerica	Commercial credit takeover	46,800
4	Edward P. Evans, Chmn.	Macmillan	Hostile takeover	31,900
5	Kenneth A. Yarnell, Pres.	Primerica	Commercial credit takeover	18,400
6	John D. Martin, Exec. V.P.	RJR Nabisco	Leveraged buyout	18,200
7	Sanford C. Sigoloff, Chmn.	Wickes	Leveraged buyout	15,900
8	Whitney Stevens, Chmn.	J.P. Stevens	West Point-Pepperell takeover	15,700
9	Philip L. Smith, Chmn.	Pillsbury	Grand Metropolitan takeover	11,000
10	Wilhelm A. Mallory, Sr. V.P.	Wickes	Leveraged buyout	7,500

SOURCE: "Executive Pay: Who Made the Most and Are They Worth It?" *Business Week*, May 1, 1989, pp. 46–52. Copyright 1989. McGraw-Hill, Inc. Reprinted by special permission.

ogy of individualism is closely related to the concept of a competitive market.

Lodge has characterized ideology as "the 'hymns' that we sing to justify and make legitimate what we are doing (or perhaps what we would like to do)." He suggested that most societies have values such as survival, justice, equality as humans, economic well being, self fulfillment, and self respect.[1] Also, as Chapter 7 suggested, these universal values lead to concepts of right and duties related to keeping secrets or confidences, keeping promises or contracts, truthfulness, and avoiding harm to others. These values are universal ideals that are cherished within the community.

The task of ideology is to connect the universal values to the "real world," of communities. Ideology provides a system of thought that uses these cherished values to justify or legitimate the realities of society. An ideology can be found in public speeches, advertisements, and themes that underlie the popular culture of television shows. In a classic study, *The American Business Creed,* Francis Sutton and others studied business advertisements and found the following such elements in the traditional American business ideology:

(1) economic teamwork based upon payment of reasonable wages to workers and business seeking a fair profit in a competitive market, (2) individual responsibility and progress through hard work, (3) limited government interference in economic affairs, and (4) a political economy based upon free enterprise and individual freedom.[2]

Ideology can also influence the general approaches to international competitiveness used by countries.[3] For example, the model of market competition outlined in Chapter 2 supports an ideology for an individualistic market-based society with a limited role for government. As discussed in Chapter 2, the conditions of a competitive market are as follows:

1. There are enough participants so that no single buyer or seller has significant market power.

2. There is freedom of entry and exit so that competitors can freely compete. There is no discrimination based upon color, race, religion, or sex.
3. There is mobility of resources according to market conditions so that investment capital, workers, and resources can flow to their most productive uses.
4. Buyers and sellers are completely knowledgeable about available offers and opportunities.
5. Buyers and sellers behave prudently in their own self-interest.
6. Decisions are based upon market-set wages, returns, and profits.
7. Market prices reflect all the costs so that there are no externalities or side effects of business not reflected in prices.
8. The needs of society are thus automatically met through market competition. The legitimate claims of people are made on business within the context of demands for goods and services in a competitive market.
9. The role of government is ideally small because the efficiency and justice of the society are brought about automatically through the "invisible hand" of market competition.

THE TRADITIONAL IDEOLOGY OF INDIVIDUALISM

Lodge has discussed the *traditional ideology* of the United States as one based upon the following core values:

1. Individualism and individual freedom
2. Equality of opportunity
3. Sanctity of contract
4. Market competition to satisfy consumer desires
5. A limited role for the state

This is the ideology that is consistent with the conditions necessary for market competition and has been increasingly challenged as the realities of the twentieth century have unfolded. As Chapter

TABLE 8–4
Ideology: A Bridge Between Values and the Real World

Values	Traditional Ideology	New Ideology	Real World
Survival	1. Individualism	1. Communitarianism	Geography
Justice	Equality (opportunity)	Equality (results) or hierarchy consensus	Demography
Economy	Contract		Economic performance
Fulfillment	2. Property rights	2. Rights and duties of membership	Technology, Scientific insights: Newton Einstein; Ecologists et al.
Self-respect	3. Competition to satisfy consumer desires	3. Community need	
etc.	4. Limited state (with interest groups)	4. Active, planning state	Traditional institutions vs. new (e.g., OPEC, Japan)
	5. Scientific specialization	5. Holism	Traditional behavior patterns

SOURCE: George Cabot Lodge, *The American Disease* (New York: Alfred A. Knopf, 1984), p. 41. Reprinted by permission.

2 suggested, markets fail when the conditions necessary for market competition do not coincide with reality. Demographic changes make evident the special needs of the young, the elderly, the uneducated, and those suffering from health problems. Advanced technology and increasing population have changed perceptions of economic progress as the quality of life is challenged by developments in the large metropolitan areas that have appeared throughout the world in this century. Science has increased the possibility of advanced health care but at great cost. The global economy linked by telecommunications and the growth of the multinational business enterprise have challenged the institution of the national economy with its role of limited government.

THE NEW IDEOLOGY AND THE VALUES OF COMMUNITY

Lodge suggests that the new realities of technologically advanced society in a globalized world economy have resulted in a new or competing ideology, as outlined in Table 8–4. The *new ideology* emphasizes the following core values:

1. *Community needs have priority over individualism.* The new ideology recognizes the interdependencies brought about by population, urbanization, technology, and globalization of competition. Thus, the community becomes more the focus of ideology as interdependence makes rugged individualism less feasible in industrialized society.

2. *Equality of results* rather than equality of opportunity. As inequalities in society increase, many argue that freedom to compete on an equal basis does not exist. Thus, equality of the distribution of status, wealth, and position becomes the focus of concern rather than assuming that such things are allocated according to relative merit through market competition. Equality of opportunity is assumed to exist in the model of market competition but may not exist in reality.

3. *Rights and duties of membership* within society rather than rights based primarily upon property ownership. An ideology based on community membership might prohibit racial discrimination and support the right to universal health care. In contrast, an ideology giving priority to property rights might allow discrimination against minorities by restaurant owners. And health care might be available only to those with sufficient wealth to pay for treatment.

4. *Community needs for employment and concerns about externalities.* This shift in ideology is brought about by growing awareness of unintended outcomes of market operations. Shifts in competitive position through the globalization of markets have been very disruptive for communities in the rust belt of the United States. Also, increased awareness of such externalities as pollution, toxic waste, and global warming have called into question the self-correcting results assumed by the invisible hand of competition. Environmental quality rather than simply satisfying the demands for goods and services within the context of market competition becomes valued.

5. *A more active role for the government* is envisaged rather than the limited role assumed in laissez-faire capitalism of the last century.

There are often strands of these two ideologies, the traditional and the new, in the many debates about business in a threefold society. Theories of economic justice outlined later in this chapter are influenced by the individualistic values of the traditional ideology or the community-oriented values of the new ideology. The debate over social responsibility of business outlined in the next chapter also can be viewed as an outgrowth of the

social changes that call into question many of the assumptions and values of the traditional ideology of individualism based upon the model of the perfect market.

TWO VIEWS OF IDEOLOGY: CYNICAL AND OPTIMISTIC

Before reviewing the major approaches to social justice currently being debated, it may be useful to comment on the two ways ideology can be interpreted, one cynical and one optimistic. The *cynical view of ideology* was first articulated by Karl Marx as outlined in Figure 8–1.[4] According to this view privileged status determines the ideals or values one holds. The primary purpose of ideology is the self-serving goal of maintaining the status and power of the privileged class. Ideology is seen as a system of values and concepts that justify the privileges and wealth of society's elite.

The cynical view of ideology suggest that where you stand on an issue depends upon where you sit. In other words, if you are sitting in the CEO's chair, the cynical view of ideology would predict a system of values that justifies the exceedingly large compensation for top management listed in Table 8–2. Those in positions of power develop self-serving ideals and ideologies that legitimate their privi-

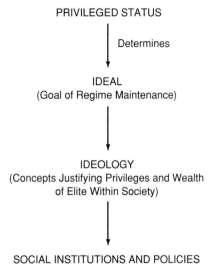

FIGURE 8–1 The Cynical View of Ideology

leged positions and maintain their status within society. Similarly, those with a cynical view would expect such executives to resist increasing the minimum wage, to push for wage concessions to keep costs down, and to oppose various social programs designed to transfer resources to the poor. The ideology supported by the elite would be expected to justify their rewards through emphasizing certain cultural values like individual responsibility and survival of the fittest, rather than values like compassion for the least advantaged, cooperation with nature, and harmonious relationships.

Ideology as the result of honest inquiry. Figure 8–2 outlines the optimistic view of ideology as honest inquiry that originates in the cultural sphere of the threefold society. According to this view, ideology is a system of values that can originate in either intellectual or spiritual inquiry. Honest persons wishing to create a good society can be guided by their thinking and by inspiration from their religion. An example of intellectual inquiry is the views of the good society found in the work of Adam Smith,[5] discussed earlier, that integrated the model of market competition with the virtues of prudence, justice, and beneficence. Another example of a contribution from philosophy was made by Immanuel Kant in his concept of the categorical imperative, discussed in Chapter 7. The work of Adam Smith is central to the individualistic ideology that uses relative merit as the basis for a theory of justice in a market system. Kant's ideas influenced John Rawls in his theory of justice in a system that combines both individualistic and community-oriented ideals.

Theologians also engage in honest inquiry to arrive at an idea or an ideology about a just society. For example, the American bishops of the Roman Catholic Church have published a letter on social justice that offers an alternative based upon the social teachings of that church. The point is that ideals can be guided by intellectual inquiry or inspired by religious concepts that later form parts of a system of sociopolitical ideals, which in turn justify social institutions and policies, as shown in Figure 8–2.

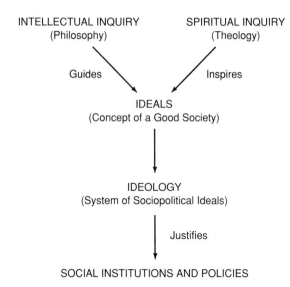

FIGURE 8–2 Ideology as Honest Inquiry

Theories of Social Justice

Business managers and entrepreneurs often have to make decisions that have consequences for customers, employees, competitors, communities, and the owners and investors in the business. Decisions are based upon their economic, ethical, political, and legal consequences. Central to the question of ethics is the concept of fairness, which poses the question of economic justice. Are the burdens and benefits resulting from a decision fair to those concerned? Are salaries fair for all concerned?

Theories of social justice explain and justify the distribution of things of value within society. These theories are used to justify decisions by managers and to determine the appropriate role of the government in economic affairs, as shown in Table 8–5. Most theories of justice are concerned with content questions about who gets what within society for what reasons? In contrast, libertarian approaches to justice consider only the processes of transfer rather than the end pattern of distribution within society. The major theories discussed in subsequent sections of this chapter include the following:

1. *Libertarian theory* is based upon the ideals of free choice and private property and considers any legal exchange to be just.
2. *Market-based systems* assume that equality of opportunity to compete exists and defines justice in terms of relative merit and individual rewards.
3. *Mixed systems* also assume there is no discrimination in access to social positions and call for a

more activist government and a society that considers the consequences experienced by the least advantaged to determine justice.
4. *Egalitarian systems* are based upon equality of distribution to all members of society.
5. *Needs-based systems* are based upon distribution according to needs but asking that contributions and productivity be based upon capability.

TABLE 8–5
Theories of Economic Justice

	Need-based	Egalitarian	Mixed System	Market-oriented	Libertarian
Type of Theory	Content	Content	Content	Content	Process
Ideology	Communitarian	Communitarian	Mixed	Individualistic	Individualistic
Assumptions	Equality in human condition	Egalitarianism: Equality in human condition	Veil of ignorance about initial position	Conditions of competition	Justice in original acquisitions
Bases of Justification	Needs should be justified	Equality for all members of society	Basic level of liberty and least advantaged	Relative merit	Private property rights, free choice, and legal exchange
Principles of Justice	Each person deserves what is needed (but is expected to contribute according to his or her capability)	Each person deserves the same holdings as other members of society	1. Each has a *right* to basic liberties 2. Inequalities are justified if they benefit the least advantaged, subject to: a. equal opportunities b. just savings	1. Each has a right to compete 2. Justice requires a. equal merit/ rewards ratios for all b. rewards should be based on relative merit	1. Justice requires legitimate original acquisition of holding 2. Justice in transfer through legal exchange 3. Principle of rectification needed if acquisition by illegal means
Is Inequality Justified?	Yes, if needs are different	No	Yes, if least advantaged benefit	Yes, if relative merit is different	Yes, if based on guiding principles
Effect on Motivation to Produce	Negative	Negative	Mixed	Positive	Unknown
Redistribution vs. Growth. Government Action to Bring about Justice	Justice through redistribution	Justice through redistribution	Justice through redistribution and growth	Justice through growth and redistribution	Justice through redistribution if transfer process illegitimate
Major Proponent of Theory	Karl Marx	Unknown	John Rawls	Aristotle	Robert Nozick

SOURCE: Based on Robert Nozick, *Anarchy, State and Utopia;* Aristotle, *Nicomachean Ethics;* John Rawls, *A Theory of Justice;* Arthur M. Okin, *Equality and Efficiency;* and Karl Marx and Friedrich Engels, *Manifesto of the Communist Party.*

The Case of the Student Movers

Jennifer Adams, a young professional living near a university, is moving to a different apartment. She hired three male students to help move the furniture in her house to a new location, promising each the standard hourly wage for professional movers in the city. One student turned out to be capable of lifting large items by himself and was both more efficient and more careful than either of the other students. Adams learned during conversation while driving the van that the second student desperately needed money, owing to a severe financial crisis that threatened his enrollment for the next semester. The third student carelessly broke two vases and scraped a table but otherwise fulfilled the conditions of the agreement, though in an undistinguished manner.

The first student deserved greater compensation on the basis of *merit,* the second *needed* a larger share of the money to be divided among them though for no reason related to performance, and the third deserved less on the basis of performance but deserved an *equal share* on the basis of the agreement (if one overlooks the problem of carelessly handled and broken items). Adams was therefore somewhat at a loss about what reward to offer each student at the end of the day. Suppose she tried to call on justice in general to tell her what ought to be done.[6]

The first two approaches are based primarily on individualistic ideologies, whereas the latter three are consistent with the community-oriented ideology, as defined above. Each theory of justice begins with certain assumptions and uses different principles to justify how things should be distributed. Some theories are indifferent to inequality of distribution within society, and some consider any inequality unjust. Also, some of these theories of justice provide incentives to individuals and businesses that are productive and some do not directly reward individual effort. Each theory has implications for the appropriate role of government in bringing about justice. Table 8–5 outlines the major concepts of these theories discussed in the following sections.

The Libertarian Approach to Justice—The Entitlement Theory

Robert Nozick, in his book *Anarchy, State, and Utopia,* has developed a libertarian approach to justice. His theory focuses on the process used to distribute things of value, rather than the characteristics of the final distribution. According to

Nozick, justice requires that a person be legally entitled to what he or she possesses. This theory is based upon the values of private property, free choice, and obeying the law when using or disposing of one's property. Legal exchange is defined by the government.

Libertarian principles of justice include the following:

1. It is assumed that the original acquisition of holdings are legitimate and legal.
2. Given this assumption, all transfers of holdings consistent with the boundaries of legal exchange are just.
3. A principle of rectification is needed if an acquisition or transfer is made by illegal means or if the original holdings are illegitimate.

JUSTICE AND THE ACQUISITION OF ORIGINAL HOLDINGS

How are original holdings developed? Libertarians draw on the social contract theory of the philosopher John Locke. According to this theory, humankind before the establishment of governments were primarily hunters and gatherers. According to Locke, agricultural society began when the first person *mixed his or her labor with the soil and thus made it private property.* Thus the original holdings were based upon "sweat equity" that philosophically came into existence *before* the government. Because there was a tendency for the strong to abuse the weak in making claims on property, the community developed a *social contract* to create the first government. The primary purpose of this government, probably a monarchy, was to protect property rights.

For Locke, the primary role of government is to insure the safety of citizens, to protect private property, and to enforce the rules of legal exchange. Because private property was *prior to* government and was the primary reason for creating government, citizens could develop new social contracts if governments fail to protect property. Governments that abuse private property or do not protect citizens were considered to be illegitimate and should rightfully be overthrown by citizens. Using this philosophy, the Founding Fathers of the United States considered it their duty to fight for independence. The violations of property rights by King George of England served as a major justification for the Revolutionary War.

Libertarian approaches to social justice typically assume that the initial holdings are just or legitimate. If this assumption is valid, then the theory of justice progresses to the second principle of legal entitlement. However, if there is a question about the initial holdings in the distant past, then the present distribution of wealth can be questioned as possibly unjust. It may be useful to consider some historical examples to see how significant the assumption of legitimate original holdings might be for current usefulness of libertarian theory.

It was assumed by those who settled the North American continent during the sixteenth through the nineteenth centuries that the land was empty, and the original holdings of property could be legally accomplished in the Lockean tradition through "sweat equity" by clearing the land and farming it. Such ventures as the Lewis and Clark expedition in the early 1800s were made to establish a legal claim to the western lands of the North American continent before any European powers could. The chapter of history concerning the treat-

ment of Native Americans was both sad and cruel and raised many questions concerning the "original holdings" concept of libertarians in America.

The Native Americans were largely ignored. However, the land was in fact already owned by them as their traditional territory. Native Americans were subsequently removed from the land and the policy of the U.S. government in the late 1800s was actually one of genocide to solve the "Indian problem." The luckier Native Americans were granted reservations rather than death. Reservations were often the least fertile lands. Many Native American groups were traditionally hunters. The slaughter of the buffalo and the increased population growth of the settlers eliminated the Native Americans' source of food. The result was starvation or subsistence granted by the federal government on Indian reservations as a treaty requirement. However, corruption was extensive in the government contracts supplying the Native Americans, particularly during the administration of President Grant, and the supplies were often spoiled or contaminated.

History abounds with stories of transfers under questionable circumstances. For example, at the close of World War II, part of Germany was transferred to Poland and much of eastern Poland was transferred to the USSR. This issue has caused some uneasiness in the discussions about German reunification, and that is why Poland wanted to be represented in the German reunification discussions of 1990.

The country of Israel came into being in 1948 because Great Britain gave the territory to the Jews that had been held by Arabs for thousands of years since the Hebrew Diaspora. Panama was created as an "independent" country whose independence was supported by the United States. The land that is now Panama had formerly been a part of Colombia, a country that was not cooperating in the construction of the Panama Canal.

Many problems exist for any theory of justice that assumes the legitimacy of original holdings. The settling of the Western Hemisphere, the creation of Panama and post–World War II Israel, territorial changes in Europe from World War II, and the boundaries of numerous other countries could be questioned. It could be argued by libertarians that the land in the Great Plains states was settled in accordance with the Homestead Act. The U.S. government established the guidelines under which a citizen could settle land in the western territories. History raises many questions about how the government obtained the claim to the land so that the original holdings could be considered legitimate. The point is that if the original holdings were illegally obtained, than all subsequent transfers are brought into question as unjust.

In technologically advanced societies, wealth is often not in the form of land but ideas. Thus intellectual property and entitlements concerning the benefits that flow from ownership of such property is central to considering justice in modern society. This was anticipated by the authors of the U.S. Constitution in that the right to a patent on an invention was guaranteed in the original Constitution, which was ratified *before* the Bill of Rights (the first ten amendments).

Consider the state of California, with its wealth based upon the intellectual and creative activity in Hollywood films and the high technology of silicon valley. What is the historical basis for these holdings? It is hardly due to the ownership of land; rather, such intellectual property as a film or a new computer is based upon the dynamics of society and technology over time in a particular location.

This issue of intellectual property further complicates any claims of justice based upon the assumptions of the original holdings. However, well-developed laws cover patents, copyrights, and registered trademarks in most industrialized societies that deal with conflicting claims. An important role of government is to develop and administer rules governing the origination and transfer of such property.

The legitimacy of original holdings of intellectual property is guided by laws, international treaties, and litigation. This is a highly dynamic, complex area. For example, the popular performer Bette Middler recently won a court suit against someone who was impersonating her singing style in a commercial. The popular film starring Eddie

Murphy, *Coming to America,* was allegedly based on someone else's ideas and was the subject of lawsuits claiming an intellectual property violation.

JUSTICE IN TRANSFER THROUGH LEGAL EXCHANGE

This principle considers any transfer based upon legal exchange to be just, assuming the exchange is freely accepted and the person transferring the holding is the rightful owner. Commitments and contracts should be fulfilled once an agreement has been reached. According to this principle, Jennifer Adams in the earlier case example agreed to pay each of the student movers a certain wage, and justice would require that she pay each student the same wage that was agreed to. All parties agreed to the moving job and to the wage rate, and so the result was justified because it was a legal exchange willingly entered into.

If an individual rightfully owns something, and exchanges or transfers are made legally, then the result is just. A rich landowner could give his property away to poor peasants; he could lease it to a multinational agricultural firm to raise coffee; he could use the property to develop a tourist resort; or he could let the land lie idle. If these acts are legal and willingly agreed to, then libertarian theory would conclude that all are just.

Several of the billionaires in *Fortune* magazine's list of the world's wealthiest individuals have wealth based on drugs. Drug cartel leaders in Colombia have amassed fortunes through illegal enterprises in both Colombia and the United States. Is this just? According to the libertarian philosophy, wealth based upon illegal transfers is inherently unjust because it violates the principle of justice in transfer through legal exchange.

PRINCIPLE OF RECTIFICATION

The last principle of justice in libertarian theory is concerned with rectification. Nozick recognized that governments have a role in bringing about justice if (1) the ownership of the thing transferred is illegal, or (2) transfers were illegal or unwillingly done.

Role of Government in Libertarian Theory

The role of government would be to protect property rights, enforce contracts, and provide for public safety. It would not be concerned about social inequalities in the distribution of wealth or with market externalities. Free exchange could result in inequalities. If a society is concerned about an externality, it would be the task of government and the public policy process to change the law.

Relative Merit and Justice in the Market System

The remaining theories of economic justice are concerned with content, that is, with the pattern of distribution of things of value within society. Market-based systems usually measure justice by the relative merit of an individual within society as determined by the market. This conception of justice integrates the theory of economic justice developed by Aristotle around 330 B.C. with the concepts of market competition developed by Adam Smith in the eighteenth century.

The major principles of justice in market-oriented systems are as follows:

1. The necessary conditions of competition must exist. Each person should have an equal opportunity to compete. Discrimination is a violation of the conditions necessary for justice in a market system.
2. All rewards should be based upon relative merit.
3. Justice requires that the merit/reward ratio be equal for all people.

Justice as Relative Merit

Aristotle defined justice as the condition when the ratio of merit to reward is equal for all persons as follows:[7]

$$\frac{\text{Merit A}}{\text{Reward A}} = \frac{\text{Merit B}}{\text{Reward B}} = \ldots = \frac{\text{Merit N}}{\text{Reward N}}$$

In this theory of justice the rewards received by different persons within society can be unequal if the merits of different individuals are proportionately unequal. From this criterion, it would be just for the student mover with the greatest strength and carefulness to earn more than students who were less careful or less productive. A statesman might be justified in receiving more income than a shopkeeper if the work of the former were more highly valued by society.

It would also be fair for the best salesperson in a company to earn more compensation than the district salesmanager who supervised a number of salespeople. Because the salesmanager may be doing a different job than sales staff in the field, it may be difficult to determine the merit of each individual. Business must somehow determine how much different activities and outcomes are valued, so that fair rewards can be based upon relative merit.

Returns in Competitive Markets

In a market-based system operating under competitive conditions, merit would be profits or market-based wages or returns. The more valuable the service to society, the more merit a person would have as measured by the market, and the result would be a higher profit or higher compensation. In microeconomic theory, prudent or rational decision makers would continue to increase the use of factor inputs as long as the marginal returns from their use were greater than or equal to the marginal costs. Assuming mobility of resources and freedom of entry and exit from the market, each factor in the production process would increase so long as it made economic sense to do so. In equilibrium, the cost-benefit ratios of all factor inputs would be equal:

$$\frac{\text{Marginal Cost A}}{\text{Marginal Returns A}} = \frac{\text{Marginal Cost B}}{\text{Marginal Returns B}} = \ldots = \frac{\text{Marginal Cost N}}{\text{Marginal Returns N}}$$

Factor inputs could include the number of employees in a certain skill category, units of equipment, building space, or any factor in the production process that could influence the output at some determined cost. If a factor input were significantly more productive than others, more would be demanded in the market. The increased quantity demanded would bid up its price and thus make it more costly to use. The operations of a market competition would result in an equilibrium in which the relative cost/return ratio for all factor inputs would be equal in value. Market efficiency would require this, because it would make sense to use less of any production factor whose cost/return ration were higher than another. Conversely, there would be a positive economic incentive to increase any factor whose marginal productivity was greater than other factors.

The high compensation for chief executive officers discussed in the introductory case would be justified if the executive increased the economic performance of the organization proportionally more than did other employees. The Disney executives who orchestrated the corporate turnaround were apparently highly valued because they were responsible for outstanding economic achievements of the corporation. Many corporations tie executive compensation to economic performance. A part of this compensation is stock options, which allow executives to buy stock at some predetermined price. Presumably, if they do an outstanding job and the price of the stock goes up, they can profit by exercising their right to the stock option. Firms with profit-sharing plans might also justify such plans for employees because they are fair and because they motivate employees to be more productive.

Markets are automatically efficient under competitive conditions if there are no barriers or constraints that impair the inclusion of a particular person or economic factor in the process. The conditions of economic efficiency parallel the conditions for justice based upon relative merit as conceived by Aristotle. Thus, *market operations are both efficient and just if competitive conditions exist.*

If a barrier causes a business to exclude certain suppliers or to discriminate against potential employees because of race, sex, or national origin, then the economic results are likely to be inefficient and unjust as well. Discrimination is inherently unjust and is likely to be inefficient because it is contrary to the conditions necessary for competition.

THE ROLE OF GOVERNMENT IN MARKET SYSTEMS

Market-based systems can be considered just even though great inequalities exist if those inequalities are consistent with the relative productivity or merit of those involved. However, if inequality exists that cannot be justified by relative merit, or if certain persons are excluded from economic activity, then social justice is called into question. As noted in Chapter 2, the role of government increases when the conditions necessary for competition are absent. Market failures can lead to inefficiency and injustice.

Thus, market failures due to insufficient competition in the United States and Canada lead antitrust laws intended to reestablish competitive conditions. Other market failures result in regulations to offset them when consumers are provided incorrect or misleading information, when discrimination results in constraints on access to jobs or fair pay by minorities, when side effects or externalities such as pollution or global warming exist, and when market power is misused.

Typically government's role to insure justice in a market-based society would include (1) restoring competitive conditions so that the invisible hand operates to balance benefit/cost ratios in the marketplace, (2) redistributing wealth when the ratios of proportional merit/rewards are out of balance, and (3) stimulating productivity and economic growth to bring about improved standards of living rather than by entitlement programs.

Political debates often center around which public policy approach to social justice is the best. Some argue for economic growth and oppose social programs that redistribute wealth or income. For example, statistics about job formation and economic growth were used by President Reagan in answer to criticisms concerning poverty and problems of the homeless during his administration. The expression "a rising tide raises all boats" argues that stimulation of economic growth is likely to be more effective than government social programs to improve the economic welfare of the country.

Others use this theory of justice to argue for programs of redistribution financed by progressive taxes. For example, if many within society argued that the high executive compensation was not justified by relative merit, taxes could be raised to the 90 percent rate of the 1960s. The proceeds of this progressive tax on the wealthy would be used to fund social programs that help those whose merit/reward ratios are out of balance. The greater the competitive market imperfections, the greater the chance that the invisible hand of the market will lead to inefficient and unjust results. Thus, market imperfections lead to arguments for redistribution through social programs based upon the theory of justice and the principle of relative merit.

JUSTICE AND THE MOTIVATION TO PRODUCE

In competitive markets, merit is determined by what customers in the marketplace are willing to buy. The more a business produces what is demanded by its customers, the more profitable it is likely to be. Under sound management, profitability results directly from customer service at competitive prices. Under competitive market conditions, there is a built-in incentive to be productive. That is why market-based economies are consistently the most productive and innovative in the world. The ideology of prosperity through growth lets market processes do the work of justice, and minimum government interference is based upon the built-in motivation of market-based societies.

Fairness in a Mixed System and the Least Advantaged

John Rawls, in A Theory of Justice, began his intellectual inquiry on justice by posing the question, What is fair? How can we come to an agreement about what is fair? His theory begins with a hypothesized veil of ignorance concerning one's position within society and goes on to develop a

set of principles that focus on the least-advantaged within society.

VEIL OF IGNORANCE CONCERNING THE INITIAL POSITION

Because there is a measure of truth to the cynical view of ideology discussed above, Rawls sought to develop a theory independent of the positions of status and wealth held by people in society. He developed the idea of a *veil of ignorance* concerning one's *initial position* within society. What system of justice would a reasonable person agree to if he or she did not know which position in society would be his or hers? Such an individual might be a wealthy businesswoman, a homeless person living in the streets of New York, a highly intelligent young man on a scholarship to an elite university, or a plumber or an electrician. If you did not know ahead of time which of these positions would be yours, then Rawls suggests that would support a theory of justice that favors the least-advantaged within society.

Rawls developed the following two major principles in the theory of justice: (1) the right to basic liberty, and (2) the difference principle.

PRINCIPLE ONE: THE RIGHT TO BASIC LIBERTIES

Each person is to have an equal right to the most extensive total system of equal basic liberties compatible with a similar amount for all.[8] The first principle is that everyone in society is entitled to a basic set of liberties compatible with the circumstances of that society. These basic liberties include both negative political rights and positive economic rights. Political liberties would include such things as freedoms of expression, religion, association, privacy, and due process under the law available in most democracies. However, the right to basic liberties proposed by Rawls also included a minimum standard of living that could include guaranteed health care, education, shelter or housing, and sufficient food. The exact makeup of basic liberties might vary from society to society, depending upon its unique economic resources and its cultural values.

Why are political liberties considered negative rights? Honoring another person's political liberties usually costs little because the major requirement is not to interfere with his or her exercise of freedom. Economic liberty is another matter. Economic rights entitle a person to things like food, shelter, work, health care, or education. For every right there is a duty. The duty that corresponds with a negative political right is the duty not to interfere.

The duty that corresponds to an economic right is the duty to provide something of value. Who is to pay for housing, health care, and a minimum living standard? For example, a publicly financed university education is a constitutional right for all individuals in France. Great Britain and Canada have government-financed universal health care. Sweden has numerous public service programs for health, education, and welfare. Economic rights almost always call for the increased role of government as the primary institution that has the duty to provide programs to fulfill such rights. Rights to health care, employment, housing, and living standards are public issues that have long been debated in the United States.

PRINCIPLE TWO:
THE DIFFERENCE PRINCIPLE

The *difference principle* is that social and economic inequalities are just if arranged so that they are to the greatest benefit of the least advantaged. Rawls conceives of a social contract based upon the original position that places a high value on equality. This principle indicated that Rawls is a qualified egalitarian because he prefers social systems that have equality of economic distribution. However, Rawls acknowledges that unequal economic distribution may benefit the disadvantaged. In such cases, the inequalities are just according to the difference principle.

For example, Lee Iacocca is credited for saving the Chrysler Corporation from bankruptcy in the early 1980s. His salary was set at one dollar plus a large number of stock options. In 1987, after the turnaround was complete, Iacocca's total compensation amounted to $19 million. Was this just? According to Rawls's difference principle, it might have been justified because thousands of automobile workers would have been unemployed had the firm gone bankrupt. If these automobile workers are considered the least advantaged, then the high compensation of Iacocca could be seen as benefiting the workers who would have otherwise lost their jobs. The large compensation of Iacocca was, in large measure, due to the exercise of stock options to purchase stock that had significantly increased in value under his leadership. Thus, his large compensation might also have been justified under the principle of relative merit, discussed earlier.

Two more subprinciples or rules govern the difference principle: (1) the equal access to position, and (2) the just savings principle. First, *every person should have equal access to positions within society.* Thus any form of discrimination is inherently unjust in Rawls's theory of justice. Second, distribution should not violate the *just savings principle,* even if such a violation would benefit the least advantaged in the short run. According to the just savings principle, society should save and reinvest in its infrastructure to maintain its productive capacity.

Infrastructure includes systems of communication, education, transportation, health care, waste disposal, sanitation, and law enforcement. The economic system and standards of living within society depend on the reinvestment in such assets if productivity is to be maintained. Furthermore, a country's overall standard of living depends on the maintenance of infrastructure. Similarly, businesses need to modernize plant, invest in new technologies, develop logistics systems, and maintain a competitive infrastructure within the firm.

Economic activity is discouraged by poor roads, unreliable or obsolete communication systems, underfinanced public education, and congested airports. If government transfers to the poor or the disadvantaged means that infrastructure is not maintained, then the benefits to the least advantaged are likely to be short-lived. Similarly, businesses that do not maintain their infrastructure lose their competitive advantage over time.

Rawls calls for a just savings principle to constrain inclinations to help the poor in the short run through massive public welfare programs that would undermine the longer-term productive capacity of society. Also, salaries or benefits to the least-advantaged employees that preclude maintaining the business's competitive position would only be short-lived. In other words, it is just to save enough resources to invest in infrastructures necessary to maintain the society in the long run.

THE ROLE OF GOVERNMENT IN A MIXED SYSTEM

Rawls's theory of justice is considered a "mixed system" because of the implied increased role of government. Under libertarian theory, the government has the minimal role of national defense, public safety, and enforcing legal exchanges and contracts. Under the market system that relies on relative merit as the criterion for justice, market-determined returns are considered just if competitive conditions prevail. When disadvantaged groups are excluded from the benefits of economic activity and from market processes, the role of government is to bring about social justice.

Approaches to economic justice under a mixed system depend upon market forces to distribute things of value within society. Mixed systems also depend upon the government to insure social justice through redistribution strategies like aid to dependent children, Medicare for the aged, and progressive tax policies. A substantial proportion of those living in poverty in the United States are children under six years of age in single-parent households. Also, a growing number of older retired persons are living in poverty. Both these groups are "outside" the market system, and thus their "merit" cannot be determined by market mechanisms. What can be done in these circumstances to bring about social and economic justice?

Although this issue is not without controversy, such situations call for a greater role of government redistribution to bring about social justice.

THE MOTIVATION TO PRODUCE UNDER MIXED SYSTEMS

Purely market-based systems are rare. Most Western countries are, in reality, mixed systems. Most of the allocations within society are the result of market forces, but the role of government in regulation and transfers can be substantial; it is a matter of degree. To the extent that market forces are used, the rewards of increased productivity and competitiveness are automatic.

Effective government regulation is difficult, but it is in principle possible for such regulations to make markets work better and to compensate for market failures like misleading advertising, discrimination, and pollution. Also, the model of market competition does not exclude any person or group from market activity. The reality is that the elderly, the very young, many single parents, the handicapped, and others are not able to work or to be engaged in market processes.

Extremely high tax rates to finance transfers to such excluded groups could discourage the economic performance of those not covered by government transfers. Also, there are cases where people could contribute to society but choose to remain unemployed because of the incentives for staying unemployed inherent in social programs.

Egalitarianism

Egalitarianism is based upon the assumption of equality in the human condition. According to Kant's categorical imperative discussed in the last chapter, people are equally deserving of respect as ends in themselves. The U.S. Declaration of Independence and the Bill of Rights form the basis for political rights and equality before the law due to all persons within society. Egalitarians question whether people can be equal in political rights, moral duties, and obligations, and yet be considered as unequal when it comes to distributing the burdens and benefits in a market economy.[9] Strict egalitarians argue that individual differences should be no more important in issues of distribution (that is, economic justice) than they are in other matters of morality.

Radical Egalitarianism

Beauchamp explained radical egalitarianism as follows:

> Distributions of burdens and benefits in a society are just to the extent they are equal, and deviations from absolute equality in distribution can be determined to be unjust without considerations of the respects in which members of society may differ. For example, the fact that roughly 20 percent of the wealth in the United States is owned by only 5 percent of the population, while the poorest 20 percent of the population controls only 5 percent of the wealth, would make American society unjust by this radical egalitarian standard, no matter how relatively deserving the people at both extremes might be (by a nonegalitarian standard of justice).[10]

Egalitarianism and Socialism

Most egalitarian systems of political economy are socialistic. A few countries with systems of democratic socialism like Sweden have developed sound economies with relative equality of distribution. However, most Communist countries like those in eastern Europe have not fared so well. Their economies collapsed because of poor performance. The joke "The government pretends to pay us and we pretend to work" aptly describes the motivation and productivity of these so-called egalitarian systems.

Okun has suggested that the major problem with egalitarian systems is motivation.[11] If everything is equally distributed regardless of performance, then the motivation to produce is eliminated for most people. Government policies of equally paying all employees and redistribution to bring about the egalitarian concept of economic justice result in reduced economic growth. Okun has suggested that attempts to insure that every-

one's slice of the pie is the same size results in the reduction in the size of the pie. Furthermore, government redistribution programs not only reduce the efficiency of production but also increase the cost that must be paid by an inefficient economy.

Need-based Concepts of Justice

The case of the student movers shows how the issue of need can enter into decisions about pay. The young professional was moved by the financial emergency faced by one of the student movers. Some extra income might make the difference that would allow the continuation of his university studies. However, these needs had nothing to do with the student's performance in the task of moving the young professional's belongings.

There are other examples of this need-based principle of justice in business organizations. Companies frequently provide health care insurance for employees as a fringe benefit. Everyone contributes a standard amount for the coverage, but only those who need health care actually receive the benefit. Medical coverage contributions by employees rarely depend upon the number of dependents. Such systems are usually considered fair by employees.

In another case, a state university with below-average salaries offered a fringe benefit of free tuition to the faculty and faculty family members who attended the university. This was considered a relatively inexpensive benefit that might encourage faculty to continue working at the university despite low salaries. The argument was made that most classes had empty chairs and most of the costs of instruction were fixed. A faculty member was paid the same whether or not the class was full. Also, the cost of light, heat, and building maintenance remains the same regardless of class size. One faculty member complained that the benefit of free tuition based upon the number of children was distribution based upon need rather than the concept of relative merit. Thus, he argued, the benefit was unjust.

Few if any systems of political economy are need-based. Marx's ideal of the Communist state was "from each according to his ability and to each according to his needs." The practical problem with this ideal is that it is hard to provide an incentive for everyone to produce as much as he or she is able while economic distribution is made according to needs. Okun's criticism of egalitarian approaches to justice would also apply to need-based systems. This criticism is supported by the economic performance of Communist countries that are now rapidly moving toward more market-oriented economies. This will no doubt correspond with the adoption of market-based rewards and the use of relative merit as the standard for justice.

Institutional Orientation, Ideology, and Approaches to Justice

When managers make decisions, the consequences affect a number of people and organizations. How should a manager go about considering which decision is the right one? Justice demands that a manager be as fair as possible. However, as Chapter 6 suggests, decisions are made within the context of organizations. Organizations have cultures, value systems or ideologies, and institutional orientations that influence decisions about justice.

INSTITUTIONAL ORIENTATION

The external institutional orientation introduced in Chapter 1 provides a framework for understanding the ideology and response patterns of business. The institutional orientation of a business can be as follows.

Type one: *reactive and defensive.* This type of firm considers the economic consequences of its decisions in terms of maximizing owners' profits. Laws are obeyed in the process, but more often legal maneuvers are used to block or delay regulation and to avoid anything that might interfere with profit acquisition. The operating mode is exploitative and anything legal is considered just.

Type two: *anticipatory and responsible.* A firm with this institutional orientation considers the broader nonmarket consequences of decisions when making economic decisions. This involves assuming some responsibility for actions that affect employees, customers, the community, the environment, as well as owners. Rather than use litigation and the courts to block responses to social change, social change is analyzed and anticipated so that appropriate actions can be incorporated into long-range plans and management decisions. Managers accept as just their responsibilities to the many constituencies that are affected by business decisions. The prevailing ideology is more community-oriented and the standards of justice are merit-based.

Type three: *proactive and responsive.* A firm with this orientation considers both the economic and the noneconomic effects of its decisions. Social changes are analyzed and forecasted. The firm is socially and politically active in the public policy process so that laws and regulations are compatible with the long-term interests of the business. Managers accept the legitimacy of nonmarket claims on the business and are willing to work with a number of constituencies to maintain the legitimacy of the business and to respond to claims on the business that are considered appropriate.

Type one firms try to maximize short-run economic results but may alienate important organizational constituencies including their customers in the long run. There is limited concern for long-term political support or for considering the fairness or justice in its decisions beyond the idea that "anything that maximizes profit within the law is fair." Type one firms follow an individualistic ideology and assume that the conditions of a perfectly competitive market exist that cause returns to be consistent with the theory of relative merit. Also, managers who think that anything that is legal is fair follow libertarian views of economic justice.

Type two firms respond to the realities of less than perfect competition and changing social expectations of business by exercising self-control in striving to be ethical and responsible to those affected by decisions, and are concerned about both the competitive and the justice implications of decisions. Managers with this orientation are likely to be more community oriented in their ideology and sensitive to a broader conception of justice than type one firms. However, their primary aim is likely to be long-term economic performance in competitive markets found in industrialized society, and thus relative merit is likely to be the standard by which justice is measured.

Type three firms are the most responsive to the political dimension and are very sensitive to the issue of legitimacy because lowered social and political support is likely to lead to undesirable laws and regulation. Political means are used to achieve or protect economic results. To be successful, such managers consider the concerns and interests of numerous stakeholder groups in the community to maintain legitimacy. Managers in such firms might be likely to adopt some of the aspects of the new ideology and community-oriented concepts of justice. However, the primary orientation of type three firms tends to be political rather than ethical.

Organizational Stakeholders

An organizational stakeholder is "any group or individual who can affect or is affected by the achievement of the firm's objectives."[12] Who are the organizational stakeholders? Managers often consider such primary stakeholders as owners and investors, customers and consumer interest groups, employees and organized labor, the community and interest groups within a pluralistic society, and the environment and environmentalists. Managers can map the various stakeholders. Any management decision is likely to affect each of these stakeholders differently. Therefore, the relations between business and stakeholders may be cordial and warm for some while hostile and cold for others. Stakeholder relations may vary with time and circumstance. For example, consider a major company that has a large number of stakeholders with extremely complex relationships between and among them.

Suppliers

Businesses obtain supplies from both domestic and international sources. The economic well-being of employees who live in the communities in which suppliers are located is often highly dependent on the economic success of these suppliers.

Local Community Groups and Significant Interest Groups

These often organize to protest the impact of some business decisions on their interests. What seems fair to environmentalists may depend upon how a business policy or practice influences the environment. Organized labor may be more interested in plant closure or expansion decisions. Civil rights organizations are more concerned with employment practices. These groups are concerned with the results of company decisions and seek to control behavior through political rather than economic processes. Business decisions may involve trade-offs where the goals and values of various interest groups are not compatible with one another.

Customers and Consumer Advocates

These call for fair prices, high-quality products, and product labeling about the effects of using products. Some have sought to control price increases or spiraling cost increases in areas like health care.

Employees

Major companies have thousands of employees located throughout many countries. Some of these employees are members of labor unions. Some are highly trained professional geologists and engineers. Others are field workers, crew members on ships, and workers in chemical factories and refineries. Decisions made by managers relating to compensation, plant closing, modernization of facilities, marketing, and distribution can have major effects on the lives of employees, and these consequences vary with decision options. For example, a plant closing may seem unfair to the displaced employees in San Antonio, Texas, in the Levi Strauss case but are favored by employees in Costa Rica.

Owners and Investors

These include stockholders, creditors, and other members of the financial community. During the 1980s there were many hostile takeovers, as will be discussed in Chapter 14. The financial community, with its stockholders, prospective stockholders, financiers attempting hostile takeovers, investment bankers supplying capital in the form of junk bonds, investment analysts, and many others form a complex network of stakeholders. Corporate restructuring has many consequences for the stakeholders in this network and for other stakeholders. There are some winners and some losers in the many changes in the economy, and the issue of justice is central.

Organizational stakeholders' claims on business are based upon their interests and institutionally defined roles that are considered legitimate. What are these concerns and interests? On what basis do stakeholders make claims on business? Are the claims just? What if the claim of one stakeholder conflicts with the claims of others? These are important problems facing the practicing manager. Like the individual context of ethical decision making discussed in Chapter 6, the context of organizational decisions is fraught with complex situations and competing stakeholder demands. Managers must strike a balance among these competing claims if they are to be just and to maintain public support while obtaining excellent economic performance.

Economic justice is primarily concerned with economic claims. However, sometimes stakeholder claims take the form of demands that legal and moral rights not be violated and that cultural values and ideology be supported. In a threefold society, stakeholder claims can be classified according to the social sphere in which they appear. The government has the role of protecting rights and maintaining justice.

Employee concerns for economic justice center around job security, just rewards or compensation, and opportunity for career development. However, employees also claim their rights of privacy, freedom of association that includes union membership, freedom of expression, the right not to be wrongfully discharged, and the right to equal opportunity and nondiscrimination in employment practices.

Investors include both the stockholders or owners and the creditors of the organization. The economic justice concerns center around the return on their investment, debt repayment, and sound management that has implications for the long-term value of their investment. Customers are concerned about prices, quality, availability of goods and services, and product safety. The legal rights claimed by customers includes honest and adequate information, fulfilled contracts, safety, and the ability to make economic choices without undue pressure or coercion. The various individuals, governments, and organizations representing the community have economic claims that relate to regional economic development, standard of living, employment, and maintenance of the tax base.

Managers need to weigh the many complex and competing claims of various stakeholders in light of the realities of competitive position, legal requirements, political pressures, and justice. As outlined in Chapter 3, the process of strategic choice includes (1) stakeholder mapping, (2) impact analysis of decision alternatives that considers the fairness of the distribution of burdens and benefits of these choices, (3) social performance assessment, and (4) strategic choice.

Summary

Justice is concerned with the fair distribution of things of value within society. Managers make decisions that have important consequences for people and communities. Therefore, managers should strive to be just because decisions about economic distribution are important to others. A knowledge of justice will help managers to understand the ethical implications of their decisions. This will enable them to justify what they are doing to themselves, to employees, and to their many stakeholders.

Justifications are often influenced by ideology. Ideology is the system of ideals or values that helps convert universal ideas about what constitutes a good society to the legitimate social institutions found in reality. Ideology can be self-serving or it can be an honest attempt to discover principles that underlie a good society. Although there may be truth in the cynical interpretation of ideology, it can be based upon sincere intellectual or spiritual inquiry and can improve our knowledge of what justice requires.

Two ideologies influence current concepts of justice, one traditional, the other newly emergent in the last 50 years. The traditional ideology is individualist, it values personal freedom and individual responsibility, it emphasizes private property and market competition, and it thinks government is best that governs least.

This new ideology is based upon community concerns rather than the rugged individual, interdependence rather than personal freedom, human rights rather than exclusively property rights, the recognition of the imperfections of market competition, a rethinking of social expectations of business and the social contract, and the support of an increased role for government in matters of justice and social affairs.

The five theories of justice may be stated as follows. (1) Libertarian theory defines justice as a process of individual free choices concerning private property in legal exchanges with limited government interference. (2) Relative merit theory defines justice as equal merit/reward ratios for everyone in a competitive market. (3) Rawls's mixed system defines justice as equal liberty and inequalities justified in terms of improving the plight of the least advantaged within society. (4) Egalitarian theory defines justice in terms of equality of political freedom and equality of economic distribution for all within society. (5) Need-based theory of justice defines justice as economic distribution based upon individual needs while holding the ideal of performance according to ability.

Managers seeking to be just in their decisions are not only faced with numerous incompatible standards of economic justice but face competing and conflicting stakeholder demands as well. A business stakeholder is anyone or any organization who affects or is affected by a decision. There are numerous stakeholders including investors, employees, consumers, communities, and the environment. Also, there is the government and numerous interest groups organized around many of the issues facing management. Each of these stakeholders makes claims on management. Some of these claims are based on what justice demands, some of these claims are market-driven, some are political, and some are linked with cultural values.

Managers seeking to make just decisions to achieve high social performance should (1) identify and map the important stakeholders, (2) analyze the impact of decision consequences for each stakeholder, (3) consider the impact significant stakeholders could potentially have for the business, (4) identify the stakeholder interests and the nature of each stakeholder claim, (5) select the decision alternative that best and most fairly responds to the conflicting stakeholder claims in order to (6) make strategic decisions that lead to high social performance by maintaining competitive position, obeying applicable laws and regulations, maintaining political support for the business and its practices, and being ethically defensible.

Conclusions for the Practicing Manager

Gone are the days, if ever there were any, when a manager could forget about matters of ethics and justice in making decisions. The consequences are too important and the interdependencies in advanced society too great to make decisions without considering the impact on stakeholders. The pressures of global competition suggest that responding to nonmarket signals should not be taken lightly or thoughtlessly done.

Furthermore, a business that is considered exploitative, unjust, and uncaring of the needs of society places its political legitimacy on the line. It is also unlikely to be considered a trustworthy supplier in the marketplace; and because all businesses are suppliers to someone, all need to be customer-driven. Thus, managers need to seriously consider the justice of their decisions, even though concepts of justice are complex and contradictory as are the varied claims of stakeholders.

Each of the theories of justice has its own appeal, and it may be possible for a manager to take the best from each theory initially. The following is meant to be suggestive rather than conclusive, to be helpful rather than demanding:

1. From *libertarian* thinking: (1) Consider the private property you manage as your own. Thus take the personal responsibility and initiative to use it in the best way possible. (2) Obey the law. (3) Invest in title insurance when purchasing property; sometimes there are problems with property transfers because of questions in initial holdings.

2. From *merit-based market systems:* (1) Strive to recognize and reward contributions. It is fair and it does motivate others to be recognized, rewarded, and empowered. (2) Select, develop, and promote according to merit. Avoid discrimination. It is immoral and unjust in every system of justice except for the libertarian approach, which leaves such decisions up to the individual.

3. From *Rawlsian Mixed System:* (1) Support equal rights for all. Also, support a minimum standard of living but remember that this standard is unique to a particular culture and situation. (2) Consider the welfare of the least advantaged in your business and in society. For example, it may be just and good business to have a company day care center for single-mother employees. But remember your core business and the basis of competitive advantage. Businesses are not particularly good at diversifying into social programs unrelated to their mission as economic institutions. Consider the role of government in a positive light here. (3) The just savings principle applies to both society and your business. It is just to reinvest in your business to maintain its advanced technology, product designs, productive facilities, and other capabilities.

4. From *egalitarian systems of justice:* (1) Equality is a good policy in fringe benefits, opportunity for career development, and base levels of compensation. (2) Equality of compensation within groups that are very interdependent helps group cooperation and productivity. Also, group-based rewards can help to develop a sense of solidarity in high-pressure competitive situations. Plantwide bonuses tied to stock options also have good results. Thus, a manager can combine features from libertarian, relative merit, and egalitarian theories if done carefully and imaginatively.

5. From *need-based systems:* Sometimes it is just to consider a person as an individual with special needs. Respecting his or her dignity and special situation can be a deeply human act. A person undergoing health problems, family difficulties, or unexpected and unwarranted financial problems may be unproductive and "undeserving" temporarily. A temporary, individualized, need-based gesture can have a very powerful moral and motivational impact. However, managers should recall the connection with generalized need-based systems that are insensitive to performance. Economic organizations need incentives based upon performance to drive them to competitive excellence.

The comments above about how practicing managers could use theories of justice to improve the moral quality of their decisions are not meant to ignore the real and profound differences among these theories of justice discussed in this chapter. Behaving in a just and ethical manner is as demanding as competing effectively in a turbulent market. Every dimension of social performance provides its challenge and complexity for managers. We hope this chapter has clarified the issues and improved readers' understanding of this important aspect of business ethics.

Discussion Questions

1. Consider the cases that have appeared earlier in this text. Was the decision fair of the City of

Detroit in Chapter 1 to condemn the area called Poletown so that a new General Motors assembly plant could be constructed? How were the property rights of the residents of Poletown considered? Evaluate the action of the City of Detroit and General Motors from the perspective of each of the theories of justice.

2. In Chapter 4, we argued that international competition has led to the closing of plants so that production could be accomplished less expensively offshore, even though it resulted in loss of jobs in the United States. Evaluate the justice of these plant closings from the perspective of relative merit and Rawls's mixed system. Are the conclusions similar or different? Who are the stakeholders in these situations? Does a broader consideration of stakeholders change your answers above?

3. In the American Cyanamid case at the beginning of Chapter 6, was the decision by the managers fair to exclude women of childbearing ages from contaminated jobs? Which theories would accept this? Which would consider this unjust?

Notes

1. George C. Lodge, *The American Disease* (New York: Knopf, 1984), p. 32.

2. Francis X. Sutton, Seymour E. Harris, Carl Kaysen, and James Tobin, *The American Business Creed* (New York: Schocken Books, 1962), p. 1.

3. George C. Lodge and Ezra F. Vogel, eds., *Ideology and National Competitiveness: An Analysis of Nine Countries* (Boston: Harvard Business School Press, 1987).

4. See Henry B. Mayo, *Introduction to Marxist Theory* (New York: Oxford University Press, 1960), especially chap. 3.

5. The concepts found in Adam Smith, *The Theory of Moral Sentiments,* are discussed in Chapters 1 and 5. According to this view a good society is based upon the balance of three virtues: prudence, justice, and beneficence. In his later work, *The Wealth of Nations,* Smith argues for a political economy based upon limited government, market competition, and prudent behavior. See Chapter 4 for an overview of the model of market competition based upon this work.

6. This case is adapted from Tom Beauchamp, "The Ethical Foundations of Economic Justice," *Review of Social Economy* 40, no. 3 (December 1982): 292–93.

7. Aristotle, *The Complete Works of Aristotle,* Revised Oxford Translation, ed. Jonathan Barnet (Princeton, N.J.: Princeton University Press, 1984).

8. John A. Rawls, *A Theory of Justice* (Cambridge, Mass.: Harvard University Press, 1971), p. 302.

9. See Tom L. Beauchamp, "The Ethical Foundations of Economic Justice," *Review of Social Economy* 40, no. 3 (December 1982): 291–300; and Thomas Donaldson, "What Justice Demands," *Review of Social Economy* 40 no. 3 (December 1982): 300–310.

10. Beauchamp, "The Ethical Foundations of Economic Justice," p. 294.

11. Arthur M. Okun, *Equality and Efficiency* (Washington, D.C.: The Brookings Institution, 1975).

12. R. Edward Freeman, *Strategic Management: A Stakeholder Approach* (Marshfield, Mass.: Pitman, 1984), p. 25.

Discussion Case 8–1 _____

The Make-up Examination

Two students in a class of 27 approached their professor to take an exam a day early because both had other exams that had been scheduled on that same day. The professor agreed to offer the special exam for these two persons. No announcement was made in class and other students were not aware of the special arrangement between the professor and the two students. Thus, other students were probably not aware that such special treatment was possible.

The course syllabus handed out in class specified that the exam would be held on the previous Monday. However, because of the timing of coverage on materials and at the urging of some

members in the class, the professor had moved the regular time from Monday to Wednesday of that same week. The class average grade after one exam and two written assignments was 81 percent or B–. The range of grades is from D (60 percent) to A (90–100 percent). The two students in question both have averages of over 95 percent.

Case Discussion Question

1. Was the decision just from the perspective of (a) libertarian, (b) relative merit of Aristotle, and (c) the mixed system proposed by Rawls?

Discussion Case 8–2 _____

The National Flood Insurance Program

Oliver Ready of Grafton, Illinois, guided his flatboat down Water Street and paused at his two-story frame house, where the Mississippi River now inhabits the first floor. When it recedes, he'll be in good shape. Ready has purchased federal flood insurance since 1975, and it's been a sweet deal. He's paid about $6,000 in premiums and collected $24,000 in payouts after floods in 1979, 1982, 1986, and last April 1993. He expects $32,000 more for this disaster in July 1993. Ready is happy to take the money, but he wonders about a government program that rewards people for living in places that are frequently underwater. "You wouldn't run a business like this," says Ready, a 53-year-old fish market owner. "If every three or four years you had to spend $10,000 to repair a business, you'd wise up and say, 'To hell with this location.'"

SOURCE: Bill Turque, John McCormick, and Daniel Glick, "On the Disaster Dole," © Newsweek, August 2, 1993, pp. 24–25. Reprinted by permission. All rights reserved.

Imagine a car insurance policy that didn't raise your rates after an accident. Or a life insurance policy that charged the same whether you were 25 years old or 70. That's the idea behind the National Flood Insurance Program (NFIP), where property near rivers or in vulnerable coastal areas is restored by the government again and again. "Repetitive loss" cases like Ready's amount to only 3 percent of all claims. But they account for more than a third of total payouts. Since 1974, the NFIP has paid nearly $2 billion to 63,000 flood-damaged properties. "Taxpayers have bought some of these people refrigerators and chain saws 10 times over," says Tom Szilasi, building commissioner of St. Charles County, Missouri, across the river from Grafton.

Although the NFIP has done well by many Midwesterners, most of the payouts actually go to the coasts, where beachfront homes are regularly inundated by storms. Federal flood insurance is effectively an entitlement for "some of the wealthiest homeowners in America," says Rep. Joe Kennedy, who is drafting legislation to tighten up the program. A 1991 measure passed by the House and stalled in the Senate after banking, real estate, and home-building lobbies mobilized. Calamities this year might provide new impetus for reform. A punishing hurricane season this fall, combined with claims from the Mississippi flood (expected to reach about $50 billion), could send the NFIP—already $18 million in the red—deeper into deficit.

Solid base: Federally subsidized flood insurance began in 1968 as a sound idea. It was a natural niche for government to fill. Private carriers won't offer it, they say, because the only buyers would be those at the worst risk. In exchange for low-cost policies, communities established rigorous building codes for new construction in flood-prone areas, limiting damage when the waters rise. That part of the program has worked. Federal officials say premiums from structures built in floodplains since 1974 have produced a net gain of $248 million for the NFIP. But Congress, reluctant to alienate property owners with older buildings in floodplains, "grandfathered" the structures. As long as flood damage is less than 50 percent of the propertys' market value, they are eligible for subsidized insurance. (Structures with more than 50 percent damage must be moved to higher ground, brought up to federal standards, or razed.) With the average flood claim totaling $10,500, NFIP continually bails out the same older, poorly built properties.

That's certainly the case in tiny Grafton (population: 918), which hugs the bottom of a bluff just above the Mississippi's edge about 40 miles northwest of St. Louis. Kathy Rulo, 37, and her husband, Ron, are filing their fourth flood insurance claim since buying their home in 1978. "I think the government has paid for our house about two times," she says. In St. Charles County north of St. Louis one homeowner received 18 separate NFIP payments before this year's two floods. Insurance is remarkably easy to get. Floodplain residents can rush to an agent at the last minute and buy a federally guaranteed policy. After that, the building need remain dry for only five days to qualify for reimbursement. Lowell Skeens, 77, a retired Grafton boat builder, says he bought insurance for his one-story house on July 2, when high crests were forecast. On July 11, floodwater reached his door.

Compounding the problem are property owners who buy no flood insurance at all. Many choose to collect federal bailout grants of up to $11,900. Banks are also culprits. The NFIP requires mortgage lenders to insist that borrowers have flood insurance. But the provision is routinely ignored. Although most homeowners do purchase a policy, many let premium payments lapse later. When mortgages are sold to other lending institutions, there is no mechanism for tracking compliance. Lax enforcement allows 250,000 policyholders to drop out of NFIP each year.

Critics say several changes would help. Those receiving disaster grants should be required to buy policies. Banks could be penalized for not enforcing insurance requirements. Washington also needs to establish more incentives for communities to raze flood-vulnerable buildings. It's not Oliver Ready's fault. But if Congress again ducks reform, he and thousands of other property owners will continue to benefit from a leaky federal program. "They set the rules," Ready says, "We didn't."

Discussion Questions

1. Is it fair for a homeowner to be subsidized by the government for flood losses over and over again?
2. Should a person be able to buy government flood loss insurance days before a flood with certain knowledge of an upcoming flood based upon forecasts of upstream water levels?
3. Should owners of expensive beachfront property be allowed to purchase flood insurance? Should low-income homeowners on floodplains be allowed to purchase flood insurance? Which theory of justice provides the best answer to these questions? Explain.
4. Under what circumstances is it fair for taxpayers, through the government NFIP program, to subsidize the losses of flood victims?
5. What reforms would you suggest in the NFIP program to make it more fair?

CHAPTER 9

Business Social Performance and Social Responsibility

1. Review the debate over the social responsibility of business.
2. Understand the difference between social responsibility as an ethical concept and social responsiveness as a political concept.
3. Show how social responsibility relates to other dimensions of business social performance.
4. Explain how the institutional orientation of business influences the views of management concerning social responsibility.
5. Describe how managers can institutionalize social responsibility and ethics throughout the organization.
6. Outline the role played by codes of ethics in social responsibility.
7. Suggest how managers might determine the limits of social responsibility.
8. Apply the concepts of corporate social responsibility (CSR) to the global environment of business.

Introductory Case _____

The Payoff from a Good Reputation

You won't find it on the balance sheet, and it's not listed in the 10K or a proxy. If you ask the wizards on Wall Street exactly how it figures into a company's net worth, be prepared for some mighty blank stares.

SOURCE: Excerpt quoted from Susan Caminiti, "The Payoff from a Good Reputation," *Fortune*, February 10, 1992, pp. 74–77. © 1992 Time, Inc. All rights reserved.

But more and more companies are now coming to realize that when managed correctly their good name can be the most valuable and enduring asset.

For small companies as well as big ones, the payoff from a good reputation is vast. For starters, it's what puts you first in the minds of customers and—no small feat—helps keep you there. A solid reputation makes a customer willing to pay more for your product or service. Want the best people working for you? A respected reputation not only helps attract and retain the top minds in your industry, but it also enables you to steal talent away from competitors. It can act as the launching pad for new-product introductions and help open doors more easily for international expansion. And contrary to what you might think, a good reputation, once lost, can be regained. . . . At the very least a great reputation is built by offering a superior product or service. "You can't skimp on quality and then pour money into marketing your reputation," explains Alan Towers, president of the consulting firm that bears his name. . . .

The companies that are winning the kudos also understand that customers are looking beyond quality for something more. If the 1980s are remembered fondly for anything, it will be that they created the sharpest, most-educated customers marketers have ever faced. Sure, these shoppers want the best you have to offer, but they are also interested in what your company stands for. Is your company one they would want to work for? Are you polluting their planet? Says Peter J. Harleman, an executive director at Landor Associates, a design and consulting firm in San Francisco: "A company with a good reputation is seen as being a member of society; that is, doing what helps the world rather than harms it."

For example, Herman Miller, the furniture maker in Zeeland, Michigan, no longer uses tropical woods, such as rosewood, from endangered rain forests in its office desks and tables. Instead it uses cherry, which does not come from the tropics. Says CEO Richard Ruch: "We thought first about the environmental aspect and then wondered if the switch would impact sales." In fact the switch has not hurt sales, which were $869 million in 1990. And it has added more luster to Herman Miller's already fine reputation. Inspired by Herman Miller's decision, the Business and Institutional Furniture Manufacturers Association now urges all its members not to use tropical wood from endangered forests.

Introduction

The notion of social responsibility of business raises a number of questions. Business, as the primary institution within the economic sphere of society, has a prime responsibility for producing the goods and services demanded by society. Does management's responsibility extend beyond its business activities? If so, what are the limits to its responsibility and how is management to determine them? If top management wants to establish a value-based culture within the organization and to accept its social responsibility, how can these views be institutionalized throughout the organization? What are the implications for social responsibility for other dimensions of business social performance, and especially the economic performance of the business? These are the questions raised by the issue of social responsibility of business, and they are the main topic of this chapter.

Many argue that the social responsibility of business should be limited to its economic activities.

Others take the position that business managers should accept a greater amount of social responsibility. The opening case suggests that social responsibility can lead to a good reputation not only for superior products and service, for advanced technology that provides unique capabilities, but also for being a good citizen. Business managers who seek to do the right thing in a visible way can raise the consciousness of others and encourage behavior that improves society. Will such actions reduce the company's economic performance, or will they be the basis for sustainable competitive advantage? What are the limits of such behavior, and how can a manager define these limits as an individual and as a representative of the business?

The Social Responsibility Debate

The end of the nineteenth century was marked by the appearance of large businesses. The dominant ideology of the time was the rugged individualism of the frontier. Government was small, markets were local or at most regional, and the impact of business decisions was relatively small. Little thought was given to the idea that business might have a responsibility beyond simply doing business. However, the idea of stewardship had been a part of American culture since the time of the Puritan communities. According to this biblical tradition humanity should be stewards of the earth. It was the duty of humanity to name the creatures, exercise dominion over creation, and care for it as good stewards. However, the exercise of dominion was usually interpreted in the context of a struggle with nature in the frontier, where land was cleared and settled and the harsh weather was often perilous.

With the advent of large-scale business the philosophy of social Darwinism and the survival of the fittest was championed by many. Wealthy individuals used this idea to justify their wealth and power because they had won the Darwinian struggle. The concentration of power led to a certain arrogance and abuse of that power. Concentration of economic power in the hands of a few large businesspeople was a source of controversy leading first to the regulation of the railroads then to the development of antitrust law, discussed in later chapters.

Business then adopted the idea of stewardship, which was sanctioned by either God or the doctrine of survival of the fittest. John D. Rockefeller, the founder of Standard Oil, was once quoted as saying, "God gave me my money." As wealthy individuals, business people sought to use their resources for the betterment of society. In 1907, J. P. Morgan stopped a panic in the banking system and averted a recession. Andrew Carnegie, the founder of U.S. Steel, donated much of his wealth to public libraries in cities throughout the country. Carnegie's ideas of stewardship were published in an essay in 1889 entitled "The Gospel of Wealth," in which he argued that business must pursue wealth but this wealth should be used to help society.

Social responsibility, beginning with the idea of business stewardship, has been controversial since the idea became popular near the turn of the century. The arguments against business assuming an expanded corporate social responsibility (CSR) was more persuasive among managers until the early 1970s. Beginning in the 1960s, major changes in the social expectations of business became visible in the form of a tidal wave of social regulation, which is discussed in Chapter 11. The legitimacy or social support for business and other social institutions began to drop, and the political environment became markedly hostile.

Businesses that resisted the new social expectations and continued to behave as though "the only business of business is business" seemed to be less able to cope with social and market changes. Arguments began to appear that widened the role of business within society beyond narrowly defined profit maximization. A social responsibility debate ensued. Opponents suggested that if business accepted social responsibility, it would undercut economic performance and lead to an abuse of power. Proponents of the idea argued that business had become a major institution within society and its efforts were both expected and needed to solve social problems. These two sides of the debate are outlined below.

THE CASE AGAINST CORPORATE SOCIAL RESPONSIBILITY

Milton Friedman has argued that corporate social responsibility (CSR) would undermine a free society.[1] He argued that managers are hired by stockholders to manage business on their behalf and the CSR is to increase profits and thus contribute to the wealth of the stockholders. If a manager owns the business or has independent wealth, then he or she can contribute to society as an individual with his or her own resources. However, if a manager uses corporate resources for the benefit of society without also contributing to the economic performance of the company, then that manager is taxing shareholders and misusing their resources without any accountability.

Thus, business managers engaged in an expansive concept of CSR are usurping the role of government, misusing the wealth of others, and undermining free society. Friedman pronounced there is one and only one social responsibility of business—to use its resources and engage in activities designed to increase its profits so long as it stays within the rules of the game, which is to say, engages in open and free competition, without deception or fraud.[2]

Theodore Levitt also argued against corporate social responsibility because it would be bad for business and bad for society.[3] He viewed society as divided into major functional areas including social, economic, and political groups. Each area had its function: organized labor supported the interests of workers, government was responsible for the general welfare, and business was responsible for maximizing profit through maintaining vigorous competition. Individual freedom was best protected by the independence of these three spheres and in the decentralization of power within society. Levitt observed that the nature of competition was warlike and thus assumed CSR and its cooperative support of society would undermine the capacity for competitiveness. It would also undermine the effectiveness of government because it would lead to the concentration of power in the hands of business leaders.

Philosophical arguments against CSR are based upon the nature of a moral agent. Can a corporation be a "moral person"? Gibson has argued that we cannot punish a corporation *as* a corporation. Individuals employed by a corporation can be blamed and punished for their actions but not the corporation itself.[4] A corporation cannot be put into prison or be put to death; only individual human beings can. Similarly, Velasquez argued that a corporation cannot act morally in the sense that a human can.[5] Organizations cannot be forgiven nor can they be said to go to heaven or hell in a religious sense.

Because organizations cannot be held morally accountable, a corporation cannot be a moral agent and cannot be held morally responsible for its actions. If a corporation cannot be held morally responsible, how can it be argued that corporate social responsibility exists? Velasquez suggests that corporations can be held legally accountable and be subject to product liability lawsuits. However,

this is not to say that a corporation is morally accountable and thus cannot be held morally responsible for anything it does. Only individual managers can be held morally accountable.

THE CASE FOR CORPORATE SOCIAL RESPONSIBILITY

There are a number of counterarguments in favor of CSR[6]: (1) corporations can be said to have a conscience and be held morally accountable for the consequences of corporate behavior, (2) a corporation is based upon an evolving social contract, (3) the social contract changes with society's expectations, (4) business has the capability and resources to improve society and thus its managers should assume CSR, (5) the solution of social problems depends upon everyone, including business, and (6) CSR is consistent with the long-term economic interests of business.

Goodpaster and Matthews have argued that corporations can have a conscience in a certain sense.[7] Organizations are social systems whose members share values and a common corporate culture. This shared value system forms the basis of a corporate conscience. Knowledge shared by several organizational units or several levels in the management hierarchy becomes organizational knowledge that transcends any single individual. Thus, a corporation can be said to have a conscience and be held morally accountable. Corporations should be held socially responsible for their behavior and should be accountable for the consequences of corporate actions.

Because corporations are chartered by the government, a contract forms the basis for their existence. In this contract, society brings the corporation legally into existence and thus the government has the power to constrain the behavior of business. Also, society has the right to change its expectations of business as an instrument of society. This social contract is an implicit social agreement based upon an evolving set of expectations.

A more historical approach to explaining CSR notes that social changes give rise to changes in social values, social needs, and the demands placed upon social institutions expressed by society. In Chapter 8 the competing ideologies were reviewed. The individualistic, market-oriented ideology emphasizes private property, rights and obligations defined by contracts, minimal government, and reliance on the invisible hand of impersonal market forces to fulfill society's needs. In this model, business has little power and is controlled by market forces.

The community-oriented activist government ideology emphasizes community membership as the basis of rights and obligations, an activist government, less reliance on market forces, government control, and social responsibility as a guide to behavior. Market forces are seen as not totally controlling behavior, and the assumption of CSR might eliminate the need for government control. Business can respond to changing social expectations and assume CSR or it can reject such expectations and lose its legitimacy as a social institution.

Many of the decisions and activities of business have consequences for the local community, for the environment, and for many aspects of society. These consequences extend beyond the marketplace and thus are of interest to the broader society that is not necessarily directly involved with a market-exchange process with business. If a business does not control the pollution from its facility, society can suffer from impure water or air. The reconfiguration of a global network of operations can cause unemployment in some communities and urban sprawl in others. For this reason, it has been argued that corporate social responsibility requires that business seriously consider the impact of its actions on society.[8]

Keith Davis has suggested that many of today's social problems would not be solvable without the knowledge, skills, and resources of business. Thus, society expects more of business, and management has a responsibility to use its resources to solve social problems and to make society a better place to live.[9]

From those who oppose corporate social responsibility, one might conclude that CSR should be limited to maximizing profits within the rules of the game, which includes abiding by the law. From those who endorse a broader interpretation of CSR, the role of business would include profits, but rather than maximizing short-term profits, business should optimize long-term profits, obey the laws and regulations, consider the nonmarket impact of its decisions or face an increase in government control, and seek ways to improve society through CSR programs.

The Pyramid of Corporate Social Responsibility

The pyramid of corporate social responsibility developed by Archie Carroll integrates the major arguments in the CSR debate into a single model.[10] It also parallels the business social performance model outlined in Chapter 1. This four-part framework defines *social responsibility* as the economic, legal, ethical, and discretionary responsibilities arising from the expectations of society, as shown in Figure 9–1.

ECONOMIC RESPONSIBILITIES

Economic performance is the foundation for the social responsibility of business. As the primary instrument within the economic sphere of society, it is the task of business to provide the needed goods and services. Market systems are characterized by interdependence—buyers and sellers need one another to satisfy their mutual needs. Business serves society by fulfilling the needs of buyers in the market and is rewarded for doing this well by profits. However, the maximization of short-term profits is often associated with irresponsibility if this means damaging long-term relations with customers through exploitation or degrading the potential of business. Failing to invest in new products, technology, or modernization of productive facilities can harm the competitive position of business.

Assuring high levels of long-term profits might better be considered a problem of optimization

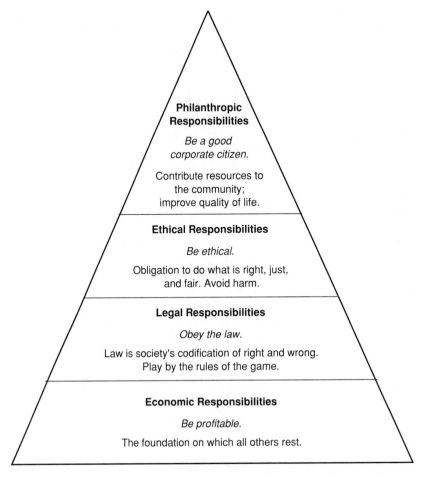

FIGURE 9–1 The Pyramid of Corporate Social Responsibility

SOURCE: Archie B. Carroll, "The Pyramid of Corporate Social Responsibility: Toward the Moral Management of Organizational Stakeholders," *Business Horizons* (July-August 1991). Copyright 1991 by the Foundation of the School of Business at Indiana University. Used with permission.

rather than maximization. If a business fails in its economic role, stockholders lose their investment, employees lose their jobs, communities lose their tax base, and customers may not have the goods and services they seek. Thus, CSR should begin with the consideration of economic performance.

LEGAL RESPONSIBILITIES

Businesses are chartered or licensed by government and are expected to comply with laws and regulations that encode society's norms for justice and fair play. Obeying the law is one of the conditions for the continued existence of business within society. It is business's responsibility to obey the law, to play by the rules of the game established by society. Businesses are expected to offer products that meet safety standards and comply with environmental regulations and the financial reporting requirements established by government. Laws are the result of the public policy process and form the legal environment in which business operates, as discussed in the next part of the book.

ETHICAL RESPONSIBILITIES

As the debate outlined above indicated, some argue that economic and legal performance are the minimum for social responsibility. Proponents of an expanded CSR call for ethical and discretionary responsibilities. As outlined in earlier chapters, ethical responsibilities include applying the concepts of utilitarian analysis, rights, duties, and justice. This requires making ethical decisions by considering the consequences of an action, by honoring the rights of others, by fulfilling duties, and by avoiding harm to others. Also, it means seeking justice and fairness in balancing the interests of various corporate stakeholders including stockholders, employees, customers, suppliers, and residents of communities in which the business operates. It requires moral imagination.

PHILANTHROPIC RESPONSIBILITIES

Philanthropic responsibilities are discretionary actions by management in response to social expectations. Such actions may include the volunteer work of executives in community programs, the providing of financial resources for college scholarship programs, or donations to local charities. They could include sponsorship of a cultural or artistic endeavor. Through these programs a corporation can obtain a reputation for being a good corporate citizen. Philanthropic programs are the most controversial dimension of CSR because it may appear that they involve trade-offs with economic performance.

Domains of Corporate Social Performance

Donna Wood revisited the CSR concept and suggested that the four dimensions of CSR principles

have three domains, as shown in Table 9-1.[11] These three domains include the institutional, the organizational, and the individual. Each of these domains spans three levels and corresponds to its own principle of CSR, as follows.

THE PRINCIPLE OF LEGITIMACY AT THE INSTITUTIONAL LEVEL

The key CSR principle at the institutional level is legitimacy. The relevant CSR principle is the *iron law of responsibility* first formulated by Keith Davis,[12] as follows: "Society grants legitimacy and power to business. In the long run, those who do not use power in a manner that society considers responsible will tend to lose it" (p. 314).

Legitimacy is relevant social and political support for business as an institution. Businesses have grown in power, resources, and size, and society has changed dramatically this century. These changes have brought about changes in social expectations that have pressed for changes in the implicit social contract between society and business. The continued legitimacy is contingent upon business meeting the changing social expectations and upon not abusing its power.

THE PRINCIPLE OF PUBLIC RESPONSIBILITY AT THE ORGANIZATIONAL LEVEL

This principle, first formulated by Preston and Post, is defined as "businesses are responsible for outcomes related to their primary and secondary areas of involvement with society."[13]

This suggests that CSR requires that organizational managers consider the consequences of their actions. They are not obliged to solve all of society's problems, but they are responsible for aiding in areas related to business operations and interests.

According to the principle of public responsibility the chemical industry should be involved in programs to reduce toxic waste, the recycling of plastics, and environmental cleanup. Secondarily, it may become involved in supporting engineering education at universities where it recruits chemical engineers. However, the support of an arts performance would be more difficult to justify with this CSR principle.

THE PRINCIPLE OF MANAGERIAL DISCRETION AT THE INDIVIDUAL LEVEL

According to this principle, "Managers are moral actors. Within every domain of CSR, they are obliged to exercise such discretion as is available to them, toward socially responsible outcomes."[14] Table 9–1 indicated how the individual decision-making discretion might enhance the moral qual-

ity of CSR across all the dimensions of social performance. This principle suggests that managers need a *moral imagination* that requires that (1) they are sensitive to the moral dimensions of their decisions, (2) they are careful to become aware of the detrimental effects of their business decisions, and (3) they are also aware of ways to increase the moral character of their decisions in ways that the social good is increased in their everyday activities.

Applying moral imagination to the levels of CSR might involve (1) producing environmentally sound products in ways that improve the competitive position, (2) taking advantage of

TABLE 9–1

Corporate Social Policy: Sample Outcomes of Acting on Corporate Social Responsibility (CSR) Principles within CSR Domains

Domains	Social Legitimacy (institutional)	Public Responsibility (organizational)	Managerial Discretion (individual)
Economic	Produce goods and services, provide jobs, create wealth for shareholders.	Price goods and services to reflect true production costs by incorporating all externalities.	Produce ecologically sound products, use low-polluting technologies, cut costs with recycling.
Legal	Obey laws and regulations. Don't expect privileged positions in public policy.	Work for public policies representing enlightened self-interest.	Take advantage of regulatory requirements to innovate in products or technologies.
Ethical	Follow fundamental ethical principles (e.g., honesty in product labeling).	Provide full and accurate product use information to enhance user safety beyond legal requirements.	Target product use information to specific markets (e.g., children, foreign speakers) and promote as a product advantage.
Discretionary	Act as a good citizen in all matters beyond law and ethical rules. Return a portion of revenues to the community.	Invest the firm's charitable resources in social problems related to the firm's primary and secondary involvements with society.	Choose charitable investments that actually pay off in social problem solving (i.e., apply an effectiveness criterion).

SOURCE: Donna J. Wood, "Corporate Social Performance Revisited," *Academy of Management Review* 16, No. 4: 710.

opportunities afforded by legal requirements to innovate products that might make a special contribution to society, (3) targeting social needs in marketing products that aid a specific group like the disabled, or (4) voluntarily using organizational resources to help resolve a social problem in areas where the organization might have special expertise.

Social Responsibility Versus Social Responsiveness

Chapter 1 discussed the institutional orientation of an organization using the three types of organizations first developed by Sethi.[15] These three types of organizations include the following:

1. *The defensive and reactive organization.* Organizations with a social obligation perspective can be characterized as defensive and reactive. These organizations are generally narrow in their view of CSR and seek to maximize profits within the law. Stakeholders considered in organizational decisions are limited to stockholders. These organizations are often seen as short-term and exploitative in their perspective and may also suffer from a poor reputation.

2. *The anticipatory and socially responsible organization.* Organizations with a social responsibility perspective anticipate changes in social expectations, develop CSR programs for various organizational stakeholders, and integrate organizational responses in the long-range planning of the organization. Stakeholder groups considered as legitimate by top management include stockholders, employees, customers, suppliers, and the local community. Their view of CSR tends to include the four factors in the CSR pyramid discussed above.

3. *The proactive and politically responsive organization.* Organizations with a politically responsive perspective are proactive and engage in strategic issues management. These firm develop a response capacity to maintain their competitiveness in economic performance and to maintain their legitimacy in political performance. While recognizing the importance of economic performance, managers in these organizations are keenly aware of the changing legal environment and the importance of being involved in the public policy process. Managers of such organizations may strive to be ethical and subscribe to the CSR pyramid outlined above, or they may be amoral in their attempts to control the development of public policy issues to accomplish their own interests.

Sethi argued that the ideologically oriented debate over the CSR issue missed the point of legitimacy. Socially responsible organizations may or may not be more ethical than defensive and reactive ones. The key point is that the socially responsible organizations are better able to respond to changing social expectations in a positive and more effective manner. Rather than be caught by surprise by new laws and regulations, the socially responsible organization monitors the environment and accepts the changes in social expectations that will eventually be manifested in new legal and regulatory requirements.

Furthermore, the proactive and politically responsive organization will probably be able to adapt to social changes even better than the socially responsible organization. The *socially responsible organization* is essentially reactive in that it monitors the environment and adapts its long-range planning to incorporate changes that are predictable in the law. As a good corporate citizen it seeks to do the right thing from an ethical perspective.

The *politically responsive organization* recognizes itself as involved as are other interest groups in the public policy process. Rather than monitor, anticipate, and plan for social changes and legal requirements, the responsive organization also communicates its needs and concerns to lawmakers and other external constituencies. Thus there is a greater chance that new laws will incorporate the interest of business and be less onerous for the socially responsive organization, which seeks to be politically adept.

Social Responsibility and Economic Performance

Ullmann reviewed a series of studies that have investigated the relationship between the disclosure of social performance by business in its annual reports and the 10K reports required by the Securities and Exchange Commission (SEC), the actual social performance, and the economic performance by business. Although the studies had mixed results, the majority found a positive relationship between social responsibility and economic performance.[16]

SOCIAL DISCLOSURE AND SOCIAL PERFORMANCE

Of seven studies reviewed, four reported no correlation, two found positive correlations, and one yielded a negative correlation. Ullmann explained the inconsistent results concerning the disclosure of social responsibility programs in two ways. He felt that managers sometimes underreport social responsibility programs because social programs are sometimes very costly and it might prove embarrassing if these costs became known, even though the programs might be favored by top management. At other times it is politically to managers' advantage to exaggerate their social programs. Companies might sometimes overstate their reports of social responsibility programs to increase their social support in politically sensitive areas.

SOCIAL RESPONSIBILITY AND ECONOMIC PERFORMANCE

Of 13 studies reviewed, 8 found positive correlations, 4 found no correlation, and one reported a negative correlation. The studies used a wide variety of methodologies and the measure used for social performance was questioned. Nine of the studies used *reputation scales* to measure social performance and four used a *pollution performance index.*

In another study of the social responsibility–economic performance relationship by Cochran and Wood, 39 firms were examined.[17] Their major conclusion was "firms with older assets have lower CSR . . . ratings." Older firms may have purchased inefficient and polluting plants before passage of environmental laws that established pollution standards. These firms may have had to spend large amounts retrofitting old and relatively inefficient facilities and thus suffered financially for their pollution control efforts. These pollution control efforts were government-mandated and thus not at the discretion of management.

To conclude their research on the social responsibility–economic performance relationship, they reiterated the conclusion of Abbott and Monsen that "being socially involved [does not appear to be] dysfunctional to the investor. Perhaps it is this latter finding that has greater significance for decision making purposes, particularly given current political and social pressures."[18]

Arlow and Gannon also reviewed the literature on social responsiveness and economic performance. They concluded that corporate social responsibility goals are subordinate to economic goals. Businesses' responses vary in different industries and depend on the size of the organization. Most studies of this relationship were done over a *short term*; the results may have varied if *long-term* performance had been considered. Lags may exist between the development of social responsibility programs and positive economic results. Economic performance remains the foundation of CSR upon which all else rests.

SOCIAL DISCLOSURE OF SOCIAL RESPONSIBILITY PROGRAMS AND ECONOMIC PERFORMANCE

Of 11 studies, 7 found positive correlations, 1 found both positive and negative correlations, and the remaining 3 found no correlations. Economic performance is often measured by considering the stock price. If we assume that financial markets are efficient, stock price should accurately reflect the value of information concerning the long-term prospects of a firm. Investors interested in socially responsible business may be willing to pay more for stock in such firm.

Social disclosures of programs by corporations may also reduce a firm's risks associated with required social improvement programs, potential fines, or social sanctions that could reflect lower levels of social legitimacy. Public disclosures by corporate public affairs may seek to influence many external stakeholders besides the stockholders of the company. However, the social and political support for a business is positively associated with its reputation. And over the long term, actions need to back up the reputation. Actions must go beyond glowing press releases from the corporate affairs office that seek to make a bad situation appear in a better light.

Institutionalizing Social Responsibility

Ethical decision making as a dimension of CSR has implications at all levels. Institutionally a firm should seek legitimacy by maintaining its public trust. This public trust is, in part, based on a business's reputation for ethical dealing. Organizationally it needs to have structures, corporate cultures, and accepted values that encourage ethical behavior. Individually, the manager is pulled in various directions by fellow employees, customers, and members of the community as ethical dilemmas are confronted daily.

A business needs to carefully institutionalize ethical responsibility if it is to be successfully implemented. A code of ethics will not work by itself, as General Electric discovered (see Box 9–1). What can business do to insure that its ethical responsibilities are being implemented? And that it will avoid wrongdoing that may result in legal problems and public embarrassment in the media?[19] Ethical responsibility needs to be organized and carefully implemented throughout the organization if it is to be successful.

Using Ethical Codes of Conduct

Formal *codes of ethics* usually form the foundation for institutionalizing business ethics within the organization. A code of ethics is a formal statement of ethical practices sanctioned by the organization. Nearly 90 percent of the *Fortune* 500, the 500 largest corporations in America, and more than one-half of all other businesses have formal codes of ethics. However, it is easy to make mistakes in developing such a code.

Codes of ethics are often misused. This may be the case when ethical codes are considered a pub-

---

BOX 9–1 **An Ethical Code Is Not Enough**

A good example is General Electric (GE). The company has long had a formal, written code of conduct that is communicated to employees and perceives itself as a leader in subscribing to ethical business practices. Yet, GE ran into trouble in 1985 for forging time cards at a Pennsylvania defense plant. This situation caused a suspension of new defense contracts for a time and much embarrassment for the firm. More recently, their Kidder Peabody subsidiary was implicated in an insider trading scandal, even though GE was assured before their June 1986 acquisition of Kidder that the firm faced no major problem with the SEC or Justice Department. These events led to a management shake-up at Kidder. GE found that it was quite difficult to implement ethics in its far-flung range of businesses.

SOURCE: Patrick E. Murphy, "Implementing Business Ethics," *Journal of Business Ethics* 7 (1988): 907–8. Reprinted by permission of Kluwer Academic Publishers.

lic relations tool directed at audiences external to the organization or to document "business practice" to avoid lawsuits. Codes used primarily for external consumption may not serve well as a guide for management behavior. Other problems with ethical codes occur when (1) codes are generally written platitudes giving little guidance for behavior, or (2) codes are a list of unethical behaviors that might reduce company profits.

Effective ethical codes should be (1) publicly available documents, (2) written in specific language that is (3) clear and realistic, (4) for internal use by the organization, and (5) periodically revised.[20] For example, receiving gifts from customers or suppliers may present a conflict of interest problem. If so, the ethical code should not use vague wording like "Only gifts of modest value are allowed." Rather, a specific amount like $25 or $100 maximum should be specified. Donnelly Mirrors uses the specific ethical guideline "If you can't eat it, drink it or use it up in one day, don't give it or anything else of greater value."

Codes should be public documents that are widely communicated to organizational employees and to external stakeholders. They should be *blunt and realistic about violations*. They should be actively enforced because the possibility of being caught is a greater deterrent of code violations than the severity of the punishment. Also, the code should tell employees what to do if they discover a violation of the code.

Ethical codes, as living documents to institutionalize CSR in a changing environment, need to be periodically revised. Controversies and scandals in the business or industry might suggest the need for new elements or a change in the relative importance of articles in the code. For example, in the wake of the insider trading scandals that occurred in the financial markets of the 1980s, companies might wish to address this issue. Highlighting its importance in response to growing awareness of the problems might be needed. However, revisions of ethical codes are not merely for public consumption; they must be realistic and focus on management behavior to be effective.

McDonnell Douglas Corporation provides a good example of a code of conduct and checklist to be used by managers to assure that their decisions are ethical and consistent with corporate social responsibility, as shown in Table 9–2. The checklist also suggests a way to encourage individual managers to engage their moral imagination in making decisions.

USING COMMITTEES, CONFERENCES, AND TRAINING

Ethical committees. These can be formed to review codes of ethics. Motorola uses an ethical committee to interpret, clarify, and communicate its code of ethics, and to serve a quasi-judicial role in its enforcement. The presence of such a committee, especially if it is visible and has access to top management, can increase the discussion of ethical issues in management meetings. A committee structure can influence the corporate culture and help to make ethical codes a living document that guides the daily life of the management and other employees.

The ethical audit. Also, a formal committee empowered to perform an ethical audit of operations periodically can increase awareness and compliance within the business. Dow Corning has had a face-to-face ethical audit in place for over a decade. Items in this audit have evolved over the years to consider needed changes. Each audit includes some eight to ten specific items tailored for each functional area or unit in this global business. For example, in sales offices, the ethical audit covers issues like kickbacks, special pricing terms, and unusual requests from customers. The audit of production facilities would be more likely to cover issues of job safety, work scheduling, and conditions.

Training modules. Ethics modules in regional sales meetings, strategic management conferences, and training sessions also can raise the consciousness of employees within the organization. One-hour sessions as a regular feature for quarterly meetings can be used to reinforce the importance of ethical

TABLE 9–2
McDonnell Douglas Ethical Code and Checklist

McDonnell Douglas Code of Ethics	Ethical Decision-making Checklist
Integrity and ethics exist in the individual or they do not exist at all. They must be upheld by individuals or they are not upheld at all. For integrity and ethics to be characteristics of McDonnell Douglas, we who make up the corporation must strive to be:	**Analysis** • What are the facts? • Who is responsible to act? • What are the consequences of action? (Benefit-Harm Analysis) • What and whose rights are involved? (Rights/Principles Analysis) • What is fair treatment in this case? (Social Justice Analysis)
• Honest and trustworthy in all our relationships • Reliable in carrying out assignments and responsibilities • Truthful and accurate in what we say and write • Cooperative and constructive in all work undertaken; • Fair and considerate in our treatment of fellow employees, customers, and all other persons • Law-abiding in all our activities • Committed to accomplishing all tasks in a superior way • Economical in utilizing company resources • Dedicated in service to our company and to improvement of the quality of life in the world in which we live.	**Solution development** • What solutions are available to me? • Have I considered all the creative solutions that might permit me to reduce harm, maximize benefits, respect more rights, or be fair to more parties? **Select the optimum solution** • What are the potential consequences of my solutions? • Which of the options I have considered does the most to maximize benefits, reduce harm, respect rights, and increase fairness? • Are all parties treated fairly in my proposed decision?
Integrity and high standards of ethics require hard work, courage, and difficult choices. Consultation among employees, top management, and the board of directors will sometimes be necessary to determine a proper course of action. Integrity and ethics may sometimes require us to forgo business opportunities. In the long run, however, we will be better served by doing what is right rather than what is expedient. (From MDC Policy 2, MDC Policy Manual.)	**Implementation** • Who should be consulted or informed? • What actions will assure that my decision achieves its intended outcome? • Implement **Follow-up** • Was the decision implemented correctly? • Did the decision maximize benefits, reduce harm, respect rights, and treat all parties fairly?

SOURCE: Reprinted by permission of McDonnell Douglas Corporation.

responsibilities. Longer sessions in the orientation training of new employees are a critical part of the socialization process an employee undergoes to internalize the culture of the organization.

CORPORATE CULTURE AND SOCIAL RESPONSIBILITY

The institutionalization of CSR through corporate culture requires that top management be aware of how behavior is influenced by culture. Corporate cultures provide the context for ethical and socially responsible behavior, as was discussed in Chapter 6. They reflect shared values and commitments of employees and can be based upon (1) fear of punishment and amoral exchange, (2) group norms and organizational policy, or (3) legitimacy through democratic processes, employee empowerment, and organizational integrity.

A candid and open culture based upon trusting relationships is important to support ethical conduct.[21] However, an organizational culture does not appear suddenly. It is the result of countless interactions among individuals within the context of shared values and organizational policies. It is the result of executive leadership and example. It is influenced by informal interaction patterns, by the stories employees tell about their company, and by the formal and informal reward systems of the organization. Thus, corporate culture provides a major dimension in the institutionalization of CSR within an organization.

An ethical corporate culture suggests that managers act as though they and the company will be around in the long term. The corporate race is a very long one and ethical violations return to haunt those who take shortcuts and make the wrong compromises. Unethical companies often have short-term perspectives embodied in their corporate culture. Such companies may have mistreated employees or have low credit ratings because of debt service practices, high customer complaints, and a poor environmental record.

In contrast, managers concerned about the long-term business social performance of their company are more likely to consider results within that time frame. This is apt to result in a greater concern for the rights and dignity of others—employees and customers alike—and fairness in their dealings with others in the marketplace within an ethical context.

Group norms can be a positive or a negative influence on ethical behavior. Hewlett-Packard is known for its high trust levels, high manager involvement by "managing by wondering around" (MBWA), and group norms based upon integrity and concern for excellence. The resulting corporate culture has a positive effect on the firm's ethical behavior. Murphy has noted that in contrast, the Anheuser Busch Company seems to suffer from a corporate culture that has paternalism, questionable group norms, and a corporate policy that seems to encourage ethical compromise.[22]

EXECUTIVE INTEGRITY AND LEADERSHIP

Executives set the tone of the organization and are of key importance in shaping corporate culture. What top managers pay close attention to quickly becomes a key organizational value. For example, top management at DuPont is known for its review of reports of any accident in DuPont facilities early each morning. The integrity of the top manager and his or her insistence on high ethical standards is a key to all other aspects of institutionalization of CSR outlined above.

On the negative side, managers quickly notice when top managers look the other way when ethical irregularities occur. A manager might encourage sales representatives by saying, "Meet your sales quota, I don't care how you do it." Or customers' needs may be ignored by shipping more than is needed. Such actions send a loud message throughout the organization. They communicate that meeting short-term objectives any way possible is the way of doing business. This leads to a corporate culture that encourages irresponsibility. It is the opposite of leadership with integrity and ethical responsibility.

The tone set by top executives is important as role managers for other managers. Lee Iacocca admitted Chrysler's mistake when it become known that the company had disconnected odometers during testing by executives. He proclaimed a recall on the company's integrity and promised to do better. And he insured that the matter had follow-through within the organization. James Burke took prompt action to recall Tylenol when product tampering was discovered that had led to the tragic death of a customer. Thus Johnson and Johnson is known as a company with great integrity and a positive reputation for its corporate social responsibility.

Global Dimensions of Social Responsibility

The framework presented above needs to be adapted to the needs of a global marketplace. Differences in culture, values, and levels of industrialization and skills provide the context of global CSR. Also, different societies express different expectations to businesses within their countries. Rather than show how to adapt each of the sections of the chapter presented above to a global context, we will address three major problems presented by global CSR. These include (1) exporting of products and technologies from the industrialized countries to the third World, (2) foreign payments as bribery or gratuities, and (3) different cultural values and CSR. Although not exhaustive, these three areas should illustrate the complexities and challenges of being socially responsible in a global market.

EXPORTING OF PRODUCTS AND TECHNOLOGIES FROM THE INDUSTRIALIZED COUNTRIES TO THE THIRD WORLD

CSR requires that managers recognize there are many differences between the conditions that exist in industrialized countries and the Third World. In developing countries, literacy and technical skills may be low, the government regulatory infrastructure may be lacking, and education in safe practices may not be available. This is in sharp contrast to conditions found in most industrialized countries.

The export of products and technologies from industrialized countries into the Third World can often endanger workers and citizens there if special precautions are not taken. Three examples of this illustrate the point: (1) the export of infant formula by Nestlé into Third World countries, (2) the export of pesticides from the United States to developing countries (see Case I–3), and (3) the use of advanced technologies to manufacture hazardous products, as was the case of the Union Carbide pesticide plant in Bhopal, India (see Case V–4). Each of these led to tragic results, were the focus of some controversy, and illustrate a breakdown in CSR.

These cases afford the opportunity to examine the CSR dimensions of economic, legal, ethical, and discretionary activities. Also, they can be considered from the perspective of the levels of institutional, organizational, and individual domains of CSR. In each case the firm or industry was pursuing its economic interests within the legal framework of the host country where its global operations were located.

Institutional Legitimacy

Unfortunately, the regulatory infrastructure in the Third World was either functioning ineffectively or it was missing entirely. Thus companies could argue that they were operating according to the prevailing legal requirements. Taking advantage of inadequate laws threatened the institutional legitimacy, as shown in Table 9–1. Rather than accepting CSR, Nestlé battled critics as agitators trying to undermine capitalism. It took an ideological position with a narrowly defined concept of social responsibility consistent with a defensive and reactive institutional orientation. This lowered its legitimacy and precipitated a worldwide boycott of its products.

Organizational Responsibility

However, many ethical questions were unanswered. Customers, workers, and local residents were not informed of dangers. Safety measures were missing and there was little provision for the required education in each of these cases. These shortcomings present organizational issues of public responsibility (see Table 9–1). Is a company or an industry responsible for solving social problems? The answer depends on (1) whether or not it had a part in creating or aggravating the problem, and (2) whether it is related to a primary or a secondary activity of the business.

In the Nestlé case, it was organizational policy to have sales representatives in white uniforms who appeared to be nurses assigned to hospitals and paid on a commission basis. Also, advertising programs of the company appeared to take advantage of low-income Third World mothers who wanted to emulate the lifestyles of more industrialized countries. On the other hand, it was true that many mothers could not provide their own milk to nurse their children and the infant formula did save some lives. Poor mothers would overdilute the formula to make it last longer and would often use contaminated water. This led to malnutrition and disease rather than the desired saving of lives.

Nestlé policies were eventually changed to be more organizationally responsible. These changes addressed questionable practices including (1) the appearance of the sales representatives who would not mislead patients into believing they were dealing with health care professionals rather than marketing employees, (2) the reward systems encouraging responsible sales rather than maximum sales, and (3) advertising that warned of the dangers of infant formula and safer alternatives.

Individual Discretion

Although little is known about the decision making of individual managers in these cases, some speculative comments might be useful. If the Union Carbide managers at Bhopal, or Nestlé in the Third World, had used an ethical checklist like the one used by McDonnell Douglas (shown in Table 9–2), they might have increased their CSR at the individual level. This could have led to changes at both the organizational and institutional domains of corporate social performance, as outlined in Table 9–2.

Institutionalization of CSR

If CSR had been institutionalized and this checklist reinforced by ethical audit committees, training conferences, and executive leadership, it is hard to imagine how these companies could have experienced such a serious breakdown in CSR and in effective responsiveness.

FOREIGN PAYMENTS

Bribery is generally illegal in most countries. However, corruption does exist in many parts of the world and it is sometimes common practice to offer bribes to public officials. A major scandal occurred in the 1970s involving Lockheed and foreign payments to Japanese officials in exchange for a large government contract. Lockheed was under severe financial stress. The U.S. aerospace industry was in disarray and many aircraft firms were facing bankruptcy. The Congress had just passed a bill for a large government guaranteed loan to bail out the company. Top management feared more layoffs.

Lockheed was competing for a major contract from the Japanese government against several other global companies. Representatives were dispatched to Japan to make a proposal for the aircraft contract. Lockheed's representative was made aware that a gratuity of around a half million dollars might be given to a number of officials including the transportation minister and the prime minister's office. Such a gesture might improve Lockheed's chances of obtaining the large government contract for aircraft. Top management approved the payment and Lockheed got the contract.

When news of the incident got out, the result was public outrage in the United States. Many complained that the government bailout funds were used to bribe foreign officials and thus the U.S. government itself was implicated in major corruption. The political firestorm eventually led to the passage of the Foreign Corrupt Practices Act. That act prohibits U.S. citizens from paying foreign officials or representatives of foreign officials to obtain business. The illegal payment could be a bribe or extortion.

A *bribe* would be the offering of funds to government policymakers, legislators, or public officials in exchange for a contract award, a law, or the passing of a government policy that would serve the economic interest of the U.S.-based business. If a public official initiated the request for funds by demanding them as a condition of a contract award, this might be viewed as extortion. It is sometimes confusing to determine the difference between extortion and bribery. Generally it depends upon who initiated the request and whether or not some negative action is threatened if money is not received. Thus a bribe is typically initiated by a person offering funds in return for a special (a usually illegal) favor. *Extortion* is a request for money in exchange for a favor or to avoid some threatened action that would be damaging.

Many countries pay lower-level public officials such low wages that the level of pay is not sufficient for subsistence. It is the practice in many countries, therefore, for users of government services to supplement the income of lower-level public servants by offering gratuities. Thus, "grease money" is often needed to obtain a prompt inspection of baggage by customs officials. Obtaining telephone service can take several months but the time can be shortened to a few weeks with the payment of a gratuity. The same is true for minor business licenses or any government service. Such practices are highly unusual by U.S. standards and would be considered public corruption here.

The CSR of the global firm needs to deal with foreign payments of all kinds. There are laws against bribery and extortion in most countries. And large payments to high-level government officials in the form of bribery and extortion are nearly universally illegal. However, laws and customs vary widely with respect to the payment of gratuities to lower-level public officials. And the actual practice often varies with the law, especially when lower-level officials are involved.

Another observation can be made here. Once a company institutionalizes the practice of kickbacks and bribery as a way of doing business, it is very difficult to change it. This is particularly the case in a global environment when dealing with corrupt government officials. It is commonly known among such officials which businesses will offer them money. Top management of global firms need to consider foreign payments of all kinds in their codes of ethics. This can affect all levels of corporate social responsibility.

DIFFERENT CULTURAL VALUES AND CSR

Global business needs to adapt its practices in management, operations, and marketing to cultural differences. A complete discussion of this is beyond the scope of this chapter, although it is very important for corporate social responsibilities. To illustrate cultural differences, consider the issue of sex and decency.[23] This issue is very controversial in the United States and is widely debated by feminist groups, business, and regulators. However, the issue is even more complex when considered in a global context.

Religious values and culture define matters of sex and decency. Boddewyn and Kunz report: (1) Islamic countries tend to oppose all kinds of sexual displays including those that are indirect; (2) Christian countries like Ireland, South Africa, Mexico, and the Philippines also have standards against most kinds of sexual display; (3) France allows seminude models on television but prohibits the advertisement of contraceptives; (4) Scandinavia and the Netherlands forbid the lewd use of women in advertisements.

In the area of human resource development, the United States has laws against discrimination. Similarly Sweden, the United Kingdom, and many other European countries hold that discrimination against women is illegal. However, discrimination against women and minorities is a common practice in Japan. Thus, the global firm needs to acquaint itself with the cultural and religious values found in the countries where they operate. Usually the laws of each country are consistent with the values held. As society changes and values and lifestyles shift, the legal environment can also be expected to change.

Thus the global firm concerned about maintaining high levels of CSR and responsiveness needs to be sensitive to local values and legal requirements. Sensitivity to these variables will enable it to have more positive relationships with consumers and employees in host countries, and that will improve its economic performance. It will also make them more aware of the ethical dimension of CSR and will afford opportunities to improve the institutional legitimacy of the global firm as well as its capacity to respond to change.

Summary

Social responsibility has been controversial since the idea was first introduced as stewardship near the turn of the century. The arguments against business assuming an expanded concept of corporate social responsibility (CSR) was more persuasive among managers until the early 1970s, when many changes in social expectations of business became the law. The legitimacy or social support for business and other social institutions began to drop and the political environment became markedly hostile.

For those who oppose CSR, one might conclude that it should be limited to maximizing profits within the rules of the game that include abiding by the law. For those who endorse a broader interpretation of CSR, the role of business would allow profits but rather than maximizing short-term profits, business should optimize long-term profits, obey the laws and regulations, consider the non-market impact of its decisions or face an increase in government control, and seek ways to improve society through CSR programs.

The pyramid of corporate social responsibility integrates the major arguments in the CSR debate into a single model and parallels the business social performance model. This four-part framework defines social responsibility as the economic, legal, ethical, and discretionary responsibilities arising from the expectations of society. Economic performance is the foundation for the social responsibility of business.

As the primary instrument within the economic sphere of society, it is the task of business to provide the needed goods and services, to maintain its competitiveness, and to operate at a profit. Legal responsibility is the second dimension of CSR. Obeying the law is one of the conditions for the continued existence of business within society. It is business's responsibility to obey the law and play by the rules of the game established by society.

Third, ethical responsibilities include applying the concepts of utilitarian analysis, rights, duties, and justice. This requires making ethical decisions by considering the consequences of an action, by honoring the rights of others, by fulfilling duties, and by avoiding harm to others. Also, it means seeking justice and fairness in balancing the interests of various corporate stakeholders. Fourth, philanthropic responsibilities are discretionary actions by management in response to social expectations. Such actions may include the volunteer work of executives in community programs, the providing of financial resources for college scholarship programs, or donations to local charities. It could include sponsorship of a cultural or artistic endeavor.

The four dimensions of CSR principles have three levels that include the institutional, the organizational, and the individual. Each of these levels corresponds to its own principle of CSR. The principle of legitimacy applies to the institutional level, the principle of public responsibility applies at the organizational level, and the principle of managerial discretion applies at the individual level. This last principle assumes that the manager is a moral agent capable of using moral imagination in daily decision making to improve society.

The institutional orientation of business influences its capacity to respond to changing social expectations. The three institutional orientations include (1) defensive and reactive, (2) anticipatory and politically responsible, and (3) proactive and socially responsive. The socially responsible organization accepts a broad view of CSR and includes projected social changes into its long-range planning. The politically responsive organization is concerned about legitimacy and seeks to influence the public policy process favorably for business interests.

Research studies found a positive relationship between social responsibility and economic performance. Of interest is the consistent finding that CSR programs do not negatively affect the economic performance of business. This is important because society increasingly expects CSR programs from business.

Business should institutionalize CSR if it is to receive consistent benefits. Codes of ethics will help guide ethically responsible behavior if they are public, specific, direct and clearly worded, and periodically revised. However, to achieve ethically responsible behavior in a dynamic environment, managers need an open culture that encourages organizational integrity. Executive leadership plays a key role in setting the ethical tone for the organization.

CSR needs to be adapted to the requirement of the global marketplace. Particularly, differences in cultural and religious values, foreign payments, and the exporting of products and technologies from industrialized countries to the Third World need special attention.

Conclusions

Corporate social responsibility is an important part of business social performance. Recent decades have brought many changes in social values and in the social expectations of business. Traditional approaches to CSR based on profit maximization within the rules of the game as expressed by law are insufficient guidance for businesses needing to adapt to a changing social environment. A broad CSR approach improves social performance, has a greater chance of sustaining high levels of social responsiveness and legitimacy, and is more likely to lead to an improved society. However, it is necessary for managers to limit the extent of their CSR programs to those areas directly or indirectly

related to business operations. Also, business should not seek to control the political process in its attempts to influence the public policy process. Such abuses of power would probably be self-defeating in the end.

Discussion Questions

1. What are the major objections to CSR programs in the social responsibility debate? Why does Milton Friedman conclude that assuming CSR would lead to undermining a free society?
2. What are the major arguments in favor of CSR?
3. Can a corporation be a moral agent? Can a corporation have a conscience? Explain.
4. What are the four levels of an expanded corporate social responsibility? Does this expanded CSR conclude that business should ignore economic performance? Why or why not?
5. What is ethical responsibility? How can codes of ethics improve an organization's ethical responsibility?
6. What is a moral imagination? What role does it play in corporate social responsibility?
7. Are there any limits to CSR? What principle can managers apply to determine the appropriate limit? Apply this principle to a specific business.
8. How should managers institutionalize CRS? Are codes of ethics enough? What more can top management do to assure that business is socially responsible?
9. What is the difference between corporate social responsibility and social responsiveness? Select a current value-oriented controversy concerning business out of a late issue of the newspaper. Apply the two concepts of social responsibility and social responsiveness to the issue selected.
10. What are the differences among the institutional, the organizational, and the individual levels of CSR?

Notes

1. Milton Friedman, "The Social Responsibility of Business Is to Increase Its Profits," *New York Times Magazine,* September 13, 1970, and Milton Friedman, *Capitalism and Freedom* (Chicago: University of Chicago Press, 1962).

2. Milton Friedman, "The Social Responsibility of Business to Increase Its Profits," in Tom L. Beauchamp and Norman E. Bowie, *Ethical Theory and Business,* 2d ed. (Englewood Cliffs, N.J.: Prentice-Hall, 1983), p. 81.

3. Theodore Levitt, "The Dangers of Social Responsibility," in *Ethical Theory and Business,* pp. 83–86.

4. Roger Gibson, "Corporations, Persons and Moral Responsibility," *Journal of Thought* (Summer 1986): 17–27.

5. Manuel Velasquez, "Why Corporations Are Not Morally Responsible for Anything They Do," *Business and Professional Ethics Journal* 2 no. 3 (Spring 1983): 1–18; the commentaries in the same journal argue the opposite side of this issue.

6. Richard J. Klonoski, "Foundational Considerations in the Corporate Social Responsibility Debate," *Business Horizons* (July–August 1991): 9–18.

7. Kenneth E. Goodpaster and John B. Matthews, Jr., "Can a Corporation Have a Conscience?" *Harvard Business Review* (January/February 1982): 132–41.

8. John L. Paluszek, *Business and Society: 1976–2000* (New York: AMACOM, 1976), p. 1.

9. Keith Davis, "The Case for and Against Business Assumption of Social Responsibilities," *Academy of Management Journal* (June 1973): 321–22.

10. Archie B. Carroll, "The Pyramid of Corporate Social Responsibility: Toward the Moral Management of Organizational Stakeholders," *Business Horizons* (July-August 1991): 39–48.

11. Donna J. Wood, "Corporate Social Performance Revisited," *Academy of Management Review* 16, no. 4 (1991): 691–718.

12. Davis, "The Case For and Against Business Assumption of Social Responsibilities," pp. 312–22.

13. Lee E. Preston and James E. Post, *Private Management and Public Policy: The Principle of Public Responsibility* (Englewood Cliffs, N.J.: Prentice-Hall, 1975).

14. Donna J. Wood, "Corporate Social Performance Revisited," *Academy of Management Review* 16, no. 4 (1991): 698.

15. S. Prakash Sethi, "Dimensions of Corporate Social Performance: An Analytical Framework," *California Management Review* (Spring 1975): 58–64.

16. Arieh Ullmann, "Data in Search of a Theory: A Critical Examination of the Relationships Among Social Performance, Social Disclosure, and Economic Performance of U.S. Firms," *Academy of Management Review* 10, no. 3 (1985): 540–57.

17. Philip L. Cochran and Robert A. Wood, "Corporate Social Responsibility and Financial Performance," *Academy of Management Journal* 27, no. 1 (1984): 42–56.

18. W. F. Abbott and R. J. Monsen, "On the Measurement of Corporate Social Responsibility: Self-report Disclosures as a Method of Measuring Social Involvement," *Academy of Management Journal* 22 (1979): 501–15.

19. This section is based on an article by Patrick E. Murphy, "Implementing Business Ethics," *Journal of Business Ethics* 7 (1988): 907–15.

20. Patrick E. Murphy, "Implementing Business Ethics: An Ethical Code Is Not Enough," *Journal of Business Ethics* 7 (1988): 907–915.

21. Michael R. Hyman, Robert Skipper, and Richard Tansey, "Ethical Codes Are Not Enough," *Business Horizons* (March-April 1990): 15–22.

22. Patrick E. Murphy, "Implementing Business Ethics," in John E. Richardson, ed., *Business Ethics 92/93,* 4th ed. (Guilford, Conn.: Dushkin), p. 108.

23. Jean J. Boddewyn and Heidi Kunz, "Sex and Decency Issues in Advertising: General and International Dimensions," *Business Horizons* (September-October 1991): 13–20.

Discussion Case 9–1

Grease Money

Many countries pay their civil servants at subsistence or below subsistence levels. Although it is usually technically illegal for these customs inspectors, passport checkers, railroad clerks, and others to receive funds for their services, they could not live without such gratuities. It is a widespread social expectation that the public will provide them with small gratuities much like waiters at good restaurants are tipped in the West for good service.

This implicit demand for money by government officials is viewed by many international managers dispatched from the United States as corruption and bribery. When they try to do the ethical thing and refuse to take part in this, they suffer poor service and unusual delays in everything from having their bags processed through customs to obtaining necessary business permits for local operations.

Case Discussion Questions

1. What is the socially responsible thing to do in these instances?
2. If a company wanted to develop a code of ethics in this situation, what would you advise?
3. When is a gratuity a bribe? When is it extortion?

Discussion Case 9–2

The Local Business Representative

In a particular oil-producing country a U.S. petroleum company representative was told by a key government official that the government of that country preferred not to deal directly with foreign business representatives. Rather, they preferred to deal through a "local" representative who would serve the interests of the global firm and would charge a fee for the service. The fee would be a small percentage of the value of all the petroleum sold to the global petroleum business. Although the percentage was rather small, it would involve the payment of millions of dollars of commissions annually to the local representative.

The government official then highly recommended a potential representative and provided the name and a means to contact the individual, who was designated as an experienced and reliable trade representative. After further checking, the manager of the global firm discovered that the person recommended was the son-in-law of the brother of the government official.

Case Discussion Questions

1. Is the suggestion to hire a local representative a bribe or is it extortion?
2. Is it merely a culturally determined way of doing business in that country?
3. What should the manager of the global firm do about the suggestion?

Case III–1

The Aircraft Brake Scandal

The B.F. Goodrich Company is what business magazines like to refer to as "a major American corporation." It has operations in a dozen states and as many foreign countries; and of these far-flung facilities, the Goodrich plant at Troy, Ohio, is not the most imposing. It is a small, one-story building, once used to manufacture airplanes. Set in the grassy flatlands of west central Ohio, it employs only about six hundred people. Nevertheless, it is one of the three largest manufacturers of aircraft wheels and brakes, a leader in a most profitable industry. Goodrich wheels and brakes support such well-known planes as the F111, the C5A, the Boeing 727, the XB70, and many others.

Contracts for aircraft wheels and brakes often run into millions of dollars, and ordinarily a contract with a total value of less than $70,000, though welcome, would not create any special stir of joy in the hearts of Goodrich sales personnel. But purchase order P-237138—issued on June 18, 1967, by the LTV Aerospace Corporation, ordering 202 brake assemblies for a new Air Force plane at a total price of $69,417—was received by Goodrich with considerable glee. And there was good reason. Some ten years previously, Goodrich had built a brake for LTV that was, to say the least, considerably less than a rousing success. The brake had not lived up to Goodrich's promises, and after experiencing considerable difficulty, LTV had written off Goodrich as a source of brakes. Since that time, Goodrich salesmen had been unable to sell so much as a shot of brake fluid to LTV. So in 1967, when LTV requested bids on wheels and

SOURCE: "Why Should My Conscience Bother Me?" "The Aircraft Brake Scandal," by Kermit Vandivier, from *In the Name of Profit*, by Robert Heilbronet et al., Copyright ©1972 by Doubleday & Co., Inc. Reprinted with permission of the publisher.

brakes for the new A7D light attack aircraft it proposed to build for the Air Force, Goodrich submitted a bid that was absurdly low, so low the LTV could not, in all prudence, turn it down.

Goodrich had, in industry parlance, "bought into the business." The company did not expect to make a profit on the initial deal; it was prepared, if necessary, to lose money. But aircraft brakes are not something that can be ordered off the shelf. They are designed for a particular aircraft, and once an airplane manufacturer buys a brake, he is forced to purchase all replacement parts from the brake manufacturer. The $70,000 that Goodrich would get for making the brake would be a drop in the bucket when compared with the cost of the linings and other parts the Air Force would have to buy from Goodrich during the lifetime of the aircraft.

There was another factor, besides the low bid, that had undoubtedly influenced LTV. All aircraft brakes made today are of the disk type, and the bid submitted by Goodrich called for a relatively small brake, one containing four disks and weighing only 106 pounds. The weight of any aircraft is extremely important: the lighter a part is, the heavier the plane's payload can be.

The brake was designed by one of Goodrich's most capable engineers, John Warren. A tall, lanky blond graduate of Purdue, Warren had come from the Chrysler Corporation seven years before and had become adept at aircraft brake design. The happy-go-lucky manner he usually maintained belied a temper that exploded whenever anyone ventured to offer criticism of his work, no matter how small. On these occasions, Warren would turn red in the face, often throwing or slamming something and then stalking from the scene. As his co-workers learned the consequences of criticizing him, they did so less and less readily, and when he submitted his preliminary design for the A7D brake, it was accepted without question.

Warren was named project engineer for the A7D, and he, in turn, assigned the task of producing the final production design to a newcomer to the Goodrich engineering stable, Searle Lawson. Just turned twenty-six, Lawson had been out of the Northrop Institute of Technology only one year when he came to Goodrich in January 1967. He had been assigned to various "paper projects" to break him in, and after several months spent reviewing statistics and old brake designs, he was beginning to fret at the lack of challenge. When told he was being assigned to his first "real" project, he was elated and immediately plunged into his work.

The major portion of the design had already been completed by Warren, and major subassemblies for the brake had already been ordered from Goodrich suppliers. Naturally, however, before Goodrich could start making the brakes on a production basis, much testing would have to be done. Lawson would have to determine the best materials to use for the linings and discover what minor adjustments in the design would have to be made.

Then, after the preliminary testing and after the brake was judged ready for production, one whole brake assembly would undergo a series of grueling, simulated braking stops and other severe trials called qualification tests. These tests are required by the military, which gives very detailed specifications on how they are to be conducted, the criteria for failure, and so on. They are performed in the Goodrich plant's test laboratory, where huge machines called dynamometers can simulate the weight and speed of almost any aircraft.

Searle Lawson was well aware that much work had to be done before the A7D brake could go into production, and he knew that LTV had set the last two weeks in June 1968 as the starting dates for flight tests. So he decided to begin testing immediately. Goodrich's suppliers had not yet delivered the brake housing and other parts, but the brake disks had arrived, and using the housing from a brake similar in size and weight to the A7D brake, Lawson built a prototype. The prototype was installed in a test wheel and placed on one of the big dynamometers in the plant's test laboratory. Lawson began a series of tests, "landing" the

wheel and brake at the A7D's landing speed and braking it to a stop. The main purpose of these preliminary tests was to learn what temperatures would develop within the brake during the simulated stops and to evaluate lining materials tentatively selected for use.

During a normal aircraft landing the temperatures inside the brake may reach 1,000 degrees, and occasionally a bit higher. During Lawson's first simulated landings, the temperature of his prototype brake reached 1,500 degrees. The brake glowed a bright cherry-red and threw off incandescent particles of metal and lining material as the temperature reached its peak. After a few such stops, the brake was dismantled and the linings were found to be almost completely disintegrated. Lawson chalked the first failure up to chance, and ordering new lining materials, tried again.

The second attempt was a repeat of the first. The brake became excessively hot, causing the lining materials to crumble into dust.

After the third such failure, Lawson, inexperienced though he was, knew that the fault lay not in defective parts or unsuitable lining materials but in the basic design of the brake itself. Ignoring Warren's original computations, Lawson made his own, and it didn't take him long to discover where the trouble lay—the brake was too small. There simply was not enough surface area on the disks to stop the aircraft without generating the excessive heat that caused the linings to fail.

The answer to the problem was obvious, but far from simple—the four-disk brake would have to be scrapped, and a new design, using five disks, would have to be developed. The implications were not lost on Lawson. Such a step would require junking the four-disk brake subassemblies, many of which had now began to arrive from the various suppliers. It would also mean several weeks of preliminary design and testing and many more weeks of waiting while the suppliers made and delivered the new subassemblies.

Yet, several weeks had already gone by since LTV's order had arrived and the date for delivery of the first production brakes for flight testing was only a few months away.

Although John Warren had more or less turned the A7D over to Lawson, he knew of the difficulties Lawson had been experiencing. He had assured the younger engineer that the problem resolved around getting the right kind of lining material. Once that was found, he said, the difficulties would end.

Despite the evidence of the abortive tests and Lawson's careful computations, Warren rejected the suggestion that the four-disk brake was too light for the job. He knew that his superior had already told LTV, in rather glowing terms, that the preliminary tests on the A7D brake were very successful. Indeed, Warren's superiors weren't aware at this time of the troubles on the brake. It would have been difficult for Warren to admit not only that he had made a serious error in his calculations and original design but that his mistakes had been caught by a green kid, barely out of college.

Warren's reaction to a five-disk brake was not unexpected by Lawson and seeing that the four-disk brake was not to be abandoned so easily he took his calculations and dismal test results one step up the corporate ladder.

At Goodrich, the man who supervises the engineers working on projects slated for production is called, predictably, the projects manager. The job was held by a short, chubby, bald man named Robert Sink. Some fifteen years before, Sink had begun working at Goodrich as a lowly draftsman. Slowly, he worked his way up. Despite his geniality, Sink was neither respected nor liked by the majority of the engineers, and his appointment as their supervisor did not improve their feelings toward him. He possessed only a high-school diploma, and it quite naturally rankled those who had gone through years of college to be commanded by a man whom they considered their intellectual inferior. But, though Sink had no college training, he had something even more useful: a fine working knowledge of company politics.

Puffing on a meerschaum pipe, Sink listened gravely as young Lawson confided his fears about the four-disk brake. Then he examined Lawson's calculations and the results of the abortive tests. Despite the fact that he was not a qualified engineer, in the strictest sense of the word, it must certainly have been obvious to Sink that Lawson's calculations were correct and that a four-disk brake would never work on the A7D.

But other things of equal importance were also obvious. First, to concede that Lawson's calcula-

tions were correct would also mean conceding that Warren's calculations were incorrect. As projects manager, not only was he responsible for Warren's activities, but in admitting that Warren had erred he would also have to admit that he had erred in trusting Warren's judgment. It also meant that, as projects manager, it would be he who would have to explain the whole messy situation to the Goodrich hierarchy, not only at Troy but possibly on the corporate level at Goodrich's Akron offices. And having taken Warren's judgment of the four-disk brake at face value, he had assured LTV, not once but several times, that about all there was left to do on the brake was pack it in a crate and ship it out the door.

There's really no problem at all, he told Lawson. After all, Warren was an experienced engineer, and if he said the brake would work, it would work. Just keep on testing and probably, maybe even on the very next try, it'll work out fine.

Lawson was far from convinced, but without the support of his superiors there was little he could do except keep on testing. By now, housings for the four-disk brake had begun to arrive at the plant, and Lawson was able to build a production model of the brake and begin the formal qualification tests demanded by the military.

The first qualification attempts went exactly as the tests on the prototype had. Terrific heat developed within the brakes, and after a few short, simulated stops the linings crumbled. A new type of lining material was ordered and once again an attempt to qualify the brake was made. Again, failure.

Experts were called in from lining manufacturers, and new lining "mixes" were tried, always with the same result. Failure.

It was now the last week in March 1968, and flight tests were scheduled to begin in seventy days. Twelve separate attempts had been made to qualify the brake, and all had failed. It was no longer possible for anyone to ignore the glaring truth that the brake was a dismal failure and that nothing short of a major design change could ever make it work.

On April 4, the thirteenth attempt at qualification was begun. This time no attempt was made to conduct the tests by the methods and techniques spelled out in the military specifications. Regardless of how it had to be done, the brake was to be "nursed" through the required fifty simulated stops.

Fans were set up to provide special cooling. Instead of maintaining pressure on the brake until the test wheel had come to a complete stop, the pressure was reduced when the wheel had decelerated to around 15 mph, allowing it to "coast" to a stop. After each stop, the brake was disassembled and carefully cleaned, and after some of the stops, internal brake parts were machined in order to remove warp and other disfigurations caused by the high heat.

By these and other methods, all clearly contrary to the techniques established by the military specifications, the brake was coaxed through the fifty stops. But even using these methods, the brake could not meet all the requirements. On one stop the wheel rolled for a distance of 16,000 feet, or over three miles, before the brake could bring it to a stop. The normal distance required for such a stop was around 3,500 feet.

On April 11, the day the thirteenth test was completed, I became personally involved in the A7D situation.

I had worked in the Goodrich test laboratory for five years, starting first as an instrumentation engineer, then later becoming a data analyst and technical writer. As part of my duties, I analyzed the reams and reams of instrumentation data that came from the many testing machines in the lab, then transcribed all of it to a more usable form for the engineering department. When a new-type brake had successfully completed the required qualification tests, I would issue a formal qualification report.

Qualification reports are an accumulation of all the data and test logs compiled during the qualification tests and are documentary proof that a brake has met all the requirements established by the military specifications and is therefore presumed safe for flight testing. Before actual flight tests are conducted on a brake, qualification reports have to be delivered to the customer and to various government officials.

On April 11, I was looking over the data from the latest A7D test, and I noticed that many irregularities in testing had been noted on the test logs.

Technically, of course, there was nothing wrong with conducting tests in any manner desired, so long as the test was for research purposes only. But qualification test methods are clearly delineated by the military, and I knew that this test had been a formal qualification attempt. One particular notation on the test logs caught my eye. For some of the stops, the instrument that recorded the brake pressure had been deliberately miscalibrated so that, while the brake pressure used during the stops was recorded as 1,000 psi (pounds per square inch)—the maximum pressure that would be available on the A7D aircraft—the pressure had actually been 1,100 psi.

I showed the test logs to the test lab supervisor, Ralph Gretzinger, who said he had learned from the technician who had miscalibrated the instrument that he had been asked to do so by Lawson. Lawson, said Gretzinger, readily admitted asking for the miscalibration, saying he had been told to do so by Sink.

I asked Gretzinger why anyone would want to miscalibrate the data recording instruments.

"Why? I'll tell you why," he snorted. "That brake is a failure. It's way too small for the job, and they're not ever going to get it to work. They're getting desperate, and instead of scrapping the damned thing and starting over, they figure they can horse around down here in the lab and qualify it that way."

An expert engineer, Gretzinger had been responsible for several innovations in brake design. It was he who had invented the unique brake system used on the famous XB70. "If you want to find out what's going on," said Gretzinger, "ask Lawson; he'll tell you."

Curious, I did ask Lawson the next time he came into the lab. He seemed eager to discuss the A7D and gave me the history of his months of frustrating efforts to get Warren and Sink to change the brake design. "I just can't believe this is really happening," said Lawson, shaking his head slowly. "This isn't engineering, at least not what I though it would be. Back in school, I thought that when you were an engineer, you tried to do your best, no matter what it cost. But this is something else."

He sat across the desk from me, his chin propped in his hand. "Just wait," he warned. "You'll get a chance to see what I'm talking about. You're going to get in the act too, because I've already had the word that we're going to make one more attempt to qualify the brake, and that's it. Win or lose, we're going to issue a qualification report!"

I reminded him that a qualification report could be issued only after the brake had successfully met all military requirements, and therefore, unless the next qualification attempt was a success, no report would be issued.

"You'll find out," retorted Lawson. "I was already told that regardless of what the brake does on test, it's going to be qualified." He said he had been told those exact words at a conference with Sink and Russell Van Horn.

This was the first indication that Sink had brought his boss, Van Horn, into the mess. Although Van Horn had said, "Regardless of what the brake does on a test, it's going to be qualified," then it could only mean that, if necessary, a fake qualification report would be issued. I discussed the possibility with Gretzinger, and he assured me that under no circumstances would such a report ever be issued.

"If they want a qualification report, we'll write them one, but we'll tell it just like it is," he declared emphatically. "No false data or false reports are going to come out of this lab."

On May 2, 1968, the fourteenth and final attempt to qualify the brake was begun. Although the same improper methods used to nurse the brake through the previous tests were employed, it soon became obvious that this too would end in failure.

When the tests were about half completed, Lawson asked if I would start preparing the various engineering curves and graphic displays that were normally incorporated in a qualification report. I flatly refused to have anything to do with the matter and immediately told Gretzinger what I had been asked to do. He was furious and repeated his previous declaration that under no circumstances would any false data or other matter be issued from the lab.

"I'm going to get this settled right now, once and for all," he declared. "I'm going to see Line [Russell Line, manager of Goodrich Technical Services Section, of which the test lab was a part] and find out just how far this thing is going to go!" He stormed out of the room.

In about an hour, he returned and called me to his desk. He sat silently for a few moments, then muttered, half to himself, "I wonder what the hell they'd do if I just quit?" I didn't answer and I didn't ask him what he meant. I knew. He had been beaten down. He had reached the point when the decision had to be made. Defy them now while there was still time—or knuckle under, sell out.

"You know," he went on uncertainly, looking down at his desk, "I've been an engineer for a long time, and I've always believed that ethics and integrity were every bit as important as theorems and formulas, and never once has anything happened to change my beliefs. Now this. . . . Hell, I've got two sons I've got to put through school and I just. . . ." His voice trailed off.

He sat for a few more minutes, then, looking over the top of his glasses, said hoarsely, "Well, it looks like we're licked. The way it stands now, we're to go ahead and prepare the data and other things for the graphic presentation in the report, and when we're finished, someone upstairs will actually write the report."

"After all," he continued, "we're just drawing some curves, and what happens to them after they leave here—well, we're not responsible for that."

I wasn't at all satisfied with the situation and decided that I too would discuss the matter with Russell Line, the senior executive in our section.

Tall, powerfully built, his teeth flashing white, his face tanned to a coffee-brown by a daily stint with a sunlamp, Line looked and acted every inch the executive. He had been transferred form the Akron offices some two years previously, and he commanded great respect and had come to be well liked by those of us who worked under him.

He listened sympathetically while I explained how I felt about the A7D situation, and when I had finished, he asked me what I wanted him to do about it. I said that as employees of the Goodrich Company we had a responsibility to protect the company and its reputation if at all possible. I said I was certain that officers on the corporate level would never knowingly allow such tactics as had been employed on the A7D.

"I agree with you," he remarked, "but I still want to know what you want me to do about it."

I suggested that in all probability the chief engineer at the Troy plant, H. G. "Bud" Sunderman, was unaware of the A7D problem and that he, Line, could tell him what was going on.

Line laughed, good-humoredly. "Sure, I could, but I'm not going to. Bud probably knows about this thing anyway, and if he doesn't, I'm sure not going to be the one to tell him."

"But why?"

"Because it's none of my business, and it's none of yours. I learned a long time ago not to worry about things over which I had no control. I have no control over this."

I wasn't satisfied with this answer, and I asked him if his conscience wouldn't bother him if, say, during flight tests on the brake, something should happen resulting in death or injury to the test pilot.

"Look," he said, becoming somewhat exasperated, "I just told you I have no control over this. Why should my conscience bother me?"

His voice took on a quiet, soothing tone as he continued. "You're just getting all upset over this thing for nothing. I just do as I'm told, and I'd advise you to do the same."

I made no attempt to rationalize what I had been asked to do. It made no difference who would falsify which part of the report or whether the actual falsification would be by misleading numbers or misleading words. Whether by acts of commission or omission, all of us who contributed to the fraud would be guilty. The only question left for me to decide was whether or not I would become a party to the fraud.

Before coming to Goodrich in 1963, I had held a variety of jobs, each a little more pleasant, a little more rewarding than the last. At forty-two, with seven children, I had decided that the Goodrich Company would probably be my "home" for the rest of my working life. The job paid well, it was pleasant and challenging, and the future looked reasonably bright. My wife and I had bought a home and we were ready to settle down into a comfortable, middle-age, middle-class rut. If I refused to take part in the A7D fraud, I would have to resign or be fired. The report would be written by someone anyway, but I would have the satisfaction of knowing I had no part in the matter. But bills aren't paid with personal satisfaction, nor house payments with ethical principles. I made my decision. The next morning, I telephoned Lawson and told him I was ready to begin on the qualification report.

I had written dozens of qualification reports, and I knew what a "good" one looked like. Resorting to the actual test data only on occasion, Lawson and I proceeded to prepare page after page of elaborate, detailed engineering curves, charts, and test logs, which purported to show what had happened during the formal qualification tests. Where temperatures were too high, we deliberately chopped them down a few hundred degrees, and where they were too low, we raised them to a value that would appear reasonable to the LTV and military engineers. Brake pressure, torque values, distances, times—everything of consequence was tailored to fit.

Occasionally, we would find that some test either hadn't been performed at all or had been conducted improperly. On those occasions, we "conducted" the test—successfully, of course—on paper.

For nearly a month we worked on the graphic presentation that would be a part of the report. Meanwhile, the final qualification attempt had been completed, and the brake, not unexpectedly, had failed again.

We finished our work on the graphic portion of the report around the first of June. Altogether, we had prepared nearly two hundred pages of data, containing dozens of deliberate falsifications and misrepresentations. I delivered the data to Gretzinger, who said that he had been instructed to deliver it personally to the chief engineer, Bud Sunderman, who in turn would assign someone in the engineering department to complete the written portion of the report. He gathered the bundle of data and left the office. Within minutes, he was back with the data, his face white with anger.

"That damned Sink's beat me to it," he said furiously. "He's already talked to Bud about this, and now Sunderman says no one in the engineering department has time to write the report. He wants us to do it, and I told him we couldn't."

The words had barely left his mouth when Russell Line burst in the door. "What the hell's all the fuss about this damned report?" he demanded.

Patiently, Gretzinger explained. "There's no fuss. Sunderman just told me that we'd have to write the report down here, and I said we couldn't. Russ," he went on, "I've told you before that we weren't going to write the report. I made my position clear on that a long time ago."

Line shut him up with a wave of his hand and, turning to me, bellowed, "I'm getting sick and tired of hearing about this damned report. Now, write the goddamn thing and shut up about it!" He slammed out of the office.

Gretzinger and I just sat for a few seconds looking at each other. Then he spoke.

"Well, I guess he's made it pretty clear, hasn't he? We can either write the thing or quit. You know, what we should have done was quit a long time ago. Now, it's too late."

Somehow I wasn't at all surprised at the turn of events, and it really didn't make that much difference. As far as I was concerned, we were all up to our necks in the thing anyway, and writing the narrative portion of the report couldn't make me more guilty than I already felt myself to be.

Within two days, I had completed the narrative, or written portion, of the report. As a final sop to my own self-respect, in the conclusion of the report I wrote, "The B.F. Goodrich P/N 2-1162-3 brake assembly does not meet the intent or the requirements of the applicable specification documents and therefore is not qualified."

This was a meaningless gesture, since I knew that this would certainly be changed when the report went through the final typing process. Sure enough, when the report was published, the negative conclusion had been made positive.

One final and significant incident occurred just before publication.

Qualification reports always bear the signature of the person who has prepared them. I refused to sign the report, as did Lawson. Warren was later asked to sign the report. He replied that he would "when I receive a signed statement from Bob Sink ordering me to sign it."

The engineering secretary who was delegated the responsibility of "dogging" the report through publication told me later that after I, Lawson, and Warren had all refused to sign the report, she had asked Sink if he would sign. He replied, "On something of this nature, I don't think a signature is really needed."

On June 5, 1968, the report was officially published and copies were delivered by hand to the Air Force and LTV. Within a week flight tests were begun at Edwards Air Force Base in California.

Searle Lawson was sent to California as Goodrich's representative. Within approximately two weeks, he returned because some rather unusual incidents during the tests had caused them to be canceled.

His face was grim as he related stories of several near crashes during landings—caused by brake troubles. He told me about one incident in which, upon landing, one brake was literally welded together by the intense heat developed during the test stop. The wheel locked, and the plane skidded for nearly 1,500 feet before coming to a halt. The plane was jacked up and the wheel removed. The fused parts within the brake had to be pried apart.

That evening I left work early and went to see my attorney. After I told him the story, he advised that, while I was probably not actually guilty of fraud, I was certainly part of a conspiracy to defraud. He advised me to go to the Federal Bureau of Investigation and offered to arrange an appointment. The following week he took me to the Dayton office of the FBI and after I had been warned that I would not be immune from prosecution, I disclosed the A7D matter to one of the agents. The agent told me to say nothing of the episode to anyone and to report any further incidents to him. He said he would forward the story to his superiors in Washington.

A few days later, Lawson returned from a conference with LTV in Dallas and said that the Air Force, which had previously approved the qualification report, had suddenly rescinded that approval and was demanding to see the raw test data. I gathered that the FBI had passed the word.

Omitting any reference to the FBI, I told Lawson I had been to an attorney and that we were probably guilty of conspiracy.

"Can you get me an appointment with your attorney?" he asked. Within a week, he had been to the FBI and told them of his part in the mess. He too was advised to say nothing but to keep on the job reporting any new developments.

Naturally, with the rescinding of Air Force approval and the demand to see raw test data, Goodrich officials were in a panic. A conference was called for July 27, a Saturday morning affair at which Lawson, Sink, Warren, and I were present. We met in a tiny conference room in the deserted engineering department. Lawson and I, by now openly hostile to Warren and Sink, ranged ourselves on one side of the conference table while Warren sat on the other side. Sink, chairing the meeting, paced slowly in front of a blackboard, puffing furiously on a pipe.

The meeting was called, Sink began, "to see where we stand on the A7D." What we were going to do, he said, was to "level" with LTV and tell them the "whole truth" about the A7D. "After all," he said, "they're in this thing with us, and they have the right to know how matters stand."

"In other words," I asked, "we're going to tell them the truth?"

"That's right," he replied. "We're going to level with them and let them handle the ball from there."

"There's one thing I don't quite understand," I interjected. "Isn't it going to be pretty hard for us to admit to them that we've lied?"

"Now, wait a minute," he said angrily. "Let's don't go off half-cocked on this thing. It's not a matter of lying. We've just interpreted the information the way we felt it should be."

"I don't know what you call it," I replied, "but to me it's lying, and it's going to be damned hard to confess to them that we've been lying all along."

He became very agitated at this and repeated, "We're not lying," adding, "I don't like this sort of talk."

I dropped the matter at this point, and he began discussing the various discrepancies in the report.

We broke for lunch, and afterward, I came back to the plant to find Sink sitting alone at his desk, waiting to resume the meeting. He called me over and said he wanted to apologize for his outburst that morning. "This thing has kind of gotten me down," he confessed, "and I think you've got the wrong picture. I don't think you really understand everything about this."

Perhaps so, I conceded, but it seemed to me that if we had already told LTV one thing and then had to tell them another, changing our story completely, we would have to admit we were lying.

"No," he explained patiently, "we're not really lying. All we were doing was interpreting the figures the way we knew they should be. We were exercising engineering license."

During the afternoon session, we marked some forty-three discrepancy points in the report; forty-three points that LTV would surely spot as occasions where we had exercised "engineering license."

After Sink listed those points on the blackboard, we discussed each one individually. As each point came up, Sink would explain that it was probably "too minor to bother about," or that perhaps it "wouldn't be wise to open up that can of worms," or that maybe this was a point that "LTV just wouldn't understand." When the meeting was over, it had been decided that only three points were "worth mentioning."

Similar conferences were held during August and September, and the summer was punctuated with frequent treks between Dallas and Troy and demands by the Air Force to see the raw test data. Tempers were short, and matters seemed to grow worse.

Finally, early in October 1968, Lawson submitted his resignation, to take effect on October 25. On October 18, I submitted my own resignation, to take effect on November 1. In my resignation, addressed to Russell Line, I cited the A7D report and stated: "As you are aware, this report contains numerous deliberate and willful misrepresentations which, according to legal counsel, constitute fraud and expose both myself and others to criminal charges of conspiracy to defraud. . .The events of the past seven months have created an atmosphere of deceit and distrust in which it is impossible to work. . ."

On October 25, I received a sharp summons to the office of Bud Sunderman. Tall and graying, impeccably dressed at all times, he was capable of producing a dazzling smile or a hearty chuckle or immobilizing his face into marble hardness, as the occasion required.

I faced the marble hardness when I reached his office. He motioned me into a chair. "I have your resignation here," he snapped, "and I must say you have made some rather shocking, I might even say irresponsible, charges. This is very serious."

Before I could reply, he was demanding an explanation. "I want to know exactly what the fraud is in connection with the A7D and how you can dare accuse the company of such a thing!"

I started to tell some of the things that had happened during the testing, but he shut me off, saying, "There's nothing wrong with anything we've done here. You aren't aware of all the things that have been going on behind the scenes. If you had known the true situation, you would never have made these charges." He said that in view of my apparent "disloyalty" he had decided to accept my resignation "right now," and said it would be better for all concerned if I left the plant immediately. As I got up to leave he asked me if I intended to "carry this thing further."

I answered simply, "Yes," to which he replied, "Suit yourself." Within twenty minutes, I had cleared out my desk and left. Forty-eight hours later, the B.F. Goodrich Company recalled the qualification report and the four-disk brake, announcing that it would replace the brake with a new, improved, five-disk brake at no cost to LTV.

Ten months later, on August 13, 1969, I was the chief government witness at a hearing conducted before Senator William Proxmire's Economy in Government Subcommittee. I related the A7D story to the committee, and my testimony was supported by Searle Lawson, who followed me to the witness stand. Air Force officers also testified, as well as a four-man team from the General Accounting Office, which had conducted an investigation on the A7D brake at the request of Senator Proxmire. Both Air Force and GAO investigators declared that the brake was dangerous and had not been tested properly.

Testifying for Goodrich was R. G. Jeter, vice-president and general counsel of the company, from the Akron headquarters. Representing the Troy plant was Robert Sink. These two denied any wrongdoing on the part of the Goodrich Company, despite expert testimony to the contrary by Air Force and GAO officials. Sink was quick to deny any connection with the writing of the report or directing of any falsifications, claiming to have been on the West Coast at the time. John Warren was the man who had supervised its writing, said Sink.

As for me, I was dismissed as a high-school graduate with no technical training, while Sink testified that Lawson was a young, inexperienced engineer.

"We tried to give him guidance," Sink testified, "but he preferred to have his own convictions."

About changing the data to figures in the report, Sink said: "When you take data from several different sources, you have to rationalize among those data what is the true story. This is part of your engineering know-how." He admitted that changes had been made in the data, "but only to make them more consistent with the overall picture of the data that is available."

Jeter pooh-poohed the suggestion that anything improper occurred, saying: "We have thirty-odd engineers at this plant . . . and I say to you that it is incredible that these men would stand idly by and see reports changed or falsified. . . . I mean you just do not have to do that working for anybody. . . . Just nobody does that."

The four-hour hearing adjourned with no real conclusion reached by the subcommittee. But the following day the Department of Defense made sweeping changes in its inspection, testing, and reporting procedures. A spokesman for the DOD said the changes were a result of the Goodrich episode.

The A7D is now in service, sporting a Goodrich-made five-disk brake, a brake that works very well, I'm told. Business at the Goodrich plant is good. Lawson is now an engineer for LTV and has been assigned to the A7D project, possibly examining why the A7D's new brakes work so well. And I am now a newspaper reporter.

At this writing, those remaining at Goodrich—including Warren—are still secure in the same positions, all except Russell Line and Robert Sink.

Line has been rewarded with a promotion to production superintendent, a large step upward on the corporate ladder. As for Sink, he moved up into Line's old job.

Case III–2 _____

Beech Nut Company and the Fake Apple Juice

In November 1986 Beech Nut Company and its two top executives pleaded guilty on 215 felony counts of fraud and admitted willful violations of food and drug laws. This was the end of a case that had started a decade earlier and saw millions of parents feeding their babies a liquid labeled "100 percent pure apple juice" that was little more than sugar water. In the process of the court cases it was revealed that not only did top executives for Beech Nut attempt to cover up the facts showing that the apple juice was fake but they intentionally stonewalled the Food and Drug Administration (FDA) and other agencies so inventories of the fake juice could be sold before a recall was forced.

Since 1891, Beech Nut had had a reputation for the finest quality and purist products. Over the years these products included Life Savers, Table Talk Pies, Tetley Tea, chewing gum, and baby food. After being taken over in 1969 by Squibb, the company was later taken private in 1973 by Frank Nicholas in a leveraged buyout. By 1973 Beech Nut sold only baby food and held a 15 percent market share compared with the 70 percent share of Gerber, the market leader. Low market performance made it extremely difficult to repay the debts that were used to buy the company and by 1978, Nicholas was deeply in debt to suppliers.

In 1977, Interjuice Trading Company, a supplier of apple juice concentrate, approached Beech Nut with an offer to supply concentrate at a price 20 percent below those of its competitors. Nicholas readily accepted the offer though rumors of adulteration of concentrate by Interjuice were widespread in the industry. Beech Nut followed the industry practice of purchasing pure apple juice concentrate and adding water to dilute it to the

SOURCE: This case was prepared by Mitch Langberg under the direction of Newman Peery. References used included "Bad Apples: In the Executive Suite," *Consumer Reports*, May 1989, pp. 294–96; James Taub, "In the Mouths of Babes," *New York Times Magazine*, July 24, 1988, pp. 18–39; and Chris Welles, "What Led Beech Nut down the Road to Disgrace," *Business Week*, February 22, 11988, pp. 124–28.

appropriate level for juice. The resulting reconstituted juice was put into jars and labeled "100% pure apple juice." However, the apple juice reconstituted from concentrate supplied by Interjuice contained little more than sugar water.

Interjuice, the supplier of the major ingredient for apple juice, had a plant in Queens, New York. In 1978, the year following the agreement with Interjuice, employees in the research and development department of Beech Nut became suspicious of the concentrate that was being used to produce the apple juice sold by the company. Chemists produced strong evidence that its primary ingredient was cane sugar. As a part of the investigation the R&D department sent two employees to the Interjuice plant in Queens, where they were shown the storage area but were not allowed to see the production facilities.

Jerome LiCari, Beech Nut's director of research and development, became increasingly concerned about the integrity of the apple juice sold to infants. He sent several samples of the concentrate to independent research laboratories, which confirmed the content as being cane sugar. John Lavery, vice president of Beech Nut, told LiCari that he was not being a "team player," and further pursuit of this issue would not be good for his career. Lavery then ordered that the "apple juice concentrate" be blended into other mixed fruit juices where adulteration of the product would be harder to detect.

In 1979 Beech Nut was in dire financial condition and was sold to the Nestlé Corporation. Neils Hoyvald became president of Beech Nut in 1981 and promised Nestlé that Beech Nut would earn $700,000 in the following year, up from the $2.5 million loss of 1978. Lavery warned Hoyvald of the risk involved if the company continued its questionable relationship with the supplier, Interjuice Trading Company. He told Hoyvald that dropping the relationship with Interjuice would mean stopping the use of cane sugar in the "pure fruit juice" sold to babies, but it would increase material costs for Beech Nut by $250,000. Hoyvald told Lavery that the budget was already too high and that Beech Nut should continue to use Interjuice as a supplier, even though they knew that the concentrate supplied by Interjuice was made of cane sugar.

In 1982, Andrew Rosenzweig, a private investigator, was hired by *Consumer Reports* to check rumors about Interjuice. Rosenzweig discovered the fraud and noticed that one of the company's trucks was destined to go to Beech Nut. He approached of Beech Nut executives assuming they were innocent victims of Interjuice and was met in a very evasive and hostile manner. The executives told Rosenzweig they wanted no part of the suit being brought against Interjuice. It was clear to him that Beech Nut was involved in the fraudulent adulteration and he informed the authorities.

Until 1982, the FDA had delayed taking any action because of the lack of any known health risks. Because the fraud now involved millions of dollars, the FDA tested four samples of Beech Nut "100% Apple Juice" and found the samples lacking in any apple juice at all. When informed of these results, Beech Nut denied any knowledge of the adulteration and refused to let the FDA examine its books.

Beech Nut had approximately $3.5 million in inventory of its "100% Apple Juice" when it was approached by the FDA in 1982. It soon notified the FDA of ten sites with adulterated juice. However, Beech Nut knew from its records that these sites had little of the adulterated product left in its inventories. That night, Beech Nut shipped 26,000 cases of "apple juice" out of the state to avoid confiscation. Mr. Hoyvald, president of Beech Nut, ordered that all stocks of "apple juice" be deeply discounted in price and sold. Much of it was sold in Puerto Rico and in the Dominican Republic, where distributors were not informed that regulators had questioned the juice's authenticity.

When the FDA visited the Beech Nut plant in Canajoharie, New York, it found 242 cases of adulterated "juice." The FDA inspectors requested that the juice not be destroyed and Beech Nut employees agreed not to destroy it. Beech Nut then proceeded to destroy the product before the FDA could get the legal authorization to seize the 242 cases. Afterward, while Beech Nut officials met with the FDA to discuss a nationwide recall of the fake juice, Beech Nut launched a promotion, "buy 12 and get 6 bottles for free," to dispose of its inventory of the adulterated juice. Finally, after Beech Nut was threatened with a nationwide seizure of its product, it agreed to a "voluntary" recall of the apple juice. The company continued to sell adulterated mixed juice as late as March 1983.

In April 1982, Hoyvald sent a message to the parent company, Nestlé S.A., stating, "It is our feeling that we can report safely now that the apple juice recall has been completed. If the recall had been effectuated in early June, over 700,000 cases in inventory would have been effected. Due to our many delays, we were only faced with having to destroy approximately 20,000 cases."

When Mr. LiCari heard executives brag of their giving the FDA the runaround, he wrote the FDA, giving details about their executives' knowledge of the adulteration and their intentional stalling. The letter was signed "Johnny Appleseed." Later LiCari served as the chief witness in the ensuing case against Beech Nut and its executives. When it was all over, Beech Nut pleaded guilty to federal charges and was fined a record $2 million. Hoyvald was found guilty of 359 felony counts and Lavery on 448. Each was sentenced to a year and a day in prison and $100,000 in fines.

Case III–3 _____

Jean François Salveson

Jean François Salveson graduated from a major university on the East Coast with an M.B.A. Subsequently he joined an investment banking firm where he was very successful. After five years he resigned his position and moved to Europe with an investment portfolio amounting to about $2 million. He wanted to own and operate his own business. After searching for business opportunities for two years, he found one in the household cleaning manufacturing industry. A friend told him of a firm that was for sale for approximately 6 million French francs.

After meeting with the owner, Kurt Lorenze, Salveson found out more about the company. This firm manufactured household cleaning products, and though its sales were nearly 10 million francs annually, the company was on the brink of bankruptcy. It had suppliers for the needed ingredients and it had an established customer base that included all the major retail organizations. The company's products had a reputation for high quality and were sold at a medium price compared with other available products.

Salveson discussed the venture possibility with friends and a number warned him about Lorenze, who had a reputation for being somewhat slippery and was not above taking advantage of others. The negotiations proceeded and it was agreed that Salveson would purchase the company for six million francs. This price included:

1. *The formulas for all products.* The products of this company were unique but not proprietary and thus no patents were owned on them. A considerable amount of money was normally spent developing new, high-quality cleaning products, and the formulas were considered to be a valuable asset. They were protected as trade secrets, and obtaining the formulas was key to the purchase.

2. *The list of suppliers and customers.* Several of the materials were hard to find and the names and

addresses of suppliers were needed to maintain the operation with the change in ownership. The same was true with respect to the list of stores and purchasing managers with whom the company had been doing business.

3. *Manufacturing facilities, warehouses, and inventory of finished goods and chemicals.* The business included one small manufacturing facility, approximately one month's supply of both chemicals used to manufacture the products and finished goods.

4. *Past due debt payments.* The company was actually on the brink of bankrukptcy, and Kurt Lorenze was trying to avoid it. He had wanted to sell the business to avoid foreclosure and to have a small amount of capital to begin anew. Of the purchase price of six million francs, four million was to go directly to the major creditors of the firm and two million was to go to Lorenze.

The terms of the buyout included an immediate payment of the long-term debt that was seriously overdue and two payments of 500,000 francs each over the next year to Lorenze.

Early difficulties. Soon after Salveson took over the company, he began to have difficulties. Supplies were running short and when he tried to reorder, he found that Lorenze had left with both the list of suppliers and the names of all the purchasing agents. Lorenze was contacted and after many promises and three weeks of delay, a list that proved to have many inaccuracies was produced. Salveson finally had his accountant go to the company archives and manually reproduce these lists from invoices that had been stored as required by tax laws.

In addition to running out of products to sell, the level of customer complaints began to rise sharply. Some complained about slow deliveries. However, the problem that concerned Salveson the most was the complaints concerning SUDZO, the best-selling product. Customers were complaining that the product *did not clean* though earlier it had been rated by a consumer reporting organization as one of the best products on the market. Salveson hired a chemist and after analysis and testing they discovered that the product indeed was useless. Apparently the formula had been altered. Thus, Salveson directed his research staff to do a chemical analysis of the product purchases from stores with low inventory turnover. After extensive searching, they found an old bottle of the product and analysis revealed that the key cleaning ingredient had been omitted from the formula. Also, a careful review of the invoices in the records storage area revealed that certain chemicals had been formerly purchased in large quantities by the firm that did not appear on any of the "updated" product formulas.

In a panic, Salveson directed his researchers to do a similar analysis of his entire product line of 42 different products. The formulas for the top 14 products had all been altered in a way that rendered them useless. After seven months of this nightmare and a cost of some 500,000 francs, the situation was corrected.

The inventory. One additional situation was with respect to the transfer of chemicals. The inventory in a warehouse located about one-half mile from the manufacturing plant should have been transferred to Salveson as part of the business agreement. This warehouse had been leased by Lorenze, who was apparently in the process of launching another cleaning products business to take advantage of the export opportunities opening in eastern Europe. (Lorenze had signed a noncompete clause in the contract that prohibited him from competing in France for a period of two years.)

On investigation, Salveson discovered that Lorenze had no wealth in his own name. He had transferred all his property to his wife's name and the title to the chemicals was being claimed by the company he had recently formed. Though the new company was controlled by Lorenze, it would be difficult for Salveson to obtain the chemicals without Lorenze's cooperation. Salveson considered a lawsuit. His attorney indicated that this would tie up the inventory for as many as six months, but because of the time and ambiguity of certain documents, he only had a 50-50 chance of winning a lawsuit. Also, the lawsuit would be very costly and require much personal attention at a time when the very survival of his business demanded his full-time efforts.

However, Lorenze's credit rating was poor and it would be difficult for him to successfully launch his new business without the use of these chemicals. Thus, Lorenze reluctantly agreed to pay for the value of the chemicals in the warehouse. Salveson agreed to accept a refund amounting to the value of the inventory from Lorenze so that he could keep the chemicals. He had paid Lorenze the first payment of 500,000 francs at the time of the purchase, and the last payment of an equal amount was due at the end of the year.

After several discussions and two visits to Lorenze by Salveson's attorney, it was agreed that two teams of employees—one team working for Salveson, the other for Lorenze—would jointly inventory the chemicals. This inventory's value would be based on the current market prices. At the appointed time of 8:00 A.M. one Wednesday morning, the two teams were to meet to accomplish the inventory. Salveson's team arrived at 7:45 A.M. eager to begin the project. When the other team failed to appear after three hours, they called Salveson at his office for guidance. Salveson instructed them to begin the inventory at 1:00 P.M., even if the other team was not available.

The inventory was accomplished by 8:00 P.M. and the supervisor took the results to the office where Salveson had been working with an important customer all day trying to smooth over some problems concerning the recall of the faulty product.

Salveson was presented with the inventory list by Mr. Justin, his plant manager, who was responsible for the inventory and valuation of the chemicals. Justin indicated that the list of chemicals was valued at 900,000 francs, and that was as accurate as they could make it, given the disorganized way that the materials were stored. Justin had become very resentful of Lorenze during the past seven months. He had supervised the recall of the faulty products, and had tried unsuccessfully to obtain accurate lists of suppliers, customers, and formulas for products from Lorenze. He was concerned because Lorenze had cost the company at least 500,000 francs and had made his own job a nightmare during the previous two quarters.

After Justin discussed the process of the inventory that day, he then produced a *second inventory* that was different from the first. The amounts of certain key chemicals were different from the first list and the total value of the inventory was exactly 500,000 francs more than the first list. Because the other team had failed to show up, Lorenze was legally bound to pay the established value of the inventory. He had the right to do his own inventory, but it seemed unlikely that he would do so. Thus, Justin reasoned, he would overcharge Lorenze to make up for all the costs

and unpleasant experiences he had caused during the past six months.

Case Discussion Question

1. What should Salveson do? Explain why you took this position.

Case III–4

Pierce vs. Ortho Pharmaceutical Corporation (A)

In May 1971 Dr. Grace Pierce accepted a position as associate director of medical research with the Ortho Pharmaceutical Corporation. She was promoted in March 1973 to director of medical research and therapeutics and was the only medical doctor on the team responsible for overseeing development and testing of therapeutic drugs that involved participating in the government review process. The development and market introduction of a new product often requires six years, beginning with test results on animals. If the initial tests are favorable, the company submits an Investigative New Drug Application to the Food and Drug Administration (FDA) that has the authority to authorize testing the drug on human beings.

Pierce served as the only medical doctor on a team researching loperamide, a drug for the treatment of diarrhea in infants and the elderly, who often have difficulty swallowing pills. The drug was very sour and had to be sweetened because it was to be taken in liquid form. Saccharin was chosen as a sweetener and each bottle of loperamide would contain 44 times the concentration permitted by the FDA in a can of diet cola.

Pierce and other members of the research team had serious concerns about the use of saccharin as a sweetener because of its carcinogenic properties. The team's toxicologist said that the saccharin was a "slow carcinogen"; it had produced benign and malignant tumors in test animals after a long period of time, and "any intentional exposure of

any segment of the human population to a potential carcinogen is not in the best interest of public health or the Ortho Pharmaceutical Corporation."

Ortho's management felt that any change in the formulation would cause a delay in the introduction of loperamide on the market and that such a delay was unacceptable. Pressure from management made all the members of the team, except Pierce, change their minds, and the team voted in March 1975 to go ahead with testing. However, Pierce continued to insist on a safer reformulation of the product. As the only medical doctor on the team, she was ultimately responsible for establishing and monitoring the tests on humans. She considered it her professional duty to resist testing unless the formula were changed to a smaller dosage of saccharin. She said, "I wanted to be on the project but I didn't want to take that high saccharin formula out to the clinical practice . . . I could not ethically take that out and give it to children."

In response to these objections, Ortho "reassigned" Pierce and removed her from all therapeutic/drug projects. Shortly afterward, she was told that management considered her unpromotable. In June 1975 Pierce submitted her resignation and later sued Ortho Pharmaceutical Corporation for wrongful discharge.

Case Discussion Questions (A)

1. In Chapter 6 we discussed the moral context of ethical behavior that included (1) the situation, (2) the individual moral and ethical standards, (3) the level of moral reasoning, and (4) organiza-

SOURCE: Adapted from *Pierce v. Ortho Pharmaceutical Corp.*, 84 N.J. 58, 417, A. 2d. 505 (1980).

tional culture and other factors influencing behavior in a particular situation. How would you characterize the context of moral behavior in the Ortho Pharmaceutical Corporation?

2. What special responsibilities did Pierce have as the only medical doctor on the drug-testing team?

3. Do you feel the company had the right to reject Pierce's expert opinion in this matter?

4. Did the management of Ortho do the right thing? Why? If you think the management should have done something different, what would you recommend and why?

Case III–5

Pierce vs. Ortho Pharmaceutical Corporation (B)

Majority Opinion of the Supreme Court of New Jersey

This case presents the question whether an employee at will has a cause of action against her employer to recover damages for the termination of her employment following her refusal to continue a project she viewed as medically unethical. . . .

Under the common law, in the absence of an employment contract, employers or employees have been free to terminate the employment relationship with or without cause. . . . Commentators have questioned the compatibility of the traditional at will doctrine with the realities of modern economics and employment practices. . . . The common law rule has been modified by the enactment of labor relations legislation. . . . The National Labor Relations Act and other labor legislation illustrate the governmental policy of preventing employers from using the right of discharge as a means of oppression. . . . Consistent with this policy, many states have recognized the need to protect employees who are not parties to a collective bargaining agreement or other contract from abusive practices by the employer.

Recently those states have recognized a common law cause of action for employees at will who were discharged for reasons that were in some way "wrongful." The courts in those jurisdictions have taken varied approaches, some recognizing the action in tort, some in contract. . . . Nearly all juris-

SOURCE: *Pierce v. Ortho Pharmaceutical Corp.*, 84 N.J. 58, 417, A.2d 505 (1980).

dictions link the success of the wrongful discharged employee's action to proof that the discharge violated public policy. . . .

In recognizing a cause of action to provide a remedy for employees who are wrongfully discharged, we must balance the interest of the employee, the employer, and the public. Employees have an interest in knowing they will not be discharged for exercising their legal rights they see fit as long as their conduct is consistent with public policy. The public has an interest in employment stability and in discouraging frivolous lawsuits by dissatisfied employees.

Although contours of an exception are important to all employees at will, this case focuses on the special considerations arising out of the right to fire an employee at will who is a member of a recognized profession. One writer has described the predicament that may confront a professional employed by a large corporation. Consider, for example, the plight of an engineer who is told that he will lose his job unless he falsifies his data or conclusions, or unless he approves a product which does not conform to specifications or meet minimum standards . . . and the predicament of an accountant who is told to falsify his employer's profit and loss statement in order to enable the employer to obtain credit.

Employees who are professionals owe a special duty to abide not only by federal and state law, but also by the recognized codes of ethics of their professions. The duty may oblige them to decline to perform acts required by their employers. However, an employee should not have the right to prevent his or her employer from pursuing its business because the employee perceives that a particular business decision violates the employee's personal morals, as distinguished from the recognized code of ethics of the employee's profession.

We hold that an employee has a cause of action for wrongful discharge when the discharge is contrary to a clear mandate of public policy. The sources of public policy include legislation; administrative rules, regulations or decisions; and judicial decisions. In certain instances, a professional code of ethics may contain an expression of public policy. However, not all such sources express a clear mandate of public policy. For example, a code of ethics designed to serve only the interests of a profession or an administrative regulation concerned with technical matters probably would not be sufficient. Absent legislation, the judiciary must define the cause of action in case-by-case determinations. . . . Unless the employee at will identifies a specific expression of public policy, he may be discharged with or without cause.

[B]efore loperamide could be tested on humans, an IND [Investigative New Drug Application] had to be submitted to the FDA to obtain the approval for such testing. The IND must contain complete manufacturing specifications, details of pre-clinical studies (testing on animals) that demonstrate the safe use of the drug, and a description of proposed clinical studies. The FDA then has 30 days to withhold approval of testing. Since no IND had been filed here, . . . it is not clear that clinical testing of loperamide on humans was imminent.

Dr. Pierce argues that by continuing to perform research on loperamide she would have been forced to violate professional ethics expressed in the Hippocratic oath. She cites the part of the oath that reads: "I will prescribe regimen for the good of my patients according to my ability and my judgment and never do harm to anyone." Clearly, the general language of the oath does not prohibit specifically research that does not involve tests on humans and that cannot lead to such tests without governmental approval.

We note that Dr. Pierce did not rely on or allege violation of any other standards, including the "codes of professional ethics" advanced by the dissent. Similarly, she did not allege that continuing her research would constitute an act of medical malpractice or violate any statute. . . . The case would be far different if Ortho had filed the IND,

the FDA had disapproved it, and Ortho insisted on testing the drug on humans.

Implicit in Dr. Pierce's position is the contention that Ortho [was] obliged to accept her opinion. Dr. Pierce contended, in effect, that Ortho should have stopped research on loperamide because of her opinion about the controversial nature of the drug.

Dr. Pierce espouses a doctrine that would lead to disorder in drug research. . . . Chaos would result if a single doctor engaged in research were allowed to determine, according to his or her individual conscience, whether a project should continue. An employee does not have a right to continued employment when he or she refuses to conduct research simply because it would contravene his or her personal morals. An employee at will who refuses to work for an employer in answer to a call of conscience should recognize that other employees and their employer might heed a different call. However, nothing in this opinion should be construed to restrict the right of an employee at will to refuse to work on a project that he or she believes is unethical. . . .

Under these circumstances, we conclude that the Hippocratic oath does not contain a clear mandate of public policy that prevented Dr. Pierce from continuing her research on loperamide. To hold otherwise would seriously impair the ability of drug manufacturers to develop new drugs according to their best judgment.

The legislative and regulatory framework pertaining to drug development reflects a public policy that research involving testing on humans may proceed with FDA approval. The public has an interest in the development of drugs, subject to the approval of a responsible management and the FDA, to protect and promote the health of mankind.

Accordingly, we reverse the judgment of the Appellate Division and remand the cause to the trial court of entry of judgment for defendant.

Judge Pashman, Dissenting Opinion

The majority's analysis recognizes that the ethical goals of professional conduct are of inestimable social value. By maintaining informed standards of conduct, licensed professionals, bring to the problems of their public responsibilities the same expertise that marks their calling. The integrity of codes of professional conduct that results from this regulation deserves judicial protection form undue economic pressure. Employers are a potential source of this pressure, for they can provide or withhold—until today, at their whim—job security and the means of enhancing a professional's reputation. Thus I completely agree with the majority's ruling that "an employee has a cause of action for wrongful discharge when the discharge is contrary to a clear mandate of public policy" as expressed in a "professional code of ethics."

The Court pronounces this rule for the first time today. One would think that it would therefore afford plaintiff with an opportunity to seek relief within the confines of this newly announced cause of action. By ordering the grant of summary judgment for defendant, however, the majority apparently believes that such an opportunity would be an exercise in futility. I fail to see how the majority reaches this conclusion. There are a number of detailed, recognized codes of medical ethics that proscribe participation in clinical experimentation when a doctor perceives an unreasonable threat to human health. Any one of these codes could provide the "clear mandate of public policy" that the majority requires. . . .

Nothing is more unfair than stating a novel principle of law for the first time on an appeal, but denying the plaintiff who sought relief under some new standard and opportunity to conform his proof to the specific requirements actually adopted. Yet it appears the majority has done precisely that. Although plaintiff might have prevailed at trial under the majority's rule by invoking one or more of the standards I have described, the majority does not acknowledge this possibility. . . .

Three other points made by the majority require discussion. . . .The first is the majority's characterization of the effect of plaintiff's ethical position. It appears to believe that Dr. Pierce had the power to determine whether defendant's proposed development program would continue at all. This is not the case, nor is plaintiff claiming the right to halt defendant's developmental efforts. Plaintiff claims only the right to her professional autonomy. She contends that she may not be discharged for expressing her view that the clinical program is unethical or for refusing to continue her participation in the project. She has done nothing else to impede continued development of defendant's proposal; moreover, it is undisputed that the defendant was able to continue its program by reassigning personnel. Thus, the majority's view that granting doctors a right to be free from abusive discharges would confer on any one of them complete veto power over desirable drug development, is ill-conceived.

The second point concerns the role of governmental approval of the proposed experimental program. In apparent ignorance of the past failures of official regulation to safeguard against pharmaceutical horrors, the majority implies that the necessity for administrative approval for human testing eliminates the need for active, ethical professionals within the drug industry. But we do not know whether the FDA would be aware of the safer alternative to the proposed drug when it would pass upon defendant's application for the more hazardous formula. The majority professes no such knowledge. We must therefore assume the FDA would have been left in ignorance. This highlights the need for ethically autonomous professionals within the pharmaceutical industry. . . .

The final point to which I must respond is the majority's observation that plaintiff expressed her opposition prematurely, before the FDA had approved clinical experimentation. . . . Essentially, the majority holds that a professional employee may not express a refusal to engage in illegal or clearly unethical conduct until actual participation and the resulting harm is imminent. This principle grants little to protect the ethical autonomy of professionals that the majority proclaims. Would the majority have Dr. Pierce wait until the first infant was placed before her, ready to receive the first dose of a drug containing 44 times the concentration of saccharin permitted in 12 ounces of soda?. . .

I respectfully dissent.

Case Discussion Questions (B)

1. Under what conditions can an employee exercise professional expertise over the objections

of management according to the majority opinion?

2. The social control of business in a market-oriented society relies on three mechanisms: the market, the government, and ethical behavior. Which of these controls does the court seem to favor in this case?

3. What is your assessment of Dr. Pierce's behavior in this case? Could she, in good conscience,

have behaved differently? What were her options? What were the likely consequences?

4. What is the implication of the majority opinion for ethical behavior of employees? Do you agree with the criticisms of the minority opinion? Explain.

5. Do you think the company's handling of this situation could affect its performance in the area of product liability?

Case III–6 _____

Safeway LBO Yields Vast Profits But Exacts a Heavy Human Toll

On the eve of the 1986 leveraged buyout of Safeway Stores, Inc., the board of directors sat down to a last supper. Peter Magowan, the boyish-looking chairman and chief executive of the world's largest supermarket chain, rose to offer a toast to the deal that had fended off a hostile takeover by the corporate raiders Herbert and Robert Haft.

"Through your efforts, a true disaster was averted," the 44-year-old Magowan told the other directors. By selling the publicly held company to a group headed by buyout specialists Kohlberg Kravis Roberts & Co. and members of Safeway management, "you have saved literally thousands of jobs in our workforce," Magowan said. "All of us—employees, customers, shareholders—have a great deal to be thankful for."

Nearly four years later, Magowan and the KKR group can indeed count their blessings. While they borrowed heavily to buy Safeway from the shareholders, last month they sold 10 percent of the company (but none of their own shares) back to the public—at a price that values their own collective stake at more than $800 million, more than four times their cash investment.

SOURCE: Reprinted with permission from "Safeway LBO Yields Vast Profits But Exacts a Heavy Human Toll," by Susan C. Faludi, *Wall Street Journal,* May 16, 1990, p. 1. David B. Hilder contributed to this article. Reprinted by permission.

Employees, on the other hand, have considerably less reason to celebrate. Magowan's toast notwithstanding, 63,000 managers and workers were terminated from Safeway, through store sales or layoffs. While the majority were reemployed by their new store owners, this was largely at lower wages, and many thousands of Safeway people wound up either unemployed or forced into the part-time workforce. A survey of former Safeway employees in Dallas found that nearly 60 percent still hadn't found full-time employment more than a year after the layoff.

James White, a Safeway trucker for nearly 30 years in Dallas, was among the 60 percent. In 1988, he marked the one-year anniversary of his last shift at Safeway this way: First he told his wife he loved her, then he locked the bathroom door, loaded his .22-caliber hunting rifle, and blew his brains out.

"Safeway was James's whole life," says his widow, Helen. "He'd near stand up and salute whenever one of those trucks went by." When Safeway dismissed him, she says, "it was like he turned into a piece of stone."

Eighties Fad

Few financial maneuvers have drawn more controversy than the leveraged buyout (LBO), a relatively old money-making tactic that was dusted off and put to extensive use in the 1980s, thanks largely to the rise of junk bond financing.

In a leveraged buyout, a small group of investors that generally includes senior management borrows heavily to buy a company from public shareholders and takes it private. The debt is to be rapidly repaid from the company's own cash flow or from sales of its assets.

The returns on some such highly leveraged investments have been astronomical, enriching such financiers as Henry Kravis, Ronald Perelman, and Nelson Peltz to a degree unheard of since the days of the robber barons. Proponents of LBOs argue that they are good for business and good for America, triggering long-overdue crash weight-loss programs for flabby corporations. By placing ownership in the hands of a small group of investors and managers with a powerful debt-driven incentive to improve productivity, the argument goes, companies can't help but shape up.

Success Story

The Safeway LBO is often cited as one of the most successful in this regard. It brought shareholders a substantial premium at the outset, and since then the company has raised productivity and operating profits and produced riches for the new investors and top management. "We could not have done what we did without going through the incredible trauma and pressure of the LBO," Magowan said in late 1988.

But while much has been written about the putative benefits of LBOs, little has been said about the hundreds of thousands of people directly affected by the past decade's buyout binge: the employees of the bought-out corporations. In the case of Safeway, a two-month investigation of the buyout reveals enormous human costs and unintended side effects. The company dropped tens of thousands of employees from its payroll, suppliers and other dependent industries laid off hundreds more, and communities lost the civic contributions of a firm whose first store had been opened by a clergyman who wanted to help his parishioners save money.

When Safeway itself selected a group of its employees to speak to this newspaper on behalf of

the company, not one of those interviewed praised the buyout. "I think LBOs are very ugly," said Carl Adkins, an inventory control clerk who described himself as happy with his job. "I think they are harmful to individual working people. I think they honestly stink."

Moreover, the evidence doesn't entirely support the argument that the LBO made Safeway a healthier institution. The supermarket chain cut plenty of muscle with the fat, both from its holdings and from its labor force, and deferred capital improvements in favor of the all-consuming debt. Many employees find the post-LBO working environment more difficult—as a company legendary for job security and fairness resorts to hardball labor policies and high-pressure quota systems.

Just before the Safeway deal was struck in 1986, Magowan's mother grew worried about the employees. The supermarket dowager wanted to be sure the LBO wouldn't damage Safeway's long-standing reputation as a benevolent employer.

Will anyone get hurt? Mrs. Magowan pressed her son at the time, according to company staff members. Will anyone lose his job?

No Mom, Magowan promised, according to the staffer's account. No one will get hurt.

"Yes, I was greatly concerned about the people," Mrs. Magowan recalls today in her mansion overlooking the San Francisco Bay. She declines to comment further.

Magowan's recollection: "Well, I don't ever remember such a conversation ever occurred. . . . I might have said things like, 'We're going to do the best we can for our employees and I'm hopeful that we are going to be able to keep the vast majority with the new owners.'"

In any event, before that summer was out, Mrs. Magowan's son had begun firing Safeway employees. Not long after, Safeway replaced its longtime motto, "Safeway Offers Security." The new corporate statement, displayed on a plaque in the lobby at corporate headquarters, reads in part: "Targeted Returns on Current Investment."

Before the LBO, Safeway was hardly a prime example of the sluggish, out-of-shape sort of company that LBO proponents like to target. Founded in 1926, it had grown under Magowan family leadership to encompass more than 2,000 stores in 29 states and in England, Australia, Canada, and Mexico. Magowan's father, Robert, had largely built Safeway, and his mother, Doris Merrill Magowan, is the daughter of a founder of Merrill Lynch & Co., which helped finance Safeway's growth.

Many companies, including Safeway, had allowed their payrolls to become bloated in certain underperforming divisions, and layoffs were common throughout large American companies during the last decade.

But Safeway was already doing—albeit at a slower pace—many of the things LBO experts advocate. It was remodeling its stores and creating the upscale "superstores" that have now proved such a big success. It was experimenting with employee productivity teams, phasing out money-losing divisions, and thinning its workforce with a program that included some layoffs but generally relied on less painful methods like attrition.

All these changes produced earnings that more than doubled in the first four years of the 1980s, to a record $231 million in 1985. The stock price tripled in three years, and dividends climbed four years in a row.

But all that wasn't enough for takeover-crazed Wall Street, where virtually no company was invulnerable to cash-rich corporate raiders. When the deep-pocketed Hafts began buying Safeway shares in the open market and then offered to buy the company for as much as $64 a share, management felt it had to take defensive action. Selling to the Hafts might have cost Chairman Magowan his job and, he felt, ultimately might have brought a breakup of the company.

Safeway considered and rejected a plan to fend off the Hafts through a so-called recapitalization. This was a move that its supermarket industry competitor Kroger Co. would use two years later to keep the same raiders at bay while allowing shareholders to realize a big one-time gain.

The decision to sell to KKR instead brought immediate benefits to some. Shareholders got $67.50 a share—82 percent more than the stock was trading at three months before—plus warrants that gave them a 5.6 percent stake in the ongoing company. Employees owned roughly 10 percent of Safeway shares at the time of the buyout.

Magowan and other directors and top executives received $28 million for their shares, $5.7 million of which went to Magowan himself. He and about 60 other top executives also got options to buy a total of 10 percent of the new Safeway at only $2 a share; those options are now valued at more than $100 million, or $12.125 a share.

The Hafts made $100 million by selling the Safeway shares they had accumulated to KKR, and as a consolation prize, they were also given options to buy a 20 percent stake in the new Safeway. The Hafts sold that option back to KKR 2½ months later for an additional $59 million.

The three investment banks that worked on the deal made a total of $65 million. Law and accounting firms shared another $25 million.

And then there are Henry Kravis, George Roberts, about a dozen other KKR employees, and the 70 investors KKR brought into the buyout. KKR itself charged Safeway $60 million in fees just to put the deal together. The five KKR partners then put up a small fraction of the equity funding—1.1 percent, or roughly $2 million—and received a 20 percent share of the eventual profits from any sale of Safeway.

KKR's investor group, half of which consists of state pension funds and which also includes banks, insurance companies, and even Harvard University, got most of the rest.

Roberts rebuts the notion that too few people really benefit in an LBO. He says that some of "our 70 limited partners represent retired teachers, sanitation workers and firemen, and 80 percent of our profits go to them."

But at the largest of those investors, Oregon's public-employee pension fund, LBO investments make up only a tiny portion of investments and thus haven't had a "significant impact" on retirees' benefits to date, according to Bob Andrews, fund manager.

The immediate gains for some triggered immediate costs for others. The first employees to be fired shortly after the buyout's completion were more than 300 staffers from Oakland corporate headquarters and a nearby division in Walnut Creek, Calif. The following spring, the entire Dallas-area division was shut down, and nearly 9,000 more employees were dismissed—employees with an average length of service of 17 years.

"This is going to kill people," transportation manager Richard Quigley says he told his boss when he learned that the layoff would take place.

On the Friday afternoon before the dismissals went into effect, Patricia Vasquez, a 14-year systems analyst, heard that her name was on the list. That evening, Vasquez, a Safeway devotee famous for her refusal to take lunch hours, packed her service citations in a cardboard box and left looking pale and drawn. The next morning her two young children found their single mother on the bathroom floor, dead of a heart attack.

That Monday, Quigley came home with the news that he himself would be fired. His worried wife's blood pressure began to rise. A diabetic who had been in good health for years, she was hospitalized by Labor Day weekend—and dead by September 5. Rightly or wrongly, Quigley blames his wife's death on his Safeway layoff: "She was very traumatized by it."

Told of these deaths and several suicides that family members and friends attribute to the Safeway layoffs, Magowan says: "I never heard of this before. If it's true, I'm obviously sorry about such a tragic thing, but any attempt to associate this directly with the LBO shows a disposition to want to believe the worst of LBOs."

For many at Safeway, firing day was only the first in a long series of financial and emotional body blows.

"The dominoes began to tumble and they crashed for a long time to come," says Ron Morrison, a former corporate systems manager. When Morrison lost his 14-year job, his fiancé announced that she couldn't marry an unemployed man.

He found work as a transportation analyst at Del Monte, but the KKR bought that company, too—and he was laid off again, just before Thanksgiving. By the time 1990 rolled around, Morrison had not only gone through two KKR-led LBOs, he had lost his second home and was unemployed again.

"Right now I pretty much live in a cocoon," Morrison says. "You begin to pull in your tentacles because you can't afford to have any more cut off."

While at Safeway, Morrison says, he helped conduct a transportation study that trimmed millions from the company transit budget. And he wasn't the only fired employee at headquarters whose work had brought the company big savings. Refrigeration engineer Mikhail Vaynberg, a Soviet émigré, says he invented a new cooling system for the stores that cut energy costs 35 percent, saved $1.6 million a year, and was copied by many suppliers. (A Safeway spokesman says the company doesn't contest these cost-saving claims.)

After he was fired, Vaynberg couldn't find work in his field and, like many other employees fired at headquarters, says he couldn't get a current letter of recommendation from Safeway; he says his boss told him he wasn't allowed to supply a written reference because "you might use it to sue the company." (A Safeway spokesman says it is company policy not to grant reference letters for "good, sound legal reasons," but maintains that managers were allowed to make exceptions for

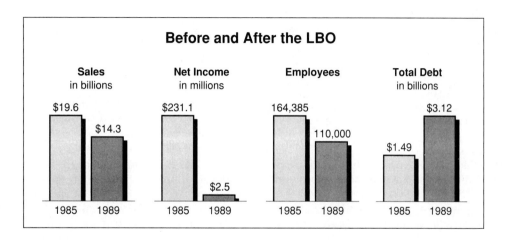

Before and After the LBO

Sales in billions	Net Income in millions	Employees	Total Debt in billions
$19.6 / $14.3	$231.1 / $2.5	164,385 / 110,000	$1.49 / $3.12
1985 / 1989	1985 / 1989	1985 / 1989	1985 / 1989

employees laid off in the 1986 firings at head-quarters.)

Vaynberg says his greatest blow came a few weeks after the layoff, when his only son dropped out of engineering school weeks shy of graduation: "The country doesn't want engineers: Look what happened to you," he told his father. Now Vaynberg, still unemployed, spends his days in a painfully clean living room, prowls the halls at night, and avoids old friends and neighbors. "I am ashamed," he says, staring at his big, empty hands. "I am like an old thrown-out mop."

Safeway fired its corporate employees with no notice, cut off their medical insurance in as little as two weeks, and provided severance pay of one week's salary for every year of service, to a maximum of just eight weeks. And to get the pay, many employees say they were told to sign a letter waiving their right to contest the severance package later. (A company spokesman says the letter wasn't a waiver but simply an "acknowledgment" that they understood the terms.)

Magowan concedes that many of the people fired at headquarters in the summer of 1986 were "very good" employees. The cuts were made in a hurry, as he later said in a court deposition, so as "to put this whole unpleasant matter behind us as soon as possible." For such haste, Safeway would wind up paying $8.2 million to settle a wrongful termination class-action suit and $750,000 to settle a separate suit for age discrimination.

One executive who left headquarters voluntarily was accorded much better treatment. Safeway president James Rowland was granted a $1 million bonus when he retired after the buyout.

Rowland advised Magowan in a memo to approve the bonus privately and divide the amount into smaller portions with labels like "paid consultant." The reason, as Rowland wrote: "Peter, I do not want to put you in an embarrassing situation." (Mr. Rowland, reached at his Arkansas home, says he never got a "million-dollar bonus. I got my regular bonus. I just don't recall what it was. I'm not going to go back and rehash all that." He then hang up. Magowan says Rowland wasn't paid a lump sum of $1 million. He was paid his previous year's bonus, which he had earned, plus an advance on consulting work he would do for Safeway, Magowan says. "It wouldn't have been some side deal under the table between Jim Rowland and me that nobody knew about. That's not my style.")

"I wouldn't be surprised if 11,000 jobs were created out of" the roughly 9,000 jobs lost, Magowan announced to the press after he closed the Dallas division. He says he assumed that the other grocery chains would expand to fill the Safeway vacuum. "What I'm talking about here is a theory of mine," he says later. "I will get right up front and say I don't have facts to support it." Magowan says he has not been back to Dallas since the closure.

When the Dallas division shut down, the state unemployment office had to open on the weekend—for the first time ever—just to accommodate the Safeway crowds. The Dallas employees had a thin financial pallet to cushion the blow. Their severance pay was half a week's pay for each year of service, up to a minimum of eight weeks.

And their severance checks didn't start arriving until July 1987, three months after the shutdown. Russell Webb, a 12-year produce clerk and single father with three children, didn't get his severance check for eight months. Vacation pay arrived even more slowly: First the union had to go to arbitration to get it; then, the company didn't start mailing the checks until February 1989. Safeway says the severance and other checks arrived late because they weren't a part of the union contract and thus "had to be negotiated."

In addition to White's suicide, at least two others tried to kill themselves. One was Bill Mayfield, Jr., a mechanic in the Safeway dairy since it opened in 1973, who slashed his wrists, then shot himself in the stomach; the bullet just missed his vital organs and he survived.

"I would say [the layoff] devastated about 80 percent of the people in the division," says Gary Jones, president of Safeway's credit union in Dallas, which eventually had to write off $4 million in loans. "Overnight we turned from a lending institution into a collection agency." At one point, more than 250 repossessed cars were sitting in his parking lot.

KKR and Safeway blame organized labor for the fall of the Dallas division. Once the leading grocer in the area, Safeway had seen its market share fall by nearly half in the 1980s. KKR and Safeway officials say the company was paying too much in wages, some 30 percent more than its rivals, thus preventing it from cutting prices, remodeling stores, and the like.

But rival Kroger was also a union shop, and it found a way to prosper and expand in Dallas by renovating stores and negotiating lower wages with the union. Its market share was on the rise. The Kroger case suggests that the Safeway layoffs might have been necessitated as much by mismanagement as by labor costs. Some company officials concede that Safeway had other problems besides wages in Dallas: Its stores were too small, too old, and poorly designed.

While grocery competitors in Dallas eventually bought more than half the 141 Safeway stores, they were less eager to pick up the unionized workers. According to a state-funded survey of the displaced workers, stores under new management typically recalled no more than half dozen of the 40 to 60 former Safeway employees who staffed each outlet.

And wages fell sharply, no matter where the workers landed: In 1988, according to the survey, ex-Safeway employees reported that their average pay had dropped to $6.50 from $12.09 an hour.

Cindy Hale, an 11-year Safeway employee, saw her wages fall to $4 an hour when she took an identical grocery clerk's job with Apple-Tree Markets, at an old Safeway store. Her new employer would only hire part-time, so Hale, a single mother, lost her medical benefits. She eventually lost her house, too, and had to send her son to live with her parents.

"But it really wasn't as bad for me as for the others," says Hale.

For Dallas employees, working for Safeway had often been a total family experience, and many households lost more than one income after the buyout. The Seabolts lost three: Husband, wife and daughter all got their pink slips on the same day. Ron Seabolt, who had worked in the company's distribution center for 17 years, searched for months before taking a job as a janitor. Now he works at the post office.

Kay Seabolt, a human resources supervisor at Safeway and a 17-year company veteran, counseled ex-employees for a year under a state job placement retraining program. The program's counselors sometimes fished into their own pockets to buy groceries for those who streamed through the counsel-ing center, an abandoned Safeway office. When Safeway sold it, the new owners evicted them.

Seared into Seabolt's memory is the day one tattered man arrived at the office. A long-timer in the Safeway bread plant, the middle-aged baker made his way to her desk with a slow, wincing limp. He apologized for his appearance, explaining that he had just walked six miles from the temporary labor pools: His car had been repossessed. He was living in a homeless shelter. "I gave him a few job leads," she recalls, "but he was pretty shabby and I didn't hold out much hope." Before he left, she slipped him some money for bus fare, she says. "I never saw him again."

When the layoff rumors first began circulating, Clara Sanchez took to praying in the parking lot of Store No. 677. Her silent pleas went unanswered. On April 24, 1987, she and her husband, Jesse, lost their jobs. She had been a checker for 12 years; he had been an order filler in the warehouse for 18 years.

Clara could find no work and is still unemployed; Jesse searched for eight months before the city hired him to cut grass for $3.55 an hour. Then he washed cars for $4.50 an hour. Two months later he was laid off. Finally, with $14,000 in unpaid bills, the Sanchezes filed for bankruptcy.

The church sent canned goods, and Mr. and Mrs. Sanchez skipped supper some evenings so their children could eat better. After a while, Mr. Sanchez was too depressed to eat anyway. "I wasn't a man; I wasn't worth anything as far as I was concerned," he says. "Why live if I can't support my kids?" One Friday night, Mr. Sanchez told his wife he was going to watch a wrestling match but went to a friend's house instead with a business proposition: "I told him I would pay him $100 to take my life. I didn't own a gun or I would've done it myself." The friend put his gun out of reach and sent Mr. Sanchez home.

When Safeway pulled out of Dallas, the shock waves didn't stop at the supermarket doors. The shutdown led to secondary layoffs at almost all the big food and beverage vendors in town, and some construction business suffered. For Harry W. Parks Co., a general contractor, Safeway represented 85 percent of annual revenues; Mr. Parks had dropped most of his other clients to assist Safeway in its big remodeling program in the early 1980s.

After the pullout, his company nearly folded, all but three employees were laid off, and Parks had a heart attack and died.

"Safeway was his whole world," says his son, Harry Jr. "That's all he cared about for 30 years. When they pulled out, it was like his whole family died."

The North Texas Food bank suffered too. It lost a founding member and its leading contributor; Safeway used to donate 600,000 pounds of food a year.

"The bottom line," food bank director Lori Palmer says, "is fewer people ate."

The layoffs in Oakland, Dallas, and elsewhere were just one part of KKR's broad-based plan to cut costs, boost profitability, and meet the stiff interest and principal deadlines set by the company's lenders and debt holders. About 1,000 of the company's stores were sold, as were 45 plants and other facilities.

Safeway put whole divisions in Kansas, Oklahoma, Arkansas and, Utah on the auction block. They were sold to a few grocery chains, many other LBO investors, and, in some cases, real estate investors.

The real estate investors didn't rehire any Safeway workers: They converted the properties to video shops, thrift stores, and in one case a bingo parlor. Some were boarded up.

While grocery chains bought some Safeway stores just to shut them down and reduce competition, other chains bought whole Safeway divisions and kept most of the workers; the British and Oklahoma divisions are examples of this. In other cases, new owners retained only selected workers. In virtually all cases, though, new ownership meant pay cuts.

In what seemed at first the best deal for employees, the grocery chain Borman's, Inc. bought the entire Utah Safeway division and hired virtually all the workers. But nine months later, those 3,000 employees lost their jobs when Borman sold the division, piece by piece, to local competitors and investors. Only a few of the stores in the Salt Lake City area still operate as supermarkets.

Don Schanche, a Safeway meat cutter in Salt Lake City for 25 years, spiraled downward from his $12.33 hourly pay at Safeway to a reduced wage scale at Borman's Farmer Jack outlet, to an unsuc-

cessful appeal for any minimum wage employment at the same store, which had been bought by his old manager. Now Schanche drives by a For Lease sign in front of the store, which is empty, having gone belly up. Schanche is making a living as a "job coach" in a state-funded displaced workers program—where he is currently counseling other ex-grocery store employees following an LBO involving their employer, Alpha-Beta.

Magowan, as Safeway's CEO but no longer the man with final decision-making authority, was at first opposed to the extent of the divestiture program, people familiar with the situation say. He liked being the head of the world's largest supermarket chain. But KKR officials gave him little choice if he wanted to stay on board, these people say.

Magowan himself says that "no one twisted my arm" over the restructuring. Still, he says he "regrets" selling promising divisions, mentioning in particular Los Angeles, El Paso, Tulsa, and Little Rock.

Still others point with regret to the loss of the company's 132-store British division—a top performer known in-house as the "jewel" of the Safeway collection—and the sale of Safeway's successful discount chain of liquor stores, Liquor Barn, which under its new owners (Majestic Wine Warehouses Ltd.) filed for Chapter 11 bankruptcy protection in 1988.

Despite such regrets, however, Magowan is now a self-professed believer in the LBO concept. For one thing, his own performance has been rewarded under KKR, which has increased his annual compensation by about 40 percent to $1.2 million, including bonus. His bonus potential has climbed to 110 percent of base pay from 40 percent before the buyout, and he has earned the highest possible bonus every year.

Many things have gone well for the buyout group. The sale of the British division alone brought $929 million, part of the $2.4 billion that KKR got from asset sales—or 40 percent more than KKR officials say they had projected.

Thanks to sales of some money-losing operations, Safeway's basic business could earn more without raising prices. The company's stores are now No. 1 or 2 in most of its markets. By 1989, operating profit per employee was up 62 percent from 1985, and operating margins had increased by nearly half. The company is producing nearly twice as much annual cash flow as it needs to cover yearly interest payments. As a result, Safeway has been able to pay bank lenders ahead of schedule and negotiate lower interest rates.

Finally, KKR and Safeway officials also credit a new combination of incentives and quotas that they say make workers more entrepreneurial and at the same time more accountable.

Magowan says that employees are thriving in this post-LBO culture: "I am convinced that today's typical Safeway employee feels better about the company than he or she has at any point since the buyout." Store managers, he says, "genuinely enjoy this extra responsibility" of meeting new quotas.

Not every part of the new Safeway picture is as rosy as Magowan portrays it, however.

The public offering completed recently didn't quite go as planned. The offering's underwriters knocked the price down to $11.25 from the $20 a share envisioned last summer. Magowan himself concedes, "I think if we had known right from the start that this was the price that we would've gotten, we probably wouldn't have come out with our offering." He blames the much publicized problems of other leveraged companies for unjustly tainting Safeway's offering and driving away stock shoppers.

But some potential investors say that it was Safeway's own financial condition that turned them off.

The company labors under an interest bill of about $400 million a year, a negative net worth of $389 million, and a remaining $3.1 billion in debt.

The Leveraged Buyout Game

Buying a company or a division with a small amount of equity and a large amount of debt is the hallmark of the LBO. The debt is repaid out of the company's cash flow. Below, the top LBOs ranked by dollar value.

Date Announced	Target Name	Acquirer Name	Amount ($ billions)
10/21/88	RJR Nabisco	Kohlberg Kravis Roberts	29.57
1/24/88	Federated Department Stores	Campeau Corp.	7.42
10/16/85	Beatrice Co. Inc.	Kohlberg Kravis Roberts	6.20
7/27/86	Safeway Stores Inc.	Acquisition group led by Kohlberg Kravis Roberts	5.65
7/3/87	Southland Corp.	Acquisition group	5.10
9/15/88	Hospital Corp. of America	Acquisition group led by management	4.91
4/12/87	Borg Warner Corp.	Acquiring group led by Merrill Lynch	4.23
3/7/88	Montgomery Ward (Mobil Corp.)	Acquisition group led by management	3.80
10/21/85	RH Macy & Co. Inc.	Acquisition group led by management	3.71
6/19/89	NEA Inc.	Wings Holdings Inc.	3.65
12/11/86	Owens Illinois Inc.	Kohlberg Kravis Roberts	3.64
6/22/88	Ford Howard Paper Co.	Acquiring group led by Morgan Stanley	3.58
9/4/86	Allied Stores Corp.	Campeau Corp.	3.47
7/5/89	Elders IXL Ltd.	Acquisition group led by management	3.37
5/21/84	Esmark Inc.	Beatrice Foods Co.	2.71
5/21/87	Burlington Industries Inc.	Acquiring group led by Morgan Stanley	2.63
3/17/88	American Standard Inc.	Kelso & Co. Inc.	2.51

SOURCE: I.I.I. Information Services, Inc.

The company's net income was only $2.5 million last year (after accounting for nonrecurring expenses), down from $31 million the year before. Safeway lost a whopping $488 million in 1987, the first year of the LBO.

A large amount of capital improvement has been postponed, with such annual spending falling from an average $600 million to $700 million in the three years before the buyout to an average of $300 million in the years since. The company estimates it must spend $3.2 billion on store remodeling and openings over the next five years. And Safeway now has few assets left that it can justify jettisoning.

When Magowan sat down in 1988 with a group of specially selected employees to tell them the story of "our growing success," the workers had a different story to tell him, as chronicled by the company's own magazine, *Safeway Today.*

"The morale in Richmond [Calif.] right now is down to rock bottom," Vince Macias, a 25-year trucker, told the boss. He added that drivers were forced to pull as much as 16-hour shifts and were so overworked they were "dangerous" on the highways.

"The morale is so bad in some of our stores," Christie Mills, a San Jose employee, told him, that it's driving away customers.

"There aren't many of us, and hours are cut back so much," said Cheryl Deniz, as a bakery clerk. "I don't let the customer see it, but inside I'm miserable. . . . I try my best, but sometimes I'm so overloaded. It's unfair to the customer, and it's unfair to the employees . . . And some of you feel the same way."

Magowan looked around the room. "I see everybody nodding their heads to what you are saying," he told her. Then he added: "I've heard this before."

(A Safeway spokesman says the company immediately followed up on the worker's complaints and that Magowan personally wrote letters to those employees who voiced concerns.)

Certainly many employees have emerged unscathed from the LBO and feel comfortable working under the new regime. A good number of them even applauded the company for its rapid surfacing from the debt depths.

But among a group of workers that Safeway supplies to this newspaper as a sampler of "happy employees," no one interviewed is praising the LBO.

"We've recovered well," says Jim Ratto, a Safeway liquor merchandiser. "But personally, I think Safeway would have been better off if we had never gone through the leveraged buyout. It definitely added some problems, and the company would have been farther ahead now if it had never happened."

"Safeway's made a beautiful comeback, we're getting on our feet again, and I have no complaints," says George Voronin, an affable wine steward, who says "I always try to look on the positive side." But even Voronin adds, "When someone comes in and takes all your funds and sells your stores, isn't that what we in the United States call dishonest?"

The new esprit de corps trumpeted in the executive suite is less apparent in the grocery aisles, where store employees say the KKR-inspired quotas—based on complex return-on-market-value formulas—create anxiety as well as productivity. And the pressure mounts as one goes down the chain from manager to checker.

While Safeway executives call the quota program an "incentive" plan, some store mangers refer to it as "the punishment system." That's because store managers say if they don't make the week's quota, they can be penalized. In some divisions they report that they must work a seven-day week as penance. Working a month without a day off isn't unusual, managers in the Washington and California divisions say. In some stores managers who miss quota say they have to pull 6 A.M. to 6 P.M. shifts.

Magowan says corporate headquarters sets no such penalties. "I have never heard of any such program," he says. "I simply do not believe for one second that this is any widespread activity." A company spokesman says that at least 50 percent of store managers are meeting their quota.

Even among the list of satisfied employees that Safeway provides, many aren't profiting from the incentive plan. Either they are too low on the totem pole to get a bonus (with few exceptions, only department heads and higher qualify) or their departments aren't generating enough sales volume to meet the demanding quotas. Vronin, whose wine department has been on the incentive plan for two years, has yet to get a bonus. Mary Wise is head of the floral department, but the company hasn't yet cut her into the plan. She says she doesn't mind: "I leave feeling good, knowing I did the job right, and for me, that's my bonus." She adds, "But I'm one of those people you look at and say, 'Oh, why is she always so happy?'"

In Seattle, only one of more than a dozen store managers in the district expects to meet quota this year, managers say. Last year, none made more than 20 percent of their bonus potential, the store heads say. A Safeway spokesman says most managers in that region are making their quota.

On Safeway's home turf in the San Francisco area, managers are "stepping down" and becoming checkers. Some have been forced to turn in their manager badges when they didn't meet quota; others say they are voluntarily taking lower status and pay—out of exhaustion.

"A number of store managers have stepped down, this year particularly," a company spokesman acknowledges. "In recent years, the job has gotten tougher."

In the wake of the LBO, the company was able to squeeze labor concessions from the unions, using the Dallas shutdown as an object lesson of what can happen when labor costs are deemed too high. With the debt hovering overhead, you could "get the labor concessions you deserve," Magowan says.

"It was like coming to the table with a gun at our heads," recalls Ed Hardy, a United Food and Commercial Workers negotiator. While the company's average hourly wage rate has risen slightly in the last three years—the exact amount is confidential, Safeway says—the small increase trails the inflation rate.

The strategy of catering to the upscale at many stores has also enabled KKR to cut service worker's wages even further. To staff trendy specialty departments, Safeway has hired "general merchandise clerks," a classification that pays as little as half the wages of food clerks.

This disparity troubles even the upbeat floral manager, Mary Wise. "Gosh, you can barely live on what they are paying them," she says. She broached the subject with Magowan at the 1988 meeting. These specialty clerks are performing a job that requires training and skill, she said, and "Safeway should pay them accordingly."

Magowan's response, as quoted in the company's magazine: "The problem, Mary, is this. The reason we got the lower GMC [general merchandising clerk] rate was to allow our labor costs to be competitive." But he reassured her that the company was taking steps to make up for the low pay. "What I've suggested from time to time is saying, 'Do you like weekends off? Do you like to work 8 to 5?' . . . We'll give you the lower rate but a better schedule.' That might make them very happy."

In one division, Safeway has extended the incentive program beyond the department manager level in an experiment aimed at letting all workers benefit from the enhanced productivity they are generating. Employees in the Denver division took a 14 percent pay cut but were assured that, on average, the new profit-sharing plan would more than make up the difference. The company acknowledges this hasn't happened in nearly half the cases; the union estimates that even fewer increased their earnings.

Store employees in Denver also complained about the way the incentive system was linked—as it is throughout the company—to grievances and work-related medical claims. "Managers have been saying to people, don't file workman's comp because it will hurt the bonus," says Charles Mercer, president of the Denver local of the United Food and Commercial Workers. Magowan concedes that the Denver bonus plan is "not very popular."

Magowan's assertion that Safeway's culture is more collegial now also doesn't always square with the view from the retail floor. In stores around the country, employees report that management is pushing out older, skilled, and well-paid employees, turning to cheap, part-time help (who don't get medical insurance and other benefits), and piling extra work on the remaining staff. Union officials estimate that the average age of the stores' workforce has dropped ten years since the buyout; a company spokesman disputes this, but says Safeway doesn't track age.

"Safeway used to be one of the best places to work of the retail grocers," says Rowena Schoos, a middle-aged Safeway meat cutter in Oregon for five years. "But after the buyout, they started cutting hours to the nitty-gritty, the store managers went into a mass panic, and Safeway just turned into a burnout company."

Schoos recently left herself, after she was cut back to 16 hours a week and lost her medical benefits. Like many of the older and well-paid meat cutters, she says, she was relegated to the "extra board," a tour of duty that can require driving more than 100 miles a day to different stores to fill in where needed.

For the older butchers, many of whom suffer physical injuries from the years of toting and carving, the assignment is the final shove out the door. Schoos, for example, has two herniated discs, which she attributes to years of lugging 100-pound carcasses.

A Safeway spokesman responds, "That's just another case of an isolated situation. She was just not performing the job adequately," and thus her hours were cut.

The company also says that meat cutters' numbers have been reduced primarily because a gradual shift to prepackaged goods in meat processing has lessened the need. Employees in the meat department argue that even with the changes, much of the work still requires a butcher's expertise and that the cutbacks have been too severe.

While on the extra-board circuit, Schoos had the opportunity to observe the LBO fallout at many stores. "It was the same thing everywhere I went," she recalls. "The managers were desperate to meet quota and the older people always got the worst. They'd bust them back to lower positions. One produce manager was told he had a 'choice'—go back to being a checker or get fired. One lady asked for a break and the manager cut her from 40 to 8 hours."

In response, Magowan produces a recent employee survey conducted in the Portland, Oregon, division that finds that more than 80 percent of employees feel Safeway offers advancement opportunity and other advantages. "These would be good scores to decertify the union, should we ever wish to do so," Magowan says, adding, "which we have no intention of doing, whatsoever."

Closer to headquarters, at the Market Street store in San Francisco, employees report a grind of tension and overwork. Some say they are shouldering as many as nine different jobs.

In the meat department, the butchers' numbers have been cut back sharply and inexperienced clerks take up the slack. "Everyone is burned out," says another employee, who points to a counter where overripe meat is on display, the result of a hasty stocking effort. "It's a whole new ball game and everyone's discontented."

In the Market Street store, employees complain that clipboard-toting managers patrol the floors, closely monitoring performance and filing a blizzard of disciplinary reports. A company spokesman disputes these accounts: "There is no ROMV [Return on Market Value] police."

Last month, at the Market Street store, food clerk Steve Dolinka lost his job after 25 years of service. His malfeasance: He says he forgot to pay for the cup of soup and toast he ate at the deli on his lunch hour. Dolinka apologized, shelled out the few dollars that his food cost, and explained why he was so distracted—his mind was on a murder trial that had ended a few weeks earlier. A gas station robber was before the court charged with slitting the throat of Dolinka's 15-year-old son in 1982 in an assault that the investigating detective called "the most brutal in my experience."

"My wife says I've been forgetting things a lot lately," Dolinka says.

"In our business, employee theft is a serious problem," a company spokesman says of Dolinka's expulsion. "And every employee is treated the same way."

Dolinka says he doesn't blame his manager for the firing. "The way it works here, I don't think any of the managers have the freedom to make these decisions. It's all coming down from company policy, and they have got to follow it like their bible."

To all such reports from the store front, Magowan says he's skeptical: "Our productivity is up," he points out. "Employees are donating more to Easter Seals, and workers' compensation claims are down," he says. "And when the earthquake hit, our employees stayed up all night cleaning up their stores."

"Are these acts of a disgruntled workforce?" he asks. "I don't think so."

George Roberts, one of KKR's two principal partners, notes that workers at many corporations are being asked to do more, whether an LBO is involved or not. Employees "are now being held accountable," Roberts says. "They have to produce up to a plan, if they are going to be competitive with the rest of the world. It's high time we did that."

Case III–7

Facing Raiders, Kroger Took Another Path

"Kroger Is Gone, Analysts Predict" was the dire headline in the *Cincinnati Post*. Hostile bidders, the Hafts and KKR, had descended on the nation's second-largest grocery chain.

When the September 1988 story came out, "people were crying in the hall," says Joseph Pichler, Kroger's president. "Make this go away," they told me. I said, 'I wish I could.'"

He did. Faced with much the same threat to its independence as rival Safeway faced two years earlier, Kroger chose a very different path. Instead of going private in a KKR-led LBO, Kroger officials countered by offering shareholders a hefty dividend and employees a significant ownership stake in what remains a public company.

While Kroger had to take on $4.1 billion in debt and it had to cut costs, it sold far fewer assets than Safeway did and reduced its workforce by about 3 percent, while Safeway reduced its by about a third. Yet today Kroger has about the same operating profit per employee as Safeway.

In some ways Kroger's story undermines two LBO articles of faith: That a company under attack from raiders has to go private to ward them off, and that, after an LBO, labor forces have to be cut severely to support the resulting interest burden.

This isn't to suggest, however, that an LBO can't be structured to share ownership more broadly or to cut costs in a less severe manner than Safeway, or that recapitalizations are panaceas. Harcourt Brace Jovanovich plunged into crisis after its recapitalization when it couldn't sell assets for enough cash to pay down its huge debt.

SOURCE: Reprinted with permission from "Facing Raiders, Kroger Took Another Path," by Susan C. Faludi, *Wall Street Journal*, May 16, 1990, p. A10.

But the recap seems to have worked so far for Kroger. "We kept asking ourselves the question, if it's so good for an outside group of investors to come in, leverage up a company, peel off underperforming assets, pay down debt, and walk off with the equity themselves, why shouldn't it be equally good for our existing shareholders to benefit from exactly the same transaction?" Pichler recalls.

Safeway says it looked at the same question two years earlier but chose to do an LBO because it would free the company from having to please shareholders with short-term profits and from future takeover threats. Certain tax breaks since rescinded also made the LBO option more attractive in 1986 than in later years.

For Kroger, the call to action came when the Hafts offered $55 a share for a "business combination." The KKR made an unsolicited bid—despite its reputation as a "white knight"—to buy out the company for $58.50 a share. When Kroger turned a cold shoulder, KKR upped its offer to $64.

Kroger quickly unfurled its plan: Shareholders would get a $40 a share cash dividend, plus an $8 junior subordinated debenture and a remaining interest in the company, called stub stock. The package was valued by Kroger at $57 to $61 a share. The recap plan also liberalized stock options so that all employees, rather than a thin slice at the top, could increase their ownership: Employees could go from owning 6 percent to more than 25 percent of Kroger's shares; corporate officers' ownership, on the other hand, could rise only from 1 percent to 3 percent.

The recap lagged by at least 5 percent to 10 percent behind KKR's $64 final bid. Even so, the board approved the recap on September 23 and the company remained public. Investors and employees reacted favorably to the offer. The value of the stub stock initially more than doubled but has since slipped to $14, still well above the initial offering price of $9.13. And Kroger workers took ample advantage of the new stock options. By 1990, Kroger increased employee ownership even more, to 35 percent.

The recap yielded them tens of millions of dollars for senior managers. Lyle Everingham, the chairman, got an estimated $10.5 million in cash and another $2.3 million in debentures. Pichler got $3.5 million in cash and $763,000 in debentures. And Goldman, Sachs & Co. made $25 million for advising Kroger.

In the aftermath, Kroger too was faced with a multibillion-dollar debt. It had laid off 314 people from headquarters, and with the subsequent asset sales, purged more than 4,000 employees from the payroll.

But the Kroger severance package was more generous than Safeway's. Fired employees received a month's salary for every year of service to a maximum of nine months, compared with a maximum of eight weeks salary at Safeway. They also got medical benefits for one year, while Safeway employees lost their benefits in as little as two weeks.

Kroger's generosity shouldn't be overstated, though: Kroger cut costs by cutting average hourly salaries of $8.12 (or $11.39 with fringe benefits) in 1985 to $7.07 (or $9.84 with benefits) in 1989. Kroger, like Safeway, saved money by paying its specialty department workers a lower rate. And Kroger has also negotiated two-tier pay scales and raised eligibility requirements for medical benefits.

In selling assets, Kroger sold less-prized properties and a total of 100 stores, only 10 percent of its operations. Safeway, on the other hand, sold 1,100 of its 2,325 stores. Kroger also turned to employees, who generated thousands of cost-saving steps.

Like Safeway, Kroger has adopted an incentive bonus plan, but it appears to be more democratic than its Oakland rival's. Kroger's new bonus system extends to secretaries and the plan adjusts for factors beyond employees' control—such as working in a store in a high-crime neighborhood.

"We're fairly excited about Kroger's bonus plan," says Ed Hardy, a national negotiator for the United Food and Commercial Workers Union. "It's more of a gain-sharing plan than a bonus based on profits."

While Kroger has improved its profit-sharing plan, Safeway stopped contributing to its plan in 1987. At the same time, Safeway also tried unsuccessfully to raid surplus funds in its employee retirement account, which provides retirees with an average pension of less than $400 a month. Retirees retained counsel to halt the raid, and Robert Van Gemert, retired Safeway general counsel, did some research and discovered that the original Safeway pension charter in fact grants surplus to the retirees.

So far, Kroger seems to be faring competitively at least as well as Safeway. In fiscal year 1989, its first year after restructuring, Kroger cash flow rose 22 percent—better than the 16 percent gain the company originally forecast at the time it restructured. Kroger, like Safeway, hasn't raised prices—and in some markets has lowered them. And Kroger, like Safeway, managed to refinance its bank-credit agreement and lower interest expenses.

But Kroger also now supports 60,000 more workers than Safeway, while maintaining similar operating profit as a percentage of sales.

Kroger also has increased its charitable contributions since the recap to $3.6 million last year from $2.1 million in 1987, while Safeway trimmed its corporate cash giving to $2.7 million last year from $3.2 million in 1986.

Thanks to the massive debt, Kroger operated at a net loss of $72.7 million in 1989; Safeway's net loss was $488 million its first year after the buyout. (The two chains are fairly comparable in number of stores and in sales.) By the first quarter of 1990, Kroger's net loss had shrunk to $10 million, a 46 percent improvement from the same period a year earlier. And analysts are estimating positive earnings for next year.

"Kroger is an extremely strong company today, with very strong cash flow and very strong markets," says Debra Levin, a retail analyst who follows Kroger for Salomon Brothers. "If they had been taken over [in an LBO], they might not look all that different from the way they look today, but I don't know that they would have gotten that same motivation level from their employees."

PART FOUR

The Legal and Regulatory Environment of Business

CHAPTER 10

The Public Policy Process and Legal Environment of Business

CHAPTER OBJECTIVES

1. Illustrate how cultural issues that get onto the public policy agenda result in public debates.

2. Explain how the public policy process results in laws and regulations that affect business practice.

3. Review the legislative process, the law-making part of the public policy process, that creates the legal environment of business.

4. Explain how two major competing ideologies shape the public policy debate.

5. Describe the court system and how litigation affects business.

6. Suggest how business, through its institutional orientation, can be affected by or can be a part of the public policy process.

7. Show how the various dimensions of the legal environment of business are created by the public policy process.

Introductory Case _____

Dragging Employers into Child Support

The statistics are alarming: Half the children born today will live in a single-parent family (usually with the mother) before reaching 18. Of children now entitled to support by court order, 25 percent

SOURCE: Jean Sensel and Diane MacDonald, "Dragging Employers into Child Support," *Nation's Business* 79, No. 10 (October 1991): 34.

receive it; another 25 percent receive only part of it; another 25 percent receive none. On average, children's standard of living declines more than two-thirds in the first year following a divorce, often casting them onto the public welfare system.

Congress passed the Family Support Act in 1988. Its object was to force parents to pay the child support they owed, to improve conditions for the children, and to relieve the welfare burden. The weapon of choice is the automatic wage deduction by employers.

In effect, the law makes employers responsible for their employees' child-support obligations. The penalties for noncompliance are severe—in some cases, the employer may become liable for the full amount of the claim against an employee plus interest, costs, and penalties.

The Family Support Act requires each state to establish standard award guidelines and make child-support payments as certain as tax payments through automatic wage deduction. All states must employ withholding for all new or revised orders processed through the state's office of support enforcement. By 1994, automatic wage withholding must be used for all support orders. Currently, in all states an employer may receive a wage garnishment order for child support in arrears.

The interplay of federal and state laws and the calculations the employer is required to make are complex. And the highly charged emotional issues of divorce and family can intrude into the normal operation of the workplace.

In one case, an employer in Seattle was startled by an anguished cry from a usually tough, competent employee: "My husband's ex-wife says she's garnishing half my wages! She can't do that, can she?" The employee—call her Janie—had never before raised personal subjects at work or displayed vulnerability.

Generally, a spouse's wages cannot be attached for the other spouse's child-support obligation. But it happens, and Janie's employer is legally obligated to withhold by the terms of an order, even when the order is in error, as Janie claimed.

Janie's employer was sympathetic and advised her to see an attorney; Janie said she could not afford one.

Before long, stress from the support issue affected her job performance. Janie became short-tempered and curt with customers, and her absenteeism skyrocketed. Her employer discharged her the fourth time she failed to show up for work without calling in. The discharge was for poor performance, but it was clearly related to anxiety over the child-support problem.

Federal law prohibits discharge for child-support withholding, garnishment, or threatened garnishment, so a sympathetic court may construe Janie's severance as unlawful. If found guilty, her employer could face his state's penalty of $2,500 in fines and liability for double lost wages and other damages.

Suppose an employer wants to be sympathetic? In another case, Dan, an employer at a construction company in Tacoma, Washington, was a friend to his employee, Jim, and he thought Jim was treated unfairly in a divorce settlement. Dan thought he'd help Jim by ignoring the child-support garnishment. First, he claimed that he did not receive it, then he said he "misread" the language of a second order: The support amount was greater than 50 percent of Jim's disposable income, so Dan deducted nothing at all instead of deducting up to the 50 percent limit. Refusing to withhold did not eliminate Jim's support obligation or Dan's responsibility for these months.

In the end, Dan had to put his legal obligations before friendship when the state pointed out that his noncompliance made him liable for the $8,000 in back support that had accumulated since the order was mailed to him—plus interest, collection costs, and penalties. Dan faced court action, with court costs and attorney fees added to his other liability, if he did not comply immediately.

The lessons are, Do not ignore an order to withhold child support, and do not ignore your employee's stress. The only way to avoid legal and emotional entanglements is to have a plan of action.

The Threefold Social Order, Public Policy, and the Legal Environment of Business

This chapter is concerned with how the public policy process and the legal environment affect business practice. It extends the discussion of Part 1, which argued that business social performance requires that business maintain legitimacy and legality. Legitimacy is the social and political support enjoyed by a policy, a practice, or an institution. Political support, mobilized through the public policy process, can lead to laws that define the legality of a particular practice. Legal performance is complying with laws and regulations.

Changes in values, lifestyles, technology, or social conditions often lead to problems or issues that are publicly debated in the public policy process, as shown in Figure 10–1. The key task of the political/governmental sphere is the protection of rights.[1] However, after a right is asserted, it must

be legitimated by society before it can be sanctioned by law and regulations. These laws and regulations become the basis for governmental control of business behavior and, taken collectively, form the legal environment of business. Business responds to the changing social expectations within the context of the social relationships shown in Figure 10–1.

As the opening case illustrates, business social performance often can be affected by public policy and laws that would, at first glance, not involve business. Cultural and lifestyle changes have led to single-parent families that have not been able to maintain an appropriate standard of living without the assistance of the second parent. Courts often award child support, and it is the legal duty to pay the amount determined by the court. However, the person responsible for providing support often refuses to pay and moves to a different state, where collection has been difficult or impossible.

Nonpayment of child support has increased poverty. Providing child support to single-parent

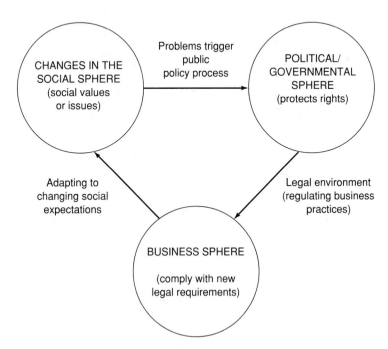

FIGURE 10–1 The Threefold Social Order, the Public Policy Process, and the Legal Environment of Business

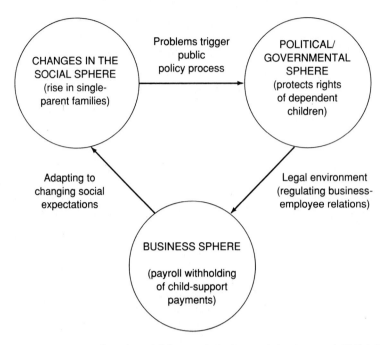

FIGURE 10–2 The Threefold Social Order and the Issue of Child Support

families became serious enough to reach public awareness. This awareness, in turn, brought the issue onto the public policy agenda where it could be debated by lawmakers. became law in 1988. Basing its actions on The Family Support Act, the government fulfills its responsibility for protecting the legal rights of children by regulating the business-employee relationship. The instrument chosen by the government to protect this right is mandatory payroll withholding of child-support payments as defined by the courts.

An employer is primarily interested in the on-the-job performance of an employee and may not want to become involved in a conflict between an employee and an ex-spouse over child support. However, the law protects the right of a child to receive economic support from a parent who does not remain with the family. By compliance with this new law a business employer meets a changing expectation of society, as shown in Figure 10–2.

It is important that those in business understand the public policy process. Both federal and state governments as well as governments of some other countries have enacted many laws affecting business over the past two decades. With the many different legal jurisdictions, it is often difficult for business to be informed of what the law is so that it can be obeyed. Furthermore, the legal standards and regulations often vary from jurisdiction to jurisdiction. A product that meets the safety standard in one country may be considered unsafe in another. Moreover, product liability and amounts of court awards vary widely from state to state within the United States. An employment practice that is legal in one country may be illegal in another. Thus the legal environment can add significant complexities and cost to business.

If business is unaware of how the public policy process works, it is unlikely that business can persuasively communicate its perspectives and problems to lawmakers when new forms of regulation are considered.[2] Also, failure to become familiar with new laws so that compliance plans can be developed can lead to legal problems. Through a knowledge of the public policy process business can become involved in public debates and help to shape government regulation of business.

Public Policy Process: From Political Debates to Legislation

The *public policy process* includes the political processes that unfold in a series of stages as shown in Figure 10–3 that establish and enforce public policy and include

1. agenda setting
2. public debates over issues leading to clarification of positions. A social problem is defined

and various interest groups express their positions relative to the issue.
3. the legislative process, in which laws are made
4. the executive processes of implementation and enforcement by government agencies or independent commissions
5. the judicial process, in which remaining disputes are resolved in the courts. Through court decisions that become precedents under common law, judges also participate in lawmaking.

WHAT IS PUBLIC POLICY?

The public policy process forms policy as the legitimate standards of behavior for society. Bertozzi and Burgunder have defined *public policy* as follows:

1. Laws (also often referred to as statutes) enacted by the U.S. Congress and the state legislatures

AGENDA-SETTING INTEREST GROUP ORGANIZATION AND POLICY DEBATES
• Social/technological change occurred
• Issue is placed on the public policy agenda
• Interest groups organize to support or to oppose policy alternatives

LEGISLATIVE PROCESS/EXECUTIVE ORDERS
• Congress passes bills that become law if signed by the president
• State legislatures pass bills that become laws if signed by the governor
• The president can sign an executive order

EXECUTIVE PROCESS AGENCY FORMATION/POLICY IMPLEMENTATION
• Laws are implemented by executive branch (federal agency)
or by independent commission

LITIGATION AND REGULATION
Administrative Law
Agency/Commission Enforcement through
• Rulings   • Regulations   • Investigations   • Hearings   • Consent decrees

FIGURE 10–3 The Public Policy Process

2. Rules and regulations adopted by administrative agencies

3. Executive orders issued by the president of the United States pursuant to his constitutional authority or authority granted him by Congress

4. Judicial opinions handed down by the federal and state courts, especially opinions by the U.S. Supreme Court and the various state supreme courts[3]

5. In addition, legal requirements sanctioned by international treaties could be considered as part of public policy.

THE CONSTITUTIONAL BASIS OF U.S. PUBLIC POLICY

The key role of the governmental sphere is to form and implement public policy and to protect the rights of people.[4] The protection of individual rights was the basis for the Declaration of Independence, which declared that all men [and women] are created equal and are endowed with certain inalienable rights including life, liberty, and the pursuit of happiness. The Revolutionary War was fought to achieve freedom so that these rights could be assured. The principle of rights was central to the United States Constitution, which provides the basis for the branches of government and for federal law.

The Bill of Rights includes the first ten amendments to the Constitution and establishes the basic political rights of expression, association, privacy, and religion, and rights to a fair trial that were discussed in Chapter 7. After the Civil War, the Fourteenth Amendment was passed to insure that

1. No government shall deny equal protection of the laws to an person regardless of race, color, or creed.

2. A person cannot be deprived of such rights as life, liberty, and property without due process of law.

The Fourteenth Amendment was intended to protect the rights of African Americans who had received their freedom with the Civil War. However, business corporations also benefited from this amendment. Soon after its passage, the Supreme Court broadened the legal definition of a person covered by this amendment to include corporations, which are legal persons under the law. Thus a corporation's right to make contracts and to be protected by due process was one result of this amendment. This helped to assure that the corporation would be a major form of business in America.

Three Branches of Government Are Constitutionally Defined

The first three articles of the U.S. Constitution authorize the three branches of the federal government including the judicial, legislative, and executive branches. Simply put, the legislative branch passes bills that become law if signed by the president, the chief executive. The executive branch, directed by the president, is responsible for implementing public policy and enforcing the laws passed by the legislative branch. The court system is responsible for adjudicating conflicts concerning the laws and disagreements between persons. This pattern of three branches of government also exists at the state level within the United States and in most countries with democratic forms of government.

The Interstate Commerce Clause

The Tenth Amendment restricts the areas of federal legislation to those specifically listed in the Constitution. Article I, section 8 states that Congress can establish laws that (1) raise revenues through taxation, (2) appropriate and spend those revenues, (3) establish treaties to regulate foreign affairs, (4) provide for the national defense, and (5) regulate interstate commerce. The interstate commerce clause was narrowly defined until the New Deal era. The Supreme Court in 1937 broadly interpreted the clause to include any area of commerce indirectly affecting goods that cross state lines.[5]

Thus if a restaurant uses food products from another state, it is considered to be involved in interstate commerce and can be regulated by federal law, even though it serves only local patrons.

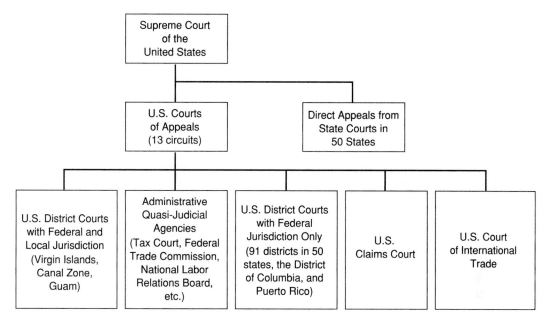

FIGURE 10–4 The Federal Court System

Also, as the introductory case of this chapter suggests, even payroll deductions for child support have been broadly considered by Congress as covered by the interstate commerce clause and thus can be regulated by federal law. The federal government can now legally enact laws to regulate virtually every aspect of business practice.

THE FEDERAL COURT SYSTEM

Article III of the Constitution establishes the Supreme Court and gives the Congress the authority to establish inferior courts. Judges are appointed by the president and confirmed by the Senate. They serve on good behavior without any specified term of office. The Constitution also vests the executive power of the United States in the executive branch.

Cases brought before the federal court system normally begin in a federal district court. There are 89 districts in the 50 states, one district court in the District of Columbia, and one in Puerto Rico, as shown in Figure 10–4. Each district has a number ranging from 1 to 27 federal judges, depending on the population served and the

amount of litigation in the district. Each district is further divided into district judgeships for a total of some 500 judgeships in the United States and the Territory of Puerto Rico. These district courts can hear two types of civil cases: (1) cases of a person residing in one state who is suing a person who resides in another state; and (2) cases that raise a constitutional question.

Also in the federal court system are administrative, quasi-judicial activities of federal agencies that enforce government regulations. *Administrative law* includes the rulings of proceedings by quasi-judicial government agencies like the Tax Court, the Federal Trade Commission, the National Labor Relations Board, and the Occupational Safety and Health Administration. These administrative law agencies are defined as those having rule-making authority that are nonjudicial and nonlegislative.

The U.S. Court of International Trade has exclusive jurisdiction over cases concerning U.S. tariff laws. The Anti-Dumping Act of 1921 grants this federal court appellate authority from customs officers. Thus, issues of alleged dumping in which foreign competitors sell products and services below cost in the U.S. market are litigated in this court.

The U.S. Supreme Court. Appeals from the lower federal trial courts normally must go to the United States courts of appeals before they can be heard by the U.S. Supreme Court. The Supreme Court has eight associate justices and one chief justice.

JUDICIAL PHILOSOPHY AND PUBLIC POLICY

Court decisions have a profound influence on defining public policy. Examples of this include (1) the Supreme Court defining the role of the federal government through its interpretation of the interstate commerce clause, (2) defining the limits of state and federal statutes by court decisions on their constitutionality of various statutes, and (3) court precedents that extend the body of common law. Court judges can define the law through the development of *common law* by making decisions concerning issues where no previous decision has been rendered. Legal precedents that form the basis of common law can be based upon any decision of state superior courts or any federal court.

Justices are appointed by the president with the confirmation of the Senate. The judicial philosophy and political ideology that prevails on the Supreme Court can have a strong effect on public policy, and thus the Senate confirmation hearings have become increasingly controversial in recent years. Judges with an activist perspective are more likely to interpret laws in ways that they feel affirm current social realities. In contrast, judges with a more conservative judicial philosophy seek to narrowly define judicial principles and are reluctant to define the law according to current social conditions or expectations. Thus, they are more likely to call upon Congress to pass a new law if the wording of present laws does not express current expectations.

Beginning with the late 1950s, the Supreme Court under Chief Justice Warren could be characterized as an activist court that sought to define the Constitution in terms of the current context of society. The Warren Court struck down the separate-but-equal doctrine that had affirmed racial segregation. That court recognized affirmative action and proportional representation to achieve equality of results to achieve economic justice. Also, the right of privacy was interpreted to mean that a woman has the right to have an abortion.

During the 1980s, President Reagan appointed a number of justices with a more conservative judicial philosophy. The more conservative Supreme Court temporarily reversed some of the civil rights cases that had affirmed affirmative action, equality of results, and the legal standards by which discrimination in employment is proved in court. More recently, confirmation hearings for appointments to the Supreme Court have been increasingly stormy, particularly over the issue of abortion and pro-choice positions. The political philosophy of the judges is a key dimension of the legal environment for business.

Setting the Public Policy Agenda

The *public policy agenda* is defined as the set of issues that have received sufficient recognition within society to be considered for government regulation. Issues can be placed on the public policy agenda by long-term changes and/or trigger events that dramatize the need for a public policy alternative. *Long-term changes* include (1) technological change, (2) lifestyle, demographic, or cultural changes within society, and (3) changing economic conditions. Cultural changes related to increased workforce diversity, an aging workforce, and the special needs of the single parent who is an employee have led to other social problems that find expression as issues on the public policy agenda.

Examples of technological changes leading to public policy issues abound in the areas of computers and software. The advent of the computer has spawned many issues concerning software copyright protection, privacy issues due to computerized databases, use of computerized telemarketing, and information relating to credit, employment, and lifestyle. The changing international competitive positions of the United States and other countries have shaped such issues as job creation, industrial policy, plant closing notification, and government economic policy.

An example of how lifestyle changes and declining economic conditions shape a public policy issue can be found in the case of child support. The opening case for this chapter points to the growing number of single-parent families in which the children do not receive sufficient support. Social changes including the move toward two-wage-earner families, increased divorce rates, children born outside a marriage relationship, and a changing international competitive position of the United States have all contributed to the problem of child support. These broad changes have been developing since the 1960s, and the pressures to move this item to the public policy agenda were both broad and deep within society.

Though a long-term change can lead to any number of major social problems, these problems may not be placed upon the public policy agenda. A "trigger event" often appears to be the immediate cause of a long-term trend being identified as an important issue that is then placed on the public policy agenda. A trigger event can be one or a combination of the following:

1. a dramatic event
2. interest group activity increasing the visibility of a situation
3. action by a political leader or opinion maker
4. the appearance of an influential book or public report that dramatizes and popularizes an issue.

DRAMATIC EVENTS AND THE PUBLIC POLICY AGENDA

An example of a trigger event is the Three Mile Island nuclear accident. The event made nuclear safety a dramatic national issue and triggered a process that has virtually stopped the development of nuclear energy in the United States over the last decade. In contrast Japan and France, which have not had similar incidents, have made substantial progress in developing nuclear energy resources during this period.

Many states have encouraged businesses to locate in their area by promising minimal state government regulations that interfere with business operations and increase operating costs. Unfortunately, there is sometimes a trade-off between an environment of minimum governmental constraints and other public values. For example, North Carolina has worked hard to develop a legal environment favorable to business. Businesses have located there because of low tax rates, favorable labor markets, and governments that are sympathetic to business concerns.

In September 1991 a disastrous fire in a chicken-processing plant resulted in 25 deaths in North Carolina. An investigation revealed that escape routes from the factory had been locked (apparently to prevent employee theft), water sprinkler systems were found to be inadequate, and the company apparently had no fire control plan. The state government had an office of occupational safety and health, but the state budget was so low that staffing levels provided only for infrequent inspections of potential accident sites.

Thus, few field inspections could be made by the state agency responsible for enforcing safety standards for occupational health and safety. This dramatic and tragic incident brought the issue of workplace safety and the possible side effects of state policies designed to attract businesses to a state onto the public policy agenda. In January 1992, the Federal Office of Safety and Health Administration moved to assume control from the state for enforcement responsibility for public policy–related work safety. Also, the public official responsible for job safety within North Carolina failed to be reelected as the controversy over job safety dominated the public policy process until the issue was resolved.

PUBLISHED DOCUMENTARY ACCOUNTS AND THE PUBLIC POLICY AGENDA

A published documentary account of a situation can raise public awareness of an issue sufficiently to place it on the public policy agenda. An early example of this is a novel written by Upton Sinclair in 1905 entitled *The Jungle*. This book vividly described the hardships of workers and the filthy conditions of the meat-packing industry in Chicago at the time. The public uproar following its publication led to the Meat Inspection Act and the Pure Food and Drugs Act passed by Congress in 1906.

The book *Unsafe at Any Speed* by Ralph Nader in 1965 brought the issue of automobile safety to the attention of the American public and led to the establishment of the Traffic Safety Act of 1966. Similarly, environmental concerns over the safety of pesticides were placed on the public policy agenda with the publication of *Silent Spring*, written by Rachel Carson in 1962. According to this documentary, the spring was silent because birds no longer sang; they no longer sang because their eggs did not hatch; and their eggs failed to hatch because of pesticide contamination in the food chain and the water supply. This book brought the problem of pesticides to public awareness and set the public policy agenda that led to the formation of the Environmental Protection Agency (EPA).

These books helped to get the issues of the environment and product safety onto the public policy agenda, launching the wave of social regulation during the 1960s. More recently, *In Search of Excess*, a book dramatizing executive salaries in the United States, shows that the average CEO in America makes around 160 times what the average worker makes. In Japan this ratio is 16. Furthermore, the highest-paid U.S. executives have a background in finance, in Germany the highest-paid executives are in science and engineering, and in Japan they are in personnel.

The compensation of executives in the United States does not seem to have a very close relationship to the economic performance of the business.[6] Considerable interest in U.S. executive compensation was expressed by activists investors in 1991, but it is unclear whether the interest will be sufficient to trigger the public policy process in this area. The issue of executive compensation has also been publicized by several documented accounts in the business press.[7] While executive compensation has been brought to public awareness, it is not clear that this issue will find its way to the public policy agenda. The issue may be handled within the context of organizational governance rather than the public policy process.

POLITICAL LEADERSHIP AND THE PUBLIC POLICY AGENDA

An influential person like the president of the United States plays an important part in setting the public policy agenda. For example, President Reagan forcefully made the overregulation of business by the government a key agenda item. He claimed that such regulation interfered with the economic performance of business and contributed to the decline of U.S. international competitiveness. He countered those who called for a U.S. competitive strategy coordinated by an activist governmental role with a definition of the issue that emphasized greater reliance on market forces and a reduced role for the government. Reagan was successful in defining the issue in the national public policy debate.

Influential senators like Edward Kennedy have helped to keep rising health care costs and the need for a publicly financed health care system on the public policy agenda.[8] Health care has been on the public policy agenda for nearly a quarter of a century. Health care costs have increased dramatically in recent years and have become a major economic threat to small businesses and consumers. Also, some 40 million Americans were without health care coverage in 1994, and most of these were employed by small businesses. Health care is normally paid through insurance coverage that is part of compensation earned by employees of business. President Clinton made this problem a major campaign issue in the election of 1992 and has kept the issue at the top of the public policy agenda during his administration.

Rising health care costs have resulted in sharply increased insurance rates for employers. Some businesses have located facilities out of the United States to avoid these costs. Many have called for a universal health care system like the government-financed system of Canada. This would result in universal access to health care for all people and would shift the cost burden away from business.

Interest Group Debates over Public Policy

An interest group is a group that organizes around some public policy issue that is of special concern to its members. Not all issues receive sufficient interest, and thus concerned organizations may not be able to affect public policy. In a *pluralistic society*, public policy is determined by the interaction of numerous interest groups that define issues and sponsor public policy alternatives based upon their special concerns. Thus, "sufficient awareness" needed to move an issue to the public policy agenda often can be determined by the relative influence of interest groups that take up an issue as a special concern or by the volatility of an issue. There are many interest groups that form around various social concerns like children's rights, product safety, the environment, women's issues, gun control, smoking, and the like.

Governmentally financed universal health care system as public policy is opposed by many interest groups including health care insurers, health care delivery professionals including the American Medical Association, and the insurance industry. Many fear that adopting the Canadian model might result in inferior service, inability of patients to choose their own physician, and a reduction in incentives to control overall health care costs. In 1994, a new health care policy that only incrementally altered the existing system seemed more likely than a radically new public policy on the Canadian model. A modified health care system that continues to rely on business- and employee-financed health care insurance to pay for privately provided health care seems likely.

Not every issue on the public policy agenda results in laws and regulations that become a part of public policy. Most public policies would affect different interest groups in very different ways. In a pluralistic society, many interest groups have dif-

ferent amounts of political power, access to lawmakers, and legitimacy, and thus the public policy outcome of an issue on the public policy agenda is never certain. Minor incremental changes are more likely to be enacted into law than a radical departure from past practice.

How Ideology Influences the Public Policy Debate

Earlier it was argued that a person's ideology influences his or her concept of justice. Ideology not only determines what people think is fair but also influences concepts of rights and the appropriate role of government in determining those rights. Rights are legally defined in society through the public policy process. Public policy debates are a major input to the policy and lawmaking process. These debates are often defined in terms of the ideology held by a person or by an interest group. The two major ideologies discussed earlier included the individually oriented traditional ideology and the community-oriented new ideology.[9]

Traditionally the two dominant political parties in the United States have been distinguished by the Democrats holding a liberal political philosophy and the Republicans holding a conservative one. These philosophies help define the role of government supported by the major sides of political debate in America. Political philosophies parallel the two major ideologies outlined in Chapter 8 and often define competing positions in public policy debates. These debates are concerned with the relative role of the government and the market in dealing with economic and social issues.

Conservatives are more likely to share an ideology that is individualistic and market-oriented, with a minimalist governmental role within society. Thus, conservatives prefer (1) a limited government role, (2) a heavy reliance on the market forces in economic matters rather than government regulation of business, (3) an emphasis on individual initiative and responsibility in social issues. This translates into a preference for limited economic regulation of business activity; monetary policy over fiscal policy in macroeconomics; "law and order" approaches to individual responsibility, with limited economic rights or entitlement to respond to social problems.

Liberals are more likely to share an ideology that is more community-oriented, with a more activist role for government, which regulates the market. Thus, liberals prefer (1) a more activist government in both economic and social matters; (2) the government regulation to supplement or control the forces of market competition; and (3) an emphasis on community support, economic rights, or entitlement in the area of social issues.

However, this dichotomy is meant to be only suggestive; there are many more ideologies than these two, and interest groups and individuals in reality have an unlimited number ideological positions that add to the complexity of the debate over the appropriate role of the economic and the political sphere in society.

As the following section suggests, ideology that parallels these political philosophies serves to guide the public policy process.

INDIVIDUALISTIC MARKET-ORIENTED IDEOLOGY

The *traditional ideology* is individualistic and market-oriented and can be characterized by the following:

1. A belief in the priority of individual freedom over the welfare of the community
2. A commitment to equality of opportunity, granting that economic and social inequality may be an acceptable outcome of freely operating market forces
3. Economic rights defined primarily through contracts made voluntarily between individuals
4. The right of private property being of central importance
5. Limiting the role of government to matters of public safety, defense, and minimal regulation of business. The government assures economic justice by providing a favorable business climate

to encourage economic growth, thus allowing the benefits to "trickle down" to everyone within the society
6. Heavy reliance on the operation of the competitive market to accomplish social goals such as economic justice and social welfare.

Those holding the traditional ideology are more likely to share a conservative political philosophy and are less supportive of an activist government to control business behavior or to achieve social goals. Also, they may not be as concerned about the failures of market competition because they believe them to be minimal. They are less likely to see monopoly or concentrated markets and anti-competitive behavior as a social problem. Also, they are less likely to be concerned about side effects or externalities as pollution or environmental harm resulting from economic activities.

Thus, those who follow the traditional ideology are more likely to argue "leave the market alone!" The invisible hand of the market will automatically accomplish social goals without government interference, the "cure" of which may be worse than the "ills" of market failures.

COMMUNITY-ORIENTED, ACTIVIST GOVERNMENT IDEOLOGY

The Great Depression of the 1930s caused many to question the value of the traditional individualistic ideology. George Cabot Lodge investigated ideologies and found an emergent ideology in the United States during the 1970s. This "new" ideology can be seen as a counterpoint to the traditional ideology. It can be traced in American history to the compacts of the Puritans, who settled the New England area in the 1600s. It is communitarian, emphasizing the community and the well-being of all members over the rights of individual members. In its new form it embraces a more activist government and can be characterized as follows:

1. Concern for the welfare of the community and its members has a higher priority than unlimited individual freedom.

2. Equality of results is more importnat than equality of opportunity. The results of the processes that distribute status and wealth within society are the best gauge of justice; these results should reflect the proportional representation of various groups within society.
3. Rights and duties are based more on the membership in society defined through the public policy process or other consensus process within society. Contracts and property ownership may no longer be the primary way to define rights within society. Certain human rights may take priority over property rights.
4. Market competition may not always be efficient and fair. Market forces do not necessarily protect the rights of people automatically while accomplishing the economic goals of society.
5. There is more reliance on the public policy process and an activist government to protect the rights of individuals through laws and regulation of business activities.
6. The government may appropriately bring about justice through redistribution of resources within society to complement policies that stimulate economic growth.

Proponents of the new ideology are more likely to argue that concentrated markets result in anticompetitive behavior. They will call for reliance on market competition but are inclined to see it as imperfect and thus in need of government regulation.

Table 10–1 provides a general overview of the two dominant social ideologies as they relate to the public policy debate. The final result of the public policy process as it relates to a particular area like consumer issues or a special issue like product labeling will be influenced by the ideological positions of those involved in the debate.

In the early 1980s there was much discussion about the need for a U.S. industrial policy that implied an enlarged role for the government in international competitiveness. Consistent with the traditional ideology, the politically conservative Reagan administration successfully redefined this issue in terms of national competitive strategy that

emphasized the mechanisms of a free market and a much more limited role for the government. Those more inclined toward the new ideology seemed to fear that this would result in a further deterioration of U.S. competitiveness. However, these ideologies need to be examined in light of existing market circumstances and economic conditions.

For example, late in 1990, General Motors had announced major layoffs owing to needed downsizing as it continued to lose market share to European and Japanese automobile producers. Lee Ioccoca of Chrysler called for a more vigorous role of government to gain access to the Japanese market. He has also called for certain protectionist measures.

The traditional ideology supporting the philosophy of free-market competition assumes the conditions of a competition outlined in Chapter 2 including such features as freedom of entry and exit from the market. If one country has trade barriers and another allows all countries the freedom to compete, then a necessary condition of a competitive market is missing. This has led to calls for an increased government role in securing free access to protectionist markets so that all competitors will be on a "level playing field." Alternatively, those losing out to foreign competitors who are frustrated because they perceive that they do not have free access to foreign markets may call for protectionist measures as a retaliation. American auto producers have recently called for quotas limiting the number of Japanese automobiles that can be imported into the United States each year.

The Legislative Process: How Laws Are Made

The legislative process is the process by which legislatures make laws. It is long and complex, beginning with an idea for resolving some social problem that is on the public policy agenda. Measures are drafted, with the help of congressional legal counsel, into bills that are introduced to either the House of Representatives or the Senate for consid-

TABLE 10–1
Ideology and the Role of Government

ISSUE	Traditional individualistic market-oriented ideology	Community oriented activist-government ideology
UNDERLYING ASSUMPTION	Market competition assumed to work well, minimum government needed.	Market competition considered imperfect, activist government needed.
GOVERNANCE ISSUES		
Hostile Takeovers	Let market forces determine ownership and control of corporations.	Regulate takeovers; require filing notification of takeover intentions. Laws are needed to protect investors.
Employee Rights	Market forces will protect workers; employment at will doctrine.	Laws are needed to protect employee rights: wrongful discharge, privacy, expression, association, etc.
INVESTOR RELATIONS	Rely on market forces; buyers and sellers are informed.	Securities exchange and banking are regulated to protect investors.
CONSUMER ISSUES		
Consumer Fraud and Misrepresentation	Fraud and misrepresentation are illegal.	Misrepresentation illegal. Other information required, labeling.
Product Safety	Require disclosure when product is unsafe; let the buyer beware.	Require disclosure of safety problems and regulate safety standards; let the seller beware.
EMPLOYEE ISSUES		
Occupational Health and Safety	Competitive forces protect workers; workers' compensation and liability insurance supplement.	Workers' compensation; child labor, job safety, and healthy working conditions all regulated.
Discrimination and Inequality	Competitive forces protect against discrimination; wages determined by labor market; equality of opportunity emphasized.	Regulate human resource policies; discrimination prohibited; affirmation action programs are appropriate; equality of results emphasized.
ENVIRONMENTAL ISSUES		
Environmental Protection	Use tax policy to encourage desired practices. Tax polluters; offer tax credits. Apply economic cost-benefit analysis to environmental regulation.	Establish standards to protect the environment. Use cost-benefit to efficiently regulate. Use market forces to induce behavior.
Energy	Abandon or limit regulation. Market forces will find new energy sources.	Subsidize new energy sources. Use tax policy to discourage energy waste.
INTERNATIONAL COMPETITIVENESS	Free trade supported. Government role is limited to removing trade barriers.	Government should support a national competitive strategy. Protect some domestic markets. Control multinational corporations.

eration. Bills are then referred to committees, which hold public hearings and later return the bills with a committee vote to Congress. If a bill passes either the Senate or the House, the process must be repeated in the other chamber. If it passes both chambers, it is sent to the president for signing before it can become law. If the president vetoes the bill, it still becomes law if each chamber votes by a two-thirds majority to override the veto.

At the national level, the Congress is responsible for this task. The Senate has 100 members, including two senators representing each state. The House of Representatives has 435 members allotted according to the population of each state. A bill can be introduced into either the House or the Senate and, if passed, is forwarded to the president before becoming law. Bills involving taxing or appropriations must originate in the House of Representatives.

Each state also has a legislature that passes statutes. The process is much the same as the federal legislative process. Businesses wishing to monitor and provide input for state-level legislation that concerns their interests should also follow this process at state and local levels.

IDEAS FOR LEGISLATION

Bills are based upon legislative ideas that can come from a variety of sources. Business is an important constituency of members of Congress, and an industry group often communicates an idea to a member of Congress for a law that would help it. The president has a legislative agenda to implement the campaign promises or program for which he or she was elected. This agenda often appears in the "State of the Union Address," which is delivered before Congress every January. Also, ideas for legislation come from the public policy agenda.

Ideas are communicated to Congress from various interest groups and constituencies. Normally such communications are directed to congressional staffs first by interest groups or the lobbyists who represent them. Members of Congress are very busy because the ideas for legislation that comes to

them number in the thousands each year. Supporters, campaign contributors, and concerned citizens in the states or districts they represent all work hard to maintain access to their congressional representatives. It is important that ideas or legislative concerns be communicated to staffers in a polite, well-documented way.

Persons interested in getting a representative to draft a bill and work hard to obtain its passage must do their homework. Has the representative already publicly expressed support for the idea or an opposing idea? Has the idea already been drafted into a bill that was defeated in an earlier session of Congress? For example, does new social or technical information further highlight the importance or workability of an idea regarding health care costs to small business or payroll withholding of child care support? If a Senator has already opposed the idea, a polite argument from a constituency may help to change his or her position.

Small businesses affected by legislation but with limited resources for introducing ideas or influencing legislation have a number of alternatives. Organizations like industry associations, chambers of commerce, and political action committees (PAC), which specialize in particular issues, can all be used to keep informed about important issues and to communicate the concerns of small business to Congress. Also, in states like California, there is often a small business advocate within a state department with the special task of monitoring and communicating small business concerns to the governor and various members of the legislature.

A bill introduced to Congress is referred to a committee that has jurisdiction over the bill's area for consideration. The Senate has 16 permanent committees and the House, 22. The chairperson of these committees are from the majority party. Members of Congress derive much power and influence from their membership on key committees and subcommittees. They are in a significant position to work for the passage or defeat of a bill.

Most of these committees have subcommittees formed to handle various areas of concern. A bill sent to a congressional committee is initially referred to a subcommittee that holds hearings. Business interested in influencing the outcome of a particular bill can communicate with the member of Congress on the committee or subcommittee or with a staff member. Also, a small business person can communicate with a trade association, chamber of commerce, or political action committee that represents the interests of the business or industry. Business can also appear at public hearings called by the subcommittee to investigate a bill.

After hearings are held on a bill, the subcommittee meets to discuss it and to make any changes they feel is appropriate. The bill, along with any amendments, is then referred to the standing committee. The committee can either approve the subcommittee's report or repeat the hearings process of deliberations and alterations of the bill. Bills coming out of committee are sometimes quite different from the version initially referred to the committee by Congress. The committee then votes on the bill and then refers it to either the Senate or the House, together with the *Committee Report* on the bill.

PASSAGE OF A BILL BY CONGRESS

The bill is then debated in Congress and voted up or down by majority vote. Before a bill can be sent to the president, both the Senate and the House must approve it in the same form. Thus the process outlined above must be repeated by the other chamber of Congress. Then a *conference committee* with members from both Senate and House committee members who have supported the bill must meet and reconcile any differences. A reconciled version is then approved by both the Senate and the House, and the bill is forwarded to the president for signing.

PRESIDENTIAL ACTION— SIGNED OR VETOED

The president can veto the bill or the bill can become law if he signs it, or if he holds the bill for ten days without a signing it. Vetoed bills may still become law if approved by two-thirds of each

chamber. However, it is very difficult to override a presidential veto. President Reagan vetoed 74 bills, of which only 9 were overridden. During President Carter's administration, only 2 of 31 vetoes were overridden.[10] Only one veto by President Bush was overridden by Congress.

Implementation of Government Regulations

Government regulations are implemented primarily by the activity of federal agencies under the auspices of administrative law. A public policy outlined by a law passed by Congress and signed by the president is often broadly worded. The agency responsible for the implementation of this public policy engages in a number of activities that begin with a broad statement of policy and end with the development and enforcement of specifically worded policy in the form of rules and regulations. This *agency* process includes (1) making and sometimes changing rules and regulations, (2) performing investigations to enforce compliance and to determine the results of regulation, (3) offering advice to business and others concerning ways to comply with existing regulations, and (4) adjudicating cases in quasi-judicial courts under the auspices of the agency.

To explain the implementation process, we need to establish a few definitions implicit in much of the earlier discussion.

A *government regulation* "is a state-imposed limitation on the discretion that may be exercised by individuals or organizations, which is supported by the threat of sanction".[11] These regulations include laws enacted by Congress or state lawmakers in legislative process and rules developed by administrative agencies that have been empowered to enforce and to implement public policy.

An *administrative agency* is a nonjudicial and nonlegislative lawmaking unit of government. Agencies can be located in the executive branch as a cabinet-level organization, as is the Department of Justice, or without cabinet-level status, as is the Environmental Protection Agency (EPA). More often, agencies are independent, as are the Equal Employment Opportunity Commission, the National Labor Relations Board, the Federal Trade Commission (FTC), the Securities and Exchange Commission, and the Federal Reserve Board.

Congress creates agencies and also must approve agency budgets annually. All agencies, whether located in the executive branch or independent, must submit their annual budgets to the Office of Management and Budget (OMB) for approval before these budgets are forwarded to Congress. Also, agencies within the executive branch must submit proposed rules or regulations to the OMB, together with an analysis of the impact analysis as a part of the agency rule-making process.

The top officials within federal agencies are appointed by the president with the confirmation of the Senate. Top officials of agencies within the executive branch, like the EPA or the Department of Justice, serve at the pleasure of the president and can be removed by him at any time. However, once top officials of independent agencies are appointed and confirmed, they cannot be removed by the president before their term expires. Thus they are somewhat independent of pressures from the president. Most administrators within these agencies are mindful of the budget process and are cautious about their relationship with the president and Congress. For example, the FTC was once threatened with a budget cut because the president and many in Congress were displeased with its handling of an issue with the cereal industry.

Employees of agencies below the levels of top administrators are governed by civil service laws, as are other government employees. Thus they cannot be removed because of political party affiliation after an election. They must be promoted and rewarded according to civil service personnel policies.

Administrative law includes the rules developed by these agencies that have been delegated the authority to implement and enforce the laws passed by Congress or other legislative bodies.

Also, these laws include court interpretation of rules and regulations.

THE AGENCY RULE-MAKING PROCESS

The Administrative Procedures Act (APA) legally defines the process by which agencies make the rule that form the greater part of government regulation of business. This process begins with the formal announcement by an agency of a proposed new rule in the *Federal Register*, as shown in Figure 10–5. After this formal announcement, the Agency begins to obtain more information concerning the effects of the proposed rule. At this point the rule making process can use guidelines for an informal process that is outlined in section 553 of the Administrative Procedures Act, or more formal procedures outlined in section 557 of the APA can be followed.

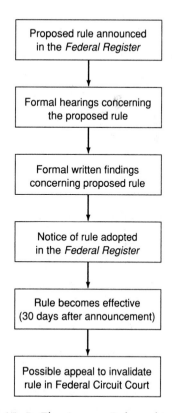

FIGURE 10–5 The Agency Rule-making Process

Informal Agency Rule Making

Businesses or other groups interested in a proposed rule have 30 days to respond in writing outlining their concerns, to state why the rule should not be adopted, or to recommend changes in the proposed rule. Also, the agency may hold hearings to provide an opportunity for interested parties to participate further in the rule-making process. Most regulations are developed by this informal process.

Formal Agency Rule Making

If the agency chooses the formal process, it uses a formal hearing that is similar to a trial. More stringent rules of evidence are used than is the case in the informal process. Parties appearing at these hearings are formally cross-examined and have the right of rebuttal to counter the claims and assertions of others opposed to their position on a proposed rule.

During the deliberations over a proposed rule, the committee obtains comments and views from business, interest groups, and often recommendations from Congress and the executive branch. It is important for businesses or their representatives to be active in the rule making process during this phase of the process.

After the formal or the informal processes, the agency can circulate findings of the formal and informal processes. These findings, together with the evidence and conclusions include the decision (1) to change the proposed rule, (2) to withdraw the rule, or (3) to proceed with the rule as originally proposed. Once the final version of a rule has been decided, the adopted rule or regulation is again announced in the *Federal Register*. A rule cannot become effective until 30 days after this last formal announcement. If business, or another interested party, wants to have the rule invalidated, it has this period to appeal to a federal circuit court.

In addition to making rules and regulations, agencies have a number of other functions, including (1) investigating and prosecuting violations of rules and regulations, (2) advising individuals and business concerning rules, (3) and adjudicating. For example, a business is required to consult with the FTC before acquiring a major competitor to assure that the acquisition would not be considered a constraint of trade by antitrust law. The FTC would offer advice concerning the acquisition, and if this advice were against the proposed merger, then the FTC would probably take the business to court if it proceeded with the acquisition.

Institutional Orientation of Business and Public Policy

As discussed in Chapter 1, business can assume three types of institutional orientation with respect to society and government. A law passed to regulate business or affect business practice as outlined in the opening case may or may not consider the particular problems of business. The policy process depends on input from all affected groups. The concerns of groups not represented in public discussions might be ignored. Business needs to be involved in the public policy process if its interests are to be represented.

DEFENSIVE AND REACTIVE ORGANIZATIONS

Type-one businesses are characterized by defensive and reactive behavior. They tend to maximize short-term profitability by exploiting a situation. They are likely to reject any concept of social responsibility and feel that their only obligation is to increase shareholder wealth, regardless of any externalities or undesirable effects on the community or the environment.

Managers of defensive and reactive organizations tend to ignore the public policy process until an onerous law or regulation is about to be implemented. At this point they tend to use legal means to block or delay its implementation. Such managers typically view government as an adversary and regulators as needlessly interfering with business interests. Because of their neglect of the public policy process and the hostile nature of relationships with government, such managers are more likely to be ineffective in managing the legal environment of business. Also, this type of orientation is likely to lead to a harmful or negative public image. This lowers public support and increases the likeliness of a hostile political climate toward business in the public policy process.

ANTICIPATORY AND RESPONSIBLE ORGANIZATIONS

Type-two businesses anticipate social responsibility and respond to changing trends and social expectations by incorporating forecasted changes into the long-range planning process. Such firms are likely to recognize a wide variety of social expectations and seek to be responsible when making decisions that affect a broader group of stakeholders. Managers of these organizations are likely to use business associations like the chamber of commerce and industry groups to monitor changes likely to affect business in the future.

Type-two firms might track human resource trends and regulations and have programs in place that enable them to employ workers with disabilities before federal laws require them to do so. For example, the anticipatory and responsive organization is likely to be well aware of the requirement of a system to use payroll deduction for child support well before the implementation date required by law. The result of such planning is less costly implementation of government requirements, fewer lawsuits, and a better public image as a socially responsible firm. These types of firms are likely to be viewed as good corporate citizens and are less of a target for hostile interest groups.

PROACTIVE AND RESPONSIVE ORGANIZATIONS

A type-three institutional orientation begins with management awareness of changing social expectations of business. Changes are anticipated but the management sometimes seeks to be proactive in influencing their direction, so that the effects of new laws and regulations on business will be desirable or at least manageable. Companies with this type of responsiveness are more likely to engage in political strategy or to interact with the environment as they communicate with the government or community groups to reach mutually agreeable solutions to social issues.

Responsiveness includes carefully reading news that might affect business in the future, monitoring issues on the public policy agenda, attending hearings to express concerns about issues under debate, and communicating with both lawmakers and enforcement agencies throughout the public policy process. Chapter 3 outlines the strategic management of public issues used by organizations with proactive and responsive institutional orientations. The result of this orientation is more likely to be high levels of public legitimacy and a greater impact on the public policy process in areas of concern to business.

The Legal Environment of Business

The legal environment of business is the net result of the public policy process. Virtually every stakeholder area has a body of laws and regulations that constrain or guide business behavior, as shown in Figure 10–6. For example, consider a person who wants to start a small business. Communities have laws that require licenses, local taxes, and building codes to assure that the building in which the business is located meets safety standards. Also, communities try to maintain the quality of life by declaring some zones in the city to be residential and others industrial. The new business must be located in an appropriately zoned area.

Employee relations are governed by labor law and employment law. If the business is to have over ten employees, the owner will have to follow federal laws against discrimination and laws that cover occupational safety and health.

If owners wish to form a corporation and offer stock, they will need to comply with securities laws. Relationships with customers are governed by contract law and the law of torts, which covers product liability matters. Consumer laws cover such matters as disclosure of product ingredients, interest charged in credit arrangements, and honesty in

FIGURE 10–6 Legal Environment of Business Shaping Major Stakeholder Relationships

advertising. Contract law and tort law also define relationships with suppliers. In sum, the legal environment includes the legal requirements and regulations that govern every dimension of business.

Summary

Changing social values, lifestyles, and technologies lead to problems or social issues that, in turn, often lead to public controversies. The breakdown of the family has led to many single-parent families. Economic pressures have required two family incomes to maintain living standards. Both these trends have led to public concern over day care, parental leave, and child support payments. Changes in technology have led to issues of product safety, job safety, concern for the environment, and a host of other issues.

If sufficient public interest is mobilized around an issue, it becomes part of the public policy agenda. Trigger events such as a dramatic accident, a well-publicized book or documentary, a charismatic opin-

ion leader, or organized interest group activities can all place an issue on the public policy agenda. Also, our pluralistic society is dominated by many diverse interest groups, many of which have conflicting interests. These interest groups compete in the public policy process to get their particular issue heard and to get society to adopt their respective view of the appropriate public policy.

The U.S. Constitution forms the basis for public policy. It authorizes the three branches of government—legislative, executive, and judicial—and outlines the responsibility of each branch. Supreme Court decisions have extended the interpretation of interstate commerce that has authorized the extensive federal regulation of business. Also, state and local-level governments also develop public policy.

Once an issue like child support or product safety has been placed on the public policy agenda, a public discourse and debate occurs. This can lead to a new public policy in the form of laws or presidential executive orders; the establishment of regulatory agencies that, in turn, develop regulations; or court decisions. Also, international agreements form an important part of the public policy affecting business.

The legislative process is an important part of the public policy process that occurs at both the state and federal levels. A public issue sparks the idea for a law in the mind of one of more lawmakers. The discussion often leads to public hearings that allows business and other interests within society to share their views of the problem and the need for a public policy. A bill is the proposed law that is based on the original idea for legislation. If this bill is passed by both branches of the legislature, it is forwarded to the chief executive for signing or a veto. Once signed, the bill becomes law. It then is enforced by the executive branch or by an independent regulatory agency as discussed.

The ideology or political philosophy of policymakers shapes the debates over public policy and the legitimized role of the government. The traditional ideology emphasizes competitive markets, individual freedom, and minimum government interference with business. The alternative ideology recognizes the imperfections of actual markets and supports a more activist government to protect individual rights and the well-being of the community. These two ideological poles serve to define the role of government and the type of legal environment for most public issues.

Business managers can have different institutional orientations with respect to the public policy process and the legal environment. The three types of institutional orientations are (1) defensive and reactive, (2) anticipatory and responsible, or (3) proactive and responsive. The defensive and reactive organization is likely to ignore the public policy process and resist unfavorable laws late in the process, when the matter finds its ways into the courts. Anticipatory and responsible businesses anticipate social changes, closely monitor the public policy process, and incorporate these new social expectations into the long-range planning process. Such organizations seek to behave in a responsible way so they can be regarded as good corporate citizens.

Proactive organizations are likely to be actively engaged in the public policy process and seek to protect and extend their interests at each stage of the process. These three institutional orientations are likely to yield very different results in terms of defining issues, supporting public policy solutions, and implementing and litigating issues concerning their interests.

Conclusions

Although the public policy process occurs within the political sphere, it is important for business to be aware of its effects. The changing expectations of society are reflected in the news stories and political debates of the time. Businesses with high social performance are likely to keep abreast of the times and are aware of trends in public policy. As an interest within a pluralistic society, it is important for business to be part of the policy process that defines the role of government, produces laws that establish standards of business behavior, and establishes the framework within which business must operate.

Discussion Questions

1. How is the public policy process part of the processes of a threefold society?
2. What is the justification for the law that requires payroll withholding of child support? Should society require that business withhold child care support even though it is not related to its business operations?
3. Briefly describe the public policy process. Identify a current event currently being discussed in a newspaper or newsmagazine and discuss in terms of the public policy process. At what stage in the process is it? How is business involved?
4. How do values enter into the public policy process?
5. Find a public statement by a business executive concerning an issue on the public policy agenda. Is the statement concerned only with

the economic impact of proposed public policies? Can you find hints of the underlying ideology of this statement?

6. What are the major ideologies that shape public policy debates? Briefly summarize one.
Select a current issue and discuss it in terms of
the ideology you have selected.

7. How do issues get on the public policy agenda?
Why do some issues appear on the public policy agenda and others do not?

8. Briefly describe the legislative process. Identify
a major law being proposed that is likely to
affect business. Where is this proposed law in
the legislative process?

9. Read the news about current Supreme Court
decisions. What major rulings were made during the past month that are important public
policy affecting business?

10. What is the likely result of a defensive and
reactive institutional orientation held by a
business? Of a business with an anticipatory
and responsible orientation? Of a business with
a proactive and responsive orientation?

Notes

1. Rudolf Steiner, *Towards Social Renewal: Basic Issues of the Social Question* (London: Rudolf Steiner Press, 1977), chap. 2.
2. Murray L. Weidenbaum, *Business, Government, and the Public,* 3d ed. (Englewood Cliffs, N.J.: Prentice Hall, 1986).
3. Dan Bertozzi, Jr., and Lee B. Burgunder, *Business, Government, and Public Policy* (Englewood Cliffs, N.J.: Prentice-Hall, 1990), p. 5.
4. Steiner, *Towards Social Renewal,* p. 64.
5. *N.L.R.B. v. Jones and Laughlin Steel Company,* 301 U.S. 1 (1937).
6. Derek Bok, *The Cost of Talent: How Executives and Professionals Are Paid and How It Affects America* (New York: Free Press, 1993).
7. For examples of executive compensation, see a series of cover stories appearing in *Business Week* issues of May 6, 1991, and March 30, 1992; and *Wall Street Journal,* March 11, 1992, p. 1; and *Economist,* February 1, 1992, pp. 13–14.
8. Martha Derthick and Paul J. Quirk, *The Politics of Deregulation* (Washington, D.C.: Brookings Institution, 1985).
9. George Cabot Lodge, *The American Disease* (New York: Knopf, 1984).
10. Bertozzi and Burgunder, *Business, Government, and Public Policy,* pp. 56–65.
11. Alan Stone, *Regulation and Its Alternatives* (Washington, D.C.: Congressional Quarterly Press, 1982), p. 10.

CHAPTER 11

Government Regulation of Business

1. Explain the control cycle of the social mechanisms that seek to insure that business behavior is consistent with social goals, values, and expectations.
2. Describe how different types of market failure lead to specific types of government regulation.
3. Distinguish economic regulation of industry from the social regulation of business functions.
4. Review the major arguments to justify the economic regulation of industry and the social regulation of business.
5. Review the historical development of government regulation of business within the United States.
6. Discuss the changing role of government in the regulation of business.
7. Examine the limitations, problems, and failures of government regulation.

Introduction

As discussed in Chapter 2, a number of social mechanisms control the behavior of business in a market-oriented society. These control mechanisms are interdependent and dynamic as the forces within society seek to assure that business and other institutions meet society's expectations. Most of the control of business in a market-oriented society is the external economic control of market competition. Governmental controls have been developed that supplement and, at times, replace market forces throughout history.[1]

This chapter provides a framework to explain the interactions between the operation and failures of market competition and the countervailing public policy process. It also chronicles the historical development of government regulation of busi-ness, the emergence of the community-oriented ideology that defined the changing role of an activist government.

Business in industrialized society operates within the context of a legal environment that is constantly changing as the public policy process responds to social issues. Many social issues are brought about by the imperfections in competition that distorts market forces.[2] Other issues, like toxic waste pollution and substance abuse, are spawned by technological and cultural changes. The governmental sphere controls business activities through laws and regulations including the following:

1. antitrust law that seeks to maintain or restore competitive conditions to markets and to prohibit anticompetitive behavior
2. economic regulation of specific industries

3. social regulation of business functions
4. litigation that resolves conflicts arising out of the legal and regulatory environment

The task of this chapter is to outline the control cycle that leads to government regulation of business, the different types of regulations that affect business operations, and the historical development of regulation that has substantially redefined the role of government during the last century.

Government Regulation and the Control Cycle

In the last chapter, we described the threefold social structure as it relates to social change and the public policy process. Changes in culture and technology result in problems that come to the awareness of sufficient numbers of people within society. This awareness triggers the public policy process, which, in turn, results in laws and regulations that govern business. The cycle ends with business adjusting to changing social expectations legitimized by the public policy process. Through complying with these new laws and regulations, business responds to the changing social expectations as expressed in public policy and the legal environment.

The *business control cycle* is the sequential process by which the various mechanisms of social control in market-oriented societies work together to assure that business activities are relatively consistent with public expectations, social goals, and social values.

The control cycle, shown in Figure 11–1, includes the following sequence of activities:

1. *Social change or market failure.* Societal problems develop, often slowly and imperceptibly at first, and then increase in difficulty until they become visible to most people. These problems could be the result of (1) changes in social values, lifestyles, or technology, (2) market forces that fail to control business behavior and then become inconsistent with social goals and val-

ues, or (3) market forces that are unstable and destructive.
2. *Problem awareness and controversy.* After the social problem involving business behavior or its consequences becomes visible to enough people, something triggers a controversy and the problem is defined as a public issue that is placed on the public policy agenda.
3. *The public policy process.* A public policy debate concerning the appropriate role and responsibility of business, of industry, and of government occurs. This debate is followed by
4. *Laws and regulations.* Government regulation of business is designed to make business practice consistent with society's goals and values.

Government Regulation Control Cycle

Government can also fail to accomplish its social role. In this case, government regulations of business can fail to accomplish expected goals and become controversial issues in themselves. If government policy or action fails to accomplish the intended social goals of control, there is likely to be another cycle of social control that mirrors the one described above: (1) regulatory failure, (2) continuing social problems, (3) renewed debate over the issue, leading to (4) privatization, regulatory reform, or deregulation.

For example, a deregulatory movement occurred both in the United Kingdom and in the United States beginning around 1975.[3] The United Kingdom has had a recent history of nationalizing industries that then show sluggish economic performance. Prime Minister Margaret Thatcher's government privatized many of these industries. In the United States, it appeared that growing regulation had sharply increased the cost of government, was hampering international competitiveness, and was not working as intended. The groundwork for deregulation was prepared during the Nixon administration and gained momentum until it became a major theme of President Reagan's administration (1980–88). This second type of control cycle that deals with public policy

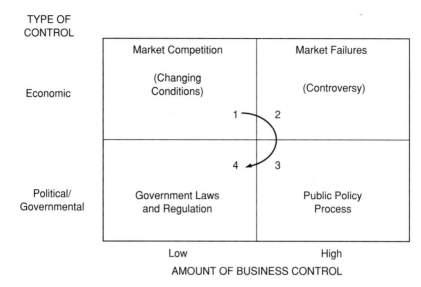

TYPE OF CONTROL

FIGURE 11–1 Government Regulation and the Control Cycle

responses to regulatory failure is addressed in the next chapter.

If social or economic problems are serious enough to come to the attention of enough people, the legitimacy of business or government can be called into question. This can activate the business control process and trigger the public policy process discussed in Chapter 10. If business fails to meet public expectations when a controversy and subsequent public policy debate develops, the likely result is government laws and regulations. If government policy fails, the cycle leads to regulatory reform.

Government regulation of business is an external political-governmental control that supplements or substitutes for the forces of market competition. Of course, many variables affect the unfolding of the control cycle, including (1) the political ideology of lawmakers, (2) the political party in control of the legislative and/or executive branches of government, (3) the resources, organizational capabilities, activities, and objectives of the interest groups, (4) the current state of the economy, and (5) the seriousness and urgency of the problem or issue.

Market Failures and the Types of Government Regulation

Competitive markets require certain conditions to be present if they are to result in economic performance that is efficient, fair, and consistent with the goals of society. When one or more of the necessary conditions is absent, a breakdown in competition or in market performance becomes likely. Each of these major types of market failure leads to different issues or social problems expressed in the control cycle and thus leads to different types of government regulation. Because social changes and economic conditions are complex and fraught with uncertainty, the regulatory response outlined in the framework below is generally true but not consistent with every public issue that involves a system failure.

THE CONDITIONS NECESSARY FOR CONTROL BY COMPETITION

Chapter 2 identified the necessary requirements for market competition, which include (1) large enough numbers of buyers and sellers so that none have sufficient market power to allow any one firm to determine prices, product/service characteristics, or terms of exchange; (2) freedom of entry and exit of buyers or sellers that suggests low barriers to entry and no discrimination against minorities in employment; (3) prudent behavior based upon self-interest; (4) knowledgeable buyers and sellers; (5) reliance on market forces to set prices, returns to factor inputs, and profitability; (6) private property; and (7) minimal government interference in the automatic functioning of the market.

The breakdown or absence of these conditions can cause a market failure. Types of market failure (introduced in Chapter 2) include (1) conditions when buyers or sellers become too powerful to be controlled by market forces, (2) anticompetitive behavior like price fixing, exclusionary practices, and conspiracies in constraint of trade, (3) unstable or destructive competition, (4) uninformed or mis-informed buyers or sellers, (5) side effects or exter-nalities of market exchange that cause pollution or harm to those not a part of the market exchange, and (6) discriminatory practices that arbitrarily exclude certain groups from economic activity. The breakdown of any of the conditions of market com-petition can result in one or more of these market failures and undermine the effectiveness of market competition. Such market failures can lead to abuses that cause business behavior to be inconsis-tent with the values and goals of society.

MARKET FAILURES AND THE REGULATORY RESPONSE

Regulatory responses by the government to control the economic behavior of business parallels these types of market failure, as shown in Table 11–1. Too little competition and anticompetitive behav-ior led to the Sherman Antitrust Law of 1890 and other antitrust laws in this century. Situations with too much competition or where competition was thought to lead to unstable, destructive, or unde-sirable consequences have led to the economic regulation of selected industries. For example, the Interstate Commerce Commission (ICC) was cre-ated in 1887 to regulate the railroad industry, and this approach to regulation was extended to other transportation industries including airlines and trucking. More recently there has been a reconsid-eration of the wisdom of this type of regulation, and the airlines, trucking industry, and railroads have all undergone deregulation.

Other market failures lead to social problems arising from information problems, side effects and externalities, unsafe work places, unsafe products, and discrimination. These failures have led to pub-lic issues that have spawned a wide variety of social regulations. Examples of social regulation responding to these types of market failure include the following:

The Federal Trade Commission (FTC), formed in 1914, and the Department of Justice enforce antitrust laws. The authority of the FTC was later extended to regulate alleged deceptive advertising by business and the need to inform customers through product labeling and other modes of disclosure.

The Environmental Protection Agency (EPA), formed in 1970, regulates side effects and externalities like pollution and toxic waste.

The Occupational Safety and Health Administra-tion (OSHA), formed in 1973, regulates the safety of the workplace.

The Consumer Products Safety Commission (CPSC), formed in 1972, and the National Highway Traffic Safety Administration (NHTSA), formed in 1966, regulate product and automobile safety, respectively.

The Equal Employment Opportunity Commission (EEOC), formed in 1973, regulates fair employ-ment practices and prohibits discrimination.

Antitrust Law, Market Power, and Anticompetitive Behavior

The first market failure identified in Table 11–1 is too little competition because of the market power of a few large businesses when industries are too concentrated. The existence of market power interferes with the ability of the forces of market competition to set prices, profit levels, and returns to suppliers. In the economic theory of industrial organization, economists have theorized that market structure is linked to market conduct, which in turn is linked to market performance as follows[4]:

market structure—>market conduct—>market performance

Market Power

According to this economic theory of industrial organization, highly competitive markets lead to competitive behaviors that ultimately result in high economic performance. A competitive market has the structural characteristic of numerous businesses in the industry or at least buyers and sellers in suffi-

TABLE 11–1
Types of Market Failure and the Regulatory Response

Type of Market Failure	Example	Regulatory Response and Enforcement
Too Little Competition	Concentrated markets Barriers to entry/exit Few buyers and sellers Monopolizing mergers	Antitrust laws
Anticompetitive Behavior	Price fixing Tying agreements Exclusive dealing Price discrimination Dumping below cost	Antitrust laws FTC and Justice Department
Too Much Competition	Natural monopoly Scarce resources Cut-throat competition	Industry regulation of entry, price, routes, broadcast frequencies, service
Unequal or Incorrect Information	Deceptive advertising Asymmetric knowledge	Social regulation FTC and deceptive advertising; required labeling
Unsafe Jobs and Products	Dangerous products/services/jobs	Social regulation OSHA
Discrimination	Sexual harassment Unequal pay Sex-dominated jobs Race or ethnic group determines access to jobs	Social regulation Equal pay acts Equal opportunity EEOC
Externalities	Pollution; toxic waste	Social regulation of environment EPA

cient number so that none has sufficient market power to set prices and terms of exchange. The result of competitive market structures is that each business makes decisions independently, consistent with the firm's best economic interest.

Prices, profit levels, and returns are established by the laws of supply and demand within the context of market competition. Competitive market conduct exists when firms vigorously compete against one another to achieve high levels of market performance. Such market performance includes readily available products and services with the qualities that customers demand at low or reasonable prices.

In contrast, markets dominated by a few large businesses are more likely to encourage anticompetitive behavior like price fixing, tying agreements, and restrictions of markets from potential competitors. Uncompetitive markets lead to behavior that more likely to be interdependent, less competitive, and predatory than a competitive market would assure.[5] Also, there may be a pattern of withholding technological change and new products in uncompetitive market situations.

Antitrust Law

Large-scale businesses in the nineteenth century sought to stabilize competition by forming, agreements, pools, trusts, and holding companies. According to these arrangements, an industry dominated by a few businesses acting in concert could set uniform rates or prices and divide markets so that they would not have to compete with one another. The use of this economic power by businesses in the railroad, steel, petroleum, and other industries resulted in a controversy over trusts.

The *trust* was an arrangement whereby the owners of businesses in a particular industry would turn over their shares of stocks and voting rights in return for trust certificates. The trustees holding most of the stock of the major businesses within an industry would set prices, divide exclusive markets or territories, and manage the industry on behalf of the businesses represented. The result was to monopolize the industry structure that provided a way to anticompetitive behavior that led to low market performance. The practice of trusts led to a market failure that precipitated a controversy leading to antitrust law.

market failure→controversy over economic power→anti-trust law

The primary regulatory tool for markets with insufficient competition has been antitrust laws. Section 1 of the Sherman Antitrust Act of 1890 prohibits anticompetitive behavior like conspiracies in constraint of trade. Section 2 of the Sherman Act prohibits monopolization or attempts to monopolize by mergers, trusts, or conspiracies. Section 1 deals primarily with anticompetitive behavior; section 2 deals primarily with market structures where too much market power exists.

Recently scholars have revisited the history of antitrust and have suggested that, in reality, antitrust laws were developed to protect small business from large business. The original intent of antitrust law was not to protect consumers against monopolistic prices of big business. Rather, small business interests influenced protectionist state legislators and Congress to pass laws to protect them from the growing number of large-scale businesses that began to appear at the end of the nineteenth century.[6] Antitrust law has come to be associated with a government policy designed to restore competitive conditions and improve market performance; it is still considered relevant.[7] Antitrust is discussed in detail in Chapter 13.

Differences Between Economic and Social Regulation

In addition to antitrust law, there are two major types of government regulation of business, including the economic regulation of specific industries and the social regulation of business functions. These types of regulations evolved over different periods and are different in concept, application, and impact on the management process. Also they are very different with respect to how much they interfere with the management of business activities. Moreover, they are based on very different situations that brought them into existence.

Economic regulation includes government guidelines or constraints on (1) prices or rates charged, (2) product or services offered including transportation routes and broadcast frequencies, (3)

standards of availability or quality, and (4) entry or license to compete in the regulated industry. Such economic regulation has been the historical response to situations where competition was viewed as destructive, unstable, or otherwise not in the public interest.

Economic regulation usually has focused upon specific industries like airlines, trucking, railroads, radio, television, public utilities, and telecommunications. For example, under regulation the trucking industry had to have its freight rates and routes approved by the ICC. The ICC granted licenses to freight carriers other than for agricultural produce, which was excluded from regulation, and also established standards that had to be met. Within general guidelines of regulation, it was up to the managers within the industry to determine how best to met regulation requirements.

Social regulation refers to regulation designed to improve social conditions or to respond to social problems such as (1) the quality of life and the environment, (2) product safety, (3) job safety and

occupational health, and (4) equal employment opportunity. These categories of social regulation are related to such market failures as externalities and incomplete information by buyers or sellers.

Social regulation usually affects specific business functions like marketing (product safety and honesty in advertising), production and operations management (job safety), human resource management (equal employment opportunity and discrimination), and environmental issues like toxic waste, air and water pollution, and other quality-of-life issues that relate to several functional areas, as shown in Figure 11–2.

Weidenbaum investigated the cost and approaches to government regulation of business and found that social regulation of business functions differed significantly from the earlier economic regulation of industries in several important ways.[8] First, economic regulation provided broad guidelines for specific industries and allowed managers to figure out how best to comply with the regulations. In contrast, social regulations could be

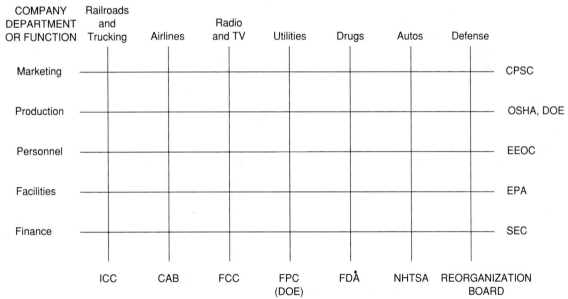

FIGURE 11–2 Economic Regulation of Industries and Social Regulation of Business Functions

SOURCE: Murray L. Weidenbaum, *Business, Government, and the Public* (Englewood Cliffs, N.J.: Prentice-Hall, 1977), p. 14.

regarded as "command and control" regulations, because they specified technologies, procedures, and every aspect of regulations in very detailed ways.

For example, OSHA regulated how to safely manufacture step ladders in a regulation that was 26 single-spaced typed pages. In another case, OSHA regulations required that guard rails in manufacturing facilities be a precise number of inches high. DuPont was reported to have spent $1 million per plant to reduce the height of guard rails and barriers, which incidentally reduced the overall safety of the facility.

Second, social regulations are much more specific than economic regulations and thus tend to be much more intrusive. Social regulations are likely to specify engineering technologies and specific processes to be used in the workplace or to control pollution emissions. Economic regulations are likely to specify a particular level of service but will leave management the discretion to meet that service level in the way managers feel to be the most cost-effective. Managers have much less discretion about how to comply with social regulations.

Third, the command and control nature of social regulations means that compliance is much more costly for the government to enforce and more costly for business to comply with the restrictive and specific requirements.[9] Much of the compliance cost is the requirement of specific technologies when other lower-cost approaches might be available. To assure compliance, regulators require extensive reporting by business that increases the cost of administration and paperwork. Also if the government is to specify specific technology or procedures, experts must be hired who are knowledgeable in the area being regulated, and resources must be spent to keep current on technological developments. When improved technologies become available, agency regulations and standards must be changed to incorporate these changes. Last, enforcing agencies need to deploy field inspectors to assure compliance.

Arguments for Economic Regulation: Can There Be Too Much Competition?

Under competitive conditions, the forces of market supply and demand determine product price, quality, the profitability of business, and who competes, that is, the entry and exit from the market. When society determines through the public policy process that market forces are unworkable or lead to socially undesirable results, it is believed to be in the *public interest* to override market forces. Under economic regulation, the price, quality, and other characteristics of products and services, profitability, entry, and exit are determined by the administrative decisions of a government regulatory agency.

It is curious to consider too much competition as a major "market failure." Alternatively, it could be asked, When is unregulated economic competition not in the public interest? A number of arguments are commonly forwarded to justify the economic regulation of selected industries. Nine arguments often used to justify the regulation of economic activities include the follwing:

1. the natural monopoly argument
2. administratively providing the opportunity for customers to complain
3. windfall profits
4. avoiding destructive or unstable competitive results
5. the need for cross-subsidy in rural areas
6. the need to allocate common property resources like the broadcast spectrum
7. the promotion of selected industries
8. controlling unfair price discrimination
9. insuring competitive fairness among different sellers.[10]

NATURAL MONOPOLIES

Some industries are considered natural monopolies because their cost structures make it most efficient for society to have only one business serving a market. For example, most communities are served by only one local telephone company because it is considered in the public interest not to have duplicate facilities. Most industries have U-shaped, long-run average cost structures. As output increases, fixed costs are absorbed by the additional units produced, leading to an overall decline in total average costs. Eventually, increases in output beyond some point result in diminishing returns to scale, causing increases in long-term average costs. This yields the typical U-shaped cost structures found in most industries.

However, U-shaped cost structures are not common to all industries. The cost structures of such industries as cable TV, public utilities, and local telephone companies are characterized by average total cost that declines indefinitely as total output increases. If more than one firm were to compete in such industries, the total social cost would increase. In the case of public utilities, competition requires duplicate facilities that are economically undesirable for society. The most efficient way to provide electricity or natural gas to a community is to have only one distribution network available to all residents. These industries are considered natural monopolies because the most efficient operation is to have only one or very few providers of the service.

In cases of natural monopoly, there is concern about the possibility of monopoly prices and poor service because customers have no alternative. Thus society grants one business organization the right to a natural monopoly in return for government regulation to protect the public. The most common type of economic regulations of natural monopoly are entry controls, price controls, and requirements of specified standards. A recognized and authorized provider becomes the only competitor allowed to enter a market such as a public utility.

Once a monopoly is granted, the forces of the market no longer control prices, profits, quality, and quantity of goods or services available to customers. Thus, a government agency regulates these variables and, in return for the monopoly status, the business is subjected to extensive regulation. Rate increases must be approved, service capacity must be increased to meet expected demand, and standards of service established by the regulatory review board must be met by the monopoly in question.

The Need to Provide an Opportunity to Voice Complaints

Market forces automatically provide information about the concerns of customers to suppliers if competitive forces exist. The competitor who can best respond to the demands of customers wins. Customers dissatisfied with the price or service level in a competitive market can withdraw from the market or seek another competitor. In cases where entry of a business into the market is controlled by regulation, the customer has no alternative. Thus prices and service levels must be set with the assistance of some nonmarket mechanism.

The Rate- or Price-setting Process Under Regulation

In the cases of the public utility and the insurance industry in some states, business sets rates or prices subject to the approval of a public agency rate-setting board. This board normally recognizes that business owners should receive a fair profit for their investment. Thus the rates usually allow for a target profit percentage based upon a cost structure or some economic return for the investment made by the owners. Because the management of these companies wants to maintain favorable profits for the owners, there can be a built-in conflict between prices and quality of service. Profit levels need to be maintained high enough for public utilities to attract investors and to maintain good relations with capital markets. Prices need to be set low enough to satisfy captive customers.

Consumers are likely to want a high level of service but will often testify at rate hearings for lower rates than those proposed by managers. Managers, in contrast, would like a rate high enough to pay operating and investment costs. If rate increases are disallowed but service levels maintained at high levels by regulators, utilities experience cost pressures. The forces of market competition are not available to keep prices down and profits fair. The rate-setting process involving negotiations among management, regulators, and public groups serves in place of market discipline.

Inefficiency and unwise investments may be encouraged because both can increase costs that then are used to justify rates based upon some percent of costs or investment. Because rate setting becomes a quasi-political process, regulatory rate-setting boards often hold public hearings so customers can have an avenue to complain about rates or service. Also, customers can file complaints or statements with regulators in an attempt to influence rate and service decisions.

WINDFALL PROFITS

The regulation of maximum prices under conditions other than natural monopolies has occurred in the case of windfall profits. Under conditions of market competition, prices are set by the forces of supply and demand. If the supply of something is fixed (often in the short run) and demand is very inelastic, that is, if price increases result in relatively little decline in the quantity demanded, price gouging becomes possible. This is particularly true in markets for things that people must have to live. Sharp price increases under these conditions lead to windfall profits that can be viewed as unfair or exploitative by consumers. In this case, the temporary short supply distorts market decisions because there is no time for competing firms to enter the market to increase supply levels and customers need the product immediately. Thus, some argue for some type of direct price control or an indirect price control in the form of a windfall profit tax to discourage exploitation.

This was the case during the 1970s when the Oil Producing and Exporting Countries (OPEC) suddenly raised the worldwide price of oil. It was

estimated that the oil companies, through taking advantage of the situation by raising prices on petroleum products, received a windfall profit of some $800 million.[11] The image of poor people in New England caught in a cold winter paying dearly to rich Texas oil barons resulted in a major political debate. The result was a Windfall Profits Tax.

A replay of the 1970s example nearly occurred just before the Persian Gulf War, when large oil companies again sharply raised prices in anticipation of a similar situation. In 1989, Saddam Hussein of Iraq invaded the neighboring country of Kuwait to gain control of its oil. Major oil companies, fearing future oil shortages, immediately raised the price of gasoline to reflect expected changes in the worldwide supply of petroleum.

Because these price changes occurred before any real change in worldwide supply, widespread protests erupted and the oil industry was accused of price gouging. Many protested the price increases and President Bush publicly warned the oil companies not to exploit their short-term economic power. Congress also began discussing passage of another excess profits tax like the one that had been used during the 1970s when OPEC had sharply raised oil prices. Most oil companies then reversed their price increases.

DESTRUCTIVE AND UNSTABLE COMPETITION

The most common justification for the economic regulation of industries, other than natural monopolies, is that uncontrolled competitive forces will lead to destructive competition or unstable markets. Such instability will lead to a "boom-and-bust" or "surplus-and-shortage" cycles in the market. Thus, it is argued, government needs to control access to markets by business to assure the public of a stable, reliable supply of product or service. We need to consider the underlying causes of the boom-and-bust cycle experienced in some industries.

Capital-intensive industries normally require large economies of scale to be efficient. The capital intensity causes the company to have high fixed costs that require high-capacity utilization to be profitable. Low-capacity utilization in capital-intensive industries results in excess capacity and low or no profitability. For example, consider a country that has enough demand to support four and one-half efficient producers. If, say, six operators are competing in this market, the result is excess capacity and some competitors operating at below their break-even point, that is, at a loss.

To increase sales volume above their break-even points, companies then engage in cutthroat price competition until several competitors are driven from the industry. In this situation, if two companies went bankrupt, the remaining four companies could not service all the demand with their efficient scale plants, even if they were operating at full capacity. The result would be supply shortages leading to high prices and excess profitability.

The high rate of profits after the industry shake-out might eventually attract other competitors into the industry. More competitors would increase industrywide capacity and market supply, driving prices down. Soon companies would be threatened again by the two evils of low capacity utilization and low price levels, both of which can result in serious business losses. Thus the process of boom-and-bust cycles over again as the market is inherently unstable over a long period of time.

The destructive competition and resulting instability was a key factor in the decision to regulate the railroads in the late 1800s. The public policy response was to establish the Interstate Commerce Commission, charged with the responsibility of regulating entry, rates, and service levels for the industry. This same argument was later used to regulate trucking, airlines, and several other industries.[12]

The theory that unstable and destructive competition requires economic regulation of specific industries has been challenged in recent years. The deregulation movement beginning in the 1970s was, in part, the result of the reconsideration of whether industry regulation is really in the public interest. Although the social performance results of industry deregulation are mixed, after the deregulation of the trucking industry in 1979, only 10 of the top 30 trucking businesses were still in business ten years later. Seventeen of the top 30 trucking companies went bankrupt and another 3 merged with other firms as a result of deregulation.[13] Perhaps the theory of unstable or destructive competition will need to be reexamined in the future.

THE NEED TO PROVIDE CROSS-SUBSIDY

It has been argued that justice requires that everyone within a society should have access to certain things, like mail delivery, electricity, transportation, and communication facilities, as a matter of economic right. However, the costs of providing electricity, telephone service, and air or rail service to areas with low population density are relatively high for each person using these services. Under the operation of a freely working competitive market, one of two things is likely under this situation: The provider of the service will be forced to charge a prohibitively high price or withdraw from the market.

Under competitive conditions, a person living in a small town like Winnemucca, Nevada, might either have to pay very dearly for air travel to other cities or the service simply would not be offered. Thus, a pattern of cross-subsidy developed in regulated industries. Regulators grant businesses the right to enter favorable markets on the condition that the business also will service a less desirable market.

For example, a regulated airline was allowed to compete in a favorable route, like the corridor from Washington, D.C., to New York City only if it also agreed to service less desirable locations at favorable rates. The rates for service to popular locations would be set high enough to cover the costs of pricing service to unpopular locations at below the actual costs of the service to those locations. Before the break up of AT&T through the 1982 consent decree, local telephone calls subsidized long-distance service, and densely populated areas subsidized the cost of service in rural areas.

COMMON PROPERTY RESOURCES

There is a limited radio wave spectrum and only one station or channel can broadcast on a given frequency within the same region if the reception is to be clearly received. Who owns these frequencies? The radio wave spectrum is considered to be a "common property resource," owned collectively by society, and it is argued that this resource is best regulated by government. Thus, the Federal Communications Commission (FCC) licenses broadcasters and regulates programming standards.

THE NEED TO PROMOTE SELECTED INDUSTRIES

This has been called the "infant industry" argument for government support of industries considered to have strategic or long-term importance to society. According to this argument, the government sponsors or promotes a particular industry through subsidizing or licensing businesses to enter it until it is strong enough to function independently.

For example, the Civil Aeronautics Board was established in 1938, in part, to promote the airline industry at a time before it had become profitable. Similarly, during the oil crisis of the 1970s, the government promoted the synfuel from oil shale industry and solar energy to encourage alternatives to petroleum. This argument for government involvement in selected industries is often connected with national security. Some industries like steel have been protected because steel was considered to be a strategically important material. In defense-related industries, the transfer of strategically important technologies has been regulated by the Department of Defense to assure that national defense would not be weakened by technology transfers. Included in this area have been computer technology, weapon systems, nuclear technology, and knowledge of mathematics that serves as the basis for secret codes.

CONTROL OF "UNFAIR" PRICE DISCRIMINATION

Price discrimination is most often regulated through the Robinson-Patman Act, which is part of antitrust law. However, the economic regulation of industry is also concerned with fair pricing, as the history of the railroads illustrates. The Interstate Commerce Act of 1887 was passed, in part, to prevent large shippers from using their greater economic power to extract lower rates than small shippers could. The ICC was empowered to approve "just and reasonable" railroad rates to protect small towns and small shippers from unjustly higher rates than those enjoyed by those with greater market power.

THE NEED TO ESTABLISH FAIRNESS AMONG DIFFERENT SELLERS

This argument includes situations of (1) cross-subsidization as a competitive tool by large business, and (2) parity in regulations among new and old providers of a good or service.

Cross-Subsidization As a Competitive Weapon

In contrast to the cross-subsidization to assure service to all areas as required by industry regulators discussed above, there are situations in which large businesses use cross-subsidization as a competitive weapon. A popular and profitable product line in which a firm has a strong competitive position can be used to supply resources to subsidize another, weaker product line. Such cross-subsidization by a large, diversified firm can be used to strengthen competitive positions and eliminate or weaken competitors in new markets. If this involves offering products or services below cost through cross-subsidization, then unfair competition can be charged.

Parity in Regulation

Sometimes a new technology or industry develops services similar to an existing regulated industry. In those situations, some argue for the regulation of the new industry so that the competition is fair.

Once the ICC was formed to regulate the railroads, other forms of transportation like trucking and airlines emerged. The railroad industry complained about unfair competition from these other industries that did not face the constraints of regulation. Thus the regulatory authorization of the ICC was extended to trucking, and Civil Aeronautics Board, another agency, was eventually formed to regulate the airlines.

Another example is the regulation of cable television. TV broadcasters had long been regulated, and the networks were fearful of unfair competition at the hands of the newly developing cable TV industry. Thus the FCC sought to achieve parity in regulation by restricting the entry and cross-ownership of programming for cable to level the competitive playing field between network television and the cable television industry. The FCC has restricted the growth of cable for some 30 years using this justification.[14]

Market Failures and Social Regulation

The market failures associated with social regulation include the following:

1. Uninformed or misinformed buyers or sellers
2. Externalities or side effects
3. Discrimination

These market failures lead to social problems and regulations in the areas of honesty in advertising, labeling requirements to inform buyers, product safety, environmental protection, and employment practices.

THE NEED TO PROHIBIT DECEPTIVE ADVERTISING AND PROVIDE FOR INADEQUATE INFORMATION

A necessary condition of a competitive market is knowledgeable buyers and sellers who are presumed to use such knowledge in their own self-interest. If they are misinformed or uninformed owing to insufficient education or lack of technical knowledge, research capabilities, or resources, buyers and sellers cannot make informed decisions in the marketplace. This situation is aggravated if one party takes advantage of the others' lack of knowledge or misinforms the public through deceptive advertising or misrepresenting a product or service.

Social regulations seeks to require adequate information by such measures as (1) requiring labels that specify certain information about product contents or dangers, (2) requiring that calculations such as financial interest charges or measures of contents be standardized and communicated in an understandable manner, and (3) prohibiting deceptive or fraudulent claims about a product or service. The FTC has primary responsibility for regulation of this area.

THE NEED TO CONTROL EXTERNALITIES OR SIDE EFFECTS

One characteristic of a market operating in a socially desirable manner is that all the costs of any transaction be internalized in each transaction. In other words, all costs should be reflected in the price charged the buyer. Figure 11–3 illustrates a hypothetical set of demand and supply curves that show the implications of externalities or social costs.

Market Supply

The market supply S for a product or a service is represented in Figure 11–3 by the distribution of quantities supplied by producers of a particular product at various prices. The supply made available would reflect the cost of producing the product plus a reasonable profit for producers. At lower prices, only a few products would be available in the market, presumably from those businesses with the most efficient cost structures. As prices increased, businesses would be induced to increase their capacity and perhaps other competing businesses would enter the market and create greater supply.

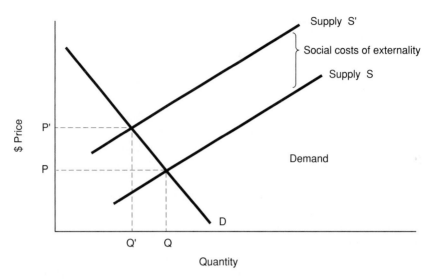

FIGURE 11–3 Social Costs or Externalities of a Market Transaction

Market Demand

The market demand *D* for a product like disposable batteries is represented in Figure 11–3 by a distribution of quantities demanded at each of the prices offered in the market. If prices are lowered, greater quantities of a product will be demanded. For example, as the price of disposable batteries is decreased, many more batteries would be purchased in the market.

Externalities and Social Costs

Note that Figure 11–3 has two supply curves labeled supply *S* and supply *S'*. The difference between *S* and *S'* is *social costs*, which are not internalized in the market exchange. These social costs are typically not considered as a part of the cost of doing business reflected in a market transaction and thus are considered *externalities*.

An example of a social cost is water pollution. If a manufacturing firm discharged waste materials into a river rather than properly disposing of them, the result could be water pollution. This pollution involves toxins that cause illness to those using the river water and kills fish and other river life. To compensate for this externality, the fishing industry would have to cover the costs to stock fish to replace those killed; local communities depending

on the river for its water supply would have to spend extra funds to purify its drinking water; and people using the river for recreation would have the burden of extra medical costs and the suffering of disease caused by the pollution. Meanwhile, the costs experienced by the manufacturer would not include any of these external social costs.

Using Figure 11–3 to interpret the economic effects of the externality, we note that the supply curve *S* would not reflect these social costs. If the social costs could be added to the manufacturing costs, the amount supplied *S'* would be a smaller quantity for each possible market price, as illustrated in Figure 11–3.

Market Price

In a competitive market the market price is subject to the forces of supply and demand and thus the equilibrium market price in Figure 11–3 is the price P where the quantity supplied *S* equals the quantity demanded *D* of a particular product or service. Note that if all costs related to a transaction, including social costs, were charged for a product, *S'* in Figure 11–3 would reflect the market supply for a given product. Thus, price P would be the market price that *does not* consider the social costs of externalities and price P' would represent the price that *does include* the social cost of the market exchange.

CASE EXAMPLE OF EXTERNALITIES: DISPOSABLE BATTERIES IN JAPAN

Another example of an externality is disposable batteries. Portable consumer electronic equipment and many children's toys require batteries. Most batteries for consumer electronic products are disposable, and thus are discarded after being used. The consumer replaces them with a new set of batteries and begins the cycle of use and disposal all over again. These disposable batteries contain toxic substances that, if disposed of in sufficient quantities, pollute water systems and soil in landfills. Thus, the cost of appropriately disposing of these batteries is a social cost external to the market transaction.

Japan, a country in which land is relatively scarce, has recognized this externality in the market exchange involving batteries. If the cost of disposing of toxic batteries were *not* included in the price of batteries quantity Q would be purchased at price P in Figure 11–3. If the externality of the social cost *were* included in the price, the price would rise to price P', but the relevant supply curve should be supply S' and thus the quantity demanded would be Q'.

In other words, the tax on batteries causes the quantity supplied automatically to be less, and the price would also automatically be adjusted higher to price P' if the externality of waste disposal costs could be incorporated into the transaction costs for the product. Thus social regulation can take advantage of the invisible hand of the market by cooperating with its underlying principles. Alternatively, regulations can be developed that ignore market forces and have implications for greater compliance costs and different levels of effectiveness.

To control this externality, the government of Japan charges a tax, estimated to be the incremental social cost, on each battery sold. The government regulates the disposal of these batteries and publicly funds this disposal process from the taxes charged from the sale of the batteries. The Japan-

ese government could have used other approaches to social regulation, for example, (1) prohibiting the sale of disposable batteries and requiring that all batteries be rechargeable, (2) requiring a deposit on all batteries that is refundable when they are returned to the store or to a recycling center, (3) establishing standards for all electric equipment to reduce the consumption of batteries because of the harmful social effects of batteries.

Other examples of externalities abound, and mention of the smoking issue may also illustrate the concept. Secondary smoke inhaled by non-smokers causes cancer and heart disease. This cost is born by the nonsmoker in the form of higher medical and insurance costs and a decreased quality of life that is hard to quantify. The government has taxed cigarettes and required warning labels to protect smokers, and smoking has been prohibited in public places to regulate this externality.

A Historical Overview of Government Regulation

Although the market failure arguments outlined above provide a rationale for economic regulation of industry, regulation developed within the context of history. Before the Civil War, the United States could be characterized as a rural society with an economy dominated by small towns and small businesses. The American frontier and the settling of the West emphasized the ideology of rugged individualism with its self-reliance, free markets, and minimal government activity. Early government activity centered around promoting the development of business rather than regulating its behavior. In the 1700s government subsidized the development of an extensive canal system in the East, and in the 1800s encouraged the development of the railroads by offering the incentive of large land grants to builders of the railroads. Also, homestead laws opened the American frontier and encouraged farmers to settle in the West.

With the Civil War period, 1861–65, came the rapid development of the railroads that linked the

United States into a single large market. Shortly afterward came large-scale enterprises like the railroads and the oil, chemicals, aluminum, and steel industries, which began to dominate the economic landscape. Urbanization and large-circulation newspapers provided the opportunity for mass markets connected by a network of railroads that could transport products nationwide from centralized production facilities. Businesses that were national in scope became economically possible.

ECONOMIC REGULATION
OF THE RAILROADS

The behavior of the railroads tested the ideology of market-oriented individualism and illustrates an early example of the control cycle. Railroads were heavily subsidized by the government through the granting of alternating sections of land along the track. This land helped to attract investors, and soon railroads were both rich and politically powerful. With their new-found market power, the railroads began to set freight rates as they pleased—to the dismay of farmers.[15] This abuse of market power led to political controversy.

Farmers responded by forming the National Grange of the Patrons of Husbandry in 1867. The Grange, a populist movement of farm interests, successfully lobbied several state legislators to regulate freight rates. In the eastern United States, the canal system offered an alternative to the railroads, and this competition effectively regulated freight rates through market forces. Thus there was little justification or political support for rigorous state-level regulation in the Eastern states. In the West, where there was no adequate substitute for the railroads, railroad companies had a great deal of market power. State legislatures in the West responded to the interest group pressure from the Grange by regulating railroads operating in their respective states. Thus, there was much variation in the existence and extent of state regulation of railroads between the Eastern and Western states.

Railroads continued to ignore the public outcry for reasonable freight rates and sued the state of Illinois, which was trying to control railroad rates through state-level regulation. This case paved the way for federal regulation in 1886, when the Supreme Court ruled in the *Wabash, St. Louis and Pacific Railway v. Illinois* case that freedom of commerce could be seriously harmed if a railroad faced different regulations in different states.[16] States were therefore not allowed to regulate enterprises predominately engaged in interstate commerce. Though the railroads won this case, it strengthened the resolve of the farmers in the Grange in their press for federal regulation because of the possibility of obtaining federal regulation implied by the Supreme Court decision. Farmers succeeded in obtaining federal legislation regulating the railroad industry.

The Interstate Commerce Act of 1887 and the formation of the ICC marked a major change toward government regulation of business. It was designed to control a single industry with a government agency rather than relying on market forces. This change was to have far-reaching implications for the dominant political philosophy in the country, and it served to reshape the role of government. This law clearly established regulation as an alternative to market forces in the control cycle of business within our market-oriented society:

> In 1887, President Grover Cleveland signed the Interstate Commerce Act, federal legislation designed to reduce private railroad power through government action. The ICC, the first independent federal regulatory commission, was empowered to set reasonable railroad rates, protect consumers from price discrimination, force the posting of rates, and prohibit a variety of anticompetitive practices.
>
> The establishment of the ICC was truly a landmark in economic regulation. With its commissioners appointed by the president and confirmed by the Senate, the ICC became a model for the structure of future agencies. Isolated from immediate pressures, commission members were given quasi-judicial power to determine a variety of policies. At last, politicians and consumers thought they had created a way to tame a huge industry that had removed itself from the public interest. In effecting this policy, government leaders abandoned the market as the best mechanism

for defining key economic and political values. Moreover, they had set a standard by which subsequent economic crises might be resolved by government regulatory responses.[17]

THE PROGRESSIVE ERA, 1887–1916

The Progressive Era was a social and political reform movement responding to the perceived anticompetitive abuses of large-scale business. After the Interstate Commerce Act of 1887, several more laws were passed and new regulatory agencies and commissions were formed, as shown in Table 11–2. This period marked the emergence of a new political ideology that recognized the role of government in remedying market failures. This development was sponsored by the administrations of popular and activist presidents including Woodrow Wilson and Theodore Roosevelt.

The laws passed during the progressive era recognized the limited role of government in the control of business in a market-oriented society. This role included (1) the reestablishment of competitive conditions in the case of antitrust law, and (2) complementing economic forces or the substitution of regulation for ineffective competition in specific industries. These were both aspects of economic regulation. The models of economic regulation developed in this era were later extended to other industries, including radio, television, telecommunications, trucking, and airlines.

Although there were several key laws passed during the Progressive Era to control business behavior, the government's intrusion into the economic sphere was limited to certain industries and decision areas. The enforcement of these economic laws and regulations was at the discretion of agency administrators and was subject to the political ideologies of those in control of government. The 1920s was a period of strong economic growth and control of both Congress and the presidency by the Republican Party, which favored probusiness policies. The dominant ideology expounded (1) an individualistic political philosophy, (2) belief in the market as an efficient, self-correcting control mechanism that assured the continued prosperity of the nation, and (3) belief in a low level of government interference in the economic affairs of business.

During this last decade of the Progressive Era there was widespread speculation in the stock market. Margin requirements for purchase of stocks were very low. Many investors borrowed heavily, rather than rely on personal resources, to take advantage of the opportunities for instant wealth in stocks. Wealth, however, was enjoyed by those already wealthy rather than by workers. Also, agriculture had been in a state of recession for most of the 1920s. Though the prosperity of the 1920s was "thinly distributed," weaknesses were not clearly visible and everything seemed to be going well until "Black Thursday," October 24, 1929, when the stock market crashed. Everything quickly collapsed like a house of cards.

THE NEW DEAL, 1932–39

The collapse of the stock market began the Great Depression of the 1930s, which challenged the traditional beliefs about the capacity of the free market to correct itself. The economic collapse that followed the stock market crash resulted in thousands of foreclosures on farms, homes, and other properties in the next few years. Unemployment rose to 25 percent and soup kitchens sprang up throughout the country to feed the many hungry or unemployed.

Those with savings deposits in banks feared their savings were not secure and tried to withdraw their savings. These bank runs led to hundreds of bank failures. Normally banks kept only a small percentage of total deposits on hand as cash. Deposits were used to make loans to businesses and consumers. Depositors trusted the bank to safeguard their money, and banks had sufficient cash to meet the withdrawal demands of customers during normal conditions. The bank panic that followed the 1929 crash became self-fulfilling prophecy because many strong and well-managed banks could not withstand the panic withdrawals of depositors.

TABLE 11–2
Federal Economic Regulation of Industries Established During the Progressive Era

Enactment Date of First-named Regulatory Body	Agency/Location	Regulatory Role
1887	Interstate Commerce Commission (independent agency)	Control over rates, entry, and exit in railways, road haulage, buses, inland waterways, and other related activities.
1890	Department of Justice (Executive Branch) and Federal Trade Commission (FTC) established 1914 (independent)	Enforced antitrust laws against monopoly and anticompetitive behavior.
1914	Clayton Antitrust Act	Amended and plugged loopholes in the Sherman Act.
1914	Federal Trade Commission Act (formed the FTC—independent)	FTC authorized to enforce antitrust laws and to regulate deceptive advertising.
1916	Federal Reserve Board (independent) and Securities and Exchange Commission (SEC is in the Executive Branch, founded 1933)	Control of margin requirements in securities dealing, supervision of security dealing on stock exchanges, and supervision of public utility holding companies.
1916	United States Shipping Board (ultimately replaced in 1961 by the independent Federal Maritime Commission)	Control of rates and service frequency of transocean freight shipments.
1920	Federal Power Commission (replaced in 1977 by the Federal Energy Regulatory Commission in the Department of Energy)	Regulation of wellhead price of natural gas and wholesale price of natural gas and electricity sold for resale in interstate commerce.
1927	Federal Radio Commission (1934—Federal Communications Commission)	Regulation of entry and price of telephone and telegraph service. Extended into radio and television broadcasting and telecommunications.
1938	Civil Aeronautics Authority (1940—Civil Aeronautics Board)	Control over entry, exit, rates, and mergers in air transport, both passenger and freight. Also extended to international operations.

And there was no way for banks to gain quick access to cash to reassure depositors that the bank was safe when these depositors were already fearful of the general economic collapse. The Federal Reserve Bank, already in existence at the time, pursued a restrictive monetary policy that added momentum to the banking collapse.[18]

Economic conditions became so bad that many questioned the assumption that the invisible hand of the market was self-correcting. The traditional, individualistic market-oriented ideology was challenged seriously by more and more people who despaired of the economic situation. As the presidential election of 1932 approached, public confidence in the market, in the existing government administration, and in the traditional ideology were badly shaken. A new ideology of an activist government began to take shape.

Franklin D. Roosevelt was elected president. Using the metaphor of a card game, he promised the people a "new deal" and ran on the platform of radical reform. His landslide victory provided him with the legitimacy to press the government into a much more activist role in the economy. The result was a new wave of economic regulation lasting until the end of the decade.

The National Recovery Administration (NRA), established by the National Industrial Recovery Act, was to serve as the central instrument for New Deal programs. It was administered by the NRA, which enforced codes of fair compensation, minimum wages, maximum hours of work, and child-labor laws. Each industry had its own set of NRA guidelines developed with input by labor unions and trade associations. A controversy soon developed when a poultry business was found to be selling sick chickens in violation of the regulation. The Schechter Poultry Corporation of New York City was covered by the NRA's Live Poultry Code, which forbade the sale of chickens ill with tuberculosis and other diseases. Schechter sued on the grounds that it sold chickens only in local New York City markets and was not a part of interstate commerce.[19]

The Supreme Court unanimously ruled in favor of Schechter Poultry and found that the NRA was an unconstitutional delegation of legislative power. In this law, the Supreme Court ruled that Congress had granted the president what the Court considered "virtually unfettered" power to regulate industries. While the Court did suggest that local commerce, which had a direct effect on interstate commerce, could be regulated by the federal government, in this case, the chickens in question were grown and sold solely within New York State.

In this decision, the Supreme Court dealt a major blow to the Roosevelt administration's program of economic reform and recovery. President Roosevelt was so angered by the decision that he sent a plan to Congress in 1937 to reform the court system. Part of this plan would be a constitutional amendment to add six more justices to the Court. With six more positions, the president would be able to appoint judges sympathetic to his administration and overturn the Court's decision. There was a public outcry at Roosevelt's attempt to undermine the Constitution and the power of the Supreme Court, and the plan was never enacted.

However, shortly after the president's attempt to pack the court, another important case found its way to the Court that was to reaffirm the activist approach of the New Deal. The National Labor Relations Act had established the National Labor Relations Board (NLRB) to regulate unfair labor practices. The NLRB attempted to regulate labor practices at the Aliquippa plant in Pennsylvania of the Jones and Laughlin Steel Company. Jones and Laughlin, the fourth-largest steel producer in the United States at the time, had suffered huge losses in the Depression and had a long history of bitter conflicts with labor. The steel company had refused to recognize the rights of employees to organize a union and had fired union organizers. When the NLRB considered these actions to be unfair labor practices, Jones and Laughlin argued that the NLRB did not have the right to regulate the plant because it was a local activity not subject to the interstate commerce clause of the Constitution.

The resulting dispute was resolved by the Supreme Court, in a 5-4 split decision, which found in favor of the NLRB. The Court found that (1) although the plant produced steel locally, the activities of the Pennsylvania facility affected interstate commerce and was subject to the interstate commerce clause, and (2) Congress had the right to delegate its constitutional right to regulate interstate commerce to the NLRB.[20] This decision was a reversal of the prohibition against congressional delegation of enforcement power to independent regulatory agencies and extended the definition of interstate commerce.

The Banking System

The Glass-Steagall Act established the Federal Deposit Insurance Corporation (FDIC), which guaranteed bank deposits so depositors would regain confidence in the banks. This also involved government oversight over bank operations by the Federal Reserve Board, including audits and regulations. The Banking Act of 1936 revised the Federal Reserve and provided a mechanism to help troubled banks and to regulate the money supply and interest rates through monetary policy. Deposits were guaranteed by the government; if a run on a bank should occur, cash would be supplied by the Federal Reserve to cover withdrawals; and banks were thereafter regularly audited by Federal Reserve Board examiners.

Securities Exchange

The Securities and Exchange Commission (SEC) was formed to regulate the exchange of public securities. Margin requirements were increased to discourage the wild speculation that had led to the crash of 1929. Also, there are extensive financial reporting requirements that must be met by all publically traded companies, including annual financial reports publicly available and the 10-K report filed with the SEC.

The regulations of the SEC have evolved since the New Deal era. Insider trading is prohibited in an attempt to assure that stock market dealing is fair. Reporting requirements changed during the hostile takeover decade of the 1980s. When a person or a business attempts to acquire another corporation, a special report must be filed with the

SEC within a ten-day period when 5 percent or more of the stock is acquired. Thus, the financial community now has better information to evaluate the relative risk involved in an investment.

Employment Practices

The NLRB was established to regulate employment practices. The Fair Labor Standards Act also served to define the standards to be enforced by the NLRB, including the use of child labor, minimum wages, and working hours. Labor laws passed later protected the right of labor to organize.

Government As Guarantor of Employment

The Works Progress Administration (WPA) and the Civilian Conservation Corps (CCC) were both formed to administer public service job programs to provide employment. Thus the government was to be the employer of last resort if the overall market failed to assure the prosperity of the country. Full employment was to become a national goal for which the government became responsible.

Even though Roosevelt's attempt to pack the Supreme Court failed, in the end, the economic regulation of the New Deal period was found to be constitutional. By 1939 the role of the government had been substantially revised, as shown by Table 11–3, which outlines the many laws passed and agencies formed during the New Deal period. The public now looked upon the government as the ultimate guarantor of the financial system and the employer of last resort, and responsible for taking action to bring about a recovery during economic downturns. Government was sanctioned as the sphere responsible for the prosperity and stability of the economy, and trust in the self-correcting forces of market competition was no longer acceptable to the public.[21]

This regulatory wave of the New Deal era ended with the growing concern over the war in Europe and ultimately the entry of the United States into World War II. The postwar period, dominated by the Cold War and a Republican administration for most of the 1950s, tempered the increasing role of the government in the economy. The New Deal

TABLE 11–3
Government Regulation of Business Established During the New Deal Period, 1933–1939

Year Established	Law/Agency	Location	Regulatory Role
1933	Glass-Steagall Act established the Federal Deposit Insurance Corporation	Independent (FDIC)	Federal government guarantees deposits and regulates banks.
1933	Department of Agriculture/ Agricultural Adjustment Act	Executive (DOA)	Farm subsidies and price supports.
1935	Banking Act of 1935	Independent Federal Reserve Bank	Changes the structure and extends the role of the Federal Reserve System in controlling the currency and in providing safeguards against bank failure.
1935	National Labor Relations Board (NLRB)/National Labor Relations Act	Independent	Enforces fair labor practices.
1933 & 1934	Securities and Exchange Commission (SEC), established by the Securities Acts of 1933 and 1934	Independent	Control of margin requirements, supervision of security dealing on stock exchanges.
1935	Social Security Act/ Administered by Social Security Administration within Department of Health and Human Services	Executive (HHS)	FICA tax withholding for retirement benefits, including pension and medical care.
1935	Works Progress Administration	Independent	Public works jobs during the Depression.
1935	Civilian Conservation Corps	Independent	Public works jobs for youth during the Depression.
1938	Fair Labor Standards Act/ Administered by Department of Labor	Executive (DOL)	Regulates minimum wage law, maximum hours, child labor laws.

period laid the groundwork for the wave of social regulation that was to come in the 1960s.

THE RISE OF SOCIAL REGULATION, 1964–75

The 1960s and 1970s were marked by a tidal wave of social regulation. For a measure of the magnitude of increase in the number of regulations, one can check the number of pages per year printed in the *Federal Register*. In the agency process, discussed in the last chapter, all new proposed regulations as well as their final versions must be published in the *Federal Register*. Thus the number of pages in this publication can be used as an indirect measure of the amount of regulations passed at any time. In 1960, the *Federal Register* was 9,562 pages long; by 1980 it had grown to 74,120 pages—a 675 percent increase!

Another way to quantify new regulation is the number of new regulatory agencies created; according to this measure, agencies increased from 27 in 1959 to 32 by 1969 and to 54 by 1979.[22] During these two decades ending in 1980, over one hundred new laws were passed by Congress and 22 new regulatory agencies were established.

Table 11–4 lists the major social regulations and regulatory agencies in the United States. With the exception of the FDA, which was established in 1906, and the FTC, established in 1915 during the Progressive Era, all the major agencies mandated to enforce social regulation were created during the two decades before 1980.

FORCES DRIVING THE SOCIAL REGULATION MOVEMENT

Many factors, both social and historical, brought about the rise of social regulation that began in the 1960s. Bertozzi and Burgunder offer a number of reasons for the sharp increase in social regulations, including the political environment, interest group activity, economic prosperity, the education level of society, mass communication technology, and technological advances that made it possible to measure the environmental effects of business activity.[23]

1. *Political environment.* The decade of the 1960s began with the inspiring administration of President John Kennedy, a charismatic leader, who said, "Think not what your country can do for you but what you can do for your country." This line, characterizing a new ideology, inspired the youthful idealism of a generation and attracted many capable young people into government service. After Kennedy's assassination, President Lyndon Johnson and the majority of Congress were ideologically the most liberal administration since Franklin D. Roosevelt's administration. Thus, the political environment was favorable for an activist government protecting the public from social problems perceived as being caused by business.

2. *Public interest groups.* Although the United States has always had many interest groups in its pluralistic society, interest groups during the 1960s were particularly well organized and active in monitoring government regulation of business. Interest groups formed around such issues as civil rights, the environment, consumer issues of product safety, and honesty in advertising. These interest groups did not trust market forces to accomplish their goals and sought government intervention through social regulation.

On the other hand, most businesses were type-one (reactive and defensive) or, at best, type-two (anticipatory and responsible) in institutional orientation, and thus were not proactive in the public policy process. Business interests, once mobilized, were an important factor in the deregulation movement that began in the late 1970s and in the election of a more conservative administration in the 1980s that sought vigorously to deregulate and to bring about regulatory reform (as discussed in Chapter 12).

3. *Public concern over quality-of-life issues.* The post–World War II period was marked by unprecedented prosperity in the United States. With high per capita income, low unemployment rates, increasing leisure time, and a shortened work week for most Americans, public interest turned to quality-of-life issues like the environment. During this period, the United States was the unquestioned leader in international competitiveness and

TABLE 11–4
Major Social Regulatory Agencies in the United States

Year Established	Law/Agency	Location	Regulatory Role
1906 (1931)	Food and Drug Administration (formerly Bureau of Chemistry in Agriculture Dept.) (FDA)	Executive Branch (Health and Human Services)	Protects public against unsafe, impure, and ineffective drugs and medical services, and to regulate hazards in foods, cosmetics, and radiation devices.
1964	Equal Employment and Opportunity Commission (EEOC)	Independent Commission	Investigates charges of job discrimination. Equal Pay and Civil Rights Acts were passed in 1963 and 1974, respectively.
1966	National Highway Executive Traffic Safety Agency (NHTSA) (formerly National Highway Safety Agency, 1966–1970)	Executive Branch (Department of Transportation)	Setting of motor vehicle safety and fuel economy standards.
1970	Environmental Protection Agency (EPA)	Executive Branch	Enforces environmental protection. Series of acts passed between 1965 and 1972 dealing with air, water, and noise pollution and automobile emissions.
1972	Consumer Product Safety Commission (CPSC)	Independent Commission	Setting of consumer product safety standards.
1973	Occupational Safety and Health Administration (OSHA)	Executive Branch (Department of Labor)	Sets and enforces workers' health and safety regulations.

had the highest productivity in the world, and corporate profits reflected high levels of performance. Confidence in continued prosperity and the concern for quality-of-life issues translated into political pressure to control the market to regulate the effects of business on the environment, quality of work life and workplace safety, and consumer concerns.

4. *Educational level of society.* The educational level of society grew dramatically during the postwar period. Soldiers returning from the Korean War in the early 1950s were eligible for the G.I. Bill, which entitled them to a college education paid for by the government. This promoted the rapid growth of higher education that was sustained by the increasing levels of prosperity. As the economy grew there was an incentive to seek more education to qualify for increasing opportunities. Also, increasing levels of education were highly correlated with interest in quality-of-life issues in society.

5. *Mass communication technology.* The growth of network television and the portable transistor radio facilitated the widespread knowledge of public events. This sharply accelerated the public policy process, because the rate of public awareness of social trends and problems increased sharply. For example, the news media was an important factor in exposing the injustices of discrimination. Television news vividly showed police using dogs and fire hoses on civil rights demonstrators. These news reports on the Civil Rights Movement helped create sympathy, heightened public awareness of the plight of minorities, and persuaded many that the government needed to do more to protect the civil rights of minorities.

6. *Books and documentary accounts.* As Chapter 10 noted, a number of books have played an instrumental role in getting issues on the public policy agenda that has resulted in the social regulation of business. This began at the turn of the century with Upton Sinclair's *The Jungle* (1905), a novel about the unhealthy conditions in the Chicago meat-packing industry. This book, and others of the muckraker era, resulted in the Meat Inspection Act of 1906, which established regulations of the meat-packing industry and the requirement of federal inspections in meat processing plants. Also, this book was an impetus for the formation of the Food and Drug Administration.

In 1962, Rachel Carson's scientific documentary, *Silent Spring*, heightened awareness of the dangers of pesticides that led to the formation of the Environmental Protection Agency. In 1965, Ralph Nader's *Unsafe at Any Speed* documented the safety problems of the Corvair automobile and characterized the manufacturer, General Motors, as unconcerned about automotive safety. This book informed the public about the automobile safety issue and led to the establishment of the National Highway Traffic Safety Administration.

7. *Technological advances.* These made it possible to measure pollution in the environment or toxic substances in products or in the workplace. Because it was technologically impossible to measure the effects of pollution, toxins, pesticides, and industrial chemicals before the 1960s, regulation was really not possible until this time. With precise measurements, standards, and engineering capabilities, environmental regulation became technically feasible, albeit a more specific and more costly approach of social regulation.

8. *Civil Rights Movement.* The Civil Rights Movement began in Birmingham, Alabama, in the early 1960s when Rosa Parks, a black woman, refused to obey the law and move to the back of a city bus. The bus driver drove the bus to the city hall, where she was arrested and jailed for not obeying the "Jim Crow" laws of the day. This arrest sparked a protest and a boycott of city buses led by a young black minister, Martin Luther King, Jr., who went on to lead demonstrations and boycotts of buses, businesses, and other facilities that practiced discrimination throughout the country. This movement ultimately led to the passage of the Equal Pay Act of 1963 and the Civil Rights Act of 1964 and the formation of the Equal Employment Opportunity Commission (EEOC) in 1972.

Government Regulation and the Management of Business

It should be clear from the earlier sections of the chapter that government regulation applies to virtually every aspect of business operations, as suggested by Table 11–5. Social regulation had been applied to every major business function including production and operations, finance, human

TABLE 11–5
Operational Decisions and Regulatory Constraints

Business Function	Decision Area	Governmental Body or Legislation
Production	Material Selection	OSHA, EPA, CPSC
	Plant Layout	OSHA
	Plant Location	EPA and Corps of Engineers
	Quality Control	CPSC
	Energy Utilization	DOE
	Production Tasks	OSHA and EPA
	Waste Materials	EPA
Marketing	Price	FTC and Department of Justice
	Promotion (Labeling and Advertising)	FTC
	Place (Distribution and Packaging)	FTC and CPSC
	Product (Recall and Liability)	FTC, CPSC, EPA, and NHTSA
Research and Development	Process Design	OSHA, EPA, DOE
	Production Design	CPSC, FTC, DOE, and EPA
Finance	Investment, Financing, and Dividends Public Disclosures	SEC
Accounting	Financial Standards	SEC
	Cost Standards	Cost Accounting Standards Board (in government contracts)
Personnel	Selection and Retention	EEOC, OFCC, and NLRB
	Employee Development	EEOC, OFCC, and NLRB
	Rewards	EEOC, NLRB, and ERISA
	Health and Safety	OSHA

Key to Regulatory Agencies:

CPSC—Consumer Product Safety Commission
DOE—Department of Energy
EEOC—Equal Employment Opportunity Commission
ERISA—Employee Retirement Income Security Act
EPA—Environmental Protection Agency
FTC—Federal Trade Commission
NHTSA—National Highway Traffic Safety Administration
NLRB—National Labor Relations Board
OFCC—Office of Federal Contract Compliance
OSHA—Occupational Safety and Health Administration
SEC—Securities and Exchange Commission

SOURCE: Henry A. Tombari, *Business and Society: Strategies for the Environment and Public Policy* (New York: CBS College Publishing, 1984), p. 439.

resource management, marketing, and logistics. Within these functions most major decisions that management make are constrained by one or more regulatory agencies and many regulations. Also, the development at the federal level was mirrored by a rapid growth in state and local levels of regulation. The public response to social issues and the failures and limitations of market forces was comprehensive.

The legal profession became a key background for successful executives in most industries as the legal environment and public policy continued to increase in strategic importance. Attention to government controls often took priority over attention to customers and to the moves of competitors by many business managers. The task of knowing and complying with all the complex and often conflicting regulations was more than many lower-level managers and other employees could accomplish.

Regulations were increasingly perceived as adding significantly to business costs, lowering business responsiveness to markets, lowering employee productivity, and adversely affecting the international competitiveness of American business. There was a growing sense that there was now too much government intervention in the economic sphere. Questions about the cost-benefit relationships of government regulation were made by increasing numbers of decision makers. Research began to appear about the high cost of regulation.[24]

By 1975 there was growing criticism of federal and state regulation of business, and a concern was developing about regulatory failure. This concern about the high cost and possible negative consequences of regulation led to two developments: (1) a movement of regulatory reform and deregulation beginning in 1975, and (2) the emergence of the strategic management of public issues by business leaders. The criticisms of government regulation of business, approaches to regulatory reform, and the deregulation movement are the subjects of Chapter 12. A framework for how business can strategically manage public issues was discussed in Chapter 3.

Summary

Society is always changing as technology, cultural values, lifestyles, and expectations change. These changes often cause problems that only slowly come to the awareness of the general public. When public issues become a major concern to a substantial number of people, the control cycle begins.

The control cycle includes social change or a perceived failure in market competition leading to general awareness of the public problem and a controversy over how to deal with it. The controversy is handled within the context of the public policy process and ends with the government laws and regulations of business.

The government laws and regulations that control the economic sphere include (1) antitrust law that seeks to maintain or to restore competitive conditions to markets and to prohibit anticompetitive behavior, (2) economic regulation of specific industries, (3) social regulation of business functions, and (4) litigation that resolves conflicts arising out of the legal and regulatory environment.

Markets fail to be self-correcting when the necessary conditions for competition are missing. These failures can occur when (1) there is too little competition because of market power or barriers to entry, (2) businesses engage in anticompetitive behavior that constrains free exchanges, (3) competition is unstable or destructive, (4) buyers or sellers are uninformed or misinformed about market conditions and opportunities, (5) externalities or side effects cause undesirable social costs, and/or (6) arbitrary discrimination exists in employment practices.

The regulatory response to market structures that have insufficient competition or when anticompetitive behavior exists is antitrust law. Section 2 of the Sherman Antitrust Act of 1890 deals with market structure and prohibits mergers or acquisitions that tend to monopolize markets. Section 1 of this law deals with conspiracies in constraint of trade and anticompetitive behavior like price fixing and predation.

When competition is considered destructive, unstable, or otherwise undesirable, the regulatory response is the economic regulation of specific industries like public utilities, railroads, trucking, airlines, radio and television, and telecommunications. Government agencies formed to regulate these industries control who is allowed to compete (that is, entry), price levels, and service standards.

The major justifications for economic regulation of industries include (1) the natural monopoly argument, (2) the need for the government to provide a nonmarket avenue for customer complaints, (3) unfair windfall profits, (4) destructive competition that leads to boom-and-bust cycles, (5) cross-subsidy of certain areas when normal market forces would not provide these services, and (6) the need to control unfair discrimination when some industries are regulated and others are not. Thus airlines and trucking were initially regulated because of complaints from the already regulated railroad industry.

Social regulation is used to regulate business when market failures lead to quality-of-life or social problems like discrimination, pollution, unsafe jobs or products, misrepresentation, or uninformed customers. The market failures associated with social regulation include (1) uninformed buyers and sellers, (2) social costs due to externalities or side effects of market exchanges, and (3) discrimination in employment or in providing services to minorities.

Before the Progressive Era, the traditional ideology of rugged individualism, laissez-faire government, and free-market competition dominated American political and economic thought. With the advent of big business and abuses of power, this ideology began to be challenged. These challenges took the form of three successive waves of regulation: (1) the Progressive Era (1887–1916), (2) the New Deal period (1933–39), and (3) the rise of social regulation (1964–75).

The role of the government was changed during the Progressive Era to include the control of power abuses in selected industries by economic regulation of entry, freight rates, and service standards.

Also, the government, through antitrust law, sought to restore competitive market structures and to prohibit anticompetitive behavior.

The New Deal era began after the stock market crash of 1929 that was followed by the collapse of the economy in the Great Depression.

The traditional ideology and the assumption that the market was self-correcting and would automatically end the Depression were discredited by its magnitude and length. Franklin Roosevelt, who campaigned with the offer of a New Deal, was elected president in 1932. He championed a comprehensive program of economic recovery spearheaded by an activist government. A number of regulatory changes were introduced: (1) the Federal Reserve Board had expanded powers and responsibilities for the banking system; (2) the Securities and Exchange Commission regulated margin requirements for stock purchases, the disclosure of financial information, and the exchange of financial securities; (3) the National Labor Relations Board guaranteed the right of workers to unionize and regulated employment practices; (4) the Social Security system was launched that provided a retirement program for most workers; (5) several programs to employ people in public jobs were launched that made the government the employer of last resort; and (6) government spending and monetary policy were used to control the overall economic climate. The government, not the self-correcting forces of the free market, became responsible for the economic conditions of the country.

By 1939, there were clearly two competing economic and political ideologies in the Unites States. The concepts of individual responsibility and market forces had been challenged by the concepts of community membership and individual rights supported by an activist government. The economic role of the government was extended well beyond the earlier limits of the Progressive Era. The targeted control of specific industries and companies through agency regulation had been substantially expanded. The use of macroeconomic approaches to regulating the overall economic climate was well established.

After nearly two decades of postwar prosperity, a third wave of government regulation began in 1963. Many factors, both social and historical, brought about the rise of social regulation, including the political environment, interest group activity, economic prosperity, the education level of society, mass communication technology, and technological advances that made it possible to measure the environmental effects of business activity.

Several social movements, each focusing on a particular type of issue, mobilized their efforts and successfully pushed to enact social legislation related to their issue, to form new government agencies, and to implement these new regulations.

Conclusions

In a pluralistic society, there are and should be competing values, competing ideologies, and competing interest groups. Effective markets require the necessary conditions of competition.

All spheres of our threefold society need to function if high levels of social and business performance are to be achieved. The business control cycle has been very active for this past century and a quarter. Market failures do occur and there are many regulatory responses for each type of response that this chapter has cataloged. Our society has evolved into a mixed system—it is not entirely market-oriented nor is it centrally planned.

By 1975, virtually every aspect of business was extensively regulated. Most major decisions in the functional areas of (1) marketing, (2) manufacturing, production and operations, (3) human resource management and employment, (4) finance, and (5) logistics were regulated by one or more government agencies. Each of the laws, government agencies, and regulations exercising control over business had a plausible rationale for its existence and responded to the public policy issues that appeared in a historical context.

Moreover, the role of government had been expanded to include guarantor of the banking system, employer of last resort, insurer of last resort, and guarantor of the overall economic prosperity of the country. But governmental action is also problematic. The 1800s demonstrated that big business can abuse power. This century may have demonstrated that the solution of government regulation needs to be provide a balance between economic performance and the protection of citizens from market failure.

Discussion Questions

1. Briefly describe the control cycle leading to regulation. Discuss a current example of this cycle, drawing facts from a current newspaper or magazine.
2. What are the major types of market failures? How are these failures related to the types of government regulation?
3. Describe the three major waves of government regulation. How was the role of government changed with each of these regulatory waves?
4. How does economic regulation differ from social regulation with respect to their relative effect on managerial discretion, government costs to administer, and business costs to comply?
5. What is the constitutional authority of government regulation of business? How is this interpreted by the Supreme Court?
6. One argument for economic regulation is that the government needs to control destructive or unstable competition. Which industries have been regulated according to this argument? Is the argument valid? Explain your position.
7. How does the economic regulation of the New Deal period differ form the economic regulation of the Progressive Era?
8. What historical events led to the revision of the traditional ideology that opposed government interference in economic processes?
9. What major operations or activities of business are now subject to regulation?

Notes

1. Jonathan R. T. Hughes, *The Government Habit: Economic Controls from Colonial Times to the Present* (New York: Basic Books, 1977).

2. Robert G. Harris and James M. Carman, "The Political Economy of Regulation: An Analysis of Market Failures," in *Scaling the Corporate Wall,* ed. S. Prakash Sethi, Paul Steidlmeier, and Cecilia M. Falbe (Englewood Cliffs, N.J.: Prentice-Hall, 1987), pp. 24–35.

3. Dennis Swann, *The Retreat of the State: Deregulation and Privatization in the UK and US* (Ann Arbor: University of Michigan Press, 1988).

4. For example, see Richard Caves, *American Industry: Structure, Conduct, Performance,* 4th ed. (Englewood Cliffs, N.J.: Prentice-Hall, 1977); and Joe Bain, *Industrial Organization* (New York: Wiley, 1959).

5. Donald J. Boudreaux, "Turning Back the Antitrust Clock: Nonprice Predation in Theory and Practice," *Regulation* 13, no. 3 (Fall 1990): 45–52.

6. Thomas J. DiLorenzo, "The Origins of Antitrust: Rhetoric vs. Reality, *Regulation* 13, no. 3 (Fall 1990): 26–34; and Lino A. Graglia, "One Hundred Years of Antitrust," *Public Interest,* no. 104 (Summer 1991): 50–66.

7. See Emil Friberg and Cecilia Thomas, "Is Antitrust Obsolete?" *Journal of Economic Issues* 25, no. 2 (June 1991): 617–24; and Walter Adams, James W. Brock, and Norman P. Obst, "Pareto Optimality and Antitrust Policy: The Old Chicago and the New Learning," *Southern Economic Journal* 58, no. 1 (July 1991): 1–14.

8. Murray L. Weidenbaum, "The Changing Nature of Government Regulation of Business," paper presented to the AACSB Conference on Business Environment/Government Regulation of Business (Summer 1979), Washington D.C. Also see Murray L. Weidenbaum and Robert De Fina, *The Rising Cost of Government Regulation* (St. Louis: Washington University Center for the Study of American Business, 1977).

9. Murray L. Weidenbaum, *Business, Government, and the Public* (Englewood Cliffs, N.J.: Prentice-Hall, 1977).

10. Douglas F. Greer, *Business, Government, and Society,* 2d ed. (New York: Macmillan, 1982), pp. 274–82.

11. Robert Stobaugh and Daniel Yergin, *Energy Future* (New York: Random House, 1979), p. 217.

12. Swann, *Retreat of the State,* chaps. 1 and 2.

13. Donald L. Barlett and James B. Steele, *America: What Went Wrong?* (Kansas City, Mo.: Andrews and McMeel, 1992), chap. 6.

14. Greer, *Business, Government, and Society,* 2d ed. (New York: Macmillan, 1987), pp. 280–81.

15. Larry N. Gerston, Cynthia Fraleigh, and Robert Schwab, *The Deregulated Society* (Pacific Grove, Calif.: Brooks/Cole, 1988), p. 23.

16. Congressional Quarterly, *Regulation: Process and Politics* (Washington, D.C.: Congressional Quarterly Corporation, 1982), pp. 11–12.

17. Gerston et al., *The Deregulated Society,* p. 23.

18. Milton Friedman and Anna J. Schwartz, *A Monetary History of the United States* (Princeton, N.J.: Princeton University Press, 1963).

19. *Schechter Poultry Corporation v. United States,* 225 U.S. 495 (1935).

20. *National Labor Relations Board v. Jones and Laughlin Steel Corporation,* 201 U.S. 1 (1937).

21. Robert L. Rabin, "Federal Regulation in Historical Perspective," *Stanford Law Review* 38 (1986): 1189–1326.

22. Kenneth W. Chilton, *A Decade of Rapid Growth in Federal Regulation* (St. Louis: Washington University Center for the Study of American Business, 1977).

23. Dan Bertozzi, Jr., and Lee B. Burgunder, *Business, Government, and Public Policy* (Englewood Cliffs, N.J.: Prentice-Hall, 1990), pp. 84–85.

24. For example, see Weidenbaum, *Business, Government, and the Public*; Arthur Anderson and Co., *Cost of Government Regulation: A Study for the Business Roundtable* (New York: Arthur Anderson, 1979); and Chilton, *A Decade of Rapid Growth in Federal Regulation.*

CHAPTER 12

Regulatory Reform and the Deregulation Movement

CHAPTER OBJECTIVES

1. Provide a framework for evaluating the effectiveness of the public policy process.
2. Apply the control cycle model to regulatory performance and failure that leads to reform and deregulation.
3. Review some of the major reasons why regulatory agencies fail to accomplish the goals of the public policy process.
4. Discuss the consequences of regulatory failure.
5. Provide an historical overview of the regulatory reform and deregulation movement.
6. Examine the strategies for reform and deregulation used by the Reagan administration during the 1980s in all areas of government regulation.
7. Question how to balance the public interest expressed in the public policy process with economic performance best accomplished through market forces.
8. Explore the politics of regulatory reform. Examine what political forces encourage or discourage successful regulatory reform.
9. Review and evaluate the success of industry deregulation.

The Public Interest and the Role of Government

An effective public policy process in a democracy defines the role of the governmental sphere and the rights and responsibilities of citizens through the public policy process. Assuring equality before the law, protecting rights, and maintaining social justice are all key responsibilities of the governmental sphere. Equality suggests a public policy process open to all.

In a threefold society the benefits of unfettered market forces striving toward economic efficiency must be balanced with the need for government intervention to protect rights or to balance the interests of citizens. When the results of market forces within the economic sphere are unfair or violate the rights of people, then government is justified in regulating the market or taking the necessary actions to bring about justice. However, the burdens of regulation can fall unevenly and affect the relative cost of small businesses more than the costs of larger firms.

Public Interest Theory

This theory assumes that the government should be the guarantor of the public good. The public good is defined by the public policy process that legitimizes the values and goals of society. When is it in the public good to regulate business? Should there be limits to such regulation? How should we determine the balance between public good expressed through political processes and material welfare derived through market exchange processes? When would it be better for the government to allow market forces to operate without governmental constraints? These are political questions that are answered in the often rough-and-tumble exchange among diverse interest groups that vie with one another in a pluralistic society. Business, including small businesses with their Small Business Legislative Council, an association of 100 trade groups, have formed interest groups to assure that their concerns are heard in public policy debates.

A democracy should have reliable processes to determine the legitimate values and interests of society, given the many competing interests in a pluralistic society. It could be argued that an effective public policy process in a democratic society has certain characteristics that parallel the conditions necessary for a competitive market in the economic sphere. Is the political process open to all people? Is it dominated by powerful narrow group interests? Are government agencies implementing public policy properly in the agency process of rule making and enforcement? Is the government involved in activities that would be better left to other spheres, like the economic sphere or the cultural sphere? Can failures occur in the governmental as well as the economic sphere? Can regulatory failures lead to results as undesirable as those experienced from market failures discussed in Chapter 11?

Social Values and Public Policy

Society does not automatically have a unified concept of justice, an ideology to guide social institutions, nor does it have a consistent set of goals and values for decision makers. Rather, like-minded individuals form interest groups that seek to influence public policy. The values and goals of various interest groups are more clearly defined than are the overall goals and values of society. Different groups often have different conceptions of economic justice, individual rights, and the appropriate role of government in regulating economic activity. Different political ideologies compete with one another. Thus, public interest is difficult to define accurately.

The Increasing Role of Government

Historically the governmental sphere has increasingly moved to constrain the economic sphere, as noted in Chapter 11. The belief that the invisible hand of the market unfettered by government interference would be self-correcting and lead to prosperity gave way to another ideology of markets controlled by the visible hand of government. To some extent the public policy process had supplanted the process of market exchange as the major instrument to achieve social goals. Each of the laws, government agencies, and regulations exercising control over business represented a public policy response to a market failure or legitimate public need. Each was based upon a rationale for its existence developed within an historical context of over a century of rapid social and technological change. The public policy process, driven by the mobilizing political forces of legitimacy, redefined the role of government.

The Control Cycle Leading to Regulatory Reform and Deregulation

Like market competition that, from time to time, fails to achieve social goals, governmental action may also have its own problems. The political process can be flawed by limitations or failures in the necessary conditions for democratic representation outlined in Table 12–1. Citizens can be uninformed or misinformed; barriers can exist that limit the opportunity to vote or to organize effec-tively; narrow interests can be so powerful that they frustrate the broader public interest; or public policy can be set by regulatory agencies or execu-tive bureaucracies rather than by the political process.

Also, the implementation of public policy can be ineffectual. The regulation of business can lead to unintended results, fail to accomplish expected goals, and become a controversial issue in itself. Changes in values, technology, lifestyle, and work can alter social goals or make established policies obsolete. Thus the public policy process frequently must refine or redefine the proper role of govern-ment in relation to business. The last chapter demonstrated the government regulatory response to market failures. This chapter seeks to show a parallel antithetical development, government or regulatory failures, leading to a control cycle within the governmental sphere.

When government policy or action fails to accomplish the intended social goals of control, its legitimacy or social support declines. This decline, reflected in public awareness of a social or politi-

TABLE 12–1
Parallel Conditions Necessary for Market Competition and Democratic Political Processes

Market Exchange Process	Political Process
Conditions necessary for competitive market exchange process:	Conditions necessary for a democratic public policy process:
Voluntary exchange	Freedom of expression and association
Prudence—self-interested buyers and sellers	Self-interested voters and interest groups
Mobility of resources (free entry and exit and no discrimination)	Open political processes (right to participate in interest group activity and right to vote)
No market power (through sufficient number of buyers and sellers)	No one interest group dominating political process
Market sets prices, profits, and returns to factors	Public policies set by voters and elected representatives
Limited government interference in market processes	Limited business interference via campaign contributions and pressure
Knowledgeable buyers and sellers	Informed voters, representatives, interest groups
Expected results of competition:	Expected results of public policy process:
Providing for the material welfare of society by the economic sphere:	Providing for the public interest by the political sphere:
economic efficiency, maximum output, economic justice	political equality, protection of rights, social justice for all citizens

cal problem, triggers another cycle of social control and includes (1) public policy expressed in government laws and regulations leading to (2) a regulatory failure made evident by social problems that (3) trigger a renewed debate leading, in turn, to (4) privatization, regulatory reform, or deregulation.

Regulatory Failure

A number of factors led to the widespread questioning of the regulation of business. Public interest theory argues that "regulation is supplied by politicians and regulators who seek the public good in response to demand by the public for correction of inefficient and inequitable outcomes in the marketplace."[1] As noted above, social values and needs change, economic conditions change, and thus the private interests of various groups within society are ever changing. Thus, the public interest is dynamic, complex, and difficult to define. Once defined, it may prove difficult for regulators to serve the public interest as legitimized by laws and other public policies.

There are several explanations why regulators fail to serve the public interest. (1) Agencies can be captured by the industry and regulate on the industry's behalf rather than on behalf of the public interest. (2) Agencies can emphasize the goals and values of narrow interest groups above theose of the general public. (3) Agencies can be administered for bureaucratic values held within the agency rather than for the values and goals of society. (4) Regulations can become obsolete as changes occur in society. These causes of failure of government regulations are discussed below.

AGENCY CAPTURE THEORY

According to the *agency capture theory* of regulations, the industry being regulated "captures" the regulating agency so that the industry is regulated for the benefit of business rather than consumers.[2] As suggested in the last chapter, some argue for economic regulation where competitiveness is

destructive and markets are unstable. The rationale for such regulation is that consumers need to be protected from the shortages, unstable prices, and inconvenience resulting from such instability.

However, businesses in such unstable industries may also want to avoid this instability. Antitrust laws prohibit businesses from forming agreements to obtain stability by (1) restraining entry of new competitors, (2) fixing prices, or (3) mutually agreeing to product or service standards if such agreements are enforced by sanctions of competitors. Industry regulators stabilize precisely those factors that are illegal for businesses, without government intervention, to control. Thus, Stigler argues that some businesses seek economic regulation to achieve private interests rather than to protect consumers.[3]

The right to compete in an industry like trucking or airlines becomes a valuable property right whose value can be sustained only by continued industry regulation. Rates set to assure a "fair profit" lower business risks when routes are assigned and entry is controlled in a way that avoids excess capacity and unstable competitive moves. Rising costs of inefficiencies or excess profits are passed on to consumers in the form of higher prices authorized by regulatory agencies.[4]

How is it possible for business to capture the regulators? One explanation assumes that regulators are individuals interested in maximizing the value of their personal careers in the following ways:

1. Regulators seek to protect or enhance their career after their term expires as regulator. Often top positions in regulatory agencies are filled with people from the industry who are experts in the field. After serving the temporary term of office, they are interested in returning to executive positions within the industries to which they, in many cases, have devoted most of their professional life.
2. Regulators seek to uphold their reputations among peers and important associates. This helps to sustain not only self-esteem; it also helps in career development.
3. Regulators, as ethical persons, try to maintain their integrity by acting consistently with what

they feel is proper. However, a regulator's view of the public interest is likely to be influenced by past experience in the industry, professional expertise, which views problems from an industry perspective, and values shared with colleagues in both the regulatory agency and industry.[5]

Despite the negative consequences of regulatory failure, regulatory reform and deregulation has often faced stiff political opposition. Economic regulation is sustained by the so-called *iron triangle* of regulators, regulated industries, and key members of Congress. Congresspersons can be influenced by the contributions from businesses in regulated industries. Entrenched interests thus provide a formidable barrier to any regulatory reform.[6]

INTEREST GROUP CONSTITUENCIES AND REGULATORY FAILURE

Similar to the iron triangle in industry regulation, social regulation is often sustained by coalitions of interest group entrepreneurs seeking the goals of narrow interests, organized labor, legislative staff, and advocacy journalists.[7] Such coalitions have been a force for the passing of new laws and have also been an obstacle to regulatory reform. When a well-organized interest group clashes with more diffused and poorly organized forces in the public policy process, the narrow interest usually wins. Interest groups become the political clientele of an agency and are allied with members of Congress who are on key committees responsible for agency oversight.

An *interest group entrepreneur* is an advocate of a particular cause or solution to a public issue or problem who forms a grass roots organization to mobilize public opinion to achieve a goal. Like a private-sector entrepreneur in search of an attractive new business opportunity, the interest group entrepreneur searches for an issue that provides a political opportunity that can be used to mobilize public sentiment. An opportunity can include publicizing a crisis, scandal, or other dramatic event.[8] Such events can be used to launch an entrepre-

neurial not-for-profit issue "start-up" that follows the following pattern:

1. Get an issue on the public policy agenda by enlisting the support of advocacy journalists.
2. Define policy approaches to solve the public problem in a manner consistent with interest group values. Seek to shape the direction of the public debate in favorable directions.
3. Use computers and electronic communication technology to raise public support with mass appeals mailing lists.
4. Develop grass roots support around an issue.
5. Develop an issue strategy based on mass demonstrations, letter writing campaigns, or litigation.

Pleas for support made by interest group organizations are expressed in terms of broadly held public values and ideologies. People on the mailing list of these not-for-profit entrepreneurs who specialize in public issues are sent fact sheets, samples of form letters, and addresses of members of Congress and are also asked to donate funds to the cause. Opponents of an issue are typically characterized polemically as uncaring, irresponsible, and evil. The choice of the dramatic event that graphically depicts the crisis, the promotion of the issue in terms that the public can relate to, and the strategy for pursuing it in the public policy process are all crucial to the success of the interest group's campaign.

Interest Groups As Clients of Regulatory Agencies

Once an interest group succeeds in getting legislation passed and agencies formed to implement the new public policy, they become clients of the agency. Through grass roots organization, interest groups seek to maintain political influence, build the legitimacy of agency resources and regulations, and develop allies for their cause in Congress. Critics argue that this results in establishing and maintaining laws and regulations that take a narrow-interest group perspective rather than a broader public interest. James Q. Wilson explains the role of interest groups in the formation and later the control of regulation in this way:

When a program supplies particular benefits to an existing or newly-created interest, public or private, it creates a set of political relationships that make exceptionally difficult further alteration of that program by coalition of the majority. What was created in the name of the common good is sustained in the name of the particular interest. Bureaucratic clientelism becomes self-perpetuating, in the absence of some crisis or scandal, because a single interest to which the program matters greatly is highly motivated and well-situated to ward off the criticism of other groups that have a broad but weak interest in the policy. . . . [A] major change is, in effect, new legislation that must overcome the same hurdles as the original law but this time with one of the hurdles—the wishes of the agency and its client—raised much higher.[9]

Many agencies, especially those that enforce social regulations, have interest groups as external constituencies. Agency dedication to more narrow issues and values is reinforced by the actions, both positive and negative, of external constituencies like an environmental group, a consumer group, organized labor, or a civil rights organization. These interest groups seek to legitimize the governmental agency charter through political support of new legislation, new regulations, or budgets.

Consumer groups politically support the Consumer Products Safety Commission. Environmental groups support the protection of the environment and seek to influence the EPA. The Civil Rights Movement supports the activities of the Equal Employment Opportunities Commission. These interest groups monitor the behavior of regulators and are quick to publicize any enforcement patterns perceived to be inconsistent with the goals and values of the interest group. Interest groups have extensive grass roots organizations and computerized mailing capabilities to launch letter-writing campaigns to oppose or support their positions.

A Case Example: Environmental Regulations and a Change in Plant Layout

An example of a controversial practice in environmental regulation is the multistage approval process to locate a plant in California. It sometimes takes as many as 60 permits from various state and local governments with a veto possible from any one of several agencies. Whereas these regulations are meant to maintain or enhance the quality of life in the state, they can cause costly delays, undercut the competitiveness of both business and the state economy, and undermine the economic health of the region. One criticism of this environmental regulation is the situation when changing economic circumstances requires a business to change the layout of its operations to enhance productivity.

However, the movement of a piece of equipment, even a move of only a few inches, requires that the business redo the multistage approval process. This situation, and others like it, have caused many businesses to move facilities out of the state or offshore.[10] Interest group activists probably are pleased that the permit process must be repeated whenever "major changes" are made in a facility formerly approved. Environmentalists would view a regulation that allowed any change in facility layout without repeating the process as a loophole that could be abused by unscrupulous businesspeople. In contrast, business and portions of the community view the requirement to repeat the permit process as a major regulatory failure.

Interest Groups As Watchdogs of Agency

Environmental groups like the Sierra Club regularly use litigation to block actions made by the EPA or the Forest Service when they disagree with a decision or to encourage them to vigorously enforce regulations when they are consistent with the goals of the organization.

Consumer groups also have investigated regulatory agencies for mismanagement, probusiness enforcement of rules, or failure to rigorously enforce social regulation. The prominent consumer advocate Ralph Nader has used investigation and litigation to press for consumer protection laws and regulations. Nader's Raiders, the name given to a number of Ivy League graduate students active in the cause, joined and studied government agencies to uncover incompetence and probusiness bias in the enforcement of regulations. They wrote a number of books exposing regulatory failure, supplied documentation for litigation against government agencies that, in their view, were not adequately enforcing regulations.

BUREAUCRATIC THEORY AND REGULATORY AGENCIES

Many regulators are highly devoted professionals committed to excellence. They have developed substantial amounts of expertise and are concerned about the issues or problem areas they are responsible for regulating. What appears to be bureaucratic inefficiency may in reality be the zeal of a dedicated professional. Professional regulators put public safety ahead of lower-cost products, put job safety ahead of the lower costs of production, and place a higher priority on the quality of life in the cities than the cost savings derived from lower environmental standards.

What is considered a regulatory failure by some would be considered a valid response to a market failure by others. Regulatory agencies are sometimes criticized when they dominate the public policy process rather than implement its results, when they embroil business in a lot of red tape that seems to be useless, when they cause time-consuming delays in permit decisions, and when they make standards and require practices that cause business to be inefficient.

For example, the Small Businesses Legislative Council, the association of 100 trade groups, complained about having to fill out 45 reports to various government agencies when one report should suffice. Like the professor who makes so many assignments that it appears he thinks the course is the only one his students are taking, sometimes agencies seem to think that the primary purpose of business is to do reports for the work of the particular agency. And there are more agencies regulating each business by far than the number of courses even the most ambitious student would ever take at one time.

Goal Displacement by Agencies

Agencies sometimes form rather than merely implement policy. According to bureaucratic theory, all organizations have a life cycle of growth, maturity, and decline.[11] In the process of organizational evolution, public agencies develop a culture and momentum of their own. Eventually, the goal to grow and to survive becomes more important to organization members than accomplishing the mission of the agency in the most cost-effective manner. Public bureaucracies ideally should implement public policy defined through the legislative process. However, they have been known to develop public policy goals of their own and to be politically active in bringing them about.[12] A regulatory failure occurs when an agency defines public policy rather than serves as its instrument.

Agency Rewards Systems Can Encourage Inefficiency

Regulatory agencies are not subject to market forces in which efficiency leads to lower cost and competitive advantage in the marketplace. Executives in bureaucracies are rewarded according to the amount of responsibility they have. Responsibility is often measured in terms of the number of staff members or budget for which an administrator is responsible. An agency administrator is thus rewarded if staff levels and budgets are increased enough so there is no chance of a wrong decision. The negative consequences for a mistake made by not monitoring a situation closely or for making a potentially harmful decision are greater in a bureaucracy than the positive consequences of being efficient in administering agency resources.

In contrast, the consequences of efficiency can actually be punished. Fewer regulators and streamlined procedures can lead to lower budget levels and thus lower status and rewards for the administrator. Employees of regulatory bureaucracies are also risk-averse because the negative consequences of a mistake are punished, whereas there are few positive consequences for a correct decision. Employees are likely to avoid negative measurable consequences that are likely to be noticed more than they seek to press for positive outcomes that are more likely to go unnoticed.

For example, it is much worse for the FDA to allow a harmful medication to be approved than to disapprove a potentially beneficial drug or speed the approval process that now requires from five to seven years. Thus, the paperwork requirements imposed upon business by the ever-growing governmental reports they are asked to make are a major part of the cost of compliance. Society is saved from the consequences of harmful drugs but may never obtain the helpful drugs that are rejected or delayed in the approval process. There is a pattern of supporting growth of the agency while discouraging timely decisions. These behavioral attributes can lead to regulatory failure and are more likely to be emphasized when there are stringent requirements of public accountability or when an organizational culture emphasizes punishing mistakes over solving problems.

CAN CHANGES IN SOCIETY MAKE REGULATION OBSOLETE?

Modern industrialized societies are not static; rather, they are subject to changes in technologies, cultural values, lifestyles, and economic circumstances. Changes call for new behaviors in both business and in government regulation. Regulations designed to control business behavior may be successful at one time only to become a source of inflexibility as conditions change. For example, it is argued by some that antitrust law is no longer relevant to today's globalized markets.

Technological change can also render regulations obsolete. The advent of satellite technology makes it possible for multiple providers to offer long-distance telephone communication. Advances in cellular telephone technology have continued this trend, causing much of the regulation in telecommunications to become obsolete. Each country has its own regulatory agency, technical standards, and agency review process. These have become a major source of inflexibility and a barrier to efficiency and service in telecommunications worldwide.

THE CONSEQUENCES OF REGULATORY FAILURE

The major consequences of regulatory failure most often mentioned are (1) rising costs of government, (2) rising costs of compliance by business, (3) declining international competitiveness by businesses who suffer increased costs and more inflexibility, (4) loss of managerial discretion by business, and (5) failure to improve the conditions for which regulations were created in the first place.

Murray Weidenbaum has suggested that every time government imposes a regulation on business that increases the cost of production, the price of the product must also rise.[13] Instead of protecting the rights of people, government regulation increases intervention into the private lives of citizens. Instead of regulating business to channel market forces in ways that are consistent with the public good, business activities become totally overwhelmed by the complexity and magnitude of government intrusion. The automatic forces of the market can no longer guide the economic sphere through the instrument of business to provide the goods and services needed by society.

The visible hand of government intrudes into the economic sphere in a way that causes the market to be less efficient, less responsive, and more costly in the form of both business and government costs. One estimate placed the costs of extra paperwork between $25 billion and $32 billion annually. Large businesses averaged more than $1 billion annually in extra costs.[14] Another study, by Arthur Anderson and Company, found that 48 large businesses spent $2.6 billion annually to comply with six major regulatory programs.[15]

Regulations have become a center of controversy, but there are major benefits of regulation. Although large cities still suffer from pollution from automobile exhaust and industrial facilities, it could be argued that air quality would be much worse without the efforts of the EPA. Similarly, discrimination against minorities, women, and the disabled would be greater without the EEOC. Products would be less safe without the CPSC.

Medicines and food would be less safe without the controls of the FDA. It is easier to estimate the costs of compliance and the greater cost of government associated with agency regulation than it is to measure the social benefits of these regulations.

Early Attempts at Regulatory Reform in the Nixon Administration

Gerston, Fraleigh, and Schwab date the antecedents of regulatory reform back to the time of the Nixon administration, which sought to bring the regulatory bureaucracies more under the control of the president.[16] Although the regulatory reform and deregulation movement did not move into full swing until President Carter's administration, important groundwork for reform was prepared by the administrations of Presidents Nixon and Ford. Nixon reorganized the White House and began a regulatory review program.

Office of Management and Budget. Congress approved a White House reorganization plan in July 1970 that changed the Office of Budget to the Office of Management and Budget (OMB). The OMB was to coordinate executive branch budget proposals, review procedures within agencies, encourage cooperation among various regulatory agencies, and review proposed new government regulations.

Quality-of-life regulatory reviews. President Nixon issued an executive order in 1971 directing the OMB to perform quality-of-life regulatory reviews of proposed regulations. These reviews were to be done 30 days prior to the official announcement of proposed new regulation in the *Federal Register.* These reviews were the result of regulated businesses lobbying the Department of Commerce for relief from impending environmental regulation.

However, quality-of-life regulatory reviews proved to be very controversial. They focused entirely on environmental regulations and were criticized by members of various interest groups,

especially environmentalists, their allies in Congress, and the professionals within the regulatory agencies. Thus, the quality-of-life reviews were terminated by the new administration with the election of President Carter in 1976.

Historical Overview of Regulatory Reform and the Deregulation Movement, 1974–84

THE FORD ADMINISTRATION— ATTEMPTING TO CONTROL INFLATION THROUGH REGULATORY REFORM

In 1974, the Oil Producing and Exporting Countries (OPEC) sharply increased the worldwide price of crude oil. This action sent a shock wave of rising prices throughout the industrialized world. Most industrialized economies were based on low-cost petroleum as the primary source of energy. However, there was also increased awareness of the inflationary effects of government regulation. Because of the oil price rise, the many new and costly government regulations, and other factors, the inflation rate reached 11 percent during the Ford administration and was perhaps President Ford's biggest problem.

The Council on Wage and Price Stability and Inflation Impact Statements

President Ford persuaded Congress to create the Council on Wage and Price Stability (COWPS) as a major instrument to dissuade business from raising prices. Then, by executive order, he established the Inflation Impact Statement (IIS) program, which required that all proposed regulations be accompanied by an inflation impact statement. The major goal of the IIS program was to curb the inflationary effect of government laws and regulations. The COWPS and the OMB jointly monitored the inflation impact statements and issued advisory statements to the various regulatory agencies concerning all new proposed laws and regulations.

Agencies often did not have the staff or the capability to do rigorous studies of the inflationary consequences of proposed regulations. Nor could they adequately interpret the implications of a regulation, even if such studies were available. Sometimes the anticipated costs of proposed regulations were carefully done but little attention was given to expected benefits. At other times, the opposite was true. Thus the studies on which the IIS were based were often poorly done and the quality varied significantly from agency to agency. The COWPS and OMB would use the studies to formulate recommendations. Because the statements were only advisory and because the IIS studies developed a reputation for being poorly done, regulatory agencies largely ignored the recommendations.

In the end, the Ford administration was not very successful in its attempts at regulatory reform and deregulation. However, both the administrations of Nixon and Ford laid much of the groundwork for the movement of deregulation and reform that was to follow.

CONGRESSIONAL SUPPORT FOR REGULATORY REFORM AND DEREGULATION

Members of Congress seek to represent their constituencies. If they can do this and at the same time achieve high levels of visibility, their political support can be enhanced. In serving the public interest, senators, representatives, and their staffs can also be allies to industry and allies to interest groups sponsoring various social movements, or they can seek to obtain favorable treatment for their home constituencies.

The Kennedy Hearings on the Civil Aeronautics Board

Beginning in 1975, Senator Edward Kennedy held hearings on the Civil Aeronautics Board (CAB) that did much to launch the deregulation movement. Kennedy had long been an advocate of social regulation for consumer issues and was searching for a way to attract attention to con-

sumer interests. His staff had prepared for one and a half years for these hearings, and much information had been prepared based upon academic studies on the anticompetitive policies of the CAB.[17] However, the dynamics of the hearings resulted in changing the focus from advocacy of social regulations to deregulating the airline industry.

The information made available at these hearings was presented in forms readily accessible to the popular press, which took on an advocacy role in the issue. Scandal was apparent when the director of the CAB committed suicide two days before he was scheduled to testify at the hearings. Dull academic presentations were avoided, the press continued to cover the study, and interest in deregulation reached an all-time high. Alfred Kahn, the new director of the CAB, favored deregulation, while the consumer movement backed deregulation. President Ford, interested in price reductions likely to come from deregulation, also supported the idea of deregulation. These hearing dramatically illustrated that Congress had now joined the deregulation movement.

THE CARTER ADMINISTRATION— DEREGULATION GAINS MOMENTUM WHILE REGULATORY REFORM FAILS

President Carter had enjoyed strong support from organized labor and the environmental movement in his election as president. While supporting social regulation, he was also strongly procompetition. He appointed people who enjoyed interest group support and who supported social regulation to key administrative posts in regulatory agencies. The result was that his administration was somewhat inconsistent: social regulation of business increased while major laws were passed to deregulate industry.

New Environmental Laws

New laws increasing social regulations, primarily environmental, were passed, including the following:

The Toxic Substances Control Act of 1976
The Resource Conservation and Recovery Act of 1976

The Surface Mining Control and Reclamation
Act of 1977
The Clean Air Act of 1978

Economic Deregulation of Industries

The Carter administration was a pivotal point in
the deregulation movement, which became the
legacy of that administration. Major laws passed
during his administration deregulated airlines,
which provided momentum and the model for the
laws passed in 1980 deregulating trucking and
financial institutions, and energy (also see Table
12–4).

Trucking: Motor Carrier Reform Act of 1980 and
the Household Goods Transportation Act of
1980
Airlines: Airline Deregulation Act of 1978 and
International Transportation Competition Act
of 1979
Energy: Natural Gas Policy Act
Finance: Depository Institutions Deregulation and
Monetary Control Act of 1980

Although these laws were passed during the
Carter administration, the results of industry
deregulation unfolded over a longer period of time.
Industry deregulation varied with each industry,
and some examples proved to be more successful
than others. Trucking deregulation resulted in
sharply lower prices and bankruptcy for most of
the top trucking firms. Airlines, probably the most
successful example of industry deregulation, saved
consumers millions of dollars in air fares. The
deregulation of the savings and loan industry
proved to be the worst debacle and will ultimately
cost the public as much as $500 billion in govern-
ment bailouts. The status of industry regulation is
discussed later in the chapter.

The Regulatory Analysis and Review Group (RARG)

President Carter also sought to bring about major
regulatory reform through the RARG, which was
created in 1978. This group was responsible for
selecting a few approximately four new and existing
regulations costing $100 million or more from each

executive branch agency annually. The group was
composed of the heads of various social regulatory
agencies within the executive branch. The agencies
were asked to submit the rules to be reviewed by
the RARG and to do the analysis of regulations
within each agency. Agencies hired economists and
scientists and developed an extensive research
capability for these reviews. This RARG, through
the use of agency provided studies, was to be the
major instrument for regulatory reform for agencies
in the executive branch of government.

Regulatory Reform

President Carter issued an executive order to provide regulatory reform guidelines for the RARG and
regulatory agencies: (1) Regulations were required
to be clearer and less burdensome to business. (2)
The review processes used to approve new regulations must consider both the costs and the benefits
of regulations, but the net benefits were not the key
factor in approving new social regulations.[18] (3) The
review process was expanded to regulations already
in existence rather than only new proposed ones.
(4) Alternatives to regulations were to be considered. Industry incentives, subsidies, use of market
forces, and alternatives to regulations were
endorsed as a part of official policy. (5) Participation
in the regulatory review process was to be opened by
requiring agencies to circulate an agenda of proposed regulations twice per year and to seek public
participation in the rule-making process.

The Cotton Dust Controversy

The RARG made recommendations to agencies for
regulatory reform but had little legal authority to
enforce them. Its authority within executive branch
agencies depended upon the leadership of the president. In a major controversy, the RARG suggested
that businesses in the textile industry be allowed to
supply individual respirators to employees rather
than be required to install more expensive ventilators. The Occupational Safety and Health Administration (OSHA) had extensively studied this issue
and insisted ventilators were the most effective
option to resolve the health problem of lung diseases from cotton dust. Individual employees would

not have to change their behavior by wearing respirators. Management would not have to provide individual respirators and train and supervise employees to assure compliance if buildings were equipped with expensive ventilators.

Carter sided with OSHA in the dispute and against RARG in the cotton dust controversy, and his position on this issue ultimately proved to be a major setback for regulatory reform. After the cotton dust incident, agencies were even more prone to resist RARG recommendations and little reform was accomplished.[19] Thus, while major strides in deregulation of industries were launched during the Carter administration, reforms of social regulations made very limited progress.

The Reagan Administration—Comprehensive Regulatory Reform and Deregulation

President Reagan was elected, in part, because of the promise "to get the government off the back of the people" and to turn around the economy. In 1978, OPEC again sharply raised worldwide oil prices, inflation continued, and interest rates were around 15 percent near the end of the Carter administration. President Reagan wanted to pursue four major goals in his administration: (1) cut taxes, stabilize monetary growth, and control inflation and high interest rates; (2) cut the cost of government and thus reduce the deficit; (3) build up military forces for defense; and (4) reduce government regulation through a comprehensive regulatory reform and deregulation program.[20]

To accomplish the objectives of his administration, Reagan adopted some earlier approaches to regulatory reform and deregulation in extended versions: (1) The influence and responsibilities of the OMB were expanded. (2) The *Task Force on Regulatory Relief* was formed. (3) Executive orders were used to provide policy guidance. (4) Cost-benefit analysis was required. (5) Staff and budget reductions were made to decrease the enforcement

of regulations. (6) Ideology was used as a litmus test for those appointed to top regulatory positions. (5) Presidential leadership was exercised. These were all management strategies to implement his political philosophy and goals for his administration were used.[21]

TASK FORCE ON REGULATORY RELIEF (TFRR)

The TFRR was headed by Vice President George Bush, with members including high-level presidential assistants and the secretaries of commerce, labor, and the treasury. Its powerful membership symbolized its key role in the Reagan reform strategy. The task forces used by previous administrations had regulatory agency heads as members and their advice had been just that—advisory, with limited backing of the president. The TFRR included more influential members of the government and had significantly more power than previous bodies. The objectives of the TFRR were more comprehensive than previous review boards and included (1) assessment of proposed new regulations, (2) assessment of existing regulations, especially those particularly costly to the economy or key industrial sectors, and (3) overseeing legislative proposals to modify the Clean Air Act and other major statutes. The TFRR killed 37 of the 100 rules reviewed in two years.

In August 1983 the TFRR was disbanded and the administration claimed a major victory by saving $150 billion in regulatory costs. A close examination of its success suggests there may have been a significant exaggeration in the amount of savings.[22] Included in its tabulation of savings were deregulatory actions taken by previous administrations and by Congress. Savings from dropping proposed regulations that were never adopted were included. Savings from the postponement of the implementation of social regulation were included, but the value of any offsetting benefits that would have resulted from such regulation was not included. Many of the standards that were eliminated to save regulatory costs were later reinstated by the courts.

EXTENDED USE OF COST-BENEFIT ANALYSIS

As indicated in Chapter 7, cost-benefit analysis is derived from utilitarian analysis and is the first step in determining the ethical desirability of a particular decision. In this analytical approach to regulatory reform, an attempt is made to quantify the social costs and social benefits of a regulation, and only those with net benefits would be considered beneficial for society.[23] President Bush required regulatory agencies to use this approach as a way to avoid unnecessary or too costly regulation of small business. Previously, as vice president in the Reagan administration and head of the Task Force on Regulatory Reform, Bush used cost-benefit analysis to stop the tide of rising social regulation that began in the 1960s.

Regulations with cost-benefit ratios less than one would be considered too costly relative to any social advantages and would be undesirable. However, as noted earlier, accurate estimates of costs and benefits are sometimes difficult or impossible to determine. This is particularly true for the benefits of social regulation in the areas of environment, occupational health and safety, and safety of foods and products.[24]

Public policy had been somewhat cautious to mixed in the application of cost-benefit analysis. The Toxic Substance Control Act requires the EPA to consider cost-benefit analysis; the Clean Air Act permits its use; and the Delaney amendments to the laws governing the FDA prohibiting carcinogenic food additives forbids the use of cost-benefit analysis in setting rules. President Nixon had attempted to use this technique selectively in evaluating environmental regulation but was strongly resisted. President Carter had indicated that the results of cost-benefit analysis would not be the determining factor in adopting social regulation.

In contrast to his predecessors, President Reagan used cost-benefit analysis as a central feature of the regulatory reform of his administration. It was required by executive order on all proposed regulations where the law did not specifically prohibit its use. To implement this guideline, cost-benefit analysis was required in the forms used to assess proposed regulations by the OMB in the Reagan administration. Regulatory cost regulations that harmed competitiveness were foremost on the minds of the administration. Thus, there was no space for the calculation of potential benefits of proposed regulation on the forms required by the OMB.[25] This potentially biased the analysis and may have led to the exaggeration of estimates of savings through regulatory reform publicized by the TFRR.

BUDGET CUTTING AND STAFF REDUCTION AS A STRATEGY FOR DEREGULATION

A key strategy to roll back the tidal wave of increasing social regulation was to reduce the staffing levels and budgets of the agencies. The threat of budget cuts was also a way for the administration to apply indirect pressure on independent regulatory agencies beyond executive branch control, as well as those agencies located within the executive branch. Actual cuts would limit their enforcement capability, which would, in turn, reduce the regulatory pressure on business. The results of this strategy are shown in Tables 12–2 and 12–3, and were perhaps the most effective strategy for holding back the tide of regulation during President Reagan's first term of office.

Kenneth Chilton at the Washington University Center for the Study of American Business has extensively studied the rise and attempted reform of government regulation.[26] Table 12–2, based upon Chilton's analysis, shows that in the five years prior to President Reagan's election, the government costs of social regulation increased by 61 percent, the costs of economic regulation increased by 80 percent, and overall regulation costs increased by 63 percent. If the effects of inflation are removed, the increase in regulatory costs are 24 percent. During President Reagan's first term the, the overall government costs of regulatory activities increased by 35 percent from 1980 to 1985. In contrast, the Reagan administration was able to reduce overall governmental expenses for regulatory activities by 3 percent after inflation. These gains were accomplished during the first three years of his

TABLE 12–2

Administrative Costs of Federal Regulatory Activities, Fiscal Years 1970–1990

		1970	1975	1980	1985	1990
Social Regulation	budget (million)	$1,116	$3,306	$5,308	$7,022	$9,143
	% change		196	61	32	30
Economic Regulation	budget (million)	$293	$554	$995	$1,483	$2,117
	% change		89	80	49	43
Total	budget (million)	$1,409	$3,860	$6,303	$8,505	$11,260
	% change		174	63	35	32
Total, 1972 dollars	budget (million)	$1,646	$3,068	$3,791	$3,680	not
	% change		86	24	−3	available

SOURCE: Adapted from Kenneth W. Chilton, *The Effects of Gramm-Rudman-Hollings on Federal Regulatory Activities* (St. Louis: Washington University Center for the Study of American Business, 1986), p. 15; and "Higher Budgets for Federal Regulators, " *Regulation: Cato Review of Business and Government* (Winter 1990): 23.

administration (1980–83), and by 1984 regulatory costs were on the rise again.

The Reagan administration was even more successful in holding down the number of full-time federal government employees involved in regulatory activities, as shown on Table 12–3. Overall growth in full-time federal employees increased by 61 percent during the 1970–75 period; this rate of increase was stopped during the next five years.

During the Reagan administration, the number of employees actually *decreased* by 7 percent during the years 1980 to 1985 and dropped by another 3 percent in the next five years ending in 1990. The major decreases were accomplished during the first three years of the Reagan administration; however, unlike the costs of regulation, employees involved in regulation continued to decrease slightly, at 1 percent annually.

TABLE 12–3

Staffing for Federal Regulatory Activities, Fiscal Years 1970–1990 (permanent full-time positions)

		1970	1975	1980	1985	1990
Social Regulation	number	54,014	95,075	92,412	87,047	83,478
	% change		76	−3	−6	−4
Economic Regulation	number	20,679	25,314	27,863	24,897	25,532
	% change		22	10	−11	3
Total	number	74,693	120,389	120,275	111,944	109,010
	% change		61	0	−7	−3

SOURCE: Adapted from Kenneth W. Chilton, *The Effects of Gramm-Rudman-Hollings on Federal Regulatory Activities* (St. Louis: Washington University Center for the Study of American Business, 1986), p. 16; and "Higher Budgets for Federal Regulators, " *Regulation: Cato Review of Business and Government* (Winter 1990): 23.

USING POLITICAL APPOINTMENTS
AS A STRATEGY OF DEREGULATION

Another management strategy for regulatory reform and deregulation used by the Reagan administration was the appointment of heads to regulatory agencies. Unlike President Carter, who appointed professionals sympathetic to social regulations to head the regulatory agencies, President Reagan appointed people sympathetic to his own political philosophy of deregulation.

The regulatory review approach was applied only to regulatory agencies located within the executive branch. The heads of these executive branch agencies were appointed by the president and could be dismissed at any time; they were closely monitored by the OMB, and were subject to the regulatory review process. Major regulatory agencies located within the executive branch include the FAA (which regulates airline safety), the EPA (the environment), the NHTSA (automobile safety), the FDA (safety of food and drugs), the Department of Justice, which enforces antitrust law, and OSHA (job safety).

However, many government regulatory agencies are independent of the executive branch and are responsible for enforcing laws based upon the authority delegated to them by Congress. Although the president can appoint the heads of independent commissions with the consent of the Senate, once appointed and confirmed, they cannot be removed until their terms of office expires. Congress is very concerned about the status of these agencies and would not tolerate the executive branch's applying its regulatory review process and cost-benefit analysis to the rules made by independent agencies. These independent agencies include the following:

The Consumer Products Safety Commission (CPSC), which regulates product safety

The Federal Trade Commission (FTC), which enforces antitrust laws and regulates anticompetitive behavior and dishonesty in advertising

The National Labor Relations Board (NLRB), which regulates unfair labor practices

The Securities and Exchange Commission (SEC), which regulates the stock exchange and financial disclosure requirements

The Equal Employment Opportunities Commission (EEOC), which enforces laws against employment discrimination

The Federal Reserve Board, which regulates the banking industry

The Interstate Commerce Commission (ICC), which regulates the trucking industry

The Federal Communications Commission (FCC), which regulates radio and television, and was responsible for cable television before it was deregulated.

Congress would have strongly resisted any direct tampering with the operations of the independent commissions and agencies by the executive branch. Direct OMB influence on independent agencies was off-limits. However, as noted above, the OMB could apply pressure on agencies indirectly through the budget approval process. Agencies that resisted the interests as voiced by the OMB could have a particularly difficult time getting their budgets approved.

President Reagan also found that he could influence the behavior of independent agencies by his choice of top administrators. Appointees were screened for their ideology, their support for the ideals of regulatory reform, and their sympathy for deregulation. By the time the president had served two terms, he had appointed all 63 of the top positions of the 15 key regulatory agencies.[27] This same ideological litmus test was applied successfully by the administration to judicial appointments. Thus, through the appointment process, the influence of a presidential administration can continue long after the administration has finished its term of office.

All presidential administrations have the dilemma of balancing appointments, rewarding those who were particularly helpful in the election campaign with appointments of knowledgeable and competent professionals. The former tend to be ideologically supportive and hardworking but may lack technical knowledge in key areas. The latter tend to be professionally dedicated to a particular issue or area of expertise but may not be totally sympathetic with the new administration's policies.

Some presidents have been even somewhat nonpartisan in their appointments that have gone to people with outstanding reputations. For example, Alfred Kahn, the head of the CAB, who strongly supported airline deregulation and presided over the phaseout of his agency, was a highly respected economist in the area of regulation. However, there was some danger in using a political ideology as a litmus test for top regulators, as the EPA case below illustrates.

POLITICAL APPOINTMENTS AND THE SCANDAL AT THE EPA

Many of those appointed to head regulatory agencies shared Reagan's vision of the proper role of government and had as their primary goals (1) stopping the growth of government and new regulations, (2) regulatory reform as a way to strengthen competitiveness, (3) slowing down or postponing the enforcement of existing regulation, and (4) dismantling regulatory agency that were considered harmful. In some cases the Reagan appointees were successful in accomplishing some, if not all, of these objectives.

Critics of President Reagan's appointments considered his appointees as probusiness, antigovernment, poorly qualified to head the regulatory agency, and, at times, too zealous in implementing the conservative political ideology. The EEOC seemed to be staffed with people against the rights of women and minorities. The Department of Labor was staffed with people with an antilabor perspective. Examples of such top-level appointments include Anne Gorsuch Burford at the EPA, Throne Auchter at OSHA, Raymond Peck at NHTSA, and the notoriously abrasive James Watt as secretary of the interior.

Anne Gorsuch Burford, head of the EPA, indicated in 1980 that the agency had become a thorn in the side of private enterprise and she began a program of opposing unnecessary environmental regulation.[28] Within three years enforcement actions of environmental regulation had dropped 84 per-

cent and EPA-initiated court cases for enforcement also dropped 78 percent.[29] Because the top administrators were not knowledgeable about the laws governing the environment nor those covering agency procedural requirements, many of their actions were later reversed in the courts.

The EPA is responsible for protecting the environment and for managing the superfund for the cleanup of old and abandoned toxic waste sites that pose a health threat and endanger the environment. In 1980, the first authorization for the superfund was $1.6 billion to clean over 2,000 identified toxic waste sites throughout the nation. EPA management of this toxic waste cleanup under Burford's leadership was highly questionable, and it was alleged that the superfund was be used politically to reward allies and to punish foes of the administration.[30] The administration tried to protect EPA documents from being subpoenaed by Congress, claiming that they were protected by executive privilege.[31] In the political firestorm that followed, Burford and most of the top management of the EPA were forced to resign in March 1982 for malfeasance and mismanagement.[32] One top EPA administrator, Rita Lavelle, was imprisoned over the scandal.

William Ruckelshaus, who had been the first head of the EPA under President Nixon, temporarily returned to the EPA, replacing Burford in an attempt to restore public confidence in the agency and to uplift the highly demoralized agency.[33] Later Lee Thomas, the new head of the EPA, requested a budget of $1 billion to finish the cleanup of toxic waste sites in 1985. Only 6 of the over 2,000 toxic waste sites were actually cleaned up in the previous five years. This budget proposal was against the advice of the top professional staff at the EPA and was strongly resisted by all the EPA regional heads and by Congress.

Accomplishments and Lessons of the Reagan Administration

What were the accomplishments and lessons of the deregulation movement during the Reagan administration? First, the OMB became an effective tool for coordinating regulatory reform and for exercising budgetary control over the process. Its use has been progressively refined by four presidential administrations.

Second, the tidal wave of rising social regulation was slowed, at least, for a time, by the Reagan administration. The reduction of the number of full-time government employees involved in regulation proved to be easier than holding down the dollar costs of regulation. Cutting regulation, in the end, proved to be as difficult a problem as balancing the federal budget.

Third, the use of cost-benefit analysis to evaluate regulations was increased. When applied correctly this analytical technique proved to be a useful tool in curbing the rising costs of regulation. However, its use in evaluating social regulation continues to be very difficult. As suggested in Chapter 7, cost-benefit analysis is an important first step to sound decisions. Dimensions of rights and justice must also be factored into the analysis, particularly into decisions to be resolved within the political sphere. In a pluralistic society with diverse interest group concerns, if any one interest is given priority, including the business interest, the result will be perceived as unjust.

Fourth, management style, executive values, and ideology can shape the organizational culture of government. Appointments, carefully made, can reinforce this. Style and executive leadership primarily affect the implementation of public policy, not its formation. Reforms based upon style and ideology can be stopped or changed quickly if an administration with different values, style, and ideology comes in power. Thus, such approach to reform can supplement, but not replace, more lasting institutional reforms that are based on changing the law.

Fifth, the alienation of Congress and external constituencies can lead to intense resistance, which makes statutory reform impossible. Most of the laws covering deregulation were accomplished during the Carter administration, when there was rapport between Congress and the executive branch. Cooperation and mutual support of leg-

islative approaches to regulatory reform declined as hostility increased between the Reagan administration and Congress. Thus, little by way of regulatory reform occurred after the first term, which ended in 1985.

By President Reagan's second term of office, the deregulation and regulatory reform movement was largely over as his attention turned to other administrative goals. Relations with Congress had become increasingly adversarial. Reagan's aggressive approach to regulatory relief had resulted in intense mistrust and widespread resistance by Congress and by the professional staff within the regulatory agencies. This resistance affected the work of the RARG, which was disbanded in 1983; it politicized the appointment process, although the administration prevailed in making most appointments consistent with its ideology; and it discredited many regulatory agencies as a probusiness bias became an election issue. As the elections for the second term of office approached, regulatory enforcement activity and litigation initiated by the administration was increased in an attempt to regain public credibility.

Industry Deregulation

Before 1975, if you wanted to make a long-distance call, it was placed with AT&T; if you wanted to fly between two major cities, two or three carriers would offer the same regulated ticket price; if you wanted to move your household, you would choose between the two or three major movers granted the routes by the ICC and the freight rates charged were regulated; and if you wanted to invest your money, savings deposit interest rates were regulated as were the broker fees on stock purchased. Within ten years, all this had radically changed. The following decade marked a wave of new laws in which the government sought to retreat from the economic sphere, as shown in Table 12–4. The deregulated industries accounted for some $250 billion dollars and deregulation was a major restructuring of the economy.[34]

TABLE 12–4
Economic Deregulation in the United States Since 1975 (key deregulatory initiatives and statutes)

1975	Securities and Exchange Commission: abolition of minimum brokerage commissions on New York Stock Exchange
	Securities Amendments Acts: development nationally of interlinked competitive securities markets
1976	Railroad Revitalization and Reform Act: increased rate-setting freedom for railroads
1977	Air Cargo Deregulation Act: progressive entry and rate deregulation
1977	Court judgment striking down antisiphoning restrictions in cable TV and subscription TV
1978	Air Passenger Deregulation Act: progressive and ultimately total deregulation of rates and entry. Sunset for CAB. In case of antitrust issues, CAB control was to be passed to Department of Justice
1978	National Gas Policy Act: gradual decontrol of gas prices, focusing mainly on newly discovered gas
1978	Department of Justice "show cause" move regarding price fixing exemption of IATA
1978	Public Utility Regulatory Policies Act: electric wheeling and interconnection powers granted to FERC. Requirement to consider rate structure reform (e.g., electricity)
1978	Presidential statement of need for increased competition in bilateral air services agreements with other countries
1979	International Air Transport Competition Act: maximum reliance on competitive market forces in international airline agreements
1979	Supreme Court: upholds termination of own programming and public interest rules imposed on cable TV
1979	FCC: radio program content rules dropped
1980	Staggers Rail Act: emphasis on more flexibility for rail carrier management
1980	Motor Carrier Act: increased entry and rate freedom and reduced role for rate-fixing bureau
1980	Household Goods Transportation Act: deregulation of household goods transport

Beginning with the Carter administration, the deregulation movement began with the removal of economic regulations:

In *transportation*, trucking, railroads, and airlines were deregulated.
In *the financial services*, minimum brokerage rates were removed, securities markets were interlinked nationally and internationally, and deposit interest rates were removed. As deregulation progressed and boundaries began to blur, the businesses of banking, savings and loans, investments, and consumer credit began to be merged into one large financial services industry.
In *telecommunications*, the FAA dropped program requirement rules within television, cable television was deregulated, and AT&T, through a consent decree, agreed to a breakup of its local

1980	Depository Institutions Deregulation and Monetary Control Act: equalization of reserve requirements among all financial institutions offering similar types of deposits; phasing out of limitation on deposit interest rates; easing of restrictions on the permitted range of lending activities
1981	FCC: approval of direct broadcasting satellite program
1981	Decontrol of Crude Oil and Refined Petroleum Products (Executive Order): complete lifting of crude oil price control. Under President Carter's National Energy Plan of 1977 control had in any case been scheduled to be lifted by October 1981
1981	Bus Regulatory Reform Act: entry and exit conditions eased, zones of rate freedom established, and role of rate bureau reduced
1982	AT&T divestiture consent decree. AT&T to divest itself of its local phone companies in return for the right to enter the computer market
1982	Garn–St. Germain Depository Institutions Act: removal of restrictions on thrift institutions both in the acceptance of deposits and in their lending and acquisition of securities
1982	U.S.–European discussions leading to introduction of zones of rate freedom on North Atlantic air routes
1983	FCC: TV program content rules dropped
1984	FCC: complete deregulation of rate and service regulation of satellites
1984	Cable Telecommunications Act: virtual completion of deregulation of cable TV
1985	Supreme Court ruling on interstate banking pacts. Agreements *between* states whereby a bank in one state may be controlled via the shareholding of a bank in another state were upheld even if New York banks were specifically excluded from benefiting from such an arrangement
1986	FRB and court rulings eroding restrictions contained in Glass–Steagall Act.

SOURCE: Dennis Swann, *The Retreat of the State: Deregulation and Privatization in the UK and US* (Ann Arbor: University of Michigan Press, 1988), pp. 34–35.

telephone companies and to the deregulation of long-distance telephone service in return for access to the computer industry.

The Savings and Loan Debacle

The savings and loan industry began with public-spirited local organizations seeking to help people fulfill the American dream of home ownership. The S&Ls received deposited savings from people for a small rate of interest set by regulation. These savings deposits were then loaned out at one or two percentage points more to home buyers. Deposits were insured for $100,000 by the Federal Savings and Loan Insurance Corporation (FSLIC), a government insurance corporation that received insurance payments from member savings and loan institutions. Also, government regulations existed over management practices, interest rates offered to depositors, and loans and investments that S&Ls could make.

The deregulation of the savings and loan industry has proved to be a major debacle that will cost taxpayers over $500 billion.[35] What went wrong? What caused a mess of such massive proportions?

Cash Management Accounts and the Decline of Savings Deposits in S&Ls

In 1977, Merrill Lynch, headed by Don Regan, who was later to be President Reagan's White House chief of staff, began to offer the cash management account. Through this account, Merrill Lynch offered investors the opportunity to invest in relatively short-term money market funds and began to compete more directly with the banking and savings and loan industries.

As noted earlier, the late 1970s were marked by a high inflation rate that translated into earnings on money market accounts of over 11 percent interest and increasing to nearly 20 percent by the beginning of the Reagan administration. Those who deposited their savings in banks or in savings and loan businesses suddenly had the opportunity to double their earnings by reinvesting their savings in Merrill Lynch's cash management accounts. Savings were invested in money market funds that were nearly as secure as the government-guaranteed savings deposit accounts.

Deregulation of Interest Rates and Investments by S&Ls

Savings and loans found that their primary source of cash, savings deposits, was suddenly drying up with the advent of the money market funds in a partially deregulated environment. The government responded in 1980 by removing the interest rate regulations on savings accounts. This allowed the savings and loans to match the money market rates so that they could continue to attract depositors' savings. Unfortunately, most of the loans on homes were 30-year fixed-rate loans at substantially lower interest rates than the new deposit rates.

The S&Ls began to lose billions of dollars and, with the belated blessings of the regulators, sought to make up the difference by loaning money for more risky projects that would also command a higher rate of interest. Also, many savings and loans tried to "grow out of the hole" by rapidly expanding by opening more branches. This increased lending also increased the need for more savings deposits. So S&Ls began to offer even higher interest rate premiums for deposits. Some began to invest in high-interest subordinated debt offerings, also called junk bonds. As discussed in Chapter 14, the 1980s was a decade of turbulent hostile takeovers financed by a mushrooming junk bond market. This climate also encouraged insider trading, fraud, and other unscrupulous and illegal practices within the S&L industry, resulting in total losses of around $150 billion before interest, as shown in Table 12–5.[36]

The Failure of Government Regulation and the S&L Mess

The behavior of government regulators also played a major part in the S&L debacle.[37] Edward Kane likened the S&Ls to zombies, those movie monsters of the living dead who managed to continue "living" after they were actually dead. Most businesses must face the discipline of the market, and thus the consequences of poor decisions that result in losses usually mean bankruptcy and the failure of the business. But the S&L is a business that cannot die; rather, it behaves more like a zombie. Why?

As noted in the last chapter, the Great Depression and the failure of the banking system led to an increase in the role of the government as the guarantor of the banking system. This role led to the extensive regulation of banking and, later, to the S&Ls, through (1) government oversight through audits, (2) the requirement for sound practices through rules and regulations enforced by bank auditors, and (3) the guarantee, by government-supported deposit insurance, of deposits that had increased to $100,000 per person by the 1980s. However, the regulatory system required all three of these factors to operate to assure prudent management within the industry.

Managers were under enormous pressure to increase savings deposit interest rates and to try to maintain the spread between the rate paid and the one received on loans made. Market forces would compel managers to respond to the pressures, decreasing this interest rate spread; but the possibility of failure should automatically control economically unsound decisions. In the absence of market forces, government regulation would need to supplement competitive pressures to protect the depositor from unsound loan decisions.

The managers of the S&Ls bought junk bonds to finance hostile takeovers. They invested in high-risk interest rate mega-projects in real estate development located in Houston and other cities without having to bear the risk. And they expanded their branch operations in an uneconomic manner. In the end, many of the junk bond schemes failed, large-scale real estate projects were overdeveloped and lost money, and the price of housing was driven up in several regions of the country and the market ultimately collapsed, resulting in numerous foreclosures.

How could the S&Ls finance all these failing endeavors and still attract money from the capital markets? The money came from depositors. Higher deposit interest rates could attract an almost unlimited amount of new deposits, because depositors knew the savings were protected by the government up to $100,000 per person. Each member of a wealthy family could invest the limit in any of a large number of S&Ls offering these high rates. And the savings deposits could be made with no risk because they were protected by the government insurance program.

TABLE 12–5
S&Ls: Where Did All Those Billions Go? ($ billion)

1. With deregulation, the 30-year fixed-rate mortgages could not support high interest on deposits	$25
2. Some S&Ls tried to make up losses on high-risk investments—and lost	28
3. Some S&Ls tried to grow out of their problems and opened unneeded branches	14
4. The increased lending caused many to offer premium interest rates to attract more deposits	14
5. Fraud	5
6. Losses on nonreal estate loans like junk bonds	6
7. Government inefficiency and mistakes made on the sell-off of insolvent S&Ls	12
8. Government allowing insolvent S&Ls to remain open	43
Total S&L losses	147
Total S&L Losses Plus Interest on Losses	647

SOURCE: Adapted from Gary Hector, "Where Did All Those Billions Go?" *Fortune*, September 10, 1990, pp. 84–85. Copyright 1990 Time, Inc. Reprinted by permission.

How could the S&L managers continue to make these unwise investments? It was during this period that the OMB was cutting the budgets and staffing of all regulatory agencies. Agencies simply did not have the staffing to audit or prosecute irregularities. Also, the S&L industry lobbied members of Congress, who intervened with the administration to reduce the pressures of regulatory oversight. This encouraged mismanagement at best, and in many cases, fraud within the S&Ls. Many were allowed to continue unsound practices as zombie institutions, costing the public billions of dollars in subsequent bailouts. Examples of some of the larger failures include the following:

Savings and Loan	Location	Cost ($ billion) to Taxpayers
American Savings	Stockton, CA	4.37
University Federal	Houston, TX	2.58
Western S&L	Phoenix, AZ	1.73
Centrust Savings	Miami, FL	1.70
United Savings of Texas	Houston, TX	1.60
Bright Bank Savings	Dallas, TX	1.38
Gill Savings	San Antonio, TX	1.24

Excesses, Fraud, and Bankruptcy As Ways to Drain S&L Resources

Many of the failures of saving and loan institutions, particularly in Texas and Lincoln Savings in California, were marked by allegations of fraud. Some high-rolling Texas managers explained, "A rolling loan gathers no loss," as they shifted bad loans from S&L to S&L to avoid the notice of bank examiners. Sunbelt Savings spent $1.3 million for Halloween and Christmas parties, which included $32,000 for orchestras.[38]

Charles Keating controlled Lincoln Savings through a holding company. Lincoln Savings made loans on overvalued property, declared an accounting profit, and paid its holding company, as owners of the S&L, huge dividends that, of course, were paid in cash from deposits. Keating made large campaign contributions to members of Congress who interceded on his behalf to reduce the level of bank auditing oversight that might have controlled his activities. In the end, Lincoln Savings was a bankrupt shell of an institution, Keating eventually went to prison, and one senator from California was censured for his behavior in the case.

The enforcement staff and budget for prosecutions were held at such low levels that much fraudulent behavior went unprosecuted and thus was encouraged by these circumstances. Sometimes unethical managers would take control of S&Ls with borrowed money, drain all the resources through fraud and questionable accounting practices, declare bankruptcy, and leave a trail of carnage.[39]

Transportation Industry Deregulation: Airlines and Trucking

Airline deregulation brought about the dismantling of the CAB but did not mean deregulating airline safety, which continues to be regulated by the Federal Aviation Administration (FAA). In the first five years of deregulation in transportation, many new firms entered the market, as predicted. Fourteen new airlines entered the market and some 10,000 new small trucking operators began operation. However, several major airlines also went bankrupt and were liquidated, including PanAm, Eastern, and Braniff. In trucking, only 10 of the top 30 firms were still operating after a decade of deregulation, and more than 150,000 workers lost their jobs. In the airline industry, wages also dropped sharply and over 50,000 employees lost their jobs as the rigors of market competition brought about efficiencies and job reduction actions. Deregulation has benefited consumers with price decreases but it has been a wrenching experience for employees.

DEREGULATING THE TRUCKING INDUSTRY

In trucking, less-than-truckload (LTL) trucking companies operate networks with regional consolidation centers that assure that trucks are filled for long hauls.[40] These consolidation centers are supplied with cargo by smaller networks of satellite terminals operated by smaller firms or

TABLE 12–6
How Deregulation Has Changed the U.S. Airline Industry

	1978	1987	1988
Millions of passengers	250	400	450
Consumer complaints	23,609	44,845	21,917
Near collisions in midair	504	1,058	480
Five largest airlines' percentage of total passenger traffic	65	55	73
Average ticket revenue per passenger mile	$.1227	$.0939	$.0979

SOURCE: Data collected from "The Frenzied Skies," *Business Week,* December 19, 1988, p. 71. Copyright 1988 by McGraw-Hill, Inc. Reprinted by special permission.

branches that operate door-to-door delivery. The use of computers and centralized dispatching systems facilitate economies-of-scale operations by assuring that trucks carry optimal loads so that overall costs decrease as total freight volume increases. In the process, the largest truckers displace smaller carriers from regional routes and put pressure on other large carriers, driving them from the industry.

As over 10,000 small operators, individuals that may own a single truck, entered the market, they were willing to work for much less than the unionized workers of the large trucking companies. Freight rates dropped sharply in the wake of desperate price wars. To counter this competition, larger trucking companies sought concessions from employees, and wages often dropped by as much as 25 percent during the decade of the 1980s, while the cost of living increased by around 28 percent.

One common approach to obtaining wage cuts was to offer the employees an employee stock ownership plan (ESOP) in return for wage concessions of 15 percent or more. The governance idea was that employees would then have a say in the management of the company. From the company perspective, ESOPs provided a way to reduce labor costs and ease cash flow strains. With the intense competition, companies often went bankrupt anyway. For example, the American Freight System, a large trucking company operating out of Overland Park, Kansas, used an ESOP but went bankrupt and was liquidated within a year after its adoption. With the failure of this firm, 9,300 employees lost their jobs and 258 truck terminals were closed and 17,000 trucking rigs idled.[41]

Unfortunately, employees often lost their retirement funds when bankruptcy occurred. This is because larger firms were often allowed to self-finance retirement funds rather than to place the deducted money into investment accounts reserved for workers upon retirement. After deregulation, freight rates did drop significantly, but labor bore much of the burden through wage cuts, lost pension funds, and massive layoffs.

DEREGULATING THE AIRLINES

During the decade of airline deregulation the total passenger load increased from 250 million passengers to 400 million by 1987, to 450 million by 1988. Service levels dropped at first and consumer complaints soared to nearly 45,000 in 1987 from 24,000 in 1978. Service then improved and customer complaints are now less than they were in the days before deregulation, even though traffic has nearly doubled, as shown in Table 12–6.

In the early 1980s an air controllers' strike was broken by President Reagan when he dismissed all striking employees. This broke the Air Controllers Union, but it also raised the question of air terminal safety. The experience level of air controllers dropped at a time when a large number of new airlines were appearing and the number of new unregulated flights threatened to overwhelm many metropolitan area airports. Near air collisions more than doubled before the situation was brought back into control by the end of the decade.

Airlines have adopted "hub-and-spoke" configurations similar to those in trucking. Each major airline developed one or more hubs through which all of its flights were funneled. The hubs were fed by many new commuter airlines that either entered the market in a symbiotic relationship with a primary carrier or were acquired by each of the major carriers to generate more passengers in the hub. These hub-and-spoke systems created economies of scale much as they did in trucking, but they also were formidable barriers to entry by new carriers and created captive traffic.

In addition to the hub-and-spoke configuration, other cost-reduction and competitive measures have been used since deregulation. While air fares between large cities generally declined, rural and sparsely populated areas did not do as well. With deregulation, the CAB-required cross-subsidization ended. Many small towns lost air service altogether, and those with service experienced sharp rate increases. For example, the rate between Pittsburgh and Philadelphia under regulation in 1978 was $86; after deregulation in 1982 the rate increased to $460.[42]

Consider American Airlines under the leadership of Robert Crandall, who characterized the business as "intensely, vigorously, bitterly, savagely competitive."[43] Under regulation, ticket prices were the same for all airlines. Immediately upon deregulation, American Airlines introduced a Super Saver fare program that offered deep cuts in ticket prices, which was the first in a series of fare wars. There have been frequent fare wars over the deregulation years, though fares did rise in 1988 (see Table 12–6). In May 1992, American Airlines again slashed fares on advance ticket purchases by 50 percent.

In 1983 a two-tier wage structure was implemented by American Airlines. Under that structure, airline pilots already employed continue to earn salaries of as high as $60,000 per year, but newly hired pilots were hired at a much lower wage scale. This system has been adopted by most airlines and extended beyond pilots to maintenance and other employees. With time and growth, American has been able to sharply reduce its labor expenses.

One unexpected result of deregulation in transportation has been a sharp increase in market concentration. This is an antitrust concern discussed in the next chapter. *Market concentration* is the percentage of total sales by the top few businesses within a particular market or industry. In airlines, the top five market concentration ratio initially decreased from 65 percent to 55 percent but has been increasing to 73 percent in recent years. Not one new entrepreneurial airline like Peoples Express has entered the airline industry in the last five years. Prices have been increasing as measured in average ticket revenue per passenger mile, as shown in Table 12–6. Recently a price-fixing case was settled through a consent decree in which American, United, Delta, and USAir agreed to pay over $400 million to former passengers. However, all deny the charge of price fixing.

At the end of 1992, the airline industry was dominated by a few large airlines. The three largest—American, Delta, and United—were all experiencing operating losses. Operating under the protection of Chapter 11 bankruptcy reorganization were TWA and Continental. USAir was close to insolvency and some observers were predicting its Chapter 11 reorganization. Only the low-cost, low-fare Southwest with $1.3 billion in revenues consistently operated at a profit throughout the decade of deregulation. Unlike the other competitors, Southwest did not use a hub-and-spoke system. It specialized in short flights, did not use advance boarding passes, offered little service with no frills, and had low fares. Its overhead expenses were substantially lower than those of other airlines, and it was in a better position to prevail in cases of cut-throat competitive price wars. Its low fares established market prices in many of its market areas that were below the cost of some other airlines.

Summary

The governmental sphere should maintain justice and protect the rights of individuals in the interests of the overall society. In accomplishing its task through the public policy process, the government must balance the needs for efficiency in the operations of the market system with the need of the government to maintain justice for all. The requirements for an effective public policy process parallel the requirements for market competition and include (1) equal access to the political process by all people, (2) limited political power so that narrow interest will not dominate the process over the will of the broader society, (3) knowledgeable citizens, (4) public policy set by citizens and their representatives, and (5) limited interference in the political process by other spheres of society. The expected result is a government that provides for the public interest, political equality, protection of legitimized rights, and social justice for all.

If the political process fails to have the necessary conditions for it to work effectively, social problems are likely. This will trigger a control cycle much like the one discussed in Chapter 11, which resulted in the rapid growth of government regulation of business. In the case of the government, public policy can fail or become obsolete if the needs of society change, industry captures the regulatory agency, narrow interests dominate the public policy process, and bureaucratic dysfunctions interfere with the accomplishment of the regulatory tasks by government agencies.

The consequences of regulatory failure are rising costs of government, rising regulatory compliance costs borne by business, loss of managerial discretion leading to lower levels of competitiveness, and failure of government policy to accomplish its primary purpose. These dysfunctions have all appeared in recent years, triggering a movement of regulatory reform and deregulation beginning with the Nixon administration in the early 1970s.

Successive presidential administrations have sought to reform regulations. The Nixon administration reorganized the White House and created the Office of Management and Budget (OMB), which worked with a quality-of-life review group to apply cost-benefit analysis and other techniques of evaluation to the regulatory process. The Ford administration was primarily concerned with the effect of regulation on inflation. During Ford's administration, Congress, industry, and several interest groups all joined in a national consensus to reform regulation and to deregulate several industries.

The Carter administration applied cost-benefit analysis but would not allow this to be the major determination of social regulation. Environmental regulation increased during this administration, but several key laws were passed that began the deregulating of industry. Included in the deregulation were trucking, airlines, and the financial services industries.

Reagan's administration embraced regulatory reform and deregulation more than any previous administration. He adopted and extended previously used approaches like (1) use of the OMB for reviewing new and existing regulations and for cutting the budgets and staffing levels of regulatory agencies, (2) instituting a regulatory review group called the Task Force on Regulatory Relief, and (3) the use of cost-benefit analysis, Also, he used the presidential appointment process to bring about a cultural change in the court system, in the top management of independent regulatory agencies, and in the management of executive branch agencies. Unfortunately his appointment approach resulted, in part, in a major scandal in the EPA, which increased mistrust and opposition in Congress. The major accomplishments of regulatory reform and industry deregulation were all but ended by the end of Reagan's first term in office in 1985.

Industry deregulation had mixed results. Airline deregulation attracted numerous new firms into the industry, followed by price wars and a shakeout resulting in increased dominance of the industry by a few large carriers. Major airlines adapted efficiency measures like the hub-and-spoke system and dropped unprofitable routes. Air fares between major cities dropped but with the dropping of cross-subsidy to less traveled cities, these fares were increased sharply or service discontinued. On balance, the traveling public saved hundreds of millions of dollars in reduced airfares during the decade.

In the savings and loan industry, interest rates and investment constraints were deregulated. However, the government continued to guarantee deposits and also sharply reduced the government audit and oversight activities in the S&Ls. The result was widespread mismanagement and fraud that will cost taxpayers over $500 billion to bail out failed S&L operations.

In the trucking industry, wages were cut by more than 25 percent during the decade, and the cost of living increased by 28 percent. Thousands of single truck operators entered the industry, resulting in a decade-long price war. Only 10 of the top 30 firms in the trucking industry survived deregulation during its first decade.

Conclusion

The issue of deregulation is more of a concern to business than ever. The opposite counterforces of two control cycles—one triggered by market failure and leading to increased government regulation of business, the other triggered by regulatory failure and leading to attempts at regulatory reform and deregulation—may have reached a stalemate. The regulatory reform approaches of OMB and control of regulatory agency budgets and staffing levels continue, but both have been increasing during the last five years.

President Reagan's administration was the most vigorous in seeking to roll back two decades of government regulation of business. The struggle was intense and so was the opposition it provoked. The issue of regulatory reform continues to be difficult, complex, urgent, and painful for both government and business. Currently there is mistrust and adversarial relationships between business and government. There is a need to work toward government-business cooperation and a need to bring

about cooperation between the executive branch and Congress within government.

Discussion Questions

1. What are the conditions necessary for the public policy process to work in a democracy? How would you know if it is working?
2. What if one or more of these conditions are missing? What is the likely result? Explain your reasons.
3. Describe the control cycle as it applies to the role of government regulations. Apply this model to an actual case you have read about in the newspaper recently.
4. What is the agency capture theory? How does it work?
5. How could a "capture" of an agency for social regulation occur?
6. Is interest group influence a "failure" of the public policy process? Describe a situation (an actual one, if you can), in which you think an interest group action caused the public policy process to fail.
7. Why do government agencies seem so inefficient and unconcerned about how much regulations cost business?
8. Describe the approaches to reforming government regulation.
9. Briefly outline the history of regulatory reform and deregulation.
10. What strategies did the Reagan administration use to halt the sharp increase government regulation of business?
11. Why did the deregulation end in 1985, at the end of the first term of the Reagan administration, rather than at the end of his second term of office? Why hasn't the deregulation movement continued until the present?
12. Did deregulation work? Use a specific example, choosing from one of the deregulated industries like the airlines, trucking, long-distance telephones, or the savings and loan industry to explain your position.

Notes

1. Dennis Swann, *The Retreat of the State: Deregulation and Privatization in the UK and US* (Ann Arbor: University of Michigan Press, 1988), p. 71. Also see Richard A. Posner, "Theories of Economic Regulation," *Bell Journal of Economics and Management Science* 5, no. 2 (Autumn 1974): 335–58.

2. Ibid., pp. 62–73.

3. George J. Stigler, "The Theory of Economic Regulation," *Bell Journal of Economics* 2 (1971): 3–21.

4. Andrew S. Carron and Paul W. MacAvoy, *The Decline of Service in the Regulated Industries* (Washington, D.C.: American Enterprise Institute for Public Policy Research, 1981), pp. 1–14.

5. M. Russell and R. B. Shelton, "A Model of Regulatory Agency Behavior," *Public Interest* 20 (1974): 47–62.

6. Martha Derthick and Paul J. Quirk, *The Politics of Deregulation* (Washington, D.C.: Brookings Institution, 1985), pp. 12–13.

7. Michael Pertschuk, *Revolt Against Regulation: The Rise and Pause of the Consumer Movement* (Berkeley, Calif.: University of California Press, 1982), pp. 5–45.

8. James Q. Wilson, *The Politics of Regulation* (New York: Basic Books, 1980).

9. James Q. Wilson, "The Rise of the Bureaucratic State," in Nathan Glazer and Irving Kristol, eds. *The American Commonwealth* (New York: Basic Books, 1976), pp. 93–94.

10. Panel on "Public Policy and Global Competitiveness," Stanford University Conference on Manufacturing, Stanford University, April 1992.

11. See Larry N. Gerston, Cynthia Fraleigh, and Robert Schwab, *The Deregulated Society* (Pacific Grove, Calif.: Brooks/Cole, 1988), pp. 72–75.

12. Francis E. Rourke, ed., *Bureaucratic Power in National Politics*, 3d ed. (Boston: Little, Brown, 1978).

13. Murray Weidenbaum, "The Consumer's Stake in Deregulation," *Vital Speeches* 5, no. 6 (January 1991): 5–11.

14. U.S. Commission on Federal Paperwork, *Final Summary Report* (Washington, D.C.: Government Printing Office, 1977).

15. Arthur Andersen and Company, *Cost of Government Regulation: Study for the Business Roundtable* (New York: Arthur Andersen, 1979).

16. Gerston et al., *The Deregulated Society*, pp. 42–61.

17. Derthick and Quirk, *The Politics of Deregulation*, p. 42.

18. Swann, *The Retreat of the State*, p. 39.

19. Gerston et al., *The Deregulated Society*, pp. 47–48.

20. Gerston et al., *The Deregulated Society*, pp. 48–61.

21. Howard Ball, *Controlling Regulatory Sprawl: Presidential Strategies from Nixon to Reagan* (Westport, Conn.: Greenwood Press, 1984); Richard M. Neustadt, "The Administration's Regulatory Reform Program: An Overview," *Administrative Law Review* 32, no. 2 (September 1980): 129–63; and George C. Eads and Michael Fix, *Relief or Reform? Reagan's Regulatory Dilemma* (Washington, D.C.: Urban Institute, 1984).

22. Gerston et al., *The Deregulated Society*, pp. 51–59.

23. E. J. Mishan, *Cost-Benefit Analysis: An Informal Introduction*, 3d ed. (New York: Praeger, 1976).

24. Robert H. Haveman and Burton A. Weisbrod, "Defining Benefits of Public Programs: Some Guidance for Policy Analysis," in *Public Expenditure and Policy Analysis*, 2d ed., Robert H. Haveman and Julius Morgolis, eds. (Chicago: Rand McNally, 1977), pp. 135–60.

25. Michael Wines, "Reagan's Reforms are Full of Sound and Fury, But What Do They Signify?" *National Journal* 14 (January 16, 1982): 96–98.

26. Kenneth W. Chilton, *The Effects of Gramm-Rudman-Hollings on Federal Regulatory Activities* (St. Louis: Washington Center for the Study of American Business, 1986).

27. "Reagan's Regulators," *National Journal* 17, no. 20 (May 18, 1985): 1188–89.

28. Gerston et al., *The Deregulated Society*, p. 230.

29. Susan J. Tolchin and Martin Tolchin, *Dismantling America* (New York: Oxford University Press, 1983), p. 92.

30. "Reagan's Toxic Turmoil," *Newsweek*, February 21, 1983, pp. 22–25.

31. "The Toxic Tar Baby at Reagan's EPA," *Newsweek*, February 28, 1983, pp. 14–15.

32. "Storm over the Environment," *Newsweek*, March 7, 1983.

33. Dick Kirschten, "Ruckelshaus May Find EPA Problems Are Budgetary as Much as Political, *National Journal*, March 26, 1983, pp. 659–60; "The Environmental Impact of the EPA's Mr. Fix-it," *Business Week*, August 22, 1983, pp. 108–9; Andy Paztor, "In Seeking to Put EPA in Order, Ruckelshaus Is Facing a Tough Job," *Wall Street Journal*, September 29, 1983, p. 1; and Lawrence Moser, "EPA Still Doesn't Know the Dimensions of the Nations's Hazardous Waste Problem, *National Journal*, April 16, 1983, pp. 796–99.

34. "Deregulating America," *Business Week*, November 28, 1983, pp. 80–96; and "Is Deregulation Working?" *Business Week*, December 22, 1986, pp. 50–54.

35. See Edward J. Kane, *The S&L Mess: How Did It Happen?* (Washington, D.C.: Urban Institute, 1989), and "The S&L Mess—and How to Fix It," *Business Week*, October 31, 1988, pp. 130–40.

36. Gary Hector, "S&Ls: Where Did All Those Billions Go?" *Fortune*, September 10, 1990, pp. 84–88.

37. Edward J. Kane, *The S&L Mess: How Did It Happen?* (Washington, D.C.: Urban Institute, 1989).

38. *U.S. News and World Report*, January 23, 1989, p. 40.

39. For several examples of this, see Donald L. Barlett and James B. Steele, *America: What Went Wrong?* (Kansas City Mo.: Andrews and McMeel, 1992), chap. 4; "The Bust of '89," *U.S. News & World Report*, January 23, 1989, pp. 36–43.

40. "Is Deregulation Working? *Business Week*, December 22, 1986, p. 50.

41. Barlett and Steele, *America: What Went Wrong?* pp. 116–20.

42. Ibid., p. 110.

43. "The Airline Mess," *Business Week*, July 6, 1992, pp. 50–55.

Discussion Case _____

The Air Bag Controversy

Should the drivers and passengers of automobiles be required to wear seat belts? Should it be an individual's responsibility to wear a seat belt while driving or riding in a car? Although it is known that seat belts save lives, many riders of automobiles do not wear them. Some argue that the responsibility for driver and passenger safety should be borne by manufacturers, who should be required to install air bags or some other type of passive restraint system in all automobiles.

An air bag is a passive restraint system that requires no action on the part of the occupant of an automobile. Unlike the seat belt that many do not wear while riding in a car, the air bag would automatically be available to protect a person in case of an accident. However, the air bag is relatively expensive to install and requiring it would increase the price of an automobile. The more active system, the seat belt, is much less expensive but is not reliable because many either forget or choose not to fasten it when they enter an automobile.

Seat belts have been required in cars by federal regulation since 1968. Many states have made the failure to use the seat belt a misdemeanor. The controversy over air bag regulation has been long and, at times, bitter.

William Coleman, Jr., secretary of transportation in the Ford administration, decided in 1976 that a rule would not be developed that required automobile manufactures to install air bags. His successor at the department, Brock Adams, reversed the decision and approved a three-year period to phase in the installation of air bags, which would be required for 1982 model automobiles. The decision was based upon an analysis that concluded that air bags would save 9,000 lives a year and prevent as many as 100,000 serious injuries.

In 1981, the Reagan administration reversed the air bag rule as a part the regulatory reform and deregulation program. The cost-benefit analysis concluded that financially troubled automobile manufactures could ill afford the estimated $1 bil-

lion cost per year to install the air bags. International competition was also causing downward pressure on automobile prices, and it was not clear that consumers would be willing to pay more for their cars.

The Reagan administration's decision was disputed by the insurance industry, which favored air bags. The estimated savings of lives and preventing of injuries resulting from increased use of air bags, whether they were voluntarily installed or not, would save a substantial amount on damage claims. In 1982, the District of Columbia Federal District Court, in *State Farm Mutual Insurance Co. v. Department of Transportation,* reversed the administration's rule not to require air bags, indicating it mattered "not whether evidence shows that usage rates would increase. . .but whether there is evidence showing that they will not."

The case was appealed all the way to the Supreme Court and in June 1983, in *Motor Vehicle Manufacturers Association of the United States v. State Farm Mutual Automobile Insurance Co. Case,* the Supreme Court upheld the decision of the court of appeals, which found the department's decision to rescind the passive restraint rule to be "arbitrary and capricious." The final department rule requiring passive restraints was issued on July 17, 1984. The rule required all automobiles marketed after 1989 to have full passive protection. However, manufacturers could choose from several passive restraint technologies available. A legal challenge to this final rule was dismissed by the D.C. Court of Appeals in 1986.

Case Discussion Questions

1. Should the use of restraints be a matter of individual choice?
2. Should the automatic forces of the market be used to make the decision?

3. Should an individual be allowed by the government to make the choice and be responsible for the risk?

4. Should automobile manufacturers be required to install costly passive restraint systems even when buyers may not want to pay for them? Would it be better to offer the passive restraint system as an optional equipment item rather than a required one?

5. What arguments can you make for the government regulation? Has the government gone too far in the passive restraint requirement?

6. What is the appropriate role of government in this case?

CHAPTER 13

Antitrust Law

CHAPTER OBJECTIVES

1. Introduce the concept of restraint of trade.
2. Review the historical context and legislative intent behind antitrust law.
3. Explain the goals of antitrust law and outline the current debate over them as they relate to competition and consumer welfare, or the newer emphasis on efficiency.
4. Provide an overview of antitrust laws.
5. Review some of the major cases that illustrate the important provisions of antitrust law.
6. Show how economists and economic theory have helped to shape antitrust law.
7. Briefly outline the different approaches to antitrust concepts, enforcement, and the role of the government.

Introduction

Antitrust law is a complex part of the legal environment of business. This area of the law applies potentially to many different decisions made by managers including pricing decisions, distribution agreements for products or services, purchasing contracts, and mergers or the acquisition of other firms. This chapter introduces the law but does not comprehensively cover the many ways that antitrust provisions affect management action.

The Sherman Antitrust Act, the first law in this area, was passed more than one hundred years ago. The act has been amended several times as new issues appeared in the public policy process, and the enforcement strategy of these laws has been subject to many changes over the years.[1] This chapter introduces readers to the basic framework within which antitrust laws apply and reviews some of the impor-

tant changes in enforcement patterns that have occurred during the past 15 years. As with all attempts by the government to regulate business, there has been considerable debate followed by attempts to change the law and deregulate business. New theories of economics about competitiveness, the increasing pressures of international competition, and the ebb and flow of different ideological orientations have all led to changes in antitrust laws. These changes in public policy in the area of antitrust are likely to have lasting effects on the economy and on the competitive process.

The purpose of antitrust law historically has been to maintain competition and to assure consumer welfare by prohibiting restraints of trade and anticompetitive behavior as defined by the courts.[2] Consumer welfare is maintained by prohibiting market constraints and unfair competition that would raise costs. In Discussion Case A at the end of this chapter, the court found that the universities were engaged in anticompetitive behavior. Their joint action was considered a type of price fixing that decreased the amount of financial aid available to students and thus increased the overall cost of education.

As briefly discussed in Chapter 11, much of the development of antitrust thought, until the 1970s, was based upon the structural economic theory of industrial organization.[3] The courts have been guided by this framework to apply antitrust law in a manner that maintains competitive market structures by dispersing economic power. This protects smaller businesses by guarding against the dominance of large-scale businesses wielding strong market power. More recently, traditional approaches to antitrust law have been challenged by those who argue that consumer welfare achieved by economic efficiency should be the sole purpose of antitrust law.[4] This debate over the proper goal of antitrust law and of government in regulating the economic sphere is a return to many concerns expressed a century ago, when antitrust law was first established in this country.[5]

Early Law, Restraints of Trade, and the Rule of Reason

Practices that restrain trade have been illegal for over five hundred years. One of the earliest reported cases against restraint of trade in common law was made against John Dyer in England in 1414.[6] Dyer had agreed not to compete in his town for six months and the court held that this agreement was invalid. The court ruled that it was important that people be able to voluntarily compete in commercial activities. While a person could freely decide not to compete, a contractual agreement not to compete was unfair.

Rule of Reason

According to the rule of reason, a practice may be found to be legal if there is a good purpose served by it. Most contractual agreements involve some sort of constraint on the terms of trade agreed upon by the parties to the contract. In another English case in 1711, *Mitchell v. Reynolds*, the court found that not all agreements in restraint of trade were illegal if they could be shown to be reasonable. In *Mitchell v. Reynolds*, a baker named Reynolds leased his business to Mitchell for five years with a contract agreement not to compete in the same area. Mitchell broke the lease and Reynolds sued for breach of contract. In his defense, Mitchell claimed the agreement was an invalid restraint of trade. The court decided in favor of Reynolds, finding that the noncompete clause was reasonable in this particular situation because it reasonably protected Mitchell for a period of time. The rule of reason has become a major principle in antitrust law.

The Per Se Rule of Illegality

In contrast to those practices that might be justified by the rule of reason, some practices have been considered as having no redeeming qualities and thus should always be considered illegal per se. In antitrust law, a *per se* offense is always illegal because its harm is presumed and proof of the act establishes illegality. The Supreme Court has described per se violations as follows:

> There are certain agreements or practices which because of their pernicious effect on competition and lack of any redeeming virtue are conclusively presumed to be unreasonable and therefore illegal without elaborate inquiry as to the precise harm they have caused or the business excuse for their use.[7]

Price fixing is a per se violation of antitrust law. In Discussion Case 13–1 at the end of this chapter, the court viewed jointly set financial aid packages as a form of price fixing and thus found the practice illegal. In responding to MIT's attempt to justify its behavior, the court seemed to be using the rule of reason rather than the per se rule against price fixing. The judge ruled that the method used to set financial aid amounts was not reasonable and the Overlap Group's practice was illegal. MIT appealed this case and has been granted another opportunity to explain its position. However, the Supreme Court has consistently ruled that any form of price fixing is a per se violation of Antitrust Law.

THE EARLY HISTORICAL CASE AGAINST MONOPOLY

An early famous English case against monopolies was *Darcy v. Allen.* In 1599 Queen Elizabeth granted Darcy the exclusive rights to import, buy, and sell playing cards in the realm.[8] Allen, without the queen's license or permission of Darcy, manufactured and imported some 180 gross of playing cards and was brought to trial. Darcy sued Allen, but the court reasoned that the effect of Darcy's monopoly was bad for society because it raised prices, reduced product quality, lessened trade, and thus created unemployment. The court also ruled that Darcy's monopoly violated the economic liberty of the individual and served to lower the wealth and welfare of the country. Therefore, the court found in favor of Allen.

Later, when Adam Smith published his *Wealth of Nations* in 1776, he criticized the monopolies that had been granted by the monarchy in his time. For example, he stated "all the other subjects of the state are taxed very absurdly in two different ways: first, by high price of goods, which, in the case of free trade, they could buy much cheaper; and, secondly, by their total exclusion from a branch of business, which it might be both convenient and profitable for them to carry on."[9] Furthermore, Smith argued that if private competitors were allowed to enter the markets then controlled by government-granted monopolies, the monopolies could not survive.

These arguments closely parallel the debate and the legislative goals given for the Sherman Antitrust Act passed in the United States a century later. Competitive rivalry in free markets protects economic liberty, results in lower prices and better goods and services, and increases the public welfare by creating national wealth.

DISTRUST OF CONCENTRATED POWER IN AMERICAN HISTORY

The history of the United States reveals a strong distrust of concentrated power. The Constitution was written with many checks and balances between the various branches of government to discourage large concentrations of political power that lead to the abuse of rights of citizens. The Founders were keenly aware of the possibility of narrow interests capturing the government and sought to minimize this possibility when they designed our constitutional government. Society at that time was agrarian and dominated by many small-scale businesses; the Founders never dreamed of the large-scale business enterprises that are commonplace in our time.

The agrarian society of that day had no large cities, no national infrastructure of communication and transportation, and no large-scale businesses. As noted in Chapter 11, major changes in the U.S. economy occurred in the eighteenth century. Technological changes in manufacturing and meat packing made economies of scale possible; the advent of the railroads linked a large national market; and the growth of cities redefined society as it changed from an agrarian to an industrial base.

When big business did appear at the end of the last century, the fear of the trusts' concentrated power was a major political issue.[10] Congress in 1890 was concerned about concentrated economic power seen as leading to political corruption and the oppression of consumers and competitors.[11] Robust competitive rivalry made possible through economic opportunity to compete was seen as the best way to achieve a balanced distribution of power and wealth in society. This process would also serve the welfare of the consumer. Antitrust law was passed, in part, to maintain competition so that large concentrations of economic power would not be a threat to society.

Interest Group Politics and the Sherman Antitrust Act

The public policy process in this complex area involved many interest groups that had different objectives with respect to antitrust policy. Interests included big business, small business operators, farmers, urban population, and thinkers of the day.

Economists of the time followed the classical economic theory of Marshall, who thought markets were self-correcting, and thus were opposed to any intervention by the government.[12] If too many firms were in a market, the most efficient firms would drive out the less efficient firms until there was no excess capacity. If a market became dominated by a few businesses so that prices rose, more firms would be attracted into the industry and competitive forces would lead to equilibrium. There was no concept of barriers to entry that might limit access to a market. This concept of the invisible hand of the self-correcting marketplace persisted until the Great Depression of the 1930s and the later development of economic theory.

Social Darwinism and Big Business

A popular social theory of the day was social Darwinism, based upon the theory of evolution developed by Darwin. According to this theory, history was a struggle for power and control among competing parties. If a person or a business was very powerful, that was evidence that it was the fittest in society and justified to rule. Applied to the economic sphere of society, this theory served to justify the concentration of economic power in the hands of large-scale enterprises in the late 1800s. Big business supported the theory of social Darwinism and the ideology of the survival of the fittest, which was popular at the time. These "captains of industry" saw themselves as the fittest, destined to control the economy and perhaps the country. Thus they opposed antitrust law, which would interfere with what they saw as the natural processes of society.

Farmers and Small Business

Farmers were mixed in their support of antitrust. They feared big business and the abuse of economic power; but farmers had already been protected from abuse of power by the railroads with the passage of the Interstate Commerce Act. As noted in Chapter 11, this act which created the ICC, the government agency that regulated the railroads, had been the result of intensive lobbying by farmers. Thus farmers enjoyed regulated freight rates and access to larger markets for their crops

afforded by the railroads; but they did not compete directly against large-scale operators.

Small businesses were in a different position than farmers. They suffered from competitive pressures from the new large-scale enterprises; thus small businesses supported the new law. Many were forced out of business and feared the loss of their ability to successfully compete. Small businesses successfully lobbied Congress, which passed the Sherman Antitrust Act in 1890. Some have argued that the real purpose of antitrust law was to protect small business interests and not to help consumers, for two reasons: (1) large-scale businesses were significantly more efficient and prices were falling; (2) a tariff bill that protected businesses from imports was passed that same year. This tariff allowed businesses to raise prices and had their support. DiLorenzo argued that the historical concern for consumer welfare and lower prices as major purposes of antitrust law is more rhetoric than reality.[13]

The Goals of Antitrust Law

Because interest groups that work together to support a public policy have diverse goals and values, it is sometimes difficult to identify clearly the goals of a public policy. When a law is not specific courts or clearly written, courts also may have difficulty defining the public interest when making judgments about a case. Thus, courts sometimes consider legislative intent when judging cases. Conservative approaches to the law oppose the law-making role of the courts if it is inconsistent with legislative intent. More progressive judges seek to adapt law to the changing demands of society.

The Constitution and laws such as the Sherman Antitrust Act were written very generally and were subject to a wide variety of interpretations. If a law is silent or unspecific concerning an issue, there are three alternatives open to the Court:

1. The Court can interpret the law in terms of current knowledge of social expectations and economics at the time a case is brought before it.

2. The Court can narrowly interpret the law in terms of its understanding of the legislative intent and specific questions addressed in the law.
3. The Court can dismiss the case and urge Congress to change or amend the law.

LEGISLATIVE INTENT AND THE GOAL OF ANTITRUST LAW

When Senator Sherman introduced the antitrust bill in 1890, he argued in favor of economic liberty and said that it would be a "bill of rights, a charter of liberty."[14] Furthermore, he said the bill had two legislative purposes, including the following:

1. To prohibit trusts and combinations that tend to "prevent full and free competition. *Free competition is needed to insure industrial liberty* defined as "the right of every man to work, labor and produce. . .on equal terms and conditions."
2. To prohibit combinations that tend to "advance the *cost to the customer.*" While Sherman recognized that large-scale businesses were more efficient, he argued that "all experience shows that this savings of cost goes to the pockets of the producer" (emphasis supplied).[15]

As suggested above, each of these goals has a history in the (1) development of laws against restraint of trade, (2) early criticisms of monopoly power, (3) and fear of concentrated power by Americans. These factors were present in the public policy debates leading to the Sherman Antitrust Act of 1890. The law clearly rejected unchecked concentrated economic power based upon the theory of social Darwinism in favor of dispersion of power. It rejected economic efficiency as its primary goal if this meant individuals would not be free to compete in the marketplace.

Antitrust law, from the beginning, sought to establish economic liberty so that small businesses and others would be free to compete and Congress considered this the best way to assure the satisfaction of consumers. There was a distrust of large-scale business even if it proved to be more effi-

cient, because the rewards of efficiency would go to big business operators and not to consumers. And it was decided that competition, and the long-term interests of the nation, would be served best by the vigorous rivalry of sufficient numbers of businesses in each industry to sufficiently disperse the economic power of the largest firms.

THE GOALS OF ANTITRUST LAW AS JUDICIAL EXPERIENCE

The great U.S. Supreme Court justice Oliver Wendell Holmes once said, "The life of the law has not been logic, it has been experience."[16] *Common law* is the collection of court precedents that are codified judicial experience. Facts in each case vary and law becomes specifically defined through the experience. Common law is distilled in the decisions that respond to the specific situations that occur within an historical context. Antitrust law reflects the experience of the courts in making judgments pursuing the social and economic goals of Congress as expressed in the law. Legislative intent is considered as important as the experience with the law over time. Antitrust law prohibits monopolization in restraint of trade and anticompetitive behavior but does not specifically define these terms. Rather, these terms have been defined by the courts.

The Supreme Court has emphasized the goal of maintaining competitiveness and echoed Senator Sherman when it suggested that American antitrust law served as the "Magna Carta of free enterprise" to protect economic liberty and the free enterprise system:

> Antitrust laws in general, and the Sherman Act in particular, are the Magna Carta of free enterprise. They are as important to the preservation of economic freedom as the Bill of Rights is to the protection of our fundamental personal freedoms. And the freedom guaranteed each and every business, no matter how small, is the freedom to compete—to assert with vigor, imagination, devotion, and ingenuity whatever economic muscle it can muster.
>
> Like the Constitution, the Sherman Act is broadly written and has been subject to varied interpretation

by the courts with the passage of time. Thus, enforcement philosophies and patterns have changed over the years and are at present undergoing a major challenge. Thus it is important to consider the underlying goals of antitrust law before reviewing the specific content.[17]

Economic Thought and the Goals of Antitrust

The necessary conditions for competition and possible market failures are enumerated in Chapter 2. Chapter 11 outlines how society has responded with either antitrust law or economic or social regulations when markets failed to have these necessary conditions. However, in antitrust law there have been four periods of economic thought concerning the meaning of competition and the role of antitrust law in sustaining it: (1) the classical period ending in the 1920s, (2) a neoclassical period ending in the 1940s, (3) a period dominated by the economic theory of industrial organization ending in the 1970s, and (4) a postmodern period sponsored by the Chicago School during the last 20 years.[18]

CLASSICAL AND NEOCLASSICAL ECONOMIC THOUGHT

During the classical and neoclassical periods, from 1880 to the 1940s, competition was viewed as a process of rivalry between both small and large firms resulting in efficient outcomes, with size seen as no advantage. In classical economic thought, the market is guided by the invisible hand, is self-correcting, and always leads to efficiency and fair allocations. Government interference is unnecessary to maintain competition. Anticompetitive behavior and violations of contract are matters of the court and common law precedents, not necessarily antitrust law.

Antitrust enforcement during this time received little guidance from economists but it was nonetheless active. Theodore Roosevelt, president during this Progressive Era, was known as a "trust buster," and antitrust laws were vigorously enforced. The Clayton Act, amending the Sherman Antitrust Act, was passed in 1914, and the Federal Trade Commission Act was passed the same year, authorizing the FTC to jointly enforce antitrust law with the Department of Justice. The goals emphasized during this period were expressed in economic terms but were not supported by economists. These goals included dispersion of economic power, economic liberty of small businesses to compete, and economic welfare of people.

Economists provided some guidance to antitrust law from 1920 to the 1940s. It became recognized that restraints of trade like price fixing, tying agreements, and artificial barriers to trade could develop in the course of market operations. Thus, the government should assume an enlarged antitrust role in maintaining competition by assuring freedom of entry and exit from markets. The government made sure artificially erected barriers to entry would not injure competition, and prohibited price fixing and tying agreements to assure that market decisions were independently made.

A *tying agreement* is a contract requirement that allows the buyer to purchase a product or service on the condition that he or she buy something else too. For example, an early case found the practice of allowing movie theaters to show popular films on the condition that they also agree to run unpopular films was an illegal tying agreement.

ECONOMIC THEORY OF INDUSTRIAL ORGANIZATION

The *economic theory of industrial organization*, briefly described in Chapter 11, dominated thinking about antitrust law during the period from 1940 through the 1970s. This theory considers the linkages among market structure, market conduct, and economic performance.[19] This school of economics supports the four historical goals of antitrust law through maintaining the vigorous rivalry among competitors outlined above. Maintaining competition is the most important purpose of antitrust law because it supports the following goals:

1. Dispersing economic power, especially the power that results from concentrated markets
2. Assuring individuals the economic liberty to compete by prohibiting barriers to entry and trade restraints
3. Maintaining market competitiveness as the major source of control, which results in
4. Market performance that enhances the welfare of the customer.

According to the theory of industrial organization, market power interferes with the ability of the forces of market competition to set prices, profit levels, and returns to suppliers. In the economic theory of industrial organization, market structure is linked to market conduct, which, in turn, is linked to market performance, as shown in Figure 13–1[20]:

Market Power

According to this economic theory of industrial organization, highly competitive markets lead to competitive behaviors that result ultimately in high economic performance. A competitive market has the structural characteristic of numerous businesses in the industry or at least enough buyers and sellers so that none has sufficient market power to control prices and output levels. The result of competitive market structures is that each business makes decisions independently, consistent with the firm's best economic interest. Prices, profit levels, and returns are established by the laws of supply and demand within the context of market competition. Competitive market conduct exists when firms vigorously compete against one another to achieve high levels of market performance. Such market performance includes readily available products and services with the qualities that customers demand at low or reasonable prices.

In contrast, markets dominated by a few large businesses are more likely to encourage anticompetitive behavior like price fixing, tying agreements, and restrictions of markets from potential competitors. Uncompetitive markets lead to behavior that is more likely to be interdependent, less competitive, and more predatory than a competitive market would assure. Also, there may be a pattern of withholding technological change and new products in uncompetitive market situations.

Market structure was defined in terms of market concentration, elasticity of demand and supply, size of market, and market shares of principal competitors. Market structure was primarily measured in the four-firm ratio of *market concentration,* which was the percent of total market sales that the top four firms received. If this ratio was in excess of 80 percent or if a single dominant firm's share exceeded 40 percent, the market structure was considered concentrated for antitrust purposes.[21]

A major aspect of antitrust enforcement was the prohibition and discouraging of monopolization as measured in terms of market concentration before 1980. Maintenance of a system of small and viable businesses was the central goal of antitrust enforcement. Also such anticompetitive restraints of trade as price fixing, tying contracts, and price discrimination were prohibited. Efficiency, consid-

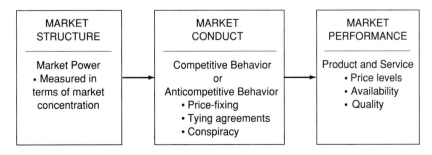

MARKET STRUCTURE	MARKET CONDUCT	MARKET PERFORMANCE
Market Power • Measured in terms of market concentration	Competitive Behavior or Anticompetitive Behavior • Price-fixing • Tying agreements • Conspiracy	Product and Service • Price levels • Availability • Quality

FIGURE 13–1 Economic Theory of Industrial Organization

ered by itself, was rejected as the goal of antitrust. However, it was assumed that efficiency and consumer welfare would be an automatic result of competition properly maintained by antitrust enforcement. Indeed, in 1975, the Court went so far as to assert that "the sole aim of antitrust legislation is to protect competition."[22]

THE "NEW LEARNING" OF THE CHICAGO SCHOOL OF ECONOMICS

During the last 20 years, "the New Learning" of the Chicago School has sought to redefine competitiveness and the goal of antitrust law.[23] This school of thought draws heavily from neoclassical price theory and develops a logic that rejects the traditional historical goals of antitrust. Bork argued that because competition and monopoly are economic concepts, only economic goals are relevant to antitrust, and the only goal of antitrust law should be consumer welfare expressed in terms of the Chicago School's economics concept of efficiency.[24] Moreover, he argued that a legislative history reveals no other appropriate goal for antitrust law.

Consistent with the classical school of the nineteenth century, this "New Learning" provides the intellectual justification for a government hands-off policy for antitrust consistent with the deregulatory movement described in Chapter 12. Faith is placed in the market to correct its failures and externalities, and government antitrust action should therefore be minimal.[25] For example, Bork has suggested that social Darwinism is consistent with competitive markets, and so long as there are at least three significant rivals in a market it can be presumed to be efficient.[26]

According to the Chicago School, antitrust enforcement should not be concerned with market power, allocation of wealth, or access to markets. It reasons that business seeks profit maximization and consumers seek to maximize their welfare. Whatever consumers choose is efficient and whatever firms produce maximizes consumer welfare. If that were not so, people would choose differently, because everyone is assumed to maximize profits or

self-interest. This type of reasoning has been criticized for being circular by Walter Adams and others, who argue that choices may not reflect a voluntary, noncoerced outcome if markets are highly concentrated.[27]

Judge Posner of the Chicago School argues that legal prohibitions against predatory pricing, price discrimination, tying contracts, and barriers to entry are poorly founded and should not be pursued by antitrust law enforcement. The rule of reason should be used over per se approaches to enforcement so that antitrust judgments can be guided by market efficiency and maximizing consumer welfare over any other purpose. Reluctantly, the Chicago School has agreed that price fixing and mergers between competitors that result in monopoly should be disallowed.[28]

The Chicago School approach supports the antitrust goal of economic efficiency rather than the maintenance of competitive market structures. Because analysis is needed to determine the efficiency trade-offs among practices under dispute, the use of the rule of reason is favored over per se interpretations of the law. This approach has strongly influenced judicial decisions since the beginning of the deregulatory movement in the mid-1970s.

The Sherman Antitrust Act of 1890, Section 1 Prohibits Anticompetitive Behavior

Section 1 prohibits conspiracy in restraint of trade. The law says, "Every contract, combination in the form of trust or otherwise, or conspiracy, in restraint of trade or commerce among the several States, or with foreign nations, is hereby declared to be illegal."

Conditions Necessary for a Violation
For a violation of this section to occur, there must be two or more people engaged in a contract or a conspiracy to restrain trade. If a contract exists or there is a written record of a conspiracy between

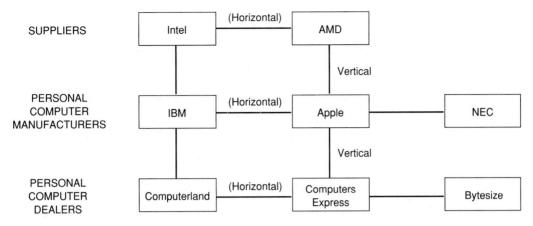

FIGURE 13–2 Horizontal and Vertical Relationships in the Personal Computer Industry

two or more people, then a violation can be proved. However, it is sometimes very difficult to determine whether a conspiracy is the cause of behavior or whether behavior is due to the independent actions of businesses all seeking their own interests. Firms may be acting in a parallel fashion according to independent self-interested business decisions without a conspiracy.

In *Theatre Enterprises, Inc. v. Paramount Film Distributors Corporation*,[29] a suburban Baltimore theater owned by Theatre Enterprises could not get first-run films because film distributors had a policy that offered all first-run films to the eight downtown theaters. After Theatre Enterprises was repeatedly rebuffed by film distributors when it sought first-run films for its suburban theater, it brought an antitrust suit against Paramount Film Distributors. The Court reasoned that because the downtown market was larger than the suburban market, distributors independently formed a policy to show first-run films in one of the eight downtown theaters and to show subsequent-run films only in the smaller suburban theaters. The Supreme Court found that the fact that all film distributors had this same policy was due to their independent assessment of the business decision and not due to any conspiracy.

Practices likely to be found illegal under this section 1 of the Sherman Act include agreements among competitors to (1) fix prices horizontally or

vertically, (2) divide geographic markets among competitors, (3) restrain trade through vertical nonprice restraints, or (4) boycott third parties.

PRICE FIXING

Price fixing is an agreement among competitors to charge the same price and is a per se violation of the Sherman Act. An early case centered on the issue of whether it was lawful for businesses to set reasonable prices jointly to avoid destructive competition. The Supreme Court rejected a rule of reason approach in price-fixing cases and held in *United States v. Trenton Potteries Company* that price fixing per se was illegal, in the following words:

> The power to fix prices, whether reasonably exercised or not, involves power to control the market and to fix arbitrary and unreasonable prices. The reasonable price fixed today may through economic and business changes become the unreasonable price of tomorrow.[30]

Horizontal division of markets is the agreement between competitors at the same level of competition to divide the geographic market. Level refers to suppliers, manufacturing, or retailing, as shown in Figure 13–2. Vertical relationships include those between buyers and sellers, that is, from sales from suppliers to manufacturers and from manufacturers to retail outlets. Horizontal relationships include relations among competitors within the same market at the same level in the vertical chain.

In *U.S. v. Topco Associates* the Supreme Court ruled that it was a per se violation of the Sherman Act to grant exclusive territories, even if such a policy would help smaller chains to more effectively compete against large supermarket chains.[31] In this case, a cooperative association of some 25 small and medium-sized regional supermarket chains served as a purchasing agent for association members. This centralized purchasing enabled the association to develop a private label at a low cost that would be competitive with the private labels of larger supermarket chains and thus could be considered procompetitive. However, Topco Associates granted exclusive territories to member chains and thus foreclosed markets to others within the designated territories. The district court found for Topco using a rule of reason concluding that the social benefit of the procompetitive effects outweighed the negative aspects of exclusive territories. Upon appeal, the Supreme Court reversed the decision of the lower court, indicating that the rule of reason could not be used for horizontal division of markets; rather, it was a per se violation.

VERTICAL NONPRICE RESTRAINTS: FROM PER SE TO RULE OF REASON

Vertical nonprice restraints include agreements between suppliers and distributors in which the buyer, as distributor of a service or product, is restricted in some way. Examples of this form of restraint include (1) exclusive geographic sales territories, (2) customer sales restrictions whereby the distributor can sell only to certain types of buyers, (3) location clauses limiting the sale of a good or service from a specified location, and (4) profit passovers that require that a distributor share profits for sales in violation of the agreement with other distributors.[32]

Antitrust enforcement in this area suggests a change by the Court from a per se violation approach to application of the rule of reason. The Supreme Court applied a per se approach in *U.S. v. Arnold Schwinn & Co.* when Schwinn, a manufacturer of bicycles, forbade its distributors to sell out-

side its assigned territory. Schwinn held title to the bicycles until they were sold to consumers and thus claimed this was not really a vertical restraint of trade. The Supreme Court found that this was indeed a vertical restraint of trade and was considered a per se violation.[33] This per se approach was overruled by the Court ten years later in the Sylvania case.

CONTINENTAL T.V., INC. v. GTE-SYLVANIA, INC.

In this case,[34] Sylvania sold its televisions to a large number of company-owned distributors who in turn "resold to a large and diverse group of retailers." Its national market share of televisions had dropped to less than 2 percent. In response to this declining market position, Sylvania adopted a franchise system designed to improve its interbrand competitive position. This marketing strategy required that its distribution system to diverse retailers be phased out, and set up a limited number franchisees within each designated area who would sell only the Sylvania brand of television sets from designated locations. This strategy was a conscious decision to limit intrabrand competition among Sylvania dealers in an effort to better compete against other brands of television.

The purpose of the change in Sylvania's strategy was to decrease the number of competing Sylvania retailers and to attract more aggressive and competent retailers necessary to improve Sylvania's position. Within three years, Sylvania's market share increased to 5 percent, suggesting that the strategy was a success.

The Continental-Sylvania Dispute

In the spring of 1965, Sylvania opened a new franchise outlet in San Francisco that was within a mile of another franchisee, Continental T.V. Continental protested the decision and asked Sylvania for an outlet in Sacramento. When Sylvania rejected the proposal, Continental opened a Sacramento outlet anyway and supplied it with televisions from Continental's warehouse in San Jose. Sylvania countered by reducing its line of credit granted Continental from $300,000 to $50,000. In the next phase of the dispute Continental refused to pay for credit purchases from Sylvania. Sylvania canceled the franchise and Continental sued Sylvania, alleging that Sylvania had engaged in an illegal nonprice vertical restraint of trade under section 1 of the Sherman Act.

Per Se Approach Used in the District Court

The lower court judge instructed the jury that if Sylvania had entered into an agreement to restrict the store outlets from which its franchisees could resell after title for the merchandise had passed to the franchisees, then Sylvania had violated section 1 of the Sherman Act. Because this would be an area guided by the per se rule, Sylvania would be guilty regardless of the reasons for the policy. The jury found for Continental. The Ninth Circuit Court of Appeals reversed, and the Supreme Court granted certiorari.

The Rule of Reason Applied by the Court of Appeals to the Sylvania Case

In the rule of reason, the Court attempts to determine the adverse and favorable effects of an action. These trade-offs are compared to determine whether or not a violation of the law is reasonable, that is, if the favorable effects outweigh the negative consequences. This process is similar to utilitarian ethical analysis discussed in Chapter 7.

Justice Powell applied the rule of reason in his opinion quoted, in part, below:

> The market impact of vertical restrictions is complex because of their potential for a simultaneous reduction of intrabrand competition and stimulation of interbrand competition. . . .
>
> Vertical restrictions reduce intrabrand competition by limiting the number of sellers of a particular product competing for the business of a given number of buyers. Location restrictions have this effect because of practical constraints on the effectiveness marketing area of retail outlets. Although intrabrand competition may be reduced, the ability of retailers to exploit the resulting market may be limited both by the ability of consumers to travel to other franchised locations and, perhaps more importantly, to purchase the competing products of other manufacturers.

> Vertical restrictions promote interbrand competition by allowing the manufacturer to achieve certain efficiencies in the distribution of his products. . . . Economists have identified a number of ways in which manufacturers can use such restrictions to compete more effectively against other manufacturers. . . . For example, new manufacturers and manufacturers entering new markets can use the restrictions in order to induce competent and aggressive retailers to make the kind of investment of capital and labor that is often required in the distribution of products unknown to the consumer. Established manufacturers can use them to induce retailers to engage in promotional activities or to provide service and repair facilities necessary to the efficient marketing of their products. Service and repair are vital for many products, such as automobiles and major household appliances. The availability and quality of such services affect a manufacturer's goodwill and competitiveness of his product. Because of market imperfections such as the so-called "free-rider" effect, these services might not be provided by retailers in a purely competitive situation, despite the fact that each retailer's benefit would be greater if all provided the services than if none did . . . .

Justice Powell recognizes that Sylvania's franchisee policy will reduce the intrabrand competition between Sylvania distributors. However, interbrand competition between Sylvania distributors and the retailers of other brands will be increased. The franchise restrictions will attract competent retailers, encourage them to promote the product, invest in service facilities, and generally strengthen the competitive position in the marketplace. Customers still have the choice of other brands or other areas and thus are not coerced. Also, it should be remembered that Sylvania was not the dominant firm in the industry. At the time of implementing this policy, its market share was between 1 and 2 percent.

Sherman Antitrust Act, Section 2 Prohibits Monopolization

Section 2 of the Sherman Act states:

> Every person who shall monopolize, or attempt to monopolize, or combine or conspire with any other person or persons to monopolize any part of the trade

or commerce among the several States, or with foreign nations, shall be deemed guilty of a felony, . . .

This section of the Sherman Act is the primary tool used by the government to restore competition in highly concentrated industries. Industries that have become very concentrated are dominated by a small number of firms. There are two major views concerning enforcement of section 2. First, the view that prevailed before 1980, supported by the economic theory of industrial organization, was that antitrust law should support competitive rivalry and discourage market dominance by a single firm. Second, the view that has prevailed since 1980 was the Chicago School's efficiency doctrine, which encourages market concentration if it is based upon competitive efficiency.

Prior to 1980, the government had vigorously enforced section 2. Examples of court action to maintain a competitive parity yielding a healthy rivalry include (1) the breakup of the Standard Oil Company into a dozen regionally dominant firms in 1911,[35] (2) the sale of aluminum war plants to new entrants in the aluminum business after World War II to assist new entrants into the market after Alcoa was found guilty of monopolizing, (3) the divestiture of the "Blue Network" by NBC, which created a competing national network, American Broadcasting Company, (4) the required divestiture of General Motors stock by a major supplier, DuPont, and (5) actions that reduced United Shoe Machinery's market share to 50 percent.

THE PROBLEM OF MARKET DOMINANCE

Competitive Rivalry Approach Before 1980
Antitrust law in the United States is seen by the industrial organization school as the fundamental industrial policy that maintains and restores competition within markets and increases economic performance.[36] According to this view, effective competition requires "a mutual striving among comparable rivals, on a basis of *competitive parity*."[37] Whenever parity is missing and firms are not comparable, competition wanes and market performance is reduced. For example, if the leading firm has over 40 or 50 percent share of market sales and no close rival exists, that firm is likely to dominate the market.

The dominance of a market by a single firm can lead to the elimination of smaller rivals through selective or predatory pricing and promotion in key market areas that can be subsidized by profits in other areas. The dominant firm is also likely to benefit from monopoly profits coming from market dominance and the misuse of market power.

In *U.S. v. Aluminum Co. of America*, the Aluminum Company of America, which controlled almost 100 percent of the market, was found guilty of monopolizing. The Court found that it had increased capacity in this capital-intensive market in anticipation of planned market growth and thus discouraged new entrants. Alcoa had over 90 percent of the market and there were no rivals. The Supreme Court indicated that a 40 percent share would be too low to be considered a monopolist, but if a firm achieved a market share in excess of 80 percent, that would be too high.[38] This case was litigated during World War II and when ALCOA was found guilty, dissolution of Alcoa was postponed. After the war, two aluminum facilities purchased by the government in the war effort were sold to competing firms who could become rivals of Alcoa. Thus Alcoa was not required to divest of any of its aluminum plants.

The Efficiency Approach: Post-1980

The Chicago School of Economics has dominated the thinking of the courts since 1980. Increasingly judges appointed by the Reagan and Bush administrations have favored deregulation, espoused the hands-off philosophy of the Reagan administration, and endorsed the Chicago School. According to this school, the efficiency doctrine should prevail as the standard for antitrust enforcement. In section 2 cases, market dominance is presumed to reflect efficient performance by the dominant firm.

Thus the market would be more competitive internationally if the government did not vigorously enforce section 2 of the Sherman Act. No new major Section 2 cases have been brought before the courts by the Justice Department Antitrust Division nor the FTC since 1980. However, two major cases have been resolved during this period: the IBM case and the AT&T case, which are briefly outlined below.

THE IBM CASE WAS DISMISSED

The IBM case was in the courts for 13 years before it was withdrawn by the Antitrust Division in 1982.[39] IBM had over 70 percent of the mainframe computer market in the 1960s. The government alleged that IBM was monopolizing to achieve the high market share by price discrimination, lease-only policies, bundling of its lease of computers with software and other system components, and by actions against various peripheral equipment firms. Also, the government alleged that IBM consciously made design changes to make obsolete competitors' peripheral attachments.[40]

IBM's new 360 family of computers in the 1960s allowed it to pool its overhead expense among many different types of computer systems, yielding efficiencies of scale economy. It practiced horizontal price discrimination by varying its price on the same computer system sold to different customers in order to obtain a sale. These deep price cuts were used to repel the incursion of competitors. Also, it rushed two money-losing "fighting lines" into market early to repel technically superior computers of smaller rival firms. These actions by IBM were violations of the *Areeda-Turner standard for predatory pricing*, which defines a predatory price as any price below short-run marginal cost (or, as a more easily ascertainable surrogate, average variable cost). A price above short-run marginal (or average variable) cost is nonpredatory.[41]

In its defense, IBM argued that the *relevant market* in the case was all computers and peripheral equipment rather than only the mainframe computer industry. The broader definition of the relevant market would serve to increase the chances of IBM's acquittal in the case because IBM's share would be substantially lower than 70 percent. The government pressed for a narrower definition of the relevant market so that IBM's share would be higher and the chances of a guilty verdict would be greater.

IBM used a tactic of delay in the case and was successful in maintaining high levels of legitimacy and favorable public sentiment. It was a highly respected firm and highly visible. High technology and computers were very important to the economy and a key to international competitiveness. It was argued that the breakup of this firm would be complex and might undercut the industry and the competitiveness of the United States. IBM's stock was widely held and if a court verdict of guilty required a breakup of this firm, many might suffer financial losses. Public sentiment was generally in support of IBM.

The IBM case dragged on for 13 years. Over the period of litigation the personal computer industry had formed and international competitors had entered the market. The new presidential administration viewed this case as another example of unnecessary government intrusion into the economic sphere. The Antitrust Division withdrew the case in 1982 and abandoned its prosecution.

THE AT&T CASE: AN ANTITRUST CASE AND AN EXAMPLE OF DEREGULATION

The AT&T case was one of the largest and most complex cases in recent years and ended in a consent decree. AT&T spun off all of its local telephone companies and kept AT&T with its Westinghouse Laboratory and long-distance lines. Technological changes in communications and satellite technology made it possible for competitors to operate in this market without expensive redundant investments. However, the arguments for natural monopoly outlined in Chapter 11 continued to exist for local telephone operations. Thus, local telephone service continues to be supplied by some seven regional regulated monopolies that were once a part of AT&T. Long-distance telephone service became a deregulated industry and MCI, Sprint, and other carriers have entered the market.

A highly skilled judge moved the case rapidly after 1977, bringing it to a clear and coherent conclusion.[42] The court had the use of an extensive economic analysis of the industry supplied by the FTC. At the time, AT&T wanted to enter the computer industry and was willing to give up its regulated monopoly status in long-distance communications to achieve that end.

The government negotiated successfully with AT&T to obtain a consent decree that (1) deregulated long-distance service and communications equipment and allowed AT&T to enter other related competitive industries in exchange for allowing competition in its major businesses, and (2) maintained the regulated monopoly status of local telephone companies that would no longer be a part of AT&T. Thus a major divestment of AT&T was accomplished.

By 1990 some of these formerly AT&T subsidiaries, now independent local companies, were also competing against AT&T in the communications equipment industry. This was generally considered to be a deregulatory success because service has improved and rates have declined for long-distance telephone service. Unfortunately for AT&T, it was not successful in its bid to enter the personal computer industry.

The Federal Trade Commission Act of 1914

The Federal Trade Commission Act of 1914 established the Federal Trade Commission (FTC) and authorized it to bring civil actions to enforce antitrust laws. Section 5 of the act prohibits unfair competition and deceptive advertising. The critical passage of the law states, "Unfair methods of competition in or affecting commerce, and unfair or deceptive acts or practices in or affecting commerce, are hereby declared illegal." The terms in section 5 are vague and not defined in the law, and unfair competition is a concept that overlaps the Sherman Act. Thus, many violations of this act are also considered violations of other antitrust laws. Later amendments to the Clayton Act have made the FTC a primary reviewer of mergers to screen and to disallow mergers that might tend to lessen competition in a market. The FTC is also the primary regulator and enforcer of consumer protection laws because of its role in prohibiting deceptive advertising.

The Clayton Act of 1914

The Clayton Act of 1914 was passed to clarify the Sherman Act and to plug a number of loopholes in the earlier law. The Clayton Act has been amended itself over the years as indicated below.

THE ROBINSON-PATMAN ACT PROHIBITS PRICE DISCRIMINATION

The Robinson-Patman Act Amendment of 1936, which amended section 2 of the Clayton Act, was meant to protect small suppliers from the market power of chain operations. However, the law does allow for quantity discounts in price if they are based on cost differences, cutting prices when perishable products are involved, and for cutting prices to meet the competition. This law is consistent with the antitrust objectives of maintaining competition and the economic liberty of small businesses.

Protecting some businesses from price discrimination is considered inconsistent with the consumer-welfare-through-market-efficiency goal that characterizes the latest approach to antitrust. According to the efficiency criterion, price discrimination is a valid way to extend a market to buyers who would not otherwise be in the market. Thus, the Antitrust Division has not prosecuted cases involving price discrimination since 1980 as a matter of policy.

Also, the courts have interpreted the interstate commerce clause of the Constitution to limit price discrimination cases that can be heard by the Supreme Court. At least one of the transactions in which price discrimination is alleged must cross a state boundary before it can be brought to court. Thus, the government has not brought price discrimination cases to court in recent years. Most price discrimination actions are private lawsuits under section 4 of the Clayton Act.

Private Suits

Section 4 of the Clayton Act allows private suits for treble damages. The working of this section also allows for reasonable attorneys' fees and thus provides an incentive to bring private suits:

> That any person who shall be injured in the business or property by reason of anything forbidden in the antitrust laws may sue therefor. . .and shall recover threefold the damages by him sustained, and the cost of the suit, including reasonable attorneys' fee.

The attraction of treble damages and attorneys' fees has provided a major incentive for a sharp increase in private antitrust lawsuits in recent years. Private lawsuits provide the following four functions:

1. They have allowed victims of price-fixing schemes or monopolies to recover their losses from overcharging. Awards in the hundreds of millions of dollars have been granted and sustained to whole classes of purchasers or even to a single injured competitor.
2. They have served as a partial check on arbitrary cutoffs of distributors, especially when the disfavored distributor has been a price-cutting maverick complained about by rival distributors.
3. They have been the main instrument for enforcing the statutory rules regarding price discrimination.
4. They have provided a remedy against the predatory form of unfair competition, particularly when carried out by a dominant firm or a small group of firms.[43]

The United States is the only country that provides multiple damages and attorneys' fees to those bringing antitrust suits. Contingency arrangements whereby an attorney's fee is based upon a percent-age of the damage award are not supported in other countries. Class-action lawsuits are rare in other countries. Thus, private antitrust actions are virtually unheard of in other countries and when they do occur, success is rare.[44]

Many private antitrust suits in the United States are follow-on suits brought to court after the Antitrust Division has successfully prosecuted a case.[45] The threat of private suits after having unsuccessfully litigated a case against the government is a powerful deterrent to violating the antitrust laws. However, the rewards to private litigators and their lawyers can also encourage out-of-court settlements by private parties, even in cases that have little merit.[46]

Section 7 Prohibits Mergers That May Lessen Competition

Section 7 of the Clayton Act prohibits mergers and acquisitions that may substantially lessen competition. This section of the act was revised in 1950.[47] It gives the FTC the authority to disallow mergers or acquisitions before they are consummated if the consequences may reduce competition. Notice that the wording of the law as indicated in Table 13–1 says "may substantially," not "will substantially," which lessens the burden of proof needed to make a case to disallow an acquisition.

Early enforcement of section 7 was highly restrictive and sought to prevent oligopoly markets from becoming more concentrated. Horizontal mergers between competing firms were disallowed even though the combined market share of merged firm would be fairly small. In *U.S. v. Pabst Brewing Co.*, the Court prevented a merger that would have resulted in a 4.49 percent share of the national beer market.[48] In the *Von's Grocery Co.* case a merger in the local Los Angeles area market that would have resulted in a 7.5 percent share of the local market was found to be unlawful.[49]

Purpose of Section 7: Competition or Efficiency?

In the Von's case, the majority opinion of the Supreme court stated that the purpose of section 7 of the Clayton Act "was to prevent economic con-

TABLE 13–1
Antitrust Laws of the United States

SHERMAN ANTITRUST ACT OF 1890

Section 1 prohibits conspiracy in restraint of trade.
> Every contract, combination in the form of trust or otherwise, or conspiracy, in restraint of trade or commerce among the several States, or with foreign nations, is hereby declared to be illegal.

Section 2 prohibits monopoly.
> Every person who shall monopolize, or attempt to monopolize, or combine or conspire with any other person or persons, to monopolize any part of the trade or commerce among the several States, or with foreign nations, shall be deemed guilty of a felony. . . .

FEDERAL TRADE COMMISSION ACT OF 1914

Section 5 prohibits unfair competition and deceptive advertising.
> Unfair methods of competition in or affecting commerce, and unfair or deceptive acts or practices in or affecting commerce, are hereby declared illegal.

CLAYTON ACT OF 1914

Section 2 ROBINSON–PATMAN ACT AMENDMENT OF 1936 prohibits price discrimination.
> It shall be unlawful for any person engaged in commerce, in the course of such commerce, either directly or indirectly, to discriminate in price between different purchasers of commodities of like grade and quality, where the effect of such discrimination may be substantially to lessen competition . . . or tend to create a monopoly in any line of commerce, or to injure, destroy, or prevent competition. . . . That nothing herein contained shall prevent differentials which make only due allowance for differences in the cost of manufacture, sale, or delivery resulting from the differing methods or quantities in which such commodities are to such purchasers sold or delivered.

Section 3 prohibits tying arrangements and exclusive dealing.
> It shall be unlawful for any person in commerce, in the course of such commerce, to lease or make a sale or contract for sale of goods, wares, merchandise, machinery, supplies, or other commodities. . .on condition, agreement, or understanding that the lessee or purchaser thereof shall not use or deal in the goods or wares of competitors of the lessor or seller, where the effect of such lease, sale, or contract for sale or such condition, agreements, or understanding may be to substantially lessen competition or tend to create a monopoly in any line of commerce.

Section 4 allows private suits for treble damages.
> That any person who shall be injured in the business or property by reason anything forbidden in the antitrust laws may sue therefor. . .and shall recover threefold the damages by him sustained, and the cost of the suit, including a reasonable attorney's fee.

Section 7 prohibits mergers and acquisitions that may substantially lessen competition.
> No corporation engaged in commerce shall acquire, directly or indirectly, the whole or any part of the stock or other share capital and no corporation subject to the jurisdiction of the Federal Trade Commission shall acquire the whole or any part of the commerce in any section of the country, where the effect of such acquisition may be substantially to lessen competition, or to tend to create a monopoly.

HART-SCOTT-RODINO ANTITRUST IMPROVEMENTS ACT OF 1976
> Requires advance notification of pending mergers.

The first antitrust law was the Sherman Act of 1890. It was followed by the Clayton Act of 1914, which amended the Sherman Act and the Federal Trade Commission Act that same year. The FTC, along with the Antitrust Division of the Department of Justice, was charged with enforcing these laws. Later the Clayton Act was amended to include prohibitions against price discrimination in 1936, prohibitions against vertical acquisitions in 1950, and in 1976, a requirement for advance FTC notification before a merger or acquisition is made.

---

centration of the American economy by keeping a large number of small competitors in business. . . . Congress sought to preserve competition among many small businesses by arresting a trend to concentration in its incipiency. . ." (pp. 275, 277).

The Procter and Gamble Case— A Product Line Extension Case

In this case, Procter and Gamble sought to acquire Clorox, the dominant firm in the liquid bleach industry, as a move to extend P&G's product line. The FTC[50] brought suit to disallow the acquisition, arguing:

1. *Liquid bleach market was concentrated.* The liquid bleach market was already concentrated and Clorox was the dominant firm, with some 70 percent of the market.

2. *Importance of advertising economies of scale.* Because all liquid bleach was essentially the same chemically, advertising was a key tool for successfully marketing. Procter and Gamble had an economy of scale in marketing and promotion, and if it acquired Clorox, its combined advertising power would overwhelm the market, leading to increased market concentration and market dominance by Procter and Gamble.

3. *Procter and Gamble was a potential market entrant* and was one of the few firms that, if it entered the market, could increase the competitive rivalry. Procter and Gamble should be encouraged to enter the liquid bleach market, but not by acquiring the leading firm in the market.

The majority opinion of the Court stated, "Possible economies cannot be used as a defense to illegality. Congress was aware that some mergers that lessen competition may also result in economies but it struck the balance in favor of protecting competition." However, the Court did very little economic analysis to establish the criteria for declaring mergers illegal in the early cases.[51] In a dissenting opinion in the Von's Grocery case, Justice Potter suggested that the only logic prevailing in these cases was that the government always won.

Merger Guidelines

In an attempt to increase economic analysis in premerger cases and to have a rational criterion for assessing the competitive effects of mergers, the Justice Department issued its first merger guidelines in 1968. These guidelines were revised in 1982 and 1984 by the Reagan administration. They relied heavily on the Chicago School and the academic research that had occurred over the pre-

vious decade. The new guidelines had the following characteristics:

1. *Market concentration.* The new guidelines continued to emphasize market concentration. However, the measure of market concentration used to evaluate mergers was changed from a four-firm ratio of 80 percent of the market to the Herfindel-Hirshman Index [HHI]. This HHI index is the sum of the squares of the market shares of firms competing in the same market. Previously, mergers were disallowed if the merger would bring the market share of the top four firms after the merger was consummated to over 80 percent. The new rule would disallow mergers that brought the Herfindel index to over 1,800.

2. *Safe harbors.* Safe harbors were those mergers where the market shares of the merged firm and changes in market concentration would be too low to warrant antitrust concern. The Justice Department indicated that mergers where combined market shares were less than 10 percent would likely not be contested. This would have excluded cases like Pabst and Von's Grocery from consideration.

3. *Efficiency factors.* Consistent with the Chicago School, the 1984 guidelines upgraded the consideration of efficiency as a defense for proposed merger. Paragraph 3.5 was added to the guidelines, which reads: "If the parties to the merger establish by clear and convincing evidence that a merger will achieve . . . efficiencies, the Department will consider efficiencies in deciding whether to challenge the merger." If the Procter and Gamble case were to be decided today using the Chicago School criterion of efficiency, the case would probably be decided differently. An economy-of-scale defense would show increased efficiency and would likely be accepted by the Court.

The Hart-Scott-Rodino Antitrust Improvements Act of 1976 Amendment to Section 7 of the Clayton Act requires advance notification of pending mergers. This amendment requires the premerger notification and assessment for competitive consequences by the FTC or Justice Department as discussed above. It also allows for the attorneys general of all 50 states to bring antitrust lawsuits to trial. This amendment has led to a significant increase in antitrust enforcement because state attorneys general tend to be more populist and to support the protection of small business and competitive rivalry as the primary goals of antitrust. Such cases at the state level have been counterbalancing reduced enforcement at the federal level. Federal-level enforcement at both the FTC and the Justice Department has adopted the philosophy and efficiency goals of the Chicago School as a guide.

Enforcement Patterns

The pattern of antitrust law enforcement is reflected in the number of cases prosecuted by the Department of Justice's Antitrust Division, the FTC, and private lawsuits as outlined in Figure 13–3. In addition to these, enforcement actions are also brought by the state attorneys general authorized by the 1976 Antitrust Improvements Act. Beginning with the Reagan administration in 1980, the Department of Justice significantly changed its approach to antitrust enforcement. Criminal cases involving bid rigging and price fixing, primarily violations of section 1 of the Sherman Act, have been sharply increased.

Justice Department prosecution of Sherman Act, section 2 cases dealing with monopolization, market power, and market concentration by a single business and Clayton Act, section 7 cases dealing with mergers that may decrease concentration have been sharply reduced. This same pattern of very low levels of enforcement of section 2 (Sherman) and section 7 (Clayton) cases is also reflected in the enforcement actions of the FTC, shown in Table 13–2.

In contrast to cases brought by the federal government, private actions have sharply increased since 1975. Private suits are often follow-on suits to Department of Justice prosecutions. More recently, they reflect a response to the perceived federal government inattention to antitrust enforcement.

As noted above, the Antitrust Division of the Department of Justice has been using merger guidelines and premerger notification to enforce antitrust laws against mergers that may be anticompetitive. However, these guidelines are not consistent with Supreme Court precedents; rather, they follow the Chicago School of Economics models. The result is very relaxed enforcement at the federal level. Many states have been unhappy with relaxed federal antitrust enforcement and are sharply increasing their activities. States have been mounting attacks on mergers and acquisitions, especially in retailing and supermarkets, that are considered anticompetitive or market-concentrating within the state borders.[52]

The National Association of Attorneys General (NAAG), representing state-level attorneys general, issued its own "Horizontal Merger Guidelines" in 1987, which are quite different from the federal government's guidelines. The NAAG guidelines reflect the precedents of the courts, do not presume that mergers lead to efficiencies, and support the earlier goals of antitrust law that seeks to maintain the competitive rivalry within markets and to protect the right of small and regional businesses to compete.

State-level antimerger activities were sharply stepped up with the appointment of William Baxter as head of the Antitrust Division by President Reagan. After 40 years of vigorous antitrust enforcement, the division began to approve large horizontal mergers in the steel and oil industries. As noted above, the 1950 amendment to Clayton Act section 7 increased the enforcement powers of the Justice Department to screen and prohibit mergers that may reduce competition. That amendment included both horizontal mergers between competitors in the same market and vertical mergers with suppliers or distributors that might foreclose markets to competing firms at another level of business.

The Antitrust Division under Baxter did not enforce the 1950 amendment; rather, it revised the merger guidelines to relax the level of enforcement. Moreover, these merger guidelines were circulated to the courts in hopes that judges would adopt the rules supported by the Justice Department rather than court precedent in subsequent cases. In some cases, the Antitrust Division took advocacy positions to encourage the courts to allow questionable mergers considered efficient. These actions dismayed many state-level attorneys general, who then took the offensive in antitrust enforcement to offset the inactivity at the federal level.[53]

THE JUSTICE DEPARTMENT AS ENFORCER OR REGULATOR

The rationale behind the merger guidelines of the Justice Department was to take antitrust enforcement out of the courts and to regulate competitiveness through out-of-court settlements and consent decrees. This marked a change in the role of

TABLE 13–2
Antitrust Case Enforcement by Department of Justice Antitrust Division, FTC, and Private Lawsuits

Year	DOJ Civil	DOJ Criminal	DOJ Total	FTC Cases*	Private Cases	Total Cases
1960	59	27	86	214	228	528
1965	33	10	43	65	472	580
1970	54	5	59	36	877	972
1975	37	35	72	30	1,375	1,477
1976	45	20	65	39	1,504	1,608
1977	34	37	71	24	1,611	1,706
1978	27	31	58	12	1,435	1,505
1979	31	27	58	37	1,234	1,329
1980	28	55	83	36	1,457	1,576
1981	25	71	96	29	1,292	1,417
1982	18	94	112	11	1,037	1,160
1983	10	98	108	10	1,192	1,310
1984	14	100	114	29	1,100	1,243
1985	11	47	58	25	1,052	1,135
1986	6	53	59	21	838	918
1987	15	92	107	14	758	879
1988	11	87	98	38	654	790

*FTC cases 1960 through 1979 are administrative complaints issued; 1980–1988 also include court actions authorized.
SOURCE: Adapted from Terry Calvani and Michael L. Sibarium, "Antitrust Today: Maturity or Decline," *Antitrust Bulletin* 35 (Spring 1990): tables 1, 2, and 3.

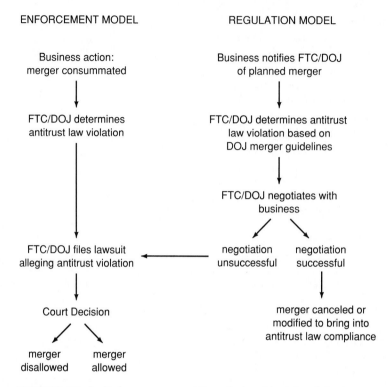

FIGURE 13–3 Enforcement and Regulation Models of Antitrust

government in antitrust. In an enforcement model, law is a rule of society that is to be obeyed. The Department of Justice is the primary prosecutor of the federal government and is responsible for enforcing laws by bringing violators to court. In this model, active enforcement of antitrust laws means litigation with offenders and the use of consent decrees in a sort of plea bargaining.

However, beginning with the use of guidelines, the role of the Justice Department has begun to shift since 1980 to one of regulator. Instead of litigating to reverse consummated mergers after they have been determined to be in violation of antitrust laws, the FTC and Justice have sought to regulate proposed mergers out of court. This regulation model relies on the premerger notification requirement of the Antitrust Improvements Act of 1976. After prenotification of a planned merger or acquisition and a filing of required competitive data with the Justice Department, a business awaits an advisory opinion.

If the opinion of the Justice Department is that the merger complies with the law, business proceeds with its planned merger or acquisition. If the opinion is that the merger is in violation of the law based on the department's merger guidelines, then the department begins a process of negotiation with business. Successful negotiations result in (1) business dropping its plan to merge, or (2) business changing its plan to bring the merger or acquisition into compliance with the department's merger guidelines.

Unsuccessful negotiations come with the implied threat that the department or the FTC will file a lawsuit to disallow the merger. Because the merger guidelines are currently much more lenient than court precedents, it is unlikely that a business would prevail in court. However, if a business feels strongly about the matter, it can litigate.

The recent pattern of the federal-level FTC and Justice Department has been to use the premerger notification requirements and the merger guidelines to regulate the types of mergers allowed under antitrust law. Few cases find their way into courts because the guidelines and the premerger negotiation serve to regulate business in this process. The department uses the regulatory model to enforce its merger guidelines that are based upon the efficiency goal of the Chicago School rather than the historical goals of competitive rivalry and protection of small business from dominant firms in regional markets. These later goals continue to be supported vigorously by many attorneys general of various states and by the state-level antitrust laws.

Lucky Food Store Acquisition

For example, in 1988, American Stores sought to acquire Lucky Stores in California. When this acquisition was apparently allowed by the federal government, the state attorney general of California brought an antitrust suit to stop the merger under both federal and California antitrust laws. American Stores was the fourth-largest chain in California, controlling 252 Skaggs and Alpha Beta stores. Lucky was the largest chain, with 340 stores and Luck Food Basket supermarkets. The FTC obtained a consent decree in this case that required American Stores to get rid of stores in geographic market areas where the Lucky–Alpha Beta combination would lead to market domination. The state attorney general was not satisfied with the FTC-initiated consent decree and filed another suit in September 1988 under federal and state antitrust laws. On April 30, 1990, the Supreme Court unanimously found that the state or a private party could obtain divestiture as a remedy for an illegal merger.

International Influence of U.S. Antitrust Law

After World War II, the United States exported antitrust law to many countries.[54]

Decartelization of Japan and Germany was an aim of the U.S. during World War II, and was in fact carried out by American experts during the period of occupation. Both Germany and Japan were influenced to adopt national antitrust laws that generally followed the U.S. pattern, though with variations. France, the Philippines and other countries aided by the U.S. during that period were also induced to adopt similar laws.[55]

As noted above, U.S. antitrust law has been subject to cycles of enforcement and the basic goals of antitrust have been much debated. Other countries that have adopted the U.S. approach to antitrust have occasionally been "out of cycle" with the United States in that enforcement patterns have increased abroad at times when U.S. enforcers have had second thoughts about certain antitrust laws. For example, Justice's Antitrust Division published a monograph calling for the repeal of the Robinson-Patman Act in 1986 at a time when European countries were debating legislation favoring price favoritism.

Merger control to prevent market concentration was resisted by Canada until 1980, when it was finally adopted. It was at this time that the U.S. government had all but abandoned merger control and had relaxed both enforcement and the merger guidelines. In most industrial countries, efficiency and international competitiveness are dominant considerations in merger control. Thus all but the most offensive horizontal mergers tend to be allowed.

The fall of Eastern Europe has led to many of these formerly Communist countries asking for assistance in moving to a market economy. Under communism the economy is dominated by state-run monopolies. A part of changing to a market economy is the move from monopoly markets with high levels of market concentration and domination by a single business to dispersed economic power. These Eastern European countries have sought ways to encourage economic rivalry and are closely examining the role of antitrust laws as they would apply to their changing economies.

Similarly, the counterpart to the U.S. deregulation movement has been a move to privatization in Europe. In privatization, formerly government-owned enterprises are sold or transferred to private ownership. A part of this process is a move from a government-owned monopoly to a regulated monopoly or to a deregulated market. This requires developing a price system by managers who have never had to respond to market forces. Thus antitrust laws have been developed to prohibit unauthorized cartels but not to interfere with the phases in the process of privatization and the move to a market economy.

The European Economic Community (EEC) Treaty for integration also has an antitrust provision in Article 85, which prohibits price fixing, control of output, or sharing markets or sources of supply that "have as their object or effect the prevention, restriction or distortion of competition within the common market. . . ." However, many restrictions have been found by the commission and the European country courts not to enforce competition, contrary to the treaty.[56] If joint ventures and territorial restrictions are seen to induce certain needed transactions and investment, they have been found to be acceptable and not in violation of the treaty. Thus, it seems that a variant of the efficiency criterion used in U.S. antitrust enforcement is also being applied in Europe in the enforcement of the EEC Treaty provisions against restricting trade.

European countries have social goals that take precedence over some of the economic goals of antitrust. Price fixing for market stability has been accepted as a social goal in much of the world. Many European countries have prohibited the "abuse of a dominant position" rather than prohibit monopolizing, which creates the dominant position in the first place.

Summary

Antitrust law can have consequences for many management decisions including mergers and acquisition, pricing, distribution, and franchise relationships. Major changes have occurred in recent years in the enforcement of antitrust law. Early enforcement patterns and much of the court precedents favor protecting small business from large-scale businesses, insuring competitive market structures, and promoting economic liberty. During the last 15 years, the courts have been strongly influenced by the Chicago School of Economics and its argument that efficiency and consumer welfare should be the sole goal of antitrust law.

There have been four major historical goals of antitrust: (1) dispersion of economic power, (2) freedom and opportunity to compete on the merits, (3) satisfaction of customers, and (4) protection of the competitive process as market governor. However, the Sherman Antitrust Act and subsequent amendments to antitrust laws were written very broadly, and thus these goals are in the legislative history but not specifically stated in the law. Like court cases that define the broadly written U.S. Constitution, the Supreme Court has had to "find antitrust law" through the its precedents expressed in its decisions in specific case situations.

Economists developing the economic theory of industrial organization began to influence legal thinking in antitrust beginning in the 1940s. This theory posited that market structures lead to market conduct that, in turn, determines market performance. Concentrated markets of oligopoly or monopoly lead to the evils of price fixing, tying agreements, price discrimination, and exclusionary practices. It is the task of the government to maintain low levels of market concentration and to disperse market power. Also, the government should prohibit the anticompetitive behavior correlated with market power if market efficiency and consumer welfare are to be achieved.

Following the theory of industrial organization, many per se rules were adopted by the courts. According to a per se rule, certain practices are considered so evil as to have no valid justification. Thus if a per se violation is found, a company is held in violation of antitrust law regardless of arguments it may try to forward defending the practice. Price fixing and monopolistic horizontal mergers are held to be per se violations.

In contrast to the per se rule is the rule of reason approach in which the Court considers the consequences of a business practice. According to the rule of reason, if the good consequences of a practice outweigh the unfavorable, then the practice may be found to be legal even if it seems to be a violation of the law. Certain vertical constraints formerly held to be per se violations have been more recently found to be legal under a rule of reason approach by the Supreme Court.

Section 2 of the Sherman Act is concerned primarily with the anticompetitive effects of market power. Early enforcement of this section was vigorous and resulted in the breakup of Standard Oil; sale of GM stock by a major supplier, DuPont; and discouraging the market dominance of Alcoa in aluminum. Since 1980 there has been very limited court enforcement of this section of the act. The two major cases during this period include a case against IBM that was dismissed and a case against AT&T that led to its breakup by consent decree in 1982. The AT&T case also led to deregulation in the long-distance telephone industry.

The premerger notification required by section 7 of the Clayton Act to the Sherman Act authorizes the Justice Department and the FTC to determine the competitive consequences of mergers before they are consummated. It the mergers are found to have likely anticompetitive effects, they are disallowed.

More recently, the Justice Department has been using merger guidelines to establish criteria for evaluating mergers. These guidelines consider market shares under 10 percent as a safe harbor unlikely to be challenged. Mergers in highly concentrated markets measured by the HHI index continue to be challenged. The new merger guidelines, particularly the 1988 international guidelines, primarily consider the effects on international competitiveness of any proposed merger.

Private antitrust lawsuits allowed by the Clayton Act serve as a deterrent to antitrust violations and supplement federal antitrust enforcement. The role of antitrust suits initiated by private and state attorneys general has increased with the decline in antitrust enforcement at the federal level. Private- and state-initiated suits are more likely to pursue the antitrust goals of protecting the rights of small business, maintaining competitive rivalry in markets, and discouraging mergers that lead to concentrated power. Federal suits following the goal of efficiency are unlikely to prosecute cases involving price discrimination, tying agreements, vertical restraints, or mergers leading to market concentration that can be defended by an efficiency argument.

Antitrust laws were exported to Japan and to Europe after World War II by U.S. experts in antitrust working in the occupied countries. Antitrust laws have been adopted by Canada. Conspiracies and contracts that restrict trade are prohibited by the EEC Treaty on European integration. As if true for the United States, social goals other than efficiency are considered in the formulation and enforcement of antitrust.

Conclusions

Although antitrust laws have not been enforced vigorously by the federal government since the Reagan administration assumed office in 1981, they continue to be an important part of the legal environment of business. Since their deemphasis by the Department of Justice and the FTC, enforcement has been supplemented by growing numbers of private lawsuits and cases filed by state-level attorneys general who were empowered to enforce these laws by the Antitrust Improvement Act of 1976.

There has been considerable controversy over the proper goals of antitrust during the past 15 years. Federal enforcers and many judges have accepted the position of the Chicago School, which argues that the only goal of antitrust is consumer welfare based on the criterion of efficiency. Private litigators and state-level enforcement have espoused the more populist goals of economic liberty of small business and regional competitors. This latter group has sought to vigorously enforce the laws against concentrated economic power, market domination, tying agreements, price discrimination, and vertical restraints.

The historical goals of antitrust offer much for society as does the economic goal of efficiency. Dispersion of market power, economic liberty of small and regional businesses to compete, and protection of the welfare of consumers will continue to be important. The level of economic knowledge now available argues against the use of simple per se rules in favor of rule of reason analysis. This will enable us to move from an either-or debate to an attempt to achieve both economic and social goals. However, such analysis should not begin with the presumption that bigness is necessarily more efficient than markets characterized by vigorous interfirm rivalry, nor does efficiency as conceived by the Chicago School necessarily lead to higher levels of consumer welfare.

The shift to the efficiency goal of the Chicago School has coincided with the decline of American international competitiveness and the deregulation movement of the 1980s. It is unlikely that U.S. antitrust law has been a factor contributing to the decline in international competitiveness. Concentrated markets of steel, automobiles, and electronics have been among the most hurt by global competition. The vigorous enforcement of antitrust should contribute to U.S. competitiveness rather than detract from it. Antitrust enforcement should consider the need for joint ventures in research and development and for strategic alliances in the international arena.[57]

Discussion Questions

1. What are the historical goals of antitrust law?
2. How does the use of per se rules differ from the rule of reason approach to antitrust?
3. Discuss the role of economics in the development of antitrust law.
4. What goals of antitrust are supported by the economic theory of organization?
5. How does the Chicago School of Economics differ from earlier approaches to antitrust?

6. What conspiracies or contracts in restraint of trade are prohibited by the Sherman Act?
7. What is meant by monopolizing under antitrust law? Has the view of the Justice Department changed with respect to monopolization? How have enforcement patterns changed since 1980?
8. What is the function of private antitrust lawsuits? Are these consistent with current enforcement approaches by the Justice Department and the FTC? Explain.
9. Compare the enforcement role with the regulator role of the Justice Department.
10. Describe the international effects of U.S. antitrust law.

Notes

1. Terry Calvani and Michael L. Sibarium, "Antitrust Today: Maturity or Decline," *Antitrust Bulletin* 35 (Spring 1990): 123–217.
2. Hans Thorelli, *The Federal Antitrust Policy: Organization of an American Tradition* (Baltimore: Johns Hopkins University Press, 1955), and Jerrold G. Van Cise, "Antitrust Past-Present-Future," *Antitrust Bulletin* 35 (Winter 1991): 985–1008.
3. For example, see William G. Shepherd, "Section 2 and the Problem of Market Dominance," *Antitrust Bulletin* 35, no. 4 (Winter 1990): 833–78.
4. Robert H. Bork, *The Antitrust Paradox: A Policy at War with Itself* (New York: Basic Books, 1978).
5. E. Thomas Sullivan, ed., *The Political Economy of the Sherman Act: The First One Hundred Years* (New York: Oxford University Press, 1991).
6. Bruce D. Fisher and Michael J. Phillips, *The Legal Environment of Business* (New York: West, 1983).
7. *Northern Pacific Railroad Company v. United States*, 356 U.S. 1, 4 (1958).
8. Walter Adams, "Some Medieval Precedents," in *Antitrust, the Market, and the State: The Contributions of Walter Adams*, ed. James W. Brock and Kenneth G. Elzinga (Armonk, N.Y.: M. E. Sharp, 1991), p. 147.
9. Adam Smith, *The Wealth of Nations*, Modern Library ed., Vol. 2, p. 712. Quoted by Walter Adams, ibid., p. 145.
10. Walter Adams, "Interview: Economic Power and the Constitution," in *Antitrust, the Market, and the State*, pp. 261–75.

11. David Millon, "The Sherman Act and the Balance of Power," *Southern California Law Review*, 1988, reprinted in *The Political Economy of Antitrust: The First One Hundred Years*, ed. E. Thomas Sullivan (New York: Oxford University Press, 1991), pp. 85–115.

12. A. Marshall, *Principles of Economics* (New York: Macmillan, 1890).

13. Thomas J. DiLorenzo, "The Origins of Antitrust: Rhetoric vs. Reality," *Regulation: The Cato Review of Business and Government* (Winter 1990): 26–35.

14. Jerrold G. Van Cise, "Antitrust Past-Present-Future," *Antitrust Bulletin* 35 (Winter 1991): 986–87.

15. Quoted in ibid., pp. 986–87.

16. Quoted in ibid., p. 985.

17. *United States v. Topco Associates, Inc.*, 405 U.S. 596, 610 (1972).

18. E. Thomas Sullivan, *The Political Economy of the Sherman Act, Part II* (New York: Oxford University Press, 1991), especially pp. 161–80.

19. For an analysis of this approach, see C. Kaysen and D. Turner, *Antitrust Policy: An Economic and Legal Analysis* (Cambridge: Harvard University Press, 1959); and more recently, W. Shepherd, *The Economics of Industrial Organization* (Englewood Cliffs, N.J.: Prentice-Hall, 1979).

20. For example, see Richard Caves, *American Industry: Structure, Conduct, Performance*, 4th ed. (Englewood Cliffs, N.J.: Prentice-Hall, 1977); and Joe Bain, *Industrial Organization* (New York: Wiley, 1959).

21. See Shepherd, "Section 2 and the Problem of Market Dominance," pp. 833–77.

22. Calvani and Sibarium, "Antitrust Today: Maturity or Decline," p. 128.

23. Bork, *The Antitrust Paradox*; and Richard Posner, "The Chicago School of Antitrust Analysis," *University of Pennsylvania Law Review* 925 (1979).

24. Bork, *The Antitrust Paradox*, pp. 20–58, 405.

25. E. Thomas Sullivan, *The Political Economy of the Sherman Antitrust Act, Part II* (New York: Oxford University Press, 1991), pp. 170–72.

26. Bork, *The Antitrust Paradox*, pp. 110–12, 219–20.

27. Walter Adams, James W. Brock, and Norman P. Obst, "Pareto Optimality and Antitrust Policy: The Old Chicago and the New Learning," *Southern Economic Journal* 58, no. 1 (July 1991): 1–14.

28. Posner, "The Chicago School of Antitrust Analysis."

29. *Theatre Enterprises, Inc. v. Paramount Film Distribution Corp.*, 346 U.S. 537 (1954).

30. *United States v. Trenton Potteries Co.*, 273 U.S. 392 (1927).

31. *United States v. Topco Associates, Inc.*, 405 U.S. 596 (1972).

32. Dan Bertozzi, Jr., and Lee B. Burgunder, *Business, Government, and Public Policy* (Englewood Cliffs, N.J.: Prentice-Hall, 1990), pp. 150–57.

33. 388 U.S. 365 (1967).

34. 433 U.S. 36 (1977).

35. *Standard Oil Company of New Jersey v. United States*, 221 U.S. 1 (1911).

36. William G. Shepherd, "Section 2 and the Problem of Market Dominance," *Antitrust Bulletin* 35 (Winter 1990): 833–77.

37. Ibid., p. 835.

38. *U.S. v. Aluminum Co. of America*, 148 F.2d 416, 421 (2d Cir. 1945).

39. *United States v. IBM*, No. 69, Civ. 200 (S.D.N.Y., dismissal filed January 8, 1982).

40. William G. Shepherd, "Efficient Profits Versus Unlimited Capture, As a Reward for Superior Performance: Analysis and Cases," *Antitrust Bulletin* 34 (Spring 1989): 121–52.

41. Philip Areeda and Donald F. Turner, "Predatory Pricing and Related Practices Under Section 2 of the Sherman Act," *Harvard Law Review* 88 (1975): 697–733.

42. *United States v. American Telephone and Telegraph Co.*, Trade Reg. Rep. (CCH) (Case No. 2416, D.D.C., Nov. 20, 1974).

43. Joel Davidow, "The Worldwide Influence of U.S. Antitrust," *Antitrust Bulletin* 35 (Fall 1990): 619–20.

44. Davidow, "The Worldwide Influence of U.S. Antitrust," pp. 620–21.

45. John J. Flynn, "Which Past Is Prologue? The Future of Private Antitrust Enforcement," *Antitrust Bulletin* 35 (Winter 1990): 897–939.

46. William F. Shughart, "Private Antitrust Enforcement: Compensation, Deterrence, or Extortion?" *Regulation: The Cato Review of Business and Government* (Winter 1990): 53–61.

47. Celler-Kefauver Act of Dec. 29, 1950, Ch. 1184, 64 Stat. 1125, 15 U.S.C. 18.

48. *U.S. v. Pabst Brewing Co.*, 384 U.S. 546 (1966).

49. *U.S. v. Von's Grocery Co.*, 384 U.S. 270 (1966).

50. *FTC v. Procter and Gamble Co.*, 386 U.S. 568 (1967).

51. Edwin M. Zimmerman, "Section 7 and the Evolving Role of Economics," *Antitrust Bulletin* 35 (Summer 1990): 447–65.

52. Seymour D. Lewis, "Why States Are Stepping Up Attacks on Large Mergers," *Mergers and Acquisitions* 25, no. 1 (June/July 1990): 35–40.

53. See Thomas E. Kauper, "The Justice Department and the Antitrust Laws: Law Enforcer or Regulator?" *Antitrust Bulletin* 35 (Spring 1990): 83–122.

54. Davidow, "The Worldwide Influence of U.S. Antitrust," pp. 603–30.

55. Ibid., p. 603.

56. Valentine Korah, "From Legal Form Toward Economic Efficiency—Article 85 (1) of the EEC Treaty in Contrast to U.S. Antitrust," *Antitrust Bulletin* 35 (Winter 1990): 1009–36.

57. Thomas M. Jorde and David J. Teece, "Innovation, Dynamic Competition, and Antitrust Policy," *Regulation: The Cato Review of Business and Government* (Winter 1990): 35–44.

Discussion Case 13–1 _____

MIT and the Overlap Group of Universities (A)

The Overlap Group, consisting of 23 of the nation's most prestigious colleges and universities, regularly met to compare the financial aid packages for students. When two or more institutions had prepared different financial aid amounts to offer the same prospective student, they compared packages and decided upon an amount that all institutions would offer that student.

The Overlap Group's practice was justified on the basis of providing need-based financial aid to the greatest number of potential students. Without an agreement on financial aid amounts, bidding wars over students would drive up the cost of individual financial aid packages. Because there was only a limited amount of financial aid available, such a bidding war would reduce the amount of money available for need-based financial aid packages.

When questioned by representatives of the Antitrust Division of the Department of Justice about the practice of comparing specific financial aid packages to set an agreed upon amount of financial aid, the Overlap Group argued that it should be exempt from antitrust laws against price fixing because financial aid was not a price but a charity. Charles M. Vest, president of MIT, said that if they were not allowed to set financial aid amounts, the ruling "would effectively erode the freedom of opportunity to get a college education regardless of income." Thus, these activities of the Overlap Group had so much social value that the Justice Department should allow them to continue.

However, others said the decision did not pose a danger to higher education, and still others said students and their families would benefit. Charles A. James, acting assistant attorney general for the Antitrust Division, issued a statement saying that students "have the right to compare prices among schools just as they do in shopping for any service."

SOURCE: Based on Scott Jaschik, "Judge Rules MIT Violated Antitrust Law as Members of 23-College 'Overlap Group',"
Chronicle of Higher Education (September 9, 1992): A23–A26.

The Justice Department started an investigation of the financial aid practices of private colleges three years ago. While the department studied the finances of dozens of higher-education institutions, it focused on the Overlap Group, which was founded in 1958 and consisted of eight Ivy League universities, MIT, and 14 other colleges in New England, New York, and Pennsylvania. When the investigation started, college officials said they were stunned because Overlap's activities had not been secret and had the support of much of the higher-education establishment. College officials said their consultations on aid packages led to more accurate aid awards and helped insure that limited aid funds went to the neediest students.

Last year, the Justice Department charged MIT and Ivy League institutions with violating antitrust laws. MIT was the sole defendant facing trial because the Ivy institutions had settled before the trial by agreeing to abandon their Overlap activities. No charges have been filed against the other 14 Overlap members, but the group effectively suspended its operations last year while negotiations with the Justice Department over a possible settlement were proceeding.

Judge Bechtle's 49-page decision rejected nearly all of MIT's arguments and prohibited MIT from continuing the practice of comparing specific students' financial aid packages. While he said that some strictly educational functions of higher education might well be exempted from antitrust laws, he said the laws would apply to anything that was "commercial in nature," and that he could "conceive of few aspects of higher education that are more commercial than the price charged to students."

Some education observers said students and their families were the big winners in the decision. Kalman A. Chany, president of Campus Consultants, Inc., a financial aid consulting service in New York City, said that Overlap would have benefited students only if the comparisons of aid awards had always led to students' receiving the more generous package from both institutions.

Chany, author of *Student Access Guide to Paying for College,* said the evidence introduced in the trial indicated that in most cases, the colleges had come up with an aid package in the middle of their two estimates or a figure closer to the less generous package. "The student is not necessarily better off with Overlap," he said.

Case Discussion Questions

1. Should the practice of jointly setting the amounts of student financial aid be allowed?
2. Is this practice different from price fixing? If not, is it reasonable and socially justified so that it should be allowed?

Discussion Case 13–2 _____

MIT and the Overlap Group of Universities (B)

Excerpts from Judge Bechtle's Ruling on MIT's Participation in Overlap Group

1. On the claim that the Overlap Group's activities are non-commercial and exempt from antitrust law: "MIT endeavors to except the Overlap process from antitrust liability based on the assertion that it solely implicated non-commercial aspects of higher education. According to MIT, Overlap had a non-commercial impact, was not commercially motivated, and was revenue neutral. . . .

"MIT provided educational services to its students, for which they pay significant sums of money. The exchange of money for services is commerce in the most common usage of that word. By agreeing on aid applicants' families expected financial contribution, the Ivy Overlap Group schools were setting the price aid applicants and their families would pay for educational services. The court can conceive of few aspects of higher education that are more commercial than the price charged to students.

"MIT's attempt to disassociate the Overlap process from commercial aspects of higher education is pure sophistry. Although MIT characterizes its financial aid as 'charity,' in essence, MIT provides a 'discount' off the price of college offered to financial aid recipients.

"Further, accepting for the moment MIT's assertion that the impetus for instituting Overlap was to distribute more fairly limited financial resources for

SOURCE: Reprinted in *The Chronicle of Higher Education,* September 9, 1992, p. A26.

financial aid, the means chosen to effectuate this goal—the elimination of merit scholarships and insuring that commonly admitted aid recipients would pay the same regardless of which institution they decided to attend—is unquestionably commercial in nature. Not only did the effects of Overlap fall within the sphere of commerce, but its existence struck at the heart of the commercial relationship between school and student."

"Not all Ivy League schools are equally powerful. . . Those on the less-selective end compete fiercely with those outside the Ivy League."

2. On the argument that the Overlap system should remain in place to prevent "bidding wars" for top students: "The message to be gleaned from MIT's defense is that the moment the Ivy Overlap Group schools are no longer able to jointly eliminate price competition, they will immediately bow to faculty pressure to enroll the very highest student at high cost and at the expense of needy students, leaving behind hallowed principles of equality of educational access and opportunity and the resultant societal benefits that they have so ardently underscored.

"William Bowen, past president of Princeton University, believes that if Overlap ends, the member schools will take 'one step back toward the economic segregation of higher education.'

"Can the Ivy Overlap Group members' purposes be so fragile that their primary goal of having the most desirable students outweighs their ability, without Overlap, to pursue diligently even an imperfect policy of promoting the virtue of student diversity and the advantages of making available to needy students the benefits of these elite educational institutions? Will there also be lost the value to be gained by signaling to all prospective students that they can in fact aspire to attend an Ivy Overlap Group institution even though their families may be of limited means? The court thinks not.

"If MIT and other Ivy League schools were to so easily abandon these objectives merely because Overlap was not in play, then the court could only conclude that their professional dedication to these ends was less than sincere.

"By the same token, if these policies are as meaningful as MIT avows, and these institutions refuse in any way to forsake admitting the 'best of the best,' then they should be willing to dedicate the necessary resources to insure the continuation of these policies.

"It is certainly true that these decisions, like nearly every important decision these schools must make, will be difficult and will have a financial impact in other areas of the schools' operations. The end of Overlap will only portend the end of need-based admissions and the schools' ability to guarantee the full need of their aid applicants if the schools decide that other financial priorities occupy a higher investment and financial plane. The dilemma over resource allocation always triggers budgetary balancing, and that is likely to be called for here.

"Such balancing is not new, nor is it unreasonable, if the suggested method of avoiding it is to act contrary to the law."

Case Discussion Questions

1. Do you agree with the court's reasoning that financial aid is simply a part of the price a university charges for the education it provides in the educational marketplace? Is financial aid charity? If so, should charity be subject to antitrust law? Explain.
2. Do you think that the overlap group's activity amounted to illegal price fixing? Explain.
3. Would a "bidding war" for financial aid be destructive to higher education? Should cooperative price setting be allowed to avoid unstable or destructive price competition?
4. What are the alternatives used by society to control unstable or destructive competition? Would these alternatives be desirable in regulating financial aid packages?

Case IV–1 _____

The Matsushita Case

Zenith claimed that defendants, 21 Japanese-controlled corporations that manufactured or sold television sets, had illegally conspired to drive U.S. firms from the American television market.[1] The gist of this conspiracy allegedly was a scheme to raise and maintain artificially high prices for television receivers sold by defendants in Japan and, at the same time, to fix and maintain low prices for television receivers exported to and sold in the United States. Zenith alleged that these low prices were at levels that produced substantial losses for defendants. They asserted violations of sections 1 and 2 of the Sherman Act and section 2(a) of the Robinson-Patman Act, and various trade law violations.[2]

After several years of discovery, defendant Japanese television manufacturers filed motions for summary judgment, claiming that the alleged conspiracy was economically irrational and practically infeasible.[3] The district court found the admissible evidence did not raise a genuine issue of material fact as to the existence of the alleged conspiracy, in large part because the evidence that bore directly on the alleged price-cutting conspiracy did not rebut the more plausible inference that the Japanese firms were cutting prices to compete in the American market and not to monopolize it. Summary judgment was entered against Zenith on all of its antitrust claims, as the court found they were functionally indistinguishable.[4]

The Court of Appeals for the Third Circuit reversed the district court, determining that a fact finder reasonably could find a conspiracy to depress prices in the American market in order to drive out American competitors, a conspiracy that

SOURCE: Reprinted from Terry Calvani and Michael L. Sibarium, "Antitrust today: Maturity or Decline," *Antitrust Bulletin* 35 (Spring 1990): 135–41. Reprinted by permission.

was funded by excess profits obtained in the Japanese market. The court relied on expert opinion suggesting that the Japanese firms sold televisions in the United States at substantial losses and on evidence of agreements among them to set supracompetitive prices in Japan and minimum prices for televisions exported to the American market, as well as evidence that the firms limited the number of distributors of their products in the United States.[5]

The Supreme Court reversed the denial of summary judgment. The Court held that "if the factual context renders respondents' claim implausible—if the claim is one that simply makes no economic sense—respondents must come forward with more persuasive evidence to support their claim than would otherwise be necessary."[6] The Court thus enumerated the summary judgment standard to include a consideration of the "plausibility" of Zenith's claim, opening wide the door to application of the McGee-Bork-Easterbrook hypothesis that predatory pricing is, at least in practical terms, almost always irrational for profit-maximizing businessmen.

"A predatory pricing conspiracy is by nature speculative," the Court wrote.[7] For predatory pricing to be a rational course of action, the conspirators must have a "reasonable expectation" of recovering, through later monopoly profits, more than the losses suffered during the price war.[8] Yet, the Court concluded, "the success of such schemes is inherently uncertain: the short-run loss is definite, but the long-run gain depends on successfully neutralizing the competition," a costly and uncertain outcome.[9]

Moreover, the Court wrote, driving out one's rivals is not a sufficient condition for earning future monopoly profits adequate to cover short-term losses; the predator must have some assurance that its anticipated monopoly pricing will not "breed quick entry by new competitors eager to share in the excess profits."[10] The success of any predatory scheme thus "depends on *maintaining* monopoly power for long enough both to recoup the predator's losses and to harvest some additional gain."[11] Because the predator must have this elusive assurance that its monopoly can be sustained for a significant period of time, "there is a consensus among commentators that predator pricing schemes are rarely tried, and even more rarely successful."[12]

Furthermore, the Court contended, the foregoing analysis shows that the adequate returns to predatory pricing are highly speculative, even for a single firm seeking monopoly power. The charge in *Matsushita* was that a large number of firms conspired over a period of many years to charge low prices in order to stifle competition. Extremely high costs of coordination among numerous firms make a conspiracy to price predatorily "incalculably more difficult to execute than an analogous plan undertaken by a single predator," the Court wrote.[13]

Applying this chiefly McGee-Bork-Easterbrook framework to the facts before it, the Court concluded that the prospects for the Japanese firms of attaining monopoly power seemed slight. Two decades after their conspiracy was allegedly commenced, they appeared to be far from achieving monopoly power; the two largest shares of the retail market in television sets were held by RCA and Zenith, not by any of the defendant Japanese electronics companies. Moreover, the market shares of RCA and Zenith, which together accounted for approximately 40 percent of sales, had not declined appreciably during the 1970s. Yet after two decades, Zenith contended that the Japanese firms were "still artificially *depressing* the market price" in order to drive the larger and well-established Zenith out.[14]

In view of the failure of the alleged predatory pricing scheme after two decades, the prospects of maintaining monopoly power long enough in the American television market to recoup such substantial losses appear especially dim, the Court reasoned.[15] Moreover, the Court found no basis to conclude that entry into the market is especially difficult, yet without barriers to entry it "would presumably be impossible to maintain supracompetitive prices for an extended time."[16] Maintaining supracompetitive prices would also depend upon the continued cooperation of the conspirators and on the numerous competitors' ability to escape antitrust liability for price fixing. Each of these factors, the Court contended, weighs more heavily as the time needed to recoup losses grows.[17] The Court thus concluded, "[T]he alleged conspiracy's failure to achieve its ends in the two decades of its asserted operation is strong evidence that the conspiracy does not in fact exist."[18]

The Court even considered and rejected the expert study offered by Zenith suggesting that defendants had sold their products in the American market below cost. The study, the Court asserted, was not based upon actual cost data but was an expert opinion based on mathematical construction that in turn rested upon assumptions about petitioners' costs. The Court found the study implausible and that its probative value was far outweighed by the "economic factors . . . that suggest that such conduct is irrational."[19] The Court apparently found the McGee-Bork-Easterbrook reasoning so compelling that even an expert study, albeit one that did not use actual cost data, could not make Zenith's predatory pricing story credible enough to raise a genuine issue of fact for trial. The Court summarized thus:

> [P]redatory pricing schemes require conspirators to suffer losses in order eventually to realize their illegal gains; moreover, the gains depend on a host of uncertainties, making such schemes more likely to fail than to succeed. These economic realities tend to make predatory pricing conspiracies self-deterring; unlike most other conduct that violates the antitrust laws, failed predatory pricing schemes are costly to the conspirators.[20]

True to the McGee-Bork-Easterbrook argument, the Court also noted the dangers of chilling price competition by imposing liability for price cutting. The Court wrote that "cutting price in order to increase business often is the very essence of competition."[21] Thus, mistaken inferences in cases attacking price cutting are especially costly, "because they chill the very conduct the antitrust laws are designed to protect."[22] While any concern about discouraging pro-competitive conduct must be balanced against the desire that illegal conspiracies be identified and punished, "[t]hat balance is . . . unusually one-sided in cases such as this one."[23]

The Court thus reversed the Third Circuit, asserting that "petitioners had no motive to enter into the alleged conspiracy"[24] and that the court of appeals in denying summary judgment "failed to consider the absence of plausible motive to engage in predatory pricing."[25] In fact, "as presumably rational businesses, [the Japanese firms] had every incentive *not* to engage in the conduct with which they are charged, for its likely effect would be to generate losses for [them] with no corresponding gains."[26] The absence of plausible motive was especially significant to the Court in view of the ambiguousness of the evidence relied upon by the court of appeals to raise an inference of "predatory pricing conspiracy." For example, evidence of agreements concerning minimum price setting and limitations on numbers of distributors in the United States was more consistent with a conspiracy by the Japanese firms to raise prices than to price predatorily. Likewise, evidence that the Japanese firms priced at levels that succeeded in taking away business from the larger and better-established Zenith was more consistent with an inference of competitive behavior than an agreement among 21 companies to price predatorily.[27] The court remanded the case, stating that "in light of the absence of any rational motive to conspire, neither petitioners' pricing practices, nor their conduct in the Japanese market, nor their agreements respecting prices and distribution in the American market, suffice to create a genuine issue for trial."[28]

Case Discussion Questions

1. How does the Matsushita case differ from the classic case of predatory pricing?
2. Why is the court reluctant to act in a case involving predatory pricing?
3. How long was the period that the alleged predatory pricing occurred? What happened to the market shares of the American firms during that period?
4. Why does the Supreme Court consider predatory pricing to be speculative or irrational in most cases? Why might predatory pricing be irrational in the Matsushita case?
5. If the Areeda-Turner principle of predatory pricing were applied in this case, what cost data would the court need to determine whether or not predatory pricing had occurred? Why was the Zenith-financed study by the expert witness unable to provide this type of data?
6. Did the Supreme Court act appropriately in granting a summary judgment in favor of Matsushita? Explain your reasons.

Case Endnotes

1. *Matsushita Electric Industrial Co. v. Zenith Radio Corporation,* 475 U.S. 574 (1986).
2. Id. p. 578.
3. See id. pp. 578, 588.
4. Id. p. 579.
5. See id. pp. 580–81.
6. Id. p. 587.
7. Id. p. 588.
8. Id. p. 589.
9. Id.
10. Id.
11. Id. (emphasis in original).
12. Id.
13. Id. p. 590.
14. Id. (emphasis in original).
15. Id. p. 592.
16. Id. p. 572, note 15.
17. Id. p. 592.
18. Id.
19. Id. p. 594, note 19.
20. Id. pp. 594–95.
21. Id. p. 594.
22. Id.
23. Id.
24. Id. p. 595.
25. Id.
26. Id. (emphasis in original).
27. Id. p. 597.
28. Id. (citation omitted).

PART FIVE

Public Policy and Strategic Management of Stakeholder Issues

CHAPTER 14

Organizational Governance and Investor Stakeholders

CHAPTER OBJECTIVES

1. Demonstrate how business organizations are social systems with a threefold social order including economic, governance, and cultural spheres.

2. Explain how business organizations use economic strategic acquisitions to implement corporate strategy.

3. Explain how business executives use judicial and legislative processes to govern organizations.

4. Outline the roles of stockholders, boards of directors, management, and external legal processes in the governing organizations.

5. Review the competition for corporate control by corporate raiders during the 1980s.

6. Distinguish the process of financially oriented hostile takeovers used by corporate raiders from the strategic acquisition process used by corporate managers.

7. Outline how corporations defend themselves against hostile corporate takeover attempts.

8. Discuss how procedural due process systems protect employee rights and can allow for liberty within business.

9. Explain how recent shareholder activism influences corporate governance.

Introductory Case _____

The Quiet Coup at ALCOA

In the 1987 annual report of Aluminum Company of America, the new chief executive officer (CEO), Paul H. O'Neil, unveiled the company's new strategic plan in a one-page message to shareholders. O'Neil told them to disregard what they had been reading about ALCOA's plans for diversification and acquisitions out of the aluminum business. ALCOA's future was now committed to concentration on its core business-Aluminum.

CHANGES IN COMPETITIVE STRATEGY. The outgoing CEO, Charles W. Parry, had spent the last four years proclaiming the new ALCOA, a major producer of new alloys and other high-technology materials, for the next century. ALCOA's new strategy was to solve the problems of a seven-year slump in the worldwide aluminum market and the boom-and-bust cycles brought on by chronic overcapacity within the industry. By 1995, ALCOA was to earn 50 percent of its revenues from acquired nonaluminum businesses and from new products made from alternative materials to be developed on its 2,300-acre research and development center.

CHANGES IN CORPORATE GOVERNANCE. Parry took early retirement at age 62 after having spent most of his career with ALCOA. His departure from the top position at ALCOA is a tale of a boardroom coup. Other members on the board of directors had become dissatisfied with Parry's leadership within two years after he began his role as CEO. Hoping to recruit a new chief executive from outside ALCOA, they had proposed a merger with Cummins Engine Company without informing Parry of their plans. Since the aluminum business does not fit well with the diesel engine business

and the corporate cultures were quite different, talks for the proposed merger collapsed.

Diversifying out of aluminum had been Parry's solution to the problem of slow growth and declining profitability in aluminum. Though Parry's plan had vision, he was unable to gain the support of other key executives within ALCOA. They feared that markets for new materials might not materialize. Many top executives resented the use of profits generated from the aluminum business to finance new product development and the acquisition of businesses in other fields. The company is a century-old producer of aluminum with annual sales of nearly $8 billion.

CORPORATE CULTURE, STRATEGIC CHANGE, AND POLITICS. The corporate culture was apparently incompatible with the more risk-oriented strategic vision of Parry, which required major changes. Executives became tired of hearing the message that ALCOA was no longer just an aluminum company. Instead of discussing his visionary strategy at meetings of the board of directors, meetings were apparently devoted to discussing the acquisitions of particular businesses. Thus, the new strategic vision held by Parry was never successfully sold to key executives. Board members could not relate to discussions about "purchasing some blue-jeans factory in Taiwan" when they were more concerned with making the aluminum business successful in a highly competitive global market.

Progress in implementing Parry's strategic vision was slow and by 1986, ALCOA had made only 12 acquisitions worth $500 million, including $330 million for TRE Corporation of Los Angeles, a producer of lightweight aerospace and defense products. This pace of change was too slow to transform the $8 billion ALCOA. When the plan did not gain sufficient support, and Parry agreed to take early retirement to make way for O'Neill as the new chief executive officer at ALCOA.

SOURCE: Adapted from "The Quiet Coup at Alcoa," *Business Week,* June 27, 1988, pp. 58–65.

Organizational Governance and the Threefold Social Order

Society is a threefold social order including the economic, political, and cultural spheres. Each sphere has its unique purpose, central idea, or unifying theme, virtue, and right.[1] Similarly, a business organization, as a social system, can be viewed as a threefold social order as illustrated in Figure 14–1. The three spheres including the economic, the governance, and the cultural spheres of a social system may be interactive with one another or they may interpenetrate.[2] Within a business organization the economic sphere is responsible for the competitive performance of the business, the political sphere is responsible for governance, and the corporate culture maintains the value system within the organization. There is considerable overlap among the top managers who perform the functions of these different spheres and between those who make and implement strategic economic decisions, govern the organization, and set the example that creates and maintains the values central to the corporation. ALCOA needed to make strategic changes in the economic activities of its core business. Successfully making these changes ultimately depended upon the nature of interactions with the governance and cultural spheres of the organization.

THE ECONOMIC SPHERE OF A BUSINESS ORGANIZATION

The economic sphere is concerned with the competitive performance of the organization. Business organizations have as a major goal the production and sale of needed goods and services at a profit within the context of a competitive market. ALCOA was seeking to move from the aluminum industry where cost efficiency was the key competitive factor to specialized materials markets where differentiation and focus strategies were more applicable. However, different rationalities and capacities were needed in these new markets if the strategies were to be implemented successfully.

Rationality is a way of thinking, usually described as instrumental, concerned with the means by which objectives are accomplished. Decision makers rationally choose those means that are perceived as the most likely to lead to desired goals.[3] Economic rationality guides economic performance but different types of thinking are needed for efficiency in relatively stable markets than for adaptability to changing market situations.

Technical rationality is concerned with efficiency, the output/input ratios of producing and distributing the goods and services of an organization at the lowest possible costs. Technical rationality is directed at increasing productivity and cost efficiency so that the cost structure of a business will be competitive. Techniques supporting technical rationality have included task specialization, mechanistic organizational structures, and investments in advanced technology to lower the cost per unit of aluminum processed.

Organizational rationality is more critical for competition based upon product differentiation and focusing on market niches because adaptability and coordination of organizational processes become more important in these situations. Organizational rationality can be achieved through management practices such as (1) team-based organizational designs that develop the capacity for coordinating fast-developing projects and organizational change; (2) management by objectives systems that focus attention on strategic goals; and (3) total quality management (TQM) systems that seek to provide high-quality service sought by customers in fast-changing markets. These management approaches facilitate the developing of distinctive, high-quality products with features that differentiate the products and services produced by a business from those of its competitors.

As the ALCOA case illustrates, organizations do not automatically achieve competitive performance. Strategy formulation that follows market analysis needs to be politically legitimated and consistent with cultural values within the organization. ALCOA was in a very price sensitive industry where efficiency was the key ingredient

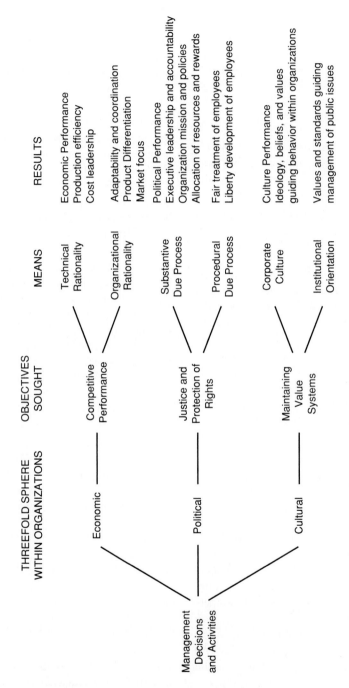

FIGURE 14–1 The Threefold Social Order of Business Organizations

for success. Alternative strategies depended upon adapting to changing technologies, pursuing new markets away from the core business of aluminum, and developing the organizational capacities needed for meeting these new opportunities. While both dimensions of economic rationality were important for competitive performance, technical rationality was more important for successful cost leadership and price-based competitive strategies in aluminum. Organizational rationality is more important for coordination and adaptability to environmental changes needed for differentiation strategies that would be needed in ceramics and other special materials industries targeted by Parry.

Parry was unable to bring about changes in the competitive strategies because he failed to effectively communicate his vision to other top managers. This was a political problem ultimately leading to his downfall as the CEO of ALCOA. His strategy would have required profound changes in the type of economic rationality and the cultural orientation historically found at ALCOA.

Key decisions affecting the economic sphere are thus interdependent with processes found in the political and cultural spheres of the organization. For this reason, an understanding of organizational governance is important for achieving economic performance. Additionally, organizational governance systems protect employee rights by treating them with dignity and maintaining justice within the organization. The principal purpose of this chapter is to discuss both aspects of organizational governance found in business, as outlined in Table 14–1.

TABLE 14–1
Due Process in Organizational Governance

Due Process	Function	Purposes	Implementation Methods
Procedural	Judicial	1. Resolve disputes over rights	1. Appeal to higher executive authority
		2. Hold employees and managers accountable	2. Appeal to a grievance system
		3. Protect rights	3. Negotiation and/or litigation
Substantive	Legislative	Resolve Issues of :	
		1. Executive succession—Who will rule?	1. Unilateral executive decisions
		2. What values will guide policy and strategy?	2. Multilateral participation in decision making
		3. Allocation of resources according to interests and justice—What will be budgeted and how much will compensation be?	3. Proxy fights, corporate takeovers, litigation, investor activism

SOURCE: Adapted from William G. Scott, "The Management Governance Theories of Justice and Liberty," *Journal of Management,* 14, no. 2 (1988): 282.

THE GOVERNMENTAL SPHERE OF A BUSINESS ORGANIZATION

Governance is concerned with the political performance of the organization. Major goals of this sphere should be justice and the protection of employee rights through substantive and procedural due processes within the organization.[4] *Substantive due process* includes (1) *executive succession,* which determines executive leadership, (2) the *legitimation* of organizational mission and policies developed by top management, and (3) the *allocation* of organizational resources and rewards. *Procedural due process* includes systems that (1) *protect employee rights,* (2) *maintain accountability* of employees and managers, and (3) *undertake dispute resolution* concerning conflicts between employee rights and management decisions.

Substantive due process in organizations sometimes is directed at regime maintenance of entrenched managers who wish to stay in power, decide policy, and receive the rewards that go with executive positions. However, in the case of ALCOA, Parry willingly left his position when it became clear that the political processes of the organization would not legitimate his vision for the future. Questions about who will rule are often very controversial and the competition for corporate control was increasingly decided through hostile takeovers during the 1980s.[5] More recently, investor activism has been an important influence on governance processes within business organizations. Investors have been influencing corporate governance through independent management committees, outside experts, and running independent candidates for the board of directors.[6]

Executives sometimes resist such attempts by investors to influence organizational governance. For example, in 1991 Sears Roebuck and Company spent $5.6 million to oppose the board membership of shareholder-activist Robert A. G. Monks. Sears also reduced the number of members on its board of directors from 15 to 10 to increase the number of votes Monks would need to be elected on the board.[7]

Though some argue that there is insufficient accountability for top executives, numerous examples exist where executives were replaced through the substantive due process mechanism. The case of Chief Executive Charles Parry of ALCOA suggests that executives must gain the political legitimacy, that is, top management support, for changes in the mission of the business. Bill Bricker, CEO of Diamond Shamrock, was removed from office because of poor economic results and a lavish executive lifestyle that seemed unjustifiable given the firm's performance.[8] The result at Diamond Shamrock was a process of accountability involving both actions by executives within the organization and by the financial community. Bricker was forced out of office under the pressure of a hostile corporate takeover launched by T. Boone Pickens.

The Traditional Model of Stockholder Governance

According to the traditional model portrayed in Figure 14–2, stockholders, as owners of the corporation, vote to elect members of the board of directors for the corporation. Board members then select the chairperson of the board who is also usually the CEO of the corporation. The board members then decide who will be included in top management, how rewards will be allocated, and what the corporate mission will be. In this model, the board is accountable to the stockholders, the top management is accountable to the board, and other managers are accountable to top management.

THE CHIEF EXECUTIVE OFFICER AND THE CHAIR OF THE BOARD OF DIRECTORS

The top executive of the corporation is the CEO and is responsible for providing leadership to the business. Usually executive leadership of a corporation is united in a single person who serves as the CEO and the chairman of the board of directors. The duties of the CEO include formulating the mission, strategy, and policy of the business that are presented to the board for approval. The

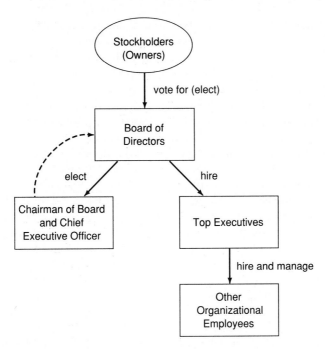

FIGURE 14–2 The Traditional Governance Model

board of directors is responsible for the top-level governance of the corporation. Board of directors (1) monitor the results of executive leadership, (2) approve the mission, strategies, and policies proposed by top management, and (3) determine executive compensation.

The board of directors, elected by a vote of the shareholders, has overall governance responsibility for policy decisions within the corporation. However, actual boards may vary in the way they operate and typically exercise different levels of power and authority:

1. *Statutory boards* fulfill the minimum legal requirements such as holding regularly scheduled meetings but exercising minimal authority.
2. *Cosmetic boards* actually derive their authority from a powerful top management rather than a mandate from stockholders. This type of board automatically approves decisions made by top management.
3. *Oversight boards* ratify or disapprove management initiatives through reviewing management

proposals, reports on performance, and strategic programs for purposes of evaluation, approval, and policy changes. In this approach to board activity, the board responds to top management's initiated programs but the board itself rarely initiates changes in missions, programs, or corporate activities.
4. *Decision-making boards* exercise more governing authority than other types of boards and sometimes exercise initiative in determining the organization's mission, strategy, and policy implementation.[9]

During the 1970s there was a trend of electing more outside board members who were not members of top management. Outsiders on the board increased the external representation and thus the legitimacy of the corporation. This was a common response to outside interest group pressures from the consumer movement, from the Civil Rights Movement, and from environmentalists. Little legal accountability to shareholders existed until the 1980s when board members began to be sued by stockholders with increasing frequency. Most companies now carry liability insurance to protect board members, but the threat of a lawsuit has served to take much of the glamor and prestige out of board membership.[10]

Though different boards may exercise differing amounts of authority and initiative in organizational governance, their legal accountability has been increasing. During the 1980s, it become increasingly difficult for corporations to keep board members who were not a part of the top management of the company, because of an increasing number of lawsuits by disgruntled shareholders. Shareholders would sue when they believed management decisions reduced the value of their investments. This was especially true in cases when top management resisted a buyout offer in which shareholders thought they could profit from the deal.

Increased litigation resulted in a change of board membership to *corporate insiders* who were a part of top management. Gone are the many part-time board members who served for social status and ceremonial reasons. *Outside board* members not a part of the management of the corporation have become more professional in years past. The increased financial liability and public scrutiny associated with board membership have significantly discouraged outsiders from accepting membership in corporate boards of directors. This has increased the proportion of top management serving as members on the board of directors. Also, as capital markets have globalized, the number of citizens of other countries serving on boards has increased. Citizens of other countries serving on U.S.-based global businesses increased 22 percent in 1991, to 186 from 152 board positions in the top one thousand largest U.S. corporations.[11]

SUBSTANTIVE DUE PROCESS: WHO RULES?

The first question that must be resolved in substance due process of business governance is who rules? Recent proposals for governance reform suggest that boards become more active in making this decision. One suggestion for board reform is that the positions of the CEO and the chairman of the board of directors (COB) be held by different

persons. Jay Lorsch of the Harvard Business School argues that the board would be better able to evaluate a COB's leadership if the chairman was not also the CEO.[12]

Boards have ousted a number of CEOs of major U.S. corporations as the ALCOA case illustrates. However, corporate performance has usually declined radically before the board took corrective action. Executive succession decisions for the top positions within corporations are chosen primarily from managers within the corporation.[13] If the new CEO selected an insider, it is justified based upon that person's past record or experience in markets or technologies critical to future competitiveness. For example, the new successor CEO for GM is an insider, John F. Smith, Jr., who had been successful in global automobile markets where GM was having severe problems. Similarly, an insider, Robert Palmer, the new CEO at Digital Equipment Corporation (DEC), was selected because of his previous performance and experience in technologies for smaller computers where DEC has been competitively weak.[14]

Outside CEOs are sought if an economic emergency exists and a turnaround in economic performance is urgent as in the recent case of IBM. Under CEO John Akers, IBM was unable to move away from its dependence upon mainframe computer technology to the networked personal computer environment required for modern information systems. IBM lost $8.7 billion and its share price dropped, resulting in a $32.3 billion drop in total market value. Akers reorganized the company and sought to cut costs by reducing jobs by 103,000 but was unable to restore investor confidence. He was forced out by the board of directors, who selected an outsider as the new CEO. Louis V. Gerstner had previously served at RJR Nabisco and Federal Express, where he was credited for turnarounds in corporate performance. The IBM board of directors felt they had to go outside IBM if the corporation was to successfully move away from its reliance on mainframe computer technology, increase efficiency, and improve the competitive position of the declining IBM.

SUBSTANTIVE DUE PROCESS— WHO GETS WHAT?

Compensation is a second key decision in substantive due process.[15] Managers and other employees of an organization are more inclined to support governance decisions if they are perceived as fair. However, like the broader society with its pluralistic interest groups, organizations have many stakeholders. An *organizational stakeholder* is anyone that is either involved or is effected by a decision or activity of an organization. When governance decisions like resource allocations that involve budgeting, pay, or other rewards are made by executives, it is easy for stakeholders to perceive injustice when they compare their received rewards relative to others. Shareholders would like to see the value of their investment grow. Employees may question wage cuts when executive pay is skyrocketing.

Differential rewards for employees depend upon factors such as types, quality and amount of work performed, level in the hierarchy, bargaining power, relative scarcity of the skill involved, and management judgments concerning these things.[16] Employees are positively motivated when they perceive that rewards are fair. Motivation, in turn, has economic outcomes in the areas of increased efficiency, coordination, adaptability, and support enjoyed by the management of an organization. Thus both the results of rationality in economic performance and legitimacy in political performance are affected by stakeholder perceptions of fair treatment within the organization.

Equity is relative. A person feels justly or unjustly treated only in relation to how other people are being treated in the same situation. If a woman is paid less for doing the same work as a man, she appropriately feels that she has suffered an injustice. However, many cases of inequitable treatment are not clearly visible. Women and minorities often experience a "glass ceiling" that is invisible but somehow blocks their advancement in organizations. An African American may feel that higher management offers the best assignments to others and thus others have greater career development opportunities. A woman manager may feel that she must prove herself more than a man before being offered a promotion. When such things occur, the fairness of substance within the organization is brought into question.

THE ISSUE OF EXECUTIVE COMPENSATION

Executive compensation has been a governance issue of growing importance. During the 1980s, corporate profits increased 78 percent, on average, while workers' pay increased only 53 percent, and CEO pay increased 212 percent.[17] Executive pay increases were often not correlated with financial performance. Although Japanese firms often were outperforming U.S. businesses, the average pay for a CEO in Japan was only one-fourth as much as a CEO in comparable U.S. corporations. Many corporations faced complaints from their shareholders, who felt the extravagant executive salaries were unjustified.[18] The SEC required shareholder proposals for pay reform to be discussed at stockholder meetings.

The compensation package for executives includes a salary, bonus for performance, and stock options. The average salary of a CEO is over $1.2 million, or about 45 times the amount received by the average worker. Stock options are the right to buy a fixed number of shares at a fixed price that is typically pegged at below market. Stock options normally increase the salary package of top executives to about $2 million per year. Perks can include a company car, the executive jet, or personal services. For example, the H.J. Heintz Company paid its CEO, Anthony O'Reily, over $470,000 from 1987 to 1990 to pay for personal financial consulting that he received.

Compensation Committees

CEO compensation levels are set by a corporate compensation committee whose members are CEOs from other corporations, consultants hired or paid by the CEO, or legal counsel on retainer by the corporation. CEOs from other businesses have been criticized for raising each other's compensa-

tion without paying much attention to performance. Furthermore, committee members such as
lawyers, investment bankers, and consultants who
receive regular fees from the corporation are influenced by the CEO. These committee members
may have a conflict of interest because they may
feel that continued contracts with the company
might be contingent on their votes on the compensation committee.

Recommended Reforms in
Executive Compensation
These include the following:

1. Reform the compensation package. Lower
salary levels to no more than $1 million. Eliminate
bonuses that are received even when performance
is poor and corporate strategic objectives are not
achieved. Eliminate expensive features that do not
encourage performance.
2. Limit perks, golden parachutes, and million-
dollar pensions. Some executives are entitled to a
golden parachute amounting to millions of dollars
(that is, two to three years' salary) if their employment contract is terminated. Also, they are often
entitled to receive huge annual pensions should
they retire.
3. Do not reprice stock options if the company
shares fall below their exercise price. Stock price
over time is an important measure of overall
strategic performance of a business. Stock options
allow executives to share in the economic wealth
that their leadership helps to create. However,
repricing stock options eliminates executive
accountability, leads to unfair compensation, and
provides the wrong signal to executives concerning
the consequences of poor performance.
4. Link pay to performance. Bonuses should be
received only if challenging performance targets are
achieved. In the past bonuses have been received
automatically by executives in many companies.
5. Encourage top executives to own shares in the
company so they will be rewarded if shareholder
wealth is increased.
6. Increase the scrutiny of the board of directors
by adding non-CEOs to the compensation com-

mittee. Exclude from the compensation committee
persons who draw fees from the corporation such
as lawyers, investment bankers, or consultants.
This proposal is designed to eliminate conflicts of
interest on compensation committees that undermine their legitimacy.[19]

Procedural Due Process—
Protecting Employees
from Arbitrary Power

INDIVIDUAL RIGHTS
WITHIN ORGANIZATIONS

How free should an employee be to do what he or
she desires as an employee of an organization?
What rights should an employee or a manager
have? How should constraints on freedom be
established? Liberty requires knowledge and freedom so that a person's actions can be based upon
informed consent. To enjoy liberty a person should
have the freedom to act but should be informed
and be willing to take responsibility for the consequences of that action.

Liberty is constrained by the recognition of
another person's rights because one party's right
limits another party's freedom. Thus an employer's
right to employee performance suggests that the
manager can do things that limit an employee's
freedom on the job. Similarly, an employee's right
to privacy might constrain the manager's freedom
to obtain certain information. Thus liberty and
rights are defined within an employment relationship by the agreed upon rights and duties of
employees and employers. Managers make decisions about promotions, assignments, and other
things affecting employees. An employee may feel
that a manager's decision is arbitrary and an abuse
of managerial authority. Also, disputes can occur
over rights because the assertion of a right often
reflects different interests.[20]

Ewing proposed a "bill of rights," which could
serve as a guide to procedural due process systems
within organizations.[21] Included are many rights

commonly accepted by democratic societies and sanctioned by law in the political and cultural sphere. These rights include the following:

1. Freedom of expression
2. Freedom of association
3. Freedom from having to obey immoral or illegal directives
4. Privacy
5. Access to one's personnel file and the right to challenge the accuracy of such information
6. Protection from slander and defamation of character
7. Written justification for a penalty received on the job
8. The right to a fair hearing to settle disputes concerning these rights.

While many of these rights remain controversial and their legal establishment in the workplace has been slow, many changes have occurred since Ewing proposed them.[22] In cases where management appeal systems and contractually required grievance systems are unavailable or are unsatisfactory, the procedural due process to protect rights are enforced by public laws.[23] Twenty-five states now require that employees have a right to know about hazardous substances in the workplace. Over 20 states protect whistle blowers, who speak out publicly about immoral or illegal activities they see occur in government or in the corporation. Federal law now requires that organizations with over 100 employees provide them with 60 days advance notice of plant closures. Some state laws limit the use of polygraph tests and protect employee privacy in other areas.

A central doctrine of the employment relationship has been *employment at will,* which allows an employer to discharge an employee at any time for any reason. A number of state laws have sharply restricted the use of this principle. If an organization has a set of published operating policies and procedures outlining employment practices, management is bound by these policies because they are an implicit contract. *Wrongful discharge* cases commonly appear in court and employees can sue employers for damages if the employee feels the employer has acted arbitrarily. If the employee wins the lawsuit the company could be forced to pay punitive damages if the court finds it has acted arbitrarily.

The California State Supreme Court has limited the amount of damages that could be awarded for wrongfully dismissing an employee to back pay.[24] If the California decision becomes the rule, only senior managers within a business would find it worthwhile to sue in cases of wrongful discharge.

PROCEDURAL DUE PROCESS AND APPEAL SYSTEMS

Procedural due process includes appeal systems that (1) protect employee rights, (2) limit the abuse of power, and (3) correct injustice within the organization.[25] Three principles underlie appeal systems:

1. Appeals systems should be available without prejudice. People want to be able to appeal without fear of reprisal.
2. The separation of power: those who make and execute the laws should not interpret these laws in the process of rendering judgments on disputes.
3. There should be a general recognition of an employee's rights and duties even though these are in dispute. A major outcome of an appeals system can be to clarify and specify the extent of a right within the workplace.

Although the three principles of a grievance system are the minimum requirements to assure that disputes are fairly adjudicated, they are infrequently found as standard organizational policy. One exception is the collective-bargaining agreements between labor and management that cover around 11 percent of private-sector employees. Union contracts generally provide union members with opportunities for appealing alleged violations of their contractual rights.

Most grievance procedures specify impartial arbitration as the final step to which unresolved issues can be submitted. There are many dimensions describing appeals systems: (1) some are formal, some are informal; (2) some are voluntarily established by management, others are required by a union-management contract; (3) some operate within the organization and others are imposed by state laws where external litigation is used to settle disputes. Increasingly employees are using the court system as an avenue of appeal.

Corporate Culture and Organizational Values

The third sphere of the social order within organizations is the corporate culture. Culture is the set of important assumptions (often unstated) and values that members of a community share in common.[26] For example, the corporate culture of Cummins Engine Company includes five important assumptions: (1) Cummins provides high quality and is highly responsive to customers; (2) things get done well and quickly; (3) informality is stressed over formal systems; (4) top management will provide instructions when problems occur; and (5) Cummins employees are part of a family.[27] Apparently these assumptions central to the corporate culture of Cummins were different from the ones within ALCOA at the time its board of directors approached Cummins about a merger. This difference, and differences in the nature of their respective businesses, caused the top management of Cummins to be uninterested in pursuing the matter with ALCOA's management.

Members of a community share the same subculture if they have internalized *beliefs* about how the world or the organization really works and hold common values. *Values* are the ideals accepted as worth striving to accomplish. For example, Borg-Warner went through an elaborate process to develop and to gain management acceptance within the company for "The Beliefs of Borg-Warner," as listed in Box 14–1. These beliefs were developed slowly through widespread management participation within Borg-Warner. Their acceptance within management established the cultural

values within the organization that encourages (1) adaptability and competitive excellence within the economic sphere, (b) respect for the dignity of the individual and a striving for fairness in the governmental sphere, and (c) key values in the cultural sphere that define appropriate attitudes and behavior within Borg-Warner. These beliefs also inspire the value of service to the community that form the basis of social responsibility.

Throughout the 1980s, merger activities were occurring with increasing regularity and hostile takeovers were becoming common. The conventional wisdom considered organizational governance as entrenched professional managers operating within the legal framework of the traditional governance model. Accountability to stockholders was expressed as the ideal, and the legal obligation was to manage corporations to increase shareholder wealth. However, most writers felt that corporations, in the end, were managed by and for professional managers in an organizational society.

The significant change that has occurred during the last decade is the intense external competition for the control of the corporation. This competition has been manifested as (1) strategic corporate acquisitions and mergers, (2) hostile takeovers by external corporate raiders who were met with (3) takeover defense strategies by corporate executives, (4) approaches to worker self-management including union attempts to influence executive leadership, (5) employee stock ownership plans (ESOPs), and (6) most recently, relationship investing by activist institutional investors.

Strategic Acquisitions

Mergers and acquisitions are often used to accomplish some strategic economic purpose.[28] A *strategic acquisition* is when a business seeks to accomplish its mission and implement its strategy through buying another business. *External growth* through acquisitions sometimes provide an easier path to market expansion and improvement of competitive position than internal expansion. *Internal*

BOX 14–1 The Beliefs of Borg-Warner: To Reach Beyond the Minimal Competition for Corporate Control

Any business is a member of a social system, entitled to the rights and bound by the responsibilities of that membership. Its freedom to pursue economic goals is constrained by law and channeled by the forces of a free market. But these demands are minimal, requiring only that a business provide wanted goods and services, compete fairly, and cause no obvious harm. For some companies, that is enough. It is not enough for Borg-Warner. We impose upon ourselves an obligation to reach beyond the minimal. We do so convinced that by making a larger contribution to the society that sustains us, we best assure not only its future vitality but our own.

This is what we believe.

WE BELIEVE IN THE DIGNITY OF THE INDIVIDUAL.

However large and complex a business may be, its work is still done by people dealing with people. Each person involved is a unique human being, with pride, needs, values, and innate personal worth. For Borg-Warner to succeed, we must operate in a climate of openness and trust, in which each of us freely grants others the same respect, cooperation, and decency we seek for ourselves.

WE BELIEVE IN OUR RESPONSIBILITY TO THE COMMON GOOD.

Because Borg-Warner is both an economic and social force, our responsibilities to the public are large. The spur of competition and the sanctions of the law give strong guidance to our behavior but alone do not inspire our best. For that we must heed the voice of our natural concern for others. Our challenge is to supply goods and services that are of superior value to those who use them; to create jobs that provide meaning for those who do them; to honor and enhance human life; and to offer our talents and our wealth to help improve the world we share.

Source: Company document. Copyright 1982. Reprinted by permission.

WE BELIEVE IN THE ENDLESS QUEST FOR EXCELLENCE.

Though we may be better today than we were yesterday, we are not as good as we must become. Borg-Warner chooses to be a leader—in serving our customers, advancing our technologies, and rewarding all who invest in us their time, money, and trust. None of us can settle for doing less than our best, and we can never stop trying to surpass what already has been achieved.

WE BELIEVE IN CONTINUOUS RENEWAL.

A corporation endures and prospers only by moving forward. The past has given us the present to build on. But to follow our visions to the future, we must see the difference between traditions that give us continuity and strength and conventions that no longer serve us—and have the courage to act on that knowledge. Most can adapt after change has occurred; we must be among the few who anticipate change, shape it to our purpose, and act as its agents.

WE BELIEVE IN THE COMMONWEALTH OF BORG-WARNER AND ITS PEOPLE.

Borg-Warner is both a federation of businesses and a community of people. Our goal is to preserve the freedom each of us needs to find personal satisfaction while building the strength that comes from unity. True unity is more than a melding of self-interests; it results when values and ideals also are shared. Some of ours are spelled out in these statements of belief. Others include faith in our political, economic, and spiritual heritage; pride in our work and our company; the knowledge that loyalty must flow in many directions, and a conviction that power is strongest when shared. We look to the unifying force and these beliefs as a source of energy to brighten the future of our company and all who depend on it.

growth is when a corporation develops a capability, expands, or moves into a new market by increasing its existing resource capabilities by hiring new employees and making new capital investments. Managers are encouraged to make strategic acquisitions by undervalued stock prices of firms that have unique capabilities in desirable markets.

STRATEGIC OBJECTIVES AND EXTERNAL GROWTH

The strategic objectives a corporation might have for merging or acquiring a target firm include (1) product and market extension, (2) complementing functions, (3) balancing the portfolio of businesses, or (4) some combination of these three.

Product or Market Extension

An example of product and market extension would be the acquisition of the Wine Group by Coca-Cola. Coca-Cola hoped to take advantage of the growth in wine sales to compensate for a slowing in the growth of soft drink sales. Although Coca-Cola was able to acquire the Wine Group in a friendly acquisition to obtain a sizable market share of the wine business, the economic performance proved to be poor under Coca-Cola. Coca-Cola was a firm with a leading position in soft drinks and was known for its strong management capabilities in that field. Unfortunately, the wine industry was very different from the soft drink business, and Coca-Cola found that its expertise in one field was not as applicable to the new industry as expected.

A more positive example of product market extension would be the purchase of Firestone by Bridgestone, a Japanese tire manufacturing firm. Bridgestone wanted to develop a position in the American market quickly. Firestone was a major U.S. tire manufacturer with a well-developed distribution system comprised of a network of tire and service centers throughout the country. Its economic performance had suffered severe losses in the years before the Bridgestone acquisition and was not able to modernize its facilities and remain competitive despite Firestone's historically advantageous market position. After the acquisition, Bridgestone was able to make a substantial capital investment that modernized the facilities to integrate product lines, and to use the acquisition to extend Bridgestone operations throughout the United States.

Complementary Functions

An acquisition for complementary functions would include a target company with similar production and product development skills. For example, General Motors acquired Hughs Electronics and IDS because the new automobiles of the future would have more electronics and computers. The technological capabilities in research and product development of these acquired businesses were expected to improve the production technology and sophistication of GM products. Another example is Pepsi Company, Inc., which acquired Frito Lay and Kentucky Fried Chicken. They could use Pepsi's marketing function to complement and strengthen their competitiveness.

Balancing the Business Portfolio by a Diversified Corporation

Acquisitions, mergers, and selling businesses are ways to implement this strategic objective of portfolio balance. Some businesses in a highly diversified corporation may be in mature markets where profitability is acceptable but growth opportunities are limited. Other businesses might be in industries that enjoy rapid market growth but the competitive capabilities are quite limited. The former type of business normally generates surplus cash for the corporation, while the latter type requires sizable capital investments to improve its competitive position and to develop newly emerging market opportunities.

A balanced portfolio should include established businesses that can generate reliable profitability to support the financing of newer businesses in need of capital to develop market opportunities and new products. Portfolio balancing can include the acquisition of an undervalued firm when the potential for improving its performance is great. Philip Morris has the strategy of becoming a diversified consumer products company. It selects companies in the food industry where they can leverage the marketing of Philip Morris and balance its portfolio of businesses. Another aspect of portfolio balancing is the selling of a low-performing business division that does not seem to "fit" into the business portfolio desired by top management. For example, Holiday Inns, Inc., sold its subsidiary, Trailways, to Greyhound because it was unprofitable and did not fit into the Holiday Inn portfolio.

THE STRATEGIC ACQUISITION PROCESS

Figure 14–3 shows the strategic acquisition process. It begins with the strategic analysis of the potential market opportunities and capabilities of the corporation. For example, a global firm may want to take advantage of a market opportunity in another country and need a local distribution system for its expansion strategy to be successful. Another company may need improved science and engineering capabilities to upgrade its products or to develop new products for the future. A cash rich corporation with extensive market capabilities may want to enter a newly emerging market like biotechnology by buying a small business with this technology already in place.

Once strategic needs are assessed, acquisition policy and guidelines are formulated by top managers who define the strategic purpose to be served by any acceptable merger or acquisition. Acquisition targets are then identified that meet the strategic criteria. Target businesses are analyzed according to their market value, strengths and weaknesses, and compatibility with the corporate culture of the buying organization. Once acceptable acquisition targets are identified, investment bankers are consulted to assist in the financial analysis and identification of other suitable targets that might be for sale, and to arrange for financing.

Managers of the target firms remaining after the screening process are then approached by the managers of the acquiring business and a "courtship" process begins. Often the meetings will

be arranged on neutral ground without the knowledge of the target country. For example, the management of the acquiring firm will identify someone within its organization who shares a common membership in a country club, local charitable organization, or sports organization with an executive in the target firm.

Before the initial meeting, the managers, products, and functional operations of the target firm are analyzed. At the initial meeting at the city golf club, the target firm's management may not have thought about selling its firm and may not have a current financial evaluation of its firm. In other words, the acquiring firm will have done considerable homework before the initial meeting with the target firm's management. If the top management teams develop a rapport and if the two corporate cultures appear compatible, negotiations for the merger begin.

An important result of the negotiation process is the *letter of* understanding, which states the precise terms of the offer. This letter is carefully written with legal and financial advice and forms the basis of a mutual agreement. It expresses the financial value of the target company and the terms of the deal that might be acceptable. If negotiations are successful, this letter serves as a tender offer and outlines the following:

1. *Financial instruments.* What is to be exchanged for what? Sometimes cash is exchanged for stock. Sometimes stock is traded for stock in the purchasing company. In leveraged buyouts, the funds are borrowed from investment bankers in the form of bonds and the money is used to purchase the target firm's shares.

2. *Terms and timing of the exchange.* What are the terms and the timing of exchanges? Can debt instruments be exchanged for stocks after a specified time? Do some shareholders receive more for their shares than others? Are some debt instruments subordinated to others?

3. *Items being exchanged.* Is the total corporation or a subsidiary of the target company being purchased? What exactly is included in the exchange? This can include all assets, trademarks and brands, debts, inventories, back orders for products and

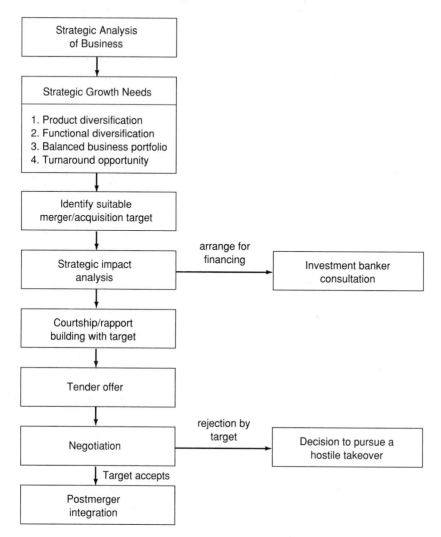

FIGURE 14–3 An Anatomy of a Strategic Acquisition

services, lists of customers and suppliers, trade secrets, patents, or other proprietary technology or intellectual property. Sometimes the most valued thing a company owns is its brand recognition or trademarks of products. Sometimes it is the patent on an important process.

Some letters of understanding are written to avoid future liabilities or management problems. For example, the purchasing business may want to exclude a subsidiary from the purchase that has had problems with product liability lawsuits, toxic spills, or a bad reputation. Some properties that are not needed but have toxic spills that would require a considerable investment to clean up would increase the liabilities in the acquisition without contributing to the value. Both the purchasing and the selling firm need to exercise due care in analyzing, evaluating, and establishing the liability involved in many areas of the business.

4. *Employment contracts and postmerger arrangements.* Often the most important capability the target firm has is its people. If a firm is acquired and

the top management promptly leaves, then the value of the firm can be substantially diminished. Thus the buying firm may want assurances that the management will remain in its present positions. Alternatively, the buying firm may want to make substantial changes in the acquired firm that might include replacing management. In these cases, the management of the selling firm may want assurances that they can remain in office for some specified period of time. Thus, the management of both the buying and the selling firm may wish to have employment contracts for managers to assure success in the postmerger period.

RESPONSIBILITY OF MANAGEMENT IN STRATEGIC ACQUISITIONS

It is the duty of management to consider the interests of the business and its stockholders. Thus both management teams consider the offers and counteroffers with this in mind during the negotiation process. If an agreement can be achieved, the executives of the two businesses conclude the merger or acquisition and combine the two management structures and operations. However, if the negotiations break down because no mutually acceptable agreement is found, the acquiring firm's offer is rejected by the target firm.

At this point, the acquiring firm can withdraw and seek out another business on its list of strategically acceptable targets. Or the acquiring firm can pursue a *hostile takeover* by attempting to buy stock from the shareholders of the target firm over the objections of its top management. If they can persuade shareholders to sell them over 50 percent of the outstanding common (voting) stock of the target firm, then the acquisition can be completed regardless of the views of the management of the target firm. The differences between a strategic acquisition and a hostile takeover are outlined in Table 14–2.

POSTACQUISITION PERFORMANCE

Once a strategic acquisition is completed, whether it is friendly or hostile, economic performance needs to be achieved. Unfortunately, mergers and acquisitions often result in decline of economic performance rather than the hoped-for results.[29] The stockholders of the target firm usually increase their wealth because of the premium paid for their shares. However, the economic performance of the merged entity is often low, and shareholders of the acquiring firms often receive no benefit from the merger.

Low postacquisition performance is more likely to result when the seven deadly sins of mergers and acquisitions are present. Mergers and acquisitions with these characteristics are likely to prove disappointing, with low postmerger economic performance. These seven deadly sins, or mistakes in acquisitions, include the following:

1. Paying too much and then assuming a boom stock market won't crash
2. Financing the takeover with too much debt that places too big of an interest burden on the corporation
3. Acquiring a firm without doing a strategic analysis
4. Diversifying beyond the core business of the acquiring firm
5. Acquiring a firm that is too big to be managed or successfully integrated into present operation by the acquiring firm
6. Acquiring a firm with a significantly different culture
7. Assuming that the top management of the target firm will stay after the acquisition is completed

Hostile Takeovers

Many takeovers do not follow the pattern of strategic acquisition outlined above.[30] Rather, many involve raiders, arbitragers, and investment bankers who play a very different role within a speculative environment. A hostile takeover is an acquisition attempt made over the objections and resistance of the top management of the business being acquired. A friendly acquisition is made with the agreement and support of the top management of the target business. A strategic acquisition can be either hostile or friendly, depending upon the outcome of the courtship and negotiation between the buying and potential selling firm, as shown in Table 14–2.

For example, Philip Morris has a strategy of diversifying out of tobacco products into the food-processing industry. Their strategic objective was to acquire the leading business in a number of selected industries. The search process identified Kraft Food Company as an ideal acquisition candidate. When they were unable to obtain agreement of top management of Kraft Foods, Philip Morris purchased Kraft in what was both a strategic acquisition and a hostile takeover. When the U.S. Steel Company, now called USX, decided to diversify into the energy industry, it acquired Marathon Oil Corporation in a friendly strategic acquisition. At the time, Mobile Oil also was attempting to acquire Marathon Oil in a hostile strategic acquisition, but Marathon's management supported the offer from U.S. Steel over Mobil's offer.

INITIAL STEPS BY RAIDER AND ARBITRAGERS

Figure 14–4, an anatomy of a hostile takeover, outlines the hostile takeover that is typically make for speculative profits rather than for the strategic reasons outlined above. The nonstrategic hostile takeover contrasts sharply with the strategic acquisition, whether the latter is friendly or hostile. A buyer who attempts this type of hostile takeover is called a *corporate raider*.

This speculative hostile takeover attempt begins when a raider identifies a target firm and acquires up to 4.9 percent of the shares in the company. Financial markets are regulated by the Securities and Exchange Commission (SEC), and one of its regulations requires that any purchase of 5 percent or more of a company's stocks must be reported within ten days. The purposes of such reporting regulations are to discourage speculative takeover attempts, allow the target firm's management a chance to respond to an offer in a rational manner, and to inform the financial community of important events that may affect the value of investments.

TABLE 14–2
Strategic Acquisitions and Hostile Takeovers

	Hostile Takeover	Friendly Acquisition
Nonstrategic Acquisition	No strategic objective drives the acquisition other than speculative profit.	No strategic objective drives the acquisition other than speculation.
	The target firm resists the acquisition.	However, the top management of the firm being purchased cooperates with the buyer.
Strategic Acquisition	A firm purchases another firm to fulfill its strategic objective.	A strategic objective is the reason for the acquisition.
	The top management of the target firm disagrees with the purchase and resists.	The top management of the selling firm agrees with the acquisition and cooperates.

Another regulation forbids the practice of "parking stock," a practice whereby a raider asks another party to buy and hold shares in a company on its behalf in order to avoid the SEC reporting requirement. The parked stock is ultimately purchased by the raider at a guaranteed profit to the party holding the parked stock. Using illegal parking and limiting the purchase of stock to 4.9 percent can result in maintaining secrecy of takeover plans at the crucial early stage of the hostile takeover process. Though illegal, stock parking is very hard to detect and enforcement of this law is difficult.

Arbitragers are persons such as investment bankers who deal in stocks in anticipation of changes in their value. They serve the purpose of absorbing risks in uncertain markets and thus can serve a positive social role in sustaining market operations. However, if arbitragers have access to insider information and practice illegal stock parking, their role becomes objectionable. Such practices are unfair to other investors and can have unjust and uneconomic consequences for the society as a whole.[31] Such illegal practices as insider trading and parking stock were a major scandal on Wall Street during the 1980s.[32]

THE TAKEOVER ROLE OF THE INVESTMENT BANKER

In the next step of a hostile takeover shown in Figure 14-4, the corporate raider makes arrangements for financing with investment bankers. Financing is commonly based on high-risk, high-yield junk bonds that were pioneered by the investment banker Drexel, Burnham, and Lambert.[33] Rumors begin to circulate in the financial community about a possible takeover of the target company. Around that time reports begin to circulate about the high value that might be obtained if the target firm were broken up and its divisions and key assets sold separately. All the rumors and attention generally makes the top management of the target firm apprehensive, and it begins to consider what might be done to defend itself against a hostile takeover attempt.

TAKEOVER DEFENSES

Early Stages of Takeover Defense
The target firm will generally retain legal advice from an attorney specializing in resisting takeovers. Investment bankers may be consulted to arrange for financing a costly defense. Sometimes preventative measures are put in place.

Golden Parachutes
These are employment contracts that specify huge payments to executives if they should leave the company before the expiration date of the contract.[34] These golden parachutes have been as much as $54 million for F. Ross Johnson, CEO, and $46 million for E. A. Horrigan of RJR Nabisco, a conglomerate that was taken over. The large termination payments made available by golden parachutes protect existing executives of the target firm and make major management changes very costly for the acquiring firm. If the takeover plan is to break up the firm or make other major changes, golden parachutes can be a deterrent to a takeover attempt.

Super Majority Vote Requirement
Top management can also change the corporate charter or bylaws in ways that make a takeover more difficult. For example, the requirement of a super majority, which requires a large-majority approval of a takeover by stockholders, has stopped some takeovers.

Encumbering Assets
Encumbering assets is the practice of borrowing huge amounts of capital and using key assets as collateral for financing. This defense against a takeover also includes selling options to purchase the asset most valued by a raider. For example, Marathon Oil defended itself against a hostile takeover attempt by Mobile Oil by selling an option to buy its largest oil field to U.S. Steel. This option could be exercised whether or not Mobile bought Marathon. When Mobile learned of this defensive move, it withdrew its offer to purchase Marathon.

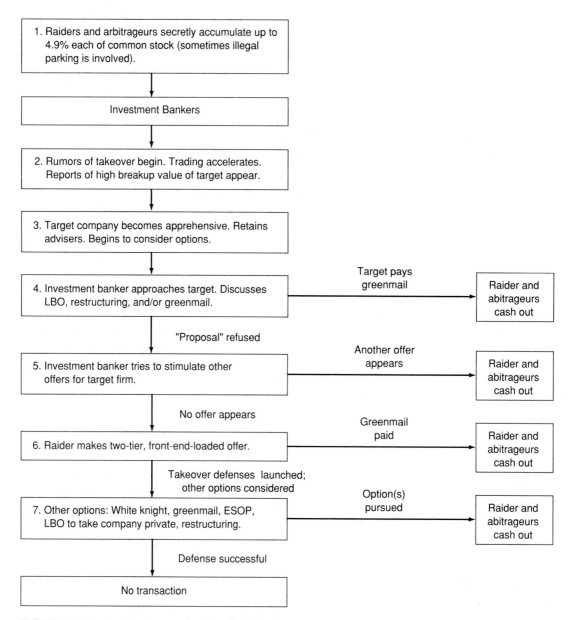

FIGURE 14–4 An Anatomy of a Hostile Takeover

SOURCE: Adapted from Bruce Atwater, "The Trouble with Takeovers," *Stanford Business School Magazine* (June 1988), pp. 13-16.

After the top management has been made somewhat apprehensive by takeover rumors, the investment banker of the raider approaches it for *greenmail*. Greenmail is the premium paid to buy back stocks of a raider so that the takeover attempt will be canceled. Sometimes this can be substantial.

Finding Another Buyer

If the management of the target firm refuses to pay the suggested greenmail, the investment banker often tries to stimulate other offers by other potential buyers of the target. If an offer appears, the raider can cash out at this time. For example, when Boone Pickens of Mesa Petroleum was unsuccessful in his attempted takeover of Gulf Oil, his profits from the attempt were approximately $750 million when Standard Oil of California served as a *white knight* and stepped in to rescue Gulf Oil. A white knight is a firm that purchases a takeover target in a friendly acquisition to rescue the target from a hostile takeover.

The Two-tiered, Front-end Loaded Tender Offer

If no likely suitors appear in step 5 of the anatomy of a hostile takeover shown in Figure 14–4, the raider then makes a *two-tiered, front-end loaded, tender offer* for the voting stock to the stockholders of the target firm. This type of offer generally involves a high premium cash offer for the first tier of stockholders needed to obtain a majority of the common voting stock. The second tier including the remainder of the common stock is made an offer of much lower value. This second tier's offer may be in terms of cash, an exchange for stock of the acquiring firm, or debt securities that are often considered high risk (including junk bonds). The problem with the two-tiered, front-end loaded, tender offer is that it is highly coercive. Stockholders who quickly respond to the offer so that they can be included in the first tier can make a huge profit for their shares; those who wait find themselves in the second tier and can lose their investment.

Takeover Defense Strategies

However, once a two-tiered, front-loaded offer is made, the takeover attempt is well underway and the target firm then can launch a number of last-minute defense strategies if it wishes to remain an independent business organization. It can seek a white knight that would be a more suitable buyer than the raider. Greenmail can be paid to call off the raid. Some companies approach an investment banker at this point to arrange for financing for a leveraged buyout to take the company private.

The Leveraged Buyout and the Junk Bond Market

A *leveraged buyout* (LBO) involves the purchasing of the target firm through the use of credit. LBOs were very popular during the 1980s because the purchaser often received as much as 40 percent return on the investment.[35] The source of the credit used in LBOs was primarily high-yield, high-risk subordinated debt called *junk bonds*. This type of credit, used in high-risk ventures, typically was not backed by collateral and was subordinated to higher-status bonds and loans that would be paid first if a default on the loan occurred. Bondholders of corporations were usually hurt by the LBO of the 1980s that added junk bonds to the corporate debt structure. Adding significantly more debt to pay for the LBO typically reduced the overall credit rating of the corporation, and the price of the original bonds dropped 20 percent or more.

Early in the 1980s a management team or group of private investors could do an LBO with as little as 5 to 10 percent of its own equity as investment. *Taking the company private* means that its stock would no longer be traded on public stock exchanges and thus would be out of the reach of potential raiders or others interested in an acquisition. In 1980, an estimated 11 LBOs occurred totaling nearly $1 billion in transactions. By 1989, over 375 companies were involved in LBOs that promised over $55 billion in debt repayment primarily in the form of junk bonds.[36] Nearly 2,500 LBOs were completed during the years 1982 to 1989, and corporate junk bond debt soared from $24 billion to $200 billion during that period.

PROBLEMS WITH LBO FINANCING

The money received from the sale of junk bonds was used to purchase enough publicly traded stock to gain control of the business. Since there was an urgent need for cash flows to repay the huge high-interest debt, the direct economic effect of the LBO on the acquired company followed a familiar and difficult pattern. Troubled LBOs, where the debt could not be serviced, included Revco, Federated Department Stores, SCI TV, and Interco, and illustrated at least one of the following problems:

1. The original transaction was often overpriced. If a significant price premium over the true economic value of the venture was paid, then the amount of credit owed on junk bonds and other forms of credit was prohibitive.
2. Cash flow projections from operations were too optimistic.
3. Debt amortization depended heavily on asset sales and cutting costs. The ability of the business to generate enough cash flow from current profitability was not possible. Thus assets were sold and expenses, like research and development needed for long-term competitiveness were slashed. Often downsizing, layoffs, and spinoffs of subsidiary operations resulted.
4. There was too little equity in the original structure. However, the LBO proved hard to undo.[37]

THE COLLAPSE OF THE JUNK BOND MARKET

By the end of 1989, the junk bond market was in a shambles. The high-yield market buckled under the effects of (1) uncertainty and a decline in economic growth, (2) declining bond prices, caused in part by the growth of the junk bond market itself, (3) the collapse of some large junk bond–financed deals, and (4) declining demand from traditional buyers.[38] The February 1990 collapse of Drexel, Burnham, Lambert signaled the decisive end of the six-year period of sustained growth in the junk bond market.

The Fall of Drexel, Burnham, Lambert

Drexel, the dominant force in the junk bond market, made $1.1 billion in pretax profit in 1986. By the end of 1988, Drexel had $1.4 billion in capital and 50 percent of junk bond underwriting. One year later, its market share had declined to 38 percent, and it was losing $86 million per month.[39] By the third quarter of 1989, Drexel's holding company held an estimated $1 billion in private junk bonds and bridge loans. In January 1990, it reported $800 million in equity, yet Drexel could not pay off $100 million of short-term loans on February 13, 1990.[40] Later that day, Drexel's holding company filed for Chapter 11 bankruptcy protection at the suggestion of the SEC, which had threatened to liquidate Drexel's assets.

Problems for Drexel came from short-term liquidity and insolvency stemming from its overwhelming dependence on junk bonds. From the speed of Drexel's demise, it is clear that the firm's doom was sealed in January 1989 when it settled with the government in a case involving fraud and other violations of securities regulations. Drexel's CEO, Peter Joseph, agreed to pay a fine of $650 million in the settlement and offered to cooperate in the investigation of Michael Milken. Milkin had been the key executive within Drexel responsible for developing the junk bond market and orchestrating Drexel's market dominance in the field.

Later during the summer of 1989, Congress passed the savings and loan bailout bill, requiring thrifts that owned junk bonds to sell them by 1994. Drexel and other investment bankers had indirectly convinced the Government Accounting Office (GAO) that junk bonds were a good investment but Congress could not be persuaded.[41] By this time many of the overleveraged corporations had begun to default on their loans. After months of erosion, the junk bond market collapsed as holders began discarding their bonds. Drexel suffered the consequences of failed deals more than anyone else because it depended so heavily on the business.

THE REVERSE LBO

After the collapse of the junk bond market, companies financed by LBOs have been struggling to service debt or refinance themselves.[42] Investors looking for a way out have had a difficult time. Undoing an LBO, that is, a *reverse LBO,* requires that a company increase its equity by issuing stock in a public offering. Going public during the recession of the early 1990s was especially difficult, as was finding another LBO buyer with a great deal of equity capital. In June 1990, the *New York Times* reported that the number of reverse LBOs (LBO companies taken public) had plummeted since the October 1987 stock market crash. Only ten were completed in 1989, with a total value of $746 million.

Less than 1 percent of all LBOs are attractive in the public marketplace because investors want to finance economic growth of a business and not simply the pay down of its debt. Some have suggested that financial managers reverse LBOs by seeking equity capital in global equity markets of Asia or Europe. However, Japan has been experiencing a recession and Europe is concentrating on integration into a single market and the move of eastern Europe to a market economy. Thus, U.S. business may have to rely on domestic sources for much of its future equity capital.

The Employee Stock Ownership Plan

Employee Stock Ownership Plans (ESOP) are profit-sharing plans that began in the United States nearly 45 years ago in which employees invest in the employing company's stock rather than in a pension plan that then invests in other securities. The benefits of an ESOP include the following: (1) employees and management gain a tax advantage, (2) it can be an important part of a benefits package, (3) employee motivation improves and productivity increases, (4) executive succession is simplified for midsized, privately held corporations,[43] (4) employees, as shareholders, will vote with management to fight a hostile takeover attempt, and (5) cash flow problems of the company can be alleviated by this employee contribution. However, the start-up costs of an ESOP can be substantial and it has been estimated that the payroll of the business should exceed $500,000 if an ESOP is to be cost-effective.[44]

In such employee benefit plans the company makes tax-deductible contributions to the ESOP and the administrator of the ESOP buys company stock. Since employees become investors in the company, they are part owners and are likely to be more motivated to increase the efficiency and economic performance of the company. Also, ESOPs can result in a change in the governance pattern of business with a greater participation by employees.[45]

Often employers use ESOPs to gain wage concessions from employees in return for ESOP participation. This usually increases the value of the company in the eyes of the financial markets if the stock is publicly traded. More often ESOPs are used by midsized companies to transfer ownership when the founder of the company retires. Often the managers who succeed the founder attempt to obtain investment capital from the ESOP and to make the executive process smoother because it does not have to deal with the many problems inherent in ownership changes. Organized labor opposed ESOPs during the 1980s because of management abuses.[46]

Management abuses of the ESOP include the following:

1. Avoiding employee participation in the governance process by offering employees a special type of common stock that carries fewer votes per share than regular common stock.
2. Management sometimes attempts to control the labor representative of the ESOP so that the person sides with management in organizational governance issues.
3. Using ESOPs as a source of investment capital in the form of wage concessions without using the increased cash flows to invest in capital improvements increases competitiveness.
4. ESOPs are frequently used as a means to raid employee pension funds by failing businesses. The money in the ESOP then becomes worthless when the company subsequently goes bankrupt.

5. Downsizing or closing plants leads to layoffs of employees who previously thought the ESOP would improve job security.

6. After installing an ESOP, management may try to issue more stock to raise more capital. This can dilute employee ownership and significantly reduce the value of their investment.[47]

An ESOP can also be used as a takeover defense.[48] For example, Shamrock Holding, Inc., made a hostile takeover bid for Polaroid Corporation. In a last-minute defense Polaroid established an ESOP for employees who voted against the takeover. This ESOP was legally contested by Shamrock but was upheld by the Delaware court. The market value of a company using an ESOP as a takeover defense usually is reduced by this strategy.[49]

The Hostile Takeover Debate

Opinions about the competition for corporate control vary widely. Strategic acquisitions contrasted with hostile takeovers suggest that some takeovers have very different circumstances than others. Thus there is a deep debate concerning whether hostile takeovers are appropriate and good for business and the economy or the reverse. The major points of this debate are listed in Table 14–3.

ARGUMENTS FAVORING HOSTILE TAKEOVERS

Those in favor of hostile takeovers suggest that they can improve our international competitiveness. For example, Tom Peters suggested that top executives of the largest U.S. firms are so complacent that they need the threat of a hostile takeover to get their attention.[50] According to this view the internationalized, rapidly changing economy of the United States calls for highly adaptive and efficient organizations.

Currently there are many organizations that are sluggish, inflexible, and unresponsive to current market needs. Government regulation limiting hostile takeovers would serve to continue the slumber of top management at a time when creativity and performance are needed. A related view considers the hostile takeover as a mechanism of the free market system that facilitates the reallocation of resources within the economy. The mergers and spinoffs, that is, the combination, separation, and recombination of capital should occur so that society's resources can be used in the most efficient manner.

Some proponents of hostile takeovers suggest that the stockholders do not get their deserved return on their investments because entrenched managers do not manage the resources under their care responsibly. In this view, takeovers force managers to increase their performance or be removed from office. Either way, the performance of an organization can be expected to increase and the shareholders would receive more on their investment.[51] Thus hostile takeovers are said to restore the accountability of corporate managers to the shareholders, which has been week since the 1930s.

Recommendations for Reform

There are some who would favor hostile takeovers if certain changes were made. For example, the two-tiered, front-end loaded tender offer central to most hostile takeovers is coercive, and it may not be fair to management of the target company or to the shareholders. Some have called for a reform that would disallow this type of offer.[52] Also, some recommend changing the SEC requirement that says that any person buying 5 percent or more shares in a company must report the purchase within two days. Because of illegal parking and manipulation, Atwater has called for changing the reporting requirement so that anyone purchasing 2 percent or more of the voting common stock must report it to the SEC within one day.[53] Such reforms, it is argued, would enable the benefits to takeovers to be realized with less stockholder coercion and market manipulation by raiders who are only after greenmail and have no interest in operating the target firm.

ARGUMENTS AGAINST HOSTILE TAKEOVERS

The arguments opposing hostile takeovers are a mirror image of the proponents' position. First, some argue that the use of junk bonds to fund takeovers simply changes the capital structure of firms from an equity-based to a debt-financed business. The high interest payments can make it difficult for businesses to weather economic downturns and may not allow for the capital investment needed to increase competitiveness. The end result is a misallocation of resources that decreases international competitiveness.

Some argue that few corporations have an entrenched top management. Rather than make such managers more accountable, the threat of a hostile takeover is a major distraction that forces much creative energy and resources to go into defenses. Defenses become a major criterion for capital investments and policy decisions. This is aggravated by the pressure to focus on short-term profitability rather than the long-run performance needed for international success.

In contrast to the argument in favor of increased shareholder returns is the complaint that greenmail is really ill-gotten gain. It is a reward for coercive and manipulative behavior that has nothing to do with the operational or strategic excellence of a business. In sum, those opposed to hostile takeovers argue that they are inefficient, reduce the capacity to compete, overload the corporation with debt, distract top management, force short-term management priorities to prevail, and lead to unjust returns for the raiders. The opposing side argues the exact opposite in nearly every case. There is a considerable amount of evidence to support each side, and there is much ambiguity over the issue of hostile corporate takeovers.

TABLE 14–3
The Hostile Takeover Debate

Arguments Favoring Hostile Takeovers	Arguments Opposing Hostile Takeovers
Facilitate needed reallocation of resources within a society consistent with market processes.	Encourage misallocation of resources within society and may be an example of market failure.
Increase international competitiveness.	Decrease international competitiveness.
Increase shareholder returns because stock values increase.	Corporations become overburdened by debt payments because junk bonds are used to finance hostile takeovers. Also, these junk bonds increase the risk and decrease the returns of other bond holders.
Increase accountability of entrenched management to shareholders.	Distract top management from the key tasks of economic performance and maintaining competitiveness.
Increase managerial efficiency in the use of corporate resources.	Result in short-term profit increases at the improvement of economic performance because long-term investments like research and development are neglected.
Increase the value of undervalued and inefficient corporations.	Result in "greenmail" as unfair rewards go to corporate raiders.

Stockholder Initiatives

In many cases, decisions concerning executive succession, strategy and policy setting, and compensation are primarily executive decisions ratified by passive boards of directors. Candidates for membership on corporate boards selected are compatible with, if not chosen by, top management. An early study by Berle and Means (1932) found that many corporations were governed by a top management that had little accountability to stockholders.[54] This brought the traditional model of corporate governance into question. Most stockholders were either incapable or not motivated to influence top management decisions through the use of proxy contests. A *proxy* is a person who casts a vote as the representative of a shareholder. A *proxy fight* is a dispute between top management and/or one or more stockholder groups that is decided by the vote of proxies (usually members of the BOD) who cast block votes on behalf of shareholders they represent.

Berle and Means found that the proxy machinery for electing board members into or out of office or for resolving shareholder issues was controlled by top corporate managers. The process was too inaccessible or cumbersome to serve as an effective mechanism for executive accountability for the purposes of substantive due process. Stockholders would rather sell their shares of stock and buy the shares of another business if they disagreed with the way an organization was governed. If enough shareholders sold stocks, then an indirect mechanism of executive accountability would pressure executives to evaluate their behavior.

Direct shareholder initiatives in corporate governance were somewhat rare prior to the advent of hostile takeovers in the 1980s. The climate of hostile takeovers and strategic acquisition changed the economic structure of American industry and served as the primary mechanism for executive accountability. If executives did not perform, boards would oust them. The threat of a hostile takeover funded by junk bonds changed the governance from a relativley passive BOD to a more decision-making board in many corporations. The threat of hostile

takeovers ended with the collapse of the junk bond market and the widespread failure of LBOs.

The 1990s have been marked by a growth in shareholder activism that has replaced the hostile takeover as a major governance alternative. Nearly 55 percent of outstanding shares in the United States are owned by institutional investors who manage the portfolios of pension and retirement funds. These institutional investors want long-term commitments in return for more say in the governance of corporations. They feel a need to have other alternatives than simply selling shares when they disagree with top management's governance of the business.

Relationship investing is a new type of approach to corporate governance based upon a long-term commitment by institutional investors in return for greater executive accountability through periodic monitoring of performance and cooperation between institutional investors and the board of directors in governance decisions.[55] The result of relationship investing is a move away from short-term orientation because the providers of capital in this model are more patient. Relationship investors became active during the 1980s when some institutional portfolio managers joined forces to oppose the payment of greenmail and corporate policies of golden parachutes and other anti-takeover measures.

For example, in 1990, Harold C. Simmons tried a hostile takeover of Lockheed. CEO Daniel Tellep sought the help of institutional investors to defend against the takeover. A long-term face-to-face dialogue was established with these major shareholders leading to relationship investors. Prior to this, many CEOs communicated with stockholders primarily by printing position statements in the *Wall Street Journal* or other business periodicals. In 1991 Lockheed stockholders agreed to a stock buyback if it could be funded by internal cash flows rather than debt. Investors were informed and the BOD sought its advice on dividend policy and strategic decisions of direct concern.

California State Teachers Retirement System, (CALPERS), has been the most activist fund interested in relationship investing. Because of the size of its investments it has direct access to the CEOs of a dozen or more major corporations. Another relationship-investing organization is United Shareholders, which relies not only on direct contact with corporate executives but also on pressure from the media to embarrass executives into responsible behavior. A poor relationship exposed in the media can have an adverse affect on stock price and market position.

Summary

This chapter has presented the business corporation as a social system with a threefold order. The economic sphere within the organization is concerned with maintaining competitiveness through rationality that enables the implementation of competitive strategies. Effective corporate governance assures executive accountability, sound policies, and resource allocations that are both effective and fair. The corporate culture sustains the values and ideals that live in the organization.

Ideally, organizational governance seeks to maintain justice and liberty and to protect the rights of employees within the organization. Organizational governance parallels the governance processes of society, with some large differences. There is little separation between the legislative and the executive functions that make up the substantive due process of the organization. Legislative functions are centered in the board of directors, which legitimate the mission, strategy, and major policies. Executive functions implement policy.

Judicial functions of government are accomplished by procedural due processes. These processes include voluntary appeal systems initiated by management, contractually required grievance systems agreed upon by management and unions, and state and federal laws that cover many aspects of the employment relationship. While some writers have proposed rights for employees, and other companies espouse values calling for respect for the dignity of the individual, there is much variability in practice.

Substantive due process is concerned with the questions (1) Who rules? (2) Who gets what? and (3) What values and ideals will guide policy? Procedural due process is concerned with protecting the rights of employees from the arbitrary use of power by managers. Due process includes appeal systems and is supplemented by state laws concerning wrongful discharge and other employee rights.

The competition for corporate control takes the form of strategic mergers and acquisitions, and hostile takeover attempts financed by junk bonds and structured as leverage buyouts (LBO). An arsenal of takeover defenses were developed that included white knights, greenmail, super majorities, management-initiated LBOs, employee stock ownership plans (ESOPs), and the support of legislation to prohibit or control hostile takeovers. The competition was intense during the 1980s, and a heated debate over hostile takeovers focused on international competitiveness and economic performance.

However, much of the motivation for hostile takeovers was financial gain that had little to do with competitiveness. The debate ended with the collapse of the junk bond market, which made the leveraged buyout much more difficult. More recently relationship investing has taken the place of hostile takeovers as the major instrument of governance for substantive due process.

Conclusions

As social systems, business organizations also have a threefold dimension and thus have economic, political, and cultural aspects. The economic sphere of an organization has the maintenance of competitiveness and market performance as its key task. This requires that top management develop competitive strategies that are congruent with market conditions and the capabilities of competitors. However, strategy determination is done within the context of the other two spheres. Economic strategies need to have political support within the organization, and the strategy needs to fit the corporate culture if implementation of the strategy is to be successful.

Organizational governance is concerned with the substance of legitimating values, goals, and objectives. It is also concerned with procedural due process so that the rights and dignity of employees can be respected. Organizational governance processes perceived as just are likely to increase the commitment of employees and lead to higher economic performance. Just organizations are likely to encourage higher levels of moral reasoning and more ethical behavior among employees. Well-designed and functioning governance processes within organizations are likely to have synergistic relationships to the other two spheres, leading to competitive economic performance and responsive corporate cultures.

Much of the activity in organizational governance in recent years has centered around strategic acquisitions, hostile takeovers, and relationship investing. Hostile takeovers require much of the energy and resources of organizations, and much of management talent was spent both in defending and in attempting to accomplish hostile takeovers. Whether this is justifiable or not depends, in part, upon whether it is positively or negatively related to international competitiveness. It appears that it was not. While most bankers and analysts agree that the LBO is not dead, most say it has faded into relative obscurity. A return to conservative capitalization policy suggests that highly leveraged transactions are a phenomenon of the 1980s.

Discussion Questions

1. Briefly describe how the three social spheres of society operate within corporations. How does the threefold sphere of society operate differently from the threefold sphere of a business organization?
2. In the ALCOA case, how did the political/governance sphere influence the implementation of the competitive strategy of the organization?

3. What is the purpose of organizational governance? How was this purpose achieved in the ALCOA case?
4. Briefly define substantive due process? How is substantive due process accomplished in the corporation according to the traditional model of governance?
5. What forms of political accountability exist for top executives?
6. What is procedural due process? What are the key factors in the design of a procedural due process system if it is to work effectively?
7. What is the role of the union procedural due process? Briefly discuss how this role has changed in recent years? What has been most responsible for the changing role of labor unions? What has served to take the place of unions in this area?
8. The chapter outlines some of the employee rights that are currently being debated. Do you think employees should have rights? If so, which ones and under what circumstances?
9. What is the difference between a strategic acquisition and a hostile takeover?
10. What are the key issues being debated in the controversy over hostile takeovers?
11. What is a two-tiered, front-loaded tender offer? How is this type of offer used in a hostile takeover? Why is the use of this offer controversial?

Notes

1. Rudolph Steiner, *The Threefold Social Order* (New York: Anthroposophic Press, 1972).
2. See Lee E. Preston and James E. Post, *Private Management and Public Policy: The Principle of Public Responsibility* (Englewood Cliffs: Prentice-Hall, 1975), chap. 2.
3. William G. Scott, Terence R. Mitchell, and Newman Peery, "Organizational Governance," in *Handbook of Organizational Design*, Vol. 2, eds. Paul C. Nystrom and William H. Starbuck (New York: Oxford University Press, 1981), p. 136.
4. Scott et al., "Organizational Governance," pp. 135–51.
5. For example, see "The Raiders," *Business Week*, March 4, 1984, pp. 80–91; H. Bruce Atwater, Jr., "The Trouble with

Takeovers," *Stanford Business School Magazine* (June 1988): 13–16; and Kimberly B. Boal and Newman S. Peery, Jr., "Corporate Acquisition Attempts, Defenses, and Outcomes," paper presented at the Western Academy of Management Meetings, March 1984, Vancouver, B.C., Canada.

6. John Pound, "Beyond Takeovers: Politics Comes to Corporate Control," *Harvard Business Review* 70, no. 2 (March/April 1992): 83–93.

7. Julia F. Siler, "Bolting the Boardroom Door at Sears," *Business Week*, May 13, 1991, pp. 86–87.

8. "The Downfall of a CEO," *Business Week*, February 17, 1987, pp. 76–84.

9. Stanley C. Vance, *Corporate Leadership: Boards, Directors, and Strategy* (New York: McGraw-Hill, 1983), p. 8.

10. "The Job Nobody Wants," *Business Week*, September 8, 1986, pp. 56–61.

11. Carrie Gottlieb, "In Search of a Better Board," *International Business* 5, no. 5 May 1992): 60–62.

12. Anonymous, "Advice and Dissent: Rating the Corporate Governance Compact," *Harvard Business Review* 69, no. 6 (Nov/Dec 1991): 136–43.

13. Newman Peery and Y. Krishna Shetty, "Are Top Executives Transferable Across Companies?" *Business Horizons* 19 (June 1976): 21–28.

14. "Requiem for Yesterday's CEO," *Business Week*, February 15, 1993, pp. 33–32.

15. William G. Scott, "The Management Governance Theories of Justice and Liberty," *Journal of Management* 12, no. 2 (1988): 277–98.

16. Scott et al., "Organizational Governance," pp. 135–51.

17. "Are CEOs Paid Too Much?" *Business Week*, May 6, 1991, pp. 90–96. See also Derek Bok, *The Cost of Talent: How Executives and Professionals Are Paid and How It Affects America* (New York: Free Press, 1993).

18. Kevin G. Salwen, "Shareholder Proposals on Pay Must be Aired, SEC to Tell 10 Firms," *Wall Street Journal*, February 12, 1992, p. 1.

19. "Executive Pay: Compensation at the Top is Out of Control, Here's How to Reform It," *Business Week*, March 30, 1992, pp. 52–58.

20. David Lyons, *Rights* (Belmont, Calif.: Wadsworth, 1979).

21. David W. Ewing, *Freedom Inside the Organization: Bringing Civil Liberties to the Workplace* (New York: McGraw-Hill, 1977), pp. 144–51.

22. For example, see "Beyond Unions," *Business Week*, July 8, 1985, pp. 72–77, and "Privacy," *Business Week*, March 28, 1988, pp. 61–68. Also see Gertrude Ezorsky, ed., *Moral Rights in the Workplace* (Albany: State University of New York Press, 1987).

23. "Beyond Unions," pp. 72–77.

24. "California Court Widens Limit on Employee Suits," *New York Times*, May 26, 1989, p. C4, and "California Court Further Restricts Right of Fired Workers to Sue Ex-Employers," *Wall Street Journal*, May 25, 1989, p. A3.

25. Scott et al., "Organizational Governance."

26. Vijay Sathe, *Culture and Related Corporate Realities* (Homewood, Ill.: Irwin, 1985), p. 10.

27. Sathe, *Culture and Related Corporate Realities*, pp. 47–62.

28. This section is based on the paper by Kimberly Boal and Newman Peery, "Corporation Acquisition Attempts, Takeover Defenses, and Outcomes," presented at the Western Academy of Management Meetings, in Vancouver, B.C., March 1984.

29. "Do Mergers Really Work?" *Business Week*, June 3, 1985, pp. 88–100; "Deal Mania," *Business Week*, November 24, 1988, pp. 122–34; and "Merger Mania," *Business Week*, March 21, 1988, pp. 122–34.

30. This section of the chapter draws from H. Bruce Atwater, Jr., "The Trouble with Takeovers," *Stanford Business School Magazine* (June 1988): 13–16.

31. For a discussion of the ethics of insider trading, see Jennifer Moore, "What Is Really Unethical about Insider Trading?" *Journal of Business Ethics* 9, no. 3 (March 1990): 171–82; and Patricia H. Werhane, "The Ethics of Insider Trading," *Journal of Business Ethics* 8, no. 11 (November 1989): 841–45.

32. "Suddenly the Fish Get Bigger," *Business Week*, March 2, 1987, pp. 28–33.

33. "The Raiders," *Business Week*, March 4, 1985, pp. 80–91.

34. "Executive Pay," *Business Week*, May 1, 1989, p. 47, lists the ten largest golden parachutes.

35. Alan Gart, "Leveraged Buyouts: A re-examination," *Advanced Management Journal* 55, no. 3 (Summer 1990): 38–46.

36. William M. Waddell, "Leveraged Buyouts: Clever Leveraging or Badly Bet Debt?" *Secured Lender* 46, no. 6 (November/December 1990): 34–40.

37. Yahya, Latif, "What Ails the Leveraged Buyouts of the 1980s," *Secured Lender* 46, no. 6 (November/December 1990): 56–60.

38. Anonymous, "The Junk Bond Fizzle," *Mergers and Acquisitions* 24, no. 6 (May/June 1990): 21–22

39. Brett Duval, "The Last Days of Drexel Burnham," *Fortune*, May 21, 1990, pp. 90–96.

40. Anonymous, "The Death of Drexel," *Economist*, February 17, 1990, pp. 81–82.

41. Benjamin J. Stein, "Watchdog in the Junkyard: The Poor Beast Couldn't even Smell a Rat," *Barron's* 70, no. 13 (March 26, 1990): 26–33.

42. Stuart Weiss, "Cashing Out of LBOs," *CFO: The Magazine of Chief Financial Officers* 6, no. 11 (November 1990): 52–54.

43. Daniel J. Ryterband, "The Decision to Implement an ESOP: Strategies and Economic Considerations," *Employee Benefits Journal* 16, no. 4 (December 1991): 19–25.

44. Joan C. Szabo, "Using ESOPs to Sell Your Firm," *Nation's Business* 79, no. 1 (January 1991): 59–60.

45. William Smith, "The ESOP Revolution: Will It Increase Employee Involvement?" *Advanced Management Journal* 57, no. 3 (Summer 1992): 14–19.

46. Roger G. McElrath and Richard L. Rowan, "The American Labor Movement and Employee Ownership: Objections to and Uses of Employee Ownership Plans," *Journal of Labor Research* 13, no. 1 (Winter 1992): 99–119.

47. Walecia Konrad, "This Is Some Way to Build Employee Loyalty," *Business Week,* March 2, 1992, p. 84.

48. "Shamrock's Polaroid Bid is Dealt a Blow as Court Upholds Employee Stock Plan," *Wall Street Journal,* January 9, 1989, p. A4.

49. Lilli A. Gordon and John Pound, "ESOPs and Corporate Control," *Journal of Financial Economics* 27, no. 2 (October 1990): 525–55.

50. Tom Peters, *Thriving on Chaos: Handbook for a Management Revolution* (New York: Harper and Row, 1987), p. 40.

51. T. Boone Pickens, Jr., "Professions of a Short-termer," *Harvard Business Review* (May-June 1986): 75–79.

52. Ira M. Millstein, "Takeover Reform: Common Sense from the Common Law," *Harvard Business Review* (July-August 1986): 16–19.

53. Atwater, "The Trouble with Takeovers."

54. Adolf A. Berle and Gardiner C. Means, *The Modern Corporation and Private Property* (New York: Macmillan, 1932).

55. "Relationship Investing," *Business Week,* March 15, 1993, pp. 68–75.

CHAPTER 15

Customer Stakeholders: Product Safety Issues, Ethics of Exchange, and Product Liability Law

CHAPTER OBJECTIVES

1. Review the development of issue life cycle (ILC) for product safety.
2. Present a framework for understanding the ethics of market exchange.
3. Show how the development of product liability law parallels ethical concepts.
4. Review some court cases that have defined product liability trends.
5. Briefly discuss the regulatory environment and government agency involvement in consumer concerns.
6. Apply the social performance model to managing the consumer stakeholder issue of product safety.

Introductory Case _____

The AUDI 5000 and the Problem of Unintended Acceleration

You get into your car, start the engine, and move the shift lever into reverse or drive. Suddenly the car takes off like a shot. You go for the brakes, but no amount of pressure will slow the car. It continues to accelerate, mowing down everything and everyone in its path—until finally it runs into something solid enough to stop it.[1]

SOURCE: The facts for this case were researched by F. Matt Gertmenian under the supervision of Newman Peery.

This is an example of the type of situation encountered during an episode of unintended or sudden acceleration. A force beyond the driver's control causes the car to lurch forward or backward, often causing injury and death. "There remains no generally accepted explanation of what unintended acceleration is, or what causes it."[2] Sudden acceleration is a problem investigated by the National Highway Traffic Safety Administration (NHTSA) in relation to several models of cars with automatic transmissions, including the Audi 5000. A heated debate as to the cause of the unintended acceleration in the Audi 5000 models has forced Audi of America, a subsidiary of Volkswagen of America, to take several measures including a number of costly product recalls. The decisions to take these measures were compounded by the media coverage, public awareness, interest group pressures, and Audi's position in the market.

When the Audi 5000 was introduced into the United States in 1978 it was hailed as an innovation in styling and engineering and remained essentially unchanged for a number of years. Within the first four years following its introduction, there were 13 complaints of unintended acceleration involving 8 accidents.[3] Initially these claims seemed to result from a problem with the driver's floor mat. The mat would slide under the accelerator, causing it to stay open. Audi promptly responded to these complaints during April 1982 with a voluntary recall of the 5000s to eliminate this interference. The design of the mat was subsequently changed in the 1983 model year.

The rate of complaints about sudden acceleration remained unchanged after the April 1982 recall. Audi's view was that the sudden acceleration accidents were primarily caused by the driver depressing the accelerator instead of the brake. The company began another voluntary recall during September 1983 to thicken the brake pedal to better differentiate it from the accelerator, which had previously been on the same level. Audi hoped that this modification would eliminate the probability of a driver pressing the wrong pedal.

Accidents continued. On February 23, 1986, the New York Times ran an article on unintended acceleration that covered many different makes of automobiles including Audi. Marian Weinstein, who had had two accidents in her Audi 5000, read this article and became convinced it was a serious problem with which Audi of America was not dealing effectively. She contacted the Center for Auto Safety (CAS), which had already received several other complaints about the Audi 5000. The CAS had originally been a part of the Nader Network organized by Ralph Nader as a consumer protection interest group. The CAS, now independent, was organized to insure that new safety standards are followed by automobile makers. It also assisted government agencies and the

automotive industry in the development of safety standards.

The CAS had contacted the New York Public Interest Research Group (NYPIRG), which, in turn, contacted the New York State attorney general, Robert Abrams. On March 19, 1986, Abrams held a press conference denouncing the Audi 5000 as unsafe and demanding a recall. Shortly after the news conference, Weinstein cofounded the Audi Victims Network (AVN) on May 28, 1986, as a support group for those who had suffered from unintended acceleration. She illustrated the problem of unintended acceleration in the following way:

> When six year old Joshua Bradosky opened the garage door for his mother's Audi 5000 in February 1986, the car suddenly accelerated forward, dragging Joshua through the family garage door and fatally crushing him against a brick wall. Audi acts as if Kristi Bradosky, Joshua's mother, recklessly ran her son down. However, hundreds of similar accidents around the country indicate the company's faulty design of the Audi 5000 is the killer, not an innocent mother.

In this widely publicized account of the accident, Weinstein failed to mention that in the official police report of the incident, the driver, Kristi Bradosky, stated that her foot had slipped off the brake onto the accelerator. This recurring type of accident had happened enough for Audi engineers to conclude that the problem was in the positioning of the brake and accelerator pedals. Stepping on the wrong pedal was most likely to occur when someone unfamiliar with the Audi 5000 was driving. Several accidents had been documented in which the spouse or friend of the primary driver of the vehicle had been involved in an unintended acceleration accident.

When explaining the problem, consumer activist groups denied driver responsibility. Audi took the position that driver error was the primary cause of such an accident. The publicized Bradosky incident brought several consumer advocate groups and the National Highway Traffic Safety Administration (NHTSA) into the issue. By March 1986 the Center for Auto Safety, the New York Public Interest Research Group, and the newly founded Audi Victim's Network began research and publicizing data regarding the unintended acceleration accidents that involved the Audi 5000s.

On May 28, 1986, a spokesperson for Audi of America met with the representatives of the Audi Victims Network and announced a recall to increase the distance between the brake and accelerator pedals. By this modification, Audi hoped to eliminate the possibility of any driver error that could cause sudden, uncontrollable acceleration. However, the Audi Victims Network denounced this action because they perceived that the recall was simply an effort to blame the drivers of the Audi 5000 for the problem.

By May 1986, nearly 250,000 Audi 5000s had been sold in the U.S. market. Despite three separate recall efforts, the reports of sudden acceleration continued to appear. Audi engineers, following the advice from NHSTA, then designed the Automatic Shift Lock (ASL). This device, to be installed on all 1984–85 Audi 5000 models, allowed the automobiles to be shifted out of park only when pressure was applied to the brakes.[4] Most of the accident reports indicated that accidents involving unintended acceleration happened during the shifting process from park to forward or reverse gear.

Tony Kirton, director of marketing for Audi of America, said, "It took headquarters a long time to understand what was happening. . .They were astonished at first because there were no reports of anything like this in Europe." The automobiles with automatic transmissions were more prone to unintended acceleration and had been much less popular in Europe than in the U.S. market. Perhaps because of this, Audi blamed the reports of unintended acceleration in the newer cars on errors due to drivers' being unfamiliar with them and media hype. The Audi 5000 model accounted for 70 percent of Audi's sales in the United States.[5]

Prior to the unintended acceleration controversy, Audi sales had been only slightly lower than those of Mercedes-Benz and BMW automobiles in the luxury performance European import segment of the market. In 1985 Audi, a subsidiary of VW, contributed 18 percent of VW's $20.8 billion in sales but 37 percent of its $236.5 million profits. Analysts in 1986 estimated that Audi's profits plunged by more than half to $38.4 million, causing VW's total profits also to plunge by 35 percent to $150 million. Also, trade-in values for the Audi 5000s dropped precipitously, making it much less desirable to purchase a new Audi. Audi of America responded by guaranteeing the trade-in value of the Audi 5000 in an effort to maintain its market position.

However, even with the ASL installation, many consumers still felt the Audi was unsafe. This fear was documented in a dramatic way on prime time television, November 23, 1986, when CBS presented a story about the Audi 5000 on "60 Minutes." The broadcast demonstrated a staged sudden acceleration accident that devastated Audi's public image. "Anti-Audi hysteria" became rampant and showroom traffic dropped by 58 percent within three months of the broadcasted show.

The broadcast noted such important statistics as the accident rate, which according to Diane Steed and Philip Davis of NHSTA, was 300 accidents including 4 deaths and 175 injuries per 250,000 cars. However, the staged unintended acceleration accident shown on "60 Minutes" had been accomplished by having the tester disable several safety valves and had "plumbing. . .rigged up to supply external pressure to the transmission." They had not been able to simulate the unintended acceleration without these modifications.

In a letter to CBS, the management of Audi complained to the CBS network and protested about the fallacies of the program's report. CBS responded by reaffirming its story and rebroadcasted the episode on September 13, 1987. After the rebroadcast, consumer complaints rose over 300 percent regarding sudden acceleration in the Audi 5000s. The rise in consumer complaints resulted in the NHSTA's requirement that Audi recall and examine the idle speed control valve on all 1985–86 models. Audi complied by recalling and replacing the valves. However, according to several experts, the valve could not cause the type of acceleration described by victims of unintended acceleration. A faulty idle speed control valve could increase the chance of pedal error, possibly leading to unintended acceleration.[6] Sensing that this latest recall had increased the damage to the company, Audi moved to reassure the public of the safety of the Audi 5000s. Audi spokesperson Tom McDonald defended the solution to the problem and told a group of consumers, "no matter what the cause of unintended acceleration, if your foot is on the brake, you're not going anywhere."[7] This theory seemed to contradict many victims who had stated that they were unable to stop their cars with their brakes. However, NHTSA found no evidence of any engine being able to override the break system.[8]

The year 1988 brought continued interest by the automotive media in the Audi 5000 controversy. Both *Car and Driver* and *Road and Track* printed articles updating studies of the long-term tests on the Audi. Both came to the same conclusion: "The common factor in these cases is pedal error. The issue now is, what causes pedal error?"[9] This view was reinforced by Csaba Csere, technical editor for *Car and Driver,* when he concluded:

> We can accept that several real, documented problems, though minor, have probably led some Audi drivers to step on the wrong pedal at the wrong time. These problems include the floor-mat-induced throttle sticking, the somewhat unusual pedal layout, and the [idle speed control] valve malfunctions. But we suspect that the number of unintended acceleration accidents actually caused by these problems have been swollen beyond its true magnitude by extensive adverse publicity.[10]

The Issue Life Cycle and Product Safety

The product safety issue has followed the pattern of the issue life cycle (ILC) described in Chapter 3. Laws protecting customers from unsafe products have had a long historical development under both contract and tort law. Contract law suggests that an implied warranty exists between the buyer and seller of a product that requires a product to be reasonably safe. Tort law requires that damages be paid when one person harms another. The trend has been a change from reliance on contract law in the nineteenth century to a greater emphasis on the tort law of product liability since the turn of the century.

The individualistic ideology, emphasizing the self-correction by market forces, shaped public policy until the 1930s. Market forces under conditions necessary for competition assume numerous knowledgeable buyers and sellers, each freely seeking his or her self-interest. The laws of market supply and demand set prices and determine profits. Contracts form the basis of free exchange between individuals. With the closing of the American frontier and the advent of large-scale businesses during the late 1800s, the first challenges of the model of market competition appeared.

The public policy response to large-scale business was the regulation of the railroad industry, the passage of the Sherman Antitrust Act in 1890, and the creation of the Federal Trade Commission (FTC) in 1914 to enforce antitrust law. The FTC was charged with the responsibility of enforcing antitrust law by restoring the structural conditions necessary for market competition and prohibiting anticompetitive behavior like price fixing, tying agreements, and conspiracies in constraint of trade. From its establishment in 1914 until the 1960s, the FTC's primary focus was on antitrust enforcement rather than on such consumer issues as product safety.

With the 1960s came a consumer movement that sought to protect consumers against market failures. It supported laws governing product labeling, truth in advertising, and product safety. The consumer movement advocated an activist government within the context of a community-oriented ideology. It believed that market forces alone would not protect the interests of consumers and pressed for numerous consumer protection laws. The FTC already had a mandate to enforce truth-in-advertising. Later, product safety became a concern of the consumer movement.

Product safety is a major public policy issue that has passed through the *six stages of the issue life cycle* in the course of its development:

1. Growing awareness of social and technological changes
2. Issue and problem definition
3. Establishment of interest groups organized around public issues

4. Growing controversy and public debate leading to laws
5. Administration of public policy by creating an agency or changing the mandate of an existing agency to develop regulations to enforce the law
6. Litigation in the courts to resolve any remaining conflict.

SOCIAL CHANGES AND GROWING AWARENESS OF PRODUCT SAFETY

The key triggering event in the growing awareness of automobile safety as a public issue was the publication of *Unsafe at Any Speed* in 1965 by Ralph Nader; it was a blistering indictment of the unsafety of automobiles.[11] Automobiles had been marketed since the turn of the century and had become the primary medium of transportation in the country. A national highway system, the suburbs, long commutes, and high traffic density had all been major social and technological changes that emerged over time. Traffic fatalities had increased to over 50,000 annually by the 1960s, but the responsibility of manufacturers for automobile safety had not been identified as a major issue in the public consciousness until the publication of this controversial book.

In the Audi 5000 case, there was an increasing number of accidents caused by unexpected acceleration in automobiles with automatic transmissions. When Audi of America finally became aware of the problem, Audi engineers extensively studied it to find the causes of the unexpected acceleration. Monitoring the environment and developing a knowledge base is normally the key to effective response in stage one of the ILC. Increased public awareness of this problem resulted from news reports like the tragic Bradosky accident, which resulted in the death of a child.

ISSUE IDENTIFICATION

Technological and social changes of the ILC stage one lead to ILC stage two, issue identification and alternative formulation of the public problem to be resolved. Under the traditional individualistic ide-

ology of market competition, the product safety issue is defined in terms of individual responsibility. Buyers were presumed to be knowledgeable about the products they purchased and to willingly accept any dangers implied by such purchases. For example, the problem of automobile safety would be defined in terms of a driver's not using a safety belt, driving carelessly, or not being sufficiently skilled to operate an automobile.

Alternatively, the problem could be defined in terms of the design defects in highways and automobiles. A more community-oriented ideology would call upon the government to insure safe conditions on the highway. This would favor the government restriction of the driving privilege to those who demonstrate the requisite skills at a government-operated licensing and testing center. The government would assume responsibility for the maintenance of a safe highway system, and the government would require safety standards to be upheld by automobile manufacturers.

During the twentieth century, consumer stakeholder problems have been redefined as market failures that require the regulation and control by an activist government. Greater legal and ethical responsibility has been placed on business and less on the individual consumer. There has been a corresponding increase in acceptance of a greater role for the government in protecting the consumer through regulations enforced by government agencies.

An early move in this direction began when Sinclair Lewis published *The Jungle,* about the unsanitary conditions in the meat-packing industry at the turn of the century. This book triggered a controversy that led to an extensive federal regulation and inspection system for meat and the creation of the precursor to the Food and Drug Administration in 1906.

The regulation of the meat-packing industry in the early 1900s was followed by the establishment of the Federal Trade Commission in 1914, and the Food and Drug Administration in 1931 to protect the public against impure and unsafe foods, drugs, and cosmetics and to regulate hazards involved with medical devices.

The collapse of the U.S. and the world economy during the 1930s challenged the faith in a self-correcting market system without large-scale government intervention. Historical events challenged the traditional individualistic ideology based upon a perfectly functioning market system. The new community-oriented ideology called for a greater role for the government in regulating economic affairs and for a greater burden of responsibility to be carried by the seller in market exchange.

The Audi 5000 unintended acceleration issue occurred within the broader historical context of the product safety issue. When this product safety crisis occurred, laws, agencies, and agency regulations were already in place. In the mini-ILC stage two of the unintended acceleration issue concerning the Audi 5000, controversy persisted over the definition of the problem. Consumers defined the issue in terms of unsafe product design. Audi defined the issue in terms of driver error.

PROBLEM IDENTIFICATION

During the second stage of the issue life cycle, the problem becomes identified, clarified, and publicly defined. A public issue can seem to "come from nowhere" and begin with ambiguous though disturbing symptoms like the tragic automobile accidents resulting from unintended acceleration. The process of converting ambiguous and disturbing experiences into a defined public problem is itself a controversy. Business is often tempted in customer stakeholder matters to define problems in terms of customer or user errors or matters of individual responsibility, rather than management or engineering problems for which the business is responsible. Issues become problems defined as they appear on the public policy agenda.

Engineers at Audi had investigated the accident complaints and made several design changes including redesign of the floor mats, changing the levels of the brake and acceleration pedals in the automobile, and eventually introducing a safety lock that would not allow the driver to shift from park unless the foot was on the brake pedal. Audi of America defined the problem in terms of driver error and made design changes to reduce the risk of such errors.

Accident victims defined the problem in terms of automobile design error. Though Audi felt that there was a scientific basis for arriving at the problem definition of driver error, this served to inflame consumers. The situation was made worse by many jokes that began to circulate, focusing on the possibility that Audi drivers must be less intelligent than drivers of automobiles manufactured by competing companies in the luxury segment of the market.

THE ESTABLISHMENT OF INTEREST GROUP ORGANIZATIONS

Organizations tend to spontaneously form around problem definitions once the interest in a public issue is heightened. After the publication of the book *Unsafe at Any Speed* in 1965, consumerism and automobile safety became major public issues in the United States. Many public interest groups began to form around this broad issue of product issue. Ralph Nader formed a highly effective consumer protection network to influence public policy in the decades following the establishment of the consumer movement:

1. *Public Citizen*, founded in 1971 as an umbrella organization to raise funds and to coordinate the activities of the other organizations within the consumer protection network
2. *Health Research Group*, founded in 1971 to engage in consumer activism and to do research on health hazards
3. *Citizen Action Group*, founded in 1971 to coordinate student public interest research groups
4. *Litigation Group*, formed in 1972 for public interest law to help to bring suits in the public interest against corporations and government agencies thought to be acting irresponsibly
5. *Tax Reform Research Group*, formed in 1972 to do research and activities for proconsumer tax reform.
6. *Congress Watch*, formed in 1973 to engage in legislative lobbying activities
7. *Critical Mass Energy Project*, founded in 1974 to engage in antinuclear activities and to encour-

age the use and development of alternative energy

8. *Open Government Project*, formed in 1984 to publicize budget cuts in consumer programs.[12]

Many other interest groups have formed around virtually every public issue, including consumer-oriented issues. In the Audi 5000 case of unintended acceleration, a consumer activist formed the Audi Victims Network as an interest group to protect the rights of Audi drivers as she saw them. This organization was successful in getting the issue on the public agenda. By this time, the public issue was "out of control" for Audi's management, which was trying to deal with the strategic management of this volatile public issue.

The key strategy of business in stage three is to seek support from available organizations to steer and guide policy alternatives in a way that is favorable to the organization. Representatives of Audi appropriately met with the Audi Victims Network to solve the problem. Despite the modification and the product recall, neither side was satisfied with the results.

MAPPING STAKEHOLDERS AND STAKEHOLDER RELATIONSHIPS

If a business is to deal effectively and justly with the many stakeholders surrounding a major decision, it can be useful to develop a stakeholder map. Such a map can clarify the network of relationships among stakeholder organizations and help to understand the likely consequences of a management decision. Usually stakeholders do not act in isolation. They have positive or negative relationships with a business and with each other. Also, some stakeholders influence other stakeholders. Sometimes the way a business action is perceived by a particular stakeholder is moderated by the organized network of stakeholder relations that can be revealed through careful mapping.

Organizations need to begin mapping stakeholders early in the issue life cycle to determine (1) who are the relevant stakeholders, (2) what are the concerns and interests of the various stake-holders, (3) whether the relationships between business and the various stakeholders with respect to the particular issue are positive or negative, (4) the important interrelationships among the various stakeholders and stakeholder groups. What is the linkage between activist groups and other interest groups? with the media? with governmental regulators? (5) how decision alternatives affect the various stakeholder groups. Whose interests are furthered? Whose concerns are perceived as being slighted? (6) whether the outcomes of the decision alternatives are consistent with the economic and political interests of stakeholders, (7) whether the consequences of the decision or policy are just. Does it honor the rights of stakeholders? Does it fulfill the duties of business in this situation?

Figure 15–1 is a stakeholder map that identifies such stakeholder groups as the following:

1. *consumers* of high performance European luxury automobiles including *Audi customers*
2. *news media*, which included newspapers, the television network CBS, the media that covered news conferences, and the automotive media including *Car and Driver* and *Road and Track.*
3. *government regulators* such as the federal government's National Highway Traffic Safety Administration and the State of New York attorney general
4. *consumer activist groups* including the Nader Network, the Center for Automobile Safety, the New York Public Interest Research Group, and the Audi Victims Network
5. *parent company*, Volkswagen of America and Volkswagen of Germany
6. *Audi dealer organizations*

Note that a network of consumer activist groups including the newly formed Audi Victims Network were all mobilized and negatively inclined toward Audi of America early in the unfolding of the ILC. These interest groups saw themselves as working on behalf of Audi customers and were effective in their relationships with government regulators and the news media. Throughout the entire development of this issue, pressure on Audi increased.

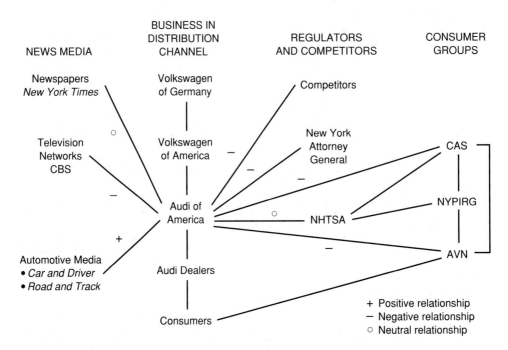

FIGURE 15–1 Stakeholder Map of Audi of America in the Unintended Acceleration Issue

The relationship with the news media was mixed. The negative CBS relationship with Audi and the coverage on the prime time television show "60 minutes" added a difficult and critically important dimension to stakeholder management. CBS had reportedly altered the Audi used in the demonstration without disclosing this fact during the broadcast and presented a very negative image of Audi. The more technical automotive media were favorably disposed to Audi's position. These magazines documented the positive actions taken by Audi and were sensitive to the technical and scientific difficulties associated with solving this problem of product safety. However, the general public is more likely to be influenced by the television networks than by the automotive media, regardless of the accuracy of the reporting.

Relationships with the government stakeholders were also mixed. The New York State attorney general opposed Audi and called for a total withdrawal of the Audi 5000s from the market. The NHTSA worked more cooperatively with Audi to solve the problem and did require certain recalls

and product modifications that, unfortunately, proved inconclusive.

THE PUBLIC POLICY AGENDA AND LEGISLATION FOR PRODUCT SAFETY

In this stage of the ILC public debates in Congress and legislatures normally lead to the adoption of legal remedies. In the area of consumer protection, the following laws have been passed:

1. *National Highway Traffic and Motor Vehicle Safety Act of 1966.* This law establishes the National Highway Traffic Safety Administration to set safety standards for motor vehicles and equipment. This agency has approximately 650 employees and a budget of $125 million to (1) set and enforce standards of automobile fuel economy; (2) establish automobile and equipment safety standards; (3) investigate safety problems in situations where no standards exist; and (4) require manufacturers to remedy safety defects.

2. *Consumer Product Safety Act of 1972.* This law established the Consumer Product Safety Commission (CPSC), which has approximately 500 employees and a budget of $35 million, to (a) develop uniform standards for safety and labeling; (b) ban hazardous products; (c) initiate and monitor product recalls; (d) assist industry in the development of voluntary safety standards; (e) help in the evaluation and publication of results concerning product safety; and (f) develop methods and conduct tests of product safety.

3. *Food and Drug Act of 1906: Food, Drug, and Cosmetic Act of 1938.* The Food and Drug Administration (FDA) was established in 1931 through enabling legislation. The FDA has nearly 7,000 employees and a budget of approximately $450 million to (a) inspect, test, and set standards for food, drugs, food colors and additives, and cosmetics, and (b) set standards for safety, labeling, and effectiveness of drugs and medical devices.

Numerous other laws govern product safety. These are specifically mentioned because they serve to establish and to define the mandates of the key government regulatory agencies in this area. Also, the FTC has been active in the area of consumer protection since 1970 in response to the negative publicity received in a scathing report published by one of Ralph Nader's consumer protection networks. The FTC enforces consumer and antitrust laws and seeks to (1) maintain competition, (2) protect competitors against unfair competition, and (3) protect consumers from deceptive advertising, unfair financial contracts, and other unfair business practices as legally defined.

The strategic objective of business in stage four of the issue life cycle is to influence policy so that the laws are consistent with organizational interests. In the Audi 5000 case the consumer issue of product safety was relatively mature by the 1980s when the unintended acceleration controversy occurred. Laws had been passed and the elaborate set of agencies mentioned above were actively regulating automobile safety. The unintended acceleration problem therefore unfolded within the

context of stage five, that is, agency regulation of the issue.

ILC STAGE FIVE, THE ADMINISTRATION OF PUBLIC POLICY

Once laws are passed, their implementation is normally delegated to various public agencies. These agencies obtain budgets, staffing, and a legal mandate to enforce the laws. Regulations are developed and enforcement patterns are implemented by the agency regulators. The key agencies in the area of consumer protection are those listed above, including (1) The Consumer Products Safety Commission, (2) The National Highway Traffic Safety Administration, (3) the Federal Trade Commission, and (4) the Food and Drug Administration.

The strategic objective of business in stage five of the ILC is to obtain a favorable administration of the formalized public policy. In the Audi 5000 case of unintended acceleration management worked closely with the NHTSA, which advised them to recall the product and change the carburetor valves. However, the cause of the problem remained a "mystery" to both Audi and the regulators. Thus, despite the cooperation with regulators, the issue was not resolved and could have been expected to continue the issue life cycle into litigation for product liability.

ILC STAGE SIX, RESOLVING ISSUE CONFLICTS THROUGH THE COURTS

Most of the litigation occurs within the context of administrative law under the jurisdiction of various regulatory agencies. Agencies monitor compliance, hold hearings, call witnesses, and levy fines in a quasi-judicial setting. Also, persons, including corporations, can sue corporations for injuries resulting from actions or practices of business. The legal standards used to judge violations and to determine damages are based upon the laws and regulations developed up to this point. In fully developed (stage six) issues, corporations seek legal compliance, or legal exceptions to the public policy through litigation. The basic approaches to product liability law are discussed later in this chapter.

The Audi case illustrates the complexity and difficulty of social performance. The issue of automobile safety was relatively mature when the controversy over unexpected acceleration appeared. Thus, consumer protection organizations, public laws, government agencies, and product safety regulations were largely in place at the time of the incident. Nevertheless, the issue proceeded through an issue life cycle that included increasing public awareness of a life-threatening problem, the formation of an activist interest group, and a public debate, followed by actions and interactions with regulatory agencies since laws were already in place. The organization seemed to try very hard to be ethical and responsive, yet its actions were ineffective.

The issue continued, Audi's market position declined, and in 1989, Audi of America discontinued sales of the Audi 5000 model car in the United States. It introduced another model, launched with an intensive advertising campaign using the theme "The Audi Advantage." The promotion campaign sought to restore public confidence in the company and position the new model based upon luxury and high performance insured by the European engineering and design. By the many recalls and ultimate withdrawal of the Audi 5000 model from the market, Audi of America may have avoided the costly and painful process likely to occur in lawsuits central to stage six of the issue life cycle.

Ethics of Exchange Under Competitive Conditions

In Chapter 1 we noted that the Declaration of Independence asserted that everyone has the basic rights to life, liberty, and the pursuit of happiness. These rights parallel the rights to safety, free choice, and property in market exchange. The way rights and their corresponding duties are defined in practice can vary, as shown in Table 15–1. In mar-

kets that are highly competitive as defined by the traditional model of perfect competition, the buyer has greater responsibility relative to the seller than under conditions of limited competition. In less competitive markets, the seller assumes greater ethical responsibility and can be expected to exercise due care in exchange relationship.

ETHICS OF EXCHANGE UNDER PERFECT COMPETITION

The ethical norm that results from the model of market competition is *caveat emptor*, "let the buyer beware." The ethical burden is on the buyer to protect his or her interest. The conditions required for a perfectly competitive market were discussed in Chapter 2 and include (1) prudent behavior by buyers and sellers, (2) enough buyers and sellers so that no single one has substantial market power, (3) mobility of resources, (4) few barriers so that freedom of entry and exit exists, (5) knowledgeable buyers and sellers, (6) market set prices, returns, and profits, (7) private property, and (8) limited government.

When these competitive requirements are present the buyer and seller are equal in power and knowledge and the buyer is responsible if he or she buys an unsafe product. The buyer is presumed to have sufficient knowledge to make a decision, is free to decide what he or she wanted, and is behaving on the basis of self-interest, and the buyer is capable and motivated to look out for his or her own interests.

MISINFORMATION AND THE ETHICS OF EXCHANGE

Even when the principle "let the buyer beware" is applied, there remains a right and duty concerning information. The buyer has the right to the necessary information that is available. Because the buyer may not depend solely on the seller as an information source, there may not be a duty to provide the buyer with all the information that may be important to make a prudent purchasing decision. However, fraud, that is, knowingly misinforming the seller about an important fact, is unethical (as well as illegal). Fraud should not be confused with *puffing,* which is the embellishment of nonfactual aspects of an exchange like emphasizing subjective elements of status, style, or glamor; this is not considered fraud.[13] For example, advertising a soft drink as enabling the buyer to become a part of "the new generation" is a subjective matter. A senior citizen in his sixties would not be expected to be misled into believing that a cola is really a "fountain of youth."

In summary, the basis for the ethics of exchange in a perfectly competitive market is the assumption that the buyer and seller are relatively equal in all important respects. Both parties to the transaction have *rights* to (1) use free choice to make agree-

ments or contracts while (2) engaging in market exchange of (3) private property in (4) the pursuit of happiness, as shown in Table 15–1. Both the buyer and the seller has the *duty* to look out for his or her interests by (1) becoming informed and (2) acting prudently. The seller has a duty not to misinform the buyer about facts concerning a good or service provided.

ETHICS OF EXCHANGE UNDER LIMITED COMPETITION

In examining the situation that influences the ethical context, rights and duties change when we can begin to relax some of the assumptions of a per-

TABLE 15–1
Ethics of Exchange: Rights and Duties Under Different Competitive Conditions

Guiding Ethical Principle	Rights and Duties Under Perfect Competition: Let the Buyer Beware	Rights and Duties Under Limited Competition: Ethics of Due Care
BASIC HUMAN RIGHT (Declaration of Independence): Pursuit of Happiness	• Right to exchange • Private property • Pursuit of self-interest	• Right to exchange • Right to be informed of danger • Right to pursue self-interest • Duty to compete fairly
Life	• Right not to be harmed • Right not to be misinformed • Duty not to defraud or to misinform • Duty to be informed • Duty to protect oneself through prudent action	• Duty not to harm others or to place another person at risk • Duty to comply with standards • Duty to test • Duty to inform buyer • Duty not to misinform • Duty to correct a dangerous product after sale
Liberty	• Free choice • Freedom of contract • Freedom of opportunity to participate in the market • Duty to become informed	• Duty not to coerce or use duress in selling • Freedom of opportunity to participate in market

fectly competitive market. Market failures occur when these elements of competition are not present: (1) when there are either few powerful buyers or sellers leading to an unbalanced condition between the buyer and seller, with respect to information and/or market power, and (2) when the transaction leads to externalities that harm persons not party to the transaction.

Asymmetrical Information and the Ethics of Exchange

In an industrialized society characterized by advanced technology, companies involved in the manufacture and sale of products and services tend to have technical and scientific information not readily available to buyers. Companies have resources to develop products, to increase technological capabilities, and to test and understand the limitations of present scientific knowledge, technological capabilities, and product and service performance limitations and dangers.

Because the resources, information, and other capabilities of manufacturing and distributing companies tend to significantly exceed those of the buyer, an out-of-balance condition with respect to information is present. The sellers tend to have better information about the nature of the product than the buyers do. This leads to an argument in favor of a *right to know*. Because the seller no longer has the resources or capability to inform himself or herself, then the right to know of the buyer calls for a corresponding *duty to inform* of the seller.

Market Power and the Ethics of Exchange

Second, many markets are oligopolistic, that is, a substantial portion of the total sales of the industry are controlled by the leading firms. As the market becomes more concentrated, barriers to entry tend to exist, products will tend to be more differentiated, and the suppliers of the products tend to have a certain amount of market power relative to buyers. When market power is out of balance in favor of the selling organizations, they may use this power by exercising discretion with respect to price, product design, and terms of sale and by fail-

ure to respond to customer complaints. Through the use of this power, the seller may have an opportunity to constrain options available to sellers and thus may use this to pressure buyers into terms, prices, and behaviors favorable to those who have market power.[14]

We cannot say that a person has a right to a certain product or to a certain design or to a certain price. However, we can argue that the buyer has a negative right to free choice in that he or she has a right not to be exposed to *undue pressure*, duress, or *exploitive prices*. The high-pressure sales tactics sometimes experienced at an automobile dealership seek to undermine the customer's free choice and is thus unethical. The seller also has a right to free choice in the decisions concerning whether or not to produce or to sell a particular product or service, to set a competitive price, and to agree or not agree to terms offered. The point is that some sort of balance in free choice is needed for an ethical exchange to occur.

THE ETHICS OF DUE CARE

We can consider the conditions of market competition to develop a conceptual scale concerning the existence of ethical duties that the seller may have. In this scale of relative competitiveness, the ethical duties of the seller may be quite limited under perfect competition but systematically increase as market competitiveness declines. As the conditions necessary for market competition are reduced with respect to information, market power and the ability of buyers to withdraw regard to sellers then there is a need for the *ethics of due care* to supplement market forces.[15] In other words, the seller should assume increased duties to the buyer such as those outlined in Table 15–1 if significant advantages exist in the area of information and market power.

According to the ethics of due care, the seller not only has more information but an ethical obligation to have more information. There is a duty to know and a duty to test products and services so that the seller knows what the limits of the products are. Once the limits of the products are known, then there is a duty to inform and a duty to warn the buyer of the dangers inherent in any limitations that may cause harm to the user. In the Audi 5000 case, Audi of America did extensive tests and engineering studies once it became aware of the problem of unintended acceleration. These tests led to a postsale correction and redesign of the automobile. Audi did not warn its customers because it believed its product was safe.

In less competitive markets, the ethical duties of due care suggest that duties are a function of the nature of the market failure. If the manufacturer has advantages with respect to information and scientific and technological resources, then there is:

1. A duty not to harm others and to existing safety standards.
2. A duty to know about your product.
3. A duty to test the product or service.
4. A duty to inform the potential buyer of the product of the potential dangers concerning the use of it.
5. The duty not to misinform continues to exist in all market conditions.
6. A duty to remedy a problem after the sale of the product or service under certain circumstances. The sixth duty is a duty to fix the product after a sale if a serious safety problem is discovered. The seller may have a duty to recall the product and fix it.
7. There is the negative duty not to pressure or coerce. In this case it is not a product liability issue, but a sales issue coming from the imbalance in power. With respect to automobiles, most states have "cooling off" laws that if you change your mind within three days you can have the contract reversed. Ethically it would be said that you shouldn't use high-pressure sales techniques, but the difference between enthusiasm and high-pressure is sometimes blurred.

From an ethical point of view, the duty not to harm implies that safety standards be followed. These standards are technical and scientific. As we move from ethics to the area of the law and regulation these technological and scientifically based standards are incorporated into the legal and regu-latory standards used in product liability cases. With respect to the auto industry, the primary regulation would be the National Highway Traffic Safety Administration and to products in general, the Consumer Product Safety Commission. The Federal Aviation Agency is responsible for regulating aircraft safety. These are the primary regulatory agencies that deal with product safety.

Product Liability: The Regulatory and Legal Environment

The development of product liability law parallels the ethical framework outlined above. The nineteenth century was marked by the traditional ideology of individual responsibility, personal freedom, and faith in the model of perfect competition.

TRADITIONAL CONTRACT APPROACHES TO PRODUCT LIABILITY LAW

Thus, the traditional theory of product liability law inspired by the cultural sphere during the nineteenth century emphasized three principles:

1. caveat emptor: "let the buyer beware"
2. freedom of contract
3. the doctrine of no liability without fault[16]

As noted above "let the buyer beware" was a principle that is reasonable under the conditions assumed in perfect competition because it was assumed that both parties were approximately equal in knowledge and power and freely entered into the contract. Thus the buyer was expected to act prudently and to be responsible for the consequences of his or her decisions. According to the principle of *freedom of contract* in the context of "let the buyer beware," contracts were a matter of free choice by both parties. Thus, unless sellers made an express warranty regarding the quality of goods sold, they were not liable for defects in those goods. The *doctrine of no liability without fault* meant that for sellers to be liable without an express warranty

TABLE 15–2
Theories of Product Liability Law

Contract-based Theories of Product Liability	Tort-based Theories of Product Liability
Classical principles	Evolving principles
"Let the buyer beware."	"Let the seller beware."

Freedom of contract between consenting parties	Behavioral standards of wrongfulness:
	    Malicious intent
	    Recklessness
	    Negligence

No liability without fault	Product standard of liability: Doctrine of strict liability
Product liability as breach of contract:	Product liability as not harming others:
Express Warranty: product liability limited to what is stated explicitly in contract	Negligent behavior as criterion. Liability is based on harm caused by inappropriate behavior
Implied Warranty: product liability extended to include what would be reasonable care in the discharge of a market relation	Doctrine of strict liability (unsafe products as criterion)
	Punitive damages used as a deterrent for callous neglect or malicious intent in the making or sale of products or services

in a contract, their conduct had to be blameworthy in some sense. Product liability during this period focused on behavior as prescribed in the contract; cases rarely focused on behavior that could be considered wrong or blameworthy. However, as industrialization continued and reality coincided with the conditions of limited competition, a shift toward tort approaches to product liability developed, as shown in Table 15–2.

TORT-BASED THEORIES OF PRODUCT LIABILITY LAW

A *tort* is a civil wrong that is not a breach of contract.[17] Typically wrongful behavior in product liability cases harms a person or results in economic dam-

ages. Tort law is concerned with correcting the results of wrongs that have resulted from negligent behavior. Tort law of product liability recognizes four different standards of wrongfulness: (1) intent, (2) recklessness, (3) negligence, and (4) strict liability.

Intent normally includes wrongful behavior willingly or intentionally done to purposefully harm or economically damage someone. More commonly, this standard is concerned with criminal assault cases rather than product liability cases. If an engineer knowingly and willingly falsifies a test result of a piece of equipment, thus endangering or harming anyone who used it, this behavioral standard of product liability would apply.

Recklessness involves intentional activity that has a high probability of harming or economically damaging another person. As Chapter 6 suggested, it is sometimes hard to determine intentional behavior and scientifically established cause-effect relationships necessary to establish a "high probability." The court must decide what a reasonable person should have known in the situation.

Negligence is legally present when a person fails to comply with an objective standard of behavior. What is an objective standard? If a business uses its strategic management of public issues capabilities to influence the regulatory standard or timing of implementation adopted by a regulatory agency, has it been negligent? In a situation involving the standards that would apply to the Pinto, the Ford Motor Company had complied with all legal standards required at the time but had influenced the NHTSA in the standard-setting process. For this and perhaps other reasons, the jury found Ford negligent in the case and handed down a $125 million punitive damages judgment against Ford.[18] A judge later reduced the punitive damages to $3.5 million.

The tort criteria of intent, recklessness, and negligence are all behavioral, that is, they are standards by which behavior is judged to determine whether product liability exists. Since the turn of this century, there has been a systematic development in the area of product liability through court cases which have shifted the risk and the burden of proof from the buyer to the seller or manufacturer of a product. The pace of change sharply increased during the past few decades. The increased risk involved for sellers and manufacturers have been significantly increased by the fourth standard for torts, that is, by the doctrine of strict liability.

Strict Liability

In this standard for torts in product liability, the court focuses on the nature of the product itself to determine the presence of a tort for product liability. Specific negligent or irresponsible behavior of the producer or seller does not have to be proven if the product or service is considered inherently unsafe. In a recent review of product liability cases, Manley reported:

> Some 46 states have mandated that manufacturers are strictly liable for product defects. Strict liability

means that you can be held liable even if you're not at fault in the traditional sense. These laws differ on many points, including the time a plaintiff has to bring a lawsuit, how much a plaintiff has to prove, and the defenses available to manufacturers. For instance, a California manufacturer may be faced with evidence of subsequent changes as proof that its product was at one time defective; in Louisiana, such evidence is prohibited in strict liability actions.

State laws not only differ from one another but are also a moving target. For example, in 1985, at least 19 states modified laws affecting manufacturer's liability. The effect of those changes is still largely untested.[19]

STRICT LIABILITY CASES

A series of landmark cases suggests an increase in the product liability risk for sellers and manufacturers that have resulted from the changing interpretations of the doctrine of strict liability used by the courts.[20] In 1963, in a California case, a manufacturer was held strictly liable for damages when the company sold a product that proved to have a defect. Previously, the plaintiff had to prove neglect that the producer had behaved unreasonably negligently in producing the product. According to the idea of strict liability plaintiffs do not have to prove negligent behavior. If the product is itself proven to be dangerous and causes injury, then the manufacturer can be held strictly liable for the product. It is not necessary to prove that reasonable management procedures or bad techniques were used in the manufacture of the product. This criterion of strict liability significantly changes the burden of proof and the risks of the producer. Business should carefully consider some of the cases that have used the principle of strict liability when they design, distribute, package, and inform customers about their products.[21]

When a Product Worsens an Injury

In a 1968 case, *Larsen v. General Motors*, it was determined that a faulty design of a product worsened an injury. The court found that the plaintiff could recover damages for the worsened part of the injury even if the design defect did not cause the injury in the first place. Later in a 1972 California case, *Cronin v. J.B.E. Olson Corporation*, the court found that a product need not be unreasonably dangerous to make the manufacturer strictly liable; it just had to be proven dangerous.

Contributory Negligence As a Defense

In 1972, *Bexiga v. Havir Manufacturing Company*, a New Jersey court found that if an injury is attributable to the lack of a safety device in the product that had been removed, the manufacturer could not base its defense on the contributory negligence on the plaintiff. If the plaintiff removes the safety device or doesn't use the safety device, the manufacturer can still be held partially liable for the unsafe product under the doctrine of strict liability.

However, this principle of contributory negligence has been applied differently by courts in other states. In 1986, in New York, Silverstein sued the Walsh Press and Die Company because of an injury suffered by a machine manufactured by it. Walsh demonstrated that when the machine had been sold 34 years previously, it had safety devices that had been removed and modified after the machine was sold. The court ruled in favor of Walsh.

Product Improvement Can Increase Liability Risk

Companies often redesign products so that through improvements they can be made safer and more useful. However, such design changes legally can work against the producer. Evidence that a manufacturer has changed or improved a product line after it was manufactured or sold has been used in some states to prove that the former design was faulty. The very fact that a business has improved the product is used as evidence that the other product shouldn't have been sold in the first place. Such court findings suggest that there may be a strong negative incentive to introducing improved designs because of the product liability implications.[22]

Mixed Results When the User Knows of the Risk

In 1976, Micallef won a product liability case in New York against Miehle Company. Evidence that an injured plaintiff obviously knew of a danger inherent in the product did not defeat his claim because the court ruled that the manufacturer could have previously guarded against the danger in designing the product. The manufacturer must show that the usefulness of the product involved in an accident outweighs the risk inherent in its design. In this radical ruling the court shifted the burden of proof from the plaintiff to the defendant.

In a related 1986 case concerning the Wysong and Miles Company, that company sold a press brake that weighed 20,000 pounds and was 9 feet high and 12 feet wide to Metal Fabricators of Jacksonville, Florida. During installation of the brake it tipped over and one of the workmen was killed. His widow sued Wysong and Miles for designing such a top-heavy brake. The court ruled in favor of Wysong and Miles because the three workers were professional installers of this type of equipment and should have known of the dangers of the brake toppling over.

When the Product Is Used Differently Than Expected

When evaluating the design of a product, the seller or manufacturer must also consider how the user may use it. In other 1976 cases, *Louisiana, Duhon v. Goodyear Tire and Rubber Co. et al.* and *Dugas v. Goodyear Tire and Rubber Co. et al.*, Ford's 1976 Mercury Cougar was equipped with a 425-horsepower engine and Goodyear radial tires. Shelby Leleux, the owner of the Cougar, drove his car over 100 miles an hour when a tire exploded, causing an accident and his death. A passenger, Floyd Dugas, was also seriously injured.

Dugas and Leleux's mother sued Ford and Goodyear for selling a defective product. Testimony indicated that the Goodyear tire had a maximum safe speed of 85 miles per hour. Both companies argued that the car had not been used as intended, and thus they were not liable. However, the judge ruled that since the Cougar, with its large engine, could be driven at 105 miles per hour, the companies should have expected that someone would drive at that speed. Thus, the car should have been equipped with tires that could withstand the maximum speed that the car could drive. Even though the owner's manual of the car warned against driving the car over 90 miles per hour, Ford and Goodyear were found strictly liable in the case. Thus, manufacturers must design products based upon how someone might use them rather than how most persons could be expected to use them.

PUNITIVE DAMAGES

Another concept in product liability is punitive damages. The idea behind punitive damages is that society needs to punish behavior that is socially undesirable so that it will be discouraged. Thus the punishment may go beyond the economic value of the damages caused by a tort to serve as a deterrence. Based upon utilitarian reasoning, punishment should be large enough to discourage undesirable social behavior.

Punitive damages judgments can be assessed when there is proof of *malicious intent and careless neglect*. In the assessment of punitive damages the court considers how the manufacturer or distributer of a product or service has *behaved*. A legal finding of product liability that calls for punitive damages shifts the criteria used by the court away from the inherent characteristic of the product or service used in the strict liability principle to a behavioral standard of gross negligence.

Prior to the 1960s product liability cases employed the criterion of reasonable behavior to determine liability. The concept of reasonable behavior is also used in punitive damages cases in that punitive damages are called for if behavior is so unreasonable as to constitute malicious intent and/or careless neglect on the part of the producer or seller of a product or service. Central to the cases involving punitive damages is the concept of actions that a reasonable business person could rightly be expected to take to insure that the product or service was safe.

From an ethical or utilitarian point of view, punitive damages as punishment should deter undesirable behavior. Thus the punishment should be severe enough to discourage persons or businesses from doing something that public policy has determined to be undesirable. Said differently, the

threat of punitive damages is meant to encourage producers of goods and services to act reasonably so that persons are not harmed unnecessarily by their activities. The key question from a utilitarian perspective is how large a punishment must be to discourage undesirable behavior.

The common image of the corporation is of businesses that are very large with virtually unlimited resources. From this perception, juries often vote for sizable punitive damages with the view that they are needed because (1) it takes a large punishment to discourage irresponsibility, (2) the company can afford the punishment and may not be deterred by a smaller amount, and (3) the behavior is so undesirable as to deserve punishment.

Another aspect of litigation in the area of product liability is the legitimacy of the company. If there is sufficient social or political support for the company, then society is likely to conclude that management is behaving in a reasonable and responsible manner. Such a conclusion may influence court decisions. However, if legitimacy is low, then society and the courts are less likely to give the corporation the benefit of the doubt. In other words, if a jury believes that the business in question is essentially exploitative, evil, and greedy, then what comes out of that is the perceived illegitimacy of the company in the minds of the jury members and is likely to lead to increased assessments of punitive damages awards.

Most companies, like most individuals, have liability insurance, but many insurance policies have exclusionary clauses. If a court finds cause for a punitive damage award against a business, then the insurance policy will not cover such losses. An additional aspect of punitive damages is that losses incurred in this way are not tax-deductible expenses. All these things provide a strong negative incentive that should discourage products or services resulting from malicious intent and callous neglect.

Criteria for Punitive Damages

Schmidt and May have identified the following five criteria used by the courts to determine malicious intent and callous neglect:

1. Did the company comply with established regulatory standards?
2. Did the company do proper testing?
3. Were users informed of dangers?
4. Did the company misrepresent the product or service?
5. Did the company take any postsale corrective action such as a recall?[23]

Note that the legal criteria used in deciding punitive damages closely parallels the ethics of due care outlined above. These five standards used to determine callous neglect and malicious intent are well established in product liability cases; the more these standards are violated, the clearer is the appropriateness of punitive damages. Of course, the amount of damages assessed also depends on the amount of harm experienced by the user of the product or service, the perceived legitimacy of the

producer or seller, and the size or perceived capacity to pay damages of the producer or seller.

International Aspects of Product Liability Law

The member states of the European Community became an economically unified market in 1992. The variations in product liability law throughout the European Community were perceived as distorting competition, impeding trade, and treating customers unequally in different countries. As part of the market integration process, the European Economic Community (EC) adopted a directive that required all member states to pass harmonizing legislation adopting the doctrine of strict liability in product-related injuries.[24]

TABLE 15–3
The Search for Uniformity in Product Liability Law in the European Community

| European Community Country | Harmonizing Legislation | | | | |
| | Derogations | | National Law | | |
	Development Risks Defense Included	Cap on Damages Included	Pain and Suffering	Punitive Damages	Strict or Near Strict Liability
Belgium	Yes	No	Yes	No	Yes
Denmark	Yes	No	Yes	No	No
France	none	none	Yes	No	Yes
Germany	Yes	Yes	Yes	No	Yes
Greece	Yes	Yes	Yes	No	No
Ireland	none	none	Yes	Yes	No
Italy	Yes	No	No	No	No
Luxembourg	No	No	Yes	No	Yes
Netherlands	Yes	No	Yes	No	Yes
Portugal	Yes	Yes	Yes	No	No
Spain	none	none	Yes	No	No
United Kingdom	Yes	No	Yes	No	No

SOURCE: Adapted from Sandra N. Hurd and Frances E. Zollers, "Desperately Seeking Harmony: The European Community's Search for Uniformity in Product Liability Law," *American Business Law Journal* 30, no. 1 (May 1992): table 1, p. 48.

Table 15–3 shows the progress made by various members of the EC in adopting the new requirements. Except for Italy, all countries will allow the victim of an injury to sue for pain and suffering as well as for economic damages. Unlike the United States, where punitive damages is relatively common, European countries do not allow for punitive damages in product liability cases with the exception of Ireland. Though several countries have now adopted the doctrine of strict liability requirement imposed by the EC, several countries have yet to do so.

One defense in product liability cases is the *developmental risk defense,* which argues that the product is as safe as the current development of technology permits. Note that all but one country listed in Table 15–3 allow for this defense. Thus most European countries do not punish companies sued in product liability cases for not adopting potentially safer technologies that do not in fact yet exist. Another criticism of variation in product liability cases is that judgments in some jurisdictions are much harsher than in others. To deal with this problem, the EC harmonizing legislation derogation also calls for a cap on product liability damages. Only Germany, Greece, and Portugal have caps on product liability damages.

Japan

The product liability system of Japan needs to be considered within the context of its culture.[25] The traditional Japanese legal precepts were based upon inequality between individuals. Conflict resolution is strongly influenced by Confucian norms and customs that call for harmonious conciliation. In Japan there are a number of extrajudicial mechanisms for resolving disputes including reconcilement, conciliation, and chotei. *Reconcilement* is when two parties confer with each other and settle the dispute privately. *Conciliation* includes mediation by a third party that makes nonbinding suggestions or arbitration where arbitration leads to a decision binding on the disputing parties.

Chotei is a quasi-judicial alternative that can be invoked prior to or at any time during litigation of a case in court. The chotei committee is often a judge plus two persons appointed by the court to work with disputing parties to reach an agreement. If accepted, the agreements become the final judgment for the court.

Because of the alternatives to litigation used in Japan, the actual court cases there are significantly fewer than the number of lawsuits filed in the United States. In 1979, there were 387,000 lawsuits filed in Japan compared with the United States, which had 155,700 lawsuits filed in federal courts and another 5.9 million filed in various state courts. With few lawyers, a clogged court system, and sanctioned alternatives to litigation, the Japanese cultural message is to settle out of court. This message is reflected in the number of lawsuits filed annually in Japan.

Summary

The chapter used the Audi 5000 and the problem of unintended acceleration to illustrate how a public issue moves through the issue life cycle. The ILC tracks the public interest in an often controversial public issue over its life as an issue, beginning with the development of social and technological changes that bring about a social problem and increasing until the issue comes to the public awareness.

In stage three of the ILC, organizations such as consumer interest groups, industry associations, and political action committees, and often prominent individuals as well, coalesce around the issue as defined in their preferred manner. These organizations become active in trying to influence management policy, public policy, and the lawmaking process, the administration of laws and regulations by agencies that may already exist. Interest groups can also bring class action lawsuits against companies, agencies, and others. Organizations need to begin mapping stakeholders early in the ILC to anticipate the consequences of their decisions so as to predict the likely reaction a decision will bring from stakeholders.

By stage four of the ILC, public interest in an issue is at its highest. In most issues relating to consumer protection, stage four occurred sometime in the 1970s.

In stage five of the ILC, the established government agencies administer and enforce compliance with the laws regulating business practices in consumer affairs. The key agencies in the area of consumer protection are those listed above, including (1) The Consumer Products Safety Commission, (2) The National Highway Traffic Safety Administration, (3) the Federal Trade Commission, and (4) the Food and Drug Administration. In stage six of the ILC, matters are litigated in the courts to resolve persisting conflicts.

The ethics of market exchanges involve rights, duties, and responsibilities that vary depending upon the nature of the competition. In perfectly competitive markets, buyers and sellers have a duty not to engage in misinformation or fraud. Because the conditions of perfect condition result in a balance of market power and equal information about offerings and product features, few duties exist. "Let the buyer beware" characterizes the duty to all because individual responsibility and capability are assumed.

There is an increase in the duties of sellers as market competition becomes less and less perfect. The adage becomes "Let the seller beware," as characterized by the ethics of due care. Duties of the seller become the duty (1) to comply with standards to insure goods and services will not harm another, (2) to know your product or service through appropriate testing, (3) to inform or warn customers of possible dangers in a product, (4) not to take advantage of market power, thus coercion, duress, or high pressure are unethical, (5) to respond justly to customer complaints and to appropriately correct problems with your products.

The development of product liability law parallels the discussion of ethics of exchange. In the last century, contract approaches dominated liability law and narrowly defined responsibilities. A tort is a wrong that harms a person or economically damages his or her interest. Product liability is determined by the courts in tort law based upon the standards of (1) intent, (2) recklessness, (3) negligence, and (4) strict liability. Intent, recklessness, and negligence are behavioral standards of wrongfulness.

Strict liability shifts the focus away from behavior and to the design, packaging, distribution, and other characteristics of the product itself. Strict liability is used as the primary standard in product liability in most of the United States through the development of this doctrine as common law. The application of the principles of strict liability varies substantially from state to state.

Punitive damages can be assessed when the court determines that the wrongful behavior in a product liability case is so severe as to show malicious intent or callous neglect of responsibility. The criteria used to determine punitive damages closely parallel the duties under the ethics of due care outlined above.

Conclusions

Managing customer stakeholder issues can be very difficult, as the Audi 5000 case illustrates. Effective social performance in customer affairs requires that companies respond to the key dimensions of social performance:

1. *Maintain competitive position* in a contested market for *economic performance.*
2. *Strategically manage public affairs for political performance.* This requires understanding the dynamics of the ILC, mapping stakeholders, and developing appropriate strategies and action plans to maintain legitimate public support for management decisions. Relationships with these agencies can be marked by cooperative interaction or contentiousness. Businesses that are respected for their honesty and technical competence are likely to be heard more clearly and sympathetically than those that are perceived as being combative, arrogant, or incompetent.
3. *Responding ethically and justly* to consumer concerns. This requires understanding the ethical

decision-making concepts and frameworks of Chapter 7 and applying them to specific stakeholder situations like customer relations and product safety. Also, this requires sensitivity to marketplace conditions. An important aspect of ethics in market exchange situations is that the duties required to be ethical increase as management discretion increases.

4. *Legal and regulatory compliance* requires knowing the relevant laws, court cases, and government agencies. Also, this may be especially difficult if you are an international corporation operating in unfamiliar jurisdictions, as may have been the case with Audi of America. Many public issues such as those in the customer stakeholder area are mature and thus are highly regulated by numerous and sometimes contradictory laws, agencies, and regulations.

Business social performance requires effectiveness in each of these four areas. Responding effectively to consumer interest groups and activists is difficult, and it is possible to be ineffective despite much hard work. The importance of knowing the local market and being alert to developments cannot be overemphasized. Missing key opportunities early in an issue can add to an already inherently volatile situation in cases of product safety.

Discussion Questions

1. Evaluate the management of the unintended acceleration by Audi of America as a public issue. What were its strong points? What went wrong? Why did Audi ultimately have to withdraw the Audi 5000 from the American market?
2. What are the stages in the issue life cycle? In the Audi 5000 case, which stage was the most crucial for management action? What factors in the situation increased or decreased the difficulty of responding effectively at each stage in the ILC?
3. What are the key elements of ethical behavior in a perfectly competitive market? Do these

change when limited competition exists? Explain.
4. What is the ethics of due care? Does this really apply in the Audi 5000 case? Why or why not?
5. What are the characteristics of the contract approach to product liability as it existed in the nineteenth century?
6. How does the tort approach to product liability differ form the contract approach?
7. What are the standards of behavior used in tort law as it applies to product liability cases?
8. Explain the doctrine of strict liability.
9. What advice can you give business concerning the design, sale, and distribution of products if you want to reduce product liability risks?
10. Apply the social performance model to the Audi 5000 case. What conclusions can you develop that might guide management decisions in other cases where managing product safety is the central problem?

Notes

1. Csaba Csere, "Audi Agonistes," *Car and Driver,* June 1987, p. 51.
2. John Tomerlin, "Solved: The Riddle of Unintended Acceleration," *Road and Track,* February 1988, p. 53.
3. Bernice Kanner, "In For Repairs," *New York Times,* October 19, 1987, p. 32.
4. Laurie McKinley, "U.S. Requests Safety Recall of Audi 5000s," *Wall Street Journal,* December 24, 1986, p. 4.
5. "Can Audi Fix a Dented Image," *Business Week,* November 17, 1989, pp. 81–82.
6. John Tomerlin, "Solved: The Riddle of Unintended Acceleration," *Road and Track,* February 1988, pp 53–56.
7. "Audi Takes the Gloves Off," *Motor Trend,* May 1987, p. 34.
8. Ted Orme, "Sudden Acceleration Stumps NHTSA," *Motor Trend,* June 1987, p. 48.
9. Tomerlin, "Solved: The Riddle of Unintended Acceleration," p. 59.
10. Csere, "Audi Agonistes," p. 57.
11. Ralph Nader, *Unsafe at Any Speed: The Designed-In Dangers of the American Automobile* (New York: Grossman, 1972 [1965]).
12. David Bollier, "15 Years," *Public Citizen,* October 1986, pp. 20–32.
13. Bruce D. Fisher and Michael J. Phillips, *The Legal Environment of Business* (New York: West, 1983), p. 476.

14. This is the key point make by Mike Porter, *Competitive Strategy* (New York: Free Press, 1980).
15. Manual Velasquez, *Business Ethics,* 2d ed. (Englewood Cliffs, N.J.: Prentice-Hall, 1988), pp. 283–87.
16. Bruce D. Fisher and Michael J. Phillips, *The Legal Environment of Business* (New York: West, 1983), chaps. 15 and 16.
17. Fisher and Phillips, *The Legal Environment of Business,* p. 451.
18. "Why the Pinto Jury Felt Ford Deserved $125 Million Penalty," *Wall Street Journal,* February 14, 1978, p. 1.
19. Marisa Manley, "Product Liability: You're More Exposed Than You Think," *Harvard Business Review* (September-October 1987), p. 36.
20. "The Devils in the Product Liability Laws," *Business Week,* February 12, 1979, pp. 72–73.
21. Manley, "Product Liability," pp. 28–40.
22. Paul A. Herbig and James E. Golden, "Inhibitor of Innovation: The Case Against Strict Product Liability," *American Business Review* 11, no. 2 (June 1993): 13–20.
23. Michael A. Schmitt and William W. May, "Beyond Products Liability: The Legal, Social, and Ethical Problems Facing the Automotive Industry in Producing Safe Products," *Journal of Urban Law* 56 (1979): 1021–50.
24. Sandra N. Hurd and Francis E. Zollers, "Desperately Seeking Harmony: The European Community's Search for Uniformity in Product Liability Law," *American Business Law Journal* 30, no. 1 (May 1992): 35–68.
25. Franklin W. Nutter and Keith T. Bateman, "The U.S. Tort System in the Era of the Global Economy: An International Perspective," *Federation of Insurance and Corporate Counsel Quarterly* 41, no. 1 (Fall 1990): 3–56.

CHAPTER 16

Employee Stakeholders: Rights, Workplace Safety, and Downsizing

CHAPTER OBJECTIVES

1. Suggest how employee stakeholder issues vary in maturity and are found in varying stages of the issue life cycle (ILC).

2. Show how employee issues are related to human needs.

3. Explain how social and technological changes spawn new employee issues like work-family conflicts and workplace diseases.

4. Explain how global competitiveness has led to corporate restructuring that includes both downsizing and employee empowerment.

5. Track the employee stakeholder issue of job safety through the ILC to illustrate how issues evolve over time.

6. Review how the Occupational Safety and Health Administration has regulated workplace safety.

Point—Work in America, 1973[1]

Significant numbers of American workers are dissatisfied with the quality of their working lives. Dull, repetitive, seemingly meaningless tasks, offering little challenge or autonomy, are causing discontent among workers at all occupational levels. This is not so much because work itself-has greatly changed; indeed, one of the main problems is that work has not changed fast enough to keep up with the rapid and wide-scale changes in worker attitudes, aspirations, and values. A general increase in their educational and economic status has placed many American workers in a position where having an interesting job is now as important as having a job that pays well. Pay is still important: it must support an "adequate" standard of living and be perceived as equitable— but high pay alone will not lead to job (or life) satisfaction.

There have been some responses to the changes in the workforce, but they have been small and slow. As a result, worker productivity is low, as measured by absenteeism, turnover rates, wildcat strikes, sabotage, poor-quality projects, and a reluctance by workers to commit themselves to

477

their work tasks. Moreover, a growing body of research indicated that, as work problems increase, there may be a consequent decline in physical and mental health, family stability, community participation and cohesiveness, and "balanced" sociopolitical attitudes, while there is an increase in drug and alcohol addiction, aggression, and delinquency.

Counterpoint—1993: Who Needs a Boss?[2]

Many American companies are discovering what may be *the* productivity breakthrough of the 1990s. The controversial innovation is called by such names as a self-managed team, cross-functional team, high-performance teams, or superteams. Corning CEO Jamie Houghton, whose company has over 3,000 teams, said, "If you believe in quality, when you cut through everything, it's empowering your people, and it's empowering your people that leads to teams." What makes superteams so controversial is that they ultimately force managers to do what they only imagined in their most Boschian nightmares: give up control. Because superteams are working right, *mirabile dictu*, they manage themselves. No boss is required. A superteam arranges schedules, sets profit targets, and may even know everyone's salary. It has a say in hiring and firing team members as well as managers. It orders material and equipment. It strokes customers, improves quality, and in some cases, devises strategy. Those who have already taken the plunge have seen impressive results:

- At a General Mills cereal plant in Lodi, California, teams schedule, operate, and maintain machinery so effectively that the factory runs with no managers present during the night shift.
- At a weekly meeting, a team of Federal Express clerks spotted—and eventually solved—a billing problem that was costing the company $2.1 million a year.

- A team of Chaparral Steel mill workers traveled the world to evaluate new production machinery. The machines they selected and installed helped make their mill one of the world's most efficient.
- 3M turned around one division by creating cross-functional teams that tripled the number of new products.
- After organizing its home office operations into superteams, Aetna Life and Casualty reduced the ratio of middle managers to workers—from 1:7 down to 1:30—all the while improving customer service.
- Teams of blue-collar workers at Johnsonville Foods of Sheboygan, Wisconsin, helped CEO Ralph Stayer make the decision to proceed with a major plant expansion. The workers told Stayer they would produce more sausage, faster than he would have ever dared to ask. Since 1986, productivity has risen at least 50 percent.

Employee Stakeholder Issues and Human Needs

Chapter 6 argued that the development of the capacity to make moral judgments parallels the need hierarchy first developed by Abraham Maslow. This need hierarchy is a series that includes physiological needs, safety needs, social or love needs, ego or esteem needs, and self-actualization. These needs become active in the order of this hierarchy as a person develops over time. A similar need hierarchy theory was developed by Alderfer, whose research produced the ERG theory of motivation that identified existence, relatedness, and growth as basic human needs.

Employee stakeholder issues parallel the employee needs found in need hierarchy theory. Employment, wrongful discharge, and job safety correspond to physiological and safety needs in the need hierarchy. These are existence needs that must be satisfied before other needs can become salient. Social needs are fulfilled by opportunities to participate, to interact with others, and to join

TABLE 16–1
Maslow's Need Hierarchy and Employee Stakeholder Issues

Motivating Needs	Employee Issue
Physiological	Employment at will Wrongful discharge Plant closure notification
Safety	Occupational safety and health Job safety
Social	Equality of opportunity Discrimination in the workplace Sexual harassment Team participation
Ego or esteem	Employee rights • Privacy • Freedom of expression • Freedom of association • Human dignity
Self-actualization	Meaningful work Participation Empowerment

work groups. Most of the employee stakeholder issues in this relatedness need category are discussed in the following chapter within the context of discrimination and employment opportunity. Many stakeholder issues relating to employee rights of privacy and freedom of expression are connected with the self-esteem needs. Meaningful work and employee empowerment fulfill the higher-order need of self-actualization and growth. Table 16–1 shows how the primary employee stakeholder issues relate to the needs of Maslow's hierarchy.

Organizations that motivate employees through need fulfillment are more likely to have higher performance in the globalized markets of contemporary business. Such organizations are more desirable places to work and can better attract talent than organizations that do not respond to human needs.

For this reason, managers often initiate programs that respond to employee concerns for competitive reasons rather than because they are legally required to do so. Thus, the ILC for employee stakeholder issues may not parallel the public policy process, as it often does in other stakeholder areas.

Emerging Employee Stakeholder Issues

Most experts in the area of human resources agree that the key issues of this decade will be driven by the trends of (1) changing workforce demographics leading to greater workforce diversity and an increasing gap between the skills available and job requirements, (2) increased globalization of competition, (3) changing technology, and (4) corporate mergers, restructuring, and downsizing. These four converging trends will spawn numerous new employee stakeholder issues and create new management challenges.

The key trends of the last decade and continuing in the 1990s suggest that employee stakeholder issues are likely to have far-reaching strategic significance for business. Wagel (1990) recently sampled human resource and management practitioners and academics and identified the following as key trends and issues:

1. Federal regulation will affect employee benefits and the mandatory retirement age.
2. Labor shortages amplified by functional illiteracy and cultural diversity will cause education to be a continuing public issue.
3. Rising health care costs will focus attention on national health insurance as a serious public policy issue.
4. Work-family conflicts will be addressed by more employers as the issues of day care, family leave, dual careers, and flexible work scheduling move to center stage.
5. Globalization and the competitive quest for the delivery of quality services will challenge human resource development.
6. The judicial arena is unlikely to enlarge employee causes.
7. Continuing drug use and other substance abuse will require employers to balance employee privacy with organizational needs for safety and productivity.
8. Individual career planning will have to have the input of both employees and employers.[3]

Similarly Rendero reported on a panel of leading human resource professionals who predicted that (1) government legislation would increase in the area of benefits, (2) lawsuits concerning privacy and defamation would be on the rise, (3) work-family issues will demand greater human resource flexibility, and (4) managers would press for the right to know more about a potential employee's work record without fear of becoming involved in a defamation suit.[4]

To the above lists, Gutteridge added the HR consequences of the merger movement, hostile takeovers, and financial restructuring of the last decade.[5] The need for corporate downsizing and a bottom-line orientation perceived by top managers to be required by the high levels of financial leverage, changing technology, and global competition increase the difficulty of formulating effective human resource development strategies to manage employee stakeholder issues.

Employee Stakeholder Issues and the ILC

Employees and employee associations are stakeholders of critical importance to business. Employee stakeholder issues are at different stages of the ILC and have followed its pattern as illustrated in Figure 16–1. Some of the issues are relatively mature and have a well-developed legal context; others are early-stage issues that are only now being defined, debated, and still await the public policy formation process.

Figure 16–1 indicates the stage of the ILC where employee stakeholder issues are likely to be found. A measure of intensity or interest in an issue would be the number of lines of newspaper or news magazine coverage each issue has, or perhaps the number of minutes of television coverage a particular issue is receiving. Early-stage ILC issues include new workplace diseases caused by computer technology, meaningful work, and conflicts between family and work. Middle-stage ILC issues include health care and the crisis over workers' compensation insurance. Mature issues include occupational safety and health, plant closing notification, and wrongful discharge cases. These mature issues are regulated by specific laws enforced by government agencies or are litigated within contract or tort law.

Technology, Work, and Empowerment

TECHNOLOGY AND WORKPLACE DISEASE

With the advent of the computer there are a host of worker illnesses and syndromes that have been appearing with increasing regularity. As a stage-one employee issue, *video display terminal (VDT) diseases* are a group of occupational illnesses caused by the extensive use of computers with radiation-emitting displays. Also, *carpel tunnel,* a condition of nerve damage and crippling that results from chronic repeated motion common to telephone operators and input clerks for computer data systems, is becoming increasingly common. Because many computer programs require clerks to input the same data repeatedly, the fingers suffer nerve and tendon

deterioration from the repeated motions. This type of work is more common because of the greater use of computers in the workplace. This "new illness" has grown in public awareness, beginning with those workers who suffer from this and the professional health community. Doctors are reporting more cases of this illness and research has been underway for several years. Stories then appear in professional medical journals. As the problem becomes more widespread, awareness grows, and a few new stories about new workplace diseases have begun to appear in more widely read news media.

While the broad issue of occupational safety and health is covered by an established set of federal and state regulations, new workplace hazards continually appear for which regulatory standards have not been developed. Rapidly changing technologies cause new workplace safety issues to appear, and thus the safety issue occasionally is

FIGURE 16–1 The Issue Life Cycle and Employee Stakeholder Issues

recycled repeatedly through the ILC. An example of this process is the repeated motion syndrome and other diseases associated with video display terminals discussed in Box 16–1.

Several of the employees in their early thirties had experienced hand surgery several times and had lost most of the use of their hands owing to this syndrome. Thus repeated motion syndrome is classified as a stage-one issue in Figure 16–1 because it is brought about by technological change that is only now entering into the awareness of the public. *Tort law* is concerned with recovering damages due to negligent behavior leading to liability. Lawsuits related to VDT diseases are beginning to be brought against producers of computerized workstations under the tort law. Thus existing social and legal remedies are being used to recover damages. However, there is a lag before safety standards are incorporated into regulations that control workplace safety.

BOX 16–1   **VDT Disease Prompts Surge of Lawsuits**

Repetitive motion injury is shaping up to be the occupational hazard of the information age—and office workers are getting ready for a fight. The injuries—which include carpal tunnel syndrome—are the subject of at least three lawsuits and several major studies. Experts say the flood of computers and the push for higher technology are causing a virtual epidemic of such injuries, and more lawsuits are inevitable.

The most recent suit was filed Friday [June 14, 1990] in federal court for $270 million by eight journalists against Atex Publishing Systems, a major supplier of word-processing systems to newspapers. The workers claim they've suffered tendinitis, nerve disorders and crippling inflammation of nerves in the wrists as a result of working at computers.

"Thousands of people are being seriously disabled," says Ellen Bravo or 9 to 5, National Association of Working Women. "These workers are frustrated because no one's willing to take responsibility."

The injuries are the leading cause of occupational illness, according to the Bureau of Labor Statistics, representing 48% of all workplace illnesses in 1988 (the latest figure available), 115,400 people had it. Susan Harrigan, 45, a former reporter of *Newsday*, says she can't write, drive, grocery shop or hug her 8-year-old daughter after developing a repetitive strain injury in both arms. She left her job a year ago, "For a long time I was in pain constantly. I'd wake up several times a night feeling like my arms were on fire."

Why the explosion now? Forty-six million people use computers at work compared with 675,000 in 1976. By the year 2000, 75% of all jobs are expected to involve computers. And there's greater awareness. Such injuries have only recently been given a label.

Though the National Institute for Occupational Safety and Health (NIOSH) is convinced there's a cause-and-effect relationship between such injuries and computer use, it's not clear where to place the blame. "Does it mean the VDT [Video Display Terminal], the table, the chair, the keyboard, poor lighting?" says Dave Le Grande, director of occupational safety and health for the Communication Workers of America.

Among studies under way: NIOSH is investigating reports of injuries at US West in Denver, where a group of phone operators filed suit two and one half years ago against Computer Consoles Inc. of Rochester, N.Y. NIOSH is also looking at the supermarket industry and the *Los Angeles Times*, where 200 of 1,100 editorial workers have filed disability claims.

Source: Julia Lawlor, "VDT Disease Prompts Surge of Lawsuits, *USA Today*, June 20, 1990, p. B1.

MEANINGFUL WORK AND
EMPLOYEE EMPOWERMENT

Empowerment is the feeling a worker has who experiences his or her work as (1) worthwhile, (2) motivating, (3) to some extent under his or her control, (4) and is consistent with self-respect and the dignity of the individual.[6] This is an experience found in self-management teams described in the "who needs a boss" counterpoint opening the chapter. The opposite of empowerment work is the experience of alienation and worker dissatisfaction reported in *Work in America*, published 20 years ago and briefly quoted at the beginning of this chapter.

There is a vast literature in sociology and management over what makes life and work meaningful, on the one hand, and the opposite experience of alienation and anomie, on the other. *Alienation* is the experience of not having control over one's life and work. *Anomie* is the experience that life and work are without importance or any inherent meaning. In contrast, *empowerment* is associated with the experience of self-control and meaning in the workplace.

Behavioral scientists, managers, and, of course, workers are aware of the high cost of wasting human potential. The quality of work issue remained early in the ILC, and it is not likely to be resolved through public policy. People-oriented productivity programs have become the key to developing competitiveness for many businesses. Total quality management (TQM) requires the empowerment of managers.[7]

Diana Meyers has suggested that we must first understand what makes life meaningful if we are to understand what makes work meaningful.[8] She argued that the feeling of self-respect precedes the experience of meaningful work. Self-respect depends upon personal integrity that requires that a person have relatively stable beliefs and feelings that are expressed in practice. A self-respecting person must be free to develop his or her potential, needs to be open-minded and have enough flexibility to grow, but should not quickly adjust beliefs and feelings or pretend to do so as the potential advantages of an immediate situation may suggest.

Integrity requires that one's actions be consistent with one's deeply held value system or deep attachment to a person or to a central principle of life. This requires self-acceptance that is enduring beyond momentary times of self-blame or self-congratulation. Self-acceptance allows the growth necessary for developing the capacity to reason morally, to behave ethically, and to overcome the self-doubts that often undermine individual growth.

A report to the secretary of health, education, and welfare entitled *Work in America* opened with the comment quoted at the beginning of this chapter. This report, published over twenty years ago, characterized work in America as providing little opportunity for individual growth and development, as undermining rather than encouraging a sense of self-respect that would support the dignity of the individual. Individuals working under such conditions are not likely to have the ingenuity, creativeness, and motivation that enable a business to remain competitive in global markets that define the new realities for business throughout the world in the 1990s.

It is ironic that this report, published the year after the high point of the American standard of living, which has been dropping each year since 1972, anticipated many of the pressing problems of concern to employee stakeholders today. Productivity increases of American workers have not kept pace with those of global competitors. Workers have had increased expectations and have wanted a measure of dignity in their work experience. Companies using self-management programs that empower employees like those cited in the counterpoint at the beginning of the chapter have benefited from the superior performance of self-managed teams that are based on the concepts of dignity and self-management at the team level. Also, the excellent companies in the international arena consistently have productivity through people programs based on respect for the dignity of the individual, worker self-management, and soundly designed reward systems.[9]

As a stakeholder issue, the meaningfulness of work or the quality of work life issue is unlikely to become a public policy matter leading to laws and regulations. Rather, the market is likely to be the final arbitrator of the meaningful work issue. Businesses that treat employees with dignity, expect personal integrity, and offer motivating assignments are likely to attract and develop more capable employees. These organizations are also likely to outperform their competitors. Self-respect and dignity are basic to the successful workplace of the future.

Employee Rights, Work-family Conflicts, and Employment

EMPLOYEE RIGHTS

Many employee rights are at the early stage of the ILC and are not defined as a problem for management or public policy. Others like privacy are hotly debated, while others are mature. The right to parental leave or the right to be informed of plant closures or of dangerous substances in the workplace are legally established as a part of public policy. However, privacy rights are often subject to debate. Drug testing is strongly resisted by most employees. What policy should management adopt? Who should be tested? Under what circumstances? How?

The Right to Privacy

Privacy relates to the inner life of the individual, and from an organizational perspective, privacy is concerned with the off-the-job life of the employee. The right of privacy from governments intrusion is a right guaranteed by the Constitution. In his or her work life an employee is concerned about unwelcome intrusions into his or her inner life and from his or her life away from the workplace. Privacy is needed for a person to experience dignity as a human being. However, sometimes what one does in private affects job performance and the safety of fellow workers. Companies have become increasingly concerned about drugs, as Box 16–2 discusses.

There is sometimes a fine line between private matters where business should not intrude and behavior that business has a right and perhaps a

responsibility to be aware of. The use of drugs by airline pilots or surgeons is a major concern because of the special responsibility those in such occupations have for public safety. Joseph Hazelwood had a substance abuse problem and was intoxicated when the *Exxon Valdez,* a supertanker under his command, went aground, causing the biggest oil spill in history. Should Exxon have tested its employees for alcohol or drugs?

Issues related to the issue of privacy as a concern of employee stakeholders include (1) substance abuse testing and treatment programs; (2) testing and programs for life-threatening illnesses like AIDS in the workplace and the question of release of information[10]; (3) release of confidential information from credit or personnel files[11]; and (4) lifestyle activities of employees that do not relate to the workplace.[12] Special interest groups have formed organizations devoted to protecting individuals' privacy in these areas. Also, many of the legislative debates of the 1990s concerning employee stakeholders will be concerned with these issues, and thus these issues are at stage four of the ILC.

BALANCING WORK AND FAMILY

The demographic characteristics of the American workforce has radically changed in the last two decades. There are record numbers of single parents, working women, two-career couples, and an aging population.[13] Employees face challenges in trying to balance the demands of work with the needs of family. Day care for children, care of elderly parents, and family leaves for care of children and parents have become important employee stakeholder issues of the 1990s. How can managers meet the special family demands created by these workforce changes and still achieve high performance? Rather than pushing for sacrifices of either family commitments or career achievement, some businesses are striving to facilitate success in both.

Economic Performance and Work-Family Issues

Global competition and economic recession both pressure business to keep costs down. Thus, accommodations of family-work issues need to be

BOX 16–2   More Top Firms Test Workers for Drugs

You could be a model employee and never have used an illegal drug in your life. But more than ever, if you work for some of the USA's largest companies, you might have to submit to a random drug test. The American Management Association says 38% of its 6,000 member firms—which are among the USA's biggest companies—now test current employees for illegal drug use. That's up from 36% last year.

New federal laws have forced random testing on industries such as transportation and defense, where safety or security is an issue. But many companies are extending random testing to all employees.

Motorola Inc. has decided to randomly test employees for illegal drugs. The company, though, guarantees that testing positive won't result in firing—the first time. "Motorola is saying if you have a problem, we'll help you," says spokeswoman Margot Brown, "but we can't allow you to affect the health of this company and of your fellow employees." All Motorola's 60,000 U.S. workers—receptionists to the company's president—will be randomly selected to submit to urine tests during three years starting in 1991. The first time an employee tests positive, he or she will be referred to counseling. The second time, the employee will be fired.

Motorola's program is a copy of Texas Instruments' (TI) program. "The majority of our employees told us through focus groups that if we were going to test defense- and transportation-related employees, they felt it was only fair to test everyone," says Sandy Christopher, TI spokeswoman.

For some, random testing signals a dangerous reversal of attitude. Says Loren Siegel of the American Civil Liberties Union, "I'd compare it to the company towns of the turn of the century, where the Rockefellers and the Morgan's thought they had the right to interfere in the personal lives of their workers. Rockefeller once hired so-called social workers to visit homes of his workers to insure they weren't gambling and they were attending church." Siegel says random testing paves the way for further intrusions into an employee's private life. "Next they will want to know if you are smoking cigarettes at home."

But private employers say they must step in where other anti-drug initiates have failed. "The philosophy is, government has been throwing money at anti-drug programs and they have not solved the problem," says Brown. "We have to be part of the solution." As random testing has increased, so have drug-education programs. The number of corporations with such programs grew by 38% last year. "Companies are now saying not only 'How do we find our drug abusers?' but 'How do we treat them?'" says Eric Greenberg of the AMA. Companies that couple education with testing find instances of drug use cut in half, he says.

Source: Ellen Neuborne, "More Top Firms Test Workers for Drugs," *USA Today*, June 21, 1990, p. B1.

formulated with the competitive and economic realities in mind. Pressure for increased productivity may be less important for business performance than flexibility in responding to employee needs and customer demands. Job sharing, compressed work weeks, and flexible work scheduling all help employees to meet family commitments while attaining high job performance.

Job sharing is when a couple share a single job. Business pays the couple a single salary and benefits package and the couple coordinate their work schedule to assure that the job is covered. A *compressed work week* is when the work week is shortened but longer hours are worked each day. For example, a 40-hour work week can be done with either five days of eight hours or with four days of ten hours work time. *Flexible scheduling* requires employees to work during a core period but allows them to begin work at different times. All employees under this approach might have to be at work between 10:00 A.M. and 2:00 P.M., but the work day may begin as early as 6:00 A.M. or as late as 10:00 A.M. The work group makes mutual adjustments to assure that the job gets done.

These flexible approaches to work scheduling allow workers to make adjustments if they need to attend a school function or a medical appointment with their child. Alternatively, employees are pressured into taking sick leave or vacation time, or arrive late to work if family responsibilities conflict with work. Flexibility allows the employee to balance work and family responsibilities. The result is reduced turnover and absenteeism, improved employee motivation, and higher productivity. Employees who do not need to worry about day care or baby sitting or meeting special family needs can be more focused on work performance. Managers who accommodate the needs of their diverse workforce can receive benefits in better economic performance.

The Johnson and Johnson Company found that helping families to resolve work-family conflicts led to improved performance. Employees who used flexible time and family leaves had a 50 percent smaller absenteeism rate than employees who did not benefit from such policies. Fifty-eight percent of employees indicated that these policies were a significant factor in their decision to remain with the company.

American Telephone and Telegraph found that providing unpaid leave for up to one year to new parents cost the company 32 percent of an annual salary compared with the 150 percent of an annual salary cost of replacing and retraining a new employee. Also, AT&T found that 60 percent of new parents returned to work within three months and 90 percent returned within six months after a child was born.

Public Policy and Work-Family Issues

As the stakeholder issue of work-family conflicts develops in the ILC, some 20 state governments have passed laws that require unpaid parental and medical leaves for employees. Also, the Family and Medical Leave Act became law in August 1993 and provides for unpaid parental leaves. Parental leave requirement was passed by the Clinton administration after being defeated in 1992 during the Bush administration. The Clean Air Act encourages flexible scheduling to reduce traffic density during peak commuting hours and also provides incentive for telecommuting. *Telecommuting* involves the use of telephone and computer technology that lets employees work at home rather than drive to work each day. However, high-performance companies do not need the pressure of government regulation to accommodate to work-family issues. Responsible companies with a type-two institutional orientation monitor workforce changes and initiate programs into their long-range planning process. Thus, work-family issues do not always proceed through the ILC by way of the public policy process. Many companies have discovered the benefits of flexibility through company-initiated programs without the need for public law to enforce flexible responses to work-family conflicts.

TRADITIONAL VS. FLEXIBLE MANAGERIAL ATTITUDES

Managers traditionally have felt that committed employees needed to sacrifice personal needs to achieve career success. Performance was measured in terms of time spent at the office and fairness required that all employees be treated the same. Accommodating unique needs of an employee requiring flexibility was considered unfair to other employees. These traditional attitudes have been challenged by the realities of work-family conflicts in an era of global competition.

Innovative managers responding to work-family challenges in competitive environments have different views concerning flexibility, performance, fairness, and sacrifice. Flexibility can be used as a competitive tool that motivates employees to perform better. Performance is measured according to value added rather than rule compliance and hours spent at the office. The economic goals of the business are often consistent with helping employees meet personal needs and family commitments. Fairness is based upon equitable treatment, which is not necessarily the uniform treatment of all employees. Cooperation and mutual adjustment in meeting the needs of the customer and balancing work-family needs is valued. Personal sacrifice to meet company expectations, rules, and policies may reflect an inflexible bureaucratic mentality rather than a true commitment to excellent performance.

DOWNSIZING AND OUTPLACEMENT PROGRAMS

Downsizing and Competitiveness

The U.S. economy has been undergoing major structural changes. To remain globally competitive, businesses have streamlined operations and cut labor costs.[14] Many are now expecting a sustained period of slow, low-inflationary expansion and global overcapacity that holds price levels down. Low-cost strategies are required and many companies are permanently downsizing their workforce and reducing the amount of capital investment needed to sustain output levels.[15] *Downsizing* is a business strategy designed to cut costs by reducing the size of business. Originally downsizing was part of a corporate turnaround or retrenchment strategy deployed when fierce competition evaporated profit margins. Currently downsizing is a major competitive weapon used by firms interested in increasing the economic value added through reduced labor costs.[16]

For example, Arvin Industries, an automotive component manufacturer, reduced its workforce by 10 percent though company profits are expected to increase at an annual rate of 20 percent through 1995. This means that downsizing is not a temporary response to economic recession; it has become a permanent strategy for many companies. Announced layoffs totaled 255,000 in the first half of 1993, and announcements by another 68 companies added nearly another 100,000 in July. Most of these jobs will never return as businesses learn to generate more productivity out of smaller-sized operations that have fewer employees and less invested capital.

Strategies to increase productivity during downsizing include consolidation and elimination of redundant administrative functions, process redesigns, and continuous improvement programs like total quality management (TQM).[17] The need to remain globally competitive provides persistent pressure on management to continuously improve productivity of technology, capital, and the workforce. Competitive pressures have affected both small business and the largest and most successful businesses in the United States. Traditionally successful and dominant companies like General Motors, IBM, and Sears have been characterized as dinosaurs that have lost their leadership positions.[18]

Corporate downsizing often translates into massive layoffs of employees. Thus job security has become a major employee stakeholder issue during the 1990s. To deal responsibly and humanely with this problem, management needs to carefully attend to the problems of those who remain within the company and those who must seek other opportunities. Many organizations have offered incentives for employees who accept early retirement. Another option is to assist employees in finding other employment opportunities through outplacement programs.

Downsizing has a serious effect on employees who survive. These remaining employees often suffer from low morale, they may distrust management, they become excessively cautious in hopes of saving their jobs in the future, and they often become less productive.[19] Security needs are among the most basic on Maslow's need hierarchy. Thus, a downsizing experience usually focuses an employee's efforts on gaining some sense of security in a very uncertain situation. Many will think, "If it happened to Frank, it could happen to me; it could happen again." Management needs to regain a sense of trust and reassure those who survive the downsizing if they are to remain productive, highly motivated employees.[20]

Management can take three actions to reassure and reestablish employees' feeling of security: (1)

provide information about company actions, (2) give the remaining employees personal attention, and (3) because managers of survivors are also survivors of a downsizing, they need also to attend to their own personal well-being.[21] When a person is well informed about why he or she was selected to remain and what can be expected in the future, feelings of security will increase. Aiding employees during the period of adjustment by providing emotional support and attending to employees' feelings can reestablish a feeling of inclusion in the organization.

A manager of downsizing survivors is also a survivor with many of the same needs as other employees. He or she often needs to discuss his or her feelings and experiences with a downsizing with the boss, with family members, and with other managers. Managers also need to restore a sense of security and to feel included in the organization. Commitments need to be renewed and a social equilibrium needs to be restored after the usual period of instability that follows a downsizing.

Management outplacement programs are designed to counsel and assist former employees to find other positions or to pursue other opportunities. There are a number of reasons why organizations should provide outplacement counseling:[22]

1. Outplacement programs free management to make decisions quickly when an individual is not working out within the organization.
2. Often it is not the employee's fault that he or she is not needed within the organization. In this case the organization may share some responsibility in the poor fit between the individual and the organization.
3. If business treats a terminated employee fairly and with compassion, the effect might be to increase the morale of those who remain employed by the organization.
4. Outplacement programs improve the positive corporate image of a business within the external community.
5. More than one-half of wrongful termination lawsuits are lost by employers. Outplacement programs reduce resentment of a termination and the likelihood of a subsequent lawsuit.

6. An outplacement program can often reduce the need for severance pay for terminated employees and thus save money.

Outplacement at Stroh's Brewery

An example of a successful outplacement program was a program implemented by Stroh's Brewery when a Detroit plant was closed in 1985. More than 1,000 jobs were eliminated including 60 management positions in this plant closure. Stroh's spent $1.5 million on a model outplacement program. It hired an outplacement firm to manage its outplacement program that included the following:

1. Employees were fully informed of the program in orientation sessions where they were provided an opportunity to ask questions.
2. Individuals were assessed for valuable skills. Psychological counseling was also provided.
3. Each individual was assisted in the development of a job-search strategy.
4. A computerized job bank was used to assist in the job-search process.
5. Each individual received job-search counseling. Such counseling is important for the maintenance of the self-esteem of individuals in the difficult relocation experience.
6. Job-search skills workshops were provided.
7. Counseling on planning for retirement, relocation, new business start-ups, and general financial planning was available.
8. Facilities were made available that included a research library, telephones, and secretarial assistance for job search process.
9. Extended severance benefits and health insurance was provided.

PLANT CLOSURES AND GLOBAL COMPETITIVENESS

Plant closure notification is an issue resolved by the Warn Act of 1989 requiring a notification of employees 60 days prior to a planned plant closure. If a business has over 100 full-time employees, management must give 60 days written notice of plant closure or mass layoff. *Plant* closure is defined as the permanent or temporary shutdown of one or more facilities or operating units within a single site. A *mass layoff* is when 500 or more employees lose their jobs or at least 33 percent of full-time employees lose their jobs. Besides supplying written notice of plant closure, managers should establish a fair way to reassign employees to other jobs whenever possible. Otherwise, a plant closure or mass layoff could lead to a spate of wrongful termination lawsuits.

The plant closure issue is, in reality, a part of the larger issue of the deindustrialization of America because of international competitiveness. Some 25 million jobs have been exported to other countries in the last 12 years, and most of these jobs have been middle-class factory positions. Since 1975 the U.S. economy has generated some 2 million new jobs per year and 800,000 new jobs were generated in the first half of 1993.[23] During this time underemployment, that is, employees working at below their normal level of skill and pay, was around 7 percent. In 1993, wages, adjusted for inflation, were at the lowest point since 1967.

In 1979, 12 percent of those employed were below the poverty level; now 18 percent of those working are below the poverty level. Many employees work part-time, though they want full-time employment. However, only 3.2 percent of college graduates are unemployed, while 11.4 percent of high school dropouts are unemployed. High-paying jobs with high-skill requirements are relatively more plentiful than low-paying, low-skill jobs in the United States. Thus the plant closure issue is part of the larger issue of economic restructuring brought about by technological change and global competition.

Occupational Health and Workplace Safety

Workplace safety relates to the occupational health and safety of employees who work with hazardous substances and/or dangerous machines. This issue is relatively mature overall and thus is considered as a stage-five issue in Figure 16–1. Laws govern-

ing workplace safety exist, a federal agency, the Occupational Safety and Health Administration (OSHA), was formed by a law passed in 1972; this agency has developed many regulations to administer this employee stakeholder issue.

The Life Cycle of an Employee Stakeholder Issue: Occupational Safety and Health

STAGE ONE: GROWING AWARENESS OF THE DANGERS IN THE WORKPLACE

The employment relationship and views of job safety prior to the twentieth century were guided by the traditional individualistic ideology of the market model discussed earlier in this book. According to this ideology, matters of employment were based upon free choice, knowledge, and individual responsibility. Free choice was reflected in the principle of employment at will, by which an employer could hire or dismiss an employee at any time with or without cause. Also, the employee could either accept or reject a job offered in the labor market. From the market model, it was assumed that both parties to the exchange of labor were fully knowledgeable of the available offers, of all aspects of the employment agreement including dangers, and that the individual accepting the job also accepted its risks.

Before the twentieth century, dangerous working conditions went largely unnoticed. Mercury was used in the processing of gold and in the tanning of beaver skins. Workers in mines, textile mills, and grinding operations suffered from respiratory illnesses but these maladies were considered a "natural" part of such occupations. Injuries were rarely systematically studied with the idea of making the workplace safer. It was very difficult for an employee to recover damages for a work-related injury or illness.

The traditional ideology of the perfect competition model was also reflected in the law concerning occupational safety and health. Courts were ineffective in providing an incentive to employers to increase the safety in the workplace, nor were the courts inclined to award damage settlements to employees. Labor was considered as a factor in the production process to be purchased on the open market. And the supply of labor was abundant because of the large numbers of immigrants who were often unskilled, illiterate, and needing employment. Those seeking employment were often at the mercy of large business organizations that seemed to be unaware of employee concerns about working conditions, workplace safety, job security, and compensation.

Increased industrialization brought steel mills, the railroad, and modern factories with machine-paced belts, blades, wheels, grinding equipment, and explosives and other hazardous chemicals. Complex technologies were often beyond the control of operators, and as work-related accidents increased, the problems of industrialized society became more visible. Many jobs were dangerous and accident rates were steadily increasing. Workers seemed to be expendable; businesses often seemed to be insensitive to occupational health and safety; and the government, through the court system, seemed ineffective in this area.

As the number of work-related injuries increased, many states implemented workers' compensation laws that entitled workers to some compensation for injuries regardless of who was responsible for causing the accident. However, employers' expenses for insurance coverage increased as the number of work-related accidents increased. Thus, for the first time, there was a clear economic incentive for the employer to make jobs safer.

Stage Two: Defining the Problem of Occupational Safety and Health

Workers' compensation laws enacted at the state level brought the insurance industry into the accident-prevention field. As these companies systematically began to study accidents in the workplace, a clearer understanding of the problem of occupational health began to emerge. As the awareness of

the need for a safer workplace became greater, the limitations of the state workers' compensation laws also become better known.

The system of state workers' compensation laws had numerous defects or limitations: (1) limited coverage of workers that often excluded certain types of claims, (2) set time limits for filing a claim that eliminated claims for occupational diseases that had time lags (as in the case of cancer-producing asbestos), (3) inadequate levels of compensation for injuries or work-related illnesses, and (4) inadequately funded state programs.

Also, most state governments did not have an effective system for establishing and updating safety standards or for monitoring safety through field inspections, nor were results of field inspections made available to employees. These problems were made public in a report by a temporary National Commission of State Workers' Compensation Laws in 1972.[24] State workers' compensation laws in only 22 of the 50 states met the federal government's Department of Labor criteria by the late 1960s. By then some 100,000 deaths per year in the United States were attributed to work-related accidents related to occupational diseases and illnesses from exposures to chemical and physical hazards.[25]

Stage Three: Organizing Around the Issue and Trigger Events

Stage three of the ILC is characterized by organizations that form around a public policy issue to get it on the public agenda. The insurance industry was instrumental in making business aware of the possibility and the importance of systematically improving workplace safety to reduce insurance costs. Also, the union movement was very active in pressing business and lawmakers for a safer workplace. The increased consciousness was particularly mobilized by a tragic event that triggered public action. In 1968, a coal mine explosion in Farmington, West Virginia, killed 78 miners. At about that same time, reports and governmental hearings concerning black lung disease also suffered by coal miners brought the plight of the miners to the front pages of newspapers and on to the top of the national public agenda.

STAGE FOUR: PUBLIC DEBATE AND LEGISLATION

The activities of labor unions, increasing awareness of the seriousness and magnitude of the problem of occupational safety and health, and the trigger events of accidents all served to focus attention on this employee stakeholder issue. The Federal Coal Mine Health and Safety Act became law in 1969, followed by the Occupational Safety and Health Act, which was signed into law by President Nixon on December 29, 1970, and took effect on April 28, 1971. The objectives of these laws were to make the workplace safe and healthy for workers and to preserve the human resources of the nation.

STAGE FIVE: ADMINISTRATION OF PUBLIC POLICY BY OSHA

Initially, OSHA covered some 57 million workers employed by about 4 million businesses engaged in interstate commerce. OSHA is administered by the Occupational Safety and Health Administration, which has over 2,000 employees and a budget of a quarter of a billion dollars to enforce the law. The Occupational Safety and Health Administration seeks to achieve the objectives of the law by (1) establishing regulatory standards (some were temporary that were to last six months while permanent standards were developed); (2) visiting workplaces to insure compliance with standards and to provide advice concerning occupational health and safety in the workplace; (3) requiring organizations of ten or more employees engaged in interstate commerce to keep records and to report to OSHA on (a) job-related injuries and accidents, (b) job hazards, (c) research on occupational safety and health, and (d) OSHA enforcement.

OSHA's First Twenty Years of Enforcement

The Occupational Safety and Health Administration has been one of the most controversial federal

agencies regulating business. During the 1970s the EEOC began the enormous task of establishing the agency, setting safety standards (temporary, interim, and permanent), and beginning field inspections for standards enforcement. The emphasis was initially on establishing safety standards, followed by field visits to assure compliance.

Business complained bitterly. Many of the standards were design-oriented and did not seek to get at the cause of workplace injuries. Thus OSHA field inspectors often knew little about safety and did not focus on the design of a safe workplace when they inspected. Rather, they searched for violations of the standards that may or may not be related to the real safety problems facing a particular business. Business thus viewed OSHA as impractical, insensitive to the real issues of safety, inflexible, and perhaps arrogant.

Because OSHA could inspect at random without a search warrant and assess fines and jail sentences for infractions, it was viewed as a major threat by business. In its first year, OSHA made 32,700 inspections and issued 23,000 citations charging nearly 103,000 violations involving $2.3 million.[26] In fact, most of the fines levied by OSHA were quite small, averaging around $16 per offense, and jail sentences were uncommon. Nevertheless, the perceived threat of inspections and fines by OSHA were a major concern of business, and opposition to this regulatory activity mounted.

Also, the paperwork burdens of OSHA reporting were considered unreasonable. Late in 1979 OSHA agreed to exempt small businesses (with fewer than ten employees) and businesses with good safety records from OSHA field inspections unless an inspection was initiated by an employee complaint. This exemption affected some 1.5 million businesses and 5 million employees.[27] The Supreme Court also ruled that business could prohibit field inspections attempted without a search warrant.[28]

In another case, the Supreme Court ruled that OSHA should not base a standard on an economic cost-benefit analysis. Thus, a feasible OSHA standard was legally defined by the court as one that substantially reduces the risk to workers but does not damage the industry, even though the standard may not be justified in terms of cost-benefit analysis. In effect, the Court said that congressional intent was to consider the legal right to a safe workplace as more important than the outcome of utilitarian analysis.[29]

The year 1980 brought in the Reagan administration, which promised "to get the government off the backs of business." During the early 1980s, inspections were limited to larger firms with poor safety records. Inspections in response to complaints were limited to the immediate area of the complaining worker rather than the entire facility.[30] Some firms were allowed have a labor-management safety committee do their routine safety inspections if the business had good safety records.[31]

Also during the 1980s, OSHA began to shift its emphasis from inspections for standards violations followed by citations and penalties to assuming more of an advisory role in accident prevention. In consultation with businesses, OSHA sought to improve safety by analysis of cause-effect relationships to eliminate safety problems rather than inflexibly searching for technical rule violations.

STAGE SIX: LITIGATION OF OCCUPATIONAL HEALTH AND SAFETY

In stage six of the occupational safety and health issue, OSHA issued citations and assesd fines without the use of a court order or it litigates in administrative law courts. These courts are part of the government agency and thus part of the executive branch of government but are the place where most of the litigation occurs in business-government-society disputes. The Supreme Court ruled that OSHA and its administrative courts could determine facts and impose fines without a jury.[32]

Several other cases involving OSHA have found their way to the Supreme Court, which has found the following: (1) Workers have the right to refuse work that they consider too dangerous, without fear of retaliation by their employer. (2) Workers have the right to know of toxic or hazardous substances in the workplace. (3) Workers

(or their designated representatives) have a right to the health and safety records of employers.

In general, litigation should be considered as a last resort for management because it is very expensive and time-consuming, and comes with all the negative aspects of adversary relationships. Issues that end in litigation are often those that were mismanaged in earlier phases of the ILC. Mismanagement of an issue can take a variety of forms: (1) an issue can be ignored while the problem increases in severity; (2) an issue can be "politically" handled by influencing legislation or the administration of the law's enforcement while failing to respond to the underlying cause of the problem; or (3) an issue can be blocked in the courts or regulations can sometimes be delayed.

In all these cases of mishandling a public issue, the basic problem is likely to increase, and thus the intensity of public interest is likely to follow, leading to the decline in a firm's political support.

Summary

This chapter begins by juxtaposing to images of the workplace an image of worker dissatisfaction and alienation found in an important 1973 report followed by an image of self-managing, high-performance teams used by high-performance companies of the 1990s. A theme of this chapter is that satisfying employee concerns in the workplace is not only the key to motivation but to performance.

Employee stakeholder issues might be better understood if viewed in the context of employee motivational needs. Major environmental trends including technological change, global competitiveness, changes in the demographic characteristics of the workforce, and corporate restructuring create newly unfolding employee issues. These issues are at differing stages of the ILC. Early ILC-stage issues include new workplace diseases caused by technological change and employee empowerment. Employee rights, work-family issues, downsizing, and plant closures are issues of intense interest at the present time. Occupational safety and health is perhaps the most mature issue because it is a broad issue with extensive regulations enforced by the Occupational Safety and Health Administration (OSHA).

Employee stakeholder issues follow the pattern of the ILC, a six-stage process including (1) increasing public awareness of social and technological changes, (2) defining concerns in terms of a public policy problem, (3) forming organizations or interest groups around problem areas, (4) public debate and legislation, (5) formation of an agency for the enforcement of laws, and (6) litigation to resolve remaining conflicts concerning an issue. Employee stakeholder issues often result in the proactive action by management that can make legislation and agency regulation unnecessary.

Organized pressure by unions and by the insurance industry together with the trigger events of a major industrial accident in the 1960s increased public attention sufficiently to result in the passage of the Occupational Safety and Health Act in the early 1970s. OSHA resulted in the formation of the Occupational Safety and Health Administration as a major enforcement agency. This agency began with establishing standards, performing field inspections, and issuing citations, fines, and jail sentences to offending businesses. It has had a controversial 20-year history and since 1980 has been doing fewer inspections, emphasizing consultation and improving the design of a safe workplace.

Conclusions

International competitiveness depends upon the empowerment and effective use of human resources. Thus employee stakeholder issues are of utmost importance to management. Businesses that attend to employee needs by effectively responding to emerging issues enjoy increased employee motivation and higher levels of performance. Also, such responses are likely to maintain high levels of legitimacy and prevent increased government regulation and litigation by employees and former employees who feel unfairly treated by business.

Discussion Questions

1. How are motivational needs related to employee stakeholder issues?
2. What are the major trends that give rise to employee stakeholder issues?
3. What are the major employee stakeholder issues? Which ones will need the most management attention in the 1990s? Explain.
4. What is the issue life cycle (ILC), and how does this concept relate to employee stakeholder issues?
5. What can management do to avoid the ILC of an issue developing through the public policy process? Provide a specific example.
6. Do you think companies should randomly test for drugs? What criteria should be used to determine whether this is appropriate? If a company decides to implement such a program, should everyone have an equal chance to be tested?
7. Why is the conflict between family and work growing in importance? How can managers manage this issue effectively?
8. Explain why flexible managers are likely to be more effective with current employee issues than traditional managers?
9. Why should a business consider an outplacement program when downsizing its operations?
10. What is the ethics of workplace safety? Can an employee accept a hazardous job? Under what conditions? Who is responsible?

Notes

1. *Work in America: Report of a Special Task Force to the Secretary of Health, Education, and Welfare* (Cambridge, Mass.: MIT Press, 1973), pp. xv–xvi.
2. Brian Dumaine, "Who Needs a Boss?" *Fortune*, May 7, 1990, pp. 52–60. Reprinted with permission.

Also see the article by Charles G. Burck, "What Happens When Workers Manage Themselves," *Fortune*, July 27, 1980, pp. 62–69.

3. William Wagel, "On the horizon: HR in the 1990s," *Personnel* 67, no. 1 (1990): 10–16

4. T. Rendero, "HR Panel Takes a Look Ahead," *Personnel* 67, no. 8 (1990): 14–24.

5. Thomas G. Gutteridge, "The HRPD Profession: A Vision of Tomorrow," *Human Resource Planning* 11. no. 2 (1988): 109–24.

6. For more information see Kenneth W. Thomas and Betty A. Velthouse, "Cognitive Elements of Empowerment, *Academy of Management Review* (October 1990): 666–81.

7. See Kaoru Ishihawa, *What is Total Quality Control? The Japanese Way* (Englewood Cliffs, N.J.: Prentice-Hall, 1985), and Marshall Sashkin and Kenneth J. Kiser, *Putting Total Quality Management to Work* San Francisco: Berrett-Koehler, 1993).

8. Diana T. Meyers, "Work and Self-Respect," in *Moral Rights in the Workplace*, ed. Gertrude Ezorsky (Albany: State University of New York Press, 1987), pp. 18–27.

9. Thomas Peters and Robert Waterman, *In Search of Excellence* (New York: Houghton-Mifflin, 1983); and Tom Peters, *Thriving on Chaos: Handbook for a Management Revolution* (New York: Harper and Row, 1987).

10. See Mary P. Rowe, Malcolm Rullell-Einhorn, and Michael A. Baker, "The Fear of AIDS," *Harvard Business Review* (July-August 1986): 28–36; and *AIDS: Employer Rights and Responsibilities*. (Chicago: Commerce Clearing House, 1985).

11. Mordechai Mironi, "The Confidentiality of Personnel Records: A Legal and Ethical View," *Labor Law Journal* (May 1974): 270–92.

12. "Privacy," *Business Week*, March 28, 1988, pp. 61–68.

13. Michele Galen, Ann Therese Palmer, Alice Cuneo, and Mark Maremont, "Work and Family," *Business Week*, June 28, 1993, pp. 80–88.

14. Louis S. Richman, "When Will the Layoffs End?" *Fortune*, September 20, 1993, pp. 54–56.

15. Shawn Tully, "The Real Key to Creating Wealth," *Fortune*, September 20, 1993, pp. 38–50.

16. See American Management Association, *Responsible Reductions in Force: An AMA Research Report on Downsizing and Outplacement* (New York: AMACOM, 1987); and Robert M. Tomasko, *Downsizing, Reshaping the Corporation for the Future* (New York: AMACOM, 1987).

17. Max Messmer, "Rightsizing, Not Downsizing," *Industry Week* 241, no. 15 (August 3, 1992): 23–26.

18. Carol J. Loomis, "Dinosaurs?" *Fortune*, May 3, 1993, pp. 36–42.

19. Dan Rice and Craig Dreilinger, "After the Downsizing," *Training and Development Journal* (May 1991): 41–44.

20. Conchita Daste, "Surviving Corporate Downsizing," *Human Resources Professional* 4, no. 2 (Winter 1992): 29–32.

21. Rice and Dreilinger, "After the Downsizing," p. 42.

22. Robert E. Karp and Nell M. Weaver, "Ethical Values Underlying the Termination Process," *Business and Society* (Spring 1991): 1–6.

23. Robert B. Reich, Secretary of Labor, "Workers of the World, Get Smart," *New York Times*, July 20, 1993, p. A19.

24. Albert L. Nichols and Richard Zeckhauser, "Government Comes to the Workplace: An Assessment of OSHA," *The Public Interest*, no. 49 (Fall 1977): 40–42.

25. *The Presidents Report on Occupational Safety and Health* (Washington, D.C.: Government Printing Office, 1972).

26. Dan Cordtz, "Safety on the Job Becomes a Major Job for Management," *Fortune*, November 1972.

27. "U.S. Agency Ends Job-Safety Paper Work of Small Firms," *Wall Street Journal*, July 20, 1977, p. 8.

28. *Marshall v. Barlow's Inc.*, 46 L. W. 4483 (1978).

29. *Marshall v. American Petroleum Institute*, 581 F.2d 493 (Fifth Circuit 1978).

30. "Business Gets a Safety Break from OSHA, *U.S. News and World Report*, October 5, 1981, p. 87.

31. Joann S. Lubin, "OSHA Weighs Allowing Some Concerns to Take Over Routine Safety Inspections," *Wall Street Journal*, January 18, 1982, p. 3.

32. "Justices Uphold Right of Job Safety Unit to Set Penalties without Going to Court," *Wall Street Journal*, July 6, 1982, p. 1.

Discussion Case 16–1 _____

The Don Gray Case

Doyle's of America is a New England restaurant chain. Don Gray had worked for Doyle's of America for ten years as an area supervisor in charge of 28 restaurants and about 500 employees. He was in line for a vice-president position within Doyle's and felt a strong loyalty to the company.

One of his employees was a company director's son who was also the godson of the president. Don Gray had refused to promote this person despite repeated requests because he considered the director's son to be incompetent. Several weeks after the requests for promotion, Gray's boss told him that someone had reported seeing him take drugs

at a party. His boss gave him two alternatives: take a polygraph test to clear his name or be fired.

Gray was very angry about being requested to take the test. He felt good about his record with the company and he had always been very loyal to the company. Also, he was hurt because his boss would not take his word that he did not use drugs. However, his boss insisted that he undergo the polygraph test and so Don Gray took the test.

Doyle's management said that the polygraph test proved that Don Gray had lied and they fired him. Doyle, a 32 year old father immediately went from his $50,000 a year job to being unemployed for the next three years. Gray said "People in the company avoided me like the plague when they spread that around, and I think I'll always carry the stigma."

Source: The names in this case have been disguised because it is based on an actual case.

Discussion Case 16–2 _____

Break Up with that Guy—or Else

Virginia Rulon-Miller had worked for the International Business Machines Corporation for the last 12 years. In her last year she won an award as a top marketing manager in the division office in San Francisco and was awarded a thirteen percent raise.

She had been dating Matt Blum, an account manager who, played with her on the IBM softball team. Matt then resigned at IBM to accept a position with a competitor. He continued to see Virginia and they continued to play softball on the IBM team. They also had a dating relationship.

IBM had a policy against higher level managers having relationships with employees of competing firms. Thus, Virginia Rulon-Miller's boss called her into his office and explained that she would have to break off her relationship with Matt Blum or accept a demotion from the company. She hesi-

tated but later that evening decided to break up with Matt because she was very committed to IBM. Before she could break off her relationship with Matt, she was fired the next day.

Virginia sued IBM for wrongful discharge. In her defense, her attorney quoted the policy of former IBM Chairman Thomas J. Watson, Jr., "we have concern with an employee's off-the-job behavior only when it reduces his ability to perform regular job assignments."

In 1984, Rulon-Miller won $300,000 in back pay and punitive damages. In explaining the emotional difficulties associated with the trial, she said "I couldn't function for four or five months." She eventually broke off her relationship with Matt Blum and accepted a position as regional director for a computer sales business. She continued to feel strong sentiments for IBM. "There was a real sense of security and a feeling of family. If I had my way, I'd still be there," she said after the ordeal.

Source: From Business Week, March 28, 1988, p. 64. (C) 1988 by Mc Graw-Hill, Inc. Reprinted by special permisiion.

CHAPTER 17

Employee Stakeholders: Equality and Discrimination

CHAPTER OBJECTIVES

1. Show how the problem of employment discrimination creates injustice within society.

2. Illustrate how discrimination includes many issues that are at different stages of the issue life cycle.

3. Differentiate between equality of opportunity and equality of results as standards for justice in employment practice and in the law.

4. Review the major laws that regulate employment practices related to discrimination.

5. Outline court precedents that define discrimination law.

6. Discuss the management of current workforce developments as they relate to discrimination in employment.

Discrimination and the Issue Life Cycle

Employee stakeholder issues have followed the pattern of the issue life cycle (ILC), which was introduced in Chapter 3. Some of the issues are relatively mature and have a well-developed legal context; others are early-stage issues only now being recognized, with the specific problem formulation still undefined, and still awaiting the public policy formation process. Figure 17–1 indicates the stage of the ILC where equality and discrimination issues are likely to be found.

The civil rights movement of the 1950s and 1960s led to the Civil Rights Act of 1964. Over the last three decades, the broadly defined issue of equality

and discrimination has passed through all the stages of the ILC. Some subissues like the issue of family-work conflict has moved into general awareness during the last few years.[1] Demographic changes in the workforce include greater diversity with more women and minorities, two income families that need day care for their children, and the need for family leave policies in the problem definition stage.

The issue of employee leave has proceeded through an awareness of discrimination against pregnant women leading to a Pregnancy Leave Act of 1978. Then it became generally recognized that with two-income families, fathers also needed the right to take leaves to care for children. After much debate and a veto by President Bush in 1992, the Parental Leave Act was passed in 1993 during the Clinton administration. This law requires employers

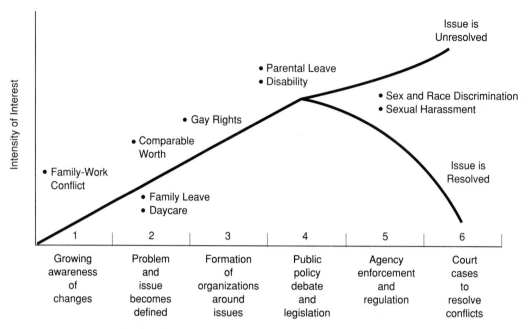

FIGURE 17–1 The Issue Life Cycle and Employee Issues Related to Equal Opportunity

to offer unpaid leaves to parents who need to be away from work to care for newborn children.

Certain subissues of employment discrimination have been recycled through the ILC a number of times as the themes of pregnancy and parental and family leaves demonstrate. The issue of leave is likely to be recycled one more time as our aging population requires more wage earners to care for their parents. We can expect the issue over leave to be redefined from parental leave to a more general family leave right as parents of the baby boomers grow old and need the care of their children who will be in midcareer.

Not all issues trigger the public policy process. Often the general awareness of a social issue is embraced by managers who develop private-sector solutions to problems. For example, many companies developed policies for pregnancy and parental leaves and for day care so that family-work conflicts could be resolved without new legislation. Many families in today's workforce have two incomes and both salaries are needed to maintain their standard of living. Some businesses recognize that employees

perform better if they do not have to worry about day care or the welfare of their parents.[2]

Ethics of Equality and Discrimination

Discrimination occurs when employment decisions are made on the basis of such nonjob-related criteria as sex, race, color, country of national origin, or religion rather than on the basis of individual merit. The result of these decisions is to unfairly affect these groups adversely.[3] Discrimination is the opposite of equal employment opportunity and leads to unequal and unfair results for those groups being discriminated against. Discrimination is morally wrong and unjust for a number of reasons outlined below.

Discrimination Violates the Categorical Imperative

According to Kant's categorical imperative, an act is moral if it (1) can be applied universally, (2) considers persons as ends and never as means only, and (3) supports or encourages autonomy and freedom of the individual. Discrimination, by definition, treats individuals in some classes differently from others in ways that are arbitrary and thus victimizes one group for the benefit of another. Because employment is central to obtaining income and thus enjoying the benefits of society in a market-oriented economy, economic discrimination has very bad and far-reaching results. This serves to make one group or class of persons a means of accomplishing another group's goals while being very destructive to the families and individual welfare of the minority group. Also, it institutionalizes an underclass that can never act with autonomy as human beings. Thus, from the perspective of the categorical imperative, discrimination is profoundly immoral.

Discrimination Violates the Utilitarian Criterion

Because efficiency and high performance require the most productive use of resources, it is important that employment decisions be made on the basis of merit. A utilitarian analysis of discrimination would measure the practice based upon the total happiness of society. Translated into economic terms, the social arrangement that maximizes the productivity and material welfare of society would be ethical. If people of a certain sex, religion, or race are excluded regardless of their capability, then all of society suffers in terms of economic prosperity and justice. Furthermore, the misery of unemployment, long-term dependency that discrimination causes, and crime brought about by people who have no other option makes discrimination indefensible by utilitarian standards.

Discrimination Violates Competitive Market Conditions

Market systems require competition if they are to result in justice based upon relative merit. If there are arbitrary barriers to entry, as is the case with discrimination, then the economic results of market activity are likely to be uncompetitive. Capable employees that are denied jobs because of their race, gender, ethnic group, or nationality are denied their opportunity to compete. Managers who discriminate according to factors other than merit are imprudent from an economic point of view. Thus discrimination violates the conditions of prudence, equal access to markets, and mobility of capital and factors of productivity. This in turn subverts the forces of supply and demand for skilled employees and thus neither prices nor returns to factors of production are based upon competitive market forces.

Discrimination Violates Principles of Justice

Discrimination violates the justice of a market system because it does not allow potential employees equal access to the market and distorts the criterion of relative merit. Discrimination also violates both principles of justice proposed by Rawls. First, a just society requires that everyone have equal liberty. Second, inequalities are justified if they improve the lot of the disadvantaged within society. Minority groups who suffer from discrimination are socially marginalized with unemployment, poverty, and lack of medical care. But even here, justice is contingent upon equal access to the positions of society by all people. Minorities are often the least advantaged with society, and discrimination works to their disadvantage rather than to their advantage as the difference principle of justice requires. Also, since discrimination is illegal; it violates libertarian concepts of justice.

Justice and Equality Without Discrimination

Discrimination is immoral and unjust because it violates the three conditions of the categorical imperative; it is indefensible through utilitarian analysis; and it deprives people of the opportunity to participate and leads to unfair results. Also, discrimination violates all the major theories of economic justice. Justice requires equality in the following ways:

1. *equal access* to career or job opportunities for all prospective employees
2. *equal pay for equal work* in the distribution of rewards

3. *equal opportunity to a positive work experience* without arbitrary pressure or harassment while doing meaningful work.

The Ideology of Equality and the Reality of Discrimination

In the Declaration of Independence, the Founding Fathers held the ideal "that all men are created equal" as a self-evident truth. Also, the individualistic traditional ideology of the nineteenth century assumed freedom and equality of opportunity as a basic tenet. However, reality has always fallen short of this ideal of democracy and the ideology of a free market. Moves in the direction of achieving our ideals of "all men are created equal" have been slow and often painful.

In the U.S. Constitution, slaves were to count as "three-fifths" of a free man for the purposes of determining representation in Congress. Slavery existed for over 200 years in America prior to its termination in 1861 by the signing of the Emancipation Proclamation by President Lincoln. Women achieved the right to vote by an amendment to the Constitution in 1920 after being introduced 47 consecutive times before it won approval.

The reality of discrimination is inconsistent with the ideals of equality of opportunity and justice articulated by the Founding Fathers. It also violates the ideals and necessary conditions for a competitive market. The ideology of the market economy includes (1) freedom to choose a profession, (2) everyone has an equal opportunity to compete for a job based upon individual merit, and (3) individuals are held responsible for their performance, which, in turn, determines rewards. These principles are not compatible with the reality of discrimination. The injustice of discrimination in spite of the ideology of freedom and competition has made the concepts of equality and discrimination a controversial public issue.

GROWING AWARENESS OF DISCRIMINATION

During the 1950s and 1960s there were bitter civil rights demonstrations across the country, leading to a series of civil rights legislation. The Birmingham bus boycott in 1955 protested a local law that required blacks to sit at the back of the bus. This protest was sparked by the arrest and jailing of a black woman named Rosa Parks, who refused to sit in the rear of a bus.

Beginning with the bus boycott in 1955, the Reverend Martin Luther King, Jr., became a prominent civil rights leader who organized many marches, boycotts, and demonstrations that increased awareness of the suffering and hardships long suffered by blacks because of discrimination in employment, in public accommodations, and education. The Supreme Court in *Brown v. Board of Education,* held in 1954 that "separate but equal" facilities were, in fact, unequal, and that the separate school systems for blacks and whites had to be integrated. Blacks had been deprived of the use of public facilities in transportation, education, restaurants, hotels, and other facilities serving the public.

Moreover, the incomes of members of minority groups were significantly lower than those for white males, and the unemployment rate for blacks remained double the rate for white males. These striking inequalities were related to being a member of a minority group rather than correlated to individual merit.

In the 1960s, the women's movement brought attention to discrimination against women. Women had increasingly entered the labor force since the days of "Rosie the Riveter" during World War II. Increasing numbers of single-parent families and a decline in per capita income since 1972 that required more families to have two incomes to maintain living standards brought increased attention to discrimination against women.

During the 1960s and 1970s, the Vietnam War was a source of much controversy in the country. Many were wounded in that war and returned home handicapped. This brought widespread awareness of the plight of the handicapped in access to public accommodations and to employment opportunities. The Vocational Rehabilitation Act of 1972 required employers with contracts over $2,500 to make reasonable accommodations for the handicapped and those with over $50,000 in contracts to use an affirmative action program to employ the handicapped. In 1974, the Vietnam Era Veterans Readjustment Assistant Act required federal contractors to employ disabled veterans. More recently, the Americans with Disabilities Act of 1990 made it illegal to discriminate against persons with disabilities.

Types of Discrimination

DISCRIMINATION IN ACCESS AND PAY

Discrimination in access to jobs, promotions, and pay are defined as follows:

1. Pay discrimination exists when *unequal pay,* usually lower, is given to a minority member or a woman for the same job done by the majority (usually white male) employee.
2. Access discrimination exists when *access is denied to minority members* or women to jobs that are available to majority members. For example, black employees have had great difficulty obtaining access to management positions, which tend to have a high proportion of white males.[4]
3. Access discrimination exists when *access is denied to persons on the basis of age, handicap, or sex.*
4. *Sexual discrimination* includes situations where (1) sexual favors are demanded in exchange for promotions or salary increases, or (2) a hostile work environment is created by sexual misconduct.
5. Some argue that another form of discrimination results when *jobs are institutionalized on the basis of gender* so that most of the people in a particular job are of the same gender.

SEXUAL HARASSMENT

Sexual harassment is an unwelcome sexual advance or request for sexual favors or verbal or physical conduct or written communication of a sexual nature. Submission to or rejection of such conduct or communication affects a person's employment status or interferes with work by creating an intimidating, hostile, or offensive environment.[5] Sexual harassment may or may not have adverse economic consequences for the victim.

Sexual harassment is an important employee stakeholder issue because it can affect the quality of work life, the sense of dignity and self respect of the individual, and may have unjust economic consequences. Victims of this type of discrimination are usually women, but they can be of either sex. Often insensitivity, macho role models, and organizational culture reinforce behavior patterns that encourage sexual harassment.

In recent years, there have been twice as many lawsuits concerning sexual harassment than any other type of discrimination. The average cost of such a lawsuit exceeds $60,000 for the business involved. It is important for a business to have a written policy explaining and prohibiting sexual harassment. Also, some type of grievance system should be implemented that allows the victim to complain to someone other than the person engaging in the harassment. Because both the meaning and the seriousness of sexual harassment are frequently misunderstood, companies should also provide training and counseling for both the victim and the person accused of harassment.

GENDER-DOMINATED OCCUPATIONS

Statistics suggest that those who work in some job categories such as office workers and nurses are primarily women. Other occupations like physicians and construction workers are primarily men. Occupations dominated by women tend to be paid less than those filled primarily by men, as suggested in Table 17–1. This raises a number of questions. Does society value work done by men more than work done by women? Are wage levels set by market forces of supply and demand? Are unique skills or backgrounds valued by the market as reflected by wage levels found in various occupa-

TABLE 17–1
Percent Female Workers and Average Hourly Pay for Selected Occupations

Occupation	Number of New Jobs in 1979–86	Percent Female	Average Pay/Hour
Registered Nurse	612,000	93	$11.79
U.S. Average Male Wage			**11.24**
U.S. Average Wage			**9.60**
Truck Driver	525,000	3	8.72
Office Clerk	462,000	80	8.11
U.S. Average Female Wage			**7.80**
Janitor/Maid	604,000	28	6.76
Nursing Aide	433,000	88	6.05
Cashier	575,000	80	5.37
Waiter/Waitress	725,000	79	5.05
Retail Sales	1,200,000	69	4.82
Food-Counter Worker	449,000	79	3.80

SOURCE: *Business Week*, February 29, 1988, p. 48. Copyright 1988 by McGraw-Hill. Reprinted by special permission.

tions? Are cultural or social forces at work that discourage women from entering certain occupations? Are the differences in wage levels explainable by (1) the economic forces of the marketplace, (2) cultural values, (3) discrimination that does not allow women to enter the more rewarding careers? Gender-dominated occupations as a form of discrimination have resulted in the issue of *comparable worth* that considers the worth of women-dominated occupations compared with similar occupations that have few women. Proponents of comparable worth suggest that the economic value of a job should be determined according to job measurement using behavioral science job techniques rather than wage levels based upon the labor market. Thus, the value placed on a job should be based on the experience and education required for the position, the motor or cognitive skills required, or the content of the tasks that make up a particular job when compared with other similar jobs.

Opponents of comparable worth say that the labor market and supply-and-demand relationships more accurately determine the worth of a job or occupation. Thus, if some jobs or occupations are institutionalized as female, opponents of comparable worth argue that the solution is not comparable worth wage surveys but the problem should be solved by (1) providing education and role models for women to make them aware of better-paying jobs, and (2) eliminating any discrimination in access to better occupations for women. Institutionalized occupations by sex with a comparable worth remedy have never been recognized in court as part of the common law of discrimination. Rather, such cases are tried as a violation of the Equal Pay Act of 1963, which requires that employers pay equal pay for equal work.

EQUALITY OF OPPORTUNITY VS. EQUALITY OF RESULTS

Equality of opportunity means that everyone has equal access to the job market and an equal chance to compete on the basis of merit for a particular position. This concept has been widely accepted as part of the prevailing ideology in the United States. It is very difficult to insure that members of minority groups really have an equal opportunity. Skills, experience, and education all can add to the capability needed to successfully take advantage of opportunities. Discrimination in education and training, and the lower self-esteem that results from general social discrimination, has complex and long-term effects. Changes in education, access to entry-level positions, apprenticeship programs, and career experience all take time before the historical effects of long-term discrimination can be overcome.

Equality of results exists when the income levels received by majority and minority groups are not significantly different and when representation in occupations is proportional across groups. *Inequality of results* exists when there is a statistically significant difference within society across groups, and within an organization when there is a significant difference between the characteristics of the labor market and a employee profile of the business. On the macro level of society there are significant differences in income levels and employment between groups. For example, for the last 20 years, the unemployment level for African Americans has been consistently double the unemployment rate for whites.

Valesquez has documented the average incomes of white males, white females, and various minority groups over the period 1970 to 1983 and has found that the gap between the incomes of white and African American families has widened in recent years.[6] The average family income for African American families as a percent of average white family income has fluctuated from 65 percent to 60 percent over the years. However, since 1980, these families have been losing approximately one percentage point per year when compared with the average income earned by white families. Similarly, the average family income received by Hispanic families has dropped approximately one percentage point per year when compared with white families since 1980. The average Hispanic family received 68 percent and the average black family received 61 percent of the average white family income of $29,875 in the year 1983.

When occupations are considered singly, white males within virtually every occupation receive significantly higher wages than women or minorities. The gap between the income of men and women has decreased over the last decade, with women earning approximately 70 percent of what men earn by 1987.[7] However, occupations dominated by women tend to receive less average pay than male-dominated occupations, as shown in Table 17–1. Of the women-dominated occupations listed, only registered nurses earned more than the average wage for men. All other female-dominated occupations in which there has been substantial job creation during the last decade earned below-average wages.

Major Laws Prohibiting Discrimination in Employment

The major laws covering discrimination in the workplace include (1) the Equal Pay Act of 1963; (2) the Civil Rights Act of 1964, as amended by the Equal Employment Opportunities Act of 1972 and the Pregnancy Discrimination Act of 1978; (3) the Vocational Rehabilitation Act of 1973; (4) the Age Discrimination Act of 1973; (5) the Americans with Disabilities Act of 1990; and (6) the Civil Rights Act of 1991. Table 17–2 briefly describes each of these laws.

THE CIVIL RIGHTS ACT OF 1964

This act prohibited employers from basing employment decisions on race, color, religion, sex, or national origin. However, the Supreme Court has allowed employers to consider these factors in certain limited circumstances when the employer is taking affirmative action to benefit traditionally disadvantaged groups.[8] Title VII of the Civil Rights Act of 1964 states that it is an

unlawful employment practice for an employer to discriminate against any individual with respect to his compensation, terms, conditions, or privileges of

TABLE 17–2
Laws Prohibiting Discrimination

Federal Law	Type of Discrimination Prohibited
Equal Pay Act of 1963	Prohibits employers from paying one sex a lower wage for equal work. Exceptions permitted based upon seniority, merit, production, or other than sex-based differential.
Civil Rights Act of 1964, Title VII	Discrimination in employment based on sex, race, color, religion, or national origin is prohibited.
Later amended by: • Equal Employment Opportunity Act of 1972	Permits the EEOC to bring enforcement actions in the federal courts. Federal, state, and local governments as well as colleges are brought under Title VII.
• Pregnancy Discrimination Act of 1978	Prohibits an employer from discharging or refusing to hire or promote a woman solely because she is pregnant.
Vocational Rehabilitation Act of 1973	Prohibits discriminating against a worker "solely by reason of handicap" in any federally funded program. Requires federal contractors to employ and promote qualified handicapped people.
Age Discrimination Act of 1973	Prohibits employers from discrimination based on age; ages 40 to 70 are covered.
Americans with Disability Act of 1990	Prohibits discrimination against those with disabilities.
Civil Rights Act of 1991	Reverses Supreme Court Cases of 1989–1990. Business necessity standard reaffirmed. Burden of proof placed on business. Punitive damages allowed.

employment, because of such an individual's race, color, religion, sex, or national origin.

Supreme Court cases, discussed later in this chapter, have allowed employers to use these factors in employment decisions when their use benefits a protected class that was underrepre-sented in the employer's workforce. Affirmative action programs are used to benefit minorities, and reverse-discrimination claims have been dismissed by the Supreme Court if certain guidelines developed in *United Steelworkers v. Weber*,[9] which are discussed later in this chapter, are followed.

LABOR MARKET STUDY

BUSINESS EMPLOYMENT PROFILE STUDY

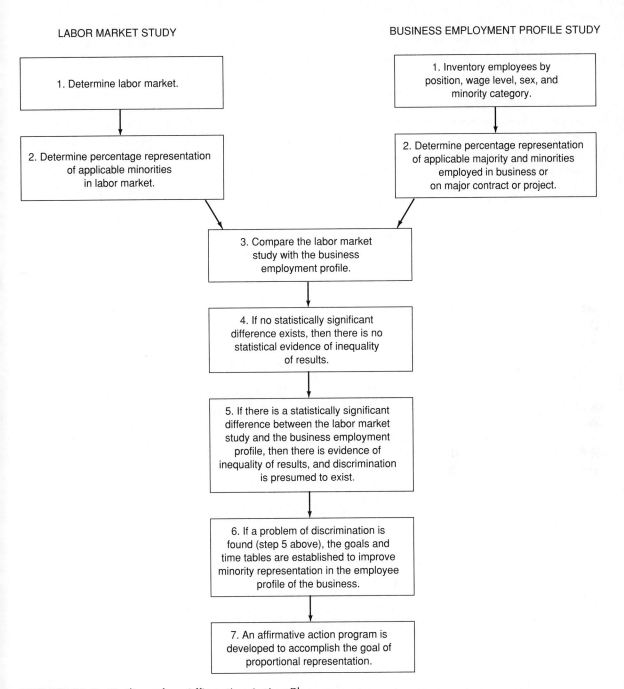

FIGURE 17–2 Outline of an Affirmative Action Plan

The enforcement of laws prohibiting discrimination in employment practices began in 1965 with an executive order signed by President Johnson that prohibited discrimination based on race, color, religion, sex, or national origin when government contracts were involved. This executive order also required federal contractors to develop *affirmative action plans* to raise the level of employment of minorities and women in their organizations. The essence of an affirmative action plan shown in Figure 17–2 includes a statistical comparison of (1) a labor market study and (2) the employee profile of a business. If a statistically significant difference is found in which sex or minorities are underrepresented, then discrimination is presumed to exist and some sort of affirmative action is required to bring about an adequate level of representation by sex or by minority group.

AMERICANS WITH DISABILITIES ACT OF 1990

Over 40 million people in the United States have one or more physical or mental disabilities. Disability can include something visible like blindness or paraplegia, or it can be less noticeable, like heart disease, diabetes, a malformed back, or AIDS. Medical problems can lower an employee's ability to perform certain tasks, or it can increase the cost of medical insurance for employers. Sometimes people have recovered from disabilities like cancer or mental or emotional disorders and have been discriminated against because of their past medical record.

The Rehabilitation Act of 1973 established the right of people with disabilities to enjoy equal employment opportunity. This right was extended by Title I of the Americans with Disabilities Act of 1990 (ADA). The ADA prohibits employers from discriminating against disabled individuals who are qualified to do the job. According to the ADA:

1. Employers may not ask individuals whether or not they have a disability. However, an employer *may* ask an individual whether he or she can perform specific job-related functions. See Box 17–1.

2. Employers are required to make *reasonable accommodations* for disabled workers who can otherwise perform the essential functions of a job.

Employers with 25 or more employees had to comply with the ADA beginning July 26, 1992. After July 26, 1994, all employers with over 14 employees must comply. The ADA requires that employers eliminate bias in hiring and also requires that employers make reasonable accommodations for disabled employees. The most obvious form of accommodation is in the area of access, which requires ramps or elevators for employees who use wheelchairs. However, another disabled employee may need a different accommodation. Employers should ask what accommodation is needed and seek to make a reasonable one. For example, a dishwasher in a wheelchair may need a special plastic apron to keep dry while sorting silverware.[10] A deaf person may need communications in writing.

Under the ADA an employer may need to make reasonable accommodation to an employee even though the employee may not be able to perform all job functions. For example, a meat cutter in a foodstore may have a back injury and be unable to carry meet from the refrigerator to the cutting boards. Prior to the ADA such a worker might not be allowed to have this job. Under the American with Disabilities Act, the store would be required to provide a cart to assist the employee with a back problem. Employers should try to improvise and work with employees to make reasonable accommodations cost-effective. However, employers are not required to make personal accommodations such as supplying hearing aids.

CIVIL RIGHTS ACT OF 1991

The Civil Rights Act of 1991 did not prescribe a set of new employment practices for business but countered seven Supreme Court decisions made between 1989 and 1990 that had reversed much of the case law that had developed since the passage of the Civil Rights Act of 1964.[11] All companies with 15 or more employees are covered by this new

---

BOX 17–1 Interviewing People with Disabilities

Employers must make sure that people with disabilities can get to the interview site and participate fully in the process. Job notices and applications should state that those needing disability-related accommodations for interviews should request them in advance.

Here are questions you can—and cannot—ask job applicants:

WHAT YOU MAY ASK

The disability act is designed to have employers focus on applicants' competencies, not disabilities. Employers may ask:

- Whether a job task can be performed with or without an accommodation.
- How the individual would perform the tasks and with what accommodations.
- To demonstrate how certain job functions would be performed, but only if every applicant for the job is required to do so, regardless of disability. If an applicant has a known disability that would seem to interfere with a job task, the employer may ask that he or she show how the task would be performed, even if others are not required to do so.
- Whether the individual can meet the job's work-hour requirements, provided the hours truly apply to the job.

Source: *Nation's Business*, June 1992, p. 31. Reprinted with permission.

WHAT NOT TO ASK

Take the following types of questions off any application forms *immediately*, and instruct your company's interviewers never to ask job applicants

- Have you ever been treated for the fofllowing listed conditions or diseases?
- Please list any conditions or diseases for which you have been treated in the past three years.
- Have you ever been hospitalized? For what?
- Have you ever been treated by a psychiatrist or psychologist? For what?
- Have you ever been treated for any mental condition?
- Is there any health-related reason that would prevent you from doing the type of work for which you are applying?
- Have you had a major illness in the last five years? Do you have any physical defects that preclude you from performing certain tasks?
- Do you have any disabilities or impairments that would affect your performance in the position for which you are applying?
- Are you taking any prescribed drugs?
- Have you ever been treated for drug addiction or alcholism?
- Have you ever filed for workers' compensation insurance?

---

law. The Civil Rights Act of 1991 has the following provisions:

1. It legally defines two types of discrimination that had been established by the Courts: *disparate treatment* and *disparate impact.*
2. The law shifts the *burden of proof* to employers in cases of disparate impact discrimination.

3. The standard in disparate impact cases will return to *business necessity*, which was established in *Griggs v. Duke Power* and was reversed in *Wards Cove v. Atonio* (which are discussed later in the chapter).
4. The *punitive damage awards* available under Title VII were extended to cover cases of sexual harassment and discrimination against individuals with disabilities.

5. The law makes clear that *on-the-job problems* like harassment, promotion, and dismissal are covered as well as discrimination in hiring.

6. The new amendment to the Civil Rights Act seems to adopt the "taint test," so that a plaintiff need only show that discrimination was a motivating factor in an employment decision that had an adverse effect to prove a violation of the law. This reverses the 1989 *Price Waterhouse v. Hopkins,* discussed below.[12] An employment decision would be unlawful even if the employer could show that the act would still have been taken for legitimate, nondiscriminatory reasons if a discriminatory factor played any part in the decision.

Disparate Treatment and Disparate Impact

Disparate treatment exists when an employer treats some people less favorably than others because of race, color, religion, sex, national origin, or disability. According to this principle, if a woman is told she may not have a position because of her gender, the employer is discriminating.

A case that was settled out of court before the Civil Rights Act of 1991 provides an example of disparate treatment in the form of a hostile work environment. In 1988 Jimmy Young, an African American truck driver, sued Von's Market in Los Angeles for race discrimination. He alleged that the hostile work environment inflicted emotional distress. Young's supervisors called him "nigger," told racist jokes, gave him inferior equipment, and took jobs away from him and gave them to junior drivers who were white. He complained to no avail. Under this extreme stress, Young, who suffered from diabetes, suffered a rapid decline in health, and eventually he became completely disabled. He sued for damages due to racial discrimination and then offered to settle for $1 million in damages.

Von's Grocery rejected Young's offer and the case went to court. A jury awarded Young $12.1 million, which included $10.7 in punitive damages. The punitive damages were reduced to $650,000, but the case was still appealed by Von's Grocery. Before the final appeal was completed, an out-of-court settlement was made that was believed to be similar.[13]

Disparate impact exists when an employer's practices, including hiring, performance appraisals, or promotions, adversely affect minorities that are in a protected class, even though no adverse reference is made to race, sex, or other protected category. Disparate impact discrimination can be totally unintentional and still be found illegal. For example, the requirement used by some police departments that all managers be over five feet eleven inches in height has the effect of eliminating most women and Asians from higher positions. Because the height requirement could not be shown to be job-related and consistent with the business necessity standard, it was unlawful.

Compensatory and Punitive Damages

Before the new law there was no limit on punitive damages involving racial discrimination, but there was no provision for punitive damages for cases involving discrimination based upon sex or disability. Victims of discrimination in the workplace are now eligible for both compensatory and punitive damages within the limits outlined in Table 17–2. In a 1989 case, a Ms. Brooms was unable to receive compensatory damages under previous civil rights law. She worked for Regal Tube Company as an industrial nurse. Her supervisor showed her obscene pictures, made sexually offensive comments, grabbed her arm, and threatened to kill her if she moved. She struggled to get free and, in the process, fell down a flight of stairs.

Brooms sued for sexual harassment and won back pay in the lawsuit. Her medical costs for the fall were covered by Regal's health plan. However, she was unable to receive payment for the cost of three years of psychotherapy for depression resulting from the incident. Compensatory damages would have covered the "pain and suffering" Bloom experienced. Punitive damages would have punished the company for the behavior of Bloom's supervisor, who was working as an agent for the company. Both compensatory and punitive damages are now available in discrimination cases involving sexual harassment and disabilities under the Civil Rights Act of 1991. Table 17–3 shows the limits placed on damages by the new law.

TABLE 17–3
Punitive Damage Limits in Civil Rights Cases of Discrimination

Number of Employees	Limit on Punitive Damages ($)
15–100	$ 50,000
101–200	100,000
201–500	200,000
over 500	300,000

SOURCE: Adapted from *Wall Street Journal*, November 4, 1991, p. B2.

Voluntary vs. Court-ordered Affirmative Action

The Civil Rights Act of 1991, Section 107(a) states that "an unlawful employment practice is established when the complaining party demonstrates that race, color, religion, sex, or national origin was a motivating factor for any employment practice, even though other factors motivated the practice."

This section of the new civil rights amendment raised some question about the legal status of voluntary affirmative action programs. As will be discussed later, the Supreme Court has twice reaffirmed the use of voluntary affirmative action programs prior to the 1991 law: first in the Weber case and secondly in *Johnson v. Transportation Agency, Santa Clara County*. However, the first federal appellate court to consider this issue since the new 1991 Civil Rights Law was passed concluded that Section 107(a) does not outlaw voluntary affirmative action programs.[14]

Complying with Discrimination Laws

AFFIRMATIVE ACTION PLANS

Affirmative action programs have been used as a major remedy to increase job access for minority group members. Affirmative action is assertive behavior to increase the representation of minorities in the workforce or in the employee profile of a particular business. Such plans have *equality of results or proportional representation* as their primary objective. Table 17–4 identifies a wide range of affirmative action plans:

TABLE 17–4
Types of Affirmative Action Programs

• Passive Affirmative Action: Advertisement of business as "An Equal Opportunity Employer."

• Affirmative recruiting of minorities to increase the pool of qualified minority applicants.

• Preferential hiring, training and development, and/or promotion of qualified minority employees to achieve "soft" goals.

• Preferential hiring, training and development, and/or promotion of minority employees to achieve "hard" quotas.

1. A passive affirmative action program uses announcements proclaiming a business as an "equal employment opportunity employer."

2. Affirmative recruiting programs increase the pool of qualified minorities for an open employment position. This may involve advertising for jobs on minority radio stations or in newspapers known to have a high minority readership.

3. Preferential treatment programs include employment decisions involving hiring, training, and development, or promotions of protected groups to achieve goals through good-faith effort by management.

4. Preferential treatment employment decisions with hard quotas go beyond good faith efforts by requiring that goals be met even if reverse discrimination results. Such programs are illegal.

Passive Affirmative Action Programs

Passively announcing that a business practices equal opportunity is a start, but it rarely produces significant results if discrimination has existed. Discrimination can be due to the informal behavior of organizational members; it can be due to an organizational policy that adversely affects the ability of a member of a minority group to qualify for a position; or it can be due to the organizational culture. Passive affirmative action programs are not likely to change these fundamental causes in discrimination.

Affirmative recruiting has the objective of enlarging the applicant pool for a job to include more minority applicants. Strategies of affirmative recruiting include advertising job openings in Hispanic or African American newspapers or on radio stations oriented to minority groups, or by recruiting more heavily at universities with large minority enrollments. Once a larger number of qualified minorities apply for open positions, selection can be based strictly on merit.

Affirmative Hiring, Training, and Promotion

This type of affirmative action normally includes affirmative recruiting, but preference is given to minority applicants if they are qualified for a job. Also, the principle can be applied to affirmative

access to training and development and affirmative promotion of qualified minorities. This practice is legal if it follows the 1979 Equal Employment Opportunity Office guidelines and the Supreme Court Guidelines established in *Weber*.

The most effective affirmative action programs go beyond the passive announcement that the business is an equal opportunity employer but fall short of the rigid use of hard quotas. This middle ground includes affirmative recruiting; preferential selection, training, and promotion; and the use of long-range goals. At the other extreme, preferential hiring with hard quotas means that an organization is committed to hire an established number or percentage of minority members. Difficulties can arise if the hard quota is higher than the number of eligible minority job applicants, or if there is a large number of exceedingly well-qualified white males relative to the number of minority applicants. *Reverse discrimination* occurs when an employment practice discriminates against the majority, usually against white males applying for a job. This is most likely to occur when an affirmative action with hard quotas is used. In 1977 the Supreme Court in the Bakke case held hard quotas to be unlawful as reverse discrimination.

EQUAL EMPLOYMENT OPPORTUNITY COMMISSION

The Equal Employment Opportunity Commission (EEOC) was formed as the primary enforcement agency for the laws prohibiting discrimination in the workplace. The Equal Employment Opportunity Act of 1972 empowered the EEOC to bring enforcement action to the courts and expanded the coverage of Title VII of the Civil Rights Act. Little progress had been made in increasing the representation of minorities in many of the better-paying occupations, despite the increasing emphasis on equality of opportunity. Though it was illegal to discriminate against minorities, the process of discrimination is often subtle, and it is difficult to identify discriminatory practices so that the law could be enforced. Thus, the EEOC used the concept of *equality of results* to define the problem for enforcement purposes.

The EEOC used consent decrees as well as lawsuits to enforce laws against discrimination. A *consent decree* is an agreement in which an alleged violator of a regulation or law agrees to stop a business practice but does not admit to any past legal violation. Once a business signs a consent decree, there is a legal requirement to comply with the agreement; the consequences of failing to do so can be substantial.

For example, in 1973 AT&T and EEOC signed a consent decree that provided for increased representation of women and minorities. After signing the agreement, AT&T prominently printed the following on their stationery and in their job announcements: "We are an equal employee opportunity employer." They also agreed to a number of goals but apparently did little to accomplish them.

A few years later, the EEOC returned and upon looking at the statistical results of its efforts, concluded there was still an inequality of results, and thus discriminatory practices were presumed to be continuing. AT&T was required to may $12 million in back pay and over $40 million in pay adjustments to minority employees and women because they had not fulfilled the consent decree. In 1975, a consent decree signed between EEOC and nine major steel companies resulted in an award of $31 million in back pay to minorities and women who allegedly had been discriminated against in previous years. The large fines and other actions connected with these consent decrees caught the notice of executives, and many companies began to implement affirmative action programs beyond the passive notice approach.[15]

The enforcement by the EEOC made it clear that affirmative action programs needed (1) the commitment of top management, (2) the support to top management-level staff and budgets, (3) a system of goals and periodic assessment of their accomplishment reported back to top management, and (4) a comprehensive program to communicate the needs for and approach to implementing affirmative action through the organization. Also

needed were management information made available to those making employment or human resource decisions concerning changes in market conditions, acceptable screening policies including the use of tests and nondiscriminatory criteria, hiring, training development and promotion policies and plans for employee layoffs.

EEOC Endorsement of Voluntary Programs

In 1979 the EEOC issued a set of guidelines under which voluntary affirmative action programs would be appropriate in the following circumstances:

1. When a self-analysis reveals an actual or potential adverse impact likely to result from existing or contemplated employment practices
2. When past discrimination has continuing effects in the form of underrepresentation of minorities or women in the employer's workforce
3. When the available pool of qualified minorities and women is artificially limited

Under any of these circumstances, an employer may adopt a *voluntary affirmative action plan* consisting of three elements:

1. A self-analysis to determine whether employment practices disadvantage previously excluded or restricted groups or tend to perpetuate the effects of past discrimination
2. A reasonable belief that affirmative action is appropriate
3. A reasonable action, such as appropriate race-, sex-, or national-origin-conscious employment practices, designed to respond to the problems identified in the self-analysis

SEXUAL HARASSMENT POLICIES IN THE WORKPLACE

Interestingly, opponents in Congress of Title VII of the 1991 Civil Rights Act added sex as a protected category of discrimination in an attempt to defeat it. The bill passed with sex as a recognized factor in discrimination, but the first sexual discrimination case was not litigated until 1977.[16] Since then a number of court cases have defined unlawful sexual discrimination in terms of (1) quid pro quo sexual harassment, and (2) hostile environment sexual harassment.

Quid Pro Quo Sexual Harassment

In *Barnes v. Costle* (1977),[17] the court recognized quid pro quo sexual harassment as a form of unlawful discrimination. In that case, the plaintiff, a female employee, refused to submit to the unwelcome sexual advances of her employer. He eliminated her job and she sued, alleging sexual discrimination. The lower court found that the supervisor's behavior was "underpinned by the subtleties of an inharmonious personal relationship" and was not unlawful discrimination. The appellate court reversed the lower court decision and noted that because the supervisor would not have subjected an employee to sexual demands unless she were female, this was a violation of Title VII.

Unlawful quid pro quo sexual harassment involves supervisors seeking sexual favors from their subordinates in exchange for employment benefits. These benefits can include continued employment, promotion, a raise, or a favorable performance appraisal. When an employment decision is affected, the Title VII prohibition against discrimination is violated. The employer is then liable to the employee for the loss of benefits plus compensatory and punitive damages because of the supervisor's misconduct.

Hostile Environment Sexual Harassment

According to the courts, a plaintiff must show that harassment was sufficiently severe or pervasive to alter the conditions of employment.[18] Factors that can define this type of illegal sex discrimination that forms a hostile working environment include (1) the nature of the unwelcome sexual acts, (2) the frequency of these acts, (3) the context in which the harassing conduct occurs, and (5) whether the behavior forms a pattern of repeated or generalized conduct.

Hostile environment was first defined as a form of unlawful sexual discrimination under Title VII by the Supreme Court in *Meritor Savings Bank v.*

Venson.[19] This type of sexual harassment is illegal even though no economic benefits are lost as a result. Also, a hostile work environment may be grounds for a sexual discrimination lawsuit even when the plaintiff is not a direct victim of unwelcome sexual conduct.

For example, in *Broderick v. Ruder,*[20] Catherine Broderick served as a staff attorney for the SEC for five years and observed numerous blatant sexual affairs. It appeared that female employees who engaged in these affairs received good performance evaluations and cash bonuses. When Broderick complained, she received poor evaluations, threats of a dismissal, and, eventually, a transfer. She was labeled a "festering morale problem" and twice received unwelcome sexual advances. The District of Columbia court held that evidence of the general work environment involving other employees could be illegal sexual discrimination under Title VII, even though the plaintiff might not have been the object of harassment. Also, it appears that both male and female employees offended by blatant sexual conduct in the workplace could be considered as victims of sexual discrimination by the courts.

Enforcing Discrimination Laws Through Court Cases

The EEOC also is empowered to enforce discrimination laws by bringing cases to court. Sample major cases concerning equality and discrimination are shown in Table 17–5. These cases represent some of the *common law,* which is the defining of the law through decisions made by judges in court cases.

A Prima Facie Case and the Burden of Proof of Unlawful Discrimination

Griggs v. Duke Power Company[21] (1971) was an important early case. In it, the Supreme Court ruled that Duke Power had unlawfully discriminated against blacks by requiring a high school education and the passing of an intelligence test for certain jobs. The company apparently had not intended to discriminate against blacks. However, the high school dropout rate was much higher for blacks than whites where Duke Power operated. Thus, the *unintentional effect* of requiring a high school diploma as a condition for being hired had a *disparate impact* on African Americans. The policy excluded a much larger proportion of African Americans than whites from the pool of eligible job candidates.

In this important case the Court ruled that:

1. Discrimination *does not have to be intentional to be unlawful.*
2. Company practices or policies, like requiring an intelligence test or a high school diploma, that have an adverse *disparate impact* on minority groups more than on the majority group are unlawful unless
3. The employer must show that it is a *business necessity* to follow such practices.
4. Employment decision criteria must be *job-related* and the employer must show that job candidates not meeting the criteria could not adequately perform the job.

Furthermore, the Duke Power Case established what was required to define a *prima facie* case of discrimination, in other words, what evidence was necessary to show, "on the face of it," that the plaintiff was guilty of unlawful discrimination unless the *plaintiff* proves otherwise. To establish a prima facie case of discrimination, a plaintiff must show that the employment practice had a significantly discriminatory impact. If that showing is made, the employer must then demonstrate "any given requirement [has] a manifest relationship to the employment in question." In other words, if a prima facie case is shown, the burden of proof and the costs of developing this evidence shifts to the defendant in the case.

Griggs v. Duke Power made it relatively easy for a minority employee or job applicant to bring a discrimination action against a business. He or she must (1) be a member of a legally covered minority group or a woman, (2) be denied a job, access to a training and development program, or promotion,

and (3) demonstrate that an inequality of results exist using readily available statistical data. The company then must show that any company decisions or policies that have caused a disparate adverse impact on minority group members were a *business necessity,* that is, the business would have difficulty continuing to operate without these needed policies. Tests and criteria must be job-related and proved by the company to be a business necessity.

Wards Cove Packing Co. v. Atonio Case

Frank Atonio spent six summers in Alaskan canneries packing fish and longing for a better job. A native of American Samoa, he worked the Alaskan salmon catches of the mid-1970s, all the while eyeing a promotion to one of the cannery's machine or carpentry shops. After submitting several unsuccessful applications for the higher-paying posts, Atonio, now 38 years old, says he figured out what was wrong: The canneries, he asserted, were allocating skilled jobs to the mostly white friends and relatives of management, while giving unskilled work to the predominantly minority members of a longshoremen's union. So Atonio, joined by nine other fish packers, sued.[22]

In the *Wards Cove* case, the Supreme Court held that those bringing a racial discrimination charge must prove that the employer had no business reason for the practice used. This decision declared that statistical disparities or racial imbalances in one segment of an employer's workforce does not, without more, establish a prima facie case. Also, this case transfers the burden (and cost) of proof from the plaintiff, who is usually a business, to the defendant, who is usually an employee or a job applicant. The company need show that there is a *reasonable cause* for a specific business practice. In this case, work in the canneries was highly seasonal, and the plaintiff argued that it was a reasonable way to do business to recruit key positions each year from friends and relatives. The Court did not require that the companies prove that the practice was a business necessity.

Because minority employees or job applicants are (1) less likely to have easy access to the com-

TABLE 17–5
Major Court Cases on Equality and Discrimination

1971 Griggs v. Duke Power Co. The U.S. Supreme Court ruled that the employer unlawfully discriminated against blacks by requiring a high school education or passing an intelligence test as conditions of employment in certain jobs. Further, it held that proof of discriminatory intent is not required to establish employment discrimination so long as discriminatory effects are shown.

1973 Hodgsen v. Robert Hall Clothes, Inc. The Third Circuit Court of Appeals held that male salespersons could be paid more than female salespersons because there was a greater profit in men's clothing. The pay differential was permitted because it was not based solely on sex, but on sales, even though women were not allowed to work in the men's clothing department, where greater profits were possible. The company argued that there was a valid reason for not allowing women to sell to men in the clothing department.

1977 Trans-World Airlines, Inc. v. Hardison. Hardison refused to work on the sabbath, a period from Friday evening through Saturday. TWA had to operate the stores department of maintenance on a 24-hour-per-day, 365-days-per-year basis. Scheduling was done on the consistent with a union-management contract on the basis of seniority. The U.S. Supreme Court ruled a bona fide seniority system does not have to give way to accommodating an individual's religion. It would be an undue hardship on TWA to bear the cost of giving Hardison Saturdays off because no one volunteered to take the assignment and it would require premium overtime paid to any replacement.

1979 Weber v. Kaiser Aluminum & Chemical. The U.S. Supreme Court endorsed right of employers and unions to adopt voluntary joint affirmative action goals to eliminate racial imbalance in a workforce. The program was temporary, no white workers were replaced or lost their jobs, whites could still advance, and a historical pattern of discrimination had existed.

1982 Connecticut v. Teal. The Supreme Court ruled that an exam used to determine eligibility for promotion was illegal. Fifty-four percent of the blacks passed the exam and 79 percent of the whites passed. The exam was found to have a disparate negative, though unintentional, impact against black employees and was thus illegally discriminatory, even though the percentage of eligible blacks exceeded the percentage of eligible whites who were promoted.

1983 Newport News Shipbuilding and Dry Dock Co. v. EEOC. The employer changed its health insurance plan to provide female employees with hospitalization benefits for pregnancy-related conditions, but the plan provided less extensive benefits for spouses of male employees. The Supreme Court ruled that the plan violated Title VII as amended by the Pregnancy Discrimination Act because it discriminated against male employees.

1984 Memphis Fire Department v. Stotts. In 1980, the city of Memphis made a settlement in a class action employment discrimination suit in federal district court, and a consent decree was approved. The purpose of the decree was to remedy the hiring and promotion practice of the Memphis Fire Department with respect to blacks. In 1981, the city announced that budget deficits made it necessary to lay off some personnel on a "last hired, first fired" basis under the citywide seniority plan. The district court ordered the city to modify its layoff plan to protect black employees hired or promoted under the consent decree. The Court of Appeals affirmed. The Supreme Court reversed the ruling, finding that layoffs could follow a bona fide seniority system.

1984 Hishon v. King & Spalding. Elizabeth Hishon accepted a position with King & Spalding, a large Atlanta law firm, and was turned down when considered as a partner after five years and her employment was terminated to following year. The U.S. Supreme Court held that Title VII was inapplicable to the selection of partners by a partnership.

1986 Meritor Savings Bank v. Vinson. The U.S. Supreme Court ruled that an employee who had been sexually harassed while on the job had suffered from sexual discrimination, which was a violation of Title VII. The employer could also be liable for civil damages resulting from the behavior.

1987 Johnson v. Transportation Agency, Santa Clara County. The U.S. Supreme Court allowed the promotion of a qualified woman over a man with slightly higher test scores in a county transportation agency. The Court decision reaffirmed the legality of a voluntary program of preferential access to a training program for women when there was evidence of historical disparity in firing and promotions.

1989 City of Richmond v. J.A. Croson Co. The city of Richmond established a set-aside program requiring that 30 percent of the subcontracts for Richmond contracts be awarded to minority firms because the city was 50% black but only .67% of the city's prime construction contracts had been awarded to minority businesses during the past five years. The U.S. Supreme Court ruled that because the city of Richmond failed to identify the need for remedial action in awarding the public construction contracts, its treatment of its citizens on a racial basis violated the dictates of the Equal Protection Clause of the Fourteenth Amendment of the Constitution.

1990 Wards-Cove v. Atonio. The U.S. Supreme Court held that those bringing a racial discrimination charge must prove that the employer has no business reason for the practice used. The new decision declares that statistical disparities or racial imbalances in one segment of an employer's workforce does not, without more, establish a prima facie case. [This case reversed *Griggs v. Duke Power Co.*]

pany records, (2) are more likely to have limited financial and other resources for developing a legal suit, and (3) the Court changed the standard to *reasonable cause* rather than the severer standard of *business necessity* in judging the business need for a practice that has a disparate and adverse effect on minority group members, *Wards Cove* is viewed as a major setback for equal opportunity and affirmative action programs in the workplace.

Griggs v. Duke Power was *reversed* in several respects by *Wards Cove.* However, the Civil Rights Act of 1991 restored the basic principles of *Griggs* including disparate impact, the business necessity standard, and the plaintiff's burden of proof in prima facie cases.

Voluntary Affirmative Action and the Court

As shown in Figure 17–2, affirmative action programs begin with a statistical analysis comparing the minority representation in the labor market with minority representation in the employee profile of a business (or nonbusiness) employer. The purpose of this is to identify inequality of results that could be used to develop a prima facie case of unlawful discrimination. Once a business identifies a potential problem with discrimination, some sort of action is necessary; this typically takes the form of an affirmative action plan. Key elements of concern to the courts are *prima facie cases of unlawful discrimination* and *legality of affirmative action plans.*

Criteria for a "Permissible" Voluntary Affirmative Action Plan

In *Weber v. Kaiser Aluminum & Chemical Co.,* an historical pattern of discrimination existed based upon statistical evidence. The company and the union entered into a voluntary agreement to end this discrimination through an affirmative action program in which blacks were selected on a preferential basis for training programs. Weber, a white employee, was eligible for the apprentice training program but not selected and thus sued on the basis of *reverse discrimination.*

The Supreme Court refused to say what a lawful affirmative program was but offered criteria for a "permissible" program that included the following:

1. An historical pattern of discrimination was proved to have existed.
2. No white employees lost their jobs.
3. Access to the training program was agreed to by both union and management.
4. The program was based on a bona fide seniority system established by the labor-management agreement with the provision that 50 percent of trainees were to be black (6 of 13 persons admitted to the program were white at the time Weber applied).
5. The program was temporary and was to be terminated when "the percentage of black skilled craftsmen in the plant approximated the percentage of blacks in the local labor force."

The criteria established in the Weber case was reaffirmed in the 1987 case, *Johnson v. Transportation Agency of Santa Clara County.*[23] The case had similar facts except that the preferential access to the skilled craft training program was designed to redress an historical pattern of discrimination against women.

"Soft Goals" or "Hard Quotas" in Affirmative Action

The U.S Supreme Court makes a distinction between goals and quotas. A *soft goal* is typically based on a standard of proportional representation that is in turn based on the comparative statistical analysis of the sex and minorities in the labor market and the profile of employees. The goal should not be arbitrary or rigid; it is to be strived for over time. A *hard quota* may also be based on a comparative statistical study but generally involves a rigidly fixed number or percentage of minority group members to be hired per year.

Hard quotas were held to be an illegal form of reverse discrimination in the *Regents of the University of California v. Bakke* case. In this 1977 case the Supreme Court reaffirmed the use of affirmative action plans to end racial discrimination but ruled that the University of California Medical School at

Davis had illegally discriminated against Bakke when it reserved a fixed number of positions for the entering class for minority group members applying for medical school. The school used the same admissions criteria for both white and minority group students but denied admission to Bakke, who had placed higher in eligibility on the list than some of the minority group applicants who were admitted to Medical School.

Partially Discriminatory Employment Decisions

Congress was dissatisfied with the Supreme Court's 1989 ruling in *Price Waterhouse v. Hopkins*[24]and included the taint test, which makes partially discriminatory employment decisions unlawful. *Price Waterhouse* gave employers an avenue to escape Title VII when a prohibited factor had been a negative consideration of any kind.[25] This case involved a "mixed motive" situation in which Price Waterhouse denied Ms. Hopkins a partnership in the CPA firm, in part because she was a woman. The employer considered both prohibited factors relating to sex and legitimate nondiscriminatory factors in denying her a partnership.

The Supreme Court held that, once the plaintiff shows that a prohibited factor was involved in an employment action to an appropriate extent, the burden of persuasion shifts to the employer to prove that it would have taken the same action, in the absence of the prohibited factor. If the same decision would have been made anyway, no discrimination violation of Title VII would be found. However, the Supreme Court could not agree on the proper standard for determining when a prohibited factor was sufficiently involved in an employment action to shift the burden of proof. Four justices adopted the taint test, according to which the plaintiff need only show that an unlawful factor played some motivating role in the employment decision. The remaining five justices representing the majority adopted a more stringent standard.

In the new Civil Rights Law of 1991, Congress adopted the standard of the taint test. Thus a plaintiff need only show that a prohibited discrimination factor was "a motivating factor in an employment decision that had adverse effect for it to be unlawful." The decision would be unlawful even if the employer could show that the act would still have been taken for legitimate, nondiscriminatory reasons.

If Section 107(a) of the Civil Rights Act of 1991 were interpreted narrowly, all affirmative action programs would be ruled illegal. In affirmative action an unlawful factor plays a role in an employment decision favoring minority members. A broad interpretation would allow affirmative action programs that the Supreme Court previously affirmed in the Weber and Johnson cases, before the 1991 law. The legislative debate on the Civil Rights Act of 1991 suggests that Congress did not wish to overturn the Weber and Johnson cases and continues to support the 1979 EEOC guidelines on voluntary affirmative action programs. However, Congress did clearly wish to overturn the *Price Waterhouse* decision by the Supreme Court, which provided an escape route for business in discrimination cases.

Recycling the Issue of Equality and Discrimination

The Supreme Court decisions between 1989 and 1990 suggest major changes in the common law that apply to employment discrimination: (1) a *prima facie* case for unlawful discrimination cannot be based solely on a statistical inequality of results; (2) the *standards of proof* required to justify a practice with a discriminatory impact shifted from a business necessity to a reasonable practice; (3) the *burden of proof* has shifted from the business plaintiff to the minority group member, who is often the defendant, or to the government regulating agency (EEOC); and (4) employment decisions that were only partially discriminatory were lawful.

These findings suggest that the new Supreme Court, which includes the conservative appointments by Presidents Reagan and Bush, had a different view of discrimination than was held by the EEOC and the courts during the 1970s and 1980s.

There was a recycling of the ILC back to stage two; that it, the problem of discrimination underwent a change by recent Supreme Court cases. A clue suggesting the problem with which the Court is struggling is found in the minority opinion in the *Johnson v. Transportation Agency of Santa Clara County.* In that opinion, Justice Scalia said the Court is replacing

the goal of a discrimination-free society with the quite incompatible goal of proportionate representation by race and by sex in the workplace. . . .The court today [March 25, 1987] completes the process of converting [the 1964 Civil Rights Act] from a guarantee that race or sex will not be the basis for employment determinations to a guarantee that it often will.

THE LOGICAL DIFFICULTY WITH AFFIRMATIVE ACTION PROGRAMS

The contradiction between the ideal of equality and the reality of discrimination leading to affirma-

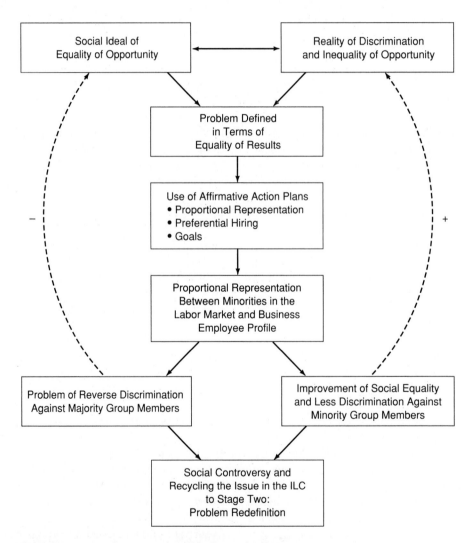

FIGURE 17–3 The Logical Difficulties of Affirmative Action

tive action programs is outlined in Figure 17–3. Growing awareness of the discrimination led to defining the public policy problem as inequality of results in the ILC. The definition of the problem led to affirmative action programs based upon proportional representation enforced by both the EEOC and a series of major court decisions. Changes in the composition of the Supreme Court resulted in a serious questioning of the way the problem of discrimination is defined. Justice Scalia was concerned with the contradiction between the proportional representation objectives in affirmative action programs and the social ideal of equality of opportunity. Equality of opportunity should logically lead to career opportunity, rewards, and promotions based upon individual merit *and not on the basis of race, color, religion, sex, or ethnic group.* Thus, any systematic attempt to use minority group (*or majority group*) status as the basis for employment decisions is inconsistent with the ideology of equality of opportunity.

The counterpoint to the concern expressed by Justice Scalia is the persistent reality of inequality of income and job opportunity available to women and minority group members. Discrimination and racism have a long, persistent history. The social changes and changes in management practice necessary to eliminate discrimination have proven very difficult to bring about. A series of laws prohibiting discrimination was passed and the EEOC was formed to enforce them. Changing the subtle behaviors resulting in discrimination was found to be very difficult. Defining the problem in terms of equality of results made enforcement and administration of the law easier. The results of this enforcement would probably lead to greater representation of women and minority group members in jobs, and the social objective of reducing or ending unjust inequalities could be accomplished quickly.

The historical record suggests that inequalities in income and job discrimination seem to have persisted despite aggressive enforcement by the EEOC using the concept of inequality of results. Affirmative action based on hard quotas was held to be illegal in 1977, but the use of such programs with soft goals has been reaffirmed several times since then.

However, the Reagan administration was adamantly opposed to affirmative action with soft goals and considered it to be essentially the same as quotas.[26] Despite slow gains in minority employment, resentment of perceived reverse discrimination was becoming a growing public issue controversy.

Although issues of equality, discrimination, and justice have long been of concern to employee stakeholders, the intensity of public interest remains high, as shown in Figure 17–1. By many standards, this is a mature issue in the ILC because of the large body of case law, the establishment of the EEOC, the well-developed regulations, and the presence of regulatory agencies. However, the Reagan and Bush administrations changed the composition of the Supreme Court, and the equality and discrimination issue was recycled as a public issue.

The public policy response to the Supreme Court decisions between 1989 and 1990 was the passage of the Civil Rights Act of 1991. This law restored the earlier concept of equality for purposes of enforcing the laws against discrimination and reversed the important changes outlined above that were made by the Supreme Court. The employee stakeholder issue of equality and discrimination, for the moment, seems to have been resolved.

Summary

Equality of opportunity is a key part of the prevailing ideology in America and is central for the working of an effective competitive market. Discrimination is inconsistent with American ideology and is immoral and unjust, according to most ethical approaches, for the following reasons: (1) discrimination violates all three tenets of Kant's categorical imperative: it is not reversible, it uses persons as means rather than ends, and it does not encourage the freedom and autonomy of the individual; (2) it is unjustifiable from a utilitarian point of view; and (3) it is grossly unfair by all theories of justice.

Awareness of the problems of discrimination was heightened by the civil rights movement of the 1950s and 1960s. This was followed by a women's liberation movement, which brought attention to injustices faced by women, and by the Vietnam War, which focused attention on the needs of the handicapped. Interest groups formed around the problems of discrimination experienced by blacks, Hispanics, women, the disabled, the gay community, and senior citizens. In the 1960s the Equal Pay Act and the Civil Rights Act (Title VII) were passed; in the 1970s these laws were amended and more laws were passed to prohibit discrimination against the disabled, pregnant women, and persons over 40 years of age.

The EEOC was formed to enforce the laws prohibiting discrimination. This agency focused on the equality-of-results concept through the use of statistical comparative analyses of labor markets and the employee profile of a business to define discrimination. This approach relied on affirmative action programs that were first required by a presidential executive order of all government contractors. Affirmative action involves positive and active approaches to increasing minority representation in employment until the proportion of minorities and women is not significantly different from their proportion in the labor market.

In stage six of the ILC, the Supreme Court has been active in developing common law, which defines unlawful discrimination and permissible voluntary affirmative action. Also, the EEOC provided guidelines for voluntary affirmative action that supplemented the criteria set forth in the Weber case. Supreme Court cases between 1989 and 1990 reversed the use of statistical evidence and inequality of results as the basis for a prima facie case in discrimination. However, the new Civil Rights Act of 1991 countered the move by the Court. Hard quotas have been ruled unlawful, but soft goals have been reaffirmed.

Conclusions

Most people spend a substantial part of their adult life in the workplace. Also, most companies need to have a motivated and capable workforce if they are to remain competitive in today's global market. Thus, issues of concern to employees are of vital interest to business, and responding to employee stakeholder issues is needed for effective business social performance.

This chapter shows that many employee stakeholder issues are mature, and thus a large body of law, regulating agencies, regulations, and common law exist to regulate the actions of business in these areas. We have moved a considerable distance from the laissez-faire days of the market model as envisioned by Adam Smith and the industrialists of the eighteenth and ninteenth centuries. The market system, when left alone, did not respond to the needs of occupational health and safety or to the injustice of discrimination. Thus the political process was activated, and many laws and regulations exist to control the behavior of business in the market. However, this chapter shows that the problems are complex and contentious.

Recent Supreme Court cases were major setbacks for affirmative action and for the enforcement of discrimination laws. This caused this key employee stakeholder issue to go unresolved, and the matter has been recycled through the ILC, resulting in new legislation. Statistical data show that social inequalities have been increasing since 1980 and the problem of discrimination has not gone away. Thus, discrimination and equality are likely to receive much public policy attention in the 1990s.

Discussion Questions

1. Why is discrimination considered to be unethical?
2. In which stage of the ILC is the issue of discrimination and equality? What does this mean for management action?
3. How have equality and discrimination issues been recycled? How is the issue of employment leave policy likely to be recycled?

4. AIDS, a life-threatening disease, is considered a disability and as such is covered by the Vocational Rehabilitation Act, which prohibits discrimination against persons with disabilities. How should business respond to the problem of AIDS in the workplace?

5. Discuss the traditional, individualistic ideology of the market model in terms of discrimination. In terms of workplace safety.

6. Suppose an employee suffering from depression needed to take medication that caused drowsiness. Because of this, the person needed close supervision and would take short naps in the afternoons. What reasonable accommodation would be required for such an employee under the Americans with Disabilities Act of 1990?

7. What are the different types of discrimination? What federal laws prohibit discrimination?

8. What is a prima facie case of discrimination?

9. What types of affirmative action programs are permissible? What types of affirmative action programs are unlawful?

10. Discuss the types of sexual discrimination in the workplace. What is the difference between sexual discrimination and sexual harassment?

Notes

1. Michele Galen, "Work and Family," *Business Week,* June 28, 1993, pp. 80–88.
2. Newman S. Peery, Jr., and Mahmoud Salem, "Strategically Managing Emerging Human Resource Issues," *Human Resource Development Quarterly* 4, no. 1 (Spring 1993): 81–96.
3. Manual Velasquez, *Business Ethics,* 2d ed. (Englewood Cliffs, N.J.: Prentice-Hall, 1988), p. 311.
4. "Progress Report on the Black Executive: The Top Spots Are Still Elusive," *Business Week,* February 20, 1984, pp. 104–105.
5. See *Meritor Savings Bank v. Vinson,* 106 S. Ct. 2399 (1986).
6. Velasquez, *Business Ethics,* chap. 7.
7. "So You Think You've Come a Long Way, Baby?" *Business Week,* February 29, 1988, p. 48.
8. James H. Coil III and Charles M. Rice, "Managing Work-Force Diversity in the Nineties: The Impact of the Civil Rights Act of 1991," *Employee Relations Law Journal* 18, no. 4 (Spring 1993): 547–65.
9. *United Steelworkers v. Weber,* 443, U.S. 193, 1979.
10. Bradford McKee, "Disability Rules Target Job Bias," *Nations Business,* June 1992, pp. 29–33.
11. Timothy Noah and Albert R. Karr, "What New Civil Rights Law Will Mean," *Wall Street Journal,* November 4, 1991, pp. B1–B2.
12. *Price Waterhouse v. Hopkins,* 490 U.S. 229, 1989.
13. Noah and Karr, "What New Civil Rights Law Will Mean," November 4, 1991, p. B1.
14. *Officers for Justice v. Civil Service Commission,* No. 91-16519, Ninth Circuit, November 5, 1992.
15. Antonia Handler Chayes, "Make Your Equal Opportunity Program Court Proof," *Harvard Business Review* (September-October 1974): 81–89.
16. Elizabeth R. Koller, "Sexual Harassment Laws: Do They Make Sense?" paper presented at the annual conference of the Academy of Legal Studies in Business, Colorado Springs, August 19, 1993.
17. *Barnes v. Costle,* 561, F. 2d 983 (D.C. Cir. 1977).
18. Carolyn Wiley, "Perspectives on Sexual Harassment in the Workplace: Cases and Recommendations for Management Practice," *Journal of Business and Economic Perspectives* 28, no. 2 (1992) 46–51.
19. *Meritor Savings Bank v. Vinson,* 477 U.S. 57, 1986.
20. *Broderick v. Ruder,* 46 FEP Cases 1272 (D.D.C., 1988).
21. *Griggs v. Duke Power Co.,* 401 U.S. 424 (1971).
22. Peter Waldman, "Affirmative Action Faces Likely Setback: Justices Seen Changing Rules on Bias Suits," *Wall Street Journal,* November 30, 1988, p. B1.
23. *Johnson v. Transportation Agency of Santa Clara County,* California, 480 U.S. 616.
24. *Price Waterhouse v. Hopkins,* 490 U.S. 228.
25. James H. Coil III and Charles M. Rice, "Managing Work-Force Diversity in the Nineties: The Impact of the Civil Rights Act of 1991," *Employee Relations Law Journal* 18, no. 4 (Spring 1993): 547–65.
26. Joe Davidson, "Jobs Debate: Quotas in Hiring are Anathema to President Despite Minority Gains," *Wall Street Journal,* October 24, 1985, pp. 1, 26.

Discussion Case _____

The Midtown Medical Clinic

The Midtown Medical Clinic was a small emergency clinic near the center of a large city. Though it handled many medical emergencies, it also had a family practice for neighborhood residents. Two doctors were on duty at all times. In addition there were three nurses, two paramedics, an X-ray technician, a small lab with two lab technicians, and a receptionist. Angela, the head nurse, supervised the two other nurses and the two paramedics.

Typically a patient would check in at the front desk with the receptionist. If it was an emergency, a paramedic who worked at the clinic would give preliminary emergency care and make referrals to one of the staff doctors. If it was a routine appointment, the patient would wait for his or her appointment before seeing a doctor. Often one of the nurses would see the patient to care for service costs, dressing, or to administer vaccinations. Also, a nurse would obtain blood or throat cultures for laboratory tests.

Bob, a paramedic, worked closely with Angela and a friendly relationship developed. After a stressful day the couple would occasionally go to a local tavern for a drink after work. Their friendship developed a romantic dimension and they had a consensual sexual relationship. Soon after this, they seemed to have disagreements both on and off the job. When Angela concluded that the relationship was not a positive experience and was interfering with their working relationship, she ended the consensual relationship. However, Bob sought to continue the relationship.

When Angela made it clear that the relationship was over, Bob became very distressed. One morning he screamed at her in front of staff and patients. After this incident Angela assigned Bob the less desirable shift assignments. When he com-plained, she said that everyone had to share the less desirable assignments. He accused her of trying to punish him because of their affair and threatened to call in sick rather than accept the late-night shifts.

Also, Bob became very concerned about who might be calling Angela. He monitored her incoming telephone calls and informed some callers that she was busy, then hung up. This behavior was observed by several co-workers. The situation deteriorated further and Angela filed a complaint against Bob with the director of the medical center. The complaint alleged sexual harassment and cited the screaming episode and the monitoring of her telephone calls as evidence.

Dr. Robertson, the director of the clinic, called a meeting with Angela and Bob upon receipt of the formal complaint. Bob seemed surprised by the complaint and retorted that he, and not Angela, was a victim of sexual harassment. Since the affair had been called off, he had been given poor assignments and had been publicly humiliated by Angela in front of his co-workers. He admitted getting angry and yelling at her in public but explained that her unfair treatment of him was unbearable.

Case Discussion Questions

1. What should Dr. Robertson do?
2. Is this case an example of illegal sexual harassment?
3. What should the manager of the medical clinic do about the complaint filed by Angela?
4. What policy should the medical clinic have concerning relationships among employees?

CHAPTER 18

Business, Ecology, and the Environment

Introduction

In times past when population was smaller and technologies less lethal, the environment was not considered in business decisions. Air and water were considered free goods that were virtually unlimited, of no real cost to society, and somehow seemed to maintain themselves. More recently there are so many waste materials from society and business, many of which are nonbiodegradable, that natural ecosystems are overwhelmed and thus become polluted. Industrialization, population growth, economic development, and changing technology all have contributed to the degradation of the environment.

It is just as important for business to know about ecological systems and the impact of business activities on them as it is to know about the traditional functions of business, economics, and technology. Failure to consider the ecological consequences of business activities and advanced technology can have negative consequences for the quality of life, lead to health problems, and reduce the planet's capacity to support life, as the opening case illustrates.

Also, the regulations protecting the environment now require business to consider the ecological consequences of management practices. Violations of regulations often carry criminal punishment involving fines and imprisonment, though enforcement of "green crimes" has been criticized.

Environmental issues have increased in importance since World War II. As the public became aware of externalities from business degrading the environment, a number of society's control mechanisms discussed in Chapter 2 were called into play:

1. The development of the "green consumer" has created a market demand for environmentally conscious products and services. Many consumers now seek out food without pesticides and recyclable products and avoid toxic products.

2. The public policy process has kept environmental issues near the top of the public policy agenda. Enforcement of existing regulations also has become a matter of public concern. Environmental violations that harm others also can be the basis of civil law suits under tort law.

3. Environmental laws have been passed to protect nearly every aspect of the environment. The Environmental Protection Agency (EPA) has been created to enforce these laws and regulations.

4. Many businesses have joined the environmental movement and have sought to become energy efficient and consider recycling in the design, manufacture, and distribution of products. Such actions by managers is strategically significant because it responds to changing market realities and is also ethically sound.

5. There has been a "greening of business" as managers seek to respond to environmental issues by institutionalizing an environmental ethic within their organizations and to identify new business opportunities.[1]

The environment is the issue that will most affect business prospects in the 1990s and beyond.[2] Many have said that the 1990s are the decade of the environment, and environmental issues will occupy even more of management's attention. This chapter reviews some basic concepts of ecology; how business, technology, and lifestyles have led to the degradation of ecological systems; how the ILC has led to public policy responses to the problems; and what business can do to manage this important stakeholder issue. Proactive man-

agement decisions consistent with ecology can improve the business social performance.

Sustainable Economic Development

Past business decisions were often made without considering the principles of ecology. Management decisions that do not take ecological principles into consideration can unintentionally degrade the natural environment. However, it is possible for business practices to generate economic growth while safeguarding the environment. *Sustainable economic development* requires business decisions to be in harmony with ecological principles. Economic growth that is inconsistent with ecological principles threatens the environment and is not sustainable in the long run.

Industrialized societies use large amounts of energy and generate growing amounts of waste material that pollutes the air and water and fills up landfills. Sustainable economic growth requires that we consider the consequences of business practices and lifestyles on the environment. This will be particularly difficult as the Third World seeks to increase its standard of living and to follow the path of the industrialized countries in economic development.

Buchholz added the dimension of justice in the long run to the concept of sustainable development and has written, "Sustainable growth is concerned with finding paths of social, economic, and political progress that meet the needs of the present without compromising the ability of future generations to meet their own needs.[3] Sustainable development could be based upon (1) boosting efficiency to use fewer resources and produce less wastes, (2) building a framework for change that considers both economics and the environment, (3) stabilizing world population, particularly the high population growth rates of the developing countries, (4) restraining consumption and energy use, particularly the consumption patterns in industrialized countries, as suggested in Figure 18–1.[4]

BOOST EFFICIENCY

Adopt innovations that slash the resources used and pollution emitted per unit of output. These include clean technology such as electric cars, energy efficiency, recycling, closed-loop production, less destructive agriculture, and designing products with less packaging, fewer materials, and longer lives.

+

BUILD A FRAMEWORK FOR CHANGE

Account for environmental costs and benefits in economic transactions and revise GNP calculations. Forge international compacts to protect common resources and address global problems. Enact taxes and other incentives to curtail destructive actions. Boost international aid for poverty alleviation, family planning, sound agriculture, and resource protection in developing nations. Liberalize trade and promote industry investment in developing nations.

+

STABILIZE POPULATION

Improve standards of living and the status of women, and make family planning widely available to help lower birth rates in developing nations.

+

RESTRAIN CONSUMPTION

Foster lifestyles that lessen the burden on the environment, especially in industrialized nations. Depend more on public transportation, less on gas-consuming cars; consume more information-based goods and services; husband consumer goods more carefully; encourage "green consumerism."

=

SUSTAINABLE DEVELOPMENT

With the cooperation of industrialized nations and developing nations alike, worldwide development might proceed without risking constraint from overpopulation, resource depletion, and ecological breakdown.

FIGURE 18–1 A Proposed Solution for Sustainable Development

SOURCE: "Growth vs. Environment: The Push for Sustainable Development," *Business Week*, May 11, 1992, pp. 68-69. Copyright 1992 by McGraw-Hill. Reprinted by special permission.

THE DIFFERENT PERSPECTIVES OF BUSINESS AND ENVIRONMENTALISTS

Business often finds itself in an adversarial relationship with environmentalists. When environmental groups are able to present arguments to business from a business perspective, managers often join the crusade of environmentalism.[5] Also, managers need to be aware of how environmental perspectives differ from those of business in important ways, as shown in Table 18–1. Because business is often seen as a threat to the environment, environmentalists often seek the government's protection and press for laws and regulations to regulate business. Thus, the political ideology of environmentalists is more likely to be community-oriented and favor an activist government. In contrast, business often subscribes to the individualistic, market-oriented ideology that views government activism with suspicion.

The ideology of environmentalism goes beyond the previous discussion of activist government discussed earlier in the book. The core values of business and environmentalism also vary dramatically. Business managers focus on business and the economy, and value economic development and growth and the sustaining of competitive advantage. Environmentalists focus on ecosystems in the natural environment. This is consistent with the core values of sustaining environmental integrity through ecological balance. While business often favors unlimited growth, environmentalists adopt a philosophy of a steady state and balance of natural systems. Thus, limiting growth for ecological principles is a core value of environmentalists.

Table 18–1 also indicates that performance objectives vary from environmentalists to managers. Managers use "the three Es" to measure performance: efficiency, return on equity, and effectiveness as demonstrated by accomplishing objectives. Environmentalists are more likely to be guided by "the four Ps," which include preservation, protection, and preventing pollution of the natural environment. Social goals from a business perspective include maintaining the standard of living and high levels of employment through economic growth and global competitiveness. Social goals from an environmental perspective focus more on the quality of life measured in terms of clean air, lower levels of traffic congestion, lower population congestion and urban sprawl, and maintenance of green belts of the natural environment.

TABLE 18–1
Business and Environmental Perspectives

	Business	Environmentalists
Focus of Attention	Business and economy	Ecosystems in the natural environment
Key Values	Sustaining competitive advantage of business Development and growth of the economy	Sustaining environmental integrity through ecological balance and steady state of natural systems
Performance Objectives for Organization	Three Es for business: efficiency (O/I), effectiveness (goal accomplishment), and equity (ROE) of the business	Four Ps: Preservation Protection Preventing Pollution of the natural environment
Goals of Society	Standard of living Full employment Economic growth	Quality of life Quality of the environment
Key Stakeholders	Stockholders, customers, and employees	Members of society, nature, and future generations

Business and environmentalists also pay attention to different stakeholder groups. Business is concerned with customers and employees as primary stakeholders. Environmentalists consider all members of society and especially future generations, as well as the natural environment, as their primary stakeholders. Thus the perspectives of business and environmentalists are very different. However, it is clear that it is increasingly important that the differences need to be reconciled. This can be done only if environmentalists become sensitive to the concepts that underlie business and business managers become sensitive and incorporate concepts of ecology in their decision making. The remainder of the chapter suggests what this might involve.

Principles of Ecology and the Environment

Ecology is the study of how plants and animals interact in their natural environment. The environment is regulated by complex, interdependent ecological cycles or relationships that can be disrupted by technology, lifestyles, and economic activities. For example, pesticides need to be carefully used and controlled or they will indiscriminately kill all living things; the predators of pests will be killed along with the pests that threaten agricultural crops and interfere with naturally balanced interrelationships. Pesticides have become a major environmental problem because they pollute water supplies, move up the food chain, and endanger animals and humans.

All living things live within a habitat.[6] When marshes are drained for urban development, the habitats for ducks and other water foul disappear. Harvesting old-growth forests has threatened the habitat of the spotted owl, resulting in a controversy between loggers and environmentalists.[7] The technology available in the timber industry produces an economy of scale for large-scale timber harvesting using clear-cutting techniques. Harvesting techniques often exceed the growth rate of

the forest, cause substantial erosion and water pollution, and otherwise destroy the environment.

The practice of sustained yield would limit the amount harvested to the amount grown annually so that the supply of wood, fish, or any other biologically based product would continue to be available indefinitely.

Within a habitat, organisms often have an ecological niche that defines their functional role within a habitat. Modern technology and economic development practices often destroy the ecological niches of living creatures. Some birds live on plants or small animals that live only when certain conditions exist that are uniquely provided by the environment. Deforestation in South America destroys habitats and eliminates ecological niches for songbirds that migrate to the United States.

Salmon have an ecological niche that requires cold water. When water temperature is decreased only a few degrees by decreased releases from reservoirs, the ecological niche of the salmon disappears. Also, the systems of reservoirs used for electric power generation make it nearly impossible for salmon to return to their spawning grounds upstream.

Living things are located in a food chain defined by what a particular animal eats and by what eats that animal. Certain plants like single-organism plankton live off nutrients in the water. Small fish may eat the plankton and are, in turn, eaten by bigger fish or birds that are eventually caught by businesses in the fishing industry. Heavy metals like mercury and many pesticides accumulate in the food chain and increase in concentration levels as they travel up the chain. Mercury has been found in Canada at levels high enough to cause blindness in Native Americans who depend upon fisheries for their livelihood. Mercury-poisoned fish have also been caught off the West Coast of the United States, and for a time certain types of fish were banned by the FDA.

Each habitat has a certain carrying capacity defined by how many of a particular type of living being it can support. For example, the natural food supply of a particular area may support a certain number of animals or fish, and if the population grows significantly above that number, starvation will occur. Also, if too many animals are allowed to graze in a given pasture, the grass cannot be replenished through natural growth. Thus, over-grazing can lead to severe soil erosion and the creation of deserts, as is the case in northern Africa and in parts of Arizona and New Mexico.

Ecological systems have interdependencies among the various organisms living in the habitat and other elements in the environment. Thus when business decisions are made without considering ecological systems, the carrying capacity of a natural system can be overwhelmed by the quest for economies of scale. For example, when sea otters were harvested nearly into extinction on the West Coast, the kelp industry suffered. Sea otters feed on sea urchins, which eat kelp. Sea otters thus control the population of sea urchins and thus protect kelp beds that grow in the coves along the coast.

Ecological systems are not only interdependent but also exist in the state of equilibrium, although many systems can achieve equilibrium or home-ostasis at different levels of functioning. The various component parts of an ecological system must be in balance, or equilibrium, although there may be a number of different possible stable equilibrium points. For example, the number of sea otters indirectly determines the size of the kelp beds that the ecosystem can support. If otters are overharvested, sea urchins, which are their primary food source, multiply and eat the kelp beds.

A fishery system can support a certain harvest level indefinitely if it is low enough to allow for the natural processes of reproduction and growth. If the habitat is overfished through large-scale harvesting, fish, lobsters, crabs, and/or clams may cease to exist in the area. For example, high-technology harvesting and processing of whales nearly drove them into extinction before international agreements controlled harvest levels. Such harvesting caused blue-fin tuna harvest levels to drop by 90 percent in 1993 in the Atlantic Ocean.

More recently, ocean drift nets have decimated the populations of salmon and other species of fish in the northern Pacific. Drift nets are light-weight nets that "drift" for as far as 25 miles in the ocean behind fishing vessels and catch large amounts of fish at very low cost. They were originally developed as a low-cost option for Third World fisheries. However, the ecological destruction due to the indiscriminate catching of sea mammals and salmon was not anticipated. The resulting destabilization of ecological systems has threatened several species. International treaties now prohibit drift nets, although frequent violations are reported.

Business Decisions and Ecology

Business decisions are normally driven by such concepts as economy of scale, efficiency, cost structures, and market growth, as outlined in Table 18–2. In contrast, ecology is determined by such concepts as carrying capacity, interdependencies, food chains, and equilibrium. When industrial and household wastes are disposed of at a rate higher than the environment can absorb and process, pollution results. Ecological cycles can only process biodegradable materials. With the advent of advanced technology, engineered organic chemicals and materials have been used to manufacture pesticides, cleaning agents, solvents, plastic materials, and many other products. These materials often become pollutants because they are resistant to the natural ecological process of decomposition and recycling.

Output/input ratios are used by managers to calculate efficiency. These calculations usually do not consider the ecological interdependencies through which output of waste materials can degrade the environment. Managers consider the cost involved in the chain of functional operations, beginning with the cost of factor inputs and continuing through manufacturing processes, outbound logistics, marketing, and postsale warranty service. Decisions based on cost factors that ignore the environmental externalities can upset the balance of nature.

For example, low-cost nitrogen fertilizers are cost-effective for agribusiness but lead to water pollution when excess fertilizer is washed away. Manufactur-

Table 18–2
Concepts of Ecology and Business Compared

Concepts of Ecology	Basis of Business Decisions
An **ecosystem** is an interdependent system of organisms with habitats.	An **economy** is an interdependent system of buyers and sellers with markets.
Habitats for a species exist within an ecosystem.	**Markets** for a product or service exist within an economy.
Biological growth rates determine the limits of population levels. **Sustained yield** harvesting practices do not exceed annual growth rates.	**Economies of scale** determine appropriate harvest or production level to achieve low costs. This may exceed biological growth rates.
Food chain determines the sequential relationship among species in terms of what species eat others. Business decisions can interfere with food chains and pesticides and pollution can poison the food chain.	**Value chain** determines sequential cost structure for functions. Business decisions are concerned about the costs of various links like purchasing, manufacturing, marketing, or logistics.
Carrying capacity determines population levels that an ecosystem can support.	**Market size** determines how many units will sell, and business often considers market potential and not ecosystem carrying capacity.
Ecological niche determines the role of a particular species within a habitat.	**Competitive position** determines basis and effectiveness among businesses competing in a market.
Pollution is waste material that an ecosystem cannot absorb or process.	**Externalities** are social costs not a part of the transaction and not paid by buyer.
Stable equilibrium is the state at which an ecosystem is in balance. This usually requires a relatively fixed ratio among interdependent populations of species.	**Efficiency** is the ratio of outputs to inputs. Increased efficiency means lowering unit costs. Seeking increased efficiency requires constant system changes.
Interdependencies within ecosystems are complex and an externality may degrade the environment in unexpected ways.	**Independent business decisions** mean that environmental impact may be ignored. This is especially true if they lead to externalities that tend to lower the costs of doing business.

ing processes designed for cost efficiency only may lead to wasteful practices if input costs are relatively low and the discharge of waste materials is uncontrolled. Thus, in recent years beaches have been polluted by chemical discharges. Raw sewage and even medical wastes have washed ashore on beaches in the eastern United States. Logistics based only upon economic considerations lead to less expensive, single-hulled supertankers for hauling petroleum rather than more expensive, double-hulled–designed ships. The massive oil spills like that from the *Exxon Valdez* in 1989 or the one in 1993 off the Shelton Islands may have been avoided by a differently designed tanker.

Environmental impact must be factored into business decisions to achieve sustained development. Failure to consider the ecological consequences of lifestyles and business decisions has resulted in a number of environmental problems. Some of these problems are outlined in the next section.

Major Environmental Problems

Pollutants and harmful waste materials from industrial processes degrade the environment, cause health problems, and threaten the capacity of the earth to support life.[8] The major environmental issues including global warming, depletion of the ozone layer, air and water pollution, toxic and hazardous wastes, and deforestation are listed in Table 18–3.

GLOBAL WARMING

The earth is heated when the energy from sunlight enters the atmosphere and partially cools when infrared radiation escapes into space. Temperatures are controlled by gases and water vapor forming a blanket around the earth that reflects infrared radiation back to the surface. Global warming refers to an overall rise in the temperature of the planet caused by the greenhouse effect of trapping solar radiation that would normally be reflected into space. This ecosystem is being changed by the continuous buildup of greenhouse gases in the atmosphere resulting from the use of fossil fuels, chlorofluorocarbons (CFCs), and the elimination of tropical rain forests.

There is some uncertainty about the extent and timing of global warming. In the ecosystem, increased heat should cause evaporation of the ocean water to form clouds. The increased cloud cover cools the earth. Oceans tend to store heat better than land areas, and the oceans may absorb enough heat to counter some of the increased heat generated by the greenhouse effect.

However, data seem to suggest that global warming is a reality.[9] The four hottest years in recorded history occurred during the 1980s. Increased heat and drought have hit many regions of the globe including the United States. In the last decade, the western United States experienced massive forest fires, the worst drought in 400 years hit California, and agricultural grain reserves have declined as crops failed with the hot, dry climate. The deserts of Africa continued to grow, and millions of people were threatened by famine.

Scientists have estimated that the earth's average temperature has increased between 0.5 and 1.5 degrees centigrade since the beginning of industrialization but could go up another three degrees by 2030. A continued trend of global warming could lead to the following:

1. Rainfall belts would shift northward, increasing Arctic precipitation 20–30 percent, leaving prairie and northern forests drier.
2. Oceans would expand. Large glaciers and ice-caps would melt, causing sea levels to rise and flooding in low-lying, populated areas.
3. Tundra would be pushed northward to Arctic islands, eventually as much as 200 to 300 kilometers, leaving insufficient time for the soils to develop to support forests.
4. Melting permafrost (frozen organic matter) would release huge amounts of methane—one of the greenhouse gases.
5. Changes in climatic conditions along the Arctic Ocean and North Atlantic coastlines would have major impacts on marine life.
6. During the first decades of warming, thousands more icebergs would appear, threatening navigation and offshore oil production.[10]

Although the danger of not acting to prevent further global warming is great, many actions can be taken, as outlined in Box 18–1. These proposed actions would require world governments to agree to eliminate CFCs within five years. Also, timber practices leading to tropical deforestation would need to be changed. Industry would need to increase fuel efficiency and market more fuel-efficient automobiles, and individuals would need to change lifestyles to conserve energy.

TABLE 18–3
Major Environmental Problems

Global problems are environmental problems that potentially affect the entire planet and whose consequences cut across national boundaries.

Global warming, or the so-called greenhouse effect. Greenhouse gases including carbon dioxide, methane, nitrous oxides, and chlorofluorocarbons (CFCs) contain heat much as does the gas in a greenhouse and gradually increase the temperatures throughout the earth. This could melt the polar ice caps and cause widespread coastal flooding.

Ozone depletion. Worldwide emissions of CFCs and other chlorine compounds last for up to 100 years and threaten to deplete upper atmospheric ozone—the substance that shields earth from harmful ultraviolet radiation.

Acid rain is rain that contains dilute solutions of nitric or sulfuric acid. It occurs when nitrogen oxides and sulfuric oxides (often produced by industrial air emissions) combine with atmospheric water vapor. Public utilities in the Midwest cause acid rain in the eastern U.S. and Canada.

Air quality is reduced by outdoor pollution caused by seven pollutants (carbon monoxide, hydrocarbons, lead, nitrogen dioxide, ozone, sulfur dioxide, and total suspended particulates) regulated by the EPA. These pollutants combine to form *smog* in urban areas, lowering air quality, causing health problems, and resulting in property damage.

Indoor air pollution often exceeds outdoor air pollution because modern buildings are tightly sealed and have air recirculation systems. Indoor air pollutants include tobacco smoke, radon, evaporation from cleaning solvents and other industrial chemicals, and airborne pathogens. This type of pollution is becoming recognized as a major health hazard.

Air pollution has to do with air quality, acid rain, and indoor air pollution. Air pollution occurs when more pollutants are dumped into the air than the ecosystem can dilute or process.

Water pollution is the degradation of water systems by sewage wastes, oxygen-demanding organic wastes, water-soluble inorganic chemicals, inorganic plant nutrients from agriculture, organic chemicals, and radioactive wastes that enter groundwater systems, streams, and lakes. Water pollution causes health problems and birth defects, and destroys the ability of water systems to support life.

Pesticides are dangerous to human health and the environment, even though they may protect crops and discourage pests. Consumers of food contaminated by pesticides, farm workers, and creatures living in natural habitats can all be harmed by pesticides.

Toxic and hazardous wastes include some 250 million tons of material produced annually. These can cause or significantly contribute to an increase in mortality or an increase in serious irreversible or incapacitating illness and pose a hazard to human health when improperly treated, transported, stored, or disposed of in the environment.

Solid wastes include household garbage and industrial waste materials that threaten to overwhelm local landfills used as waste disposal sites.

Deforestation and elimination of species. Forests, especially tropical forests, are not being managed with sustained yield practices; nearly 10 million hectares of forestland are cleared annually. This destroys habitat, and eliminates thousands of species. Also, deforestation contributes to the global warming problem because trees process carbon dioxide naturally in the ecosystem.

SOURCE: Adapted from G. Tyler Miller, Jr., *Living in the Environment: An Introduction to Environmental Studies,* 6th ed. (Bemont, Calif.: Wadsworth, 1990), and Russell Wild, *The Earth Care Annual 1990* (Emmaus, Pa.: Rodale Press, 1990).

DESTRUCTION OF THE OZONE LAYER

The ozone layer in the stratosphere stops ultraviolet rays from reaching the surface of the earth. If the ozone layer were destroyed, the planet would cease to support life. Deterioration in the ozone layer would sharply reduce crop yields in peas, beans, squash, cabbage, soybeans, and other crops. The EPA has predicted that the thinning ozone layer will cause 200,000 skin cancer deaths in the United States by the year 2050 and imperil crops and ecosystems.[11] Each 1 percent drop in

---

BOX 18–1 Ten Steps to Turn Off the Heat

Used in combination, the following steps could take the world from the abyss of environmental despair to a realistic Promised Land, with virtually zero pollution. And it could do so by 2050, or even earlier, using existing technologies and actions—if only we have the will.

1. Switch to natural gas where possible. It cuts all three of the critical air pollutants, halving carbon dioxide, the main greenhouse gas. When natural gas is burned in one of the new superturbines already available, air pollution is reduced still further.

2. Burn coal more efficiently. Switching to a new technology such as pressurized, fluidized-bed combustion cuts sulfur pollution by 94 percent and oxides by 30 percent over conventional coal-burning power-plant operations.

3. Cleanse the stack gases. Pollution controls added to existing coal-fired power plants cut sulfur dioxides and oxides of nitrogen by up to another 90 percent. One technology has already been installed on 400 power plants abroad.

4. Don't waste the heat. Instead of burning fuel in one place to generate electricity and another to manufacture products, combine these processes. Cogeneration boosts total efficiency to 85–90 percent, dropping air pollution by another 40–50 percent.

5. Build better cars. In the United States alone, a five-mile-per-gallon improvement in auto mileage would cut carbon dioxide pollution by nearly 200 billion pounds a year. Fuel-efficient cars would cut automotive carbon dioxide by up to 70 percent.

6. Phase out freons. Chlorofluorocarbons (CFCs) could be virtually eliminated in five years if governments mandated that existing alternatives be used. An additional ban on CFC spraycan use would cut this gas by 25 percent. [These have been banned in the United States since 1976.]

7. Make homes more efficient. Replacing current generation, energy-hungry water heaters, air conditioners, furnaces, and light bulbs would cut household energy consumption—and air pollution from homes by 50–56 percent.

8. Halt tropical deforestation. New schemes that allow multiple harvesting, sustainable development, and replanting of certain species—instead of burning virgin jungle—can cut air pollution from a given acre by 90 percent.

9. Curtail industry energy consumption. Industries in the United States and Canada gobble twice as much energy per unit of production as their Japanese counterparts. Put them on a par and industrial air pollution is cut by 50 percent in North America.

10. Use hydrogen fuel. Over the long term, development of radically different technologies, including those that use hydrogen, is the answer, because interim phaseout of dirty cars and power plants may be offset by population and economic growth.

Source: Curtis A. Moore, "Ten Steps to Turn Off the Heat," *International Wildlife*, May/June 1989. All rights reserved.

ozone is likely to result in a 4 to 6 percent increase in skin cancer.

The major cause of ozone depletion is CFCs, inert chemicals that are so stable that they exist in the environment for 75 to 100 years before breaking down. CFCs were discovered by chemists working for General Motors during the 1920s who were searching for a stable, safe, and nontoxic substance that could be used for refrigeration. Because of their unique properties, many other uses were found for CFCs, including as solvents to remove glue, as a major component in foam packaging, as solvents for soldering microcomputers, and as a propellant in aerosol cans. In 1974, two University of California chemists discovered that CFCs could eventually find their way to the ozone layer, where a single CFC molecule could lead to the destruction of thousands of ozone molecules. Ultraviolet rays separate chlorine molecules from the CFCs that, in turn, destroy ozone. CFCs were banned for use in aerosol cans in the United States in 1976, though they continue to be used for this purpose in many other countries.

On April 4, 1991, the EPA announced that measurements from a NASA satellite revealed that the fragile ozone layer had shrunk as much as 5 percent over the United States in the past ten years, at least 50 percent more than previously estimated. Some 67 nations have signed the updated Montreal protocol, which agreed to ban CFCs and other chlorine-containing compounds that destroy ozone by the year 2000. The Clean Air Act of 1990 calls for phasing out interim substitutes, in favor of entirely harmless ones, by 2015.

ACID RAIN

The news media first reported rain and snow containing acid in the 1970s. Acid-forming pollutants captured in weather systems was found to travel hundreds of miles from their sources to pollute waters across state and national boundaries. Primary sources of acid rain are sulfur dioxide from power plants that burn coal high in sulfur, and nitrogen oxides from industrial furnaces and gasoline-burning automobiles.

These pollutants enter the air and chemically interact to form nitric and sulfuric acids that then are born by the winds until dissolved with rain or snow as they return to the earth. When the acidic water enters the soil, it robs plants of nutrients by breaking down certain minerals that later form to poison the waterways. The result is the pollution of waterways that destroys forests and kills wildlife in lakes and streams. Also, its corrosiveness damages buildings and water systems.[12]

AIR POLLUTION

The ecosystem can dilute and eliminate large amounts of chemicals that are emitted into the air. However, modern industrial processes and the automobile dump such large quantities into the environment that the purifying capacity of the ecosystem is overwhelmed. The result is air pollution.

Outdoor Air Quality

Air pollution has long been a major environmental problem. Eighteenth-century London and other cities experienced severe air pollution from coal-burning factories and home heating systems. More recently, the automobile exhaust released in large cities has interacted through photosynthesis to form ozone, a major ingredient of smog. London experienced a major air pollution incident in 1952 in which 4,000 people died. Such air pollution is particularly bad in cities where atmospheric inversions trap it, forming high concentrations that can be lethal.

The major air pollutants, their sources, and health effects are listed in Table 18–4. Although 99 percent of the air is gaseous nitrogen and oxygen, the seven pollutants, even in relatively small quantities, can cause major health problems. The EPA has set ambient air quality standards for these seven pollutants without regard to the cost or availability of control technology.

The Clean Air Act of 1970 authorized the EPA to establish 247 air quality control regions with a goal of achieving the air quality standards by 1975. Amendments to the act extended the target dates until 1982 except for transportation system pollu-

TABLE 18–4
Major Air Pollutants and Their Health Effects

Pollutant	Major Sources	Characteristics and Effects
Carbon monoxide (CO)	Vehicle exhaust	Colorless, odorless poisonous gas. Replaces oxygen in red blood cells, causing dizziness, unconsciousness, or death.
Hydrocarbons (H C)	Incomplete combustion of gasoline; evaporation of petroleum fuels, solvents, and paints	Although some are poisonous, most are not. Reacts with NO_2 to form ozone or smog.
Lead (Pb)	Antiknock agents in gasoline; also in lead-based paints	Accumulates in the bone and soft tissues. Affects blood-forming organs, kidneys, and nervous system. Suspected of causing learning disabilities in young children.
Nitrogen dioxide (NO_2)	Industrial processes, vehicle exhausts	Causes structural and chemical changes in the lungs. Lowers resistance to respiratory infections. Reacts in sunlight with hydrocarbons to produce smog. Contributes to acid rain.
Ozone (O_3)	Formed when hydrocarbons and (NO_2) react	Principal constituent of smog. Irritates mucous membranes, causing coughing, choking, and impaired lung function. Aggravates chronic asthma and bronchitis.
Sulfur dioxide (SO_2)	Burning coal and oil, industrial processes	Corrosive, poisonous gas. Associated with coughs, colds, asthma, and bronchitis. Contributes to acid rain.
Total suspended particulates (TSP)	Industrial plants, heating boilers, auto engines, dust	Larger visible types (soot, smoke, or dust) particles can pass into the bloodstream. Often carry carcinogens and toxic metals, and impair visibility.

SOURCE: *Environmental Health,* 2d ed. (Washington, D.C.: Congressional Quarterly Inc., 1982) p. 21.

tants of carbon monoxide and ozone that were to be controlled by 1987. Each state was required to develop specific plans for attaining the required air quality standards for the regions within the state jurisdiction. More recently, the 1990 Clean Air Act seeks to reduce air pollution from stationary sources like manufacturing facilities through the use of a permitting system discussed later in the chapter.

Indoor Air Pollution
The EPA has released reports that indicate that indoor air pollution may be worse than what is found outdoors. Indoor air pollution includes formaldehyde, tobacco smoke, radon, combustion products from furnaces and appliances, and chemicals from household items like cleaning products, paints, solvents, and pesticides.[13] Formaldehyde is

used in particle board and a variety of other building products; it can cause irritation, headaches, and possibly cancer. Secondary smoke is a major cause of lung cancer, as is radon, a naturally occurring radiation. Other forms of indoor pollution have been linked to a variety of health problems. As buildings are made more air-tight to conserve energy, the problems with indoor air pollution become worse.

WATER POLLUTION

The supply of fresh water is collected, purified, and distributed in the ecosystem by a process of evaporation from surface water into clouds that are moved by air currents and later precipitated. Precipitation and surface runoff slowly enter porous, water-bearing underground rock called aquifers, which become the major source of groundwater. This system functions as long as water is not withdrawn faster than it can be resupplied and as long as it does not become polluted from overloading with waste materials.[14]

Another aspect of carrying capacity is the capacity of an ecosystem to "carry" or decompose waste materials. Oxygen in water systems is needed to convert biological wastes into inorganic salts.[15] The biological oxygen demand (BOD) is a measure of the amount of oxygen required to break down waste; if this exceeds the amount available in a lake, eutrophication results. The waste material that exceeds the BOD capacity of the water becomes water pollution and, if the levels increase beyond some point, ultimately destroys the ecosystem. The waterway then ceases to provide pure water for human use, to support fish, or to supply safe recreation.

Major sources of water pollution include point sources from identifiable locations, including sewage and wastes from industrial facilities. Nonpoint sources cannot be located and include runoff from agricultural regions, urban settings, open-pit mining, and construction sites. From these sources pollution includes sediments, pesticides, and fertilizers from agriculture, organic waste from sewage, phosphates from household detergents, and toxic substances from industry and synthetic chemicals.

There have been a number of major laws that regulate water pollution beginning in 1899 as outlined in Table 18–5. These laws sought initially to control the pollution of navigable waters and shores. As awareness of the problems of pollution increased, the regulation of water pollution was extended to cover free-flowing waters and watersheds used for drinking. Initially pollution control was attempted at the local level, then at the local level enforced by a federal agency, and then federal water standards were established and regulated by a federal agency located within the Department of Health, Education, and Welfare. Later enforcement authority was transferred to the EPA.

PESTICIDES AND TOXIC SUBSTANCES

Pesticides can be a dangerous source of pollution. There are many types of pesticides, including herbicides for killing weeds, insecticides for killing insects, fungicides for killing fungi, and rodenticides for killing rodents. Some 3 billion pounds of pesticides—nearly one pound for each person on earth—are used annually by agriculture, industry, forestry, government, and home gardeners. Modern agriculture depends heavily on pesticides to control pests so that food can be produced.[16]

However, pesticides are by nature toxic and can be dangerous to human health. Pesticides used to kill pests move up the food chain from insects and plants, to animals, and to humans. Pesticides dumped on land can contaminate it, and when dissolved in water, pesticides find their way into aquifers to contaminate groundwater. Rachel Carson, in her book *Silent Spring*, dramatically documented how DDT accumulated in the food chain and was responsible for killing bird life . The resulting controversy ultimately led to the banning of DDT and the control of pesticides by the EPA.

SOLID WASTE DISPOSAL
AND SCARCITY OF LANDFILLS

The United States is running short of landfill capacity, and local communities, states, and regions face mounting costs and critical environmental choices.[17] Americans produce roughly 160 million tons of solid waste each year. About 80 percent of it is dumped into a shrinking pool of sanitary landfills. It is estimated that 25 percent of the nation's major cities will run out of landfill space within by 1996.[18] The largest category of garbage produced in the United States is consumer product containers and packaging, much of it plastic. Sales of plastic products exceed $150 billion a year. Plastic eventually turns into garbage, and it degrades extremely slowly. Plastics account for roughly 25 percent of all solid waste measured by volume, versus 40 percent for paper.[19]

The options to deal with the solid-waste crisis are to (1) reduce the amount of plastics manufactured and used, (2) recycle them, (3) incinerate them, and (4) dump them into landfills. Business is coming under increasing pressure to use less material for packages, make packages out of recycled material, and ensure that packages are recyclable or degradable. Pressures are mounting from the environmental movement, consumers, and government for businesses to respond to the solid-waste crisis.

Environmentalists have long fought for such "green" packages that are made of recycled material or can be recycled, and more consumers are now demanding them. Consumers have even indicated they would be willing to pay up to 5 percent more for such recycled, recyclable, or degradable packages. State and local governments are also concerned about a waste disposal crisis and are not content to let market forces guide the development of green packages. Many new laws are being considered by state and local governments that are likely to be enacted if businesses do not act responsibly.

TOXIC AND HAZARDOUS SUBSTANCES

Chemicals are used in a wide variety of products and contribute to the high standards of living in the industrialized world. Although most chemicals do not pose a threat, exposure to some can cause hazards such as birth defects, cancer, and serious environmental degradation.[20] The slightest exposure to some chemicals poses a major threat to public health. A major goal of the government regulatory process is to reduce exposure to hazardous substances.

The Toxic Substances Control Act (TSCA) requires that the EPA be notified of any new chemical before its manufacture, and authorizes

TABLE 18–5
Major U.S. Water Pollution Laws

Rivers and Harbors Act of 1899	Prohibits discharge of pollutants or refuse into or on the banks of navigable waters without a permit.
Oil Pollution Act of 1924	Prohibits the discharge of refuse and oil into or upon coastal or navigable waters of the United States.
Water Pollution Control Act of 1948	Requires the U.S. Public Health Service to provide information and to help coordinate local efforts to control pollution.
Water Pollution Control Act of 1956 (amended 1961)	Provides for federal jurisdiction in enforcement of water pollution control actions brought by state-level water pollution agencies.
Water Quality Act of 1965	Creates the Water Pollution Control Administration within HEW. (now HHS). Provides for setting water quality standards.
Clean Water Restoration Act of 1966	Imposes fines on polluters who fail to file required reports.
Water Quality Improvement Act of 1970	Prohibits discharge of harmful amounts of oil into or upon navigable waters or on the shores of the United States.

the EPA to regulate production, use, or disposal of a chemical.[21] This act provides a "cradle-to-the-grave" regulatory environment that subjects toxic substances to government regulation throughout its environmental life cycle. Under this regulatory approach, the EPA assesses the risks of new chemicals before they are manufactured or imported into the United States. If the risks are considered too high, a chemical can be denied entry. Toxic substances that pose an acceptable level of risk are tracked through the manufacturing process and on to their commercial use. Eventually the regulation controls the safe disposal of the substance.

In 1977, hazardous chemicals were discovered leaking from an abandoned dump site in Niagara Falls, New York, causing the contamination of Love Canal, a suburban development. Elected officials had bought a contaminated site from Hooker Chemical for the price of one dollar and had converted it into a city park. The discovery of the toxic contamination in a children's playground became a major controversy and heightened public awareness of the dangers posed by buried toxic substances.

The EPA estimates that some 264 tons of toxic wastes are produced each year. Most of this waste material is produced by business and is stored or treated on site. However, if the property becomes contaminated, the business involved is legally liable for the cleanup of the material and for any subsequent contamination of groundwater caused by the migration of toxic wastes. The Resource Conservation and Recovery Act (RCRA) was passed in 1976 to control the generation, transportation, storage, and disposal of toxic wastes. Some 3,000 facilities manage 275 million metric tons of wastes covered by this law annually. The RCRA provides for the following:

1. Federal classification of wastes as ignitable and thus potentially a fire hazard, as corrosive acid, as reactive and thus explosive, and as toxic and thus a potential threat to human health or the environment.

2. The EPA is responsible for the cradle-to-the-grave tracking of toxic substances.

3. The EPA is responsible for the development of standards throughout the cradle-to-the-grave environmental life cycle of toxic substances. This includes standards for generators, transporters, treatment, storage, and disposal of toxic substances.

4. The EPA is empowered to enforce its standards through a permitting system. This system permits business to produce and process toxic substances during its environmental life cycle.

5. State regulations are allowed to replace the federal programs if they meet the standards.

DEFORESTATION AND THE ELIMINATION OF SPECIES

Forests, as ecological systems, are a renewable resource if managed according to the principle of sustained yield. According to this principle, the upper limit on timber harvest levels is the amount that can be replaced by its natural growth during the year. Unfortunately, forest resources are mismanaged throughout the world. Controversies in this area abound. Clearing old-growth timber and endangering the habitat of threatened species like the spotted owl is a controversy in the northwestern United States. Tropical rain forests are subjected to a slash-and-burn process to create grasslands for agricultural use and to raise beef for sale to fast-food chains in industrialized countries.

Timber is cleared in Malaysia and other Pacific Rim countries by Japanese-based MNCs that do not follow sustained yield or reforestation management practices.

The elimination of the rain forests contributes to global warming, to extensive soil erosion, and to the collapse of local economies. For example, forest mismanagement practices in Central America has caused soil erosion that is so severe during the rainy season that most good agricultural land has been destroyed. The rural peasants are thus driven from their lands by poverty and move to the cities, where huge slums are created. Also, because the rain forest is the habitat for most of the planet's animal species, its elimination is driving thousands of species to extinction each year.

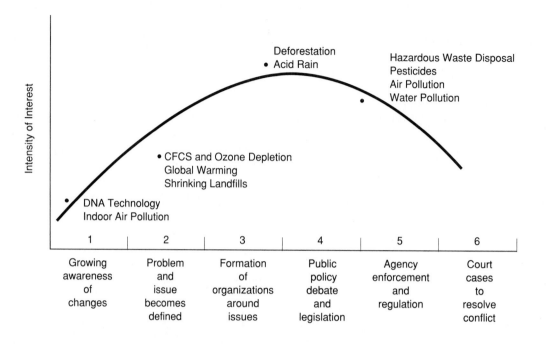

FIGURE 18–2 The Issue Life Cycle and Environmental Issues

Business, Ecology and the Issue Life Cycle

Environmental issues, taken as a whole, are relatively mature in the ILC. Because economic development, population growth, and technological change have continued, new issues concerning the environment continually appear. Figure 18–2 identifies a number of environmental issues and their ILC stage.

Government Regulation of the Environment

The EPA was formed in 1970 to protect the environment and to enforce environmental laws passed beginning early in that decade. The EPA is the major enforcer of environmental law, although the Department of the Interior is responsible for enforcing the 1973 Endangered Species Act, and

the Nuclear Regulatory Commission licenses and regulates nuclear power plants. The Council on Environmental Quality, established in 1969, does analysis and recommends national policy in the area of environmental regulation. In all some 21 agencies are involved in the regulation of the environment. There are also local regulatory agencies at the state, regional, and city levels of government. Major laws exist for every one of the environmental problems outlined above.

Approaches to Environmental Regulation

The government uses a number of approaches to environmental regulation, including (1) setting standards, (2) using incentives to encourage business to reduce pollution, (3) charging for pollution, and (4) allowing for a market to be established for the buying and selling of pollution rights.

Banning a Substance

Sometimes a toxic substance is viewed as a danger to public health and no standard for its use is considered in the public interest. For example, the insecticides DDT and cloradane have both been banned in the United States, as have been lead additives for regular gasoline. Since these substances have been banned, public exposure has been nearly eliminated.

The Best Available Technology Standard

Regulatory standards are often based on technological and economic feasibility. In command-and-control approaches to regulation, a particular technology might be mandated by the regulatory agency. The Clean Air Act of 1970 as amended in 1977 prescribed two different standards for choosing emission control technology, including the best system of continuous emission reduction and the lowest achievable emission rate. Similarly, the Clean Water Act sets standards based upon the best available technology (BAT). Because air and water pollution occur in a large number of settings with a wide variety of technological processes, determining the best available technology is often a complicated matter. This type of regulation requires that the EPA keep track of available technologies so that standards can be kept current.

USING MARKET INCENTIVES TO REGULATE THE ENVIRONMENT

The idea behind market incentives is to use the profit motive guiding the private interests of business to accomplish the public policy of environmental control. While the idea might have wide applicability, it has been used primarily in the area of air pollution control. The two major approaches use offsets in which low levels of pollution attainable in some areas can offset the EPA standards in other areas where it is less feasible to reduce pollution to the EPA standard. The offset concept has been used in different forms in the so-called bubble concept and in the creation of a market for the buying and selling of pollution rights.

The Bubble Concept

According to the bubble concept, a business that owns an industrial complex with several sources of air pollution is viewed by the EPA as a "bubble," and the air quality standard is set for the entire complex rather than for each smokestack or other source of pollution. Thus, if a business can sharply reduce the emissions from some sources but cannot meet the EPA standard for others within the same complex, the overall standard for the complex might still be met. This bubble concept provides an incentive for business managers to take a larger systems viewpoint and find the best way to reduce pollution overall. This avoids spending an unreasonable amount on pollution control for an older facility when the same investment might reduce the overall level of pollution much more if applied to other potential sources of pollution.

Providing a Market for Pollution Rights

The 1990 Clean Air Act provides for the buying and selling of pollution rights. According to this law, a polluter has the right to emit pollutants up to the pollution standard set by the EPA. If a business reduces its pollution level below the allowable standard, it can sell the right to emit the remaining pollutants up to the level of the EPA standard. Other businesses that are sources of pollution in the same area may not be able to economically meet the EPA standard by making technological changes in their facility. These polluters over the EPA standard can buy the right to pollute from businesses operating under the standard.

The creation of a market for pollution rights authorized by the Clean Air Act of 1990 has been criticized by those who object to such a legal right. However, this approach leaves it up to managers to find the most cost-effective way to meet environmental standards set by the EPA. It might be cost-effective for businesses to develop new technologies to reduce pollution if they can obtain a good price for their pollution rights. The hope is that this approach will make the regulatory process more efficient and improve the overall quality of the environment by using market incentives to accomplish public policy.

GOVERNMENT DEVELOPMENT OF A MARKET FOR RECYCLED PRODUCTS

The government, with its massive purchasing power, is creating markets for those products and for recycled tires, re-refined oil, insulation containing recycled cellulose or other recovered materials, and cement made with fly ash left over from garbage incineration. Responding to public pressures and legislative mandates, federal, state, and local government agencies are buying such products as recycled paper and lumber made from plastic milk containers.[22]

Thirty-nine states and the District of Columbia, representing nearly 93 percent of the U.S. population, have some policy favoring recycled products. Governments at all levels are generating regulations and guidelines for their purchasing agents to encourage markets that are sensitive to the environment. The EPA is the key federal agency issuing guidelines. Any government agency that buys $10,000 or more per year of products covered in EPA guidelines must buy items that meet requirements for recovered-material content.

The Greening of Business

The institutional orientation of business has shifted from defensive to proactive in the last two decades. Businesses need to understand thoroughly how social pressures affect their markets and to adapt accordingly. Many large corporations have launched environmental initiatives:

IBM has slashed its use of ozone-depleting CFCs by 31 percent and has dedicated a research center in Bergen, Norway, to study climate.

General Electric evaluates new products according to environmental criteria and invested some $200 million in environmental projects in 1990.

DuPont has the goal of reducing air emissions by 60 percent between 1990 and 1993, and toxic wastes by 35 percent by the year 2000. It is phasing out CFCs and is developing an alternative.

Monsanto will reduce toxic air emissions by 90 percent by 1992 from its 1988 levels and plans to spend $600 million on environmental programs by 1992.

Union Carbide will spend $310 million per year from 1990 to 1994 on the environment and recycling programs. It recycles or reuses 50 percent of its hazardous solid wastes.[23]

Institutionalizing the Environmental Ethic

A successful environmental policy should be based on a sound environmental strategy that has the following components:

1. Top management commitment
2. Empowerment of employees
3. Communication of environmental policy to all employees and company constituencies
4. Involvement with all kinds of audiences
5. Cooperation with government and communities.[24]

Suzanne Gauntlett has consulted a number of businesses on the implementation of an environmental ethic within the organization and uses the following approach:

1. Obtain the support of the chief executive officer (CEO) and top management. It is a major mistake for the CEO to recognize that there is an environmental necessity and then to delegate action to an environmental department or to a staff department within the organization. If an environmental program is seen within the organization as a staff-initiated project, it is likely to receive little middle-management support.

2. Form a steering committee or task force whose members include middle managers, engineers, suppliers, and workers from various departments.

3. The task force should visit plants and facilities to determine the concrete business problems that affect the environment and environmental regulation. The task force does an environmental assessment and selects areas for operating environmental programs. It is important to get ideas from various areas within the organization to identify environmental problems and formulate projects with a high likelihood of success, with sufficient enthusiasm and commitment from within the organization.

4. Develop a companywide model for environmental improvement based on the results of the first few projects. Incorporate more people into the effort so that the environmental ethic can have an impact on the corporate culture.

5. Implement the environmental improvement model in each organizational unit, tailoring its implementation to the particular needs found in each particular department. A common mistake at this point is to try to institutionalize an environmental program simply by using posted slogans or by a series of training programs. The key to success is the hands-on implementation of environmental programs in operations throughout the organization. Also, if the departmental managers and employees at the operational level are not involved in adapting a program to their unique needs, implementation will likely be resisted. Then if top management, or worse, a staff unit tries to impose a program by directive, the program will probably not work. Then the environmental project director will return to the CEO and proclaim that he or she does not know how to make an environmental program work successfully.

6. Top management should maintain interest in the program by requiring regular reporting of progress. Follow-through should be closely monitored, and the successes in implementation of the environmental model for the business should be reflected in the reward system.[25]

Managing the Environmental Product Life Cycle

The EPA and Congress are making efforts to persuade business to act responsibly and, in some cases, pressure businesses to minimize their generation of toxic and hazardous waste. Because of the increasing demands of the regulatory system, the cost to industry of controlling toxic and hazardous waste is skyrocketing. The generation of toxic and hazardous waste results in liability under the regulatory statutes or produce adverse publicity for the company under public reporting requirements.

Business traditionally used "end of pipe" to deal with environmental problems. According to this approach, the output of environmentally hazardous wastes was measured and, if necessary, treated. If treatment was not possible, the generated waste was managed through a disposal program sanctioned by the EPA. An alternative adopted by business recently is a systems approach in environmental programs that utilizes the environmental product life cycle, as shown in Figure 18–3.

Recycling of disposed equipment parts is unlikely because it is usually not possible. Once a

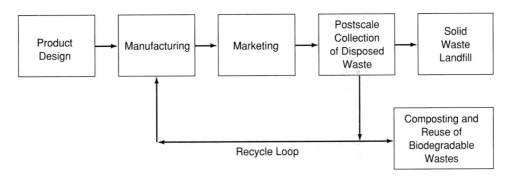

FIGURE 18–3 The Environmental Product Life Cycle

piece of equipment has ended its useful life, parts are hard to disassemble, and comingled materials are not recyclable. Often no market exists for material that has been collected after the natural useful life of a piece of equipment. Sound environmental practices begin with engineering and product design. If recycling is to be a reality, then products must be designed with this in mind so that at the end of the useful product life, they can be easily disassembled and different types of components separated. Different types of plastics vary from one another, and each major type of plastic must be sorted together. Also, metal component parts must be sorted.

SOURCE REDUCTION

Waste Minimization Programs

Corporate waste minimization programs may offer a competitive advantage to the extent that pollution prevention can help avoid or significantly reduce pollution control costs or provide a marketing edge for a product. A number of large manufacturers have taken leadership positions in redundancy waste and pollution prevention.[26] The 3M Corporation operates Pollution Prevention Pays, a program that has saved the company millions of dollars in disposal and related costs by reducing wastes. Procter and Gamble minimizes waste by selling detergents in containers that can be refilled rather than disposed of after one use (see Box 18–2).

DESIGN AND MANUFACTURING FOR REUSE

The General Electric Corporation

The General Electric Plastics Group uses the environmental life cycle in its product design, manufacturing, and recycling system. Products are manufactured using a stacking technique that isolates different types of material from each other while still enabling a piece of equipment to accomplish its purpose, like lawn mowing or transporting people. GE engineers design products for recycling and negotiate agreements with suppliers and downstream manufacturers who are their primary customers for GE plastics. Negotiations with customers established responsibility for disassembling, sorting, and recycling of the plastics and metal parts of equipment. This total systems approach based upon the environmental life cycle of its product facilitates environmentally sound management.

Eastman Kodak and the Single-use Camera

Kodak recently introduced a single-use camera. Initially it was criticized for encouraging waste because the camera was marketed as "disposable." However, the product was designed with the environmental life cycle concept. The camera holds a single role of film that is turned in to authorized developers after the pictures are taken. The film is separated from the plastic cameras. The cameras are then disassembled and plastic parts are reused up to six times. The remaining plastic is ground up and recycled to make other cameras. Nearly one million of the single-use cameras have been recycled in this manner.

Managing Relationships with Regulators

Companies have a lot to gain by fostering a smooth working relationship with regulators.[27] Obstacles to a positive relationship between business and environmental regulators include conflicting priorities and perspectives of business and the environmental perspective of regulators. This leads to a mutual underlying distrust, agency skepticism of business, and top management impatience with government interference. Rapport with regulators by management allows companies to avoid unpleasant surprises, obtain faster decisions from regulators, reduce costs of regulation to business, and avoid the risks of public debate.

BOX 18–2 P&G Tries Hauling Itself Out of America's Trash Heap

Garbage. That's one of the top concerns of Ed Artzt, Procter & Gamble Co.'s new chairman. "We want to be among the leaders," says Artzt, "in dealing with this problem."

It's easy to see why. P&G sells $21 billion a year worth of everything from toothpaste to tissue. Indirectly, that makes it a big contributor to the 160 million tons of household garbage America throws out each year, which has landfills brimming. To critics, P&G's Pampers and Luvs disposable diapers are code words for environmental profligacy. So, with public opinion running against conspicuous waste, it's in P&G's interest to find a way, as Artzt puts it, "to make our products environmentally friendly."

Downy Refills. P&G has handed the job to its operating managers, who are told to treat like any consumer demand, "similar to if we needed a better detergent," says Research Vice-President Geoffrey Place, the company's self-styled "head garbageman." Already, P&G has quit using inks and pigments containing heavy metals that might show up in incinerator ash and, buried, contaminate groundwater. The company has begun to reduce excess packaging, redesigning Crisco oil bottles to use 28 percent less plastic and compressing Pampers into smaller plastic packs. It also now sells superconcentrated detergents requiring 15 percent less packaging. And in a test in Baltimore, P&G is trying to get Downy fabric softener buyers to use just one plastic container, over and over. Taking a leaf from its approach in Europe, the company sells Downy refills in milk-style cartons that use less space in landfills.

Even more ambitious are P&G's efforts to support plastics recycling. The company will soon be using up 80 million recycled milk, water, and soft-

drink bottles a year. It is about to begin selling some sizes of Liquid Tide, Cheer, Era, Dash, and Downy in bottles made of at least 25 percent recycled polyethylene. And Spic 'n Span Pine will be sold in containers made entirely from preowned pop bottles.

P&G will thus pump life into the market for recycled plastics—and set an important example. The question soon arises: "If P&G can do it, why can't you?" says Jeanne L. Wirka, solid-waste policy analyst at the Environmental Action Foundation. Robert M. Viney, an associate advertising manager for the company's Packaged Soap & Detergent Div., says he would like to see competitors copy P&G so that the industry can avoid regulation. He guesses that within seven years, half of detergent bottles will be recycled.

As it makes such changes, P&G is steering clear of exaggerated claims. Indeed, it has campaigned against "biodegradable" products, many of which don't break down in landfills. "We're not trying to outgreen everyone with advertising slogans," says Viney. So far, in fact, P&G has found that "at the level of concern most people have about the environment, they're not willing to make sacrifices in convenience, value, and performance."

Diaper Data. Take disposable diapers. They still sell well, despite the critics and the rebound of cloth diaper services. And P&G is all for that. A study it commissioned from Arthur D. Little Inc. concludes that disposables have more advantages than cloth, considering every effect of using each one.

Yet, this is where critics most fault the company. Some 17 percent of P&G's worldwide sales come from diapers, including the 8 billion it sells each year in the United States, where it holds about half the market. Those numbers alone mean P&G is "working on environmental problems, but working on them so it doesn't affect the bottom line," argues Jill McIntyre, a member of Colorado's Citizens for Cloth Diapers. Bills have been offered in more than a dozen states to tax or regulate dispos-

Source: Zack Schiller, "P&G Tries Hauling Itself Out of America's Trash Heap," *Business Week*, April 23, 1990, p. 101.

BOX 18–2   (continued)

ables, though few have passed, partly because of P&G's aggressive lobbying.

The company argues that diapers get too much play, since they're only 2 percent of solid waste. But it is trying to keep them out of landfills anyway. One way is to recycle diapers into drywall backing. In another test, industrial composters have turned diapers into humus. Although some

see this as mere public relations, Place believes that industrial composting will start to pay once landfill fees reach $50 a ton, as they already have in some areas. Still, it may be that no matter what P&G tries, there will always be more to do. Maybe the company that put the first plastic bottle in U.S. supermarkets—Ivory Liquid in 1959—gave birth to a creature it can't control.

A business can take practical steps to build a good regulatory relationship by signaling the change to the agencies that are likely to affect the environment or the current permit status. Frequently any change in process or layout of a facility requires that management obtain from the EPA either a change in an environmental permit or a new permit. Business can also be proactive by finding out what environmental problems the company's activities are causing. Once a problem has been discovered, business should establish an action plan to deal effectively with the problem. The details of this plan should be communicated to the appropriate regulators as a part of a proposal or reports required by the regulators. Also, business should monitor its relationship, new regulations being considered, and enforcement trends by regulators.

Five general principles can help companies build productive regulatory relationships:

1. Submit accurate and quality reports to regulators to develop credibility.
2. Be proactive in investigating environmental problems and in developing responsive action plans.
3. Be responsive rather than avoid responsibility for the company's role in the environment.
4. Communicate openly and frequently with regulators and other key constituencies. The more that critical publics know about the responsible actions taken by a business, the more trust

develops and the less the pressure for punitive actions against the business.
5. Encourage agency input in environmental plans and seek to provide input for agency decisions. Seek to build a cooperative partnership with regulators.

Summary

Industrialization, population growth, economic development, and changing technology all have contributed to the degradation of the environment. In times past, when population was smaller and technologies less lethal, the environment was not considered in business decisions. Air and water were considered virtually unlimited free goods of no real cost to society, and they somehow seemed to maintain themselves. More recently society and business have spawned so many waste materials, many of which are nonbiodegradable, that the natural ecosystem has been overwhelmed and thus becomes polluted.

Environmental issues have increased in importance since World War II. As the public became aware of externalities from business's degrading the environment, a number of society's control mechanisms were called into play: (1) The development of the green consumer has created a market demand for environmentally friendly products and services. Many consumers now seek out food without pesticides and products that are recyclable, and avoid toxic products. (2) The public policy process has kept environmental issues near the top of the public agenda by the environmental movement and an aware society. Laws and regulations now control nearly every aspect of the environment. Enforcement of existing regulations also has become a matter of public concern. Environmental violations that harm others also can be the basis of civil lawsuits under tort law. (3) Environmental laws have been passed to protect nearly every aspect of the environment. The EPA was created to enforce these laws and regulations. (4) Many businesses have joined the environmental movement; they have sought to become energy-efficient and to consider recycling when they design, manufacture, and distribute products. Such actions by managers is both strategically significant because it responds to changing market realities but also ethically sound. There has been a "greening of business" as managers seek to respond to environmental issues by institutionalizing an environmental ethic within their organizations and to identify new business opportunities.

Sustainable economic development requires business decisions to be in harmony with ecological principles. Economic growth that is inconsistent with ecological principles threatens the environment and is not sustainable in the long run. Business often finds itself in an adversarial relationship with environmentalists. When environmental groups are able to present arguments to business from a business perspective, managers often join the crusade of environmentalism.[28] Also, managers need to be aware of how environmental perspectives differ from those of business in important ways.

Ecology is concerned with ecosystems of interdependent organisms and habitats, biological growth rates, food chains, and carrying capacity that limits the perpetual yield rates of any ecosystem. It is also concerned with niches that serve as habitats for various species and with the problem of environmental degradation brought about by pollution.

In contrast, business decisions are based on such concepts as market size and growth rates,

economies of scale, and value chains that determine cost structures through the sequence of business functions. Business is also concerned with efficiency, returns on investments, and competitive position. The environment has been a blind spot for business managers because they do not normally consider concepts of ecology in the decision-making process. This has led to a wide variety of environmental problems, including international problems like global warming, the destruction of the ozone layer, and deforestation and species elimination. Regional environmental problems include acid rain, water and air pollution, toxic wastes, and overcrowded landfills.

Extensive environmental laws and regulations cover every major environmental problem. The EPA is the primary agency responsible for protecting the environment, by setting standards, monitoring for compliance of standards and regulations, issuing permits to businesses involved in polluting, and fining violators. It also seeks to use market incentives wherever possible to encourage business to protect the environment and comply with environmental law. Environmental protection is one of the fastest-growing parts of the government.

Many businesses have joined environmentalists in programs that encourage recycling and discourage waste, and by designing products that are friendlier to the environment. A major concept is the environmental product life cycle, which offers a total systems approach for environmentally sound business practice. Many businesses are also systematically institutionalizing an environmental ethic within their organizations.

Conclusions

The environment and problems related to its degradation by business activities in the process of economic development have become major stakeholder issues in recent decades. These issues affect the quality of life, the habitability of the planet, and the public health of everyone. Thus the environment continues to be very controversial as both government and business seek to develop sound approaches to sustainable development.

The magnitude of the problems facing the international community is staggering. Global warming and ozone destruction threaten the life on our planet. Water pollution and toxic waste threaten the health of our citizens. Technology is so complex that the consequences of industrial processes for the environment are both serious and hard to control. Therefore, the environment is likely to remain a major stakeholder issue demanding much attention by government, business, and society in general for the foreseeable future.

The government is using market-based incentives to control business in the protection of the environment. Business is increasingly trying to incorporate ecological concepts into its decision-making processes. Also, the general awareness within our society of environmental problems is increasing as citizens seek to participate in recycling campaigns and to curtail consumption that adds to our solid waste problems. These hopeful signs suggest that we may be able to develop an environmentally friendly civilization.

Discussion Questions

1. How do the values inherent in business differ from those of environmentalists?
2. Discuss how the basic concepts of ecology compare with those of business and economic decision making.
3. What are the most troublesome environmental problems at the current time?
4. Is continued economic growth possible without further degrading the environment? Discuss what is required for sustainable development.
5. What are the causes of global warming? Should the government do anything about this phenomenon?
6. Explain the controversy surrounding CFCs. What should businesses in the computer and air-conditioning industries do in view of the Montreal Protocol, which calls for reducing CFC use?

7. What is the "greening of business?" What are businesses doing to become more environmentally conscious?
8. Explain the environmental product life cycle. How is this model used by business to manage the environment?
9. Explain how a business can implement an environmental ethic. What are the common mistakes in this process?
10. What approaches exist to regulate the environment? How can the government use market incentives in the process of regulation? Explain using examples.
11. What guidelines should business use in dealing with regulators?
12. What is meant by "source reduction"? How can business use this concept?

Notes

1. See Rogene A. Buchholz, *Principles of Environmental Management: The Greening of Business* (Englewood Cliffs, N.J.: Prentice-Hall, 1993); "The Greening of Corporate America," *Business Week*, April 23, 1990, pp. 96–103; and David Kirkpatrick, "Environmentalism: The New Crusade," *Fortune*, February 12, 1990, pp. 44–55.
2. David T. Buzzelli, "Time to Structure an Environmental Policy Strategy," *Journal of Business Strategy* 12, no. 2 (Mar/Apr 1991): 17–20.
3. Rogene A. Buchholz, "Corporate Responsibility and the Good Society: From Economics to Ecology," *Business Horizons* 34 (July-August 1991): 29.
4. "Growth vs. Environment: The Push for Sustainable Development," *Business Week*, May 11, 1992, pp. 66–75.
5. David Kirkpatrick, "Environmentalism: The New Crusade," *Fortune*, February 12, 1990, pp. 44–55.
6. Buchholz, *Principles of Environmental Management*, chap. 2.
7. Mark A. Stein, "Loggers See Spotted Owl As a Harbinger of Doom," *Los Angeles Times*, July 7, 1989, and Jonathan B. Levine, "The Spotted Owl Could Wipe Us Out," *Business Week*, September 18, 1989, p. 99.
8. For a complete discussion of these problems, see Buchholz, *Principles of Environmental Management*.
9. Stephen H. Schneider, "Cooling It: The Global Warming Debate," *World Monitor* (July 1990): 30–38.
10. Mark Stevenson and Victor S. Godden, "Ethics and Energy Supplement," *Journal of Business Ethics* 10 (1991): 641.
11. John Carey, "A Red Alert over the Ozone," *Business Week*, April 22, 1991, pp. 88–89.

12. Buchholz, *Principles of Environmental Management*, pp. 170–77.
13. Mike Lipske, "How Safe Is the Air Inside Your Home?" *National Wildlife* 25, no. 3 (April-May, 1987): 36–37.
14. G. Tyler Miller, *Living in the Environment*, 6th ed. (Belmont, Calif.: Wadsworth, 1990), p. 238.
15. Barry Commoner, *The Closing Circle* (New York: Bantam, 1972), p. 94.
16. Buchholz, *Principles of Environmental Management*, pp. 231–34.
17. George C. Lodge and Jeffrey F. Rayport, "Knee-Deep and Rising: America's Recycling Crisis," *Harvard Business Review* 69, no. 5 (September-October 1991): 128–39.
18. Jay Stuller, "The Politics of Packaging," *Across the Board* 27, no. 1 (January-February 1990): 40–48.
19. Stratford P. Sherman, "Trashing a $150 Billion Business," *Fortune* 120, no. 5 (August 28, 1989): 90–98.
20. Buchholz, *Principles of Environmental Management*, pp. 250–65.
21. Environmental Protection Agency, *Environmental Progress and Challenges: EPA Update* (Washington, D.C.: Government Printing Office, 1988), p. 113.
22. Kate Bertrand, "Government Boosts Market for Recycled Products," *Business Marketing* 75 no. 11 (November 1990): 3.
23. Emily T. Smith and Vicki Cahan, "The Greening of America, *Business Week*, April 23, 1990, pp. 96–103.
24. Buzzelli, "Time to Structure an Environmental Policy Strategy," pp. 17–20.
25. Suzanne Gauntlett, the Gauntlett Group, interview during a conference sponsored by *Business Week* and World Resources Institute, *Environmental Responsibility: Corporate Accountability and Business Opportunity in the Decade of Global Awakening*, broadcast December 5–6, 1990.
26. J. Winston Porter and Jonathan Z. Cannon, "Waste Minimization: Challenge for American Industry," *Business Horizons* 35, no. 2 (March-April 1992): 46–49.
27. Allan Prager and John J. Cala, "Coexisting with Regulators," *Journal of Business Strategy* 11, no. 1 (January-February 1990): 22–25.
28. David Kirkpatrick, "Environmentalism: The New Crusade," *Fortune*, February 12, 1990, pp. 44–55.
29. Anonymous, "Africa: The Wastebasket of the West," *Business and Society Review* 67 (Fall 1988): 48–50.

Discussion Case

Exporting Toxic Wastes to the Third World

As industrialized countries become aware of the potential for environmental degradation and harm to public health from toxic wastes, they have passed increasingly stringent regulatory controls over the shipment and disposal of toxic substances. This has significantly increased the business costs associated with many chemical products. One approach to dealing with these costs is to use the environmental life cycle concept and reduce the generation of toxics at the source rather than continue with an "end of pipe" approach to toxic waste management.

Often contracts are made with toxic waste management companies that are then responsible for disposing of these highly regulated substances. The toxic waste companies seek cost-effective disposal sites. Often the use of toxic sites in industrialized countries is very expensive and subject to expensive controls over transportation and storage as well as disposal. The companies have discovered that it is often more cost-effective to ship these toxic wastes to countries where the regulatory requirements are less stringent.

Many Third world countries, especially in Africa, have limited knowledge of toxic waste, do not have a well-developed system of environmental regulation, and have little experience in administering toxic waste programs. Often these countries urgently need foreign exchange to finance economic development. In other cases, corrupt government officials are eager to increase their personal wealth by agreeing to use their country as a disposal site for toxic substances. Thus the cost of disposal of toxic waste is considerably lower in the Third world than it is in the industrialized world.

The U.S. Congress, State Department, and Environmental Protection Agency are investigating the acceptance of toxic wastes generated in Western countries by African nations.[29] International press reports have alleged that deals have been made between American and European waste disposal firms and African nations, including Guinea-Bissau, Guinea, Benin, Congo, Equatorial Guinea, and Niger. Guinea and Guinea-Bissau were named as storage sites for toxic waste from abroad at an

Organization of African Unity summit. Later, Guinea-Bissau's minister of natural resources and industry said the country had abandoned the plan altogether.

Reports of specific incidents of toxic waste disposal in Africa often cause political controversy or denial. For example, when reports of the burial of 15,000 tons of toxic U.S. waste in Guinea were made public, President Lansana Conte set up an inquiry commission. It was later reported that the waste was dug up and packaged for reshipment. In response to another case, the government of the Congo denied a report that it had agreed to store one million tons of toxic waste from Europe. However, it is generally believed that the practice is common and only now coming to the public's attention.

Case Discussion Questions

1. Do the governments of the industrialized nations have any responsibility for regulating the disposal of toxic wastes in the Third world? Why?
2. Should Third World nations provide storage sites for hazardous and toxic substances for the industrialized world? Discuss.
3. What responsibility does the business that generates the toxic waste have in its disposal? Does this responsibility end when it signs a contract with a toxic waste management company?
4. What should be done about this global problem of toxic waste storage practices?

Case V–1 _____

Macmillan Tried Many Defenses to Stop Suitors

How far will managers go to prevent an outsider from buying their company? How far can they go? The case of Macmillan, Inc., may provide some answers.

Few management groups have thrown up as many takeover defenses as the one running Macmillan, a publishing and information-services company based in New York City. Although many of the strategies Macmillan used have become commonplace in recent years, it tried more of them—and pushed them further—than almost any other company in recent memory.

Macmillan granted its managers hundreds of thousands of restricted shares for which they paid nothing; it borrowed millions of dollars to buy shares for an employee stock-ownership plan, then made management the plan's trustees; and it funded a mammoth "golden parachute" plan for executives. Most audacious of all was the company's restructuring plan, which would have preserved Macmillan's independence by giving management ownership of the company's best assets at very little cost to themselves.

Although Macmillan rejected several bids that would have profited shareholders handsomely, investors who held on to their shares would be richly rewarded for management's recalcitrance.

Yesterday, Macmillan's board finally surrendered, recommending to shareholders that they tender their stock to Maxwell Communication Corp. Meanwhile, Kohlberg Kravis Roberts & Co. withdrew its rival offer. Maxwell last night completed its tender offer and will pay $90.25 a share, or $2.62 billion. That price is 80 percent higher than when

SOURCE: Cynthia Crossen and Karen Blumenthal, "An Anti-takeover Arsenal That Failed," *Wall Street Journal*, November 4, 1988, p. B1.

Macmillan's six-month-long battle to retain independence began.

Harbir Singh, an associate professor of management at the University of Pennsylvania's Wharton School, says one of the only restraints on a management's defensive excesses is the company's board of directors, who are vulnerable to shareholder lawsuits. Macmillan's board, however, approved almost every plan management devised to remain independent, even when those plans could have been costly to shareholders.

The board also voted itself two raises, to $30,000 a year from $20,000, and granted itself a retirement plan guaranteeing $30,000 a year for life for most of its outside members—as well as benefits for their spouses. The board eventually asked the final two bidders for the company to indemnify the members against shareholder suits.

Edward P. Evans, Macmillan's proud and stubborn chairman and chief executive officer, contends that the maneuvers were meant only to protect shareholders. He also maintains that he has been more a hapless victim than an active player in the struggle. I didn't mean to do it, he says. "It was more or less done to me."

Even critics who say Mr. Evans's efforts were excessive concede that he deserved more than a gold watch for his work at Macmillan. When he took over in 1980, it was an overly diversified concern whose earnings and stock price were sagging. Mr. Evans cut expenses and refocused the company, on three core businesses—publishing, information services, and instruction. The company's per share earnings and stock price soared.

Mr. Evans has been well compensated for this. In addition to a respectable salary—$420,000 in 1987—he now controls at least 739,000 Macmillan shares. Many came through option plans, but

549

at least 230,000 shares were an outright gift from a grateful board of directors. His stock is now valued at more than $65 million.

Though Macmillan's stock price was rising, Mr. Evans was acutely aware that the company was takeover bait, a prosperous and growing company in a glamor industry. Macmillan had already put its board of directors on staggered terms, which made the board much less vulnerable to a change of control instituted by an outsider. It also had a by-law provision prohibiting the calling of a special meeting without a 75 percent shareholder vote.

But in May 1987, another publishing company, Harcourt Brace Jovanovich, Inc., narrowly escaped a takeover by Robert Maxwell. Fearful of being the British press baron's next target, Macmillan launched its unprecedented campaign to ward off trespassers.

GOLDEN PARACHUTES. In July 1987, Macmillan's board approved golden parachute severance agreements for 21 executives, backed by a $60 million letter of credit. If the executive actually received any golden parachute payments—some of which could be triggered if anyone acquired as little as 20 percent of the company—Macmillan agreed to pay all income or other taxes on the payments.

POISON PILL. The company also adopted a shareholder rights, or "poison pill," plan. Under the plan, if anyone acquired 30 percent of Macmillan's stock, the other stockholders could exchange their rights for the common stock at half price. The effect would be to dilute severely the investment of the potential buyer, thus deterring all stock acquisitions above the 30 percent "trigger" level.

Although many of the strategies Macmillan used have become commonplace in recent years, it tried more of them—and pushed them further—than almost any other company in recent memory. Moreover, Macmillan's board approved almost every plan management devised to remain independent.

VOTING RIGHTS. A $60 million loan was approved for the company's employee stock-ownership plan, which was to be used to buy a million

Macmillan shares. The company ousted the ESOP's trustee, replacing it with management members, who would have had voting control of all unallocated shares deposited in the plan. The company was also authorized to issue up to 50 million new "blank check" preferred shares with potentially disproportionate voting rights to be set by the board.

RESTRUCTURING. Of all the company's defenses, the most extreme was its restructuring plan. Although management weighed several approaches, all shared one aspect: They would leave Mr. Evans and a few other top managers owning a sizable chunk of the revamped company. Management would acquire that stake not by investing new capital at prevailing market prices but by trading in previously granted restricted shares and stock options.

Under the chosen plan, Macmillan would be split into two companies, one containing the publishing businesses, the other the information services businesses, considered the crown jewels of the company. At first, management, which just a year earlier owned only 1.2 percent of Macmillan, decided to trade its restricted shares and stock options for a 55 percent stake in the information services business. But the company's advisers pointed out that such a hefty stake would be considered a change of corporate control from public stockholders to management. So management's stake in the information businesses was reduced to 39 percent.

The restructuring not only thwarted unwanted suitors and gave a huge share of the company to management but also avoided the necessity of a shareholder vote because, management argued, control of the company wasn't changing. In fact, shareholders first heard of the restructuring on May 31, the day after the board approved it—and just ten days before it was to be consummated. There was no time for shareholders to organize a protest.

Only a legal challenge filed by Robert M. Bass Group, which was trying to acquire Macmillan, stood between management and its plan. A Delaware court stopped the restructuring cold. In a stinging opinion, the court ruled that not only did the plan "offer interior value to shareholders, it also forced them to accept it."

With its restructuring plan quashed—and both Bass Group and Maxwell vying for the company—investors hoped that management would stop fighting to stay independent and start looking for a buyer willing to pay a premium price. Management did neither and refused to negotiate terms, disclose financial information, or discuss price with either bidder.

WHITE KNIGHT. Meanwhile, management thought it had found a way to sell the company while keeping a large stake. It struck a deal with Kohlberg Kravis Roberts, the leveraged buyout specialists, in which management would end up with 20 percent equity in the company. Macmillan's board quickly endorsed KKR's first offer without giving either Bass Group or Maxwell a chance to top it.

Maxwell was not deterred. It topped KKR's bid, ultimately forcing management to do what it had been resisting, hold an auction. But when the auction was over KKR had won even though Maxwell was prepared to pay more. Furthermore, Macmillan took steps to prevent anyone else from getting the company, granting KKR the right to buy four of its best assets if the KKR merger fell through.

Once again, a suitor—Maxwell, in this case—took Macmillan to court, and once again the suitor won. The Delaware Supreme Court ruled that the auction was "neither evenhanded nor neutral" and that management had tainted the process by getting involved, even though it had a personal interest in the outcome.

Now that Maxwell has succeeded in buying Macmillan, it appears that the company's elaborate defenses, which cost almost an entire quarter's profits for fees and expenses, only delayed the inevitable. "No takeover defense is impenetrable," says Wharton's Mr. Singh. But as fast as they're knocked down, he adds, managements will find new ones to take their place.

Case Discussion Questions

1. What takeover defenses did the management of Macmillan use?
2. Under what conditions, if any, should top management resist a takeover attempt?
3. Were corporate raiders justified in their attempts to acquire Macmillan?
4. What would it be like to work for Macmillan in the post-takeover period?

Case V–2 _____

The Suzuki Samurai

"People absolutely flip over the Samurai."[1] The author of this 1986 article did not know the irony of his statement in the review of the Suzuki Samurai shortly after it arrived in U.S. showrooms. The Samurai, a small, four-wheel-drive jeep, was a success as Suzuki's first entry into the U.S. automobile market. Although this was Suzuki's first U.S. car, it was based upon an eighteen-year-old design that had been selling in Third World countries for over

SOURCE: This case is based on the research of Cindy Philofsky and Sona Bray under the direction of Newman Peery, University of the Pacific.

15 years. The smaller Suzuki is a common sight in such places as Sri Lanka and Puerto Rico. Suzuki then decided to enter the U.S. market and fill a niche undiscovered by other automakers. It was going to build an off-road vehicle that was also economical. The most attractive feature of the vehicle was its base price of $6,500. Over 90 enticing accessories were offered, driving the price up to well over $8,500, which was still slightly under the base price of the next in line, the Jeep Wrangler.[2] In 1986 the Suzuki Samurai received rave reviews and sales skyrocketed as it became the hottest car on the road. It looked as if Suzuki

was heading for a superb success with its first U.S. auto entry.

THE MARKETING OF THE SUZUKI SAMURAI

Before the Samurai rolled on to American roadways, Suzuki had done its marketing homework well. Suzuki planned for each new dealership to have a freestanding showroom and a complete service system. Suzuki then developed ways for Americans to express their individuality. The dealers would not just have parts but also "personalization centers" with the available accessories on display so that buyers could mix and match as desired. Prior to introducing the Samurai, Suzuki printed a multipaged color accessory catalog with everything from wheels to windows in it. Suzuki also opted for an alternative advertising approach. Many off-road vehicles were geared toward the macho man. "The key was not insisting that you had to be a Marlboro man to get into a Samurai," said Leonard Pearlstein, president of keye/donna/pearlstein, which handled the Suzuki of America account.[3] The commercials mocked those of similar vehicles with mach stereotypes.

For example, in one, a Suzuki Samurai is passed by several faster-moving cars and a safety "brake test" turns out to be a lunch break. It helped that it was hard to classify the Samurai in any one auto category. Although it was originally intended to be a small, off-road vehicle, it managed to take on a variety of other identities partly owing to the advertising campaign. "The safe thing to do would have been to market it as a sport utility vehicle," said Doug Mazza, Suzuki's general Manager.[4] But Suzuki checked sales in nearby U.S. markets like Canada and Puerto Rico, and discovered it wasn't only the macho types that bought their product. Women and first-time car buyers were interested in them as well. Many perceived the vehicle as a light pickup, subcompact, or just a fun convertible. The Samurai's versatility was a boon to the image-conscious—and had the advantages of being economical and tough as well as fun.

INITIAL REVIEWS AND SALES

When the Samurai was introduced, auto magazines enthusiastically reviewed it. They liked the versatility, durability, and, most of all, its low price, which was nearly one-half of the next-lowest-priced four-wheel drive vehicle. *Motor Trend Magazine* reported:

> It could be beginners luck that Suzuki is having such instant success with its new little Samurai. But it looks like the company has done its market research well and come up with a winner. . . . As long as you understand the limits of what it can do, this is a great little 4x4. . . .The Samurai is just overall fun. For the price, that's a lot.[5]

Sales reflected the enthusiasm; they increased from the expected 2,000 Samurai per month when it was first introduced to over 8,000 per month within two years. The total for the first two years was approximately 100,000 cars and $1 billion in sales. Many dealers were charging a premium price well above the posted sticker price because of these high demand levels. Suzuki was one of only two Japanese automobile manufacturers that did not have to resort to factory rebate sales incentives in 1987. Because of the booming sales, Suzuki had to restructure its entire marketing scheme. Originally Suzuki had planned to introduce the Samurai in California in November 1985, followed by introductions into Florida and Georgia in December and into the rest of the United States over the next three years. Less than two years after the Samurai's introduction, the car was in 170 showrooms across thirty states.

Feeling confident with its first U.S. entry, Suzuki made plans to extend its product line. It planned to sell a larger sport/utility vehicle, now known as the sidekick, in the United States by late 1988, followed by a car line with the four-wheel drive option. However, storms were brewing by early 1988 over the safety of the Samurai.

THE CRISIS

On Thursday, June 2, 1988, Consumers Union, the consumer testing organization that publishes *Consumer Reports,* announced that it was giving the Suzuki Samurai its first "not acceptable" rating in a decade because of what the group said were basic design flaws that could lead to deadly rollover accidents.[6] Consumers Union also called for the recall of all 160,000 Samurais, for the withdrawal of the product from the market, and for the full refund to all Samurai owners.

At a news conference, the nonprofit testing group called the vehicle's design "inherently dangerous" and said that "it could not be modified to rectify the problems."[7] The Samurai's design flaws were considered to be so serious that the car was the first of 349 models reviewed by Consumers Union over the past ten years to receive an unacceptable rating. The last models rated unacceptable were the Plymouth Horizon and Dodge Omni.

During the first three years after its introduction, the federal government had received 44 reports of roll-over accidents involving Samurais, which had reportedly caused 16 deaths and 53 injuries.[8] Utility vehicles, such as the Samurai, have higher centers of gravity and a narrower wheel configuration than most passenger cars, making them more likely to tip over when unbalanced. Consumers Union petitioned the federal regulators to set performance standards requiring such sports/utility vehicles to pass a test measuring vehicle stability.

In addition to the controversy already raging with consumer groups, Suzuki Motor Company was faced with a class-action lawsuit demanding that Samurai owners get their money back. The suit, which was filed in Illinois State Court, came a day after *Consumer Reports* announced its "not acceptable" rating for the Samurai. The suit contended that all 150,000 U.S. owners should get refunds because of charges that the vehicles were dangerously unstable. Suzuki was also charged with fraudulently withholding information about alleged design defects that gave the Samurai a propensity to roll over in certain abrupt maneuvers.[9]

THE CONSUMERS UNION TEST

In the Consumers Union test, the group attempted to simulate a routine situation in which a driver would have to swerve sharply to avoid an obstacle and then reenter the driving lane. Three competing utility vehicles were also tested: the Jeep Wrangler, the Jeep Cherokee, and the Isuzu Trooper, plus two versions of the Samurai. The two smaller vehicles, the Samurai and the Jeep Wrangler, carried outriggers in the tests to prevent the vehicles from either falling over to the side or rolling owing to a swerve or sharp turn.

During the tests, Consumers Unions' drivers veered to the left 50 feet before an obstacle and moved back into the driving lane no more than 60 feet beyond the obstacle. Moving at about 40 miles an hour, the two jeep models and the Trooper remained stable, but both Samurai models went over onto the outriggers and would have rolled had the outriggers not stopped them.

After acquiring a copy of the test results, Suzuki accused Consumers Union of having put the Samurai through a second, more difficult maneuvering test, after it had passed the usual routine test to which hundreds of other vehicles had been subjected. "The magazine changed its test for the first time in history," said Doug Mazza, an American Suzuki vice president. "It appears as though the magazine wants the Samurai to fail."[10] When Consumers Union announced its test results and asked the federal government to require a recall of the Samurai, the testing organization acknowledged that the four-wheel-drive vehicle had passed its standard test before tipping over during a second test that required sharper turns.

THE SUZUKI DEFENSE STRATEGY

Unlike Audi and other automakers that had been faced with similar attacks of controversy, Suzuki did not ignore the mounting negative publicity. Instead, the Suzuki Motor Company took an immediate combative stance. With badly slumping sales, Suzuki's defense strategy turned into an all-out aggressive nationwide campaign to combat the tidal wave of negative publicity facing Samurai.

Suzuki's counteroffensive actually began the night before the Consumers Union June 2 press conference to announce its findings on the Samurai. After hearing from reporters that *Consumer Reports* was planning a press conference the following day, Suzuki feverishly started buying advertising time on the next evening's local and national network television news shows. Even though it still did not know exactly what *Consumer Reports* planned to say, Suzuki wanted to have a place to air its rebuttal.

Suzuki and its public relations agency, Rogers and Associates of Los Angeles, created a five-member "crisis group" that included Suzuki engineers and outside advertising and public relations staffers, who planned the advertising campaign and media response to the allegations.[11]

During the following ten days, Suzuki spent $1.5 million over its normal advertising budget to air ads quoting positive reviews of the Samurai from auto-motive trade publications. Although some net-works refused to air the ads on their news pro-grams at a time when Suzuki was such a hot news story, the ads did find their way onto the air in major market areas where Suzuki had dealerships.

During a press conference in Los Angeles, Suzuki general manager Doug Mazza showed video tapes once used by American Motors to defend its jeep utility vehicles against lawsuits. These videos showed that almost any car or truck can be made to roll over. Mazza also made veiled warnings that Suzuki planned to investigate ties between Consumers Union and the Center for Auto Safety, and might take legal action against them.

In defense of allegations that its Samurai sports vehicle was unsafe, Suzuki changed the tone of its advertising. Instead of the "laugh-a-minute" com-mercials that appealed mostly to younger con-sumers, the company now adopted a more serious approach. The new ads, shot almost entirely in black and white, featured quotes of praise from car enthusiast magazines like this from *Off-Road Maga-zine*: "We gave the Samurai good points for maneuverability, engine performance, and chassis balance."[12]

A month after the Samurai controversy began, the Suzuki Motor Company and some of its deal-ers resorted to extraordinary measures, including huge discounts and free life insurance, to reverse the Samurai model's sales plunge.[13] Suzuki began giving dealers $2,000 incentives on the now $7,995 base price of the Samurai. Suzuki dealers in Ohio went a step further by giving Samurai buy-ers a free $1 million life insurance policy.

SAMURAI BOUNCES BACK

The promotions worked, and by the end of August 1988, sales of the Samurai reached a one-month record of 12,208.[14] In September 1988, the National Highway Traffic Safety Administration turned down petitions to investigate and recall the Suzuki Samurai, contending that the four-wheel drive sports vehicle made by Suzuki was not any more dangerous than similar vehicles made by other manufacturers. In a report explaining why it had turned down the recall request, the NHTSA criticized the roll-over tests conducted by Con-sumers Union, stating that they did not have a sci-entific basis and could not be "linked to real-world crash avoidance needs."[15] The agency, however, approvingly cited Suzuki's tests of the Samurai, saying they demonstrated that the vehicle "satisfac-torily completed industry accepted tests which might be used to assess a vehicle's roll-over propensity." Suzuki officials said the NHTSA ruling was a major victory and should "put to rest the inaccurate and misleading attacks on the vehicle."

In March 1989, American Suzuki Motor Corpo-ration agreed to pay $200,000 to California and six other states and to include a warning statement about the handling of its Samurai sport utility vehi-cle in all future advertising. The settlement also required that Suzuki's new Sidekick model carry a warning label that stated, "This vehicle handles dif-ferently from ordinary passenger cars. Federal law cautions to avoid sharp turns and abrupt maneu-vers."[16] Suzuki entered the agreement without admitting any guilt or safety problems with its products. The $200,000 payment was to cover the states' investigative costs over this controversy.

Case Discussion Questions

1. Why was the product safety issue unexpected for Suzuki's management?
2. Explain how Suzuki managed its media rela-tions during this product safety crisis? How did Suzuki's actions differ from Audi's actions when the "60 Minutes" program was broadcasted?
3. Was the test by the Consumer Union fair?
4. What is your overall assessment of the way the product safety crisis was managed in this case? What conclusions or generalizations can you provide for future managers who face a product safety crisis?

Case V–3 _____

City of Richmond v. J.A. Croson Company

In April 1983, the City of Richmond, Virginia, adopted a Minority Business Utilization Plan. The plan, which passed on a 6-to-2 vote with one abstention, called for prime contractors to subcontract at least 30 percent of the dollar amount of each contract to one or more minority business enterprises (MBEs).[17] According to the plan, businesses anywhere in the country in which at least 51 percent is owned and controlled by Black, Spanish-speaking, Oriental, Indian, Eskimo, or Aleut citizens is considered a minority-owned business. The plan, which was designed by a black-majority city council, granted a waiver of the 30 percent set-aside level only after it was evident that every attempt had been made to demonstrate that a qualified, sufficient, relevant MBE was unavailable to participate in the contract.

In addition to the plan, a procedure had been established for purchasing contracts. Prime contractors were provided with a Minority Business Utilization Plan Commitment Form. Within ten days of the opening of bids, the lowest otherwise responsive bidder was required to submit a commitment form naming the MBEs to be used on the contract and the percentage of the total contract price awarded to the minority firm or firms. The commitment form or request for a waiver of the 30 percent set-aside was then referred to the City of Richmond Human Relations Commission. The Human Relations Commission then verified the minority ownership of the identified MBEs. The commitment form was then either approved or a recommendation regarding the prime contractor's request for a partial or complete waiver of the 30 percent set-aside level was given.

On September 6, 1983, the city issued an invitation to bid on a project to install plumbing fixtures at the city jail. The J.A. Croson Company, a mechanical plumbing and heating contractor, received the bid forms through its regional man-

ager, Eugene Bonn. Products of one of two manufacturers (Acorn Engineering Company and Bradley Manufacturing Company) were named by the city. Bonn was aware of the 30 percent set-aside requirement and later contacted about six potential MBEs, yet no MBE expressed an interest in the project.

The day bids were due, Bonn again contacted more MBEs, this time with more success. Melvin Brown, president of Continental Metal Hose, a local MBE, indicated that he was interested in the project. Brown proceeded to contact two suppliers to obtain price quotes, one of which had been specified by the city. Bradley Manufacturing Company was not familiar with Continental Metal Hose and indicated that a credit check, which would require 30 days to complete, would be necessary before an agreement could be made. On October 13, 1983, bids were opened and J.A. Croson was the sole bidder with a bid of $126,530. Brown could not submit a bid because of the difficulty in obtaining credit approval.

By October 19, 1983, Croson had not yet received a bid from Continental. Subsequently Croson submitted a request for a waiver of the 30 percent set-aside requirement on the grounds that Continental was unqualified and that the other MBEs were unresponsive. In response to the waiver application, Brown contacted the Acorn Engineering Company, the other specified fixture manufacturer. From their discussion, Brown submitted a bid on the fixtures to Croson. Continental's bid was $7,663 higher than what Croson had included in its bid to the city for fixtures.

On November 2, 1983, the City of Richmond denied Croson's waiver and warned the company that it had ten days to submit a commitment form naming an MBE to be used on the contract. Failure to do so would result in loss of the contract. Croson responded with two letters to the city.

In the first letter, Croson indicated (1) Continental Metal Hose was not an authorized supplier for either of the two specified manufacturers. (2)

SOURCE: This case was written by Cherese Newborne under the direction of Newman Peery, University of the Pacific.

Acorn Engineering Company's quote was higher than any other quote received for the fixtures, and it was contingent upon receipt of credit approval. (3) Continental Metal had submitted its quote 21 days after the bids were due for prime contractors.

In the second letter, Croson detailed the additional costs that would be required if an MBE were used on the project. He asked that the contract price that Croson had submitted on the bid day be increased to reflect the additional costs.

In response to these two letters the City of Richmond denied the request for a waiver of the MBE requirement and also denied the request to raise the contract price. Also, the city indicated that it would rebid the project. Croson then asked the city to review the decision to deny the waiver. The city said there was no appeal available to its decision and proceeded with the plans to rebid the project. Croson then brought action in the federal district court, claiming that the Minority Business Utilization Plan was unconstitutional.

The federal district court upheld the City of Richmond's set-aside plan fully. On appeal, the Fourth Circuit Court of Appeals upheld the district court's decision, and Croson appealed the case to the U.S. Supreme Court.[18] The Supreme Court vacated the opinion of the appellate court, sending the case back to the court of appeals for further review in light of the 1986 decision in *Wygant v. Jackson Board of Education*. In that case, the Court had held that a program that laid off workers according to race was unconstitutional.

In 1987, the Fourth Circuit Court of Appeals struck down the City of Richmond set-aside program as unconstitutional because the city failed to prove that it had discriminated against minority contractors in the past. The City of Richmond then appealed to the Supreme Court. On January 23, 1989, the Supreme Court concurred with the Court of Appeals, ruling with a 6-to-3 vote. The Supreme Court held that the set-aside law denied whites a fair chance to compete. It also ruled that all cities and states with set-aside laws must be able to present evidence of past discrimination by the government to justify hardships imposed on whites.

Justice Sandra Day O'Connor, who wrote the majority opinion, stated that all affirmative action programs must be based on precise findings of past discrimination and must be "narrowly tailored" to overcome only that wrong. The majority opinion found that the 30 percent set-aside level is purely arbitrary, with no basis for justification. The city did not make certain how many minority construction businesses existed in the industry nor the level of their participation. The city also failed to demonstrate that minority contractors were being bypassed for city contracts or subcontracts.

In the dissenting opinion, Justice Thurgood Marshall remarked that the Court's decision marked a giant step backward in the area of affirmative action. He stated that in one city's effort to redress the effects of past racial discrimination in one industry, the Court's decision was an attack on race-conscious remedies in general. It appeared to Marshall that the Court regarded racial discrimination as a phenomenon of the past.

In defense of Richmond's set-aside program, John Payton, the city's lawyer, argued that less than 1 percent of the $124 million in construction contracts signed by the City of Richmond over a five-year period were awarded to minority firms. This was before the set-aside law was established in Richmond. After the law was in effect, construction contracts going to minority-owned firms rose to the mandated 30 percent level. When the court of appeals struck down the law in 1987, the number of contracts going to minority firms dropped to 2 percent. According to Payton, the 30 percent set-aside level was established as a midpoint between the 1 percent minority-awarded contracts and the City of Richmond's 52 percent minority population.

Other supporters of affirmative action are confused and worried. They say that they are not sure what kind of discrimination warrants affirmative action plans. Justice O'Connor, in the majority opinion, said that a city could impose an affirmative action plan only if there is a "strong basis in evidence" that minorities were purposely excluded from doing business with the city.

Case Discussion Questions

1. William Beer has observed that the idea of affirmative action has changed over the years. Originally it referred to honest efforts to recruit qualified members of designated groups into universities, professions, and other respected

positions within American society. In fact, affirmative action has been translated into a series of quotas that benefit certain groups at the cost of others. This deviation from original intent has given birth to reverse discrimination lawsuits.[19] How does the City of Richmond MBE law relate to this observation?

2. How do affirmative action plans designed for employees (like the one used by Kaiser in the Weber case) differ from set-aside programs such as the one used by the City of Richmond?

3. Do you agree with the Court that the 30 percent figure for the set-aside program was arbitrary?

4. What if the City of Richmond had required affirmative action plans from all businesses contracting with the city? What difference would this have made if its concern was to employ minority workers within Richmond? What is the implication of focusing on minority-owned businesses, both contractors and manufacturers of fixtures, rather than on employees?

Case V–4 _____

Union Carbide in Bhopal

On December 3, 1984, a deadly methyl isocyanate (MIC) gas leaked from the Union Carbide plant in Bhopal, India, over the sleeping city. MIC was a volatile, highly toxic chemical (500 times more poisonous than cyanide) used to make pesticides. It reacts explosively with almost any substance, including water.[20] The gas that floated over the city claimed more than 2,000 lives, leaving 500 children without parents and killing over 20,000 of the city's livestock.[21]

Union Carbide Corporation (UCC) is one of the largest companies in America. It has several plants throughout the United States and in foreign countries. Union Carbide managers from the United States built the Bhopal plant in 1969 with the blessing of the Indian government, which was anxious to increase production of the pesticides it desperately needed to raise food for India's huge population. Over the next 15 years pesticides enabled India to cut its annual grain losses from 25 percent to 15 percent, a saving of 15 million tons of grain, or enough to feed 70 million people for a year.

Indian officials willingly accepted the technology, skills, and equipment that Union Carbide provided, and Indian workers were thankful for the company jobs without which they would have had to beg or starve because India has no welfare system. In return, India offered the company cheap labor, low taxes, and few laws requiring expensive environmental equipment or costly workplace protections. Managers insisted that responsibility for the plant's operations rested with the local Indian managers; they hastened to say that all cost-cutting measures had been justified.

Management of the company had a very relationship-oriented style. "As long as you were good and loyal, you did well. You did not have to be efficient," said Brij Kapur, executive director of the Asian Centre for Organization Research and Development. Yet most business executives in India agree that Carbide was well respected there, and making products that involved hazardous substances is difficult in a developing country that lacks a highly educated pool of workers, a reliable source of parts, and other basic services.

In 1982 an inspection of the Bhopal pesticide plant revealed serious equipment and safety problems. Inspectors said they had found ten "major" deficiencies. These included a potential for materials to leak poison gas from storage tanks, the possibility of dust explosions in the system, problems with safety valves and instruments,

SOURCE: This case was written by Barbara Zears under the direction of Newman S. Peery, Jr.

and a high degree of personnel turnover at the plant. Union Carbide Corporation said the Indian subsidiary had rectified most of the problems by June.

One of the problems that remained in June involved the adequacy of a valve on a tank used in producing highly toxic gas. The valve was designed to relieve "a runaway reaction." After the ten major safety deficiencies were found at the plant, the company concedes that American safety experts had not returned to Bhopal. A few days after the accident a company spokesman said that he did not know whether the relief valve had been replaced or repaired before the accident. But the spokesman said, "we have no reason to believe" that the work was not completed.[22]

The final report by the subsidiary, which was dated June 26, 1984, said that virtually all the problems at the plant had been corrected. It said that a potential safety problem remained in the operation of a safety valve used in its methyl isocyanate manufacturing process. The final report also said that the work on the two remaining deficiencies was "almost complete and only awaiting delivery of a control valve." It said the valve was expected to be delivered in July.[23]

Late at night on December 2, 1984, the MIC stored in a tank at the Bhopal factory started boiling violently when water accidently entered the tank. A cooling unit that should have switched on automatically had been disabled for at least a year. Both the manager and the senior operator on duty at the time distrusted the initial readings on their gauges in the control room. "Instruments often didn't work," the manager said later. "They got corroded, and crystals would form on them."[24]

By 11:30 P.M. the eyes of workers at the plant were burning. But they remained unconcerned because, as they later reported, minor leaks were common at the plant and were often first detected in this way. Many of the illiterate workers were unaware of the deadly properties of the chemical. Not until 12:40 A.M., as workers began choking on the fumes, did they realize something was drastically wrong. Five minutes later emergency valves on the storage tank exploded and white toxic gas began shooting out of a pipestack and drifting toward the shantytowns downwind from the plant.

An alarm sounded as the senior operator shouted into the factory loudspeaker that a massive leak had erupted and workers should flee the area. Meanwhile, the manager ordered company firetrucks to spray the escaping gas with water to neutralize the chemical. But water pressure was too low to reach the top of the 120-foot-high pipestack. The senior operator then rushed to turn on a vent scrubber that should have neutralized the escaping gas with caustic soda. Unfortunately, the scrubber had been shut down for maintenance 15 days earlier. As white clouds continued to pour out of the pipestack, the manager shouted to workers to turn on a nearby flare tower to burn off the gas. The flare, however, would not go on because its pipes had corroded and were still being repaired.

Panicked workers poured out of the plant and the lethal cloud settled over the neighboring shantytowns of Jayaprakash Nagar and Chola. Hundreds died in their beds, choking helplessly in violent spasms as their burning lungs filled with fluid. Thousands were blinded by the caustic gas, and thousands of others suffered burns and lesions in their nasal and bronchial passages. The majority of the dead were squatters who had built huts illegally next to the factory. Surviving residents of the slums, most of them illiterate, declared afterward that they had built their shacks there because they did not understand the danger and thought the factory made healthy "medicine for plants."[25]

Union Carbide immediately offered aid and relief to the reeling city of Bhopal by contributing $1 million to the relief effort. The president of the company personally made a trip to Bhopal and was immediately arrested by state authorities. He was charged with criminal liability in the gas leak. Immediately following the disaster, the managers of the Indian plant were placed under house arrest.[26] Early reports were that unskilled maintenance workers—lacking the required supervision—had somehow caused the accident. Charges of negligence were quick to follow.

The company's executives faced a string of management problems: how best to aid the victims, how to be sure whatever happened at Bhopal didn't happen again somewhere else, how to help employees keep up morale, how to assure investors about the corporation's financial stability, and how to begin protecting the company from excessive legal liability.

UCC lacked a preexisting corporate plan for coping with a catastrophe of this magnitude. Like most chemical companies, Carbide had disaster plans for all its plants, with details about evacuation routes and hospitals tailored to each area. Just what kind of plan Carbide had provided for Bhopal is still murky. Though Carbide provided the specifications for the plant, its final design and construction was Indian, at the insistence of the Indian government. Danbury, Connecticut, headquarters never had a copy of the blueprints and seems not to have had detailed knowledge of whatever evacuation plan was on hand. Questions about whether the plant was built properly, whether workers were adequately trained, and whether the plant had adequate safety provisions will become crucial in fixing responsibility and in judging whether Union Carbide management was doing its job in the years before the accident.[27]

The chemical industry has one of the best safety records in U.S. manufacturing, and Carbide is considered one of the best in the industry. Its reputation has helped prevent a rush to judgment against Carbide in the court of public opinion. However, the first lawsuit focused on the culpability of employees of the American-based parent, Union Carbide, not on the conduct of the Indian subsidiary that operated the plant in Bhopal. This suit claims that the corporation was negligent in designing the Bhopal plant and that it failed to warn the area's residents adequately about the dangers presented by the stored gas.

Other lawsuits charged that Carbide acted "willfully and wantonly," with utter disregard for the safety of Bhopal residents.[28] It notes that the Bhopal plant lacked a computerized early-warning system of the kind that had been installed in the plant in Institute, West Virginia, which Carbide said was identical to the Bhopal facility.

Some chemical companies contend that pesticides similar to those produced by Carbide in India can be made without large stockpiles of methyl isocyanate. Other companies produce such pesticides with other chemical reactions, and Mitsubishi Chemical Industries Ltd. of Japan uses a continuous process that consumes methyl isocyanate as fast as it is made. A Union Carbide pesticide plant in France stores methyl isocyanate in many small cylinders, rather than in the huge tanks used in Bhopal.[29]

The Indian government's investigation into the Bhopal disaster identified a combination of design flaws, operating errors, and managerial mistakes that helped cause the accident and intensified its effects. After seven weeks of investigation, the Indian government concluded four main reasons for this disaster.[30]

Plant safety procedures were inadequate to deal with a large-scale leak of the deadly MIC, despite the fact that the dangers such a leak would pose were known. Nor had any precautions been taken to protect people living near the plant site. Although a safety survey conducted by experts from Union Carbide headquarters in 1982 identified major hazards that could lead to serious incidents, no procedures were developed for alerting or evacuating the population that would be affected by an accident.

Leaky valves were a constant problem at the plant. Six serious accidents occurred at the Bhopal installation between 1978 and 1982, and three, one of which was fatal, involved gas leaks. Some important safety systems were not working at the time of the accident. Refrigeration units designed to keep the highly reactive MIC cool so that it could not vaporize had been shut down before the accident. Other equipment, including devices designed to vent and burn off excess gases, was so inadequate, investigators hinted, that it would have been ineffective even if it had been operating at the time of the accident.

Plant workers failed to grasp the gravity of the situation as it developed, allowing the leak to go unattended for about an hour. Brief and frantic efforts to check the leak failed. As the situation deteriorated, the workers panicked and fled the plant.

The chairman of Union Carbide has been said to be personally devastated by the accident. "Union Carbide has a moral responsibility in this matter," he said.[31] He had stated that his company intends to compensate the victims, and says that it is trying to work out a plan for doing that as soon as possible.

Case Discussion Questions

1. What should the chairman of Union Carbide do now?

2. What is the central problem of this case? What caused the disaster? What could management do to prevent a similar situation from recurring?

3. How would you rank the business social performance of Union Carbide in Bhopal?

4. What social control mechanisms were present in this case? Did they fail? Does the government have any responsibility in this case? If so, which government?

5. Should industries develop standards of conduct for global operations with facilities located in the Third World? Explain.

6. Should the governments of the industrialized world have a role in the export of dangerous technologies or products to Third World countries? Explain.

7. Should victims of the Bhopal disaster be able to bring lawsuits against Union Carbide in the United States? Why or why not?

8. What is your assessment of the moral and legal responsibility of Union Carbide in this case?

Case Endnotes

1. "Off Road Warriors," *Popular Mechanics,* September 1986, p. 78.

2. Michael Brockman, "Suzuki Samurai," *Motor Trend,* June 1986, p. 122.

3. Jerry Flint, "Buy Two, They're Cheap," *Forbes,* November 2, 1987, p. 193.

4. Ibid.

5. Brockman, "Suzuki Samurai."

6. James Risen, "Consumer Reports Throw Cold Water on Hot Suzuki Samurai," *Los Angeles Times,* June 3, 1988, p. IV–1.

7. Robert Daniels, "Suzuki Urged to Recall Samurai Vehicles As Consumer Group Calls Them Unsafe," *Wall Street Journal,* June 3, 1988, p. 4.

8. *Los Angeles Times,* June 3, 1988.

9. "Samurai Owners File Suit Against Suzuki for Refunds," *Wall Street Journal,* June 7, 1988, p. 12.

10. Doron P. Levin. "Test Change Draws Fire from Suzuki," *New York Times,* June 11, 1988, p. 37.

11. James Risen. "Suzuki Shifted into High Gear When Crisis Hit," *Los Angeles Times,* June 27, 1988, p. IV–1.

12. *Wall Street Journal,* March 3, 1988, p. 22.

13. Bradley A. Stertz, "Suzuki Takes Extraordinary Measures to Halt Sales Plunge of Samurai Model," *Wall Street Journal,* July 15, 1988, p. 20.

14. *Los Angeles Times,* September 7, 1988.

15. Bob Davis, "U.S. Turns Down Petitions to Investigate and Order Recall of Suzuki's Samurai," *Wall Street Journal,* September 2, 1988, p. 3.

16. John Tighe, "Suzuki Will Put Safety Warnings in Samurai Ads," *Los Angeles Times,* March 24, 1989, p. IV–1.

17. *Supreme Court Reporter,* February 15, 1989, p. 706.

18. Tom Ichniowski, "Supreme Court Rejects the Richmond MBE Plan," *ENR,* January 26, 1989, p. 9.

19. William R. Beer, "Resolute Ignorance: Social Science and Affirmative Action," *Society,* May-June 1987, pp. 63–69.

20. William K. Stevens, "Indians Worry Over Poison Chemical Still in Plant," *New York Times*, December 11, 1984, p.8.

21. Manuel G. Velasquez, *Business Ethics: Concepts and Cases* (Englewood Cliffs, N.J.: Prentice-Hall, 1988 [1982]), p.3

22. Ibid.

23. Ibid.

24. Velasquez, *Business Ethics: Concepts and Cases.*

25. Ibid., p.4.

26. Thomas J. Lueck, "1982 Report Cited Safety Problems at Plant in India." *New York Times,* December 11, 1984, sec. 1, pp. 1, 8.

27. Richard I. Kirkland, Jr., "Union Carbide: Coping with Catastrophe," *Fortune,* January 7, 1985, pp. 50-52.

28. Judith H. Dobrzynski, William B. Glaberson, Resa W. King, William J. Powell, Jr., and Leslie Helm, "Union Carbide Fights for Its Life," *Business Week,* December 24, 1985, pp. 53-56.

29. Ibid.

30. Peter Stoler and K. K. Sharma, "Frightening Findings at Bhopal," *Time,* February 18, 1985, p.78.

31. Alan Hall, "The Bhopal Tragedy Has Union Carbide Reeling," *Business Week,* December 17, 1984, p.32

INDEX OF NAMES AND COMPANIES

SUBJECT INDEX

A

Abortion, 55
Access discrimination, 501
Acid rain, 531, 533
Act utilitarianism, 204
Administrative law, 315, 325
Administrative Procedures Act (APA), 325
Affirmative action, 18, 316, 506
  logical difficulties of, 518-519
  plan outline, 505
  and reverse discrimination, 504, 510, 516-517
  Supreme Court on, 510, 516-517, 555-557
  types of plans, 509-510
  voluntary v. court-ordered, 509, 516
Age Discrimination Act of 1973, 504
Agent Orange, 83
Agricultural Adjustment Act, 351
Agriculture, global competitiveness of, 113
Air bag rule, 388
Aircraft brake scandal, 277-285
Airline industry
  deregulation of, 376, 383-386
  regulation of, 341, 342
Air pollution, 531
  indoor, 534-535
  outdoor, 533-534
Alienation, 483
Aluminum industry, 426
American Business Creed, The (Sutton), 233
American Management Association, 485
American Revolutionary War, 7, 218, 239
Americans with Disability Act of 1990, 504, 506
Anarchy, State, and Utopia (Nozick), 238
Anomie, 483
Anticipatory/socially responsible orientation, 14-16, 17-18, 247, 263, 327, 329
Anticompetitive behavior, 398-340
Anti-Dumping Act of 1921, 315-316
Antitrust law, 44, 222, 242, 331, 335, 391- 421, 458
  anticompetitive behavior under, 398-340
  in college financial aid, 416-418
  and economic theory, 396-398, 412
  efficiency approach to, 398, 402-404, 407, 414
  enforcement of, 408-411, 413, 414
  and Federal Trade Commission (FTC), 404
  goals of, 336, 391-392, 394-396, 412, 413-414
  historical background of, 392-393
  and interest groups, 393-394
  international influence of, 411-412, 413
  mergers under, 405-410, 413
  monopolization under, 401-402
  in predatory pricing case, 419-421
  price discrimination under, 404-405
  private suits under, 405, 408, 413
Appeal systems, employee, 435-436

B

Arbitragers, 443
Areeda-Turner standard for predatory pricing, 403
Asbestos industry, 77-80
Asbestos Litigation Group, 79
Asbestos Litigation Reporter, 79
Asbestos Victims of America, 79
Audi 5000 unintended acceleration case, 455-458, 459, 460, 461-462, 463, 464
Audi Victims Network (AVN), 456, 457, 461
Australia, 92, 110, 129
Authoritarian capitalism, 34
Authoritarian society, 32
Automobile industry, 111, 130, 321
  Audi 5000 case, 455-458, 459, 460, 461-462, 463, 464
  competitive strategies in, 115
  and passive-restraint system, 388
  and plant closings/relocations, 3-4, 19, 224-225
  safety issues in, 73-76, 455-458, 459, 460, 461-462, 463, 464, 469, 470-471, 551-554
  Suzuki Samurai case, 551-554

B

Baby-boom generation, 103
Baby food industry, adulterated juice in, 286-287
Balance of payments, 110
Banking Act of 1936, 350, 351
Banking system
  failure of, 347, 349, 380
  regulation of, 350, 380
Bankruptcy protection, 79-80, 384
Belgium, 140, 472
Beneficence, 8, 182, 184, 222
Beta video players, 39
Bexiga v. Havir Manufacturing Company, 470
Bhopal disaster, 269, 557-559
Bill of Rights, 314
Biological growth rates, 529, 545
Board of directors, 431-432, 450, 549
Brazil, 86, 110, 129
Bribery, 270-271
Britain, 34, 36, 92, 102, 105, 110, 244, 271, 472
  antitrust law in, 392, 393
  deregulation in, 332
Broadcasting industry, regulation of, 342, 378
Broderick v. Ruder, 512
Brown v. Board of Education, 500
Bubble concept, 539
Budget deficit, 120
Bureau of Labor Statistics, 77, 482
Business
  and ecological decision making, 528-530
  environmental policy of, 540-541, 543-544
  market control of, 36-44, 46
  perspective of, 525-527
  role in threefold society, 5, 7, 28, 132